# Contents

*Doing Business 2013* is the 10th in a series of annual reports investigating the regulations that enhance business activity and those that constrain it. *Doing Business* presents quantitative indicators on business regulations and the protection of property rights that can be compared across 185 economies—from Afghanistan to Zimbabwe—and over time.

Regulations affecting 11 areas of the life of a business are covered: starting a business, dealing with construction permits, getting electricity, registering property, getting credit, protecting investors, paying taxes, trading across borders, enforcing contracts, resolving insolvency and employing workers. The employing workers data are not included in this year's ranking on the ease of doing business.

Data in *Doing Business 2013* are current as of June 1, 2012. The indicators are used to analyze economic outcomes and identify what reforms of business regulation have worked, where and why.

Doing
Business
THE WORLD BANK · IFC
2013

# DOING BUSINESS 2013

## Smarter Regulations for Small and Medium-Size Enterprises

2007 2012 2011 2005 2009 2004 2008 2006 2010 2013

**COMPARING BUSINESS REGULATIONS FOR DOMESTIC FIRMS IN 185 ECONOMIES**

A COPUBLICATION OF THE WORLD BANK AND THE INTERNATIONAL FINANCE CORPORATION

## RESOURCES ON THE *DOING BUSINESS* WEBSITE

### Current features
News on the *Doing Business* project
*http://www.doingbusiness.org*

### Rankings
How economies rank—from 1 to 185
*http://www.doingbusiness.org/rankings/*

### Data
All the data for 185 economies—topic rankings,
indicator values, lists of regulatory procedures and
details underlying indicators
*http://www.doingbusiness.org/data/*

### Reports
Access to *Doing Business reports* as well as
subnational and regional reports, reform case
studies and customized economy and regional
profiles
*http://www.doingbusiness.org/reports/*

### Methodology
The methodologies and research papers underlying
*Doing Business*
*http://www.doingbusiness.org/methodology/*

### Research
Abstracts of papers on *Doing Business* topics and
related policy issues
*http://www.doingbusiness.org/research/*

### *Doing Business* reforms
Short summaries of DB2013 business regulation
reforms, lists of reforms since DB2008 and a
ranking simulation tool
*http://www.doingbusiness.org/reforms/*

### Historical data
Customized data sets since DB2004
*http://www.doingbusiness.org/custom-query/*

### Law library
Online collection of business laws
and regulations relating to business and
gender issues
*http://www.doingbusiness.org/law-library/*
*http://wbl.worldbank.org/*

### Contributors
More than 9,600 specialists in 185 economies
who participate in *Doing Business*
*http://www.doingbusiness.org/contributors/*
*doing-business/*

### NEW! Entrepreneurship data
Data on business density for 130 economies
*http://www.doingbusiness.org/data/exploretopics/*
*entrepreneurship/*

### More to come
Coming soon—information on good practices
and data on transparency and on the distance
to frontier

# Preface

This is the 10th edition of the *Doing Business* report. First published in 2003 with 5 indicator sets measuring business regulation in 133 economies, the report has grown into an annual publication covering 11 indicator sets and 185 economies. In these 10 years *Doing Business* has recorded nearly 2,000 business regulation reforms in the areas covered by the indicators. And researchers have produced well over 1,000 articles in peer-reviewed journals using the data published by *Doing Business*—work that helps explore many of the key development questions of our time.

*Doing Business 2013* holds new information to inspire policy makers and researchers. One finding is that Poland improved the most in the *Doing Business* measures in 2011/12, while Singapore maintains its top spot in the overall ranking. Another finding is that European economies in fiscal distress are making efforts to improve the business climate, and this is beginning to be reflected in the indicators tracked by *Doing Business*, with Greece being among the 10 economies that improved the most in the *Doing Business* measures in the past year. Part of the solution to high debt is the recovery of economic growth, and there is broad recognition that creating a friendlier environment for entrepreneurs is central to this goal. But perhaps the most exciting finding is that of a steady march from 2003 to 2012 toward better business regulation across the wide range of economies included. With a handful of exceptions, every economy covered by *Doing Business* has narrowed the gap in business regulatory practice with the top global performance in the areas measured by the indicators. This is a welcome race to the top.

Collecting the more than 57,000 unique *Doing Business* data points each year and placing them in a broader context of economic policy and development is a major undertaking. We thank the team and the *Doing Business* contributors for their efforts. Data collection and analysis for *Doing Business 2013* were conducted through the Global Indicators and Analysis Department under the general direction of Augusto Lopez-Claros. The project was managed by Sylvia Solf and Rita Ramalho, with the support of Carolin Geginat and Adrian Gonzalez. Other team members included Beatriz Mejia Asserias, Andres Baquero Franco, Karim O. Belayachi, Iryna Bilotserkivska, Mariana Carvalho, Hayane Chang Dahmen, Rong Chen, Maya Choueiri. Dariga Chukmaitova, Santiago Croci Downes, Fernando Dancausa Diaz, Marie Lily Delion, Raian Divanbeigi, Alejandro Espinosa-Wang, Margherita Fabbri, Caroline Frontigny, Betina Hennig, Sarah Holmberg, Hussam Hussein, Joyce Ibrahim, Ludmila Jantuan, Nan Jiang, Hervé Kaddoura, Paweł Kopko, Jean Michel Lobet, Jean-Philippe Lodugnon-Harding, Frédéric Meunier, Robert Murillo, Joanna Nasr, Marie-Jeanne Ndiaye, Nuria de Oca, Mikiko Imai Ollison, Nina Paustian, Galina Rudenko, Valentina Saltane, Lucas Seabra, Paula Garcia Serna, Anastasia Shegay, Jayashree Srinivasan, Susanne Szymanski, Moussa Traoré, Tea Trumbic, Marina Turlakova, Julien Vilquin, Yasmin Zand and Yucheng Zheng.

More than 9,600 lawyers and other professionals generously donated their time to provide the legal assessments that underpin the data. We thank in particular the global contributors: Advocates for International Development; Allen & Overy LLP; American

Bar Association, Section of International Law; Baker & McKenzie; Cleary Gottlieb Steen & Hamilton LLP; Ernst & Young; Ius Laboris, Alliance of Labor, Employment, Benefits and Pensions Law Firms; KPMG; the Law Society of England and Wales; Lex Mundi, Association of Independent Law Firms; Panalpina; PwC; Raposo Bernardo & Associados; Russell Bedford International; SDV International Logistics; and Security Cargo Network. The efforts of all these contributors help maintain the distinctive voice of *Doing Business* and its annual contribution to business regulation reform.

Ten years marks a good time to take stock of where the world has moved in business regulatory practices and what challenges remain. We welcome you to give feedback on the *Doing Business* website (http://www.doingbusiness.org) and join the conversation as we shape the project in the years to come.

Sincerely,

Janamitra Devan
Vice President and Head of Network
Financial & Private Sector Development
World Bank Group

# Executive summary

2007 2012 2011
2005 2009
2004
2008 2006 2010 2013

This 10th edition of the *Doing Business* report marks a good time to take stock—to look at how far the world has come in business regulatory practices and what challenges remain. In the first report one of the main findings was that low-income economies had very cumbersome regulatory systems. Ten years later it is apparent that business regulatory practices in these economies have been gradually but noticeably converging toward the more efficient practices common in higher-income economies (box 1.1). How much has the gap narrowed? Did some regions close the regulatory gap more rapidly than others? This year's report tells that story. It points to important trends in regulatory reform and identifies the regions and economies making the biggest improvements for local entrepreneurs.

And it highlights both the areas of business regulation that have received the most attention and those where more progress remains to be made.

The report also reviews research on which regulatory reforms have worked and how. After 10 years of data tracking reforms and regulatory practices around the world, more evidence is available to address these questions. The report summarizes just some of the main findings. Among the highlights: Smarter business regulation supports economic growth. Simpler business registration promotes greater entrepreneurship and firm productivity, while lower-cost registration improves formal employment opportunities. An effective regulatory environment boosts trade performance. And sound

## BOX 1.1 MAIN FINDINGS SINCE 2003 AND THE FIRST *DOING BUSINESS* REPORT

- Over these 10 years 180 economies implemented close to 2,000 business regulatory reforms as measured by *Doing Business*.
- Eastern Europe and Central Asia improved the most, overtaking East Asia and the Pacific as the world's second most business-friendly region according to *Doing Business* indicators. OECD high-income economies continue to have the most business-friendly environment.
- Business regulatory practices have been slowly converging as economies with initially poor performance narrow the gap with better performers. Among the 50 economies with the biggest improvements since 2005, the largest share—a third—are in Sub-Saharan Africa.
- Among the categories of business regulatory practices measured by *Doing Business*, there has been more convergence in those that relate to the complexity and cost of regulatory processes (business start-up, property registration, construction permitting, electricity connections, tax payment and trade procedures) than in those that relate to the strength of legal institutions (contract enforcement, insolvency regimes, credit information, legal rights of borrowers and lenders and the protection of minority shareholders).
- Two-thirds of the nearly 2,000 reforms recorded by *Doing Business* were focused on reducing the complexity and cost of regulatory processes.
- A growing body of research has traced out the effects of simpler business regulation on a range of economic outcomes, such as faster job growth and an accelerated pace of new business creation.

## MAIN FINDINGS IN 2011/12

- Worldwide, 108 economies implemented 201 regulatory reforms in 2011/12 making it easier to do business as measured by *Doing Business*.

- Poland improved the most in the ease of doing business, through 4 reforms—making it easier to register property, pay taxes, enforce contracts and resolve insolvency as measured by *Doing Business*.

- Eastern Europe and Central Asia once again had the largest share of economies implementing regulatory reforms—88% of its economies reformed in at least one of the areas measured by *Doing Business*.

- European economies in fiscal distress are working to improve the business climate, and this is beginning to be reflected in the indicators tracked by *Doing Business*. Greece is one of the 10 most improved globally in 2011/12.

- Reform efforts globally have focused on making it easier to start a new business, increasing the efficiency of tax administration and facilitating trade across international borders. Of the 201 regulatory reforms recorded in the past year, 44% focused on these 3 policy areas alone.

financial market infrastructure—courts, creditor and insolvency laws, and credit and collateral registries—improves access to credit (see the chapter "About *Doing Business*").

## WHAT ARE SMART RULES FOR BUSINESSES?

Just as good rules are needed to allow traffic to flow in a city, they are also essential to allow business transactions to flow. Good business regulations enable the private sector to thrive and businesses to expand their transactions network. But regulations put in place to safeguard economic activity and facilitate business operations, if poorly designed, can become obstacles to doing business. They can be like traffic lights put up to prevent gridlock—ineffective if a red light lasts for an hour. Most people would run the red light, just as most businesses facing burdensome regulations will try to circumvent them to stay afloat.

Striking the right balance in business regulation can be a challenge. It becomes an even greater challenge in a changing world, where regulations must continually adapt to new realities. Just as traffic systems have to adjust when a new road is being constructed, regulations need to adapt to new demands from the market and to changes in technology (such as the growing use of information and communication technology in business processes).

This challenge is one focus of this report. Through indicators benchmarking 185 economies, *Doing Business* measures and tracks changes in the regulations applying to domestic small and medium-size companies in 11 areas in their life cycle. This year's aggregate ranking on the ease of doing business is based on indicator sets that measure and benchmark regulations affecting 10 of those areas: starting a business, dealing with construction permits, getting electricity, registering property, getting credit, protecting investors, paying taxes, trading across borders, enforcing contracts and

resolving insolvency. *Doing Business* also documents regulations on employing workers, which are not included in this year's aggregate ranking or in the count of reforms.

The economies that rank highest on the ease of doing business are not those where there is no regulation—but those where governments have managed to create rules that facilitate interactions in the marketplace without needlessly hindering the development of the private sector. In essence, *Doing Business* is about SMART business regulations—Streamlined, Meaningful, Adaptable, Relevant, Transparent—not necessarily fewer regulations (see figure 2.1 in the chapter "About *Doing Business*").

*Doing Business* encompasses 2 types of indicators: indicators relating to the *strength of legal institutions* relevant to business regulation and indicators relating to the *complexity and cost of regulatory processes*. Those in the first group focus on the legal and regulatory framework for getting credit, protecting investors, enforcing contracts and resolving insolvency. Those in the second focus on the cost and efficiency of regulatory processes for starting a business, dealing with construction permits, getting electricity, registering property, paying taxes and trading across borders. Based on time-and-motion case studies from the perspective of the business, these indicators measure the procedures, time and cost required to complete a transaction in accordance with relevant regulations. (For a detailed explanation of the *Doing Business* methodology, see the data notes and the chapter "About *Doing Business*.")

Economies that rank high on the ease of doing business tend to combine efficient regulatory processes with strong legal institutions that protect property and investor rights (figure 1.1). OECD high-income economies have, by a large margin, the most business-friendly regulatory environment on both dimensions. Regions such as East Asia and the Pacific and the Middle East and North Africa have

relatively efficient regulatory processes but still lag in the strength of legal institutions relevant to business regulation. Good practices around the world provide insights into how governments have improved the regulatory environment in the past in the areas measured by *Doing Business* (see table 1.4 at the end of the executive summary).

## WHO NARROWED THE REGULATORY GAP IN 2011/12?

As reflected in the ranking on the ease of doing business, the 10 economies with the most business-friendly regulation are Singapore; Hong Kong SAR, China; New Zealand; the United States; Denmark; Norway; the United Kingdom; the Republic of Korea; Georgia; and Australia (table 1.1). Singapore tops the global ranking for the seventh consecutive year.

A number 1 ranking on the ease of doing business does not mean that an economy ranks number 1 across all 10 regulatory areas included in this aggregate measure. Indeed, Singapore's rankings range from 1 in trading across borders to 36 in registering property. Its top 3 rankings (on trading across borders, dealing with construction permits and protecting investors) average 2, while its lowest 3 (on registering property, getting credit and enforcing contracts) average 20. Similarly, Guatemala's top 3 (on getting credit, registering property and getting electricity) average 22, and its bottom 3 (on paying taxes, protecting investors and starting a business) average 151. So while the ease of doing business ranking is a useful aggregate measure, analysis based on this measure should also take into account the dispersion of regulatory efficiency across the areas measured by *Doing Business* (figure 1.2).

In the past year 58% of economies covered by *Doing Business* implemented at least 1 institutional or regulatory reform making it easier to do business in the areas measured, and 23 undertook reforms in 3 or more areas. Of these 23 economies, 10 stand out as having jumped

## TABLE 1.1  Rankings on the ease of doing business

| Rank | Economy | DB2013 reforms | Rank | Economy | DB2013 reforms | Rank | Economy | DB2013 reforms |
|---|---|---|---|---|---|---|---|---|
| 1 | Singapore | 0 | 63 | Antigua and Barbuda | 0 | 125 | Honduras | 0 |
| 2 | Hong Kong SAR, China | 0 | 64 | Ghana | 0 | 126 | Bosnia and Herzegovina | 2 |
| 3 | New Zealand | 1 | 65 | Czech Republic | 3 | 127 | Ethiopia | 1 |
| 4 | United States | 0 | 66 | Bulgaria | 1 | 128 | Indonesia | 1 |
| 5 | Denmark | 1 | 67 | Azerbaijan | 0 | 129 | Bangladesh | 1 |
| 6 | Norway | 2 | 68 | Dominica | 1 | 130 | Brazil | 1 |
| 7 | United Kingdom | 1 | 69 | Trinidad and Tobago | 2 | 131 | Nigeria | 0 |
| 8 | Korea, Rep. | 4 | 70 | Kyrgyz Republic | 0 | 132 | India | 1 |
| 9 | Georgia | 6 | 71 | Turkey | 2 | 133 | Cambodia | 1 |
| 10 | Australia | 1 | 72 | Romania | 2 | 134 | Tanzania | 1 |
| 11 | Finland | 0 | 73 | Italy | 2 | 135 | West Bank and Gaza | 1 |
| 12 | Malaysia | 2 | 74 | Seychelles | 0 | 136 | Lesotho | 2 |
| 13 | Sweden | 0 | 75 | St. Vincent and the Grenadines | 0 | 137 | Ukraine | 3 |
| 14 | Iceland | 0 | 76 | Mongolia | 3 | 138 | Philippines | 0 |
| 15 | Ireland | 2 | 77 | Bahamas, The | 0 | 139 | Ecuador | 0 |
| 16 | Taiwan, China | 2 | 78 | Greece | 3 | 140 | Sierra Leone | 2 |
| 17 | Canada | 1 | 79 | Brunei Darussalam | 2 | 141 | Tajikistan | 1 |
| 18 | Thailand | 2 | 80 | Vanuatu | 0 | 142 | Madagascar | 1 |
| 19 | Mauritius | 2 | 81 | Sri Lanka | 4 | 143 | Sudan | 0 |
| 20 | Germany | 2 | 82 | Kuwait | 0 | 144 | Syrian Arab Republic | 1 |
| 21 | Estonia | 0 | 83 | Moldova | 2 | 145 | Iran, Islamic Rep. | 1 |
| 22 | Saudi Arabia | 2 | 84 | Croatia | 1 | 146 | Mozambique | 0 |
| 23 | Macedonia, FYR | 1 | 85 | Albania | 2 | 147 | Gambia, The | 0 |
| 24 | Japan | 1 | 86 | Serbia | 3 | 148 | Bhutan | 0 |
| 25 | Latvia | 0 | 87 | Namibia | 1 | 149 | Liberia | 3 |
| 26 | United Arab Emirates | 3 | 88 | Barbados | 0 | 150 | Micronesia, Fed. Sts. | 0 |
| 27 | Lithuania | 2 | 89 | Uruguay | 2 | 151 | Mali | 1 |
| 28 | Switzerland | 0 | 90 | Jamaica | 2 | 152 | Algeria | 1 |
| 29 | Austria | 0 | 91 | China | 2 | 153 | Burkina Faso | 0 |
| 30 | Portugal | 3 | 92 | Solomon Islands | 0 | 154 | Uzbekistan | 4 |
| 31 | Netherlands | 4 | 93 | Guatemala | 1 | 155 | Bolivia | 0 |
| 32 | Armenia | 2 | 94 | Zambia | 1 | 156 | Togo | 1 |
| 33 | Belgium | 0 | 95 | Maldives | 0 | 157 | Malawi | 1 |
| 34 | France | 0 | 96 | St. Kitts and Nevis | 0 | 158 | Comoros | 2 |
| 35 | Slovenia | 3 | 97 | Morocco | 1 | 159 | Burundi | 4 |
| 36 | Cyprus | 1 | 98 | Kosovo | 2 | 160 | São Tomé and Príncipe | 0 |
| 37 | Chile | 0 | 99 | Vietnam | 1 | 161 | Cameroon | 1 |
| 38 | Israel | 1 | 100 | Grenada | 1 | 162 | Equatorial Guinea | 0 |
| 39 | South Africa | 1 | 101 | Marshall Islands | 0 | 163 | Lao PDR | 3 |
| 40 | Qatar | 1 | 102 | Malta | 0 | 164 | Suriname | 0 |
| 41 | Puerto Rico (U.S.) | 1 | 103 | Paraguay | 0 | 165 | Iraq | 0 |
| 42 | Bahrain | 0 | 104 | Papua New Guinea | 0 | 166 | Senegal | 0 |
| 43 | Peru | 2 | 105 | Belize | 1 | 167 | Mauritania | 0 |
| 44 | Spain | 2 | 106 | Jordan | 0 | 168 | Afghanistan | 0 |
| 45 | Colombia | 1 | 107 | Pakistan | 0 | 169 | Timor-Leste | 0 |
| 46 | Slovak Republic | 4 | 108 | Nepal | 0 | 170 | Gabon | 0 |
| 47 | Oman | 1 | 109 | Egypt, Arab Rep. | 0 | 171 | Djibouti | 0 |
| 48 | Mexico | 2 | 110 | Costa Rica | 4 | 172 | Angola | 1 |
| 49 | Kazakhstan | 3 | 111 | Palau | 0 | 173 | Zimbabwe | 0 |
| 50 | Tunisia | 0 | 112 | Russian Federation | 2 | 174 | Haiti | 0 |
| 51 | Montenegro | 2 | 113 | El Salvador | 1 | 175 | Benin | 4 |
| 52 | Rwanda | 2 | 114 | Guyana | 0 | 176 | Niger | 1 |
| 53 | St. Lucia | 0 | 115 | Lebanon | 0 | 177 | Côte d'Ivoire | 0 |
| 54 | Hungary | 3 | 116 | Dominican Republic | 0 | 178 | Guinea | 3 |
| 55 | Poland | 4 | 117 | Kiribati | 0 | 179 | Guinea-Bissau | 0 |
| 56 | Luxembourg | 0 | 118 | Yemen, Rep. | 0 | 180 | Venezuela, RB | 0 |
| 57 | Samoa | 0 | 119 | Nicaragua | 0 | 181 | Congo, Dem. Rep. | 1 |
| 58 | Belarus | 2 | 120 | Uganda | 1 | 182 | Eritrea | 0 |
| 59 | Botswana | 1 | 121 | Kenya | 1 | 183 | Congo, Rep. | 2 |
| 60 | Fiji | 1 | 122 | Cape Verde | 0 | 184 | Chad | 1 |
| 61 | Panama | 3 | 123 | Swaziland | 1 | 185 | Central African Republic | 0 |
| 62 | Tonga | 0 | 124 | Argentina | 0 | | | |

*Note:* The rankings for all economies are benchmarked to June 2012 and reported in the country tables. This year's rankings on the ease of doing business are the average of the economy's percentile rankings on the 10 topics included in this year's aggregate ranking. The number of reforms excludes those making it more difficult to do business.

*Source: Doing Business* database.

## FIGURE 1.1 OECD high-income economies combine efficient regulatory processes with strong legal institutions

Average ranking on sets of *Doing Business* indicators

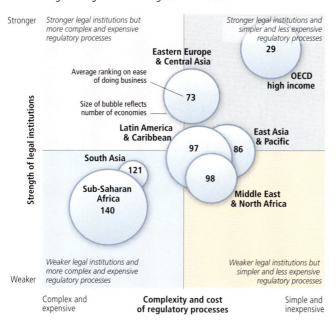

Note: **Strength of legal institutions** refers to the average ranking on getting credit, protecting investors, enforcing contracts and resolving insolvency. **Complexity and cost of regulatory processes** refers to the average ranking on starting a business, dealing with construction permits, getting electricity, registering property, paying taxes and trading across borders.

Source: *Doing Business* database.

ahead the most in the relative ranking (table 1.2). Others in this group advanced less in the global ranking because they already ranked high. Two are Korea and the Netherlands. Already among the top 35 in last year's global ranking, both implemented regulatory reforms making it easier to do business in 4 areas measured by *Doing Business*.

Four of the 10 economies improving the most in the ease of doing business are in Eastern Europe and Central Asia—the region that also had the largest number of regulatory reforms per economy in the past year. Four of the 10 are lower-middle-income economies; of the rest, 1 is low income, 3 are upper middle income and 2 are high income. And for the first time in 7 years, a South Asian economy—Sri Lanka—ranks among those improving the most in the ease of doing business.

Eight of the 10 economies made it easier to start a business. Kazakhstan, Mongolia and Ukraine reduced or eliminated the minimum capital requirement

| | Economy | Ease of doing business rank | Reforms making it easier to do business | | | | | | | | | |
|---|---|---|---|---|---|---|---|---|---|---|---|---|
| | | | Starting a business | Dealing with construction permits | Getting electricity | Registering property | Getting credit | Protecting investors | Paying taxes | Trading across borders | Enforcing contracts | Resolving insolvency |
| 1 | Poland | 55 | | | | ✔ | | | ✔ | | ✔ | ✔ |
| 2 | Sri Lanka | 81 | ✔ | | | ✔ | ✔ | | | ✔ | | |
| 2 | Ukraine | 137 | ✔ | | | ✔ | | | ✔ | | | |
| 4 | Uzbekistan | 154 | ✔ | | | | ✔ | | | ✔ | | ✔ |
| 5 | Burundi | 159 | ✔ | ✔ | | ✔ | | | | ✔ | | |
| 6 | Costa Rica | 110 | ✔ | ✔ | | | ✔ | | ✔ | | | |
| 6 | Mongolia | 76 | ✔ | | | | ✔ | ✔ | | | | |
| 8 | Greece | 78 | | ✔ | | | | ✔ | | | | ✔ |
| 9 | Serbia | 86 | ✔ | | | | | | | | ✔ | ✔ |
| 10 | Kazakhstan | 49 | ✔ | | | | ✔ | | | | | ✔ |

**TABLE 1.2 The 10 economies improving the most across 3 or more areas measured by *Doing Business* in 2011/12**

Note: Economies are ranked on the number of their reforms and on how much they improved in the ease of doing business ranking. First, *Doing Business* selects the economies that implemented reforms making it easier to do business in 3 or more of the 10 topics included in this year's aggregate ranking. Regulatory reforms making it more difficult to do business are subtracted from the number of those making it easier to do business. Second, *Doing Business* ranks these economies on the increase in their ranking on the ease of doing business from the previous year. The increase in economy rankings is not calculated using the published ranking of last year but by using a comparable ranking for DB2012 that captures the effects of other factors, such as the inclusion this year of 2 new economies in the sample, Barbados and Malta. The choice of the most improved economies is determined by the largest improvement in rankings, among those economies with at least 3 reforms.

Source: *Doing Business* database.

FIGURE 1.2  An economy's regulatory environment may be more business-friendly in some areas than in others

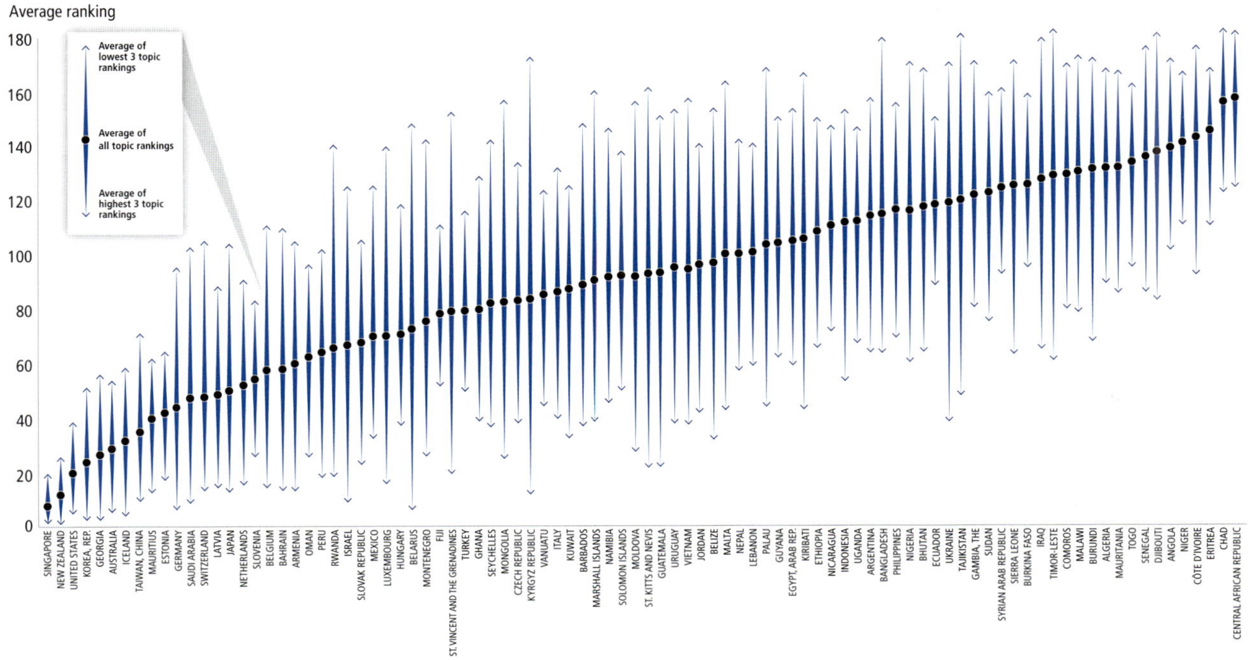

*Note:* Rankings reflected are those on the 10 *Doing Business* topics included in this year's aggregate ranking on the ease of doing business. Figure is for illustrative purposes only; it does not include all 185 economies covered by this year's report. See the country tables for rankings on the ease of doing business and each *Doing Business* topic for all economies.
*Source: Doing Business* database.

for company incorporation. Sri Lanka computerized and expedited the process for registering employees. Burundi eliminated 3 requirements: to have company documents notarized, to publish information on new companies in a journal and to register new companies with the Ministry of Trade and Industry.

Five of the 10 made it easier to resolve insolvency, and 2 of these also strengthened their systems for enforcing contracts. Serbia strengthened its insolvency process by introducing private bailiffs, prohibiting appeals of the court's decision on the proposal for enforcement, expediting service of process and adopting a public electronic registry for injunctions. The new private bailiff system also increased efficiency in enforcing contracts. Poland introduced a new civil procedure code that, along with an increase in the number of judges, reduced the time required to enforce a commercial contract. Poland also made it easier to resolve insolvency,

by updating the documentation requirements for bankruptcy filings.

Four economies made it easier to register property. Poland increased efficiency in processing property registration applications through a series of initiatives in recent years. These included creating 2 new registration districts in Warsaw and, in the past year, introducing a new caseload management system for the land and mortgage registries and continuing to digitize their records.

Five economies improved in the area of getting credit. Costa Rica, Mongolia and Uzbekistan guaranteed borrowers' right to inspect their personal credit data. Sri Lanka established a searchable electronic collateral registry and issued regulations for its operation. Kazakhstan strengthened the rights of secured creditors in insolvency proceedings.

Greece, driven in part by its economic crisis, implemented regulatory reforms in 3 areas measured by *Doing*

*Business*—improving its regulatory environment at a greater pace in the past year than in any of the previous 6. It made construction permitting faster by transferring the planning approval process from the municipality to certified private professionals, strengthened investor protections by requiring greater disclosure and introduced a new prebankruptcy rehabilitation procedure aimed at enhancing the rescue of distressed companies.

Costa Rica, the only economy in Latin America and the Caribbean in the group of 10, implemented regulatory changes in 4 areas measured by *Doing Business*. It introduced a risk-based approach for granting sanitary approvals for business start-ups and established online approval systems for the construction permitting process. Costa Rica also guaranteed borrowers' right to inspect their personal data and made paying taxes easier for local companies by implementing electronic payments for municipal taxes.

While these 10 economies improved the most in the ease of doing business, they were far from alone in introducing improvements in the areas measured by *Doing Business* in 2011/12. A total of 108 economies did so, through 201 institutional and regulatory reforms. And in the years since the first report was published in 2003, 180 of the 185 economies covered by *Doing Business* made improvements in at least one of these areas—through nearly 2,000 such reforms in total.

In 2011/12 starting a business was again the area with the most regulatory reforms. In the past 8 years the start-up process received more attention from policy makers than any other area of business regulation tracked by *Doing Business*—through 368 reforms in 149 economies. These worldwide efforts reduced the average time to start a business from 50 days to 30 and the average cost from 89% of income per capita to 31%.

In the past year Eastern Europe and Central Asia once again had the largest share of economies registering improvements, with 88% of economies implementing at least 1 institutional or regulatory reform making it easier to do business and 67% implementing at least 2 (figure 1.3). This region has been consistently active through all the years covered by *Doing Business*, implementing 397 institutional and regulatory reforms since 2005. At least some of this regulatory reform push reflects efforts by economies joining the European Union in 2004 to continue to narrow the gap in regulatory efficiency with established EU members—as well as similar efforts among economies now engaged in EU accession negotiations.

## WHO HAS NARROWED THE GAP OVER THE LONG RUN?

To complement the ease of doing business ranking, a relative measure, last year's *Doing Business* report introduced the distance to frontier, an absolute measure of business regulatory efficiency. This measure aids in assessing how much the regulatory environment for local entrepreneurs improves in absolute terms

over time by showing the distance of each economy to the "frontier," which represents the best performance observed on each of the *Doing Business* indicators across all economies and years included since 2005. The measure is normalized to range between 0 and 100, with 100 representing the frontier. A higher score therefore indicates a more efficient business regulatory system (for a detailed description of the methodology, see the chapter on the ease of doing business and distance to frontier).

Analysis based on the distance to frontier measure shows that the burden of regulation has declined since 2005 in the areas measured by *Doing Business*. On average the 174 economies covered by *Doing Business* since that year are today closer to the frontier in regulatory practice (figure 1.4). In 2005 these economies were 46 percentage points from the frontier on average, with the closest economy 10 percentage points away and the furthest one 74 percentage points away. Now these 174 economies are 40 percentage points from the frontier on average, with

FIGURE 1.4 Almost all economies are closer to the frontier in regulatory practice today than they were in 2005

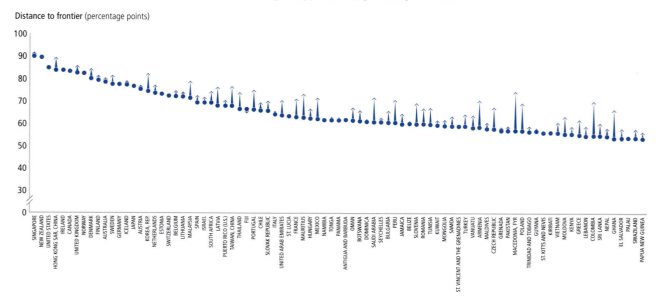

*Note:* The distance to frontier measure shows how far on average an economy is from the best performance achieved by any economy on each *Doing Business* indicator since 2005. The measure is normalized to range between 0 and 100, with 100 representing the best performance (the frontier). The data refer to the 174 economies included in *Doing Business 2006* (2005). Eleven economies were added in subsequent years.

*Source: Doing Business* database.

FIGURE 1.3  Eastern Europe and Central Asia had the largest share of economies reforming business regulation in 2011/12

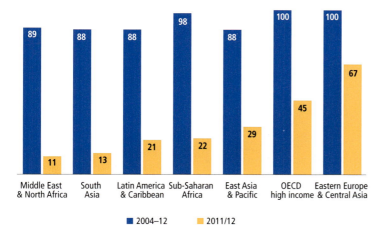

Share of economies with at least 2 *Doing Business* reforms making it easier to do business (%)

■ 2004–12    ■ 2011/12

*Source: Doing Business database.*

the closest economy 8 percentage points away and the furthest economy 69 percentage points away.

OECD high-income economies are closest to the frontier on average. But other regions are narrowing the gap. Eastern Europe and Central Asia has done so the most, thanks to about 17 institutional and regulatory reforms per economy since 2005 (figure 1.5). Economies in the Middle East and North Africa and Sub-Saharan Africa have implemented more than 9 institutional and regulatory reforms on average—and those in East Asia and the Pacific, Latin America and the Caribbean and South Asia about 8. With its faster pace of improvement, Eastern Europe and Central Asia overtook East Asia and the Pacific as the second most business-friendly region according to *Doing Business* indicators.

But the variation within regions is large. In Latin America and the Caribbean, for example, Colombia implemented 25 institutional and regulatory reforms in the past 8 years, while Suriname had none. In East Asia and the Pacific, Vietnam implemented 18 reforms, and Kiribati none. In a few economies (such as República Bolivariana de Venezuela and Zimbabwe) the business environment deteriorated as measures added to the complexity and cost of regulatory processes or undermined property rights and investor protections. Within the European Union, 4 Southern European economies have recently accelerated regulatory reform efforts (box 1.2).

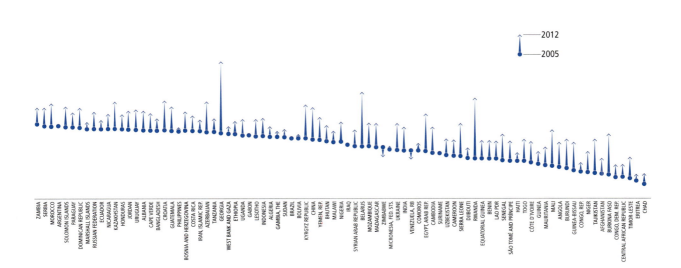

FIGURE 1.5  Doing business is easier today than in 2005, particularly in Eastern Europe and Central Asia and Sub-Saharan Africa

Average distance to frontier (percentage points)

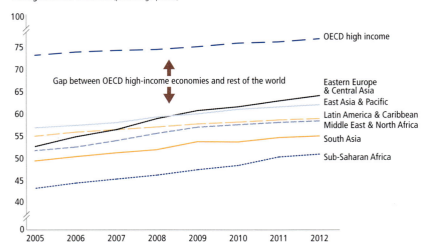

Note: The distance to frontier measure shows how far on average an economy is from the best performance achieved by any economy on each Doing Business indicator since 2005. The measure is normalized to range between 0 and 100, with 100 representing the best performance (the frontier). The data refer to the 174 economies included in Doing Business 2006 (2005) and to the regional classifications that apply in 2012. Eleven economies were added in subsequent years.

Source: Doing Business database.

FIGURE 1.6  Globally, reform efforts have focused more on reducing the complexity and cost of regulatory processes than on strengthening legal institutions

Average distance to frontier (percentage points)

Note: Figure illustrates the extent to which average regulatory practice across economies has moved closer to the most efficient practice in each area measured by Doing Business. The distance to frontier measure shows how far on average an economy is from the best performance achieved by any economy on each Doing Business indicator since 2005. The measure is normalized to range between 0 and 100, with 100 representing the best performance (the frontier). The data refer to the 174 economies included in Doing Business 2006 (2005). Eleven economies were added in subsequent years.

Source: Doing Business database.

Improvements happened across all regulatory areas measured by Doing Business between 2005 and 2012. But governments were more likely to focus their reform efforts on reducing the complexity and cost of regulatory processes—the focus of 1,227 reforms recorded by Doing Business since 2005—than on strengthening legal institutions—the focus of close to 600 (figure 1.6).

Improving business regulation is a challenging task, and doing it consistently over time even more so. Yet some economies have achieved considerable success since 2005 in doing just that (table 1.3). A few of these economies stand out within their region: Georgia, Rwanda, Colombia, China and Poland.

Georgia is the top improver since 2005 both in Eastern Europe and Central Asia and globally. With 35 institutional and regulatory reforms since 2005, Georgia has improved in all areas measured by Doing Business. In the past year alone it improved in 6 areas. As just one example, Georgia made trading across borders easier by introducing customs clearance zones in such cities as Tbilisi and Poti. These one-stop shops for trade clearance processes are open all day every day, allowing traders to submit customs documents and complete other formalities in a single place. Georgia also strengthened its secured transactions system. A new amendment to its civil code allows a security interest to extend to the products, proceeds and replacements of an asset used as collateral.

Georgia has also distinguished itself by following a relatively balanced regulatory reform path. Many economies aiming to improve their regulatory environment start by reducing the complexity and cost of regulatory processes (in such areas as starting a business). Later they may move on to reforms strengthening legal institutions relevant to business regulation (in such areas as getting credit). These tend to be a bigger challenge, sometimes requiring amendments to key pieces of legislation rather than simply changes in

## BOX 1.2  FISCAL IMBALANCES AND REGULATORY REFORM IN SOUTHERN EUROPE

The 2008–09 global financial crisis contributed to rapid increases in public debt levels among high-income economies. The recession depressed tax revenues and forced governments to increase spending to ease the effects of the crisis. Governments used public sector stimulus to cushion the impact of the sharp contraction in output, and many were also forced to intervene to strengthen the balance sheets of commercial banks and prop up industries struck particularly hard by the crisis. The fiscal deterioration in the context of weak global demand contributed to greater risk aversion among investors, complicating fiscal management in many economies, particularly those with already high debt levels or rapidly growing deficits.

Greece, Italy, Portugal and Spain were among those most affected by the crisis and associated market pressures. Aware that the resumption of economic growth would be key to returning to a sustainable fiscal position, authorities in these economies moved to implement broad-ranging reforms.

Business regulation reforms were an integral part of these plans, as reflected in the *Doing Business* data. While Greece is among the 10 economies with the biggest improvements in the ease of doing business in the past year, the other 3 economies also made important strides. Italy made it easier to get an electricity connection and to register property. Portugal simplified the process for construction permitting, for importing and exporting and for resolving insolvency. Spain made trading across borders simpler and amended its bankruptcy law. All 4 economies reformed or are also in the process of reforming their labor laws with the aim of making their labor market more flexible.

*Doing Business* reforms are not new to these economies. Since 2004, Portugal has implemented 25, Spain and Greece 17, and Italy 14 institutional or regulatory reforms. The impact of these reforms has helped these 4 economies narrow the business regulatory gap with the best performers in the European Union (see figure).

### In Southern Europe, an acceleration in the pace of regulatory reform

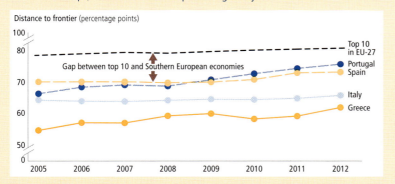

*Note:* The distance to frontier measure shows how far on average an economy is from the best performance achieved by any economy on each *Doing Business* indicator since 2005. The measure is normalized to range between 0 and 100, with 100 representing the best performance (the frontier). The top 10 in EU-27 are the 10 economies closest to the frontier among current members of the European Union.

*Source: Doing Business* database.

| Rank | Economy | Region | Improvement (percentage points) |
|---|---|---|---|
| 1 | Georgia | ECA | 31.6 |
| 2 | Rwanda | SSA | 26.5 |
| 3 | Belarus | ECA | 23.5 |
| 4 | Burkina Faso | SSA | 18.5 |
| 5 | Macedonia, FYR | ECA | 17.4 |
| 6 | Egypt, Arab Rep. | MENA | 16.3 |
| 7 | Mali | SSA | 15.8 |
| 8 | Colombia | LAC | 15.3 |
| 9 | Tajikistan | ECA | 15.2 |
| 10 | Kyrgyz Republic | ECA | 14.8 |
| 11 | Sierra Leone | SSA | 14.7 |
| 12 | China | EAP | 14.3 |
| 13 | Azerbaijan | ECA | 12.9 |
| 14 | Croatia | ECA | 12.8 |
| 15 | Ghana | SSA | 12.7 |
| 16 | Burundi | SSA | 12.6 |
| 17 | Poland | OECD | 12.3 |
| 18 | Guinea-Bissau | SSA | 12.2 |
| 19 | Armenia | ECA | 12.2 |
| 20 | Ukraine | ECA | 12.0 |
| 21 | Kazakhstan | ECA | 11.9 |
| 22 | Senegal | SSA | 11.5 |
| 23 | Cambodia | EAP | 11.1 |
| 24 | Angola | SSA | 11.0 |
| 25 | Mauritius | SSA | 10.9 |
| 26 | Saudi Arabia | MENA | 10.7 |
| 27 | India | SAS | 10.6 |
| 28 | Guatemala | LAC | 10.4 |
| 29 | Madagascar | SSA | 10.3 |
| 30 | Morocco | MENA | 10.1 |
| 31 | Yemen, Rep. | MENA | 10.1 |
| 32 | Peru | LAC | 10.1 |
| 33 | Mozambique | SSA | 10.0 |
| 34 | Czech Republic | OECD | 9.8 |
| 35 | Timor-Leste | EAP | 9.7 |
| 36 | Côte d'Ivoire | SSA | 9.5 |
| 37 | Togo | SSA | 9.5 |
| 38 | Slovenia | OECD | 9.5 |
| 39 | Mexico | LAC | 9.4 |
| 40 | Niger | SSA | 9.4 |
| 41 | Nigeria | SSA | 9.0 |
| 42 | Portugal | OECD | 9.0 |
| 43 | Solomon Islands | EAP | 8.9 |
| 44 | Uruguay | LAC | 8.8 |
| 45 | Dominican Republic | LAC | 8.8 |
| 46 | Taiwan, China | EAP | 8.8 |
| 47 | São Tomé and Príncipe | SSA | 8.7 |
| 48 | France | OECD | 8.6 |
| 49 | Bosnia and Herzegovina | ECA | 8.4 |
| 50 | Albania | ECA | 8.3 |

**TABLE 1.3  The 50 economies narrowing the distance to frontier the most since 2005**

*Note:* Rankings are based on the absolute difference for each economy between its distance to frontier in 2005 and that in 2012. The data refer to the 174 economies included in *Doing Business 2006* (2005). Eleven economies were added in subsequent years. The distance to frontier measure shows how far on average an economy is from the best performance achieved by any economy on each *Doing Business* indicator since 2005. The measure is normalized to range between 0 and 100, with 100 representing the best performance (the frontier). EAP = East Asia and the Pacific; ECA = Eastern Europe and Central Asia; LAC = Latin America and the Caribbean; MENA = Middle East and North Africa; OECD = OECD high income; SAS = South Asia; SSA = Sub-Saharan Africa.

*Source: Doing Business* database.

administrative procedures. Georgia has followed this pattern, focusing initially on reducing the complexity and cost of regulatory processes and later on strengthening legal institutions. But among a group of 5 top regional improvers, Georgia has improved the most along both dimensions (figure 1.7).

Rwanda, the number 2 improver globally and top improver in Sub-Saharan Africa since 2005, has reduced the gap with the frontier by almost half. To highlight key lessons emerging from Rwanda's sustained efforts, this year's report features a case study of its reform process. But Rwanda is far from alone in the region: of the 50 economies advancing the most toward the frontier since 2005, 17 are in Sub-Saharan Africa.

Worldwide, economies at all income levels are narrowing the gap with the frontier on average—but low-income economies more so than high-income ones. This is an important achievement. Indeed, while business regulatory practices in all lower-income groups are converging toward those in high-income economies on average, low-income economies have reduced the gap the most, by 4 percentage points since 2005. Lower-middle-income economies have closed the gap with high-income economies by 3 percentage points, and upper-middle-income economies by 2 percentage points. This convergence is far from complete, however.

While the Arab Republic of Egypt is the top improver in the Middle East and North Africa since 2005, its improvement was concentrated in the years before 2009. In the past 4 years there was no visible improvement in the areas measured by *Doing Business*. Regionally, there was less focus on reforming business regulation in the past year than in any previous year covered by *Doing Business*, with only 11% of economies implementing at least 2 regulatory reforms (box 1.3).

Colombia, the economy narrowing the gap with the frontier the most in Latin America and the Caribbean, is also featured in a case study this year. Between 2006 and 2009 Colombia focused mostly on improving the efficiency of regulatory processes, with an emphasis on business registration and tax administration. But in 2010 it began reforming legal institutions, such as by strengthening the protection of minority shareholders and by improving the insolvency regime.

Two of the "BRICs" rank among the top 50 improvers—China and India, each also the top improver in its region since 2005. Both implemented regulatory reforms particularly in the early years covered by *Doing Business*. China established a new company law in 2005, a new credit registry in 2006, its first bankruptcy law

in 2007, a new property law in 2007, a new civil procedure law in 2008 and a new corporate income tax law in 2008. After establishing its first credit bureau in 2004, India focused mostly on simplifying and reducing the cost of regulatory processes in such areas as starting a business, paying taxes and trading across borders.

Five OECD high-income economies make the list of top 50 improvers: Poland, the Czech Republic, Slovenia, Portugal and France. Poland in the past year alone implemented 4 institutional and regulatory reforms, among the 20 recorded for it by *Doing Business* since 2005. It improved the process for transferring property, made paying taxes more convenient by promoting the use of electronic facilities, reduced the time to enforce contracts and

strengthened the process of resolving insolvency.

## IN WHAT AREAS IS THE GAP NARROWING THE MOST?

Since 2005 there has been a convergence in business regulatory practices in two-thirds of the areas measured by *Doing Business*: starting a business, paying taxes, dealing with construction permits, registering property, getting credit and enforcing contracts. This means that laws, regulations and procedures in these areas are more similar across economies today than they were 8 years ago. Overall, more convergence has occurred in the areas measured by *Doing Business* that relate to the complexity and cost of regulatory processes than in those that relate to the strength of legal institutions.[1]

**FIGURE 1.7** Different economies have followed a variety of regulatory reform paths

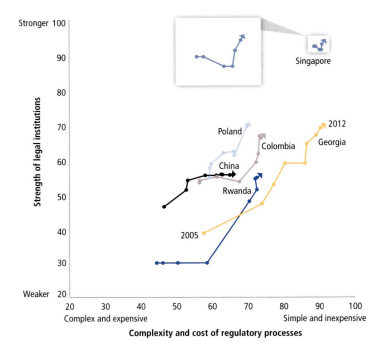

Average distance to frontier in sets of *Doing Business* indicators (percentage points)

*Note: Strength of legal institutions* refers to the average distance to frontier in getting credit, protecting investors, enforcing contracts and resolving insolvency. *Complexity and cost of regulatory processes* refers to the average distance to frontier in starting a business, dealing with construction permits, registering property, paying taxes and trading across borders. Each dot refers to a different year, starting in 2005 and ending in 2012. The reform progress of Singapore, the economy with the most business-friendly regulation for the seventh year in a row, is shown for purposes of comparison. For visual clarity the series for Singapore starts in 2007. The distance to frontier measure shows how far on average an economy is from the best performance achieved by any economy on each *Doing Business* indicator since 2005. The measure is normalized to range between 0 and 100, with 100 representing the best performance (the frontier).
*Source: Doing Business* database.

The greatest convergence in regulatory practice has occurred in business start-up. Among the 174 economies covered by *Doing Business* since 2005, the time to start a business in that year averaged 112 days in the worst quartile of the economies as ranked by performance on this indicator, while it averaged 29 days for the rest (figure 1.8). Since then, thanks to 368 reforms in 149 economies, the average time for the worst quartile has fallen to 63 days, getting closer to the average of 18 for the rest. Similar but less strong patterns are observed for indicators of time, procedures and cost for paying taxes, dealing with construction permits and registering property.

But in 3 areas the trend runs weakly in the other direction. In protecting investors, trading across borders and resolving insolvency the realities in different economies have slowly drifted apart rather than converged. This does not mean that in these 3 areas the average regulatory environment is worse today than in 2005; it is actually better (see figure 1.6). But it does mean that economies that were in the best 3 quartiles of the distribution in these 3 areas in 2005 have strengthened practices and institutions somewhat faster than those in the worst quartile.

## WHAT IS THE IMPACT ON ECONOMIC OUTCOMES?

Beyond what *Doing Business* measures, have the business regulation reforms undertaken by governments since 2005 had an impact? In presenting analysis of this question, earlier editions of *Doing Business* focused on cross-country analyses linking business regulation to economic variables such as corruption or rates of informality in the economy.

With more years of data now available, previous research on the impact of reforms in the areas measured by *Doing Business* can be extended over time and linked to more economic outcomes. Using several years of data for the same economy makes it possible to take into account country characteristics that

remain constant over time when doing analysis across economies—something not possible in the earlier cross-country analyses. Based on a 5-year panel of economies, one such study finds that in low-income economies that implemented reforms making it easier to do business, the growth rate increased by 0.4 percentage point in the following year.[2] Emerging evidence from analysis based on 8 years of *Doing Business* data and building on the earlier studies shows that improvements in business entry and other aspects of business regulation matter for aggregate growth as well. Credibly pinning down the magnitude of this effect is more difficult, however.[3]

Research on the effect of regulatory reforms is advancing especially rapidly around the question of business start-up. A growing body of research has shown that simpler entry regulations encourage the creation of more new firms and new jobs in the formal sector. Economies at varying income levels and in different regions saw noticeable increases in the number of new firm registrations after implementing such reforms (figure 1.9). Within-country studies have confirmed the positive association between improvements in business registration and registration of new firms in such countries as Colombia, India, Mexico and Portugal. These studies have found increases of 5–17% in the number of newly registered businesses after reforms of the business registration process (for more discussion, see the chapter "About *Doing Business*").

Better business regulation as measured by *Doing Business* is also associated with greater new business registration. Ongoing research by *Doing Business* using 8 years of data shows that reducing the distance to frontier by 10 percentage points is associated with an increase of 1 newly registered business for every 1,000 working-age people, a meaningful result given the world average of 3.2 newly registered businesses for every 1,000 working-age people per year.[4]

**FIGURE 1.8  Strong convergence across economies since 2005**

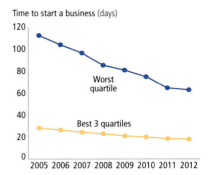

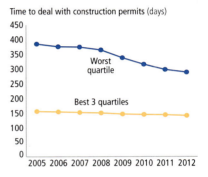

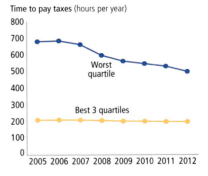

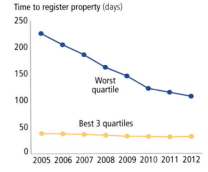

*Note:* Economies are ranked in quartiles by performance in 2005 on the indicator shown. The data refer to the 174 economies included in *Doing Business 2006* (2005). Eleven economies were added in subsequent years.
*Source: Doing Business* database.

## BOX 1.3  BUSINESS REGULATION IN THE MIDDLE EAST AND NORTH AFRICA—THE CHALLENGES AHEAD

Earlier editions of the *Doing Business* report highlighted substantial efforts by governments in the Middle East and North Africa to improve business regulation for local entrepreneurs. But the reform momentum has slowed since the beginning of the Arab Spring in January 2011, as some countries have entered a complex process of transition to more democratic forms of governance. The post–Arab Spring governments have had a broad range of economic, social and political issues to address, and this in turn has resulted in a slower overall reform process, as new governments have struggled to adjust to important shifts in the political and economic landscape.

The region faces structural challenges that can impede private sector activity. A history of government intervention has created more opportunities for rent seeking than for entrepreneurship. Firm surveys show that manufacturing firms as well as their managers are older on average than those in other regions, indicating weaker entry and exit mechanisms. Firm entry density in the Middle East and North Africa is among the lowest in the world.[1]

Moreover, the region suffers from a crisis of governance and trust: businesses do not trust officials, and officials do not trust businesses. Business managers in the region rank corruption, anticompetitive practices and regulatory policy uncertainty high on their list of concerns. At the same time 60% of public officials interviewed across the region perceive the private sector as rent seeking and corrupt. And banks cite lack of corporate transparency as among the main obstacles to extending more finance to small and medium-size enterprises.[2]

Some governments in the region have tried to aggressively reform the business environment in the past, but have seen the impact of their efforts lessened by a lack of sustained commitment to in-depth changes and the related risk of upsetting the established order. A common view is that only connected entrepreneurs are successful, suggesting a dual set of rules with preferential treatment for those close to the ruling elites. This suggests a need for governments to invest in governance structures and increase transparency in parallel with efforts to improve the business regulatory environment. The case study on transparency in this year's report points to one area where they could start: the Middle East and North Africa is one of the regions with the most constrained access to basic regulatory information such as fee schedules.

Although economies in the region have made some strides in reducing the complexity and cost of regulatory processes, entrepreneurs across the region still contend with weak investor and property rights protections (see figure). With an average ease of doing business ranking of 98, the region still has much room for making the life of local businesses easier through clearer and more transparent rules applied more consistently. Such rules would facilitate rather than impede private sector activity in economies where the state has traditionally had an outsized presence in the national economy and in a region where the need to encourage entrepreneurship is thus perhaps more intense than in any other.

All these challenges notwithstanding, the recent political changes in the region—fast, hectic, unpredictable, far-reaching in their effects—provide a unique opportunity for governments to substantively address many of the impediments to private sector development that have plagued the region in recent decades. Moving to a system of more transparent and sensible rules—rules that are better able to respond to the needs of the business community and that provide incentives to narrow the gap between the law as written and the law as practiced—will go a long way toward creating the conditions for more equitable economic growth and a faster pace of job creation.

**Entrepreneurs across the Middle East and North Africa face relatively weak investor and property rights protections**

Average ranking on sets of *Doing Business* indicators by economy and global income group

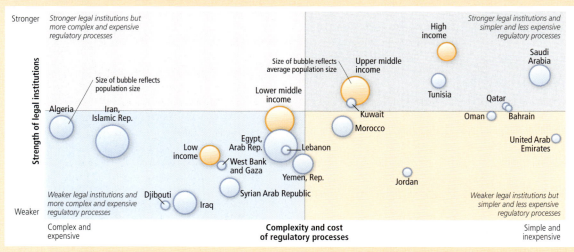

*Note: Strength of legal institutions* refers to the average ranking on getting credit, protecting investors, enforcing contracts and resolving insolvency. *Complexity and cost of regulatory processes* refers to the average ranking on starting a business, dealing with construction permits, getting electricity, registering property, paying taxes and trading across borders. The global income groups exclude economies in the Middle East and North Africa.

*Source: Doing Business* database.

1. World Bank, *From Privilege to Competition: Unlocking Private-Led Growth in the Middle East and North Africa* (Washington, DC: World Bank, 2009). *Firm entry density* is defined as the number of newly registered limited liability companies per 1,000 working-age people (ages 15–64).

2. Roberto Rocha, Subika Farazi, Rania Khouri and Douglas Pearce, "The Status of Bank Lending to SMEs in the Middle East and North Africa Region: The Results of a Joint Survey of the Union of Arab Banks and the World Bank" (World Bank, Washington, DC; and Union of Arab Banks, Beirut, 2010).

**TABLE 1.4  Good practices around the world, by *Doing Business* topic**

| Topic | Practice | Economies[a] | Examples |
|---|---|---|---|
| Making it easy to start a business | Putting procedures online | 106 | Hong Kong SAR, China; FYR Macedonia; New Zealand; Peru; Singapore |
| | Having no minimum capital requirement | 91 | Kazakhstan; Kenya; Kosovo; Madagascar; Mexico; Mongolia; Morocco; Portugal; Rwanda; Serbia; United Arab Emirates; United Kingdom |
| | Having a one-stop shop | 88 | Bahrain; Burkina Faso; Georgia; Republic of Korea; Peru; Vietnam |
| Making it easy to deal with construction permits | Having comprehensive building rules | 135 | Croatia; Kenya; New Zealand; Republic of Yemen |
| | Using risk-based building approvals | 86 | Armenia; Germany; Mauritius; Singapore |
| | Having a one-stop shop | 31 | Bahrain; Chile; Hong Kong SAR, China; Rwanda |
| Making it easy to obtain an electricity connection | Streamlining approval processes (utility obtains excavation permit or right of way if required) | 104[b] | Armenia; Austria; Benin; Cambodia; Czech Republic; Panama |
| | Providing transparent connection costs and processes | 103 | France; Germany; Ireland; Netherlands; Trinidad and Tobago |
| | Reducing the financial burden of security deposits for new connections | 96 | Argentina; Austria; Kyrgyz Republic; Latvia; Mozambique; Nepal |
| | Ensuring the safety of internal wiring by regulating the electrical profession rather than the connection process | 40 | Denmark; Germany; Iceland; Japan |
| Making it easy to register property | Using an electronic database for encumbrances | 108 | Jamaica; Sweden; United Kingdom |
| | Offering cadastre information online | 50 | Denmark; Lithuania; Malaysia |
| | Offering expedited procedures | 16 | Azerbaijan; Bulgaria; Georgia |
| | Setting fixed transfer fees | 10 | New Zealand; Russian Federation; Rwanda |
| Making it easy to get credit | **Legal rights** | | |
| | Allowing out-of-court enforcement | 122 | Australia; India; Nepal; Peru; Russian Federation; Serbia; Sri Lanka |
| | Allowing a general description of collateral | 92 | Cambodia; Canada; Guatemala; Nigeria; Romania; Rwanda; Singapore |
| | Maintaining a unified registry | 67 | Bosnia and Herzegovina; Ghana; Honduras; Marshall Islands; Mexico; Montenegro; New Zealand |
| | **Credit information** | | |
| | Distributing data on loans below 1% of income per capita | 123 | Brazil; Bulgaria; Germany; Kenya; Malaysia; Sri Lanka; Tunisia |
| | Distributing both positive and negative credit information | 105 | China; Croatia; India; Italy; Jordan; Panama; South Africa |
| | Distributing credit information from retailers, trade creditors or utilities as well as financial institutions | 55 | Fiji; Lithuania; Nicaragua; Rwanda; Saudi Arabia; Spain |
| Protecting investors | Allowing rescission of prejudicial related-party transactions[c] | 73 | Brazil; Mauritius; Rwanda; United States |
| | Regulating approval of related-party transactions | 60 | Albania; France; United Kingdom |
| | Requiring detailed disclosure | 53 | Hong Kong SAR, China; New Zealand; Singapore |
| | Allowing access to all corporate documents during the trial | 46 | Chile; Ireland; Israel |
| | Requiring external review of related-party transactions | 43 | Australia; Arab Republic of Egypt; Sweden |
| | Allowing access to all corporate documents *before* the trial | 30 | Japan; Sweden; Tajikistan |
| | Defining clear duties for directors | 28 | Colombia; Malaysia; Mexico; United States |
| Making it easy to pay taxes | Allowing self-assessment | 156 | Argentina; Canada; China; Rwanda; Sri Lanka; Turkey |
| | Allowing electronic filing and payment | 74 | Australia; Colombia; India; Lithuania; Malta; Mauritius; Tunisia |
| | Having one tax per tax base | 48 | FYR Macedonia; Namibia; Paraguay; United Kingdom |
| Making it easy to trade across borders[d] | Allowing electronic submission and processing | 149[e] | Belize; Chile; Estonia; Pakistan; Turkey |
| | Using risk-based inspections | 133 | Morocco; Nigeria; Palau; Vietnam |
| | Providing a single window | 71[f] | Colombia; Ghana; Republic of Korea; Singapore |
| Making it easy to enforce contracts | Making all judgments in commercial cases by first-instance courts publicly available in practice | 121[g] | Chile; Iceland; Nigeria; Russian Federation; Uruguay |
| | Maintaining specialized commercial court, division or judge | 82 | Burkina Faso; France; Liberia; Poland; Sierra Leone; Singapore |
| | Allowing electronic filing of complaints | 19 | Brazil; Republic of Korea; Malaysia; Rwanda; Saudi Arabia |
| Making it easy to resolve insolvency | Allowing creditors' committees a say in insolvency proceeding decisions | 109 | Australia; Bulgaria; Philippines; United States; Uzbekistan |
| | Requiring professional or academic qualifications for insolvency administrators by law | 107 | Armenia; Belarus; Colombia; Namibia; Poland; United Kingdom |
| | Specifying time limits for the majority of insolvency procedures | 94 | Albania; Italy; Japan; Republic of Korea; Lesotho |
| | Providing a legal framework for out-of-court workouts | 82 | Argentina; Hong Kong SAR, China; Latvia; Philippines; Romania |

a. Among 185 economies surveyed, unless otherwise specified.

b. Among 151 economies surveyed.

c. Rescission is the right of parties involved in a contract to return to a state identical to that before they entered into the agreement.

d. Among 181 economies surveyed.

e. Thirty-one have a full electronic data interchange system, 118 a partial one.

f. Eighteen have a single-window system that links all relevant government agencies, 53 a system that does so partially.

g. Among 184 economies surveyed.

*Source: Doing Business* database; for starting a business, also World Bank (2009b).

FIGURE 1.9 More new firms are registered after reforms making it simpler to start a business

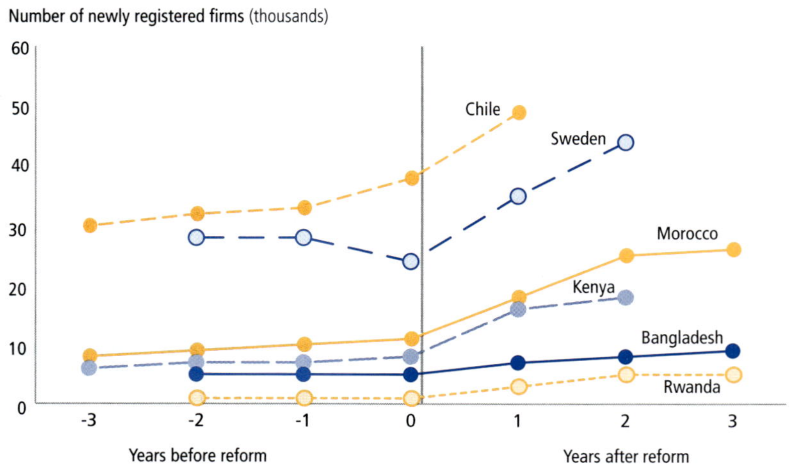

Number of newly registered firms (thousands)

*Note:* All 6 economies implemented a reform making it easier to start a business as measured by *Doing Business*. The reform year varies by economy and is represented by the vertical line in the figure. For Bangladesh and Rwanda it is 2009; for Chile, 2011; for Kenya, 2007; for Morocco, 2006; and for Sweden, 2010.

*Source:* World Bank Group Entrepreneurship Snapshots, 2012 edition.

Yet another finding relates to the relationship between foreign direct investment and business regulation. A case study in this year's report shows that although the *Doing Business* indicators measure regulations applying to domestic firms, economies that do well in this area also provide an attractive regulatory environment for foreign firms. Again using multiple years of data, the case study shows that economies that are closer to the frontier in regulatory practice attract larger inflows of foreign direct investment.

## WHAT'S NEW IN THIS YEAR'S REPORT?

This year's report, like last year's, presents country case studies. These feature Colombia, Latvia and Rwanda. In addition, the report presents a regional case study on Asia-Pacific Economic Cooperation

(APEC), focusing on peer-to-peer learning. And for the first time the report presents thematic case studies, on foreign direct investment and on transparency in business regulation.

This year's report also reintroduces the topic chapters. But it presents them in a different format, as shorter "topic notes" that focus on the changes in the data from the previous year and over all years covered by *Doing Business*. The topic notes also discuss the most prominent reforms from the past year. Full information for each topic, including examples of good practices and relevant research, is available on the *Doing Business* website.[5] The website also presents the full list of good practices by topic summarized in table 1.4.

## NOTES

1. To measure convergence, *Doing Business* calculated the change in the variance of distance to frontier across 174 economies since 2005 for each topic. The results suggest that the largest convergence has been in starting a business, with the variance decreasing by 49% since 2005. The topics with the next largest convergence are paying taxes (with a change in variance of −24%), dealing with construction permits (−23%), registering property (−19%), getting credit (−12%) and enforcing contracts (−4%). Several other topics show a small divergence: trading across borders (7%), protecting investors (2%) and resolving insolvency (1%). The overall change in the variance is −16%, suggesting an overall convergence in all *Doing Business* topics.

2. Eifert 2009.

3. The analysis, by Divanbeigi and Ramalho (2012), finds that narrowing the distance to frontier in the indicator sets measuring the complexity and cost of regulatory processes by 10 percentage points is associated with an increase of close to 1 percentage point in the GDP growth rate. Since the distance to frontier improves by 1 percentage point a year on average, these simulations are based on expected results for a 10-year period. Results are based on Arellano-Bond dynamic panel estimation to control for economic cycle and time-invariant country-specific factors. Following Eifert (2009) and Djankov, McLeish and Ramalho (2006), the analysis controls for government consumption, institutional quality and corruption perception. It also controls for total trade openness and rents from natural resources.

4. This research follows Klapper and Love (2011a). The analysis controls for government consumption, institutional quality and corruption perception. It also controls for total trade openness and rents from natural resources.

5. http://www.doingbusiness.org.

# About *Doing Business*: measuring for impact

The private sector provides an estimated 90% of jobs in developing economies.[1] Where government policies support a dynamic business environment—with firms making investments, creating jobs and increasing productivity—all people have greater opportunities. A growing body of evidence suggests that policy makers seeking to strengthen the private sector need to pay attention not only to macroeconomic factors but also to the quality of laws, regulations and institutional arrangements that shape daily economic life.[2]

This is the 10th *Doing Business* report. When the first report was produced, in 2003, there were few globally available and regularly updated indicators for monitoring such microeconomic issues as business regulations affecting local firms. Earlier efforts from the 1980s drew on perceptions data, but these expert or business surveys focused on broad aspects of the business environment and often captured the experiences of businesses. These surveys also lacked the specificity and cross-country comparability that *Doing Business* provides—by focusing on well-defined transactions, laws and institutions rather than generic, perceptions-based questions on the business environment.

*Doing Business* seeks to measure business regulations for domestic firms through an objective lens. The project looks primarily at small and medium-size companies in the largest business city. Based on standardized case studies, it presents quantitative indicators on the regulations that apply to firms at different stages of their life cycle. The results for each economy can be compared with those for 184 other economies and over time.

Over the years the choice of indicators for *Doing Business* has been guided by a rich pool of data collected through the World Bank Enterprise Surveys. These data highlight the main obstacles to business activity as reported by entrepreneurs in well over 100 economies. Among the factors that the surveys have identified as important to businesses have been taxes (tax administration as well as tax rates) and electricity—inspiring the design of the paying taxes and getting electricity indicators. In addition, the design of the *Doing Business* indicators has drawn on theoretical insights gleaned from extensive research literature.[3] The *Doing Business* methodology makes it possible to update the indicators in a relatively inexpensive and replicable way.

The *Doing Business* methodology is also responsive to the needs of policy makers. Rules and regulations are under the direct control of policy makers—and policy makers intending to change the experience and behavior of businesses will often start by changing rules and regulations that affect them. *Doing Business* goes beyond identifying that a problem exists and points to specific regulations or regulatory procedures that may lend themselves to regulatory reform. And its quantitative measures of business regulation enable research on how specific regulations affect firm behavior and economic outcomes.

The first *Doing Business* report covered 5 topics and 133 economies. This year's report covers 11 topics and 185 economies.

Ten topics are included in the aggregate ranking on the ease of doing business, and 9 in the distance to frontier measure.[4] The project has benefited from feedback from governments, academics, practitioners and reviewers.[5] The initial goal remains: to provide an objective basis for understanding and improving the regulatory environment for business.

## WHAT *DOING BUSINESS* COVERS

*Doing Business* captures several important dimensions of the regulatory environment as they apply to local firms. It provides quantitative measures of regulations for starting a business, dealing with construction permits, getting electricity, registering property, getting credit, protecting investors, paying taxes, trading across borders, enforcing contracts and resolving insolvency. *Doing Business* also looks at regulations on employing workers. Pending further progress on research in this area, this year's report does not present rankings of economies on the employing workers indicators or include the topic in the aggregate ranking on the ease of doing business. It does present the data on the employing workers indicators. Additional data on labor regulations collected in 185 economies are available on the *Doing Business* website.[6]

The foundation of *Doing Business* is the notion that economic activity, particularly private sector development, benefits from clear and coherent rules: Rules that set out and clarify property rights and facilitate the resolution of disputes. And rules that enhance the predictability of economic interactions and provide contractual partners with essential protections against arbitrariness and abuse. Where such rules are reasonably efficient in design, are transparent and accessible to those for whom they are intended and can be implemented at a reasonable cost, they are much more effective in shaping the incentives of economic agents in ways that promote growth and development. The quality of the rules also has a crucial bearing on how societies distribute the

benefits and bear the costs of development strategies and policies.

Consistent with the view that rules matter, some *Doing Business* indicators give a higher score for more regulation and better-functioning institutions (such as courts or credit bureaus). In the area of protecting investors, for example, higher scores are given for stricter disclosure requirements for related-party transactions. Higher scores are also given for a simplified way of applying regulation that keeps compliance costs for firms low—such as by allowing firms to comply with business start-up formalities in a one-stop shop or through a single online portal. Finally, *Doing Business* scores reward economies that apply a risk-based approach to regulation as a way to address social and environmental concerns—such as by imposing a greater regulatory burden on activities that pose a high risk to the population and a lesser one on lower-risk activities.

Thus the economies that rank highest on the ease of doing business are not those where there is no regulation—but those where governments have managed to create rules that facilitate interactions in the marketplace without needlessly hindering the development of the private sector. In essence, *Doing Business* is about smart business regulations, not necessarily fewer regulations (figure 2.1).

In constructing the indicators the *Doing Business* project uses 2 types of data. The first come from readings of laws and regulations in each economy. The *Doing Business* team, in collaboration with local expert respondents, examines the company law to find the disclosure requirements for related-party transactions. It reads the civil law to find the number of procedures necessary to resolve a commercial sale dispute before local courts. It reviews the labor code to find data on a range of issues concerning employer-employee relations. And it plumbs other legal instruments for other key pieces of data used in the indicators, several of which have a large legal dimension.

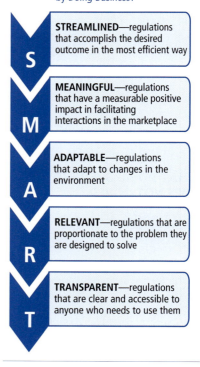

FIGURE 2.1 What are SMART business regulations as defined by *Doing Business*?

**S** STREAMLINED—regulations that accomplish the desired outcome in the most efficient way

**M** MEANINGFUL—regulations that have a measurable positive impact in facilitating interactions in the marketplace

**A** ADAPTABLE—regulations that adapt to changes in the environment

**R** RELEVANT—regulations that are proportionate to the problem they are designed to solve

**T** TRANSPARENT—regulations that are clear and accessible to anyone who needs to use them

Indeed, about three-quarters of the data used in *Doing Business* are of this factual type, reducing the need to have a larger sample size of experts in order to improve accuracy. The local expert respondents play a vital role in corroborating the *Doing Business* team's understanding and interpretation of rules and laws.

Data of the second type serve as inputs into indicators on the complexity and cost of regulatory processes. These indicators measure the efficiency in achieving a regulatory goal, such as the number of procedures to obtain a building permit or the time taken to grant legal identity to a business. In this group of indicators cost estimates are recorded from official fee schedules where applicable. Time estimates often involve an element of judgment by respondents who routinely administer the relevant regulations or undertake the relevant transactions.[7] These experts have several rounds of interaction with the *Doing Business* team, involving conference calls, written correspondence and visits by the team until there is convergence on the final answer. To construct the time indicators, a regulatory process such as starting a business is broken down into clearly defined steps and procedures (for more details, see the discussion on methodology in this chapter). Here *Doing Business* builds on Hernando de Soto's pioneering work in applying the time-and-motion approach in the 1980s to show the obstacles to setting up a garment factory on the outskirts of Lima.[8]

## WHAT *DOING BUSINESS* DOES NOT COVER

The *Doing Business* data have key limitations that should be kept in mind by those who use them.

### Limited in scope

The *Doing Business* indicators are limited in scope. In particular:

- *Doing Business* does not measure the full range of factors, policies and institutions that affect the quality of the business environment in an economy or its national competitiveness. It does not, for example, capture aspects of security, the prevalence of bribery and corruption, market size, macroeconomic stability (including whether the government manages its public finances in a sustainable way), the state of the financial system or the level of training and skills of the labor force.

- Even within the relatively small set of indicators included in *Doing Business*, the focus is deliberately narrow. The getting electricity indicators, for example, capture the procedures, time and cost involved for a business to obtain a permanent electricity connection to supply a standardized warehouse. Through these indicators *Doing Business* thus provides a narrow perspective on the range of infrastructure challenges that firms face, particularly in the developing world. It does not address the extent to which inadequate roads, rail, ports and communications may add to firms' costs and undermine competitiveness. *Doing Business* covers 11 areas of a company's life cycle,

**TABLE 2.1  *Doing Business*—benchmarking 11 areas of business regulation**

| Complexity and cost of regulatory processes | |
|---|---|
| Starting a business | Procedures, time, cost and paid-in minimum capital requirement |
| Dealing with construction permits | Procedures, time and cost |
| Getting electricity | Procedures, time and cost |
| Registering property | Procedures, time and cost |
| Paying taxes | Payments, time and total tax rate |
| Trading across borders | Documents, time and cost |
| **Strength of legal institutions** | |
| Getting credit | Movable collateral laws and credit information systems |
| Protecting investors | Disclosure and liability in related-party transactions |
| Enforcing contracts | Procedures, time and cost to resolve a commercial dispute |
| Resolving insolvency | Time, cost, outcome and recovery rate |
| Employing workers[a] | Flexibility in the regulation of employment |

a. The employing workers indicators are not included in this year's ranking on the ease of doing business nor in the calculation of any data cn the strength of legal institutions included in figures in the report.

through 11 specific sets of indicators (table 2.1). Similar to the indicators on getting electricity, those on starting a business or protecting investors do not cover all aspects of commercial legislation. And those on employing workers do not cover all areas of labor regulation; for example, they do not measure regulations addressing health and safety issues at work or the right of collective bargaining.

- *Doing Business* does not attempt to measure all costs and benefits of a particular law or regulation to society as a whole. The paying taxes indicators, for example, measure the total tax rate, which in isolation is a cost to the business. The indicators do not measure, nor are they intended to measure, the benefits of the social and economic programs funded through tax revenues. Measuring business laws and regulations provides one input into the debate on the regulatory burden associated with achieving regulatory objectives. Those objectives can differ across economies.

### Limited to standardized case scenarios

A key consideration for the *Doing Business* indicators is that they should ensure comparability of the data across a global set of economies. The indicators are therefore developed around standardized case scenarios with specific assumptions.

One such assumption is the location of a notional business in the largest business city of the economy. The reality is that business regulations and their enforcement very often differ within a country, particularly in federal states and large economies. But gathering data for every relevant jurisdiction in each of the 185 economies covered by *Doing Business* would be far too costly.

*Doing Business* recognizes the limitations of the standardized case scenarios and assumptions. But while such assumptions come at the expense of generality, they also help ensure the comparability of data. For this reason it is common to see limiting assumptions of this kind in economic indicators. Inflation statistics, for example, are often based on prices of a set of consumer goods in a few urban areas, since collecting nationally representative price data at high frequencies may be prohibitively costly in many countries. To capture regional variation in the business environment within economies, *Doing Business* has complemented its global indicators with subnational studies in some economies where resources and interest have come together (box 2.1).

Some *Doing Business* topics include complex and highly differentiated areas. Here the standardized cases and assumptions are carefully considered and defined. For example, the standardized case scenario usually involves a limited liability company or its legal equivalent. The considerations in defining this assumption are twofold. First, private limited liability companies are, empirically, the most prevalent business form in many economies around the world. Second, this choice reflects the focus of *Doing Business* on expanding opportunities for entrepreneurship:

investors are encouraged to venture into business when potential losses are limited to their capital participation.

## Limited to the formal sector

The *Doing Business* indicators assume that entrepreneurs have knowledge of and comply with applicable regulations. In practice, entrepreneurs may not know

what needs to be done or how to comply and may lose considerable time in trying to find out. Or they may deliberately avoid compliance altogether—by not registering for social security, for example. Where regulation is particularly onerous, levels of informality tend to be higher (figure 2.2).

Informality comes at a cost. Compared with their formal sector counterparts, firms in the informal sector typically grow more slowly, have poorer access to credit and employ fewer workers—and these workers remain outside the protections of labor law.[9] All this may be even more so for female-owned businesses, according to country-specific research.[10] Firms in the informal sector are also less likely to pay taxes.

*Doing Business* measures one set of factors that help explain the occurrence of informality and give policy makers insights into potential areas of reform. Gaining a fuller understanding of the broader business environment, and a broader perspective on policy challenges, requires combining insights from *Doing Business* with data from other sources, such as the World Bank Enterprise Surveys.[11]

## WHY THIS FOCUS?

Why does *Doing Business* focus on the regulatory environment for small and medium-size enterprises? These enterprises are key drivers of competition, growth and job creation, particularly in developing economies. But in these economies up to 65% of economic activity takes place in the informal sector, often because of excessive bureaucracy and regulation—and in the informal sector firms lack access to the opportunities and protections that the law provides. Even firms operating in the formal sector might not have equal access to these opportunities and protections. Where regulation is burdensome and competition limited, success tends to depend on whom one knows. But where regulation is transparent, efficient and implemented in a simple way, it becomes easier for aspiring entrepreneurs to compete, innovate and grow.

---

**BOX 2.1 COMPARING REGULATIONS AT THE LOCAL LEVEL: SUBNATIONAL *DOING BUSINESS* REPORTS**

Subnational *Doing Business* reports expand the indicators beyond the largest business city in an economy. They capture local differences in regulations or in the implementation of national regulations across cities within an economy (as in Colombia) or region (as in South East Europe). Projects are undertaken at the request of central governments, which often contribute financing, as in Mexico. In some cases local governments also provide funding, as in the Russian Federation.

Subnational indicators provide governments with standard measures, based on laws and regulations, that allow objective comparisons both domestically and internationally. As a diagnostic tool, they identify bottlenecks as well as highlight good practices that are easily replicable in other cities sharing a similar legal framework.

Governments take ownership of a subnational project by participating in all steps of its design and implementation—choosing the cities to be benchmarked, the indicators that can capture local differences and the frequency of benchmarking. All levels of government are involved—national, regional and municipal.

Subnational projects create a space for discussing regulatory reform and provide opportunities for governments and agencies to learn from one another, through the report and through peer-to-peer learning workshops. Even after the report is launched, knowledge sharing continues. In Mexico 28 of 32 states hold regular exchanges.

Repeated benchmarking creates healthy competition between cities to improve their regulatory environment. The dissemination of the results reinforces this process and gives cities an opportunity to tell their stories. Fifteen economies have requested 2 or more rounds of benchmarking since 2005 (including Colombia, Indonesia and Nigeria), and many have expanded the geographic coverage to more cities (including Russia). In Mexico each successive round has captured an increase in the number of states improving their regulatory environment in each of the 4 indicator sets included—reaching 100% of states in 2011.

Since 2005 subnational reports have covered 335 cities in 54 economies, including Brazil, China, the Arab Republic of Egypt, India, Kenya, Morocco, Pakistan and the Philippines.[1]

This year studies were updated in Indonesia, Kenya, Mexico, Russia and the United Arab Emirates. Studies are ongoing in Hargeisa (Somaliland) as well as in 23 cities and 4 ports in Colombia, 15 cities and 3 ports in Egypt and 13 cities and 7 ports in Italy. In addition, 3 regional reports were published:

- *Doing Business in OHADA,* comparing business regulations in the 16 member states of the Organization for the Harmonization of Business Law in Africa (Benin, Burkina Faso, Cameroon, the Central African Republic, Chad, the Comoros, the Republic of Congo, Côte d'Ivoire, Equatorial Guinea, Gabon, Guinea, Guinea-Bissau, Mali, Niger, Senegal and Togo).

- *Doing Business in the East African Community,* covering 5 economies (Burundi, Kenya, Rwanda, Tanzania and Uganda).

- *Doing Business in the Arab World,* covering 20 economies (Algeria, Bahrain, the Comoros, Djibouti, Egypt, Iraq, Jordan, Kuwait, Lebanon, Mauritania, Morocco, Oman, Qatar, Saudi Arabia, Sudan, the Syrian Arab Republic, Tunisia, the United Arab Emirates, West Bank and Gaza, and the Republic of Yemen).

1. Subnational reports are available on the *Doing Business* website at http://www.doingbusiness.org/subnational.

FIGURE 2.2 Higher levels of informality are associated with lower *Doing Business* rankings

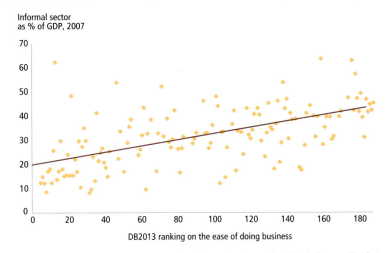

*Note:* The correlation between the 2 variables is 0.57. Relationships are significant at the 5% level after controlling for income per capita. The data sample includes 143 economies.

*Source: Doing Business* database; Schneider, Buehn and Montenegro 2010.

Do the focus areas of *Doing Business* matter for development and poverty reduction? The World Bank study *Voices of the Poor* asked 60,000 poor people around the world how they thought they might escape poverty.[12] The answers were unequivocal: women and men alike pin their hopes, above all, on income from their own business or wages earned in employment. Enabling growth—and ensuring that all people, regardless of income level, can participate in its benefits—requires an environment where new entrants with drive and good ideas can get started in business and where good firms can invest and grow, thereby generating more jobs. In this sense *Doing Business* values good rules as a key to social inclusion.

In effect, *Doing Business* functions as a barometer of the regulatory environment for domestic businesses. To use a medical analogy, *Doing Business* is similar to a cholesterol test. A cholesterol test does not tell us everything about our health. But our cholesterol level is easier to measure than our overall health, and the test provides us with important information, warning us when we need to adjust our behavior. Similarly, *Doing Business* does not tell us everything we need to know about the regulatory environment for domestic businesses. But its indicators

cover aspects that are more easily measured than the entire regulatory environment, and they provide important information about where change is needed. What type of change or regulatory reform is right, however, can vary substantially across economies.

To test whether *Doing Business* serves as a proxy for the broader business environment and for competitiveness, one approach is to look at correlations between the *Doing Business* rankings and

other major economic benchmarks. The indicator set closest to *Doing Business* in what it measures is the set of indicators on product market regulation compiled by the Organisation for Economic Co-operation and Development (OECD). These are designed to help assess the extent to which the regulatory environment promotes or inhibits competition. They include measures of the extent of price controls, the licensing and permit system, the degree of simplification of rules and procedures, the administrative burdens and legal and regulatory barriers, the prevalence of discriminatory procedures and the degree of government control over business enterprises.[13] These indicators—for the 39 countries that are covered, several of them large emerging markets—are correlated with the *Doing Business* rankings (the correlation here is 0.53) (figure 2.3).

There is a high correlation (0.83) between the *Doing Business* rankings and the rankings on the World Economic Forum's Global Competitiveness Index, a much broader measure capturing such factors as macroeconomic stability, aspects of human capital, the soundness of public institutions and the sophistication of the business community (figure 2.4).[14] Self-reported experiences with business regulations, such as those captured by the

FIGURE 2.3 A significant correlation between *Doing Business* rankings and OECD rankings on product market regulation

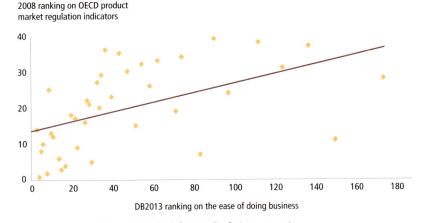

*Note:* Relationships are significant at the 5% level after controlling for income per capita.

*Source: Doing Business* database; OECD data.

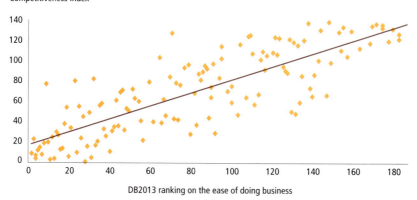

2012/13 ranking on Global
Competitiveness Index

DB2013 ranking on the ease of doing business

*Note:* Relationships are significant at the 5% level after controlling for income per capita.
*Source: Doing Business* database; WEF 2012.

Global Competitiveness Index, often vary much more within economies (across respondents in the same economy) than across economies.[15] A high correlation such as this one can therefore coexist with significant differences within economies.

## DOING BUSINESS AS A BENCHMARKING EXERCISE

By capturing key dimensions of regulatory regimes, *Doing Business* provides a rich opportunity for benchmarking. Such a benchmarking exercise is necessarily incomplete, just as the *Doing Business* data are limited in scope. It is useful when it aids judgment, but not when it supplants judgment.

Since 2006 *Doing Business* has sought to provide 2 perspectives on the data it collects: it presents "absolute" indicators for each economy for each of the 11 regulatory topics it addresses, and it provides rankings of economies for 10 topics, by topic and also in the aggregate. Judgment is required in interpreting these measures for any economy and in determining a sensible and politically feasible path for regulatory reform.

Reviewing the *Doing Business* rankings in isolation may reveal unexpected results. Some economies may rank unexpectedly high on some topics. And some

economies that have had rapid growth or attracted a great deal of investment may rank lower than others that appear to be less dynamic.

As economies develop, they may add to or improve on regulations that protect investor and property rights. Many also tend to streamline existing regulations and prune outdated ones. One finding of *Doing Business* is that dynamic and growing economies continually reform and update their business regulations and the implementation of those regulations, while many poor economies still work with regulatory systems dating to the late 1800s.

For reform-minded governments, how much the regulatory environment for local entrepreneurs improves in an absolute sense matters far more than their economy's ranking relative to other economies. To aid in assessing the absolute level of regulatory performance and how it improves over time, this year's report again presents the distance to frontier measure. This measure shows the distance of each economy to the "frontier," which represents the highest performance observed on each of the indicators across all economies included in *Doing Business* since 2003.

At any point in time the distance to frontier measure shows how far an economy is from the highest performance. And comparing an economy's score at 2 points in time allows users to assess the absolute change over time in the economy's regulatory environment as measured by *Doing Business*, rather than simply the change in the economy's performance relative to others. In this way the distance to frontier measure complements the yearly ease of doing business ranking, which compares economies with one another at a point in time.

Each topic covered by *Doing Business* relates to a different aspect of the business regulatory environment. The rankings of each economy vary, sometimes significantly, across topics. A quick way to assess the variability of an economy's regulatory performance across the different areas of business regulation is to look at the topic rankings (see the country tables). Guatemala, for example, stands at 93 in the overall ease of doing business ranking. Its ranking is 12 on the ease of getting credit, 20 on the ease of registering property and 34 on the ease of getting electricity. At the same time, it has a ranking of 124 on the ease of paying taxes, 158 on the strength of investor protections and 172 on the ease of starting a business (see figure 1.2 in the executive summary).

## WHAT 10 YEARS OF DATA SHOW

A growing body of empirical research shows that particular areas of business regulation, and particular regulatory reforms in those areas, are associated with vital social and economic outcomes— including firm creation, employment, formality, international trade, access to financial services and the survival of struggling but viable firms.[16] This research has been made possible by a decade of *Doing Business* data combined with other data sets. Some 1,245 research articles published in peer-reviewed academic journals, and about 4,071 working papers available through Google Scholar, refer to the *Doing Business* data.[17]

Determining the empirical impact of regulatory reforms is not easy. One possible approach is cross-country correlation analysis. But with this method it is difficult to isolate the effect of a particular regulatory reform because of all the other factors that may vary across economies and that may not have been taken into account in the analysis. How then do researchers determine whether social or economic outcomes would have been different without a specific regulatory reform? A growing number of studies have been able to investigate such questions by analyzing regulatory changes within a country over time or by using panel estimations. Others have focused on regulatory reforms relevant only for particular firms or industries within a country. The broader literature, using a range of different empirical strategies, has produced a number of interesting findings, including those described below.

*Smarter business regulation promotes economic growth.* Economies with better business regulation grow faster. One study found that for economies in the best quartile of business regulation as measured by *Doing Business*, the difference in business regulation with those in the worst quartile is associated with a 2.3 percentage point increase in annual growth rates.[18] Another found that regulatory reforms making it easier to do business in relatively low-income economies are associated with an increase in growth rates of 0.4 percentage point in the following year.[19]

*Simpler business registration promotes greater entrepreneurship and firm productivity.* Economies that have efficient business registration also tend to have a higher entry rate by new firms and greater business density.[20] Faster business registration is associated with more businesses registering in industries with the strongest potential for growth, such as those experiencing expansionary global demand or technology shifts.[21] And easier start-up is associated with more investment in industries often sheltered from competition, including transport, utilities and communications.[22] Empirical evidence also suggests that more efficient business entry regulations improve firm productivity and macroeconomic performance.[23]

*Lower costs for business registration improve formal employment opportunities.* Because new firms are often set up by high-skilled workers, lowering entry costs often leads to higher take-up rates for education, more jobs for high-skilled workers and higher average productivity.[24] And by increasing formal registration, it can also boost legal certainty—because the newly formal firms are now covered by the legal system, benefiting themselves as well as their customers and suppliers.[25]

Country-specific studies confirm that simplifying entry regulations can promote the establishment of new formal sector firms:

• In Colombia the introduction of one-stop shops for business registration in different cities across the country was followed by a 5.2% increase in new firm registrations.[26]

• In Mexico a study analyzing the effects of a program simplifying municipal licensing found that it led to a 5% increase in the number of registered businesses and a 2.2% increase in employment. Moreover, competition from new entrants lowered prices by 0.6% and the income of incumbent businesses by 3.2%.[27] A second study found that the program was more effective in municipalities with less corruption and cheaper additional registration procedures.[28] Yet another found that simpler licensing may result in both more wage workers and more formal enterprises, depending on the personal characteristics of informal business owners: those with characteristics similar to wage workers were more likely to become wage workers, while those with characteristics similar to entrepreneurs in the formal sector were more likely to become formal business owners.[29]

• In India a study found that the progressive elimination of the "license raj"—the system regulating entry and production in industry—led to a 6% increase in new firm registrations.[30] Another study found that simpler entry regulation and labor market flexibility were complementary: in Indian states with more flexible employment regulations informal firms decreased by 25% more, and real output grew by 18% more, than in states with less flexible regulations.[31] A third study found that the licensing reform resulted in an aggregate productivity increase of 22% among the firms affected.[32]

• In Portugal the introduction of a one-stop shop for businesses led to a 17% increase in new firm registrations. The reform favored mostly small-scale entrepreneurs with low levels of education operating in low-tech sectors such as agriculture, construction and retail.[33]

*An effective regulatory environment improves trade performance.* Strengthening the institutional environment for trade—such as by increasing customs efficiency—can boost trade volumes.[34] In Sub-Saharan Africa an inefficient trade environment was found to be among the main factors in poor trade performance.[35] One study found that a 1-day reduction in inland travel times leads to a 7% increase in exports.[36] Another found that among the factors that improve trade performance are access to finance, the quality of infrastructure and the government's ability to formulate and implement sound policies and regulations that promote private sector development.[37] The same study showed that the more constrained economies are in their access to foreign markets, the more they can benefit from improvements in the investment climate. Yet another study found that improvements in transport efficiency and the business environment have a greater marginal effect on exports in lower-income economies than in high-income ones.[38] One study even suggests that behind-the-border measures to improve logistics performance and facilitate trade may have a larger effect on trade, especially on exports, than tariff reduction would.[39]

Other areas of regulation matter for trade performance. Economies with good contract enforcement tend to produce and export more customized products than those with poor contract enforcement.[40] Since production of high-quality output is a precondition for firms to become exporters, reforms that lower the cost of high-quality production increase the positive effect of trade reforms.[41] Moreover, reforms removing barriers to trade need to be accompanied by other reforms, such as those making labor markets more flexible, to increase productivity and growth.[42]

*Sound financial market infrastructure— including courts, creditor and insolvency laws, and credit and collateral registries— improves access to credit.* Businesses worldwide identify access to credit as one of the main obstacles they face.[43] Good credit information systems and strong collateral laws help overcome this obstacle. An analysis of reforms improving collateral law in 12 transition economies concludes that they had a positive effect on the volume of bank lending.[44] Greater information sharing through credit bureaus is associated with higher bank profitability and lower bank risk. And stronger creditor rights and the existence of public or private credit registries are associated with a higher ratio of private credit to GDP.[45]

Country-specific studies confirm that efficient debt recovery and exit processes are key in determining credit conditions and in ensuring that less productive firms are either restructured or exit the market:

- In India the establishment of specialized debt recovery tribunals had a range of positive effects, including speeding up the resolution of debt recovery claims, allowing lenders to seize more collateral on defaulting loans, increasing the probability of repayment by 28% and reducing interest rates on loans by 1–2 percentage points.[46]

- Brazil's extensive bankruptcy reform in 2005 was associated with a 22% reduction in the cost of debt and a 39% increase in the aggregate level of credit.[47]

- Introducing streamlined mechanisms for reorganization has been shown to reduce the number of liquidations because it encourages more viable firms to opt for reorganization. Indeed, it reduced the number of liquidations by 14% in Colombia and by 8.4% in Belgium.[48] One important feature of Colombia's new system is that it better distinguishes between viable and nonviable firms, making it more likely that financially distressed but fundamentally viable firms will survive.

- Improving investor protections, developing financial markets and promoting more active markets for corporate control reduce the persistence of family-controlled firms over time, expanding opportunity for firms with more diversified capital structures.[49]

## HOW GOVERNMENTS USE *DOING BUSINESS*

*Doing Business* offers policy makers a benchmarking tool useful in stimulating policy debate, both by exposing potential challenges and by identifying good practices and lessons learned. The initial debate on the results highlighted by the data typically turns into a deeper discussion on the relevance of the data to the economy and on areas where business regulation reform is needed, including areas well beyond those measured by *Doing Business*.

Reform-minded governments seeking success stories in business regulation refer to *Doing Business* for examples (box 2.2). Saudi Arabia, for example, used the company law of France as a model for revising its own law. Many African governments look to Mauritius—the region's strongest performer on *Doing Business* indicators—as a source of good practices to inspire regulatory reforms in their own countries. Governments shared knowledge of business regulations before

the *Doing Business* project began. But *Doing Business* made it easier by creating a common language comparing business regulations around the world.

Over the past 10 years governments worldwide have been actively improving the regulatory environment for domestic companies. Most reforms relating to *Doing Business* topics have been nested in broader reform programs aimed at enhancing economic competitiveness, as in Colombia, Kenya and Liberia. In structuring reform programs for the business environment, governments use multiple data sources and indicators. This recognizes the reality that the *Doing Business* data on their own provide an incomplete roadmap for successful business regulation reforms.[50] It also reflects the need to respond to many stakeholders and interest groups, all of whom bring important issues and concerns to the reform debate.

When the World Bank Group engages with governments on the subject of improving the investment climate, the dialogue aims to encourage the critical use of the *Doing Business* data—to sharpen judgment and promote broad-based reforms that enhance the investment climate rather than a narrow focus on improving the *Doing Business* rankings. The World Bank Group uses a vast range of indicators and analytics in this policy dialogue, including its Global Poverty Monitoring Indicators, World Development Indicators, Logistics Performance Indicators and many others. The open data initiative has made data for many such indicators conveniently available to the public at http://data .worldbank.org.

## METHODOLOGY AND DATA

The *Doing Business* data are based on domestic laws and regulations as well as administrative requirements. The data cover 185 economies—including small economies and some of the poorest economies, for which little or no data are available in other data sets. (For a detailed explanation of the *Doing Business* methodology, see the data notes.)

## *Doing Business* respondents

Over the past 10 years more than 18,000 professionals in 185 economies have assisted in providing the data that inform the *Doing Business* indicators. This year's report draws on the inputs of more than 9,600 professionals.[51] Table 20.2 in the data notes lists the number of respondents for each indicator set. The *Doing Business* website shows the number of respondents for each economy and each indicator. Respondents are professionals who routinely administer or advise on the legal and regulatory requirements covered in each *Doing Business* topic. They are selected on the basis of their expertise in the specific areas covered by *Doing Business*. Because of the focus on legal and regulatory arrangements, most of the respondents are legal professionals such as lawyers, judges or notaries. The credit information survey is answered by officials of the credit registry or bureau. Freight forwarders, accountants, architects, engineers and other professionals answer the surveys related to trading across borders, taxes and construction permits. Certain public officials (such as registrars from the commercial or property registry) also provide information that is incorporated into the indicators.

## Information sources for the data

Most of the *Doing Business* indicators are based on laws and regulations. In addition, most of the cost indicators are backed by official fee schedules. *Doing Business* respondents both fill out written questionnaires and provide references to the relevant laws, regulations and fee schedules, aiding data checking and quality assurance. Having representative samples of respondents is not an issue, as the texts of the relevant laws and regulations are collected and answers checked for accuracy.

For some indicators—for example, those on dealing with construction permits, enforcing contracts and resolving insolvency—the time component and part of the cost component (where fee schedules are lacking) are based on actual practice rather than the law on the books. This introduces a degree of judgment. The *Doing Business* approach has therefore been to work with legal practitioners or professionals who regularly undertake the transactions involved. Following the standard methodological approach for time-and-motion studies, *Doing Business* breaks down each process or transaction, such as starting a business or registering a building, into separate steps to ensure a better estimate of time. The time estimate for each step is given by practitioners with significant and routine experience in the transaction. When time estimates differ, further interactions with respondents are pursued to converge on one estimate that reflects the majority of applicable cases.

The *Doing Business* approach to data collection contrasts with that of firm surveys, which capture perceptions and experiences of businesses. A corporate lawyer registering 100–150 businesses a year will be more familiar with the process than an entrepreneur, who will register a business only once or maybe twice. A bankruptcy attorney or judge dealing with dozens of cases a year will have more insight into bankruptcy than a company that may undergo the process once.

## Development of the methodology

The methodology for calculating each indicator is transparent, objective and easily replicable. Leading academics collaborate in the development of the indicators, ensuring academic rigor. Eight of the background papers underlying the indicators have been published in leading economic journals.[52]

*Doing Business* uses a simple averaging approach for weighting component indicators and calculating rankings and the distance to frontier measure. Other approaches were explored, including using principal components and unobserved components.[53] They turn out to yield results nearly identical to those of simple averaging. In the absence of a strong theoretical framework that assigns different weights to the topics covered for the 185 economies by *Doing Business*, the simplest method is used: weighting all topics equally and, within each topic, giving equal weight to each of the topic components (for more details, see the chapter on the ease of doing business and distance to frontier).[54]

## Improvements to the methodology

The methodology has undergone continual improvement over the years. For enforcing contracts, for example, the amount of the disputed claim in the case study was increased from 50% of income per capita to 200% after the first year of data collection, as it became clear that smaller claims were unlikely to go to court.

Another change related to starting a business. The minimum capital requirement can be an obstacle for potential entrepreneurs. *Doing Business* measured the required minimum capital regardless of whether it had to be paid up front or not. In many economies only part of the minimum capital has to be paid up front. To reflect the relevant barrier to entry, the paid-in minimum capital has been used rather than the required minimum capital.

This year's report includes an update in the ranking methodology for paying taxes. Last year's report introduced a threshold for the total tax rate for the purpose of calculating the ranking on the ease of paying taxes. This change came as a result of consultations on the survey instrument and methodology for the paying taxes indicators with external stakeholders, including participants in the International Tax Dialogue. All economies with a total tax rate below the threshold (which is calculated and adjusted on a yearly basis) now receive the same ranking on the total tax rate indicator. This year's threshold is set at the 15th percentile of the total tax rate distribution, which translates into a threshold for the total tax rate of 25.7%.

## Data adjustments

All changes in methodology are explained in the data notes as well as on the *Doing Business* website. In addition, data time series for each indicator and economy are available on the website, beginning with the first year the indicator or economy was included in the report. To provide a comparable time series for research, the data set is back-calculated to adjust for changes in methodology and any revisions in data due to corrections. The data set is not back-calculated for year-to-year revisions in income per capita data (that is, when the income per capita data are revised by the original data sources, *Doing Business* does not update the cost measures for previous years). The website also makes available all original data sets used for background papers.

Information on data corrections is provided in the data notes and on the website. A transparent complaint procedure allows anyone to challenge the data. If errors are confirmed after a data verification process, they are expeditiously corrected.

---

## NOTES

1. World Bank 2005; Stampini and others 2011.

2. See, for example, Alesina and others (2005); Perotti and Volpin (2005); Fisman and Sarria-Allende (2010); Antunes and Cavalcanti (2007); Barseghyan (2008); Klapper, Lewin and Quesada Delgado (2009); Freund and Bolaky (2008); Chang, Kaltani and Loayza (2009); Helpman, Melitz and Rubinstein (2008); Klapper, Laeven and Rajan (2006); World Bank (2005); and Ardagna and Lusardi (2010).

3. This includes Djankov and others (2002); Djankov, McLiesh and Shleifer (2007); Djankov, La Porta and others (2008); Djankov, Freund and Pham (2010); Djankov and others (2003); Djankov, Hart and others (2008); Botero and others (2004); and Djankov and others (2010).

4. For more details on how the aggregate ranking is created, see the chapter on the ease of doing business and distance to frontier.

5. This has included a review by the World Bank Independent Evaluation Group

(2008), input from the International Tax Dialogue and regular input from the Indicators Advisory Group.

6. http://www.doingbusiness.org.

7. Local experts in 185 economies are surveyed annually to collect and update the data. The local experts for each economy are listed on the *Doing Business* website (http://www.doingbusiness.org) and in the acknowledgments at the end of this report.

8. De Soto 2000.

9. Schneider 2005; La Porta and Shleifer 2008.

10. Amin 2011.

11. http://www.enterprisesurveys.org.

12. Narayan and others 2000.

13. OECD, "Indicators of Product Market Regulation," http://www.oecd.org/. The measures are aggregated into 3 broad families that capture state control, barriers to entrepreneurship and barriers to international trade and investment. The 39 countries included in the OECD market regulation indicators are Australia, Austria, Belgium, Brazil, Canada, Chile, China, the Czech Republic, Denmark, Estonia, Finland, France, Germany, Greece, Hungary, Iceland, India, Ireland, Israel, Italy, Japan, Korea, Luxembourg, Mexico, the Netherlands, New Zealand, Norway, Poland, Portugal, Russia, the Slovak Republic, Slovenia, South Africa, Spain, Sweden, Switzerland, Turkey, the United Kingdom and the United States.

14. The World Economic Forum's *Global Competitiveness Report* uses *Doing Business* data sets on starting a business, employing workers, protecting investors and getting credit (legal rights), representing 7 of a total of 113 different indicators (or 6.19%).

15. Hallward-Driemeier, Khun-Jush and Pritchett (2010), analyzing data from World Bank Enterprise Surveys for Sub-Saharan Africa, show that de jure measures such as *Doing Business* indicators are virtually uncorrelated with ex post firm-level responses, providing evidence that deals rather than rules prevail in Africa. The authors find that the gap between de jure and de facto conditions grows with the formal regulatory burden. The evidence also shows that more burdensome processes open up more space for making deals and that firms may not incur the official costs of compliance but still pay to avoid them.

16. Much attention has been given to exploring links to microeconomic outcomes, such as firm creation and employment. Recent research focuses on how business regulations affect the behavior of firms by creating incentives (or disincentives) to register and operate formally, to create jobs, to innovate and to increase productivity. For details, see Djankov and others (2002); Alesina and others (2005); Banerjee and Duflo (2005); Perotti and Volpin (2005); Klapper, Laeven and Rajan (2006); Fisman and Sarria-Allende (2010); Antunes and Cavalcanti (2007); Barseghyan (2008); Eifert (2009); Klapper, Lewin and Quesada Delgado (2009); Djankov, Freund and Pham (2010); Klapper and Love (2011a); Chari (2011); and Bruhn (2011).

17. According to searches for citations of the 9 background papers that serve as the basis for the *Doing Business* indicators in the Social Science Citation Index and on Google Scholar (http://scholar .google.com).

18. Djankov, McLiesh and Ramalho 2006.

19. Eifert 2009.

20. Klapper, Lewin and Quesada Delgado 2009. *Entry rate* refers to newly registered firms as a percentage of total registered firms. *Business density* is defined as the total number of businesses as a percentage of the working-age population (ages 18–65).

21. Ciccone and Papaioannou 2007.

22. Alesina and others 2005.

23. Loayza, Oviedo and Servén 2005; Barseghyan 2008.

24. Dulleck, Frijters and Winter-Ebmer 2006; Calderon, Chong and Leon 2007; Micco and Pagés 2006.

25. Masatlioglu and Rigolini 2008; Djankov 2009.

26. Cardenas and Rozo 2009.

27. Bruhn 2011.

28. Kaplan, Piedra and Seira 2007.

29. Bruhn 2012.

30. Aghion and others 2008.

31. Sharma 2009.

32. Chari 2011.

33. Branstetter and others 2010.

34. Djankov, Freund and Pham 2010.

35. Iwanow and Kirkpatrick 2009.

36. Freund and Rocha 2011.

37. Seker 2011.

38. Portugal-Perez and Wilson 2011.

39. Hoekman and Nicita 2011.

40. Nunn 2007.

41. Rauch 2010.

42. Chang, Kaltani and Loayza 2009; Cuñat and Melitz 2007.

43. http://www.enterprisesurveys.org.

44. Haselmann, Pistor and Vig 2010. The countries studied were Bulgaria, Croatia, the Czech Republic, Estonia, Hungary, Latvia, Lithuania, Poland, Romania, the Slovak Republic, Slovenia and Ukraine.

45. Djankov, McLiesh and Shleifer 2007; Houston and others 2010.

46. Visaria 2009. In a follow-up study, von Lilienfeld-Toal, Mookherjee and Visaria (2012) found that the average effects identified by Visaria (2009) differ between wealthy and poor borrowers when the credit supply is inelastic (because of limits in such resources as funds, staff and information). In particular, they found that in the short term after the debt recovery tribunals are introduced, borrowers with less collateral may experience a reduction in access to credit while those with more collateral may experience an increase. But the authors also point out that this short-term effect disappears over time as banks are able to increase their resources and the credit supply becomes elastic.

47. Funchal 2008.

48. Giné and Love (2010) on Colombia; Dewaelheyns and Van Hulle (2008) on Belgium.

49. Franks and others 2011.

50. One recent study using *Doing Business* indicators illustrates the difficulties in using highly disaggregated indicators to identify reform priorities (Kraay and Tawara 2011).

51. While about 9,600 contributors provided data for this year's report, many of them completed a survey for more than one *Doing Business* indicator set. Indeed, the total number of surveys completed for this year's report is more than 12,000, which represents a truer measure of the inputs received. The average number of surveys per indicator set and economy is just under 6. For more details, see http://www .doingbusiness.org/contributors/ doing-business.

52. All background papers are available on the *Doing Business* website (http://www .doingbusiness.org).

53. For more details, see the chapter on the ease of doing business and distance to frontier.

54. A technical note on the different aggregation and weighting methods is available on the *Doing Business* website (http://www.doingbusiness.org).

# Colombia: sustaining reforms over time

- Colombia's experience shows the importance of sustaining reform efforts over time and adjusting them to the changing needs of the economy, whether at the national or local level.

- Colombia is a regional leader in narrowing the gap with the world's most efficient regulatory practice.

- Over time, the focus of Colombia's reform efforts has shifted from reducing the cost and complexity of business regulation to strengthening legal institutions.

- Colombia's most notable regulatory improvements have been in the areas of starting a business, paying taxes, protecting investors and resolving insolvency.

- While development hurdles remain, Colombia's regulatory reforms have increased its competitiveness and have had local and regional "spillover" effects.

Over the past several decades Colombia has pursued a broad range of structural and institutional reforms. The emphasis has shifted over the years, reflecting the priorities of different administrations and the perceived needs of the economy. In the 1980s and early 1990s much of the focus was on macroeconomic management.[1] As progress was made in laying a firm foundation of macroeconomic stability, the focus shifted to other areas. The government gave particular emphasis to policies and institutions seen as central to enhancing productivity and growth and boosting the country's competitiveness. As part of this, it set in motion reforms aimed at improving the regulatory framework and the rules underpinning private sector activity. The Ministry of Commerce, Industry and Tourism led a coordinated reform effort bringing together government agencies, the Congress and the judiciary as well as the private sector.

In 2007 Colombia's government further institutionalized its commitment to regulatory reform by establishing the Private Council for Competitiveness. A public-private partnership, the council is made up of business associations and private sector players working closely with the government to promote sound, business-friendly regulatory practices.[2]

Recent administrations have continued to use national development plans to establish a clear economic agenda. In 2009 President Alvaro Uribe highlighted Colombia's progress and his government's plans for new regulatory reforms aimed at further gains in competitiveness.[3] And since the change of legislature

in August 2010, the new government, led by President Juan Manuel Santos, has been pushing forward an economic reform agenda through the "Prosperity for All" national development plan for 2010–14. The plan's overall goals are to reduce poverty, increase income, generate employment, improve security, ensure the sustainable use of natural resources and improve the quality of the business environment.[4]

## SUSTAINED EFFORT AT THE NATIONAL LEVEL

As Colombia has improved its business regulatory environment, results have shown in *Doing Business* indicators—including those on starting a business, paying taxes, protecting investors and resolving insolvency. Indeed, thanks to its sustained efforts, Colombia has made greater progress toward the frontier in regulatory practice since 2005 than any other Latin American economy (figure 3.1).

Other indicators also reflect the improvements. The total number of newly registered businesses in the country rose from 33,752 in 2006 to 57,768 in 2011.[5] Colombia's performance on several relevant measures compiled by the Worldwide Governance Indicators project improved between 2002 and 2010—including the Rule of Law Index (reflecting perceptions of the extent to which firms have confidence in and abide by the rules of society) and the Regulatory Quality Index (capturing perceptions of the government's ability to formulate and implement sound policies and regulations that permit and promote private sector development).[6]

FIGURE 3.1  Colombia has outpaced the region in advancing toward the frontier in regulatory practice

Progress in narrowing distance to frontier since 2005 (percentage points)

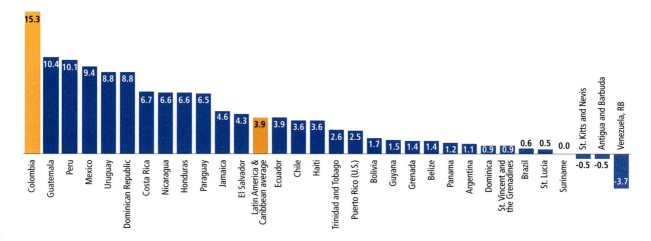

*Note:* The distance to frontier measure shows how far on average an economy is from the best performance achieved by any economy on each *Doing Business* indicator since 2005. The measure is normalized to range between 0 and 100, with 100 representing the best performance (the frontier). The figure shows the absolute difference for each economy between its distance to frontier in 2005 and that in 2012. No data are shown for The Bahamas and Barbados, which were added to the *Doing Business* sample after 2005.

*Source: Doing Business* database.

And Colombia's ranking on the ease of doing business rose from 79 among the 175 economies included in 2006 to 45 among the 185 included in 2012.

FIGURE 3.2  A trend toward stronger legal institutions and less expensive regulatory processes in Colombia

Average distance to frontier in sets of *Doing Business* indicators

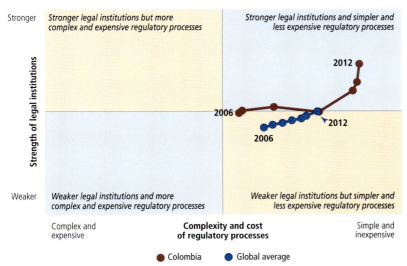

*Note: Strength of legal institutions* refers to the average distance to frontier in getting credit, protecting investors, enforcing contracts and resolving insolvency. *Complexity and cost of regulatory processes* refers to the average distance to frontier in starting a business, dealing with construction permits, registering property, paying taxes and trading across borders. The distance to frontier measure shows how far on average an economy is from the best performance achieved by any economy on each *Doing Business* indicator since 2005.

*Source: Doing Business* database.

## Choosing a reform path

While Colombia simultaneously pursued very different types of regulatory reforms, it first completed those aimed at streamlining business regulation and reducing its cost to companies. Until 2008 the focus was largely on reducing transactions costs, such as by simplifying business start-up procedures or tax administration. These types of reforms have continued since 2008, but the focus has shifted toward strengthening legal institutions such as bankruptcy systems and investor protections (figure 3.2).

This sequencing of reforms is not unusual. Many economies have focused first on simplifying regulatory transactions for businesses, then moved on to more complex and time-consuming reforms aimed at improving legal institutions such as court systems. Such reforms require more sustained efforts, often over a period of several years.

## Encouraging business start-ups

Regulatory reforms implemented by Colombia in recent years have made a clear difference in the ease of starting a business as measured by *Doing Business*. They have reduced the time required to start a business from 60 days to 14, the cost from 28% of income per capita to

8% and the number of procedures from 19 to 9 in 2011 (figure 3.3).

The introduction and subsequent upgrades of one-stop shops for business registration at chambers of commerce account for much of the change. The first one-stop shops started to operate in May 2003. As the changes in the start-up process yielded positive results, the government continued to improve it. In 2005, for example, Law 962—the "*antitrámites*" ("antipaperwork") law—eliminated around 80 bureaucratic processes required to start a business and introduced a provision preventing government agencies from creating new procedures. It also simplified the procedures required by allowing electronic submission of documents and eliminating the need to have signatures notarized.

More improvements came in 2010. A new public-private health provider, Nueva EPS, replaced the previous provider administered by the Social Security Institute. The new system enables employers and employees to register for health services in just 1 week. In addition, Colombia introduced online preenrollment for new companies, making registration faster and simpler.

New regulations recently introduced a progressive fee schedule for new companies.[7] The fee schedule exempts new firms from up-front payment of regulatory fees during their first few years of operation. And the start-up fee associated with the commercial license is no longer required.

## Simplifying tax compliance

Over the years Colombia has greatly improved its tax and social security compliance processes. In 2002, as the government realized that about a third of its potential revenue from corporate income, personal income and value added taxes went uncollected, it decided to introduce an electronic payment system in an attempt to lower tax evasion.[8]

In 2009 the government lowered corporate income tax rates and introduced an online form for social contribution

**FIGURE 3.3** Starting a business is now faster and less costly in Colombia

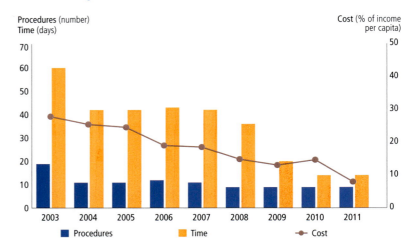

Source: *Doing Business* database.

payments. This form simplified tax compliance for Colombian businesses by combining into a single online payment all contributions for social security, the welfare security system and labor risk insurance.

To further improve and simplify tax compliance, in 2010 the government made electronic filing of corporate income tax and value added tax mandatory for firms with annual sales exceeding 500 million Colombian pesos (about $280,000) in or after 2008.

Thanks to these continued efforts, paying taxes as measured by *Doing Business* became considerably easier between 2004 and 2010. The number of payments fell from 69 a year to 9, and the time needed to prepare and file taxes from 456 hours a year to 193. And the total tax rate declined from 82.1% of profit to 74.8% in this period (figure 3.4).

## Enhancing investor protections

Starting in 2005, Colombia implemented 3 major legal reforms aimed at strengthening investor protections. In 2005 Colombia enacted Law 964, providing

**FIGURE 3.4** Colombia has made tax compliance simpler for businesses

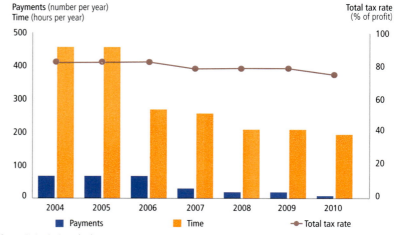

Source: *Doing Business* database.

FIGURE 3.5  Legal and regulatory changes have strengthened investor protections in Colombia

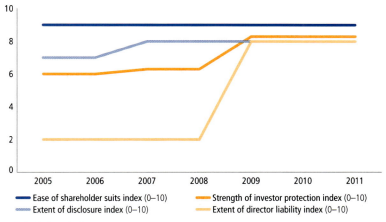

- Ease of shareholder suits index (0–10)
- Extent of disclosure index (0–10)
- Strength of investor protection index (0–10)
- Extent of director liability index (0–10)

*Source: Doing Business database.*

a modern framework for capital market activity. The law encourages better corporate governance practices by requiring greater transparency and disclosure, equitable treatment of minority shareholders and more effective boards of directors.

In 2007 the government amended Colombia's securities regulation. Decree 3139 requires listed companies to report more information to investors. Before, listed companies had to report any "relevant" or "extraordinary" event—a subjective standard open to abuse. Although the decree still includes the broad "relevant" requirement, it lists specific events that must be disclosed to the financial authorities. It also requires companies to report extensive information before going public.

In 2010 the government made further progress by amending the company law. The amendments clarified the liability regime for company directors involved in related-party transactions that harm the company. Now directors can be forced to pay damages and disgorge profits made from such transactions.

As a result of these changes, Colombia's scores have improved on both the extent of director liability index (which measures the liability of company executives for abusive related-party transactions) and the extent of disclosure index (which

measures the approval and disclosure regime for related-party transactions; figure 3.5).

## Making insolvency proceedings more efficient

Colombia's insolvency reforms began almost 2 decades ago. In 1995 the enactment of Law 222, allowing debtors and creditors to resolve disputes before the Superintendence of Companies, helped ease the burden on the judiciary. In 1999 changes to the reorganization law improved the existing corporate reorganization proceedings and introduced new time limits for negotiations. These changes increased the efficiency of the bankruptcy system and improved its capacity to distinguish between viable and nonviable businesses.[9]

Another series of insolvency reforms took place in the past 6 years. Thanks to these reforms, creditors' recovery rate rose from 56 cents on the dollar to 76 and the time to complete a liquidation proceeding fell from 3 years to 1.3.

The reforms began with a comprehensive revision of the insolvency proceedings available. In 2007 authorities introduced 2 new proceedings: a reorganization procedure to restructure insolvent companies and a mandatory liquidation procedure. And a new insolvency law

imposed more stringent time limits for negotiating reorganization agreements.

In 2009 the government issued several decrees as part of continued efforts to better regulate the profession of insolvency administrators. In addition, it introduced an electronic filing system to make insolvency proceedings faster and more efficient. And it eliminated the requirement to submit financial statements to request reorganization in cases where these statements had previously been submitted to the Superintendence of Companies.

## Improving other areas of regulation

Colombia has also made improvements in other areas of regulation. In 1995 the country undertook a complete overhaul of its construction approvals. It moved the administration of building permits out of the state-run planning office into the private domain, becoming the first economy in Latin America to privatize the review process. This move carried risks, but public and private stakeholders in the country were calling for comprehensive change.

Bogotá's mayor first appointed 5 ad hoc "urban curators," all architects or engineers with construction experience, to review building permit applications. Soon after, a more transparent, merit-based hiring system was established that is still in place. Potential curators now undergo a selection process that includes exams and interviews with public and private sector experts. Privatizing the issuance of building permits improved timeliness and freed up the planning office's resources.

In other regulatory areas, introducing electronic systems made processes easier. When registering property, a business can now obtain online certification of valuation, ownership and good standing for property taxes. And for properties with no liens, it can submit online certificates directly to the land registry. Certificates have no cost if requested online.

An electronic data interchange system was introduced for exports, making it possible to centralize electronic data. The new system also allows traders to pay duties electronically, eliminating the need to go to a bank to submit payments. And it allows shippers to share information with customs electronically, so that customs declarations can be processed before the vessel even arrives at the port. Most importantly, since 2008 Colombia has implemented improvements to the Single Window for Foreign Trade (VUCE) system. The system now connects over a dozen government agencies that are involved in import and export procedures.

## SPILLOVER TO THE LOCAL LEVEL

Colombia has been actively reforming its regulatory environment at the local as well as the national level. Local efforts have been inspired in part by a subnational study. Carried out through the National Department of Planning, the 2008 study was designed to analyze the regulatory environment in different regions with the aim of improving regional competitiveness across the country. The study was also intended to enable Colombian cities to learn from one another and adopt good practices from elsewhere in the country.

The subnational *Doing Business* report resulting from the study was soon followed by another, and work on a third began in 2012.[10] The second report showed that all 12 cities included in the first one had improved on at least one *Doing Business* indicator.

Among these 12 cities, Neiva made the most progress in improving the ease of doing business. Local authorities took several measures to increase the city's competitiveness, including creating an anti-red-tape committee to reduce the regulatory burden on the private sector. The committee encompassed wide representation, with participants from the municipality, the chamber of commerce, business associations and national agencies such as police and tax authorities.

Neiva's local government also set up one-stop shops for registering new companies. This eliminated 11 procedures and reduced the time required to register a business from 32 days to 8. The success of the one-stop shops has been due largely to cooperation between municipal and national government departments.

Medellín is another city that substantially improved its business regulatory environment. The city government cut 3 procedures required to start a business by improving one-stop shops and eliminating the requirement for a land use certificate. And it made registering property easier by merging 2 certificates and eliminating a stamp previously required as proof of registration tax compliance.

## CONCLUSION

Colombia's commitment to regulatory reform has led to substantial improvements in the quality of the business environment and a more solid foundation for private sector development. Its experience shows the importance of sustaining reform efforts over time and adjusting them to the changing needs of the economy. Initially, most of the regulatory reforms took place at the national level. But as the business environment continued to improve, the reforms spilled over to the local level.

Colombia's experience is having "spillover" effects in the region as well. Bolivia has shown an interest in learning more about Colombia's experience with business entry. Paraguay has sought to learn from Colombia's innovations in construction permitting. And both Costa Rica and El Salvador intend to learn from Colombia's trade logistics reforms.

Colombia's experience also shows the importance of setting out economic policy objectives. The government's commitment to well-defined, long-term economic goals has helped drive implementation of the reforms. Having made major strides in safeguarding macroeconomic stability, the government widened the focus of its policies to include a range of institutional and economic reforms aimed at boosting productivity. The steady pace of change led to the development of the broader competitiveness agenda and the creation of a public-private partnership aimed at promoting business-friendly regulatory practices.

Yet despite the government's sustained efforts, and its success in improving the business climate and implementing an ambitious competitiveness agenda, a number of challenges remain. Addressing income inequality remains a key priority, in part because it would strengthen support in the business community and in civil society for the government's overall development strategies.

While the country has more development hurdles to overcome, the measures taken over the past years have greatly improved its competitiveness. The regulatory reforms may take more time to show full results in all areas of doing business, but they have already led to substantial immediate benefits. Colombia's reform agenda is expected to continue to expand—and to inspire further improvements in the region.

### NOTES

This case study was written by Valentina Saltane and Hayane Chang Dahmen.

1.  According to the International Monetary Fund, average annual inflation in Colombia fell from 23% in the 1980s to 6% by the 2000s. Management of public finances also improved, with public deficits in recent years lower as a percentage of GDP. Colombia's general government public debt was 35.9% of GDP in 2009, low by international standards ("IMF Data Mapper," http://www.imf.org/).

2.  Consejo Privado de Competitividad, http://www.compite.com.co/site/sistema-nacional-de-competitividad/.

3.  Remarks delivered before the Americas Society/Council of the Americas, September 24, 2009. Available at http://www.as-coa.org/article.php?id=1908.

4.  International Fund for Agricultural Development, "Rural Poverty Portal," http://www.ruralpovertyportal.org/.

5.  *Doing Business* database; World Bank

Group Entrepreneurship Snapshots database.

6. World Bank, Worldwide Governance Indicators, "2011 Update," http://www .govindicators.org. The Rule of Law Index and the Regulatory Quality Index both range from −2.5 (weak) to 2.5 (strong). On the Rule of Law Index Colombia's score rose from −0.84 in 2002 to −0.33 in 2010. On the Regulatory Quality Index its score rose from 0.05 in 2002 to 0.31 in 2010.

7. Law 1429 of 2010 and Decree 545 of 2011.

8. Sohn 2008.

9. Giné and Love 2010.

10. Subnational *Doing Business* reports are available at http://www.doingbusiness .org/reports/subnational-reports.

2007 2012 2011 2005 2009 2004 2008 2006 2010 2013

# Latvia: maintaining a reform state of mind

- For Latvia, accession to the European Union has been among the main motivations for improving business regulation.
- Latvia's reform agenda has benefited from strong public support for economic integration.
- Since 2004 the country has made positive changes across all areas measured by *Doing Business*.
- Despite being substantially affected by the financial crisis starting in 2008, Latvia continued its reform agenda, adapting it to the new challenges the country was facing.

Latvia has made substantial economic progress since its transition to a liberal market economy in the 1990s. Income per capita has more than tripled over the past 15 years despite a deep recession following the global financial crisis.[1] Exports grew by almost 7% a year in the 2000s, and the share of the population living on less than $4 a day fell from 25.8% in 1998 to 3.4% in 2008, the latest year for which this information is available.[2]

Economic reforms have been a central part of this process. Structural reforms have increased competitiveness and facilitated integration with the world economy. Reforms to business laws and regulations have substantially improved the investment climate. Since the late 1990s successive governments have held a regular dialogue with the private sector and international organizations to identify and implement ways to streamline business registration, improve the tax system and increase the efficiency of international trade, among many other such reforms.[3]

These reform efforts have been sustained through changing domestic and international conditions. They began as part of a process to join the European Union (EU). They continued during a period of rapid growth in the mid-2000s. And they have persisted during the significant economic downturn following the financial crisis. Throughout this transition there were many changes in political leadership—but the commitment to legislative and regulatory reform endured.

What enabled this continued commitment to reform? How has Latvia made such

significant improvements to its regulatory environment—advancing further toward the frontier in regulatory practice than almost all other EU member economies (figure 4.1)? And what lessons can be learned about this "reform state of mind" demonstrated by Latvia?

## REFORMING FOR THE EUROPEAN UNION

Broad consensus for reform emerged in Latvia in the late 1990s, as the country transitioned to a liberal market economy after regaining independence in 1991. Integration into the world economy was a commonly held goal, and the Latvian government and business community began a dialogue on how to achieve it. Latvia joined the World Trade Organization in 1999, then targeted membership in the European Union.

The goal of EU accession provided a structure for an array of legislative and regulatory reforms. The EU membership requirements, known as the Copenhagen criteria, provided a series of general directives for reforms centered on democratic governance, human rights, a market economy and commitment to European integration. Latvia also began harmonizing its laws with the body of EU legislation, the *acquis communautaire*, including in ways to reduce administrative barriers to investment. In 1999 the Latvian Cabinet of Ministers adopted an action plan to improve the business environment and welcomed support from international financial institutions to implement the reforms.[4]

These reform efforts proved very successful: by 2003, 91 of 106 reforms

FIGURE 4.1  Latvia has made big advances toward the frontier in regulatory practice

Progress in narrowing distance to frontier since 2005 (percentage points)

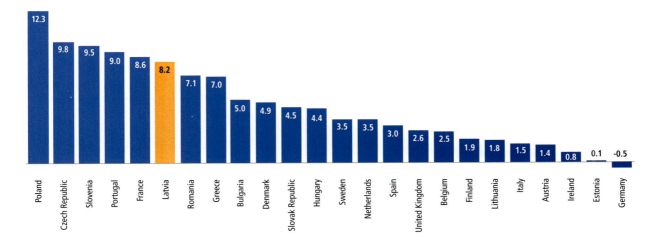

*Note:* The distance to frontier measure shows how far on average an economy is from the best performance achieved by any economy on each *Doing Business* indicator since 2005. The measure is normalized to range between 0 and 100, with 100 representing the best performance (the frontier). The figure shows the absolute difference for each economy between its distance to frontier in 2005 and that in 2012. It shows data for all current EU members except Cyprus, Luxembourg and Malta, which were added to the *Doing Business* sample after 2005.

*Source: Doing Business* database.

initially identified in 1999 had been implemented.[5] During this initial reform phase the government focused on improving aspects of the investment climate that had been raised as issues by the Latvian business community.

One focus was streamlining business registration. The government simplified the procedures required, such as by combining company and tax registration. By 2004 starting a business in Latvia took only 5 procedures and 16 days—less time than in all but 21 economies covered by *Doing Business 2005.* The change was dramatic: in 1999 opening a business in Latvia had required 17 procedures and 114 days.

The government also improved business inspections. Most business inspectorates in Latvia were perceived as obstructing rather than enabling legitimate business in their enforcement of government regulations. The government requested that inspectorate reform be included as a conditionality of financing from the World Bank.[6] Later efforts provided new instruction on the rights and responsibilities

of government inspectors and private firms, introduced a requirement for written reports after all inspections and developed performance indicators for inspectorates.[7]

Construction permitting was another target of regulatory reform. In 2001 it took Latvian businesses 2 years to obtain all the licenses and inspections required to build a warehouse. By 2004 the government had reduced the time required to obtain a building permit by 2 months, simply by preparing a flowchart showing what offices to visit and which documents to take.[8] Further improvements followed, including amendments to the construction code and the establishment of a public register for construction companies.

The government improved tax administration by amending the laws on value added and corporate income tax to resolve specific issues identified by businesses. Draft tax legislation was posted online for public comment, and an appeals body was established in the State Revenue Service.[9]

Latvia enjoyed significant growth during this initial reform period. From 2000 to 2004 GDP growth averaged 7.5%, and unemployment fell from 14.2% to 9.9%.[10] In May 2004 Latvia achieved its goal of joining the European Union.

## CONTINUING THE AGENDA

Latvia's strong economic performance continued after the country became an EU member. From 2005 to 2007 economic growth averaged nearly 11% a year. The number of newly registered firms rose from around 7,000 a year to 12,000. And exports of goods and services grew by more than 5% a year, with a peak in growth of 20% in 2005.[11]

Business regulation reforms continued as well. Rather than relaxing the reform agenda after becoming an EU member, Latvia continued working to enhance its competitiveness by bringing its economic laws, regulations and institutions further into line with those of Western European countries.[12] The action plan initially established in 1999 was regularly amended to identify new areas to target with regulatory reforms. *Doing Business* has tracked the success of many of these reforms over time.

One set of improvements made property registration faster and easier. Businesses trying to expand were being hindered by complex administrative procedures to access land, leading to long delays and considerable uncertainty. The government responded by installing electronic terminals at the land registry, enabling businesses to pay fees and stamp duties at the same time that they registered property. It also granted the land registry electronic access to municipal tax databases, eliminating the requirement to obtain the property tax status in paper format. As a result, the time required to transfer property fell from 55 days in 2004 to 18 in 2012 (figure 4.2).

Construction permitting, a focus of earlier efforts, received renewed attention in response to investors' complaints that unclear fee schedules were a burden to construction activity. The government established a more transparent set of construction fees and duties, reducing the cost associated with completing the procedures to legally build a warehouse from 43.5% of income per capita in 2006 to 18.6% in 2012.

Even after Latvia's accession to the European Union, some regulatory reforms were still driven by the integration process. One was the adoption of an electronic customs system, triggered by the implementation of EU regulations in 2009. Entry and exit declaration forms can now be submitted electronically, and a requirement to submit customs information in advance allows the system to perform computerized risk analysis before goods are presented to customs.

Continuing its improvements in tax administration, Latvia introduced a process for electronic submission and acceptance of tax declarations in 2005 and 2006. This reduced the number of tax payments as measured by Doing Business from 29 a year to 7 in 2006.

**FIGURE 4.2  Latvia made transferring property simpler and faster**

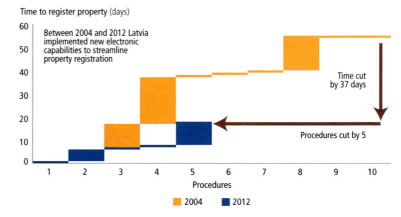

Source: Doing Business database.

More recently, Latvia made getting electricity easier by streamlining the approval process for connection designs for straightforward projects. Before 2011 an entrepreneur in Riga had to wait more than 6 months to connect a warehouse to the electricity network. Reducing the number of approvals that were required shortened the wait by almost 3 months— a change that earned Latvia recognition in Doing Business 2012 as having made the biggest improvement in the ease of getting electricity in the year covered by the report.

## CONFRONTING THE CRISIS WITH REFORMS

The global financial crisis brought Latvia's strong economic growth to a halt. Much of the growth had been driven by increased domestic demand enabled by substantial inflows of foreign capital, and when the capital inflows ceased, the economy went into a deep recession starting in 2008.[13] Latvia responded by undertaking significant structural reforms, including reductions in public spending and wage moderation in the public sector. The public broadly supported the main thrust of the authorities' response to the crisis, and election results in October 2010 endorsed the government's reform efforts.[14]

Despite the economic turmoil associated with the financial crisis—or perhaps because of it—Latvia also implemented

a series of new business regulation reforms. The crisis highlighted the need for greater resilience to such shocks in the future and for greater access to finance. It also underscored the need to reduce administrative barriers to investment. The Latvian authorities responded with reforms targeting the insolvency regime, the credit information system and corporate governance.

The insolvency law was amended in 2008 to ensure a better balance between the interests of debtors and creditors and to facilitate the recovery of companies experiencing financial problems. The changes included allowing easier access to insolvency and restructuring procedures, introducing faster procedures for selling a debtor's assets and implementing stricter qualification standards for insolvency administrators. In 2009 further amendments to the insolvency law introduced a mechanism for settling insolvencies out of court to ease pressure on the judiciary. As a result of these reforms, the recovery rate for creditors rose from 32 cents on the dollar to 56 between 2010 and 2011, leading to the biggest improvement in the ease of resolving insolvency worldwide according to Doing Business 2012.

Another focus was expanding the credit information system. In 2008 the Bank of Latvia's registry of debtors was transformed into a full-fledged credit registry.

FIGURE 4.3  More and better credit information in Latvia

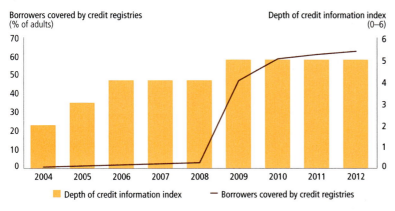

Source: Doing Business database.

It now collects both positive and negative information on borrowers, borrower guarantors and their obligations. The registry is also able to record more precise information, such as the type of settlement of the borrower's obligations and the date on which settlement of a delayed payment is registered. And the registry expanded its coverage from 3.5% of adults in 2008 to 63.8% in 2012 (figure 4.3).

With the goal of increasing investors' confidence in the market, Latvia also introduced more robust corporate governance measures. The government amended the company law to harmonize with the EU *acquis communautaire*, including by improving disclosure mechanisms and increasing transparency.[15] And in 2010 the Riga Stock Exchange issued corporate governance principles and recommendations related to disclosure requirements, remuneration policy and conflicts of interest, further strengthening corporate governance rules for listed companies.

## WHAT ARE THE LESSONS?

Latvia has sustained a clear commitment to business regulation reform over more than a decade, under changing political leadership and through economic booms and downturns. What factors have enabled this impressive commitment?

One is the structural incentive provided by economic integration. The EU requirements of committing to democratic institutions and processes, strengthening the institutional underpinnings of a free market and harmonizing laws with EU legislation provided an actionable roadmap. Results are reflected in Latvia's improvement on the Worldwide Governance Indicators between 2000 and 2005, including on the Regulatory Quality Index.[16] In addition, the potential economic benefits of joining the European Union created strong public support for the reform agenda. This combination of EU requirements and potential economic benefits made it possible to sustain the implementation of both broad structural reforms and specific business regulation reforms.

Similar support for economic reform after the crisis can be linked to a desire for further integration with the European Union, including as a future full member of the euro zone. Devaluation of the Latvian currency against the euro was a policy option for mitigating the effects of the crisis, and it might arguably have implied lower short-term economic costs than cuts in public spending. But the government opted instead to intensify the pace of structural reforms; it viewed maintaining the currency peg less in terms of the purely macroeconomic effects and more as part of its long-term strategy for strengthening links with the European Union, particularly the members of the euro zone.[17] This approach was broadly endorsed by the business community and the population.

That economic integration can provide useful incentives is not a new lesson: *Doing Business 2012* identified a similar association between successful reforms in FYR Macedonia and its preparations ahead of eventual EU entry. But the case of Latvia provides another example of how economic integration can serve as a powerful stimulus for economic and institutional reforms—and how integration and reform together can create a virtuous circle of development.

The case of Latvia also shows that local circumstances matter as well. Latvia has benefited from a high-quality technocratic bureaucracy through which pro-reform civil servants were able to provide competent support to the reform process over time. The presence of a stable cadre of well-qualified civil servants, maintained through changes in political leadership, almost certainly aided the development and implementation of what has been a largely successful reform agenda. In addition, the ability to establish an ongoing dialogue between the government and the business community may have helped build and sustain the broad political consensus for the reform process.

Whatever the combination of causes, Latvia has maintained a state of mind focused on reform of the business environment and the broader economy. *Doing Business* measures just one component of the reforms that Latvia has implemented. But the results are clear: in the areas tracked by *Doing Business* indicators, the quality of the business environment has improved substantially over the past decade and a half.

## CONCLUSION

Latvia's reform process is likely to continue. The authorities have signaled their determination to continue to implement cautious macroeconomic policies that will support continued investments in infrastructure, education and training, seen as key elements of an ambitious competitiveness agenda.[18] Further business regulatory reforms are planned as well, as part of Latvia's program to implement the "Europe 2020" strategy.[19] The objectives include, among others, the reduction of administrative barriers and the strengthening of access to finance as well as support for access to external markets and encouragement of greater inflows of foreign direct investment to export-oriented sectors. These reforms should enable Latvia to fully overcome the economic effects of the financial crisis and allow it to continue on its path toward successful long-term development.

## NOTES

This case study was written by Caroline Frontigny and Betina Tirelli Hennig.

1. World Bank, World Development Indicators database, http://data .worldbank.org/. The income measure is gross national income (GNI) per capita at purchasing power parity.

2. Export growth data are from the World Bank's World Development Indicators database (http://data.worldbank.org/). Poverty data are based on the poverty headcount ratio at purchasing power parity and are from PovcalNet, the online tool for poverty measurement developed by the World Bank's Development Research Group (http://iresearch .worldbank.org/PovcalNet).

3. See, for example, Coolidge, Grava and Putnina (2003).

4. Liepina, Coolidge and Grava 2008.

5. Liepina, Coolidge and Grava 2008.

6. World Bank 2001.

7. Coolidge, Grava and Putnina 2003.

8. World Bank 2007.

9. Liepina, Coolidge and Grava 2008.

10. World Bank, World Development Indicators database, http://data .worldbank.org/.

11. World Bank, World Development Indicators database, http://data .worldbank.org/.

12. Liepina, Coolidge and Grava 2008.

13. Latvia, Ministry of Economics 2011.

14. EBRD 2011.

15. EBRD 2011.

16. The Regulatory Quality Index captures perceptions of the government's ability to formulate and implement sound policies and regulations that permit and promote private sector development. It ranges from -2.5 (weak government performance) to 2.5 (strong government performance). Latvia's score rose from 0.74 in 2000 to 0.94 in 2005, then rose to 0.98 in 2010.

17. See, for example, Åslund (2009). Another consideration in the government's policy choice may have been a desire to protect the significant share of the population with debt in euros and other foreign currencies from the consequences of a devaluation.

18. EBRD 2011.

19. Latvia, Ministry of Economics 2011.

# Rwanda: fostering prosperity by promoting entrepreneurship

Emerging from a decade marked by civil war and political instability, Rwanda began a comprehensive and ambitious campaign in 2000 to rebuild, foster national reconciliation and drastically reduce poverty. The government's agenda gave priority to health, education, infrastructure, and private and financial sector development, showing a commitment to improving citizens' living conditions and building a solid foundation for reconciliation.

Starting early on in the reform campaign, Rwanda has implemented many business regulation reforms. These have transformed the life of the private sector and made it noticeably easier to do business. While challenges remain, the country has achieved much success in its reform agenda since the early 2000s. This success stems from many factors, and Rwanda's experience may provide useful lessons for other nations seeking to improve their business climate, particularly for those coming out of conflict.

## DESIGNING A STRATEGY

Between 2005 and 2011 Rwanda's real GDP per capita grew by 4.5% a year, reflecting a sustained expansion of exports and domestic investment, with inflows of foreign direct investment also increasing substantially.[1] In addition, the government strengthened the foundations of macroeconomic stability by implementing cautious fiscal policies supported by a number of structural and institutional reforms. Underpinning this policy stance was a strong and sustained commitment by national authorities to private sector development.

Building on a 2-year consultation process, the government designed a long-term development strategy, *Rwanda Vision 2020*, aimed at transforming Rwanda into a middle-income economy by raising income per capita from $290 to $900 before 2020.[2] Introduced in 2000, the strategy recognized and sought to overcome Rwanda's multiple development challenges—including past civil war, poor governance, weak infrastructure, underdeveloped financial and private sectors, unemployment, overwhelming public debt, a poorly developed education system, HIV and the rapid growth of a population expected to reach 13 million by 2020.

In 2001 the World Bank set up the Competitiveness and Enterprise Development Project, designed to help the government establish an environment conducive to private sector growth and the emergence of a more competitive investment climate. The project focused on developing and updating the commercial law and supporting the government's privatization program through technical assistance, capacity building and advice on bank restructuring. This program contributed to an overhaul of the country's financial sector that led to the recapitalization of banks, the establishment of an insurance market and the introduction of microfinance lenders. In addition, the Competitiveness and Enterprise Development Project collaborated with the World Bank's Rwanda Investment Climate Reform Program to develop a robust reform agenda. The project helped establish the Doing Business Unit, the institution responsible for spearheading Rwanda's reform initiatives, while the investment

- Rwanda's commitment to private sector development has facilitated growth in exports, domestic investment and foreign direct investment inflows—and the implementation of effective fiscal policies supported by structural and institutional reforms.

- Starting in 2000, Rwanda developed a strong institutional pipeline for designing and implementing business regulation reforms.

- Since 2004 Rwanda has substantially improved access to credit, streamlined procedures for starting a business, reduced the time to register property, simplified cross-border trade and made courts more accessible for resolving commercial disputes.

- Rwanda is among more than 35 economies where the executive branch has made private sector development a priority by establishing institutions whose main purpose is to design and implement business regulation reforms.

climate reform program provided technical assistance and expertise to support the implementation of planned legal, regulatory and institutional reforms.

Rwanda's 2007 Economic Development and Poverty Reduction Strategy, like its *Vision 2020*, emphasized private sector development as the key to creating jobs, bringing peace, generating wealth and ultimately eliminating poverty.[3] In addition, aware of its scarce natural resources and landlocked location, Rwanda has focused on business regulation reform to attract foreign investment.

Dubbed "Africa's new Singapore" by *The Economist* for its positive economic reforms,[4] Rwanda has been effectively learning from the success stories of economies like Singapore since the early 2000s. And in 2007 it started using the *Doing Business* report as a tool to identify and learn from good practices in business regulation and to monitor improvement.

Several elements of a successful reform program were present, including political will and commitment at the highest level and a broadly appropriate set of macroeconomic policies that created room in the budget to invest in reforms and gained strong support from the donor community.

## BUILDING AN EFFECTIVE REFORM PIPELINE

Government responsibility for improving the investment climate in Rwanda and driving through the reforms has shifted over time. The responsibility was initially assigned to the Rwanda Investment Promotion Agency. In August 2008 this agency was joined by 7 others to create the Rwanda Development Board.[5]

The board's creation marked not only a change in name and gains in size, resources and efficiency but also a fundamental increase in political will and support. The president of Rwanda made business regulation reform a priority, as did the leaders of more than 35

other economies—including economies that have made some of the biggest improvements in the ease of doing business, such as Burundi, Colombia and Georgia.[6] The approach has proved effective in triggering reforms. In Rwanda it helped put investment climate reforms at the top of the economic policy agenda for promoting private sector development and helped consolidate and unify the multiple reform efforts.

Since reforms to the investment climate require changes across many areas of government, the Doing Business Steering Committee, bringing together representatives from different ministries, was created in early 2009 to lead the reform efforts at the cabinet level. While other countries have created similar institutions to promote reform, Rwanda has made effective use of the steering committee in implementing successful regulatory reforms (as detailed in the following section).

Below the steering committee is a technical task force made up of 6 working groups focusing on business entry, licensing reform, legislative changes, taxes and trade logistics, construction permits and property registration. One key to the working groups' effectiveness has been their inclusion of private sector representatives. This has helped ensure private sector buy-in and allowed participants to share their experiences during discussions about reform design.

To ensure success, the organizational structure still needed something to bring all the pieces together. For this purpose the Doing Business Unit was created. A small, full-time team, this unit links the working groups to the steering committee, coordinates with donors providing technical support, manages development funding to ensure proper use and promotes efforts to improve the investment climate. It also advises agencies, explains the reforms to the private sector and monitors progress through internal indicators.

The Doing Business Unit identifies reform opportunities; the technical task force and the steering committee approve the reform proposals. The annual plan for regulatory reforms is then communicated to the cabinet. The steering committee and the technical task force commit to the new priorities that are agreed on at the national leadership's annual retreats.[7] The Doing Business Unit monitors implementation and reports to the steering committee and to the prime minister, who is ultimately responsible for ensuring the execution of goals.[8] Besides reporting directly to the Rwanda Development Board, the unit also periodically informs the head of the Strategy and Policy Unit in the Office of the President about reform progress.

Far from being rigid, this structure has been further improved by the involvement of other stakeholders. Ahead of the promulgation of major pieces of legislation, the Rwanda Development Board has worked closely with the parliament and the judiciary, both of which have helped in meeting targets and deadlines. Civil society, development partners and institutions such as the Presidential Advisory Council have also provided crucial input in shaping the reform agenda.[9]

## LAUNCHING REGULATORY REFORMS

Even as the internal organization was evolving, the government was enacting reforms: since 2005 Rwanda has implemented 26 business regulation reforms as recorded by *Doing Business*.

### Improving access to credit

A series of changes improved conditions for getting credit. In 2005 the public credit registry expanded its database of financial institutions and improved the content of its credit reporting system. In 2009 a new secured transactions law was introduced, allowing a wider range of assets to be used as collateral and permitting out-of-court enforcement proceedings.[10]

In 2010 the legislature passed a law regulating the distribution of information from credit bureaus. This led to the creation of the country's first private credit bureau, which provides wider coverage than the public registry because it includes information from utilities. In addition, the public registry expanded coverage to loans of all sizes. In December 2011 the public registry stopped issuing credit reports, and now only the private bureau shares credit information. The public registry still collects information from regulated financial institutions but only for supervisory purposes.

## Streamlining regulatory processes

Other changes streamlined regulatory processes. In 2006 the introduction of hundreds of new notaries made starting a business faster. Before, only 1 notary had been available countrywide, and the high volume of requests meant a long wait for entrepreneurs wanting to register a new business. After an overhaul of the company law in 2009, entrepreneurs no longer needed to use the services of a notary; they could use standard forms instead. An online system for publishing the registration notice replaced requirements for physical publication. And a new one-stop shop streamlined business registration by reducing the number of interactions required from 9 to 2 (figure 5.1). The time required to start a business fell from 18 days to 3, and the cost from 235% of income per capita to 4%.

Rwanda also made it easier to transfer property. In 2008 it eliminated mortgage registration fees and shifted from a 6% transfer tax to a flat rate of 20,000 Rwandan francs (about $33). In 2010 the government decentralized the Office of the Registrar and Land Titles and created 5 branches throughout the country, purging the backlog of cases in Kigali. It also introduced strict time limits for some procedures. One was the issuance of tax clearance certificates, which had been the lengthiest part of the process.

The administrative reorganization and the statutory time limits reduced the time required to transfer property by 346 days—from more than a year in 2004 to less than a month (figure 5.2). And the changes in the transfer fees reduced the cost from 10.3% of the property value to 5.6%.[11]

Changes over several years made trading across borders faster. In 2005 Rwanda made it possible to submit customs declarations electronically. In 2007 the customs authority introduced more acceptance points for customs declarations, reducing the waiting time to submit them. In 2008 the government extended operating hours for border posts and implemented an electronic data interchange system and risk-based inspections. And in 2010 it streamlined trade documentation requirements and improved border cooperation.

Results are clear. In 2006 exporting goods in Rwanda required 14 documents and 60 days (figure 5.3). Today it takes only 8 documents and 29 days. The story is similar for importing.

## Strengthening laws and the judiciary

The new company law adopted in 2009 introduced several concepts into Rwanda's

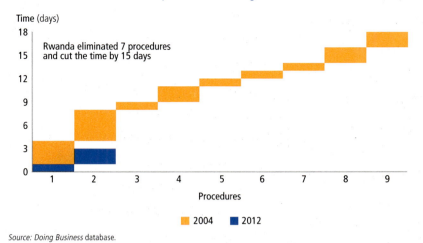

FIGURE 5.1  Rwanda streamlined the procedures for starting a business

Time (days)

Rwanda eliminated 7 procedures and cut the time by 15 days

Procedures

■ 2004  ■ 2012

Source: Doing Business database.

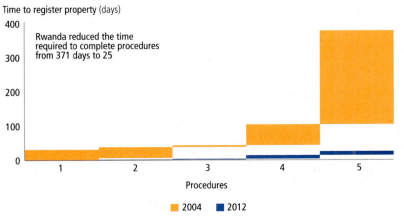

FIGURE 5.2  Rwanda cut the time for property transfers by almost a year

Time to register property (days)

Rwanda reduced the time required to complete procedures from 371 days to 25

Procedures

■ 2004  ■ 2012

Source: Doing Business database.

FIGURE 5.3  Big reduction in time and documents to trade across borders in Rwanda

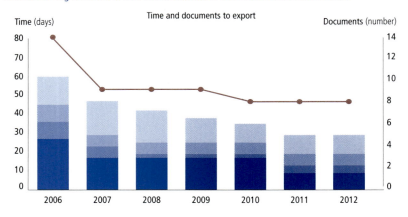

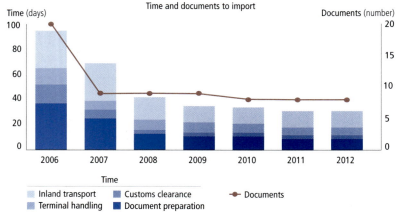

Source: Doing Business database.

corporate legal system for the first time: minority shareholder rights, regulation of conflicts of interest, extensive corporate disclosure and directors' duties. The new law introduced rules requiring approval by the board of directors for related-party transactions representing less than 5% of the company's assets and by shareholders for those representing more than 5%. The law strengthened the director liability regime for breach of fiduciary duties and for related-party transactions that harm the company. And it increased corporate transparency by improving disclosure requirements and minority shareholders' access to corporate information.

In 2005 the government made contract enforcement more of a reality by establishing more commercial courts[12] and creating the Business Law Reform Cell, whose review of 14 commercial

laws proved crucial for the approval of important legal reforms. The government further enhanced the court system in 2008 by creating lower commercial courts.

Consistent with its emphasis on bringing in the skills and expertise needed to ensure the success of the reform process, the government also hired non-Rwandan expatriate judges: 2 Mauritian judges to help local judges run the new commercial courts during the first 3 years of operation.[13] In addition, the government has provided incentives for Western-educated members of the diaspora to repatriate and has promoted an exchange of skills by opening the job market to immigrants from neighboring countries, including Burundi, Kenya, Tanzania and Uganda.[14] Moreover, the Capacity Strengthening Program

(financed by the Competitiveness and Enterprise Development Project) and the Institute for Legal Practice are training judges, legal officers and lawyers to work in a mixed legal system, where the civil law tradition dominates but common law and customary law tendencies are also evident.[15]

With the aim of increasing efficiency in resolving corporate insolvencies, the government enacted a new insolvency law in 2009. But resolving insolvency remains the one area among all those included in the ease of doing business index in which Rwanda still has great room for improvement. Achieving widespread use of the law in insolvency cases has been among the greatest regulatory reform challenges in this area.[16]

## SEEING MEASURABLE RESULTS
The ultimate goal of the reform program is a private sector that promotes economic growth and job creation.[17] And the program is achieving measurable progress toward this goal.

After Rwanda simplified formalities for business registration in 2006, 77% more firms registered in the following year.[18] In 2008 more than 3,000 firms registered, up from an average of 700 in previous years. In 2009 the number rose to 6,905. And in 2010 the government managed to register 18,447 new businesses—nearly achieving its goal of registering 20,000 that year.[19] The jump in registration numbers cannot be attributed solely to the simplification of the start-up process; the business registration reforms were part of a wider government agenda to promote private sector growth and entrepreneurship in Rwanda. Even so, the increase points to a positive trend.

Good results are also showing up in the area of contract enforcement: the commercial courts started operating in Kigali in May 2008 and had fully cleared the case backlog by the end of 2009.[20]

Rwanda's consistent reforms to make trade easier improved the productivity of customs officials, who increased the number of documents they cleared annually by 39% between 2006 and 2009. And according to the Ministry of Trade and Industry, Rwanda's exports rose from $147 million in 2006 to $193 million in 2009.

Rwanda recently adjusted some of the targets set in *Vision 2020*. Most notably, it raised the income per capita target from $900 to $3,500. This brings the target into line with levels in middle-income economies today and reflects Rwanda's recent growth, which increased income per capita to around $570 in 2011.[21]

## CONCLUSION

Every country faces different development challenges. But Rwanda's ambitious and complex reform program may offer lessons for others seeking to reform through private sector development.

One key to its achievements has been the strong commitment to reform shown by Rwanda's leaders and its citizens. The government has established structures for building a foundation for private sector development and coordinating government-wide reform efforts. And it has created a well-defined, long-term reform strategy that informs all of the country's short-term development goals.

The government entities involved in the process have had clearly defined roles and responsibilities, and they have respected the goals set in initial implementation strategy documents. The Doing Business Unit has played a pivotal role not only in ensuring coordination within the government and between the government and donors but also in coordinating development funding initiatives so as to avoid duplication.

The government has worked to meet the needs of entrepreneurs by streamlining regulatory processes involved in starting, operating and closing a business. Beyond undertaking legal and administrative reforms, the government has invested in training for professionals—including

lawyers and judges—to ensure proper administration of the reforms. Recognizing the benefits of a diverse knowledge base, Rwanda has also imported technical expertise from other countries, to replicate good practices and build capacity. And the government has involved the private sector in the reform process and maintained an open line of communication to keep entrepreneurs, civil society and other stakeholders apprised of developments.

All these efforts are showing results in Rwanda's regulatory performance. And Rwanda's dedication to private sector development, in triggering positive legal reforms, has contributed substantially to its overarching goal of promoting national reconciliation and prosperity.

## NOTES

This case study was written by Moussa Traoré, Adrian Gonzalez, César Chaparro Yedro, Jean Michel Lobet and Jonathan Bailey.

1. World Bank, World Development Indicators database, http://data .worldbank.org/.

2. Rwanda, Ministry of Finance and Economic Planning 2000.

3. Rwanda, Ministry of Finance and Economic Planning 2007.

4. "Africa's New Singapore?" *The Economist*, February 25, 2012, http://www.economist.com/.

5. The 7 agencies were Tourism and Conservation, the Registrar General's Office, the Privatization Unit, Human and Institutional Development, the Center for the Support to Small and Medium-Sized Enterprises (CAPMER), the IT Agency and the National Environment Management Authority.

6. See box 2.2 in the chapter "About *Doing Business*" for a list of economies using this approach.

7. These retreats, which gather about 300 top members of the administration, have included *Doing Business* reforms on the agenda since 2007.

8. Presentation by Emmanuel Hategeka, permanent secretary, Ministry of Trade and Industry, Kigali, March 16, 2011; Karim 2011.

9. In particular, the U.K. Department for International Development's multiyear

program to support the Rwanda Revenue Authority is considered a success, enabling the agency both to improve its tax collection rate and to simplify its interactions with businesses.

10. Legal changes often require only modest investments. For the secured transactions law, for example, Rwanda invested $55,320 (excluding technical assistance from donors) in the validation and translation of the new law as well as in the legislative process.

11. World Bank 2010a.

12. World Bank 2006.

13. Hertveldt 2008.

14. "Africa's New Singapore?" *The Economist*, February 25, 2012, http://www.economist.com/.

15. The Institute for Legal Practice was established by an organic law in 2006 and started to operate in May 2008.

16. "Rwanda: Country Struggles on Insolvency Law," *East African Business Week*, May 13, 2012, http://allafrica .com/.

17. Edmund Kagire, "New Reforms Set Up to Boost Doing Business," *New Times* (Kigali), April 18, 2010.

18. World Bank 2010a.

19. Frank Kanyesigye, "Rwanda Development Board Targets to Register 20,000 New Businesses," *New Times* (Kigali), May 14, 2010.

20. Interview by *Business Times* (Kigali) with Benoit Gatete, vice president of the commercial high court, January 12, 2010, http://allafrica.com/.

21. "Government to Adjust Vision 2020," *New Times* (Kigali), February 25, 2010; World Bank, World Development Indicators database, http://data .worldbank.org/.

# APEC: sharing goals and experience

- Asia-Pacific Economic Cooperation (APEC), a regional forum of 21 member economies, has as its primary goal to ensure sustainable economic growth and prosperity through voluntary cooperation.

- A key focus is promoting regulatory reforms, and in 2009 the APEC Ease of Doing Business Action Plan was launched as a way to set collective targets and measure progress.

- Using 5 *Doing Business* indicator sets, the action plan targets an APEC-wide aspirational goal of making it 25% cheaper, faster and easier to do business by 2015, with an interim target of 5% improvement by 2011.

- Between 2009 and 2012 APEC members improved their performance on the 5 indicator sets by 11.5% on average. But much variation remains among APEC members in the ease of doing business and in the rate of progress being made.

- Consistent with APEC's view of capacity building as central to enhancing cooperation and accelerating progress, the action plan identifies "champion economies" to share information and experience and to assist other members through tailored diagnostic studies.

Many factors can drive reforms in an economy's business regulatory environment—from domestic factors such as financial crises to international ones such as binding agreements in the World Trade Organization (WTO). For economies in the Asia-Pacific region, regional factors play a part, including commitments made in Asia-Pacific Economic Cooperation (APEC). Improving the region's business regulatory environment is a focus of APEC, and member economies have pledged to carry out regulatory reforms both collectively and unilaterally.

To help monitor and assess members' progress toward these commitments, APEC sets measurable targets with specific timelines. While these targets are set at the regional level, APEC also encourages members to draft plans for their own economy that will aid in achieving APEC-wide targets. One set of targets that APEC has chosen for this purpose is based on *Doing Business* indicators.

APEC also encourages capacity building activities among members in support of its goals. Toward the goal of improving the region's regulatory environment, APEC has selected "champion economies" to provide capacity building assistance to other members.

## A HISTORY OF COLLECTIVE GOAL SETTING

Established in 1989, APEC is a forum for supporting economic growth, cooperation, trade and investment in the Asia-Pacific region. APEC operates on a voluntary and consensual basis, with activities and work programs centered on 3 main pillars: trade and investment

liberalization, business facilitation, and economic and technical cooperation.[1]

Meeting in Bogor, Indonesia, in 1994, leaders of APEC members committed to achieving free and open trade and investment by 2010 for developed economy members and by 2020 for developing economy members—targets that became known as the Bogor Goals. Today APEC's 21 members account for about 54% of world GDP and about 44% of world trade.[2] APEC members' total trade grew by 10% a year on average between 1989 and 2010. This rate, though impressive, only slightly exceeded the world's overall trade growth rate of 9%.[3] On the other hand, APEC members reduced their average applied tariff from 16.9% to 5.8% over this period.[4]

As tariffs declined in APEC members, attention shifted to addressing the structural and regulatory obstacles that inhibit cross-border trade and investment by removing behind-the-border barriers to doing business.[5] At the same time, economic integration between APEC members highlighted difficult new challenges—such as how to ensure that growth and economic integration are sustainable and shared by all APEC members in a constantly changing economic environment.

To address these challenges, in 2010 APEC leaders embraced the APEC Growth Strategy, which takes into consideration new global realities—including energy and environmental constraints, human security concerns and disparities in opportunity across and within economies. APEC leaders also endorsed the

FIGURE 6.1  Milestones in the APEC Ease of Doing Business Action Plan

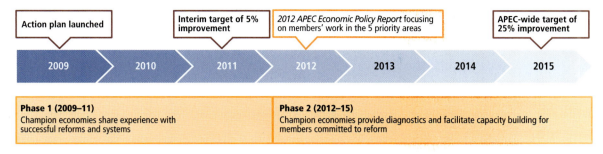

*Source:* Based on information from APEC Policy Support Unit.

New Strategy for Structural Reform, a broad work program that calls on each member economy to undertake demonstrable and significant structural reform, consistent with the objective of achieving strong, inclusive and balanced growth. Recognizing the importance of capacity building to assist members in undertaking structural reform, APEC is supporting workshops, peer-to-peer events and knowledge sharing tools in such areas as regulatory reform and public sector governance.

## AN ACTION PLAN FOR MAKING IT EASIER TO DO BUSINESS

Another APEC initiative focuses more closely on improving the business regulatory environment. To provide a pragmatic way of addressing priorities, senior government officials of APEC members agreed to put in place the APEC Ease of Doing Business Action Plan in 2009.[6] The action plan uses *Doing Business* indicators to set collective targets and encourage measurable progress in regulatory reform. The overall goal is to make it 25% cheaper, faster and easier to do business in the region by 2015, with an interim target of 5% improvement by 2011.

The action plan focuses on 5 priority areas. These were identified through a survey asking APEC members to rank by priority the 11 areas measured by *Doing Business*. The 5 priority areas are starting a business, getting credit, trading across borders, enforcing contracts and dealing with construction permits.

The action plan has highlighted the importance of measuring results since the beginning. And the APEC Secretariat has agreed to regularly assess progress toward the targets set (figure 6.1).[7]

## Encouraging early results

Early results are encouraging. Among the 5 areas covered by the action plan, APEC members made the biggest improvements in starting a business between 2009 and 2012. On average, they reduced the number of procedures to start a business by 19.3% (from 7.9 to 6.4), the time by 22.5% (from 28.1 days to 21.8), the cost by 16.5% (from 8.8% of income per capita to 7.4%) and the paid-in minimum capital requirement by 35.3% (from 9.8% of income per capita to 6.4%). Economies in the rest of the world made smaller improvements on average on 3 of these indicators, reducing the number of procedures by 8.2%, the time by 17.7% and the paid-in minimum capital requirement by 32.4%. But they improved more than APEC members on the cost to start a business, reducing it by 29.1%.

Overall, APEC members improved the ease of starting a business by 23.4% on average, while non-APEC economies improved it by 21.9%. Beyond the differences with the rest of the world, what makes these improvements by APEC particularly impressive is that in 2009 the region already performed better on

FIGURE 6.2  APEC members have advanced furthest toward the frontier in regulatory practice for starting a business

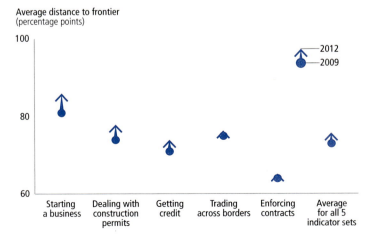

*Note:* The distance to frontier measure shows how far on average an economy is from the best performance achieved by any economy on each *Doing Business* indicator since 2005. The measure is normalized to range between 0 and 100, with 100 representing the best performance (the frontier).

*Source: Doing Business* database.

average on the *Doing Business* indicators for starting a business than on those for the other 4 areas (figure 6.2).

Over the same period APEC members also improved their performance on the *Doing Business* indicators for dealing with construction permits (by 15.8% on average, compared with 13.9% in non-APEC economies) and for getting credit (by 16.1%, compared with 23.9%). Their performance on the trading across borders indicators improved only slightly (by 2.3%, compared with a decline of 0.7% in non-APEC economies), while that on the enforcing contracts indicators remained nearly unchanged (improving by 0.1%, compared with no improvement in non-APEC economies). Across all 5 priority areas, APEC members improved their performance on the *Doing Business* indicators by 11.5% on average.

## Wide discrepancies between APEC members

Despite the good start, the ease of doing business still varies sharply among APEC members. Consider the process for starting a business. In New Zealand it requires only 1 procedure and 1 day and costs 0.4% of income per capita; in the Philippines it takes 16 procedures and 36 days and costs 18.1% of income per capita. Similarly, while dealing with construction permits in Singapore takes 26 days and costs 16.7% of income per capita, in Russia it takes 344 days and in Mexico it costs 322.7% of income per capita.

Indeed, APEC's high-income members perform substantially better in all 5 priority areas as measured by *Doing Business* than its middle-income members do. And on the aggregate ease of doing business they rank 59 places higher on average than middle-income members (figure 6.3).

Moreover, while APEC as a whole is making improvements, its members are progressing at very different rates. Among APEC members, China has made the most progress toward the frontier in regulatory practice (figure 6.4). In the past 8

years China implemented 16 reforms in 8 areas of business regulation measured by *Doing Business*. These changes included a new company law in 2005, a new credit registry in 2006, a new law regulating the bankruptcy of private enterprises in 2007 and a new corporate income tax law in 2008.

FIGURE 6.3 APEC members' performance on *Doing Business* indicators varies widely

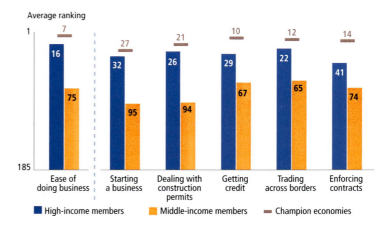

*Note:* Champion economies as defined by the APEC Ease of Doing Business Action Plan are Hong Kong SAR, China; Japan; Korea; New Zealand; Singapore; and the United States.
*Source: Doing Business* database.

FIGURE 6.4 Which APEC economies have advanced the most in narrowing the gap with the frontier?

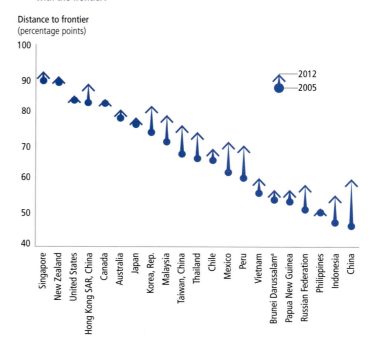

*Note:* The distance to frontier measure shows how far on average an economy is from the best performance achieved by any economy on each *Doing Business* indicator since 2005. The measure is normalized to range between 0 and 100, with 100 representing the best performance (the frontier).

a. Because Brunei Darussalam was first included in the aggregate ranking in *Doing Business 2008* (2007), its distance to frontier in 2012 is compared with that in 2007.

*Source: Doing Business* database.

What does all this mean for APEC's prospects of meeting its ambitious goal? APEC's 2011 interim report on the initiative delivered a clear message: if APEC is to improve the ease of doing business by 25% by 2015, it must intensify and accelerate its efforts, including through capacity building programs.[8]

## Sharing of information and experience

While APEC members advocate building capacity and sharing experience as a way of enhancing cooperation in a range of areas, such efforts feature strongly in the initiative to improve the ease of doing business. The action plan identifies champion economies with strong performance in each of the 5 priority areas to lead capacity building activities in those areas.

In phase 1 (2009–11) the focus was on building awareness through seminars and workshops to share information and experience in each of the 5 priority areas. The APEC Secretariat and the champion economies organized 6 topic-specific seminars and workshops.[9]

In phase 2 (2012–15) the focus is on developing more customized capacity building programs for economies seeking specific assistance in their regulatory reform efforts. In these programs technical experts conduct diagnostic studies of an economy's priority area and develop practical recommendations for improvement. While designed to directly benefit the participating economies, the programs also help move APEC closer to its collective goal of making it 25% cheaper, faster and easier to do business by 2015.[10]

Several programs focus on the area of starting a business. One is in Indonesia, where an expert from New Zealand and another from the United States made a joint visit in July 2010 to collect data and information. The diagnostic report, issued in August 2010, contains 8 concrete recommendations. Among them is a recommendation to consolidate the procedure for labor and social insurance registration with those for issuing the trade license and registering the business at the one-stop shop.[11]

In Thailand an assessment by U.S. experts in July 2011 went beyond the aspects of business start-up measured by *Doing Business*, resulting in a comprehensive report and policy recommendations. The study found that Thailand, by creating a customer-friendly and demand-driven system for business registration, had made it substantially easier to start a business as measured by *Doing Business*. It also recommended that the government broaden the focus of its efforts to improve business registration beyond the aspects captured by the *Doing Business* indicators.[12]

Korea, a champion for the topic of enforcing contracts, is assisting Indonesia and Peru in developing customized solutions. A Korean delegation visited Indonesia in January 2011 and Peru in July 2011 to review the systems and procedures in place for enforcing contracts. In addition, international seminars were held in the 2 countries on ways to improve such systems. Together, these attracted more than 100 participants, including judges, attorneys, professors and government officials. In October 2011 the Korean government brought together legal experts and high-level policy makers from Indonesia and Peru to discuss the future of both countries' systems for enforcing contracts.[13]

Japan, a champion for the topic of getting credit, is preparing a study on financing for small and medium-size enterprises in Thailand. Singapore is preparing a diagnostic study on trading across borders for Peru and planning similar ones for Mexico and Vietnam. Singapore is also planning diagnostic studies on dealing with construction permits for Indonesia, Peru and Thailand.[14]

The next phase of capacity building activities will focus on converting the diagnostic studies' recommendations into actions. Champion economies will again play a role, by assisting other member economies in implementing regulatory reforms.

## CONCLUSION

APEC has focused on institutional, regulatory and policy reforms to encourage efficient functioning of markets and reduce barriers to regional trade since the early 2000s. The APEC Ease of Doing Business Action Plan represents only one set of targets that APEC uses to encourage regulatory reforms. But it provides a useful example of the application of *Doing Business* indicators in setting concrete collective targets and in monitoring and assessing progress.

The framework of capacity building activities created through the action plan has proved useful in promoting exchanges between member economies. Here, the diversity of APEC's 21 member economies—with different income levels and located in different geographic regions—has contributed to success. By sharing experience and providing assistance to other APEC members, those identified as champions in each of the priority areas can lift the APEC-wide performance.

Other regional bodies can learn from this model of capacity building. *Doing Business 2012* found that in many economies the degree to which regulations and institutions are business-friendly varies fairly widely across areas of regulation.[15] Regional bodies can take advantage of these differences, encouraging each member economy to capitalize on its strengths by providing assistance in areas of strong performance to members with weaker performance.

APEC appears poised to continue its capacity building efforts, with talks already under way on a new phase related to policy implementation. Because APEC is a voluntary and nonbinding forum, sustained engagement by top government officials from every APEC member is needed to accelerate progress toward the goals it has set for itself.

## NOTES

This case study was written by Mikiko Imai Ollison, Paula Garcia Serna and Anastasia Shegay.

1. APEC 2010a.
2. APEC 2010b. The founding members of APEC are Australia, Brunei Darussalam, Canada, Indonesia, Japan, Korea, Malaysia, New Zealand, the Philippines, Singapore, Thailand and the United States. China; Hong Kong SAR, China; and Taiwan, China, joined in 1991. Mexico and Papua New Guinea followed in 1993, Chile in 1994 and Peru, Russia and Vietnam in 1998—bringing the current membership to 21.
3. WTO Statistics Database, Trade Profile, http://stat.wto.org/.
4. WTO Statistics Database, Tariff Profile, http://stat.wto.org/.
5. APEC 2005.
6. APEC 2011a.
7. As Doing Business 2013 was going to press, the 2012 APEC Economic Policy Report was scheduled to be released in early October 2012.
8. APEC 2011b.
9. Based on information provided by the APEC Policy Support Unit as of June 2012.
10. APEC 2011b.
11. USAID and New Zealand Ministry of Foreign Affairs and Trade 2010.
12. APEC 2012.
13. Republic of Korea, Ministry of Justice 2011.
14. Based on information provided by the APEC Policy Support Unit as of June 2012.
15. World Bank 2011a, p. 7.

# Does *Doing Business* matter for foreign direct investment?

Many people who use *Doing Business* data—particularly in policy-making circles and in the private sector—associate better performance on the *Doing Business* indicators with greater inflows of foreign direct investment (FDI), even though the methodology is not explicitly designed for this purpose. Since the launch of last year's report nearly 2,000 articles in the international press have drawn a connection between FDI and *Doing Business*. Such articles often suggest that higher *Doing Business* rankings will be associated with more foreign investment, which is believed to create jobs, bring in new technologies and processes and have other beneficial collateral effects on the real economy. And many senior government officials have suggested that a better ranking for an economy implies that its investment climate is more favorable to foreign investors.

The case studies underpinning the *Doing Business* indicators focus on small to medium-size domestic firms, so the laws, regulations and practices tracked by the project are not necessarily relevant to larger foreign-owned firms. But the quality of the laws and regulations, and the extent to which this quality is reflected in their implementation, may be a useful

signal to foreign investors of the overall quality of the business environment. And some laws may indeed affect foreign-owned firms in the same way that they affect domestic firms.

Given the interest of so many governments in attracting more foreign investment, this raises an important question: does *Doing Business* actually matter for FDI? If so, does this suggest that *Doing Business* indicators reflect the quality of the investment climate at a broader level? This case study presents evidence suggesting that they do—supporting a broader claim that economies that provide a good regulatory environment for domestic firms tend to also provide a good one for foreign-owned firms.

## A FIRST LOOK AT THE LINK

There is certainly a correlation between the overall ease of doing business and FDI flows. Grouping economies by the *Doing Business* distance to frontier score for 2011,[1] table 7.1 shows that those closest to the frontier in regulatory practice received substantially more FDI than those in the middle, which in turn received substantially more than those furthest from the frontier. Figure 7.1 demonstrates this

- Even though *Doing Business* indicators focus on small to medium-size domestic firms, many policy makers have associated improvements in the indicators with greater inflows of foreign direct investment (FDI).

- Cross-country correlations show that FDI inflows are indeed higher for economies performing better on *Doing Business* indicators, even when taking into account differences across economies in other factors considered important for FDI.

- Results suggest that on average across economies, a difference of 1 percentage point in regulatory quality as measured by *Doing Business* distance to frontier scores is associated with a difference in annual FDI inflows of $250–500 million.

- Although this correlation does not imply causation, the evidence suggests that *Doing Business* reflects more about the overall investment climate than what matters only to small and medium-size domestic firms.

- In particular, these findings support the claim that economies that provide a good regulatory environment for domestic firms tend to also provide a good one for foreign firms.

TABLE 7.1 Average FDI inflows and stocks by tiers of economies grouped by their distance to frontier, 2011

| Economies grouped by distance to frontier | Average FDI inflows (US$ millions) | Average FDI stocks (US$ millions) | Average distance to frontier (percentage points) |
|---|---|---|---|
| Top 10 | 50,384 | 768,496 | 86.0 |
| Middle 10 | 14,362 | 89,776 | 58.9 |
| Lowest 10 | 1,257 | 8,179 | 34.2 |

*Note:* The distance to frontier measure is normalized to range between 0 and 100, with 100 representing the best performance (the frontier).

*Source: Doing Business* database; United Nations Conference on Trade and Development, UNCTADstat database.

FIGURE 7.1  Better overall regulation is correlated with more FDI inflows per capita

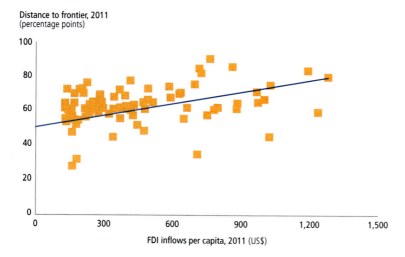

*Note:* The distance to frontier measure is normalized to range between 0 and 100, with 100 representing the best performance (the frontier). Sample includes 157 economies with positive 2011 FDI inflows per capita of $1,500 or less. This includes all economies covered by *Doing Business 2012* for which data are available, excluding outliers with negative inflows or inflows greater than $1,500 per capita. Dropping these outliers does not significantly affect the trend line.
*Source: Doing Business* database; United Nations Conference on Trade and Development, UNCTADstat database.

graphically, using a different measure of FDI: it shows that FDI inflows per person in 2011 were higher for economies that were closer to the frontier.

But these are simple statistical correlations looking at the relationship between performance on the distance to frontier measure and FDI at a particular point in time. What does more robust research say about the determinants of FDI flows?

## RESEARCH ON FDI DETERMINANTS

A large body of research has looked at the question of what the key drivers of FDI are. One approach in the literature sees FDI as being market-seeking (driven by economy size and country location), efficiency-seeking (driven by human capital or infrastructure quality) or resource-seeking (driven by the availability of natural resources or other strategic assets). Numerous studies have measured the significance of these and other explanatory variables.[2]

Many studies use a "gravity model," which seeks to explain what causes FDI flows between 2 specific countries. This research confirms that such factors as

the size of the market and its growth prospects, distance to important markets, relative labor endowments and openness to trade tend to be important drivers of FDI. For example, the larger the market, the greater the scope for economies of scale in production and thus the greater the chances for producing at competitive prices. Economies in Central and Eastern Europe have received large inflows of FDI over the past couple of decades because they are seen as entry points into the huge European market and also because they have relatively well-educated labor forces.

The institutional and regulatory framework has also been shown to be an important determinant of FDI. One study finds that judicial independence and labor market flexibility are significantly associated with FDI inflows, depending on the sector of the investment.[3] Another finds that corruption is a significant deterrent to FDI, having an effect comparable to the impact of substantial increases in the tax rate on foreign firms.[4] Indirect taxes on foreign investors, which are higher than the direct foreign income taxes in many countries, also significantly reduce FDI inflows.[5] Business regulations matter as

well. Using a data set of regulations specific to foreign investment, a study finds that the number of procedures required to start a foreign-owned business and the strength of the arbitration regime both have a significant and robust effect on FDI.[6]

What about *Doing Business*? Using 4 years of *Doing Business* data, a recent study finds that a better *Doing Business* ranking is significantly associated with larger FDI inflows[7]—strong support for the claim that higher *Doing Business* rankings are a broad indicator of an attractive investment climate. But the study is unable to find evidence for smaller subsets of economies, such as for developing economies.[8] Related research finds that business regulations as measured by *Doing Business* influence the impact of FDI inflows: economies with more effective regulations for starting a business benefit more from the FDI flows that they receive.[9]

## WHAT DO THE DATA TELL US?

To expand on this existing body of research, *Doing Business* conducted its own econometric analysis of the relationship between *Doing Business* indicators and FDI flows. The analysis generally follows the model established by an earlier study,[10] considering the relationship between an economy's performance on *Doing Business* indicators and total FDI inflows from all other economies and taking into account differences in macroeconomic and governance conditions. But it also adds to prior analysis in several ways. It uses distance to frontier scores rather than economy rankings, as a more precise measure of how far business regulations are from the most efficient practice. Most specifications use 1 year of distance to frontier scores to explain subsequent years of FDI inflows, rather than panel data over time. The analysis considers differences in natural resource exports, and it covers a larger sample of between 145 and 160 economies across specifications.[11]

The basic model considers whether distance to frontier scores in 1 year are associated with total FDI inflows in the following year. When taking into account differences in income, inflation, population size, governance measures, openness to trade and exports of primary goods, the analysis finds significant results: a better distance to frontier score is significantly associated with larger inflows of FDI. To account for potential fluctuations in annual FDI flows, a different model examines the distance to frontier score for 2005 and average FDI inflows for the subsequent 5 years, and finds similar results. When considering population and income levels, as well as when using several other model specifications, the analysis finds a significant positive association between the distance to frontier score and FDI inflows. Other research has shown that *Doing Business* reforms are associated with greater domestic investment and GDP growth,[12] supporting the general finding that reforms that improve the quality of the regulatory environment are positively associated with FDI inflows.

In general, these results need to be interpreted cautiously. Correlation of course does not imply causation. But the estimated magnitudes suggest that the laws, regulations and practices captured by *Doing Business* may have a strong influence on FDI flows. Results suggest that for an economy with an average distance to frontier score, moving 1 percentage point closer to the frontier regulatory environment is associated with $250–500 million more in annual FDI inflows. These strong correlations, if upheld by further and more refined research, would have significant policy implications: they suggest that relatively modest improvements in the regulatory environment could potentially attract substantial increases in foreign investment. Consider the example of Costa Rica. If causation is proven, the correlations suggest that improving its score by just a percentage point—to a regulatory environment comparable to that of Uruguay—would

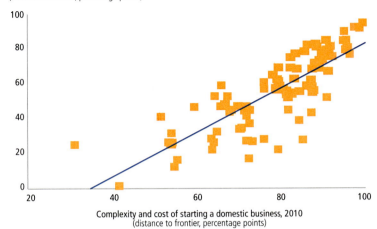

FIGURE 7.2 Complexity and cost of starting a domestic business are strongly correlated with complexity of starting a foreign one

Complexity of starting a foreign business, 2010
(distance to frontier, percentage points)

*Note:* Figure plots the distance to frontier in starting a (domestic) business as measured by *Doing Business* and the distance to frontier in starting a foreign business as measured by *Investing Across Borders*. The distance to frontier measure is normalized to range between 0 and 100, with 100 representing the best performance (the frontier). Scores are shown for the 92 economies for which *Investing Across Borders* collected data in 2010.

*Source: Doing Business* database; *Investing Across Borders* database.

be associated with a 21% increase in its annual FDI inflows.[13]

## GOOD REGULATIONS ALL AROUND

The strong and statistically significant relationship between FDI and the overall level of regulation as measured by *Doing Business* indicators supports the claim that *Doing Business* data reflect more about the overall investment climate than what matters only to small and medium-size local firms. These findings also support the more general claim that governments that regulate well in one area, such as domestic business, tend to also regulate well in other areas, such as foreign investment. For example, a working paper on transparency for this year's report highlights the positive correlation between a transparent approach to governance in one regulatory area and efficient regulation in other areas.[14]

Comparing the *Doing Business* indicators with other measures of the regulatory environment also supports this perspective. For example, some *Doing Business* indicators are strongly correlated with

similar indicators from the *Investing Across Borders* project, which focuses on regulation of foreign direct investment.[15] The correlation between the distance to frontier measures of the 2 sets of indicators is 57%.

This general relationship also holds for comparable individual indicators from *Doing Business* and *Investing Across Borders* (figure 7.2). The correlation between the complexity and cost of starting a local company as measured by *Doing Business* and the complexity of starting a local subsidiary of a foreign firm as measured by *Investing Across Borders* is 81%.[16] This correlation does not imply that the level of complexity is identical, however—indeed, while it takes 8 procedures and 26 days on average to start a local business in the economies covered by *Investing Across Borders*, it takes 10 procedures and 41 days on average to start a foreign-owned company in those economies.

## CONCLUSION

This case study presents evidence of a significant correlation between the *Doing Business* indicators and flows of FDI.

Although this does not imply causation, the findings do support the claim that *Doing Business* reflects more about the overall investment climate than what matters only to small and medium-size domestic firms. More definitive conclusions about the relationship between *Doing Business* indicators and FDI will require more refined research. One initial step could be to disaggregate FDI by sector—for example, to compare the effect of business regulations on manufacturing FDI with their effect on resource extraction FDI. If such research supports the association between regulatory quality as measured by *Doing Business* and the size of FDI flows, government officials and business analysts will have even stronger justification for claims that better *Doing Business* rankings should attract more FDI.

## NOTES

This case study was written by John Anderson and Adrian Gonzalez.

1. The *Doing Business* indicators can be aggregated in multiple ways to create composite measures of the investment climate. One approach is the ease of doing business index, which ranks economies from 1 to 185. Another is the distance to frontier, which measures how far an economy is from the most efficient practice or highest score achieved by any economy since 2005 for each *Doing Business* indicator. This case study uses the distance to frontier measure to capture not only how an economy ranks relative to others but also how far it is from the most efficient business regulatory practices identified by *Doing Business*. For more details, see the chapter on the ease of doing business and distance to frontier.

2. For an overview of such studies, see, for example, Blonigen and Piger (2011); and Hornberger, Battat and Kusek (2011).

3. Walsh and Yu 2010.

4. Wei 2000.

5. Desai, Foley and Hines 2003.

6. Waglé 2011.

7. Jayasuriya 2011.

8. This suggests that the results may be driven by differences between higher- and lower-income economies, not by variation within groups of economies.

9. Busse and Groizard 2008.

10. Jayasuriya 2011.

11. Jayasuriya (2011) estimates the influence of *Doing Business* rankings across 84 economies, noting that this smaller sample of economies is due to the use of an unbalanced panel.

12. See, for example, Eifert (2009); and Haidar (2012).

13. These calculations were made using distance to frontier scores for 2009 and data on FDI inflows in 2010 from the United Nations Conference on Trade and Development's UNCTADstat database. The calculation for Costa Rica uses a lower-end estimate of $300 million in FDI flows being associated with a 1 percentage point difference in the distance to frontier score.

14. Geginat, Gonzalez and Saltane 2012.

15. The *Investing Across Borders* database launched by the World Bank Group in 2010 presents indicators of FDI regulation across economies. The *Investing Across Borders* indicators referenced in this case study are based on data for 87 economies published in the 2010 *Investing Across Borders* report plus 5 additional economies for which data were collected but not included in that report.

16. This correlation is calculated between the distance to frontier in starting a business as measured by *Doing Business* and the distance to frontier in starting a foreign business as measured by *Investing Across Borders*, the same data as those shown in figure 7.2.

# How transparent is business regulation around the world?

Nobel Prize–winning economist Amartya Sen wrote in 2009 that lack of transparency in the global financial system was among the main factors contributing to the financial crisis that began in 2008.[1] Had there been greater disclosure of information, regulatory authorities could have more effectively monitored the explosive growth of increasingly sophisticated and opaque financial instruments—and the crisis might have been less severe.

An institutional environment characterized by openness and transparency is of central importance not only for private markets but also for the effective and efficient management of public resources.[2] Lack of transparency around the decisions made by policy makers and government officials can lead to resource misallocation as funds, rather than being directed toward their most productive ends, are instead captured for private gain. Lack of transparency can also undermine the credibility of those who are perceived as being its beneficiaries and thus sharply limit their ability to gain public support for economic and other reforms.

Access to information can empower citizens to monitor the quality of government services and the use of public resources. Because government markets are usually monopolistic, the consumers of public services have no "exit" option—they cannot "vote with their feet" by going to a competitor for better services. Access to information is therefore critical if citizens are to exercise their "voice" in demanding greater accountability from public servants.[3] The government of Uganda demonstrated this by having newspapers publish data on monthly transfers of school grants to local governments. By improving the ability of schools and parents to monitor how local officials handled the grants, the program reduced the share of grant funding lost to corruption from 80% to 20%.[4] With more information, people can better evaluate different options and manage risks more effectively.[5]

How much can transparency and access to information affect the quality of the government services relevant for businesses? A sizable body of literature already attests to the importance of information in ensuring the quality of public services in such areas as health, sanitation and education.[6] But thus far little attention has been paid to this role of information in the administrative branches of government that implement business regulation, such as company and property registries, building departments and power distribution utilities.

Yet the World Bank Enterprise Surveys suggest that there is much room for improvement in service quality and accountability in business regulation. The companies surveyed report that in a typical week their senior managers spend on average 11% of their time dealing with government regulations. More than 50% of them disagree with the notion that regulations are implemented consistently and predictably. And what's worse, companies often have to pay a bribe to get things done. Worldwide, 19% of firms report having had to pay bribes in connection with their application for an operating license or electricity connection.[7]

- It is in OECD high-income economies that businesses can expect the most consistently easy access to regulatory information through websites or printed brochures.

- Access to fee schedules for regulatory processes is most limited in Sub-Saharan Africa and the Middle East and North Africa, where it is more common to have to meet with an official to obtain this information.

- The accessibility of regulatory information varies with income level and internet penetration, but resources are not the only explanation.

- Access to regulatory information is easier in economies that are characterized by greater political accountability and that guarantee greater political and civil rights.

- Economies providing greater access to regulatory information tend to have more efficient regulatory processes and lower regulatory compliance costs.

About two-thirds of these are small or medium-size firms.

This year's report presents new data that speak to the efforts at transparency made by government agencies tasked with implementing business regulation. The data capture how governments make basic regulatory information such as fee schedules available to businesses. Because agencies in many developing economies may be unable to rely on online solutions, the data also consider other ways of making information available, such as brochures and notice boards (see box 8.1 for a description of the new data and the *Doing Business* website for detailed data at the economy level).[8]

## HOW TRANSPARENT IS BUSINESS REGULATION?

Company registries, property registries, building departments and power distribution utilities in too many economies make it difficult to access basic information such as fee schedules for their services. In only 25% of economies do all 4 agencies make fee schedules easily accessible through their websites or through brochures or notice boards. These are mostly higher-income economies, but they also include low- and lower-middle-income economies such as Armenia, Burkina Faso, El Salvador, Georgia and Tanzania. Around the world company registries are most likely to make information available online or through brochures or notice boards, and building departments least likely to do so (figure 8.1). On the brighter side, in only 7 of 176 economies do all 4 of these agencies require that customers meet with an official to obtain fee schedules.

Access to fee schedules is most limited in Sub-Saharan Africa and the Middle East and North Africa. Of the 7 economies globally where fee schedules cannot be obtained from any of the agencies surveyed without meeting with an official, 6

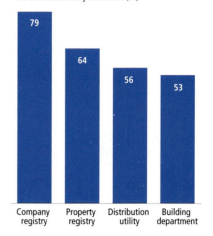

FIGURE 8.1 Which agencies are more likely to make information accessible?

Share of economies where agency makes fee schedules easily accessible (%)

Source: *Doing Business* database.

are in Sub-Saharan Africa and the other in the Middle East and North Africa.[9] On average in these regions businesses are unable to find fee schedules online or in a brochure for 2 of the 4 agencies. But there are notable exceptions. In Sub-Saharan Africa, Burkina Faso, Mauritius, South Africa and Tanzania guarantee easy access to information in all 4 regulatory areas. In the Middle East and North Africa, Oman and the United Arab Emirates provide the easiest access: in both these countries 3 of the 4 agencies provide information without a need for a meeting with an official.

Businesses can expect consistently easy access to information in OECD high-income economies. More than 60% of these economies make it easy to access information in all 4 regulatory areas covered by the new data. In Australia, Belgium, Denmark, Finland, Sweden and the United States, for example, company registries, property registries, building departments and power distribution utilities all make fee schedules associated with their services available on the internet or through brochures. Greece, Hungary and Luxembourg are the only OECD high-income economies where businesses still have to meet with an official at 2 of the 4 agencies to get this information.

---

### BOX 8.1  HOW IS THE ACCESSIBILITY OF REGULATORY INFORMATION MEASURED?

The new data on the accessibility of regulatory information, collected between January and August 2012, measure how easy it is to access fee schedules for 4 regulatory processes in the largest business city of an economy: incorporating a new company, obtaining a building permit, connecting a business to electricity and transferring property. Fee schedules are considered easily accessible if they can be obtained either through the website of the relevant agency or through public notices (brochures or notice boards) available at that agency or a related one, without a need to meet with an official. They are considered not easily accessible if they can be obtained only by meeting with an official.

For incorporation fees the relevant agency is the company registry; for building permit fees, the building department; for electricity connection fees, the distribution utility or electricity regulator; and for property transfer fees, the property registry.

For each regulatory area, economies where information is easily accessible are assigned a score of 1; those where information is not easily accessible are assigned a score of 0.

Computed as a simple average of the scores for these 4 areas, an aggregate accessibility of information index is constructed for a sample of 176 economies for which the data are available for all 4 (see table). The index illustrates how consistent governments are in their transparency efforts across different agencies and branches of government.

| Sample sizes for accessibility of information data | |
|---|---|
| **Measure** | **Sample** |
| Accessibility of information on incorporation fees | 185 economies |
| Accessibility of information on building permit fees | 176 economies |
| Accessibility of information on electricity connection fees | 185 economies |
| Accessibility of information on property transfer fees | 185 economies |
| Accessibility of information index | 176 economies |

FIGURE 8.2  Accessibility of regulatory information varies with economies' income level and internet penetration

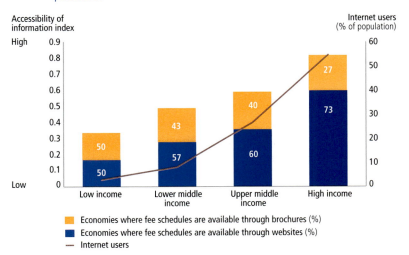

Economies where fee schedules are available through brochures (%)
Economies where fee schedules are available through websites (%)
Internet users

*Note:* For an explanation of the accessibility of information index, see box 8.1. Relationships are significant at the 5% level after controlling for income per capita.

*Source: Doing Business* database; World Bank, World Development Indicators database (2008 data).

## WHO MAKES REGULATORY INFORMATION EASY TO ACCESS?

The accessibility of regulatory information varies with income level and internet penetration: low-income economies have the least regulatory transparency on average, and high-income economies the most (figure 8.2). In OECD high-income economies the accessibility of regulatory information as measured by *Doing Business* is 38% higher than the average for the sample. Is the reason simply that richer economies have more resources to invest in online solutions and in other ways to make information easily accessible to the public?

Variation within income groups suggests that making information easily accessible may not be entirely a question of resources; for many governments it may also be a question of choice. Tanzania, a low-income economy, makes more information easily accessible than such high-income economies as Greece, Kuwait and the United Arab Emirates. Cape Verde and Georgia, two lower-middle-income economies, also have higher accessibility levels than some richer economies. Moreover, as figure 8.2 illustrates, there

are multiple ways in which governments can share information with the public. Where internet access might be difficult, for example, information can be distributed though brochures and notice boards. Low-income economies such as Burkina Faso and Tanzania show that brochures can be an effective means of creating more transparency around regulatory information.

The new data show that even when differences in income per capita are

taken into account, economies with easy access to regulatory information are more likely to be democratic, to be generally more transparent and to guarantee greater political and civil rights (figure 8.3). Governments that provide greater transparency in their business regulatory environment are also more transparent in other areas. To take 2 examples, they disclose more budgetary information (as measured by the Open Budget Index of the International Budget Partnership), and they make greater efforts to publicize laws and make them comprehensible to the wider public (as measured by the Rule of Law Index of the World Justice Project).[10]

## MORE INFORMATION, BETTER BUSINESS REGULATION?

Greater access to regulatory information is also associated with more efficient regulatory processes. Economies that make fee schedules consistently easy to access rank higher on the ease of doing business—and they keep regulatory compliance costs for firms significantly lower.

Take the cost of starting a business. The global average is a significant 31% of income per capita. Entrepreneurs in lower-income economies face even higher costs, reaching 87% of income per capita in Sub-Saharan Africa. But regardless of income levels, official incorporation fees

FIGURE 8.3  Access to regulatory information is greater where democracy and political rights are greater

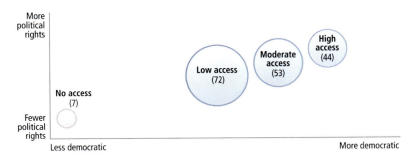

*Note:* The 176 economies in the sample are divided into 4 groups based on the accessibility of information index, and averages are taken for the economies in each group on institutionalized democracy ratings (for 2012) and political rights ratings (for 2010). Numbers in parentheses are the number of economies in each group. Relationships are significant at the 5% level after controlling for income per capita.

*Source:* Freedom House 2012; Center for Systemic Peace, Integrated Network for Societal Conflict Research; *Doing Business* database.

FIGURE 8.4 Incorporation and electricity connection fees are lower in economies with greater disclosure of fee schedules and structures

Average cost to start a business
(% of income per capita)

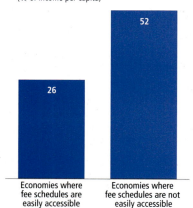

| Economies where fee schedules are easily accessible | Economies where fee schedules are not easily accessible |

Average cost to connect to electricity
(% of income per capita)

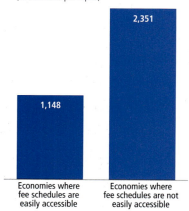

| Economies where fee schedules are easily accessible | Economies where fee schedules are not easily accessible |

*Note:* Fee schedules are considered easily accessible if they can be obtained through the website of the relevant authority or another government agency or through public notices, without a need for a meeting with an official. The data sample includes 185 economies. Relationships are significant at the 5% level after controlling for income per capita.

*Source: Doing Business* database.

FIGURE 8.5 Greater access to regulatory information is associated with greater trust in regulatory quality

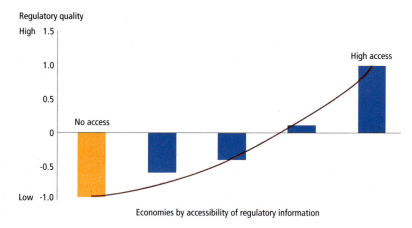

*Note:* The 176 economies in the sample are divided into 5 groups based on the accessibility of information index, and averages are taken for the economies in each group on the Regulatory Quality Index ranking of the Worldwide Governance Indicators for 2009. The Regulatory Quality Index, ranging from -2.5 (weak) to 2.5 (strong), measures public perception of government's ability to formulate and implement sound policies. Relationships are significant at the 5% level after controlling for income per capita.

*Source:* World Bank, Worldwide Governance Indicators; *Doing Business* database.

tend to be significantly lower in economies where fee schedules are easily accessible (figure 8.4).[11] Starting a business costs 26% of income per capita on average in economies where fee schedules are publicly available, but 52% where they are not. Similarly, getting a new electricity connection costs more than twice as much in economies where information on the connection fees is more difficult to

access. Similar results were found for the fees to register property and to obtain a construction permit.

Moreover, access to basic regulatory information is also positively associated with the trust the public places in its government. Where regulatory information is more consistently accessible, businesses perceive their government as being better able to formulate and implement sound policies and regulations that permit and promote private sector development (figure 8.5).

## CONCLUSION

A growing body of empirical research suggests that while transparency alone might not be enough to increase government accountability, it is certainly necessary.[12] A study of Brazilian municipalities shows that mayors are less corrupt where citizens can gain access to municipal budget reports, but only in the municipalities where electoral rules stipulate the possibility for reelection of a mayor. Where mayors cannot be reelected, access to budgetary information has no effect in reducing corruption.[13] Similarly, a study in India found evidence that local governments' responsiveness

to newspaper reports on drops in food production and flood damage to crops is more pronounced where elections loom close, political competition is strong and voter turnout high.[14] In short, information is more powerful when it is complemented by incentives that hold officials accountable.

The data and analysis presented here suggest that easier access to regulatory information such as fee schedules is associated with greater regulatory efficiency, lower compliance costs and better regulatory quality for businesses. This seems to confirm the findings of others who have shown that more transparency and better-quality government tend to go hand in hand.[15]

The correlations cannot answer the question whether greater transparency might lead to better governments or whether better governments might also simply be more transparent. Yet it seems that improving transparency could at least be a good start in increasing the accountability of public agencies charged with implementing regulations. Only when citizens have access to information do they also have a chance to act on the information and use it to pressure for greater accountability of public agents. The effort appears to be worth making, and as the data here show, it need not always be costly. Sometimes printing a simple brochure might be enough.

## NOTES

This case study was written by Carolin Geginat.

1. Amartya Sen, "Adam Smith's Market Never Stood Alone," *Financial Times*, March 11, 2009, http://www.ft.com/.
2. Hirschman 1970; Paul 1992; Stiglitz 2003; Kaufmann 2003.
3. *Exit* and *voice* are terms introduced by Hirschman (1970) in his discussion on how consumers can respond to poor-quality provision of goods and services.
4. Reinikka and Svensson 2005.
5. Akerlof 1970; Stiglitz and Weiss 1981; Hirshleifer 1980; Stigler 1971.
6. See, for example, World Bank (2004); Reinikka and Svensson (2005); Deininger and Mpuga (2005); and Besley and Burgess (2002).
7. In addition, research suggests that enterprise surveys in corrupt countries tend to understate the gravity of the corruption problem. Jensen, Li and Rahman (2010) find that enterprises in countries with less press freedom are more likely to provide no responses or false responses on the issue of corruption. Corruption is understated in such countries.
8. Fee schedules are generally made available by implementing agencies and are not part of national legislation. The accessibility of this type of regulatory information therefore speaks directly to the openness and transparency efforts of particular government agencies.
9. These economies are Botswana, the Republic of Congo, Equatorial Guinea, Eritrea, Gabon and Mauritania in Sub-Saharan Africa and Iraq in the Middle East and North Africa.
10. Geginat, Gonzalez and Saltane 2012.
11. The correlations were calculated on the basis of official regulatory compliance costs only. Bribes that might have to be paid as well in some economies are not captured by the cost estimates.
12. See Olken (2007); Besley and Burgess (2002); and Ferraz and Finan (2011).
13. Ferraz and Finan 2011.
14. Besley and Burgess 2002.
15. See, for example, Islam (2006); and Williams (2009). Islam (2006) finds that governments that are timelier in releasing important political and macroeconomic data also rank better on various measures of good governance. Using Granger causality regressions, Williams (2009) shows that the release of information by governments has a positive short-term effect on the quality of bureaucracy. The analysis uses data similar to those employed by Islam (2006) as well as measures of corruption, the size of government and education, along with trade variables as control variables.

2007 2012 2011
2005 2009 2004
2008 2006 2010 2013

# Starting a business

- **Starting a business is easiest in New Zealand, where it takes 1 procedure, 1 day, less than 1% of income per capita and no paid-in minimum capital.**

- **From June 2011 to June 2012 *Doing Business* recorded 36 reforms making it easier to start a business.**

- **Burundi made the biggest improvement in the ease of starting a business in the past year.**

- **Madagascar is among the economies advancing the furthest toward the frontier in regulatory practice in starting a business since 2005.**

- **Simplifying company registration formalities was the most common feature of business start-up reforms in the past 8 years.**

- **Among regions, Eastern Europe and Central Asia has improved the business start-up process the most since 2005.**

*For more information on good practices and research related to starting a business, visit http://www .doingbusiness.org/data/ exploretopics/starting-a-business. For more on the methodology, see the section on starting a business in the data notes.*

Entrepreneurs around the world face a range of challenges. One of them is inefficient regulation. *Doing Business* measures the procedures, time, cost and paid-in minimum capital required for a small or medium-size limited liability company to start up and formally operate. To make the data comparable across 185 economies, *Doing Business* uses a standardized business that is 100% domestically owned, has start-up capital equivalent to 10 times income per capita, engages in general industrial or commercial activities and employs between 10 and 50 people within the first month of operations.

According to a recent review, evidence from several studies shows that reforms making it easier to start a formal business are associated with increases in the number of newly registered firms and sustained gains in economic performance, including improvements in employment and productivity.[1] For example, in both Canada and the United States empirical research finds that economic growth is driven by the entry of new formal businesses rather than by the growth of existing firms.[2] In Mexico the number of registered businesses increased by 5% and employment by 2.2% after business registration was simplified in different municipalities.[3]

## WHO REFORMED IN STARTING A BUSINESS IN 2011/12?

In 2011/12, 36 economies made it easier to start a business (table 9.1). Five others made the process more difficult. Among those making it easier, some created online

| TABLE 9.1  Who made starting a business easier in 2011/12—and what did they do? | | |
|---|---|---|
| **Feature** | **Economies** | **Some highlights** |
| Simplified registration formalities (seal, publication, notarization, inspection, other requirements) | Albania; Benin; Bulgaria; Burundi; China; Colombia; Comoros; Democratic Republic of Congo; Republic of Congo; Lesotho; FYR Macedonia; Netherlands; Romania; Slovak Republic; Tanzania; Togo; Ukraine; Uzbekistan; Vietnam | Albania made the notarization of incorporation documents optional, cutting procedures by 1, time by 1 day and cost by 7% of income per capita. The Netherlands eliminated the requirement for a declaration of nonobjection before incorporation, cutting procedures by 1, time by 3 days and cost by €91. |
| Abolished or reduced minimum capital requirement | Kazakhstan; Kosovo; Mexico; Mongolia; Morocco; Norway; Serbia | Mexico eliminated its minimum capital requirement for limited liability companies. Norway reduced its requirement by 70%. |
| Created or improved one-stop shop | Burundi; Chad; Guinea; Lao PDR; Lesotho; Madagascar; Thailand | Guinea created a one-stop shop for business start-up, cutting 6 procedures and 5 days from the start-up process. |
| Cut or simplified postregistration procedures (tax registration, social security registration, licensing) | Costa Rica; Sri Lanka; United Arab Emirates | Sri Lanka computerized and expedited the process of obtaining registration numbers with the Employees Provident Fund and Employees Trust Fund. This cut time by 29 days. |
| Introduced or improved online procedures | Ireland; Lithuania | Ireland introduced an online facility for business registration, reducing time by 3 days and cost by a third. |

*Source: Doing Business database.*

FIGURE 9.1 Burundi made starting a business easier in 2011/12 by setting up a one-stop shop

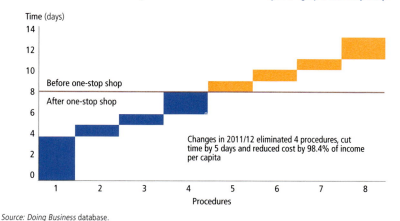

*Source: Doing Business database.*

services and standard registration documents, which go a long way in facilitating swift and legally sound incorporation.

Lithuania introduced an online facility for business registration. Sri Lanka computerized and expedited the process of obtaining registration numbers with the social security agencies. Other economies—including Mongolia and Serbia—eliminated the paid-in minimum capital requirement. Norway reduced it. To encourage entrepreneurship among youth, Italy created a new type of limited liability company with a simplified incorporation process for people under age 35. Now it is working to extend this option to all entrepreneurs.

Globally, Burundi improved the most in the ease of starting a business in the past year. The government reduced tax registration costs and created a one-stop shop at the Burundi Revenue Authority, bringing together representatives from several agencies involved in the business start-up process (figure 9.1).

## WHAT HAVE WE LEARNED FROM 8 YEARS OF DATA?

In the past 8 years *Doing Business* recorded 368 business registration reforms in 149 economies (figure 9.2). Globally since 2005, the average time to start a business has fallen from 50 days to 30—and in low-income economies the average has been reduced by half. Many economies

have abolished the paid-in minimum capital requirement (figure 9.3).

In 2005 only 2 low-income economies made it easier to start a business. Seven years later 9 did so. As a result, today 2 low- or lower-middle-income economies rank among the top 10 globally on the ease of starting a business (table 9.2).

Madagascar is among the economies advancing furthest toward the frontier in regulatory practice in starting a business since 2005 (table 9.3). This is thanks to 6 reforms making business start-up easier. The country set up a one-stop shop and improved its services over time. It also simplified registration formalities and the publication requirement. Finally, it reduced and then progressively eliminated the paid-in minimum capital requirement. Other economies also made steady progress over time: Guinea-Bissau and Tajikistan both implemented a one-stop shop and simplified business registration procedures.

Introducing information and communication technology has been a common feature of start-up reforms, and today 106 economies use it for services ranging from name search to full online business registration. Of these, more than 40 offer electronic registration services. Several economies with the fastest business start-up offer electronic

FIGURE 9.2 Sub-Saharan Africa and Eastern Europe & Central Asia still lead in start-up reforms

Number of *Doing Business* reforms making it easier to start a business by *Doing Business* report year

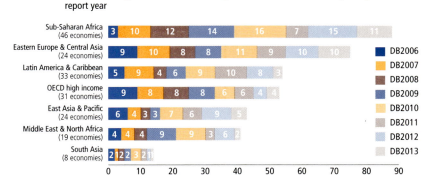

*Note:* An economy can be considered to have only 1 *Doing Business* reform per topic and year. The data sample for DB2006 (2005) includes 174 economies. The sample for DB2013 (2012) also includes The Bahamas, Bahrain, Barbados, Brunei Darussalam, Cyprus, Kosovo, Liberia, Luxembourg, Malta, Montenegro and Qatar, for a total of 185 economies.
*Source: Doing Business database.*

FIGURE 9.3  Worldwide, big cuts in the time and paid-in minimum capital requirement to start a business

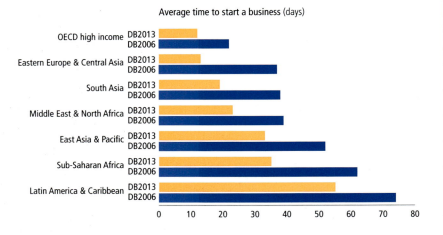

Average time to start a business (days)

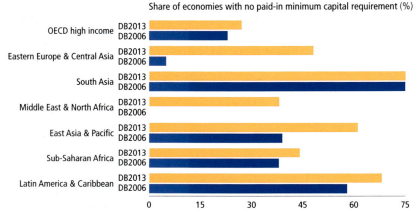

Share of economies with no paid-in minimum capital requirement (%)

*Note:* To ensure an accurate comparison, the figure shows data for the same sample of 174 economies for both DB2006 (2005) and DB2013 (2012) and uses the regional classifications that apply in 2012. The economies added to the *Doing Business* sample after 2005 and therefore excluded here are The Bahamas, Bahrain, Barbados, Brunei Darussalam, Cyprus, Kosovo, Liberia, Luxembourg, Malta, Montenegro and Qatar. DB2006 data are adjusted for any data revisions and changes in methodology.

*Source: Doing Business* database.

TABLE 9.2  Where is starting a business easiest—and where most difficult?

| Easiest | RANK | Most difficult | RANK |
|---|---|---|---|
| New Zealand | 1 | Côte d'Ivoire | 176 |
| Australia | 2 | Iraq | 177 |
| Canada | 3 | Suriname | 178 |
| Singapore | 4 | West Bank and Gaza | 179 |
| Macedonia, FYR | 5 | Congo, Rep. | 180 |
| Hong Kong SAR, China | 6 | Chad | 181 |
| Georgia | 7 | Equatorial Guinea | 182 |
| Rwanda | 8 | Eritrea | 183 |
| Belarus | 9 | Haiti | 183 |
| Ireland | 10 | Djibouti | 185 |

*Note:* Rankings are the average of the economy's rankings on the procedures, time, cost and paid-in minimum capital for starting a business. See the data notes for details. Economies shown with the same number are tied in the ranking.

*Source: Doing Business* database.

TABLE 9.3  Who has narrowed the distance to frontier in starting a business the most since 2005?

| Most improved | Improvement in distance to frontier (percentage points) |
|---|---|
| Guinea-Bissau | 63 (0→63) |
| Yemen, Rep. | 57 (17→74) |
| Tajikistan | 55 (30→85) |
| Angola | 53 (7→60) |
| Madagascar | 52 (43→95) |
| Saudi Arabia | 50 (31→81) |
| Egypt, Arab Rep. | 46 (42→88) |
| Timor-Leste | 45 (16→61) |
| Mali | 41 (26→67) |
| Mozambique | 41 (40→81) |

*Note:* The distance to frontier measure shows how far on average an economy is from the best performance achieved by any economy on each *Doing Business* indicator since 2005—in this case for the starting a business indicators. The measure is normalized to range between 0 and 100, with 100 representing the best performance (the frontier). The data refer to the 174 economies included in *Doing Business 2006* (2005). Eleven economies were added in subsequent years. The first column lists the top 10 most improved economies in order; the second shows the absolute improvement in the distance to frontier between 2005 and 2012.

*Source: Doing Business* database.

registration—New Zealand, Australia, Singapore, Canada, Portugal, Denmark and Estonia (table 9.4). And online services are increasingly being offered in developing economies.

Eighty-eight economies have some sort of one-stop shop for business registration, including the 58 that established

or improved theirs in the past 8 years. Ninety-one economies require no paid-in minimum capital, and many others have lowered the requirement. The average paid-in minimum capital requirement has fallen from 183% of income per capita to only 44% since 2005.

## TABLE 9.4  Who makes starting a business easy—and who does not?

| Procedures (number) | | | | Cost (% of income per capita) | | | |
|---|---|---|---|---|---|---|---|
| Fewest | | Most | | Least | | Most | |
| Canada | 1 | Honduras | 13 | Slovenia | 0.0 | Côte d'Ivoire | 130.0 |
| New Zealand | 1 | Suriname | 13 | Denmark | 0.2 | Ethiopia | 135.3 |
| Australia | 2 | Algeria | 14 | Ireland | 0.3 | Micronesia, Fed. Sts. | 144.2 |
| Georgia | 2 | Argentina | 14 | South Africa | 0.3 | Comoros | 150.0 |
| Kyrgyz Republic | 2 | Bolivia | 15 | Canada | 0.4 | Djibouti | 150.7 |
| Macedonia, FYR | 2 | Brunei Darussalam | 15 | New Zealand | 0.4 | Gambia, The | 158.7 |
| Madagascar | 2 | Uganda | 15 | Sweden | 0.5 | Central African Republic | 172.6 |
| Rwanda | 2 | Philippines | 16 | Singapore | 0.6 | Chad | 202.0 |
| Slovenia | 2 | Venezuela, RB | 17 | Kazakhstan | 0.6 | Congo, Dem. Rep. | 284.7 |
| Armenia | 3 | Equatorial Guinea | 18 | Australia | 0.7 | Haiti | 286.6 |

| Time (days) | | | | Paid-in minimum capital | | |
|---|---|---|---|---|---|---|
| Fastest | | Slowest | | Most | % of income per capita | US$ |
| New Zealand | 1 | Zimbabwe | 90 | Chad | 289 | 1,997 |
| Australia | 2 | Lao PDR | 92 | Guinea | 325 | 1,428 |
| Georgia | 2 | Timor-Leste | 94 | Mauritania | 328 | 3,279 |
| Macedonia, FYR | 2 | Brunei Darussalam | 101 | Mali | 332 | 2,025 |
| Hong Kong SAR, China | 3 | Haiti | 105 | Guinea-Bissau | 338 | 2,028 |
| Rwanda | 3 | Brazil | 119 | Burkina Faso | 354 | 2,017 |
| Singapore | 3 | Equatorial Guinea | 135 | Togo | 366 | 2,047 |
| Albania | 4 | Venezuela, RB | 144 | Djibouti | 384 | 5,627 |
| Belgium | 4 | Congo, Rep. | 161 | Central African Republic | 444 | 2,087 |
| Canada | 5 | Suriname | 694 | Niger | 573 | 2,062 |

*Note:* Ninety-one economies have no paid-in minimum capital requirement.

*Source: Doing Business* database.

## NOTES

This topic note was written by Karim O. Belayachi, Paula Garcia Serna, Hussam Hussein and Frédéric Meunier.

1. Motta, Oviedo and Santini 2010.
2. Klapper and Love 2011b.
3. Bruhn 2011.

# Dealing with construction permits

- **Dealing with construction permits is easiest in Hong Kong SAR, China, where it takes 6 procedures and 67 days to complete this process.**

- **From June 2011 to June 2012 *Doing Business* recorded 20 reforms making it easier to deal with construction permits.**

- **Taiwan, China, made the biggest improvement in the ease of dealing with construction permits in the past year.**

- **FYR Macedonia has advanced the furthest toward the frontier in regulatory practice in construction permitting since 2005.**

- **Among regions, Eastern Europe and Central Asia has made the biggest improvements in the ease of dealing with construction permits since 2005.**

- **Introducing or improving one-stop shops was among the most common features of construction permitting reforms in the past 8 years.**

*For more information on good practices and research related to dealing with construction permits, visit http://www.doingbusiness .org/data/exploretopics/dealing-with-construction-permits. For more on the methodology, see the section on dealing with construction permits in the data notes.*

Construction regulation matters for public safety. If procedures are too complicated or costly, builders tend to proceed without a permit.[1] By some estimates 60–80% of building projects in developing economies are undertaken without the proper permits and approvals.[2] Construction regulation also matters for the health of the building sector and the economy as a whole. According to a recent study, the construction industry accounts on average for 6.5% of GDP in OECD economies.[3] Good regulations help ensure the safety standards that protect the public while making the permitting process efficient, transparent and affordable.

To measure the ease of dealing with construction permits, *Doing Business* records the procedures, time and cost required for a small to medium-size business to obtain all the necessary approvals to build a simple commercial warehouse and connect it to water, sewerage and a fixed telephone line (table 10.1). The case study includes all types of inspections and certificates needed before, during and after construction of the warehouse. To make the data comparable across 185 economies, the case study assumes that the warehouse is located in the periurban area of the largest business city, is not in a special economic or industrial zone and will be used for general storage activities.

## WHO REFORMED IN DEALING WITH CONSTRUCTION PERMITS IN 2011/12?

From June 2011 to June 2012 *Doing Business* recorded 20 reforms making it easier to deal with construction permits (table 10.2). Six others made the process

| TABLE 10.1 | Where is dealing with construction permits easiest— and where most difficult? | | |
|---|---|---|---|
| **Easiest** | **RANK** | **Most difficult** | **RANK** |
| Hong Kong SAR, China | 1 | Montenegro | 176 |
| Singapore | 2 | Azerbaijan | 177 |
| Georgia | 3 | Russian Federation | 178 |
| Marshall Islands | 4 | Serbia | 179 |
| St. Vincent and the Grenadines | 5 | Tajikistan | 180 |
| New Zealand | 6 | China | 181 |
| Bahrain | 7 | India | 182 |
| Denmark | 8 | Ukraine | 183 |
| Taiwan, China | 9 | Albania[a] | 185 |
| Grenada | 10 | Eritrea[a] | 185 |

*Note:* Rankings are the average of the economy's rankings on the procedures, time and cost to comply with formalities to build a warehouse. See the data notes for details.

a. Albania and Eritrea are both "no practice" economies with barriers preventing private builders from legally obtaining a building permit. They are tied in the ranking.

*Source: Doing Business* database.

longer and costlier. East Asia and the Pacific, Latin America and the Caribbean, OECD high-income economies and Sub-Saharan Africa had the largest number making it easier, all with 4, followed by Eastern Europe and Central Asia with 3 and South Asia with 1. The Middle East and North Africa implemented no major regulatory improvements in the area of dealing with construction permits in 2011/12.

Taiwan, China, made the biggest improvement in the ease of dealing with construction permits in the past year (figure 10.1). By early 2012 the city of Taipei had finished implementing a single window for preconstruction approvals and

| TABLE 10.2 | Who made dealing with construction permits easier in 2011/12—and what did they do? | |
|---|---|---|
| Feature | Economies | Some highlights |
| Streamlined procedures | Burundi; China; Costa Rica; Netherlands; Panama; Peru; Portugal; Russian Federation | Burundi eliminated the requirement to obtain a clearance from the Ministry of Health and reduced the cost of the geotechnical study. |
| Reduced time for processing permit applications | Benin; Burundi; Greece; India; Malaysia; Norway; Portugal | India implemented strict time limits at the municipality for processing building permits. |
| Introduced or improved one-stop shop | Brunei Darussalam; Malaysia; Taiwan, China | Taiwan, China, introduced a risk-based, self-regulatory inspection system and improved operational features of its one-stop shop for building permits. |
| Reduced fees | Republic of Congo; Guinea; Montenegro | The Republic of Congo reduced the cost of first-time registration of the building. |
| Improved electronic platforms or online services | Costa Rica; Netherlands | The Netherlands merged several types of approvals and implemented online application systems. |
| Introduced risk-based approvals | Guatemala; Turkey | Guatemala introduced a risk-based approval system for building permits. |

*Source: Doing Business database.*

another for postconstruction approvals in its one-stop shop. In addition, authorities issued new rules on private inspections. These allow builders to perform inspections during the construction of lower-risk commercial buildings with fewer than 5 floors. The changes eliminated 14 procedures and 31 days from the process of dealing with construction permits.

## WHAT HAVE WE LEARNED FROM 8 YEARS OF DATA?

In the past 8 years 83 economies around the world implemented 146 reforms making it easier to deal with construction permits (figure 10.2). Eastern Europe and Central Asia had the most, with 39, followed by Sub-Saharan Africa (33), Latin America and the Caribbean (22), OECD high-income economies (22), East Asia and the Pacific (16), the Middle East and North Africa (13) and South Asia (1).

Economies in Eastern Europe and Central Asia have achieved the biggest time savings since 2005, reducing the time to deal with construction permits by 88 days on average (figure 10.3).

| TABLE 10.3 | Who makes dealing with construction permits easy—and who does not? | | |
|---|---|---|---|
| **Procedures (number)** | | | |
| Fewest | | Most | |
| Hong Kong SAR, China | 6 | Azerbaijan | 28 |
| New Zealand | 6 | Guinea | 29 |
| St. Lucia | 7 | Philippines | 29 |
| Sweden | 7 | Poland | 29 |
| Colombia | 8 | Kazakhstan | 32 |
| Denmark | 8 | Czech Republic | 33 |
| Jamaica | 8 | El Salvador | 33 |
| Spain | 8 | India | 34 |
| St. Vincent and the Grenadines | 8 | Malaysia | 37 |
| Thailand | 8[a] | Russian Federation | 42 |
| **Time (days)** | | | |
| Fastest | | Slowest | |
| Singapore | 26 | Mozambique | 377 |
| United States | 27 | Venezuela, RB | 381 |
| Korea, Rep. | 29 | Barbados | 416 |
| Bahrain | 43 | Suriname | 461 |
| Colombia | 46 | Brazil | 469 |
| United Arab Emirates | 46 | Côte d'Ivoire | 475 |
| Vanuatu | 54 | Zimbabwe | 614 |
| Qatar | 62 | Cambodia | 652 |
| Finland | 66 | Cyprus | 677 |
| Hong Kong SAR, China | 67 | Haiti | 1,129 |
| **Cost (% of income per capita)** | | | |
| Least | | Most | |
| Qatar | 1.1 | Congo, Dem. Rep. | 1,582.7 |
| Brunei Darussalam | 4.0 | Niger | 1,612.8 |
| Trinidad and Tobago | 5.3 | Zambia | 1,679.1 |
| St. Kitts and Nevis | 5.4 | Burundi | 1,911.9 |
| Hungary | 5.7 | Djibouti | 2,023.6 |
| Slovak Republic | 7.3 | Mauritania | 2,796.6 |
| Palau | 7.6 | Kosovo | 2,986.0 |
| Dominica | 7.6 | Afghanistan | 4,308.6 |
| Maldives | 8.2 | Zimbabwe | 4,423.4 |
| Barbados | 8.3 | Chad | 5,106.8 |

a. Five other economies also have 8 procedures for dealing with construction permits: Belize, Grenada, Guyana, Maldives and the Marshall Islands.

*Source: Doing Business database.*

FIGURE 10.1  Taiwan, China, made dealing with construction permits faster and easier

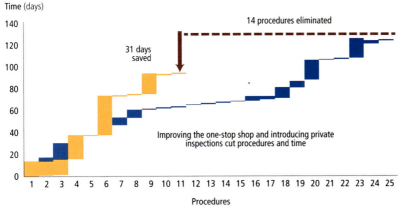

Source: Doing Business database.

**FIGURE 10.2** Eastern Europe and Central Asia keeps up its fast pace in construction permitting reforms

Number of *Doing Business* reforms making it easier to deal with construction permits by *Doing Business* report year

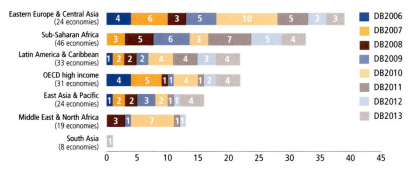

*Note:* An economy can be considered to have only 1 *Doing Business* reform per topic and year. The data sample for DB2006 (2005) includes 174 economies. The sample for DB2013 (2012) also includes The Bahamas, Bahrain, Barbados, Brunei Darussalam, Cyprus, Kosovo, Liberia, Luxembourg, Malta, Montenegro and Qatar, for a total of 185 economies.
*Source: Doing Business* database.

| TABLE 10.4 Who has narrowed the distance to frontier in dealing with construction permits the most since 2005? | |
|---|---|
| **Most improved** | **Improvement in distance to frontier (percentage points)** |
| Macedonia, FYR | 46 (36→82) |
| Kyrgyz Republic | 42 (39→81) |
| Tajikistan | 41 (11→52) |
| Burkina Faso | 39 (43→82) |
| Nigeria | 34 (44→78) |
| Georgia | 31 (61→92) |
| Equatorial Guinea | 30 (45→75) |
| Hong Kong SAR, China | 30 (67→97) |
| Guatemala | 26 (51→77) |
| São Tomé and Príncipe | 26[a] (53→79) |

*Note:* The distance to frontier measure shows how far on average an economy is from the best performance achieved by any economy on each *Doing Business* indicator since 2005—in this case for the dealing with construction permits indicators. The measure is normalized to range between 0 and 100, with 100 representing the best performance (the frontier). The data refer to the 174 economies included in *Doing Business 2006* (2005). Eleven economies were added in subsequent years. The first column lists the top 10 most improved economies in order; the second shows the absolute improvement in the distance to frontier between 2005 and 2012.

a. The Democratic Republic of Congo and Croatia also have an improvement of 26 percentage points.
*Source: Doing Business* database.

Among the most difficult changes to implement is the introduction or improvement of a one-stop shop. Construction approval systems usually involve many different agencies. To prevent overlap in their roles and ensure efficiency, many economies have opted to put representatives from many agencies in a single location. These one-stop shops improve the organization of the review process—not by reducing the number of checks needed but by better coordinating the efforts of the agencies involved. In the past 8 years 18 regulatory reforms were implemented to set up or improve one-stop shops, including the efforts made by Brunei Darussalam, Malaysia and Taiwan, China, in 2011/12. The 2 regions with the most such reforms are East Asia and the Pacific (with 5) and Eastern Europe and Central Asia (with 5).

Introducing risk-based approval systems is also a complex yet important change. Not all building projects are associated with the same economic or environmental risks. It therefore makes sense to differentiate construction permitting processes to treat buildings according to their risk level and location. This saves time for both entrepreneurs and authorities and allows them to direct their efforts and resources more efficiently. Seventeen regulatory reforms introduced risk-based approvals

**FIGURE 10.3** Biggest time savings in Eastern Europe and Central Asia

Average time to deal with construction permits (days)

| | OECD high income | East Asia & Pacific | Middle East & North Africa | Sub-Saharan Africa | South Asia | Eastern Europe & Central Asia | Latin America & Caribbean |
|---|---|---|---|---|---|---|---|

■ Before construction (including building permit)
■ During and after construction, utility connections

*Note:* To ensure an accurate comparison, the figure data includes 172 practice economies for both DB2006 (2005) and DB2013 (2012) and uses the regional classifications that apply in 2012. The economies added to the *Doing Business* sample after 2005 and therefore excluded here are The Bahamas, Bahrain, Barbados, Brunei Darussalam, Cyprus, Kosovo, Liberia, Luxembourg, Malta, Montenegro and Qatar. DB2006 data are adjusted for any data revisions and changes in methodology.
*Source: Doing Business* database.

in the past 8 years, including those in Guatemala and Turkey in 2011/12. Eastern Europe and Central Asia led the way with 7 such reforms, followed by Latin America and the Caribbean with 4.

Many economies have gone particularly far in closing the gap with the most efficient regulatory systems for dealing with construction permits, such as those in Hong Kong SAR, China, and Georgia (table 10.3). Those making the greatest progress toward the frontier in regulatory practice in this area have been able to do so thanks to a continual effort to improve regulations. FYR Macedonia has advanced the furthest toward this frontier since 2005 (table 10.4).

Authorities in Skopje implemented 4 reforms making it easier to deal with construction permits, including passing new construction laws, privatizing part of the inspection process and reducing several fees. The changes made a difference for builders in FYR Macedonia. In 2005 complying with all regulatory requirements for constructing the standard warehouse took 20 procedures and 244 days and cost the equivalent of 2,439% of income per capita. Today it takes 10 procedures and 117 days and costs 518% of income per capita.

## NOTES

This topic note was written by Marie Lily Delion, Anastasia Shegay, Alejandro Espinosa-Wang and Yucheng Zheng.

1. Moullier 2009.
2. De Soto 2000.
3. OECD 2010.

# Getting electricity

Infrastructure services, particularly electricity, are a concern for businesses around the world. World Bank Enterprise Surveys show that managers in 109 economies, 71 of them low or lower middle income, consider electricity to be among the biggest constraints to their business. In addition, managers estimate losses due to power outages at an average 5.1% of annual sales.[1]

*Doing Business* measures the procedures, time and cost for a small to medium-size business to get a new electricity connection for a warehouse. To make the data comparable across 185 economies, *Doing Business* uses a standardized case study of a newly established warehouse requiring a connection 150 meters long and with a power need of 140 kilovolt-amperes (kVA). The warehouse is assumed to be located in the largest business city, in an area where warehouses usually locate and electricity is most easily available.

## WHO REFORMED IN GETTING ELECTRICITY IN 2011/12?

Economies where getting an electricity connection is easy have several good practices in common (table 11.1). Other economies are adopting some of these practices. From June 2011 to June 2012 *Doing Business* recorded 13 reforms that made getting electricity easier (table 11.2). Two economies introduced changes that made connections costlier.

Improving process efficiency within the utility and streamlining approvals with other public agencies are the most common features of reforms making it easier to get electricity. These are also among the most effective ways to reduce

| TABLE 11.1 Where is getting electricity easiest—and where most difficult? | | | |
|---|---|---|---|
| Easiest | RANK | Most difficult | RANK |
| Iceland | 1 | Sierra Leone | 176 |
| Germany | 2 | Kyrgyz Republic | 177 |
| Korea, Rep. | 3 | Nigeria | 178 |
| Hong Kong SAR, China | 4 | Malawi | 179 |
| Singapore | 5 | Senegal | 180 |
| Taiwan, China | 6 | Tajikistan | 181 |
| United Arab Emirates | 7 | Guinea-Bissau | 182 |
| Switzerland | 8 | Madagascar | 183 |
| Sweden | 9 | Russian Federation | 184 |
| Thailand | 10 | Bangladesh | 185 |

*Note:* Rankings are the average of the economy's rankings on the procedures, time and cost to get an electricity connection. See the data notes for details.
*Source: Doing Business* database.

connection delays and the duplication of formalities. In Canada a more efficient process for obtaining the excavation permit and materials needed for the connection reduced the time to get a new electricity connection by 26 days. In Indonesia in 2011 the utility PT PLN set up a call center enabling customers to request a new electricity connection by phone. It further simplified the application process by eliminating the requirement to bring in a copy of a neighbor's bill to help determine the exact address of the new customer's business.

As these examples show, small adjustments can lead to big gains in time and efficiency. Other economies have adopted broader approaches. Armenia and Georgia streamlined procedures and revised connection costs through several amendments to the regulations

**TABLE 11.2  Who made getting electricity easier in 2011/12—and what did they do?**

| Feature | Economies | Some highlights |
|---|---|---|
| Improved process efficiency | Canada; Indonesia; Italy; Liberia; Mexico; Namibia; United Arab Emirates | In Italy the utility Acea Distribuzione reorganized its departmental workflow, increasing efficiency and reducing the time to complete external connection works. In Liberia the materials needed for an electricity connection are now readily available in the utility's stock, reducing the time to obtain a connection. The purchase of materials was facilitated by increased donor funding. |
| Streamlined approval process | Angola; Armenia; Georgia; Guinea | In Armenia the Public Services Regulatory Commission adopted resolutions giving customers more technical options for connecting to electricity. As a result, customers no longer have to wait for a permit from the State Energy Inspectorate. The commission also revised its fee structure, reducing the costs customers pay for a new connection. |
| Improved regulation of connection costs and processes | Republic of Korea; Rwanda | In Rwanda the installation cost that a customer must pay the Energy, Water and Sanitation Authority for the external connection works was reduced from 30% of the materials cost to 15% when the customer provides the materials. |

*Source: Doing Business database.*

**TABLE 11.3  Who makes getting electricity easy—and who does not?**

**Procedures (number)**

| Fewest | | Most | |
|---|---|---|---|
| Comoros | 3 | Nigeria | 8 |
| Germany | 3 | Senegal | 8 |
| Japan | 3 | Sierra Leone | 8 |
| Micronesia, Fed. Sts. | 3 | Azerbaijan | 9 |
| St. Vincent and the Grenadines | 3 | Bangladesh | 9 |
| Sweden | 3 | Mozambique | 9 |
| Switzerland | 3 | Tajikistan | 9 |
| Timor-Leste | 3 | Uzbekistan | 9 |
| Afghanistan | 4 | Russian Federation | 10 |
| Iceland | 4 | Ukraine | 11 |

**Time (days)**

| Fastest | | Slowest | |
|---|---|---|---|
| Germany | 17 | Cyprus | 247 |
| St. Kitts and Nevis | 18 | Hungary | 252 |
| Iceland | 22 | Nigeria | 260 |
| Austria | 23 | Czech Republic | 279 |
| Taiwan, China | 24 | Russian Federation | 281 |
| St. Lucia | 25 | Ukraine | 285 |
| Korea, Rep. | 28 | Bangladesh | 404 |
| Rwanda | 30 | Madagascar | 450 |
| Chile | 31 | Guinea-Bissau | 455 |
| Puerto Rico (U.S.) | 32 | Liberia | 465 |

**Cost (% of income per capita)**

| Least | | Most | |
|---|---|---|---|
| Japan | 0.0 | Djibouti | 7,776.4 |
| Hong Kong SAR, China | 1.6 | Guinea | 8,377.7 |
| Qatar | 3.9 | Malawi | 8,854.9 |
| Norway | 6.5 | Madagascar | 9,056.7 |
| Trinidad and Tobago | 6.6 | Chad | 11,017.6 |
| Australia | 8.7 | Central African Republic | 12,603.6 |
| Panama | 13.6 | Burkina Faso | 12,662.0 |
| Israel | 13.8 | Benin | 14,343.1 |
| Uruguay | 14.3 | Burundi | 21,481.7 |
| Iceland | 14.9 | Congo, Dem. Rep. | 27,211.6 |

*Source: Doing Business database.*

governing the process of connecting new customers. In Armenia the new connection process eliminated 1 procedure while a revised fee structure reduced the cost of new connections. In Georgia the National Commission on Energy and Water Regulation, through a resolution adopted in November 2011, also introduced a new process and a revised fee structure. The changes reduced the number of procedures by 1, the time by a quarter and the cost by a fifth (figure 11.1).

In the United Arab Emirates the Dubai Electricity and Water Authority introduced a "one window, one step" application for getting electricity as the latest enhancement to its SAP system. The new system allows customers to both submit and track their application online. It also streamlines their interactions with the utility and with their electrical contractor by offering a single interface. Implementation of the new system reduced the time to get a new connection by 15 days.

Other utilities have reduced connection costs and wait times by improving procurement practices. The Liberia Electricity Corporation reduced the time to get a new connection by 120 days by ensuring that the materials needed for the connection are readily available in its stock. The utility of the Namibian city of Windhoek

**FIGURE 11.1  Georgia made obtaining an electricity connection faster and cheaper**

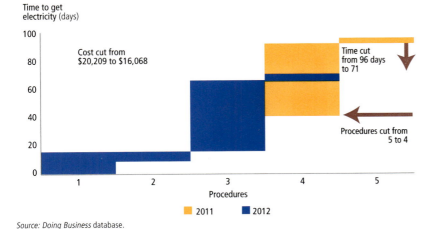

Time to get electricity (days)

Cost cut from $20,209 to $16,068

Time cut from 96 days to 71

Procedures cut from 5 to 4

Procedures

■ 2011   ■ 2012

*Source: Doing Business database.*

FIGURE 11.2  Sub-Saharan Africa had the most reforms in getting electricity in the past 3 years

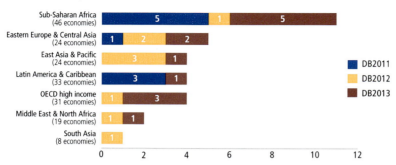

Number of *Doing Business* reforms making it easier to get electricity by *Doing Business* report year

*Note:* An economy can be considered to have only 1 *Doing Business* reform per topic and year. The data sample for DB2011 (2010) includes 176 economies. The sample for DB2013 (2012) includes a total of 185 economies.
*Source: Doing Business* database.

TABLE 11.4  Who has narrowed the distance to frontier in getting electricity the most since 2010?

| Most improved | Improvement in distance to frontier (percentage points) |
|---|---|
| Vanuatu | 19 (48→67) |
| Gambia, The | 17 (46→63) |
| Central African Republic | 15 (13→28) |
| Zimbabwe | 13 (40→53) |
| Afghanistan | 12 (55→67) |
| Latvia | 12 (61→73) |
| Georgia | 12 (72→84) |
| Kyrgyz Republic | 11 (33→44) |
| Congo, Rep. | 11 (35→46) |
| Angola | 10 (55→65) |

*Note:* The distance to frontier measure shows how far on average an economy is from the best performance achieved by any economy on each *Doing Business* indicator—in this case for the getting electricity indicators since 2010. The measure is normalized to range between 0 and 100, with 100 representing the best performance (the frontier). The data refer to the 176 economies included in the getting electricity sample in 2010. Nine economies were added in subsequent years. The first column lists the top 10 most improved economies in order; the second shows the absolute improvement in the distance to frontier between 2010 and 2012.
*Source: Doing Business* database.

took several steps aimed at reducing connection times and costs. First, the utility created a new template for calculating commodity prices, enabling it to provide customers with a cost estimate for a new connection more easily and thus more quickly. Second, the utility selected a more effective, efficient and experienced civil contractor through an open tender process. Together, these 2 measures reduced the connection time by 17 days. Finally, the utility began acquiring materials and equipment through an open tender process held every 2 years. This led to more competition and lower prices, reducing the connection cost by 77.8% of income per capita.

Many economies put an emphasis on making it easier to get a connection to the distribution network as a way to increase the electrification rate and stimulate business growth. Rwanda is an example. Its process for obtaining a connection is among the fastest in the world (table 11.3). The government improved it further by reducing installation costs. Customers still provide the materials for the connection, but rather than paying an additional 30% of that cost to the utility for installation, they now pay only half that.

## WHAT WERE THE TRENDS IN THE PAST 3 YEARS?

In the past 3 years 30 economies around the world implemented 31

regulatory reforms making it easier to get a new electricity connection. Sub-Saharan Africa accounts for the largest number of such reforms, with 11. Eastern Europe and Central Asia follows (figure 11.2). Among the most common and effective features of regulatory reforms in this area have been improving process efficiency within the utility, streamlining procedures and approvals with other public agencies, making information on connection fees and costs more readily available to customers, regulating the electrical profession to ensure the quality

FIGURE 11.3  In economies where utilities make the connection process cheap and efficient, supply is likely to be more reliable

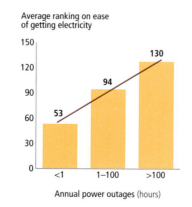

Average ranking on ease of getting electricity

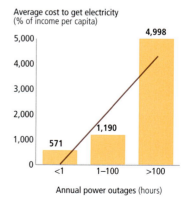

Average cost to get electricity (% of income per capita)

*Note:* Data refer to outages per low- or medium-voltage customer in the largest business city. The sample includes 86 economies. South Asia is excluded because of lack of data. Relationships in the first graph are significant at the 5% level after controlling for income per capita. Relationships in the second graph are significant at the 1% level after controlling for income per capita.
*Source: Doing Business* database.

of internal wiring and lessening the burden of security deposits.

Making it easier to get an electricity connection pays off. Since 2010 Vanuatu and The Gambia have advanced the furthest in narrowing the gap with the regulatory systems of economies with the most efficient practices in connecting new customers (table 11.4).

## WHAT DO THE INDICATORS SUGGEST ABOUT QUALITY OF SUPPLY?

Studies have shown that poor electricity supply adversely affects the productivity of firms and the investments they make in their productive capacity.[2] It is therefore essential for businesses to have reliable, good-quality electricity supply. But whether electricity supply is reliable or not, the first step for customers is to get a new connection, the process measured by the getting electricity indicators. This process represents only a small part of electricity services. Yet the indicators offer information on a number of issues for which data were previously unavailable, complementing indicators measuring such outcomes as outages.

Analysis of data for 140 economies suggests that the getting electricity indicators can serve as a useful proxy for the broader performance of the electricity sector.[3] Greater time and cost to get an electricity connection are associated with lower electrification rates. Additional connection procedures are more likely to occur in economies where the electricity supply is weak as a result of high losses in the transmission and distribution systems. New analysis of data for 86 economies suggests that where utilities make the connection process cheap and efficient as measured by the getting electricity indicators, supply is likely to be more reliable as measured by the total hours of power outages per customer per year (figure 11.3).[4]

## NOTES

This topic note was written by Maya Choueiri, Caroline Frontigny, Anastasia Shegay, Jayashree Srinivasan and Susanne Szymanski.

1. The surveys are for various years in 2002-10. The data sample includes 113 economies.
2. Calderon and Servén 2003; Dollar, Hallward-Driemeier and Mengistae 2006; Reinikka and Svensson 1999; Eifert 2007; Iimi 2011.
3. This analysis, by Geginat and Ramalho (2010), was done in 2009, when the data sample for the getting electricity indicators included only 140 economies. For 2012 the indicators cover 185 economies.
4. The price paid by a customer to get a new connection is not necessarily a measure of the operational performance of the electricity utility but of the existing regulatory framework and the policy to expand electricity access (partial or total subsidization of the costs incurred to build the connection). Besides efficient distribution companies, generation capacity and proper transmission infrastructure also play a critical part in reducing power outages.

The analysis was based on data collected from distribution utilities and regulators on the total hours of outages per customer in the largest business city. The analysis distinguished connection type by low or medium voltage (based on the getting electricity case study) and outages for the respective voltage level. The data analysis included the System Average Interruption Duration Index (SAIDI), the System Average Interruption Frequency Index (SAIFI) and the Customer Average Interruption Duration Index (CAIDI). Many utilities do not use these measures but provided other indices and statistics on power outages.

2007 2012 2011 2005 2009 2004 2008 2006 2010 2013

# Registering property

- As measured by *Doing Business*, registering property is easiest in Georgia.

- From June 2011 to June 2012 *Doing Business* recorded 17 reforms making it easier to register property.

- Malaysia made the biggest improvement in the ease of registering property in the past year.

- Angola, Burkina Faso, Côte d'Ivoire, Mauritius, Rwanda and Sierra Leone rank among the 10 economies making the biggest improvements since 2005, giving Sub-Saharan Africa the largest representation in this group.

- Economies making effective cuts in the procedures to register property have centralized procedures in a single agency. And they use information and communication technology or better caseload management systems to make the process faster and less costly.

*For more information on good practices and research related to registering property, visit http://www.doingbusiness.org/data/exploretopics/registering-property. For more on the methodology, see the section on registering property in the data notes.*

*Doing Business* records the procedures necessary for a business to purchase a property from another business and to formally transfer the property title to the buyer's name. The process starts with obtaining the necessary documents, such as a copy of the seller's title, and ends when the buyer is registered as the new owner of the property. Every procedure required by law or necessary in practice is included, whether it is the responsibility of the seller or the buyer and even if it must be completed by a third party on their behalf. As measured by *Doing Business*, formally transferring and registering property is easiest in Georgia (table 12.1).

## WHO REFORMED IN REGISTERING PROPERTY IN 2011/12?

In 2011/12, 17 economies made it easier for local businesses to register property by reducing the procedures, time or cost required (table 12.2). The most common improvements were introducing time limits or expedited procedures, increasing administrative efficiency, streamlining procedures and computerizing cadastres and registries. Nine other economies made it more difficult to transfer property by increasing the procedures, time or cost involved.

Malaysia made the biggest improvement in the ease of registering property in the past year by introducing a new caseload management system at the land registry. Inspired by Toyota's effective supply chain management strategy, the registry reduced registration time from 41 days in 2011 to 7 days in 2012 for nonstrata properties (those that are not part of a

subdivision or common-interest community). Malaysia is now working to bring registration times for strata properties, still in the range of 90–100 days, down to a similar time frame.

The OECD high-income group had both the largest share of economies with a property registration reform and the largest number of such reforms in 2011/12, accounting for 6 of the 17 such reforms recorded worldwide (figure 12.1). Poland, with the biggest improvement in the group, increased the efficiency of its land and mortgage registries through a series of coordinated changes. These included creating 2 new registration districts in Warsaw, introducing a new caseload management system and digitizing the records of the registries. Thanks to the changes, the time to process property applications at the registries fell from 3–6

| TABLE 12.1 Where is registering property easiest—and where most difficult? | | | |
|---|---|---|---|
| **Easiest** | **RANK** | **Most difficult** | **RANK** |
| Georgia | 1 | Belgium | 176 |
| New Zealand | 2 | Trinidad and Tobago | 177 |
| Belarus | 3 | Liberia | 178 |
| Armenia | 4 | Bahamas, The | 179 |
| Lithuania | 5 | Guinea-Bissau | 180 |
| Denmark | 6 | Eritrea | 181 |
| Norway | 7 | Nigeria | 182 |
| Slovak Republic | 8 | Marshall Islands | 185 |
| Azerbaijan | 9 | Micronesia, Fed. Sts. | 185 |
| Iceland | 9 | Timor-Leste | 185 |

*Note:* Rankings are the average of the economy's rankings on the procedures, time and cost to register property. See the data notes for details. Economies shown with the same number are tied in the ranking.

*Source: Doing Business* database.

| TABLE 12.2  Who made registering property easier in 2011/12—and what did they do? | | |
|---|---|---|
| Feature | Economies | Some highlights |
| Introduced effective time limits | Burundi; Israel; Mauritius; Ukraine | *Average time saved: 39 days*<br>Israel introduced a 20-day time limit for tax authorities to process capital gains self-assessments on property transfers, saving about 2 months. Burundi, Mauritius and Ukraine introduced time limits at their land registries and, while full compliance has not yet been achieved, have already cut registration time by 30 days, 7 days and 48 days, respectively. |
| Increased administrative efficiency | Malaysia; Panama; Poland; Sierra Leone; Trinidad and Tobago | *Average time saved: 38 days*<br>Malaysia implemented a new caseload management system in the land office, enabling clerks to process property transfer applications 34 days faster. The increase of the number of operating hours of the Public Registry of Panama until 11pm has cut 4 days in time. Poland cut 98 days from the time to register property by introducing a new caseload management system for land registries. Sierra Leone increased efficiency at the Ministry of Lands by digitizing records and hiring more personnel, reducing the time to register property by 19 days. The Water Authority (WASA) of Trinidad and Tobago, reduced the time needed to obtain its clearance certificate by 35 days, from 42 days to 7 days. |
| Computerized procedures | Bosnia and Herzegovina; Cyprus; Italy; Mauritius; Poland | *Average time saved: 32 days*<br>Bosnia and Herzegovina computerized its commercial registries, cutting registration time by 8 days. Cyprus reduced time by 14 days by computerizing its land registry. Mauritius implemented an electronic information management system at the Registrar-General's Department to allow different branches of the department to share information, cutting 7 days from the processing of property transfers. Italy merged all due diligence procedures performed by notaries through a secure portal, Notartel, which gives notaries access to the databases of the land registry, cadastre and commercial registry. |
| Reduced taxes or fees | Comoros; Ireland | *Cost reduction: up to 6% of the property value*<br>Ireland introduced a single stamp duty rate for transfers of nonresidential properties and reduced the rate by 4% of the property value, from 6% to 2%. The Comoros reduced the transfer tax from 15% of the property value to 9%. |
| Combined or reduced procedures | Czech Republic; Italy | *Procedures cut: 1*<br>The Czech Republic cut 1 procedure by giving the cadastral office online access to the database of the commercial registry. Italy gave notaries online access to all cadastral plans, eliminating the need to request the plans from the cadastre. |
| Put procedures online | Denmark | *Time saved: 6 days*<br>Denmark's land registry introduced electronic filing of property transfers and now accepts property transfer applications only online, cutting 6 days. |

*Source: Doing Business database.*

months in 2011 to as little as 14–60 days in 2012. Other OECD high-income economies improving their property registration process were the Czech Republic, Denmark, Ireland, Israel and Italy.

## WHAT HAVE WE LEARNED FROM 8 YEARS OF DATA?

In the past 8 years *Doing Business* recorded 185 reforms, undertaken in 121 economies, which increased the efficiency of procedures for transferring property (see figure 12.1). Globally, the average time to transfer property fell by 35 days, from 90 to 55, and the average cost by 1.2 percentage points, from 7.1% of the property value to 5.9% (figure 12.2).

| TABLE 12.3  Who has narrowed the distance to frontier in registering property the most since 2005? | |
|---|---|
| Most improved | Improvement in distance to frontier (percentage points) |
| Maldives | 49 (0→49) |
| Belarus | 42 (54→96) |
| Burkina Faso | 39 (23→62) |
| Rwanda | 38 (36→74) |
| Mauritius | 37 (33→70) |
| Bosnia and Herzegovina | 32 (36→68) |
| Côte d'Ivoire | 30 (22→52) |
| Angola | 27 (27→54) |
| Sierra Leone | 24 (28→52) |
| Slovenia | 24[a] (47→71) |

*Note:* The distance to frontier measure shows how far on average an economy is from the best performance achieved by any economy on each *Doing Business* indicator since 2005—in this case for the registering property indicators. The measure is normalized to range between 0 and 100, with 100 representing the best performance (the frontier). The data refer to the 174 economies included in *Doing Business 2006* (2005). Eleven economies were added in subsequent years. The first column lists the top 10 most improved economies in order; the second shows the absolute improvement in the distance to frontier between 2005 and 2012.

a. Burundi and the Solomon Islands also have an improvement of 24 percentage points.

*Source: Doing Business database.*

**FIGURE 12.1**  Sub-Saharan Africa leads in number of property registration reforms

Number of *Doing Business* reforms making it easier to register property by *Doing Business* report year

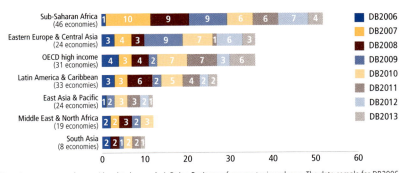

*Note:* An economy can be considered to have only 1 *Doing Business* reform per topic and year. The data sample for DB2006 (2005) includes 174 economies. The sample for DB2013 (2012) also includes The Bahamas, Bahrain, Barbados, Brunei Darussalam, Cyprus, Kosovo, Liberia, Luxembourg, Malta, Montenegro and Qatar, for a total of 185 economies.

*Source: Doing Business database.*

FIGURE 12.2 Property transfers have become faster in all regions

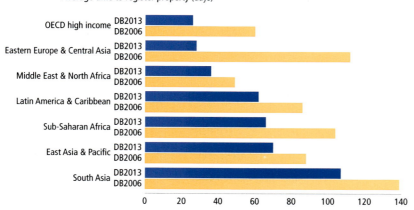

Average time to register property (days)

*Note:* To ensure an accurate comparison, the figure shows data for the same sample of 170 practice economies for both DB2006 (2005) and DB2013 (2012) and uses the regional classifications that apply in 2012. The economies added to the *Doing Business* sample after 2005 and therefore excluded here are The Bahamas, Bahrain, Barbados, Brunei Darussalam, Cyprus, Kosovo, Liberia, Luxembourg, Malta, Montenegro and Qatar. DB2006 data are adjusted for any data revisions and changes in methodology.
*Source: Doing Business database.*

FIGURE 12.3 Burkina Faso made transferring property faster and easier

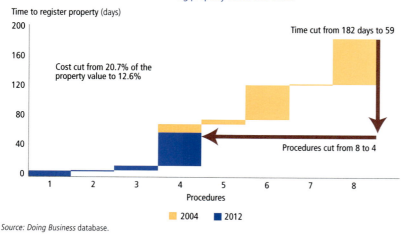

Time to register property (days)

Cost cut from 20.7% of the property value to 12.6%

Time cut from 182 days to 59

Procedures cut from 8 to 4

■ 2004  ■ 2012

*Source: Doing Business database.*

| TABLE 12.4 Who makes registering property easy—and who does not? | | | |
|---|---|---|---|
| **Procedures (number)** | | | |
| Fewest | | Most | |
| Georgia | 1 | Algeria | 10 |
| Norway | 1 | Ethiopia | 10 |
| Portugal | 1 | Liberia | 10 |
| Sweden | 1 | Ukraine | 10 |
| Bahrain | 2 | Eritrea | 11 |
| Belarus | 2 | Greece | 11 |
| New Zealand | 2 | Uganda | 12 |
| Oman | 2 | Nigeria | 13 |
| Thailand | 2 | Brazil | 14 |
| United Arab Emirates | 2 | Uzbekistan | 15 |

| **Time (days)** | | | |
|---|---|---|---|
| Fastest | | Slowest | |
| Portugal | 1 | Angola | 184 |
| Georgia | 2 | Puerto Rico (U.S.) | 194 |
| New Zealand | 2 | Suriname | 197 |
| Thailand | 2 | Guinea-Bissau | 210 |
| Lithuania | 3 | Bangladesh | 245 |
| Norway | 3 | Afghanistan | 250 |
| Iceland | 4 | Togo | 295 |
| Kyrgyz Republic | 5 | Brunei Darussalam | 298 |
| Nepal | 5 | Haiti | 301 |
| Taiwan, China | 5 | Kiribati | 513 |

| **Cost (% of property value)** | | | |
|---|---|---|---|
| Least | | Most | |
| Saudi Arabia | 0.00 | Côte d'Ivoire | 13.9 |
| Belarus | 0.03 | Guinea | 14.2 |
| Kiribati | 0.04 | Tonga | 15.1 |
| Slovak Republic | 0.05 | Maldives | 16.1 |
| Georgia | 0.06 | Chad | 17.9 |
| New Zealand | 0.08 | Cameroon | 19.1 |
| Kazakhstan | 0.08 | Senegal | 20.2 |
| Armenia | 0.16 | Nigeria | 20.8 |
| Russian Federation | 0.18 | Congo, Rep. | 21.3 |
| Qatar | 0.25 | Syrian Arab Republic | 27.8 |

*Source: Doing Business database.*

Among regions, Sub-Saharan Africa had the largest number of property registration reforms in the past 8 years. As a result, it also cut the cost to register property the most, though the regional average remains the highest. Among the biggest cost cutters was Angola, whose government slashed the property transfer cost from 11.5% of the property value to 3.2% in 2011 by reducing both the transfer tax, or *sisa* (from 10% to 2%), and the stamp duty (from 0.8% to 0.3%).

Thanks to effective efforts to increase efficiency, Burkina Faso ranks among the 10 economies making the biggest improvements in property registration since 2005 (table 12.3). By introducing a one-stop shop for property issues and eliminating the need to obtain a consent to the transfer from the municipality, Burkina Faso cut the number of procedures from 8 to 4 and the time from 182 days to 59 (figure 12.3). It also reduced the property transfer tax 2 years in a row—from 15% of the property value to 10% in 2008, then to 8% in 2009. This helped bring down the total cost from 20.7% of the property value in 2004 to 12.6% in 2012.

Worldwide, economies making effective cuts in the number of procedures have reviewed the efficiency of their property transfer process, then designed regulatory reforms that centralized procedures in a single agency—such as due diligence, signing of the contract, payment of taxes and registration. One is Italy, which centralized most procedures at the notary office by introducing an electronic platform

(Notartel). Now notaries can electronically access the databases of all agencies involved in property transfers.

Economies making effective reductions in time have reorganized the workflow of their registries, introduced time limits (taking into account the capacity of the institutions involved) or paired the computerization of their registries with the introduction of efficient caseload management systems. Portugal made its land registry one of the world's most efficient by introducing an effective 1-day time limit for urgent transfers and a 10-day time limit for others (table 12.4).

---

## NOTE

This topic note was written by Dariga Chukmaitova, Nuria de Oca and Moussa Traoré.

# Getting credit

- Malaysia, South Africa and the United Kingdom remain tied at the top of the ranking on the ease of getting credit.

- Between June 2011 and June 2012 *Doing Business* recorded 5 reforms strengthening legal rights of borrowers and lenders and 16 improving credit information systems.

- Cambodia improved the most in the ease of getting credit in the past year.

- Guatemala is among the 10 economies advancing the furthest toward the frontier in regulatory practice in the area of getting credit since 2005. Of the rest, 5 are in Eastern Europe and Central Asia.

- Among regions, Sub-Saharan Africa had the most reforms strengthening legal rights of borrowers and lenders in the past 8 years, while Eastern Europe and Central Asia had the most improving credit information systems.

- Among reforms strengthening legal rights in the past year, the most common feature was implementing collateral registries. Among those improving credit information systems, the most common was guaranteeing by law borrowers' right to inspect their own credit data.

*For more information on good practices and research related to getting credit, visit http://www.doingbusiness.org/data/exploretopics/getting-credit. For more on the methodology, see the section on getting credit in the data notes.*

The United Nations Commission on International Trade Law (UNCITRAL), in its *Legislative Guide on Secured Transactions*, emphasizes the importance the international community places on secured credit: "All businesses, whether engaged in mining, lumbering, agriculture, manufacturing, distributing, providing services or retailing, require working capital to operate, to grow and to compete successfully in the marketplace. It is well established that one of the most effective means of providing working capital to commercial enterprises is through secured credit."[1]

In that spirit *Doing Business* measures 2 types of institutions and systems that can facilitate access to finance and improve its allocation: credit registries or credit bureaus and the legal rights of borrowers and lenders in secured transactions and bankruptcy laws. These institutions and systems work best together.[2] Information sharing through credit registries or bureaus helps creditors assess the creditworthiness of clients (though it is not the only risk assessment tool), while legal rights can facilitate the use of collateral and the ability to enforce claims in the event of default. Creditors' rights and insolvency regimes are fundamental to a sound investment climate and can help promote commerce and economic growth.[3]

These 2 types of institutions are measured by 2 sets of indicators. One set analyzes the legal framework for secured transactions by looking at how well collateral and bankruptcy laws facilitate lending. The other looks at the coverage, scope and quality of credit information

| TABLE 13.1 Where is getting credit easiest—and where most difficult? | | | |
|---|---|---|---|
| **Easiest** | **RANK** | **Most difficult** | **RANK** |
| Malaysia | 1 | Congo, Dem. Rep. | 176 |
| South Africa | 1 | Iraq | 176 |
| United Kingdom | 1 | Malta | 176 |
| Australia | 4 | Syrian Arab Republic | 176 |
| Georgia | 4 | Djibouti | 180 |
| Hong Kong SAR, China | 4 | Eritrea | 180 |
| Latvia | 4 | Madagascar | 180 |
| Montenegro | 4 | São Tomé and Príncipe | 180 |
| New Zealand | 4 | Tajikistan | 180 |
| Poland | 4[a] | Palau | 185 |

*Note:* Rankings on the ease of getting credit are based on the sum of the strength of legal rights index and the depth of credit information index. See the data notes for details. Economies shown with the same number are tied in the ranking.

a. The United States is also tied in the ranking at 4.

*Source: Doing Business* database.

available through credit registries and credit bureaus.

Rankings on the ease of getting credit are based on the sum of the strength of legal rights index and the depth of credit information index (table 13.1).

## WHO REFORMED IN GETTING CREDIT IN 2011/12?

In 2011/12, 5 economies improved access to credit by reforming their secured transactions legislation or strengthening the rights of secured creditors during bankruptcy proceedings (table 13.2).

Three of the 5 reforming economies are in Eastern Europe and Central Asia. Considered one of the success stories of collateral reform in the 1990s, Romania

**TABLE 13.2  Who strengthened legal rights of borrowers and lenders in 2011/12— and what did they do?**

| Feature | Economies | Some highlights |
|---|---|---|
| Expanded range of movable assets that can be used as collateral | Georgia; Romania | In Romania a new civil code repealed the previous legal framework for secured transactions while maintaining most of its modern principles. The new code introduced the concept of *hypothèque*, allowing security interests in immovable as well as movable property. |
| Created a unified registry for movable property | Australia; Sri Lanka | In Australia the Personal Property Securities Act 2009 and associated regulations came into effect, and a single, national online registry began operating. The web-based registry allows creditors to conduct searches and register security interests in personal property at any time.[a] |
| Strengthened rights of secured creditors during reorganization procedures | Kazakhstan | In Kazakhstan a new law introduced changes to the regulation of the rehabilitation procedure under bankruptcy legislation, specifying several conditions under which secured creditors can apply for relief during the procedure. |

a. Accessible at http://www.ppsr.gov.au.
*Source: Doing Business* database.

**TABLE 13.4  Who has the most legal rights for borrowers and lenders— and who the least?**

Strength of legal rights index (0–10)

| Most | | Least | |
|---|---|---|---|
| Australia | 10 | Eritrea | 2 |
| Hong Kong SAR, China | 10 | São Tomé and Príncipe | 2 |
| Kyrgyz Republic | 10 | Timor-Leste | 2 |
| Latvia | 10 | Yemen, Rep. | 2[b] |
| Malaysia | 10 | Bolivia | 1 |
| Montenegro | 10 | Djibouti | 1 |
| New Zealand | 10 | Palau | 1 |
| Singapore | 10 | Syrian Arab Republic | 1 |
| South Africa | 10 | Venezuela, RB | 1 |
| United Kingdom | 10[a] | West Bank and Gaza | 1 |

a. Kenya also has a score of 10 on the strength of legal rights index.
b. Four other economies also have a score of 2 on the strength of legal rights index: Jordan, Madagascar, Tajikistan and Uzbekistan.
*Source: Doing Business* database.

went a step further in harmonizing its secured transactions legislation. It adopted a new civil code, entering into force in October 2011, that repealed the previous legal framework for secured transactions. Inspired in part by the law of the Canadian province of Quebec, the new code introduces the concept of *hypothèque* to cover security interests in movable and immovable assets. While positive overall, this reform also rendered out-of-court enforcement procedures more formalistic. Kazakhstan introduced new grounds for relief from an automatic stay for secured creditors during rehabilitation proceedings. Georgia amended its civil code to allow a security interest to extend to the products, proceeds and replacements of an asset used as collateral.

Sixteen economies improved their credit reporting system in the past year (table 13.3); 1 economy made access to credit information more difficult. Seven of these economies—Costa Rica, Ethiopia, Mongolia, Montenegro, Oman, Uzbekistan, and West Bank and Gaza— introduced new laws or regulations guaranteeing the right of borrowers to inspect their personal data.

Cambodia established its first private credit bureau, which began operating in March 2012. The bureau collects and distributes both positive and negative credit information on individuals and includes all loans in its database, regardless of size. In addition, a regulation on credit information sharing issued in May 2011 guarantees the right of borrowers to inspect their own data. The country made the biggest improvement in the ease of getting credit in 2011/12.

Mauritius also improved access to credit information in the past year. Its credit registry now reports both positive and negative data and collects payment information from retailers.

## WHAT HAVE WE LEARNED FROM 8 YEARS OF DATA?

Several economies have incorporated good practices in their legal framework for secured transactions with the aim of improving access to finance for small and medium-size enterprises. Such reforms are usually reflected in a change in score on the strength of legal rights index (table 13.4).

**TABLE 13.3  Who improved the sharing of credit information in 2011/12—and what did they do?**

| Feature | Economies | Some highlights |
|---|---|---|
| Guaranteed by law borrowers' right to access data | Costa Rica; Ethiopia; Mongolia; Montenegro; Oman; Uzbekistan; West Bank and Gaza | In West Bank and Gaza a new ordinance gave borrowers the right to inspect their credit data. |
| Improved regulatory framework for sharing credit information | El Salvador; Hungary; New Zealand | New Zealand adopted a legal framework for expanding the set of information collected by credit bureaus. |
| Provided online access to data at credit registry or bureau | Bangladesh; Ethiopia; Syrian Arab Republic | Ethiopia introduced a new online system for sharing credit information. |
| Expanded set of information collected in credit registry or bureau | Ethiopia; Mauritius | In Mauritius the public credit registry developed a new format for credit reports that includes on-time payments and unpaid installments and also began collecting data from retailers. |
| Created a new credit registry or bureau | Cambodia; Sierra Leone | Cambodia's first private credit bureau started operations, covering more than 1.1 million individuals. |
| Lowered or eliminated threshold for loans reported | Algeria | Algeria eliminated the minimum threshold for loans included in the database. |

*Source: Doing Business* database.

FIGURE 13.1 Sub-Saharan Africa leads in number of legal rights reforms

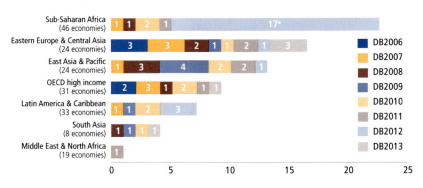

Number of *Doing Business* reforms strengthening legal rights of borrowers and lenders by *Doing Business* report year

Legend:
- DB2006
- DB2007
- DB2008
- DB2009
- DB2010
- DB2011
- DB2012
- DB2013

*Note:* An economy can be considered to have only 1 *Doing Business* reform per topic and year. The data sample for DB2006 (2005) includes 174 economies. The sample for DB2013 (2012) also includes The Bahamas, Bahrain, Barbados, Brunei Darussalam, Cyprus, Kosovo, Liberia, Luxembourg, Malta, Montenegro and Qatar, for a total of 185 economies.

a. During the period covered by *Doing Business 2012*, amendments to the Uniform Act on Secured Transactions strengthened legal rights in the 16 member economies of the Organization for the Harmonization of Business Law in Africa (OHADA).

*Source: Doing Business* database.

| TABLE 13.5 Who has narrowed the distance to frontier in getting credit the most since 2005? [*] | |
|---|---|
| **Most improved** | **Improvement in distance to frontier (percentage points)** |
| Cambodia | 69 (0→69) |
| Georgia | 63 (31→94) |
| Rwanda | 56 (25→81) |
| Croatia | 44 (31→75) |
| Ghana | 43 (38→81) |
| Guatemala | 38 (50→88) |
| Kyrgyz Republic | 38 (50→88) |
| Kazakhstan | 37 (19→56) |
| India | 31 (50→81) |
| Russian Federation | 31[a] (19→50) |

*Note:* The distance to frontier measure shows how far on average an economy is from the best performance achieved by any economy on each *Doing Business* indicator since 2005—in this case for the getting credit indicators. The measure is normalized to range between 0 and 100, with 100 representing the best performance (the frontier). The data refer to the 174 economies included in *Doing Business 2006* (2005). Eleven economies were added in subsequent years. The first column lists the top 10 most improved economies in order; the second shows the absolute improvement in the distance to frontier between 2005 and 2012.

a. Afghanistan, Mauritius, the Solomon Islands, Uganda and Zambia also have an improvement of 31 percentage points.

*Source: Doing Business* database.

One example is Guatemala, which enhanced its secured transactions regime by issuing a decree in 2007 that broadened the range of movable assets that can be used as collateral and created a registry for movable property that began operating in January 2009. In addition, Guatemala strengthened its credit information system in 2009 through a decree guaranteeing the right of borrowers to inspect their own data in any public institution. Thanks to these changes, Guatemala ranks among the 10 economies advancing the furthest toward the frontier in regulatory practice in the area of getting credit since 2005 (table 13.5).

Guatemala is far from being the only example. In the past 8 years *Doing Business* recorded 72 reforms strengthening legal rights of borrowers and lenders in 58 economies. Sub-Saharan Africa and East Asia and the Pacific are among the regions with the most such reforms (figure 13.1).

The data also reflect a difference in focus. Governments in East Asia and the Pacific focused more on aspects relating to the creation and publicity of security interests in movable property (figure 13.2). Those in Sub-Saharan Africa gave greater emphasis to aspects relating to the enforcement of security interests. For example, the new Uniform Act on Secured Transactions adopted by the Organization for the Harmonization of Business Law in Africa (OHADA) introduced a novel provision allowing out-of-court enforcement between "professionals."

Worldwide, creating a collateral registry was among the most common features of legal rights reforms. While there are different types of collateral registries, notice-based registries are widely considered the most effective.[4] Since 2005 a number of economies have tried to unify the information on collateral under some sort of centralized registry: Australia, Chile, France, Georgia, Ghana, Guatemala, Honduras, the Marshall Islands, Mexico, the Federated States of Micronesia, Peru, Rwanda, the Solomon Islands, Sri Lanka, Vanuatu and Vietnam. Some of these new registries, accompanied by legal reform, have proved to be a real success story. One example is Mexico's registry, which began operating in September 2010. By April 2012 the number of filings had increased by 4 times, and the secured amounts registered totaled $172 billion.[5]

The past 8 years also saw 171 regulatory reforms to improve credit information systems, implemented in 99 economies—more than half of the 146 economies with a credit reporting system as recorded by *Doing Business* (figure 13.3). Eastern Europe and Central Asia had the largest share of economies with improvements: 85% implemented at least 1 such reform, for a total of 43. And 14 of the 18 economies with 100% coverage of borrowers are in the OECD high-income group (table 13.6).

The efforts to improve credit reporting should be no surprise: responsible finance is much in the news these days. But since the onset of the financial crisis in 2008, consumer protection issues have also received attention worldwide. In the past year, for the first time since 2005, the most common feature of credit information reforms as recorded by *Doing Business* was guaranteeing by law borrowers' right to access their data. The main objective is to balance the ability of institutions to exchange credit information with the protection of individuals' right to privacy.

Today 104 economies guarantee by law consumers' right to access their credit information. In 72 of them the law guarantees this access at no cost.[6] Among the rest, consumers can obtain a credit report at no cost in 9 economies in practice, at little cost in 7 economies ($2.60 on average) and at a relatively high cost in 14 economies ($13.30 on average). In 100 of the 146 economies with a credit reporting system the law guarantees the right of consumers to dispute erroneous data.[7] And in 55 economies regulations require the bureau or registry to either flag the disputed data or block their distribution.[8]

In the past 8 years 30 economies adopted legislation providing borrowers with the right to access data held on them. Efforts also focused on expanding the sources of information collected by credit registries or bureaus: 28 credit information reforms were aimed at having these entities distribute both positive and negative information, collect alternative data from utilities or retailers or report historical information (figure 13.4). In 2005 credit registries and credit bureaus in 42 economies around the world included credit information from sources other than banks. Today those in 55 economies do so.

The other main focus was expanding the coverage of borrowers, such as by lowering or eliminating the minimum threshold for the loans included in a credit bureau or registry's database. Where these thresholds are high, retail and small business loans are more likely to be excluded. In 2005, 79 economies had a minimum loan

**TABLE 13.6  Who has the most credit information—and who the least?**

Depth of credit information index (0–6)

| Most | | Least | |
|---|---|---|---|
| Argentina | 6 | Benin | 1 |
| Canada | 6 | Burkina Faso | 1 |
| Germany | 6 | Burundi | 1 |
| Japan | 6 | Djibouti | 1 |
| Korea, Rep. | 6 | Guinea-Bissau | 1 |
| Lithuania | 6 | Liberia | 1 |
| Malaysia | 6 | Mauritania | 1 |
| Mexico | 6 | Niger | 1[b] |
| United Kingdom | 6 | Guinea | 0 |
| United States | 6[a] | Madagascar | 0 |

Borrowers covered by credit registries or bureaus (% of adults)

| Most | | Least | |
|---|---|---|---|
| Argentina | 100 | Bangladesh | 0.82 |
| Australia | 100 | Haiti | 0.70 |
| Canada | 100 | Sierra Leone | 0.68 |
| Iceland | 100 | Mauritania | 0.53 |
| Ireland | 100 | Nepal | 0.47 |
| New Zealand | 100 | Burundi | 0.26 |
| Norway | 100 | Djibouti | 0.23 |
| Sweden | 100 | Madagascar | 0.10 |
| United Kingdom | 100 | Ethiopia | 0.07 |
| United States | 100[c] | Guinea | 0.01 |

*Note:* The rankings on borrower coverage reflected in the table include only economies with a credit registry or credit bureau (146 in total). Another 39 economies have no credit registry or bureau and therefore no coverage (see http://www.doingbusiness.org). See the data notes for details.

a. Twenty other economies also have a score of 6 on the depth of credit information index: Armenia, Austria, Bolivia, Costa Rica, the Dominican Republic, Ecuador, Egypt, El Salvador, Georgia, Guatemala, Honduras, FYR Macedonia, Panama, Paraguay, Peru, Poland, Rwanda, Saudi Arabia, South Africa and Uruguay.

b. Four other economies also have a score of 1 on the depth of credit information index: Côte d'Ivoire, Mali, Senegal and Togo.

c. Eight other economies also have coverage of 100% of the adult population: Croatia, Germany, Israel, Italy, Japan, Korea, Serbia and Uruguay.

*Source: Doing Business* database.

**FIGURE 13.2  East Asia and the Pacific made the biggest improvement in laws on the creation of security interests in movable property**

Regional averages in strength of legal rights

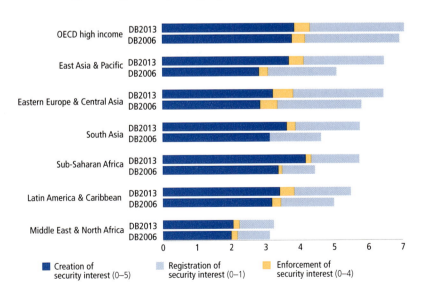

*Note:* To ensure an accurate comparison, the figure shows data for the same sample of 174 economies for both DB2006 (2005) and DB2013 (2012) and uses the regional classifications that apply in 2012. The economies added to the *Doing Business* sample after 2005 and therefore excluded here are The Bahamas, Bahrain, Barbados, Brunei Darussalam, Cyprus, Kosovo, Liberia, Luxembourg, Malta, Montenegro and Qatar. DB2006 data are adjusted for any data revisions and changes in methodology. *Creation of security interest* refers to the first 5 components of the strength of legal rights index. *Registration of security interest* refers to the component relating to the existence of a collateral registry. *Enforcement of security interest* refers to the last 4 components. See the data notes for details.

*Source: Doing Business* database.

**FIGURE 13.3** Eastern Europe and Central Asia leads in number of credit information reforms

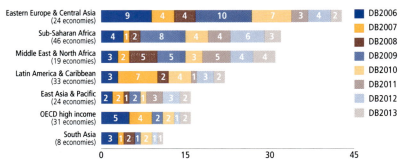

Number of *Doing Business* reforms improving credit information systems by *Doing Business* report year

*Note:* An economy can be considered to have only 1 *Doing Business* reform per topic and year. The data sample for DB2006 (2005) includes 123 economies. The sample for DB2013 (2012) includes a total of 146 economies.
*Source: Doing Business* database.

**FIGURE 13.4** Guaranteeing by law borrowers' right to access data was the biggest focus of credit information reform worldwide in the past 8 years

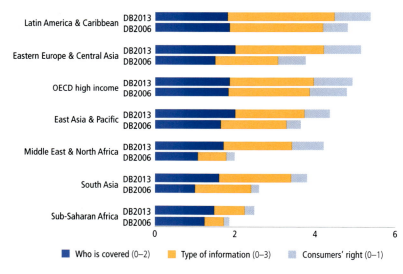

Regional averages in depth of credit information

*Note:* To ensure an accurate comparison, the figure shows data for the same sample of 123 economies for both DB2006 (2005) and DB2013 (2012) and uses the regional classifications that apply in 2012. DB2006 data are adjusted for any data revisions and changes in methodology. *Who is covered* refers to whether both individuals and firms are covered by a bureau or registry and whether loans below 1% of income per capita are included. *Type of information* refers to the availability of information from retailers or utilities, distribution of positive and negative information and availability of historical data. *Consumers' right* refers to whether the law guarantees borrowers' right to inspect their own data.
*Source: Doing Business* database.

threshold below 1% of income per capita (including those in which loans of all sizes are reported). Today 123 economies do.

An encouraging trend over the past 8 years has been the establishment of new credit bureaus or registries in economies that previously had none—25 in total, mainly in Eastern Europe and Central Asia. Credit information is still hardly shared in Sub-Saharan Africa, despite the pickup in efforts to develop credit information systems starting in 2008. Since then Ghana, Liberia, Rwanda, Sierra Leone, Uganda and Zambia have established new credit reporting systems. In East Asia and the Pacific 10 of 24 economies still have no credit bureau or registry. But things are improving. Brunei Darussalam, Lao PDR, Samoa, the Solomon Islands, Tonga and Vanuatu are all working to get their credit reporting systems operating.[9]

## NOTES

This topic note was written by Santiago Croci Downes, Hayane Chang Dahmen and Joanna Nasr.

1. UNCITRAL 2007, p. 1.
2. Djankov, McLiesh and Shleifer 2007.
3. World Bank 2011b.
4. Alvarez de la Campa, Croci Downes and Tirelli Hennig 2012.
5. Estimates were provided by the Mexican government.
6. No data are available for 2 economies.
7. No data are available for 7 economies.
8. No data are available for 13 economies.
9. As of June 1, 2012, the credit bureaus in Tonga and Vanuatu had loaded the information into their systems but the databases were not yet accessible to banks.

2007 2012 2011
2005 2003 2009 2004
2008 2006 2010 2013

# Protecting investors

Corporations are instruments of entrepreneurship and growth. They can also be abused for personal gain. In July 2012 authorities in Korea imposed a $30 million fine on SK Group, the country's third-largest conglomerate, for illicit related-party transactions. The transactions were priced significantly above market averages and allegedly allowed the group's founder to misappropriate $87 million. The group's market capitalization declined sharply as a result.[1] Korea's strong institutions and extensive disclosure requirements played an essential part in addressing this situation and protecting minority investors.

*Doing Business* measures the strength of minority shareholder protections against directors' misuse of corporate assets for personal gain. The indicators distinguish 3 dimensions of investor protections: approval and transparency of related-party transactions (extent of disclosure index), liability of company directors for self-dealing (extent of director liability index) and shareholders' ability to obtain corporate documents before and during litigation (ease of shareholder suits index). The standard case study assumes a related-party transaction between Company A ("Buyer") and Company B ("Seller") where "Mr. James" is the controlling shareholder of both Buyer and Seller and a member of both their boards of directors. The transaction is overpriced and causes damages to Buyer.

Protecting minority investors matters for companies. Without adequate regulations, equity markets fail to develop and banks become the only source of the finance that companies need to grow,

innovate, diversify and compete. A recent study shows that in economies with stronger investor protections, investment in firms is less sensitive to financial constraints and leads to greater growth in revenue and profitability.[2] Another study shows that regulating conflicts of interest is essential to successfully empowering minority shareholders.[3]

New Zealand provides the strongest minority investor protections as measured by *Doing Business*, ranking highest in this area for the eighth year in a row (table 14.1).

## WHO IMPROVED INVESTOR PROTECTIONS IN 2011/12?

In the past year 13 economies strengthened investor protections as measured by *Doing Business*. OECD high-income economies, with 4 legal changes, continue to

- New Zealand has the strongest minority investor protections in related-party transactions, for the eighth year in a row.

- From June 2011 to June 2012 *Doing Business* recorded 13 legal changes strengthening the protections of minority investors.

- Kosovo made the biggest improvement in the strength of investor protections in the past year.

- Tajikistan has advanced the furthest toward the frontier in regulatory practice in protecting investors since 2005.

- Improving disclosure was the most common feature of investor protection reforms in the past 8 years.

- Among regions, Eastern Europe and Central Asia has strengthened investor protections the most since 2005—and is quickly catching up with OECD high-income economies.

*For more information on good practices and research related to protecting investors, visit http://www.doingbusiness.org/data/exploretopics/protecting-investors. For more on the methodology, see the section on protecting investors in the data notes.*

| TABLE 14.1 | Where are investors most protected—and where least? | | |
|---|---|---|---|
| Most protected | RANK | Least protected | RANK |
| New Zealand | 1 | Haiti | 176 |
| Singapore | 2 | Gambia, The | 177 |
| Hong Kong SAR, China | 3 | Guinea | 177 |
| Canada | 4 | Micronesia, Fed. Sts. | 177 |
| Malaysia | 4 | Palau | 177 |
| Colombia | 6 | Djibouti | 181 |
| Ireland | 6 | Venezuela, RB | 181 |
| Israel | 6 | Suriname | 183 |
| United States | 6 | Lao PDR | 184 |
| United Kingdom | 10 | Afghanistan | 185 |

*Note:* Rankings are based on the strength of investor protection index. See the data notes for details. Economies shown with the same number are tied in the ranking.

*Source: Doing Business* database.

FIGURE 14.1 Kosovo's new Law on Business Organizations strengthened investor protections

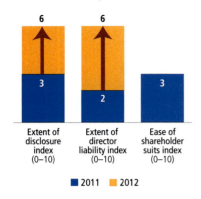

■ 2011 ■ 2012

Source: Doing Business database.

TABLE 14.2 Who strengthened investor protections in 2011/12—and what did they do?

| Feature | Economies | Some highlights |
|---|---|---|
| Made it easier to sue directors | Armenia; Republic of Korea; Kosovo; Lesotho; Peru; Taiwan, China; Tajikistan | Korea clarified directors' duties in its commercial code. Now negligent directors can be held liable for damages caused by prejudicial related-party transactions. |
| Increased disclosure requirements | Armenia; Greece; Islamic Republic of Iran; Kosovo; Lesotho; Mongolia; Taiwan, China | Lesotho enacted a new company law that requires company directors to disclose to the board the full extent of any conflict of interest they may have relating to a proposed transaction. |
| Regulated approval of related-party transactions | Armenia; Kosovo; Netherlands; Peru; Slovenia; Taiwan, China | Kosovo amended its Law on Business Organizations. Now only disinterested shareholders can approve related-party transactions. |
| Allowed the rescission of prejudicial related-party transactions | Kosovo; Moldova | Moldova amended its law on joint stock companies. Shareholders can now petition the court for a rescission of transactions approved despite major conflicts of interest when such transactions cause damages to the company. |

Source: Doing Business database.

provide the strongest protections. Eastern Europe and Central Asia, also with 4, remains the most improved region and the most active in making legal changes, with 24 recorded in 16 economies since 2005.

Kosovo improved minority shareholder protections the most in the past year, through a comprehensive revision of its Law on Business Organizations (figure 14.1). The amended law requires shareholder approval of related-party transactions and mandates greater disclosure both by directors to their board and by companies in their annual reports. In addition, the law allows shareholders to petition a judge for rescission of a prejudicial related-party transaction and clarifies the liability of directors. If found liable, directors must now pay damages and disgorge any profit made from the transaction.

Economies in other regions were active as well. In Greece the Hellenic Capital Market Commission issued a circular clarifying the concept of material transactions for purposes of disclosure by listed companies—helping to instill more transparency in an economy looking to restore confidence in its market.

Peru now requires that the terms of transactions between interested parties be reviewed by an independent external auditor certified by the securities commission.

Continuing a trend in Sub-Saharan Africa of upgrading company law, Lesotho adopted a new one setting out duties of care, diligence and skill for directors. Breach of these duties constitutes a cause of action for shareholders (table 14.2).

## WHAT HAVE WE LEARNED FROM 8 YEARS OF DATA?

In the past 8 years 68% of economies in Eastern Europe and Central Asia implemented at least 1 reform strengthening investor protections (figure 14.2). Among OECD high-income economies 48% did, and in East Asia and the Pacific and the Middle East and North Africa 33% did. Of all these reforms captured by Doing Business, 49% improved the extent of disclosure index. But OECD high-income economies had a much higher share that did so, at 78%, followed by the Middle East and North Africa with 60% and Eastern Europe and Central Asia with 54%. In Sub-Saharan Africa the priority was increasing director liability. In East Asia and the Pacific and Latin America and the Caribbean the approach was more balanced.

While many economies have strengthened investor protections, Tajikistan, Albania and Rwanda have made the biggest improvements since 2005 (table 14.3). Two of them did so through one major overhaul of their company law,

FIGURE 14.2 Eastern Europe and Central Asia still leading in number of investor protection reforms

Number of Doing Business reforms strengthening investor protections by Doing Business report year

| | |
|---|---|
| Eastern Europe & Central Asia (24 economies) | 1 1 2 5 3 3 5 4 |
| OECD high income (31 economies) | 5 6 4 2 1 1 4 |
| East Asia & Pacific (24 economies) | 5 2 2 1 3 2 2 |
| Latin America & Caribbean (33 economies) | 2 3 1 2 1 2 1 |
| Middle East & North Africa (19 economies) | 1 3 3 1 1 1 |
| Sub-Saharan Africa (46 economies) | 1 1 1 3 1 1 1 |
| South Asia (8 economies) | 1 1 1 |

■ DB2006  ■ DB2007  ■ DB2008  ■ DB2009  ■ DB2010  ■ DB2011  ■ DB2012  ■ DB2013

0  5  10  15  20  25

Note: An economy can be considered to have only 1 Doing Business reform per topic and year. The data sample for DB2006 (2005) includes 174 economies. The sample for DB2013 (2012) also includes The Bahamas, Bahrain, Barbados, Brunei Darussalam, Cyprus, Kosovo, Liberia, Luxembourg, Malta, Montenegro and Qatar, for a total of 185 economies.
Source: Doing Business database.

FIGURE 14.3 Strongest investor protections in OECD high-income economies

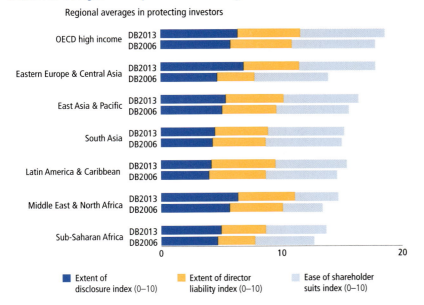

Regional averages in protecting investors

**Extent of disclosure index (0–10)** ▪ (dark blue)
**Extent of director liability index (0–10)** ▪ (yellow)
**Ease of shareholder suits index (0–10)** ▪ (light blue)

*Note:* To ensure an accurate comparison, the figure shows data for the same sample of 174 economies for both DB2006 (2005) and DB2013 (2012) and uses the regional classifications that apply in 2012. The economies added to the *Doing Business* sample after 2005 and therefore excluded here are The Bahamas, Bahrain, Barbados, Brunei Darussalam, Cyprus, Kosovo, Liberia, Luxembourg, Malta, Montenegro and Qatar. DB2006 data are adjusted for any data revisions and changes in methodology.
*Source: Doing Business* database.

TABLE 14.3 Who has narrowed the distance to frontier in protecting investors the most since 2005?

| Most improved | Improvement in distance to frontier (percentage points) |
|---|---|
| Tajikistan | 52 (17→69) |
| Albania | 48 (29→77) |
| Rwanda | 38 (29→67) |
| Georgia | 31 (41→72) |
| Burundi | 29 (34→62) |
| Tunisia | 28 (35→63) |
| Colombia | 26 (44→69) |
| Azerbaijan | 25 (57→82) |
| Kazakhstan | 25 (57→82) |
| Mexico | 25[a] (37→63) |

*Note:* The distance to frontier measure shows how far on average an economy is from the best performance achieved by any economy on each *Doing Business* indicator since 2005—in this case for the protecting investors indicators. The measure is normalized to range between 0 and 100, with 100 representing the best performance (the frontier). The data refer to the 174 economies included in *Doing Business 2006* (2005). Eleven economies were added in subsequent years. The first column lists the top 10 most improved economies in order; the second shows the absolute improvement in the distance to frontier between 2005 and 2012.

a. Swaziland also has an improvement of 25 percentage points.
*Source: Doing Business* database.

Albania in 2008 and Rwanda in 2009. Tajikistan achieved similar results by amending its law incrementally—in 2007, in 2009 (twice) and in 2011.

OECD high-income economies may have the strongest investor protections as measured by *Doing Business*, but Eastern Europe and Central Asia is quickly catching up, having passed East Asia and the Pacific in 2007 (figure 14.3). Policy makers in the region have emphasized stricter disclosure requirements and better standards for company directors.

Sub-Saharan Africa has had some of the most comprehensive investor protection reforms. Besides Lesotho, such economies as Burundi and Rwanda have also updated their company laws following global good practices. East Asia and the Pacific has focused mostly on strengthening disclosure requirements and

directors' duties (as in Taiwan, China, and in Thailand).

Investor protection reforms have been sparse in Latin America and the Caribbean, with Chile, Colombia and Mexico among the few economies implementing them. In the Middle East and North Africa, despite some improvements (as in Morocco and Saudi Arabia), protections are often weak because of limited access to corporate information during litigation. South Asia has been the least active in strengthening investor protections. Over the past 8 years *Doing Business* recorded 3 investor protection reforms among the region's 8 economies—in India, Pakistan and Sri Lanka.

Improving disclosure was the most common feature of investor protection reforms in the past 8 years, accounting for 46

of the total. But in the past year, for the first time, the most common feature was increasing director liability (accounting for 8 of the 13 reforms).

Overall, smart, comprehensive regulations have had the strongest lasting impact (table 14.4). Economies undertaking a complete overhaul of their corporate, securities and civil procedure laws—including Albania, Burundi, Kosovo, Mexico, Rwanda, Swaziland, Tajikistan and Thailand—have improved the most on the strength of investor protections as measured by *Doing Business*.

**TABLE 14.4  Who provides strong minority investor protections—and who does not?**

**Extent of disclosure index (0–10)**

| Most | | Least | |
|---|---|---|---|
| Bulgaria | 10 | Afghanistan | 1 |
| China | 10 | Bolivia | 1 |
| France | 10 | Cape Verde | 1 |
| Hong Kong SAR, China | 10 | Croatia | 1 |
| Indonesia | 10 | Honduras | 0 |
| Ireland | 10 | Maldives | 0 |
| Malaysia | 10 | Micronesia, Fed. Sts. | 0 |
| New Zealand | 10 | Palau | 0 |
| Singapore | 10 | Sudan | 0 |
| Thailand | 10[a] | Switzerland | 0 |

**Extent of director liability index (0–10)**

| Most | | Least | |
|---|---|---|---|
| Albania | 9 | Afghanistan | 1 |
| Cambodia | 9 | Barbados | 1 |
| Canada | 9 | Belarus | 1 |
| Israel | 9 | Benin | 1 |
| Malaysia | 9 | Bulgaria | 1 |
| New Zealand | 9 | El Salvador | 0 |
| Rwanda | 9 | Marshall Islands | 0 |
| Singapore | 9 | Micronesia, Fed. Sts. | 0 |
| Slovenia | 9 | Palau | 0 |
| United States | 9[b] | Suriname | 0 |

**Ease of shareholder suits index (0–10)**

| Easiest | | Most difficult | |
|---|---|---|---|
| Kenya | 10 | Lao PDR | 2 |
| New Zealand | 10 | Senegal | 2 |
| Colombia | 9 | Syrian Arab Republic | 2 |
| Hong Kong SAR, China | 9 | United Arab Emirates | 2 |
| Ireland | 9 | Venezuela, RB | 2 |
| Israel | 9 | Yemen, Rep. | 2 |
| Panama | 9 | Afghanistan | 1 |
| Poland | 9 | Guinea | 1 |
| Singapore | 9 | Djibouti | 0 |
| United States | 9[c] | Iran, Islamic Rep. | 0 |

a. The United Kingdom also has a score of 10 points on the extent of disclosure index.

b. Trinidad and Tobago also has a score of 9 points on the extent of director liability index.

c. Canada, Kazakhstan, Mauritius, Mozambique and Nepal also have a score of 9 points on the ease of shareholder suits index.

*Source: Doing Business* database.

**NOTES**

This topic note was written by Hervé Kaddoura and Jean Michel Lobet.

1.  Sangim Han and Seyoon Kim, "SK Group Units Fall After Chairman Questioned by Prosecutors," *Bloomberg News,* December 18, 2011.

2.  Mclean, Zhang and Zhao 2012.

3.  Hamdani and Yafeh 2012.

# Paying taxes

Jean-Baptiste Colbert, French philosopher and minister of finance to King Louis XIV, once remarked that "the art of taxation consists in so plucking the goose as to obtain the largest possible amount of feathers with the smallest possible amount of hissing." How taxes are collected and paid has changed a great deal since then. But governments still face the challenge of maximizing revenue collection while minimizing distortions.

*Doing Business* records the taxes and mandatory contributions that a medium-size company must pay in a given year and also measures the administrative burden of paying taxes and contributions. It does this with 3 indicators: number of payments, time and total tax rate for the *Doing Business* case study firm. The number of payments indicates the frequency with which the company has to file and pay different types of taxes and contributions, adjusted for the way in which those filings and payments are made.[1] The time indicator captures the number of hours it takes to prepare, file and pay 3 major types of taxes: profit taxes, consumption taxes, and labor taxes and mandatory contributions. The total tax rate measures the tax cost (as a percentage of profit) borne by the standard firm. The indicators do not measure the fiscal health of economies, the macroeconomic conditions under which governments collect revenue or the provision of public services supported by taxation. The ranking on the ease of paying taxes is the simple average of the percentile rankings on its component indicators, with a threshold applied to the total tax rate (table 15.1).[2]

## WHO REFORMED IN PAYING TAXES IN 2011/12?

From June 2011 to June 2012 *Doing Business* recorded 31 reforms making it easier or less costly for firms to pay taxes (table 15.2). Sixteen economies mandated or enhanced electronic filing, eliminating the need for 196 separate tax payments and reducing compliance time by 134 days (1,070 hours) in total. In Uruguay small and medium-size companies can now file and pay corporate income tax, value added tax and capital tax online. This option was available only for large taxpayers until 2011. Seven other economies implemented electronic filing for the first time, raising the number offering this option from 67 in 2010 to 74 in 2011.[3] Thanks to improvements in electronic systems for filing and paying social security contributions, Saudi Arabia

### TABLE 15.1 Where is paying taxes easiest—and where most difficult?

| Easiest | RANK | Most difficult | RANK |
|---|---|---|---|
| United Arab Emirates | 1 | Cameroon | 176 |
| Qatar | 2 | Mauritania | 177 |
| Saudi Arabia | 3 | Senegal | 178 |
| Hong Kong SAR, China | 4 | Gambia, The | 179 |
| Singapore | 5 | Bolivia | 180 |
| Ireland | 6 | Central African Republic | 181 |
| Bahrain | 7 | Congo, Rep. | 182 |
| Canada | 8 | Guinea | 183 |
| Kiribati | 9 | Chad | 184 |
| Oman | 10 | Venezuela, RB | 185 |

*Note:* Rankings are the average of the economy's rankings on the number of payments, time and total tax rate, with a threshold imposed on the total tax rate. See the data notes for details.
*Source: Doing Business* database.

- Firms in the United Arab Emirates face the lightest administrative burden in paying taxes. They must make only 4 payments a year and spend 12 hours doing so.
- From June 2011 to June 2012 *Doing Business* recorded 31 reforms making it easier and less costly for companies to comply with taxes.
- Liberia made the biggest improvement in the ease of paying taxes in the past year.
- Belarus has advanced the most toward the frontier in regulatory practice in paying taxes since 2004.
- The most common feature of tax reforms in the past 8 years was to reduce profit tax rates, often in the context of parallel efforts to improve tax compliance. But in the past 2 years more economies focused on introducing electronic systems.
- Among regions, Eastern Europe and Central Asia had the biggest improvement in the ease of paying taxes in the past 8 years.

*For more information on good practices and research related to paying taxes, visit http://www.doingbusiness.org/data/exploretopics/paying-taxes. For more on the methodology, see the section on paying taxes in the data notes.*

| TABLE 15.2 Who made paying taxes easier and lowered the tax burden in 2011/12—and what did they do? | | |
|---|---|---|
| Feature | Economies | Some highlights |
| Introduced or enhanced electronic systems | Albania; Belarus; Bosnia and Herzegovina; Costa Rica; Czech Republic; Georgia; Germany; Kenya; Panama; Russian Federation; Saudi Arabia; Slovak Republic; Slovenia; Ukraine; United Arab Emirates; Uruguay | Ukraine introduced an online filing and payment system and made its use mandatory for medium-size and large enterprises. |
| Reduced profit tax rate by 2 percentage points or more | Belarus; Brunei Darussalam; Fiji; Japan; Republic of Korea; Lao PDR; Liberia; Mali; Puerto Rico (U.S.); Slovenia; Thailand; United Kingdom | The United Kingdom reduced 2 corporate income tax rates: the main rate from 28% to 26% and the small-company rate from 21% to 20%. |
| Merged or eliminated taxes other than profit tax | Albania; Hungary; Liberia | Liberia abolished the turnover tax. |
| Simplified tax compliance process | Jamaica; Mali; Panama; Poland | Jamaica introduced joint filing and payment of all 5 types of social security contributions that firms must make. |
| Reduced labor taxes and mandatory contributions | Croatia | Croatia made paying taxes less costly by reducing health insurance contributions. |
| Introduced change in cascading sales tax | Swaziland | Swaziland introduced value added tax to replace its cascading sales tax. |

Source: *Doing Business* database.

| TABLE 15.3 Who makes paying taxes easy and who does not—and where is the total tax rate highest? | | | |
|---|---|---|---|
| **Payments (number per year)** | | | |
| Fewest | | Most | |
| Hong Kong SAR, China | 3 | Antigua and Barbuda | 57 |
| Saudi Arabia | 3 | Guinea | 58 |
| Norway | 4 | Senegal | 59 |
| Qatar | 4 | Panama | 60 |
| Sweden | 4 | Congo, Rep. | 61 |
| United Arab Emirates | 4 | Sri Lanka | 61 |
| Georgia | 5 | Côte d'Ivoire | 62 |
| Singapore | 5 | Serbia | 66 |
| Chile | 6 | Tajikistan | 69 |
| Malta | 6 | Venezuela, RB | 71 |

| **Time (hours per year)** | | | |
|---|---|---|---|
| Fastest | | Slowest | |
| United Arab Emirates | 12 | Cameroon | 654 |
| Bahrain | 36 | Ecuador | 654 |
| Qatar | 48 | Senegal | 666 |
| Bahamas, The | 58 | Mauritania | 696 |
| Luxembourg | 59 | Chad | 732 |
| Oman | 62 | Venezuela, RB | 792 |
| Switzerland | 63 | Vietnam | 872 |
| Saudi Arabia | 72 | Nigeria | 956 |
| Seychelles | 76 | Bolivia | 1,025 |
| Hong Kong SAR, China | 78 | Brazil | 2,600 |

| **Total tax rate (% of profit)** | |
|---|---|
| Highest | |
| Colombia | 74.8 |
| Palau | 75.7 |
| Bolivia | 83.4 |
| Tajikistan | 84.5 |
| Eritrea | 84.5 |
| Uzbekistan | 98.5 |
| Argentina | 108.3[a] |
| Comoros | 217.9[a] |
| Gambia, The | 283.5[a] |
| Congo, Dem. Rep. | 339.7[a] |

*Note:* The indicator on payments is adjusted for the possibility of electronic or joint filing and payment when used by the majority of firms in an economy. See the data notes for more details.

a. As a result of assumptions about the profit margin used to standardize the financial statements of the case study company, in 4 economies the amount of taxes due would exceed the profit of the company. To be able to comply with its tax obligations in these economies, the company would therefore have to charge more for its products and generate a higher profit. The methodology does not allow for price adjustments and assumes a standard cost markup of 120%. See the data notes for more details.

*Source: Doing Business* database.

this year ranks among the 10 economies with the fewest payments and lowest tax compliance time (table 15.3).

Electronic systems for filing and paying taxes eliminate excessive paperwork and interaction with tax officers. They can reduce the time businesses spend on complying with tax laws, increase tax compliance and reduce the cost of revenue administration.[4] But achieving these results requires effective implementation and high-quality security systems.

Twelve economies reduced profit tax rates in 2011/12: 6 high-income economies (Brunei Darussalam, Japan, Korea, Puerto Rico [territory of the United States], Slovenia and the United Kingdom), 4 middle-income ones (Belarus, Fiji, Lao PDR and Thailand) and 2 low-income ones (Liberia and Mali). Reductions in profit tax rates are often combined with efforts to widen the tax base by removing exemptions and with increases in the rates of other taxes, such as value added tax (VAT). Liberia improved the most in the ease of paying taxes. It reduced the corporate income tax rate from 35% to 25% and abolished the turnover tax. The total tax rate fell from 43.7% of profit to 27.4%.

Eleven economies introduced new taxes (Cambodia, Costa Rica, Cyprus, El Salvador, Ethiopia, Japan, Malawi, Maldives, Mali, Nigeria and República Bolivariana de Venezuela). Others increased profit or income tax rates (Botswana, the Dominican Republic and Moldova)[5] or social security contributions (Hungary and Poland).

## WHAT HAVE WE LEARNED FROM 8 YEARS OF DATA?

Since 2005 *Doing Business* has recorded 296 tax reforms in 142 economies (figure 15.1). Some of these reforms introduced online filing, added in 29 economies in the past 8 years. These and other improvements to simplify tax compliance reduced the time required to comply with the 3 major taxes measured (profit, labor and consumption taxes) by 54 hours on average, and the number of payments by 7. Eastern Europe and Central Asia had the biggest improvement, with the time reduced by 181 hours and the number of payments by 24 (figure 15.2). Upper-middle-income economies have advanced the most toward the frontier in regulatory practice in paying taxes, followed by lower-middle-income economies (figure 15.3).

FIGURE 15.1 Tax reforms implemented by more than 75% of economies in the past 8 years

Number of *Doing Business* reforms making it easier to pay taxes by *Doing Business* report year

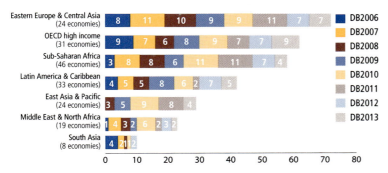

Note: An economy can be considered to have only 1 *Doing Business* reform per topic and year. The data sample for DB2006 (2004) includes 174 economies. The sample for DB2013 (2011) also includes The Bahamas, Bahrain, Barbados, Brunei Darussalam, Cyprus, Kosovo, Liberia, Luxembourg, Malta, Montenegro and Qatar, for a total of 185 economies.
*Source: Doing Business* database.

FIGURE 15.3 Middle-income economies have advanced the most toward the frontier in paying taxes

Average distance to frontier (percentage points)

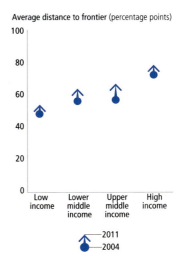

Note: The distance to frontier measure shows how far on average an economy is from the best performance achieved by any economy on each *Doing Business* indicator—in this case for the paying taxes indicators since 2004. The measure is normalized to range between 0 and 100, with 100 representing the best performance (the frontier). The data refer to the 174 economies included in *Doing Business 2006* (2004). Eleven economies were added in subsequent years. The figure shows data for the financial years 2004 (measured by the paying taxes indicators in *Doing Business 2006*) and 2011 (measured in *Doing Business 2013*).
*Source: Doing Business* database.

Besides lessening the administrative burden of taxes, many economies also reduced tax rates, often from relatively high levels and with complementary efforts to improve tax compliance. Sub-Saharan Africa had the largest reduction in the total tax rate, 13.3 percentage points on average since 2005. Some of this reduction came from the introduction of VAT, which replaced the cascading sales tax.[6] Burundi, Djibouti, Mozambique, Sierra Leone and Swaziland all introduced VAT systems. In Sierra Leone tax revenue remained relatively stable as a percentage of GDP, rising only from 10.8% in 2005 to 11% in 2009. But the share of revenue coming from taxes on goods and services increased from 11.9% to 24.6%.[7]

Many African economies also reduced profit tax rates in the past 8 years, reducing the share of profit taxes in the total tax rate by 0.9 percentage point on average in the region. But the biggest reduction in this share occurred in OECD high-income economies, where it fell by 4.1 percentage points on average. Over the same period tax revenue increased slightly as a percentage of GDP in Sub-Saharan Africa and remained relatively stable in OECD high-income economies.[8]

Such reforms have had positive effects. Matching the data available since 2005 on total tax rates with investment data indicates that a reduction of 1 percentage point in the total tax rate is linked to an increase in investment equivalent to 1% of GDP.[9]

Belarus has advanced the furthest toward the frontier in regulatory practice in paying taxes since 2004 (table 15.4). Embarking on an ambitious tax reform in

FIGURE 15.2 Tax compliance simplified the most in Eastern Europe and Central Asia

Average payments (number per year)

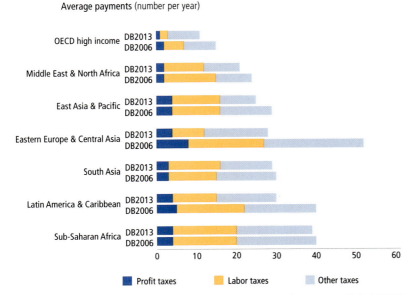

Note: To ensure an accurate comparison, the figure shows data for the same sample of 174 economies for both DB2006 (2004) and DB2013 (2011) and uses the regional classifications that apply in 2012. The economies added to the *Doing Business* sample after 2004 and therefore excluded here are The Bahamas, Bahrain, Barbados, Brunei Darussalam, Cyprus, Kosovo, Liberia, Luxembourg, Malta, Montenegro and Qatar. DB2006 data are adjusted for any data revisions and changes in methodology.
*Source: Doing Business* database.

| TABLE 15.4 Who has narrowed the distance to frontier in paying taxes the most since 2004? | |
|---|---|
| **Most improved** | **Improvement in distance to frontier (percentage points)** |
| Belarus | 61 (0→61) |
| Colombia | 47 (13→60) |
| Georgia | 47 (39→86) |
| China | 42 (19→61) |
| Azerbaijan | 37 (38→75) |
| Ukraine | 31 (16→47) |
| Argentina | 30 (14→44) |
| Sierra Leone | 30 (34→64) |
| Uruguay | 30 (31→61) |
| Yemen, Rep. | 30 (33→63) |

*Note:* The distance to frontier measure shows how far on average an economy is from the best performance achieved by any economy on each *Doing Business* indicator—in this case for the paying taxes indicators since 2004. The measure is normalized to range between 0 and 100, with 100 representing the best performance (the frontier). The data refer to the 174 economies included in *Doing Business 2006* (2004). Eleven economies were added in subsequent years. The first column lists the top 10 most improved economies in order; the second shows the absolute improvement in the distance to frontier between financial years 2004 and 2011.

*Source: Doing Business* database.

FIGURE 15.4  Broad tax reform in Belarus reduces payments, time and total tax rate

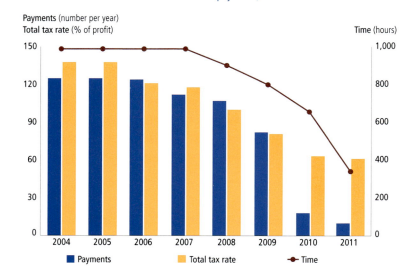

*Source: Doing Business* database.

2005, Belarus abolished several taxes, reduced tax rates, broadened the tax base, simplified filing forms and the tax law and invested in electronic systems that make it easier to file and pay taxes. These changes reduced the number of annual payments from 125 to 10, the time from 987 hours a year to 338 and the total tax rate from 137.5% of profit to 60.7% (figure 15.4). The efforts to make tax compliance easier and less costly are paying off. While 1,681 new limited liability corporations registered for the first time in 2005 in Belarus, 6,142 did so in 2011. Indeed, the total number registered in this period increased by 68.9% (from 27,619 to 46,653).[10]

## NOTES

This topic note was written by Nan Jiang, Pawel Kopko, Nina Paustian, Momodou Salifu Sey and Tea Trumbic.

1. Companies sometimes prefer more frequent payments, to smooth cash flow, and less frequent filing.

2. The threshold is set at the 15th percentile of the total tax rate distribution, and this year is 25.7%. All economies with a total tax rate below this level receive the same percentile ranking on this component. The threshold is not based on any economic theory of an "optimal tax rate" that minimizes distortions or maximizes efficiency in the tax system of an economy overall. Instead, it is mainly empirical in nature, set at the lower end of the distribution of tax rates levied on medium-size enterprises in the manufacturing sector as observed through the paying taxes indicators. This reduces the bias in the indicators toward economies that do not need to levy significant taxes on companies like the *Doing Business* standardized case study company because they raise public revenue in other ways—for example, through taxes on foreign companies, through taxes on sectors other than manufacturing or from natural resources (all of which are outside the scope of the methodology).

3. One of the economies added to the sample in this year's report, Malta, has offered electronic filing for several years and so is included in the count for 2010.

4. Mexico, for example, has relied heavily on technology and the use of electronic

systems to lessen the administrative burden for taxpayers. These efforts simplified requirements for firms, reducing the number of annual tax payments recorded by *Doing Business* from 27 in 2007 to 6 in 2011 and the time to comply with major taxes from 549 hours to 337.

5. At the same time Moldova reduced the withholding tax for dividends from 15% to 6% and lowered the withholding tax for payments other than dividends from 15% to 12%. In addition, it introduced a new tax regime for small and medium-size enterprises under which small companies pay a single tax of 3% of revenues from operational activities.

6. VAT is collected by the firm and its cost is fully passed on to the consumer. Because the firm has to make the payments and spend time filling out the returns, VAT is included in the indicators on payments and time. But the amount of VAT paid is not included in the total tax rate. Cascading sales tax, which is paid at every point of the supply chain, is included in the total tax rate, because the firm cannot deduct the sales tax it pays on its supplies from the amount it owes on its sales. Economies introducing VAT regimes to replace the sales tax regime have therefore seen a reduction in their total tax rate.

7. World Bank, World Development Indicators database, http://data .worldbank.org/.

8. World Bank, World Development Indicators database, http://data .worldbank.org/.

9. Following Eifert (2009) and Djankov, McLiesh and Ramalho (2006), the analysis controls for government consumption, institutional quality and corruption perception. It also controls for total trade openness and rents from natural resources.

10. World Bank Group Entrepreneurship Snapshots. The full data set is availab e on the *Doing Business* website (http://www.doingbusiness.org).

# Trading across borders

- Trading across borders remains easiest in Singapore.

- From June 2011 to June 2012 *Doing Business* recorded 22 reforms making it easier to trade across borders.

- South Africa made the biggest improvement in the ease of trading across borders in the past year.

- Georgia has made the greatest progress toward the frontier in regulatory practice in trading across borders since 2005. Among the 10 economies making the most progress, 4 are in Sub-Saharan Africa.

- The most common feature of trade facilitation reforms in the past 8 years was the introduction or improvement of electronic submission and processing.

- Economies in Latin America and the Caribbean have made the biggest reductions in the time to trade across borders since 2005. Those in the Middle East and North Africa have made the biggest reductions in the documents required to export and import.

*For more information on good practices and research related to trading across borders, visit http://www.doingbusiness.org/data/ exploretopics/trading-across-borders. For more on the methodology, see the section on trading across borders in the data notes.*

"Inefficiencies in processing and clearing goods put traders in developing countries at a competitive disadvantage," declared the heads of the World Bank and regional development banks in a statement urging the international community to commit to a new WTO trade facilitation agreement. "Developing countries stand to gain the most from improving trade facilitation. The right support will help traders in poorer countries compete and integrate into global supply chains."[1]

To shed light on the bureaucratic and logistical hurdles facing traders, *Doing Business* measures the time and cost (excluding tariffs) associated with exporting and importing by sea transport and the number of documents necessary to complete the transaction.[2] The indicators cover documentation requirements and procedures at customs and other regulatory agencies as well as at the port. They also cover logistical aspects, including the time and cost of inland transport between the largest business city and the main port used by traders. As measured by *Doing Business*, trading across borders remains easiest in Singapore (tables 16.1 and 16.2).

Outdated and inefficient border procedures, inadequate infrastructure and lack of reliable logistics services often mean high transactions costs and long delays, particularly for landlocked economies.[3] The more costly and time consuming it is to export or import, the more difficult it is for local companies to be competitive and to reach international markets. Indeed, a study in Sub-Saharan Africa shows that reducing inland travel time by 1 day increases exports by 7%.[4]

| TABLE 16.1 | Where is trading across borders easiest—and where most difficult? | | |
|---|---|---|---|
| **Easiest** | **RANK** | **Most difficult** | **RANK** |
| Singapore | 1 | Niger | 176 |
| Hong Kong SAR, China | 2 | Burundi | 177 |
| Korea, Rep. | 3 | Afghanistan | 178 |
| Denmark | 4 | Iraq | 179 |
| United Arab Emirates | 5 | Chad | 180 |
| Finland | 6 | Congo, Rep. | 181 |
| Estonia | 7 | Central African Republic | 182 |
| Sweden | 8 | Kazakhstan | 182 |
| Panama | 9 | Tajikistan | 184 |
| Israel | 10 | Uzbekistan | 185 |

*Note: Rankings are the average of the economy's rankings on the documents, time and cost required to export and import. See the data notes for details. Economies shown with the same number are tied in the ranking.*

*Source: Doing Business database.*

## WHO REFORMED IN TRADING ACROSS BORDERS IN 2011/12?

In 2011/12 South Africa improved the most in the ease of trading across borders as measured by *Doing Business*. Through its customs modernization program it implemented measures that reduced the time, cost and documents required for international trade (figure 16.1). Improvements in South Africa have effects throughout southern Africa. Since overseas goods to and from Botswana, Lesotho, Swaziland and Zimbabwe transit through South Africa, traders in these economies are also enjoying the benefits.

South Africa was not alone. *Doing Business* recorded reforms making it easier to trade across borders in 21 other economies in the past year, for a total of 22 (table 16.3). Latin America and the

| TABLE 16.2 | Who makes exporting easy— and who does not? | | | | Who makes importing easy— and who does not? | | | |
|---|---|---|---|---|---|---|---|---|
| **Documents (number)** | | | | | **Documents (number)** | | | |
| Fewest | | Most | | | Fewest | | Most | |
| France | 2 | Afghanistan | 10 | | France | 2 | Chad | 11 |
| Canada | 3 | Burkina Faso | 10 | | Denmark | 3 | Niger | 11 |
| Estonia | 3 | Côte d'Ivoire | 10 | | Korea, Rep. | 3 | Russian Federation | 11 |
| Japan | 3 | Iraq | 10 | | Panama | 3 | Tajikistan | 11 |
| Korea, Rep. | 3 | Angola | 11 | | Sweden | 3 | Bhutan | 12 |
| Panama | 3 | Cameroon | 11 | | Hong Kong SAR, China | 4 | Cameroon | 12 |
| Sweden | 3 | Congo, Rep. | 11 | | Israel | 4 | Eritrea | 12 |
| Finland | 4 | Nepal | 11 | | Netherlands | 4 | Kazakhstan | 12 |
| Hong Kong SAR, China | 4 | Tajikistan | 11 | | Singapore | 4 | Uzbekistan | 14 |
| Singapore | 4 | Uzbekistan | 13 | | United Kingdom | 4 | Central African Republic | 17 |
| **Time (days)** | | | | | **Time (days)** | | | |
| Fastest | | Slowest | | | Fastest | | Slowest | |
| Denmark | 5 | Zimbabwe | 53 | | Singapore | 4 | Niger | 64 |
| Estonia | 5 | Central African Republic | 54 | | Cyprus | 5 | Kazakhstan | 69 |
| Hong Kong SAR, China | 5 | Niger | 59 | | Denmark | 5 | Venezuela, RB | 71 |
| Singapore | 5 | Kyrgyz Republic | 63 | | Estonia | 5 | Tajikistan | 72 |
| Netherlands | 6 | Tajikistan | 71 | | Hong Kong SAR, China | 5 | Zimbabwe | 73 |
| United States | 6 | Afghanistan | 74 | | United States | 5 | Kyrgyz Republic | 75 |
| Germany | 7 | Chad | 75 | | Netherlands | 6 | Afghanistan | 77 |
| Luxembourg | 7 | Iraq | 80 | | Sweden | 6 | Iraq | 82 |
| Norway | 7 | Uzbekistan | 80 | | United Kingdom | 6 | Uzbekistan | 99 |
| United Kingdom | 7 | Kazakhstan | 81 | | Luxembourg | 7 | Chad | 101 |
| **Cost (US$ per container)** | | | | | **Cost (US$ per container)** | | | |
| Least | | Most | | | Least | | Most | |
| Malaysia | 435 | Afghanistan | 3,545 | | Malaysia | 420 | Kazakhstan | 4,665 |
| Singapore | 456 | Iraq | 3,550 | | Singapore | 439 | Kyrgyz Republic | 4,700 |
| Finland | 540 | Niger | 3,676 | | Hong Kong SAR, China | 565 | Uzbekistan | 4,750 |
| Hong Kong SAR, China | 575 | Congo, Rep. | 3,818 | | Israel | 565 | Rwanda | 4,990 |
| Morocco | 577 | Kyrgyz Republic | 4,160 | | São Tomé and Príncipe | 577 | Burundi | 5,005 |
| China | 580 | Uzbekistan | 4,585 | | United Arab Emirates | 590 | Zimbabwe | 5,200 |
| Philippines | 585 | Kazakhstan | 4,685 | | Vietnam | 600 | Central African Republic | 5,554 |
| Thailand | 585 | Central African Republic | 5,491 | | China | 615 | Congo, Rep. | 7,709 |
| Latvia | 600 | Chad | 5,902 | | Finland | 620 | Chad | 8,525 |
| Vietnam | 610 | Tajikistan | 8,450 | | Fiji | 635 | Tajikistan | 9,800 |

*Source: Doing Business database.*

FIGURE 16.1 Modernizing customs made importing faster in South Africa

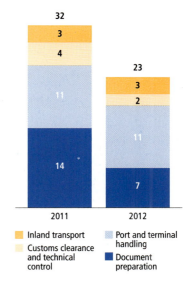

Time to import (days)

*Source: Doing Business database.*

Caribbean and Sub-Saharan Africa had the most, with 6 each, followed by OECD high-income economies (5) and Eastern Europe and Central Asia (2). One reform each was also recorded in East Asia and the Pacific, the Middle East and North Africa and South Asia. Six economies made trading across borders more difficult as measured by *Doing Business*—4 in Latin America and the Caribbean and 2 in Sub-Saharan Africa.

Automation has continued to play an important part in facilitating the processing and clearance of goods in many economies. In the past year 6 economies—Belize, Dominica, Grenada, Lao PDR, Sri Lanka, and Trinidad and Tobago—implemented computerized customs management systems that allow web-based submission of customs declarations.

## WHAT HAVE WE LEARNED FROM 8 YEARS OF DATA?

In the past 8 years *Doing Business* recorded 212 trade facilitation reforms around the world (figure 16.2). Eastern Europe and Central Asia and the Middle East and North Africa had the largest share

| TABLE 16.3 Who made trading across borders easier in 2011/12—and what did they do? | | |
|---|---|---|
| **Feature** | **Economies** | **Some highlights** |
| Introduced or improved electronic submission and processing | Belize; Botswana; Burundi; Czech Republic; Dominica; Grenada; Hungary; Lao PDR; Niger; Qatar; South Africa; Spain; Sri Lanka; Trinidad and Tobago; Uruguay | Lao PDR launched the ASYCUDA electronic data interchange system at the Thanaleng–Friendship Bridge border crossing. |
| Improved customs administration | Georgia; Jamaica; Malawi; South Africa | Jamaica facilitated overnight processing of customs declarations by extending the hours for lodging customs entries. |
| Introduced electronic single window | Benin; Portugal; Uzbekistan | Benin implemented an electronic single-window and unique payment system integrating customs, control agencies, port authorities and other service providers at the Cotonou port. |
| Introduced or improved risk-based inspections | Botswana; Lao PDR | Botswana introduced a scanner at the Kopfontein–Tlokweng border crossing, replacing physical inspections. Trucks are selected for scanning on the basis of their risk. |
| Improved port procedures | Netherlands; Uruguay | The Netherlands introduced a new web-based system for cargo release at the port terminals in Rotterdam. |

*Source: Doing Business database.*

| TABLE 16.4 Who has narrowed the distance to frontier in trading across borders the most since 2005? | |
|---|---|
| **Most improved** | **Improvement in distance to frontier (percentage points)** |
| Georgia | 49 (28→77) |
| France | 31 (57→88) |
| Rwanda | 30 (0→30) |
| Thailand | 28 (52→80) |
| Djibouti | 25 (50→75) |
| Madagascar | 25 (38→63) |
| Senegal | 23 (48→71) |
| Romania | 20 (50→70) |
| Kenya | 19 (26→45) |
| Korea, Rep. | 17 (74→91) |

*Note: The distance to frontier measure shows how far on average an economy is from the best performance achieved by any economy on each Doing Business indicator since 2005—in this case for the trading across borders indicators. The measure is normalized to range between 0 and 100, with 100 representing the best performance (the frontier). The data refer to the 174 economies included in Doing Business 2006 (2005). Eleven economies were added in subsequent years. The first column lists the top 10 most improved economies in order; the second shows the absolute improvement in the distance to frontier between 2005 and 2012.*
*Source: Doing Business database.*

of economies with such reforms: in both regions 83% implemented at least 1. Latin America and the Caribbean had the next largest share, with 73% of economies implementing at least 1, followed closely by Sub-Saharan Africa with 72%. The share in East Asia and the Pacific was 63%, in South Asia 50% and among the OECD high-income economies 42%.

Thanks to these efforts, trading across borders as measured by *Doing Business* has become faster and easier around the world. In 2006 it took 26.0 days on average to export and 30.4 days to import

a standardized cargo of goods by ocean transport (with every official procedure recorded but actual time in the ocean excluded). Today it takes only 22.2 days on average to export and 25.0 to import (figure 16.3). Analysis shows that such gains have had positive effects. Matching the data available since 2005 on the time to trade across borders with GDP per capita growth data indicates that a reduction of 4 days in the time to import or export is linked to an increase in the per capita growth rate of 0.1 percentage point.[5]

While many economies have made strides in improving international trade practices, Georgia has made the greatest progress toward the frontier in regulatory practice in trading across borders since 2005 (table 16.4). It did so through improvements over several years. In 2006 Georgia enacted a new customs code, simplifying the customs clearance process and better aligning it with international good practices. Three years later it reduced the cost to trade and simplified the documentation requirements for imports and exports. And in the past year Georgia created customs clearance zones—one-stop shops for different clearance processes.

The most common feature of trade facilitation reforms in all regions over the past 8

FIGURE 16.2  Sub-Saharan Africa leads in number of trade facilitation reforms

Number of *Doing Business* reforms making it easier to trade across borders by *Doing Business* report year

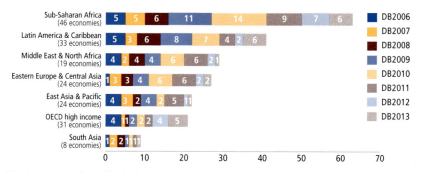

*Note: An economy can be considered to have only 1 Doing Business reform per topic and year. The data sample for DB2006 (2005) includes 174 economies. The sample for DB2013 (2012) also includes The Bahamas, Bahrain, Barbados, Brunei Darussalam, Cyprus, Kosovo, Liberia, Luxembourg, Malta, Montenegro and Qatar, for a total of 185 economies.*
*Source: Doing Business database.*

FIGURE 16.3  Large decline in document preparation time across regions

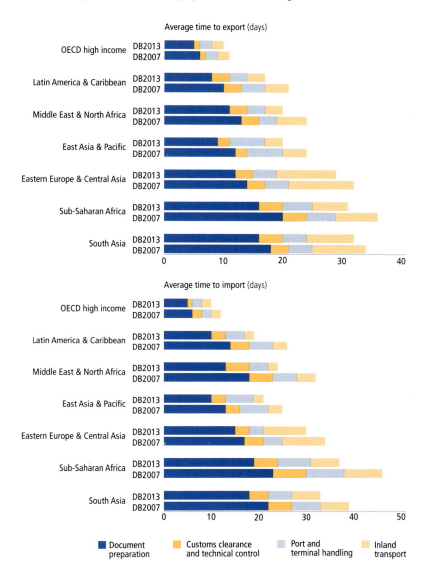

Average time to export (days)

Average time to import (days)

■ Document preparation   ■ Customs clearance and technical control   ■ Port and terminal handling   ■ Inland transport

*Note:* To ensure an accurate comparison, the figure shows data for the same sample of 174 economies for both DB2007 (2006) and DB2013 (2012) and uses the regional classifications that apply in 2012. The economies added to the *Doing Business* sample after 2006 and therefore excluded here are The Bahamas, Bahrain, Barbados, Brunei Darussalam, Cyprus, Kosovo, Liberia, Luxembourg, Malta, Montenegro and Qatar. DB2007 data are adjusted for any data revisions and changes in methodology.

*Source: Doing Business* database.

years was the introduction or improvement of electronic submission and processing of customs declarations—implemented in 110 economies. The improvement of customs administration was the second most common feature, undertaken by 61 economies. Improving port procedures was the third most common among economies in Sub-Saharan Africa and the Middle East and North Africa. By contrast, among other economies, including those in Eastern Europe and Central Asia, Latin America and the Caribbean and the OECD high-income group, introducing or improving risk-based inspection systems was more common.

## NOTES

This topic note was written by Iryna Bilotserkivska, Robert Murillo and Mikiko Imai Ollison.

1. Zoellick and others 2012.

2. To ensure comparability across economies, the *Doing Business* methodology assumes that trade is by sea transport and therefore may not capture regional trade in some regions, such as Sub-Saharan Africa and Eastern Europe and Central Asia. While sea transport still accounts for the majority of world trade, regional trade is becoming increasingly important for small and medium-size enterprises.

3. Arvis, Marteau and Raballand 2010.

4. Freund and Rocha 2011. The authors use a modified gravity equation that controls for importer fixed effects and exporter remoteness to understand whether different types of export costs affect trade differently. All 3 techniques used to analyze the effect on trade values of export times for key components lead to the same conclusion: that inland transit delays have a robust negative effect on export values.

5. Results are based on Arellano-Bond dynamic panel estimation to control for economic cycle and time-invariant country-specific factors. Following Eifert (2009) and Djankov, McLiesh and Ramalho (2006), the analysis controls for initial level of education, initial level of income per capita and institutional quality. It also controls for total trade openness and rents from natural resources.

# Enforcing contracts

- Enforcing contracts is easiest in Luxembourg, where it takes 321 days and 26 procedures and costs 9.7% of the value of the claim.

- From June 2011 to June 2012 *Doing Business* recorded 11 reforms making it easier to enforce contracts.

- In the past year Poland improved the most in the ease of enforcing contracts.

- Bhutan has advanced the furthest toward the frontier in regulatory practice in contract enforcement since 2005. Among the 10 economies making the greatest progress in this period, 6 are in Sub-Saharan Africa.

- Introducing specialized commercial courts or divisions was the most common feature of reforms making it easier to enforce contracts in the past 8 years.

*For more information on good practices and research related to enforcing contracts, visit http://www .doingbusiness.org/data/ exploretopics/enforcing-contracts. For more on the methodology, see the section on enforcing contracts in the data notes.*

A judicial system that provides effective commercial dispute resolution is crucial to a healthy economy.[1] Without one, firms risk finding themselves operating in an environment where compliance with contractual obligations is not the norm. While using alternative dispute resolution systems may have benefits, *Doing Business* focuses on how public institutions function in the case of a commercial dispute.[2] *Doing Business* measures the time, cost and procedural complexity of resolving a commercial lawsuit between 2 domestic businesses. The dispute involves the breach of a sales contract worth twice the income per capita of the economy. The case study assumes that the court hears arguments on the merits and that an expert provides an opinion on the quality of the goods in dispute. This distinguishes the case from simple debt enforcement. The time, cost and procedures are measured from the perspective of an entrepreneur (the plaintiff) pursuing the standardized case through local courts.

Efficiency in this process matters. A study in Eastern Europe found that in countries with slower courts, firms on average tend to have less bank financing for new investment. The study shows that reforms in other areas, such as creditors' rights, help increase bank lending only if contracts can be enforced before the courts.[3] Another recent study, analyzing 98 developing economies, suggests that foreign direct investment tends to be greater where the cost of contract enforcement in debt collection and property eviction cases is lower, particularly when the host economy is more indebted.[4]

Among the 185 economies covered by *Doing Business*, Luxembourg has the top ranking on the ease of enforcing contracts (table 17.1). But contract enforcement is fastest in Singapore, where it takes only 150 days to resolve the standardized case measured by *Doing Business* (table 17.2).

## WHO REFORMED IN ENFORCING CONTRACTS IN 2011/12?

From June 2011 to June 2012 *Doing Business* recorded 11 reforms making it easier to enforce contracts and 1 making it more difficult (table 17.3). Brazil, Rwanda and Saudi Arabia improved electronic systems in their courts. Such systems offer multiple benefits. By allowing litigants to file complaints electronically in commercial cases, they can speed up the filing and service process. They can prevent the

| TABLE 17.1 | Where is enforcing contracts easiest—and where most difficult? | | |
|---|---|---|---|
| **Easiest** | **RANK** | **Most difficult** | **RANK** |
| Luxembourg | 1 | Syrian Arab Republic | 176 |
| Korea, Rep. | 2 | Central African Republic | 177 |
| Iceland | 3 | Benin | 178 |
| Norway | 4 | Honduras | 179 |
| Germany | 5 | Suriname | 180 |
| United States | 6 | São Tomé and Príncipe | 181 |
| Austria | 7 | Bangladesh | 182 |
| France | 8 | Angola | 183 |
| Finland | 9 | India | 184 |
| Hong Kong SAR, China | 10 | Timor-Leste | 185 |

*Note:* Rankings are the average of the economy's rankings on the procedures, time and cost to resolve a commercial dispute through the courts. See the data notes for details.

*Source: Doing Business* database.

## TABLE 17.2 Who makes enforcing contracts easy—and who does not?

### Procedures (number of steps)

| Fewest | | Most | |
|---|---|---|---|
| Ireland | 21 | Armenia | 49 |
| Singapore | 21 | Guinea | 49 |
| Rwanda | 23 | Kuwait | 50 |
| Austria | 25 | Belize | 51 |
| Belgium | 26 | Iraq | 51 |
| Luxembourg | 26 | Oman | 51 |
| Netherlands | 26 | Timor-Leste | 51 |
| Czech Republic | 27 | Kosovo | 53 |
| Hong Kong SAR, China | 27 | Sudan | 53 |
| Iceland | 27 | Syrian Arab Republic | 55 |

### Time (days)

| Fastest | | Slowest | |
|---|---|---|---|
| Singapore | 150 | Sri Lanka | 1,318 |
| Uzbekistan | 195 | Barbados | 1,340 |
| New Zealand | 216 | Trinidad and Tobago | 1,340 |
| Bhutan | 225 | Colombia | 1,346 |
| Korea, Rep. | 230 | India | 1,420 |
| Rwanda | 230 | Bangladesh | 1,442 |
| Azerbaijan | 237 | Guatemala | 1,459 |
| Kyrgyz Republic | 260 | Afghanistan | 1,642 |
| Namibia | 270 | Guinea-Bissau | 1,715 |
| Russian Federation | 270 | Suriname | 1,715 |

### Cost (% of claim)

| Least | | Most | |
|---|---|---|---|
| Bhutan | 0.1 | Comoros | 89.4 |
| Iceland | 8.2 | Malawi | 94.1 |
| Luxembourg | 9.7 | Cambodia | 103.4 |
| Norway | 9.9 | Papua New Guinea | 110.3 |
| Korea, Rep. | 10.3 | Zimbabwe | 113.1 |
| China | 11.1 | Indonesia | 139.4 |
| Slovenia | 12.7 | Mozambique | 142.5 |
| Portugal | 13.0 | Congo, Dem. Rep. | 147.6 |
| Finland | 13.3 | Sierra Leone | 149.5 |
| Russian Federation | 13.4 | Timor-Leste | 163.2 |

*Source: Doing Business database.*

FIGURE 17.1 Sub-Saharan Africa continues to lead in number of contract enforcement reforms

Number of *Doing Business* reforms making it easier to enforce contracts by *Doing Business* report year

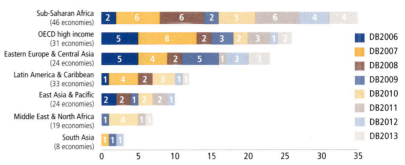

*Note:* An economy can be considered to have only 1 *Doing Business* reform per topic and year. The data sample for DB2006 (2005) includes 174 economies. The sample for DB2013 (2012) also includes The Bahamas, Bahrain, Barbados, Brunei Darussalam, Cyprus, Kosovo, Liberia, Luxembourg, Malta, Montenegro and Qatar, for a total of 185 economies.

*Source: Doing Business database.*

which involves monitoring and managing cases in the court docket from the filing of the claim until the judgment is issued, has proved to be an effective tool for reducing procedural delays at court and for monitoring the performance of judges and court officers.

Increasing the specialization of judges, divisions or courts in commercial cases has been a common feature of reforms to increase court efficiency in recent years. Two economies implemented such reforms in the past year. Liberia launched a specialized commercial court in November 2011 and has already appointed 3 new judges for the court. Cameroon created specialized commercial divisions within its courts of first instance. Benin appointed more judges and bailiffs in commercial courts. And it introduced the

FIGURE 17.2 Contract enforcement has become faster in most regions

Average time to enforce contracts (days)

■ Filing and service ■ Trial and judgment ■ Enforcement

*Note:* To ensure an accurate comparison, the figure shows data for the same sample of 178 economies for both DB2008 (2007) and DB2013 (2012) and uses the regional classifications that apply in 2012. The economies added to the *Doing Business* sample after 2007 and therefore excluded here are The Bahamas, Bahrain, Barbados, Cyprus, Kosovo, Malta and Qatar. DB2008 data are adjusted for any data revisions and changes in methodology.

*Source: Doing Business database.*

loss, destruction or concealment of court records. And they can increase transparency and limit opportunities for corruption in the judiciary. Even more beneficial is the use of computerized systems for case management. Case management,

**TABLE 17.3  Who made enforcing contracts easier in 2011/12—and what did they do?**

| Feature | Economies | Some highlights |
|---|---|---|
| Increased procedural efficiency at main trial court | Georgia; Poland; Slovak Republic; Turkey | The Slovak Republic amended its civil procedure code to simplify and speed up proceedings and to limit obstructive tactics by the parties to a case. |
| Introduced or expanded computerized case management system | Brazil; Rwanda; Saudi Arabia | Saudi Arabia expanded the computerization of its courts and introduced an electronic filing system for commercial cases, allowing attorneys to submit a summons online through a dedicated website. |
| Significantly increased number of judges | Benin; Liberia; Poland | Poland appointed more judges and bailiffs in commercial courts. |
| Made enforcement of judgment more efficient | Poland; Serbia | Serbia introduced private bailiffs. |
| Introduced specialized commercial court | Cameroon; Liberia | Liberia launched a specialized commercial court in November 2011 and has appointed 3 new judges for the court. |

*Source: Doing Business database.*

concept of managing judges as well as enforcement judges.

Serbia made it easier to enforce contracts by introducing a private bailiff system, providing competitive options for enforcing a binding decision. The winning party in a commercial case may now choose between private and court bailiffs to carry out enforcement proceedings.

Georgia, Poland, the Slovak Republic and Turkey amended the procedural rules applying to commercial cases, mainly to simplify and speed up proceedings and to limit obstructive tactics by the parties to a case. New legislation adopted in January 2012 by the Slovak Republic imposes new individual deadlines on the parties at different stages of the proceedings. For example, courts are now obliged to

deliver a complaint to the defendant in less than 60 days.

## WHAT HAVE WE LEARNED FROM 8 YEARS OF DATA?

In the past 8 years *Doing Business* recorded 116 reforms that helped improve court efficiency in commercial dispute resolution. Sub-Saharan Africa had the most reforms, with 35 (figure 17.1). But Eastern Europe and Central Asia, the region where contract enforcement is the fastest on average (figure 17.2), had the largest share of economies with such reforms: 15 of 24 economies in the region implemented at least 1.

Some economies introduced specialized commercial courts. Others overhauled the organization of their courts or their system of judicial case management for commercial dispute resolution. In the past

year the implementation of electronic filing systems was among the most common improvements recorded by *Doing Business*. Today 19 economies allow electronic filing of complaints, including 12 OECD high-income economies. Among all OECD high-income economies, the average time for filing and service fell by 9 days between 2007 and 2012 (see figure 17.2).

Specialized courts tend to improve efficiency.[5] Creating specialized commercial courts can result in faster and less costly contract enforcement, particularly where the commercial caseload is large. Today 82 of the 185 economies covered by *Doing Business* have a dedicated stand-alone court, a specialized commercial section within an existing court or specialized judges within a general civil court. In 7 Sub-Saharan African economies that introduced commercial courts or sections in the past 10 years—the Democratic Republic of Congo, Ghana, Lesotho, Mauritania, Mozambique, Nigeria and Rwanda—the average time to resolve the standardized case measured by *Doing Business* dropped by more than 5 months.

Poland improved the most in the ease of enforcing contracts in the past year and is also among the 10 economies advancing the furthest toward the frontier in regulatory practice in this area since 2005 (table 17.4). In 2003 resolving a commercial dispute in Warsaw took 1,000 days. Today, thanks to extensive efforts, it takes 685 (figure 17.3).

What did Poland do? In 2007 it started deregulating the bailiff profession, increasing the number of service providers. That same year it created its first electronic court, in Lublin; the new court, which processes cases and assigns them to judges in only 2–3 weeks on average, has already dealt with more than 3 million cases. In a parallel effort Poland launched an information technology system in 2003, then the Praetor software in 2007, improving the internal operations of courts over time. The software system facilitates the circulation of documents

**FIGURE 17.3  How Poland cut the time to enforce contracts by a third in Warsaw**

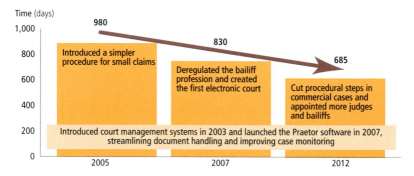

*Source: Doing Business database.*

| TABLE 17.4 Who has narrowed the distance to frontier in enforcing contracts the most since 2005? ||
|---|---|
| Most improved | Improvement in distance to frontier (percentage points) |
| Bhutan | 35 (31→66) |
| Gambia, The | 14 (50→64) |
| Poland | 13 (50→63) |
| Botswana | 11 (56→67) |
| Georgia | 11 (59→70) |
| Mozambique | 10 (29→39) |
| Nigeria | 8 (48→56) |
| Lesotho | 7 (44→51) |
| Mali | 6 (43→49) |
| Portugal | 6[a] (64→70) |

*Note:* The distance to frontier measure shows how far on average an economy is from the best performance achieved by any economy on each *Doing Business* indicator since 2005—in this case for the enforcing contracts indicators. The measure is normalized to range between 0 and 100, with 100 representing the best performance (the frontier). The data refer to the 174 economies included in *Doing Business 2006* (2005). Eleven economies were added in subsequent years. The first column lists the top 10 most improved economies in order; the second shows the absolute improvement in the distance to frontier between 2005 and 2012.

a. Ethiopia, FYR Macedonia and Malaysia also have an improvement of 6 percentage points.

*Source: Doing Business* database.

within the court and allows users to trace the history of the decision stage for particular documents. By 2007 the implementation of these court management systems had already reduced the backlog of cases by 36% compared with 2004.

Efforts are ongoing. In May 2012 Poland amended its civil procedure code, eliminating separate procedural steps in commercial cases. Poland also appointed more judges and bailiffs to the district and regional commercial courts, expanded the role of judges in managing processes (particularly in the introduction of evidence), expanded the responsibilities of assistant judges (such as in overseeing bailiffs and enforcing court judgments), allowed new electronic processes and introduced economic incentives for debtors to comply with judgments.

## NOTES

This topic note was written by Joyce Antone Ibrahim and Julien Vilquin.

1. Ramello and Voigt 2012.
2. World Bank Facility for Investment Climate Advisory Services 2011.
3. Safavian and Sharma 2007.
4. Ahlquist and Prakash 2010.
5. Botero and others 2003.

2005 2007 2012 2011 2004 2008 2009 2006 2010 2013

# Resolving insolvency

- Creditors of firms facing insolvency benefit from the highest recovery rate in Japan.

- From June 2011 to June 2012 *Doing Business* recorded 17 reforms aimed at improving insolvency proceedings.

- Poland is among the 10 economies advancing the furthest toward the frontier in regulatory practice in resolving insolvency since 2005.

- Common features of insolvency reforms in the past 8 years include passing new bankruptcy laws, promoting reorganization proceedings, shortening time limits, regulating the qualifications of insolvency administrators and strengthening the rights of secured creditors.

- Eastern Europe and Central Asia had the biggest increase in the recovery rate in the past 8 years, while OECD high-income economies had the most insolvency reforms.

*For more information on good practices and research related to resolving insolvency, visit http://www.doingbusiness.org/data/exploretopics/resolving-insolvency. For more on the methodology, see the section on resolving insolvency in the data notes.*

Driven by steeper labor costs and the high fuel prices and dampened travel demand resulting from the global financial crisis, American Airlines, the third largest U.S. carrier, filed for Chapter 11 bankruptcy in November 2011. Its core business is still viable, and if allowed to reorganize its finances and operations the company could avoid failure—to the benefit of its creditors, shareholders and employees. Thanks to the solid insolvency laws in the United States, American Airlines had the opportunity to file for restructuring, and if the company's viability is proven, it is expected to survive.[1] This does not happen in the many economies that lack restructuring frameworks.

*Doing Business* measures the time, cost and outcome of insolvency proceedings involving domestic entities. The time required for creditors to recover their credit is recorded in calendar years. The cost of the proceedings is recorded as a percentage of the value of the debtor's estate. The recovery rate for creditors depends on whether the case study company (a hotel business) emerges from the proceedings as a going concern or its assets are sold piecemeal. The rate is recorded as cents on the dollar recouped by creditors through reorganization, liquidation or debt enforcement (foreclosure) proceedings. If an economy had zero insolvency cases a year over the past 5 years, it receives a "no practice" classification. This means that creditors are unlikely to recover their money through a formal legal process (in or out of court). The recovery rate for "no practice" economies is zero. The ranking on the ease of resolving insolvency is based on the recovery rate, which is affected by the key variables of time, cost and outcome (tables 18.1 and 18.2).

Whether insolvency proceedings are efficient matters not just for firms that are struggling. A recent study shows that Brazil's 2005 bankruptcy reform, which strengthened the rights of secured creditors, led to a significant reduction in the cost of debt and an increase in both short- and long-term debt.[2] However, an analysis of Italy's 2005–06 reform of its bankruptcy law shows that excessive use of reorganization proceedings increases interest rates on loan financing because it reduces the incentives for entrepreneurs to act prudently.[3] Another study, focusing on U.S. airlines, shows that bankruptcies reduce the collateral value of other firms in the same industry, increasing the cost

| TABLE 18.1 Where is resolving insolvency easiest—and where most difficult? | | | |
|---|---|---|---|
| **Recovery rate** | | | |
| **Easiest** | | **Most difficult** | |
| Japan | 92.8 | Angola | 8.0 |
| Singapore | 91.3 | Venezuela, RB | 6.4 |
| Norway | 90.8 | São Tomé and Príncipe | 5.2 |
| Canada | 90.7 | Philippines | 4.9 |
| Finland | 89.7 | Micronesia, Fed. Sts. | 3.4 |
| Netherlands | 88.8 | Rwanda | 3.1 |
| Belgium | 88.7 | Congo, Dem. Rep. | 1.6 |
| United Kingdom | 88.6 | Zimbabwe | 0.1 |
| Ireland | 87.5 | Central African Republic | 0.0 |
| Denmark | 87.1 | Eritrea | 0.0[a] |

*Note:* Rankings are based on the recovery rate: how many cents on the dollar creditors recover from an insolvent firm as calculated by *Doing Business*. See the data notes for details.

a. Sixteen economies have a recovery rate of 0, including 14 "no practice" economies.

*Source: Doing Business* database.

| TABLE 18.2 | Who makes resolving insolvency easy—and who does not? | | |
|---|---|---|---|
| **Time (years)** | | | |
| **Fastest** | | **Slowest** | |
| Ireland | 0.4 | Congo, Dem. Rep. | 5.2 |
| Japan | 0.6 | Ecuador | 5.3 |
| Canada | 0.8 | Micronesia, Fed. Sts. | 5.3 |
| Singapore | 0.8 | Indonesia | 5.5 |
| Belgium | 0.9 | Haiti | 5.7 |
| Finland | 0.9 | Philippines | 5.7 |
| Norway | 0.9 | Cambodia | 6.0 |
| Australia | 1.0 | Angola | 6.2 |
| Belize | 1.0 | São Tomé and Príncipe | 6.2 |
| Denmark | 1.0[a] | Mauritania | 8.0 |

| **Cost (% of estate)** | | | |
|---|---|---|---|
| **Least** | | **Most** | |
| Norway | 1 | Dominican Republic | 38 |
| Singapore | 1 | Marshall Islands | 38 |
| Armenia | 4 | Micronesia, Fed. Sts. | 38 |
| Bahamas, The | 4 | Philippines | 38[c] |
| Belgium | 4 | Sierra Leone | 42 |
| Brunei Darussalam | 4 | Ukraine | 42 |
| Canada | 4 | Liberia | 43 |
| Denmark | 4 | Rwanda | 50 |
| Finland | 4 | Chad | 60 |
| Georgia | 4[b] | Central African Republic | 76 |

a. Four other economies also have a time of 1 year: Iceland; Palau; the Solomon Islands; and the United Kingdom.

b. Eleven other economies also have a cost of 4% of the estate value: Iceland; Japan; Korea; Maldives; the Netherlands; New Zealand; Oman; Pakistan; Slovenia; Switzerland; and Taiwan, China.

c. Four other economies also have a cost of 38% of the estate value: Samoa; the Solomon Islands; Vanuatu; and República Bolivariana de Venezuela.

*Source: Doing Business* database.

of external debt financing for all firms in the industry.[4] In the aftermath of the financial crisis, researchers, practitioners and policy makers have been emphasizing the importance of efficient bankruptcy regimes to strengthen local economies while also discussing the challenges of implementing bankruptcy reforms.[5]

| TABLE 18.3 | Who made resolving insolvency easier in 2011/12—and what did they do? | |
|---|---|---|
| **Feature** | **Economies** | **Some highlights** |
| Established or promoted reorganization, liquidation or foreclosure procedures | Belarus; Germany; Greece; Kazakhstan; Lithuania; Moldova; Poland; Serbia; Slovak Republic; Spain; Uzbekistan | Germany amended its insolvency law to facilitate in-court restructuring of distressed companies, providing new opportunities for creditors and debtors. |
| Eliminated formalities or introduced or tightened time limits | Belarus; Georgia; Kazakhstan; Republic of Korea; Lithuania; Slovenia; Uganda; Uzbekistan | Georgia streamlined all insolvency procedures, introducing a deadline for the creditors' first meeting and shorter time limits for the submission of documentation and creditors' claims, for decisions on the outcome of insolvency proceedings and for the duration of the auction. |
| Regulated profession of insolvency administrators | Kazakhstan; Moldova; Poland; Slovenia; Uganda; Zambia | Zambia established qualification requirements, professional duties and provisions on pay for liquidators and receivers. |
| Granted priority to secured creditors | Kazakhstan; Slovak Republic | The Slovak Republic strengthened the rights of secured creditors, prioritizing their claims and granting them voting power over the restructuring plan. |
| Increased transparency of insolvency system | Lithuania; Serbia | Serbia introduced an online public registry, making public all injunctions issued by the court. |
| Introduced framework for out-of-court restructurings | Portugal; Spain | Spain improved its framework for out-of-court restructuring by facilitating the approval of an agreement between creditors and debtors. |

*Source: Doing Business* database.

## WHO REFORMED IN RESOLVING INSOLVENCY IN 2011/12?

From June 2011 to June 2012 *Doing Business* recorded 17 reforms making it easier to resolve insolvency (table 18.3). Most were in Eastern Europe and Central Asia, where 29% of economies had such reforms, and in OECD high-income economies, of which 26% did.

Germany promoted its reorganization proceedings by streamlining insolvency procedures and introducing a debt-for-equity swap remedy. It also strengthened the rights of secured creditors by involving creditors in the restructuring process and establishing a preliminary creditors' committee. The Slovak Republic adopted a new amendment to its bankruptcy and restructuring law that clearly defines the roles and powers of creditors, secured creditors and trustees with the aim of increasing the efficiency of the insolvency process.

FIGURE 18.1 Eastern Europe & Central Asia and OECD high-income economies keep up fast pace in insolvency reforms

Number of *Doing Business* reforms making it easier to resolve insolvency by *Doing Business* report year

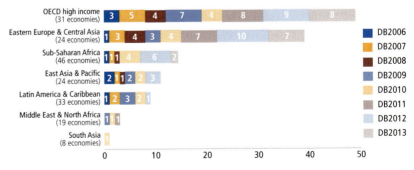

*Note:* An economy can be considered to have only 1 *Doing Business* reform per topic and year. The data sample for DB2006 (2005) includes 174 economies. The sample for DB2013 (2012) also includes The Bahamas, Bahrain, Barbados, Brunei Darussalam, Cyprus, Kosovo, Liberia, Luxembourg, Malta, Montenegro and Qatar, for a total of 185 economies.

*Source: Doing Business* database.

FIGURE 18.2  Big increase in recovery rate in Eastern Europe and Central Asia

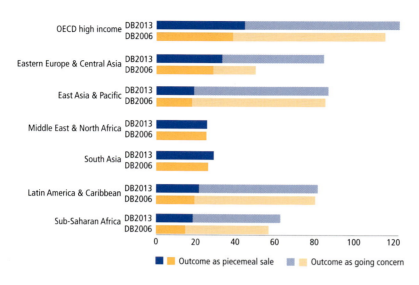

Average recovery rate by type of outcome (cents on the dollar)

■ Outcome as piecemeal sale   ☐ Outcome as going concern

*Note:* To ensure an accurate comparison, the figure shows data for the same sample of 174 economies for both DB2006 (2005) and DB2013 (2012) and uses the regional classifications that apply in 2012. The economies added to the *Doing Business* sample after 2005 and therefore excluded here are The Bahamas, Bahrain, Barbados, Brunei Darussalam, Cyprus, Kosovo, Liberia, Luxembourg, Malta, Montenegro and Qatar. DB2006 data are adjusted for any data revisions and changes in methodology. All outcomes are recorded as piecemeal sales for economies in the Middle East and North Africa and South Asia.
*Source: Doing Business* database.

| TABLE 18.4  Who has narrowed the distance to frontier in resolving insolvency the most since 2005? | |
|---|---|
| Most improved | Improvement in distance to frontier (percentage points) |
| Czech Republic | 40 (20→60) |
| Afghanistan | 29 (0→29) |
| Uzbekistan | 29 (12→41) |
| Latvia | 27 (37→64) |
| Colombia | 26 (55→81) |
| Belarus | 23 (23→46) |
| Côte d'Ivoire | 23 (17→40) |
| Poland | 23 (35→58) |
| Burkina Faso | 22 (8→30) |
| Senegal | 22 (13→35) |

*Note:* The distance to frontier measure shows how far on average an economy is from the best performance achieved by any economy on each *Doing Business* indicator since 2005—in this case for the resolving insolvency indicator. The measure is normalized to range between 0 and 100, with 100 representing the best performance (the frontier). The data refer to the 174 economies included in *Doing Business 2006* (2005). Eleven economies were added in subsequent years. The first column lists the top 10 most improved economies in order; the second shows the absolute improvement in the distance to frontier between 2005 and 2012.
*Source: Doing Business* database.

Kazakhstan further developed its rehabilitation process by introducing an accelerated proceeding, setting clear time limits for developing a rehabilitation plan and clearly defining the roles and powers of the court in the process. Lithuania also specified time limits for some insolvency procedures, including for creditors to file their claims and for the court to hear an appeal of the ruling to initiate bankruptcy proceedings or dismiss the administrator.

## WHAT HAVE WE LEARNED FROM 8 YEARS OF DATA?

In the past 8 years *Doing Business* recorded 126 insolvency reforms in 74 economies (figure 18.1). While economies focused their efforts on different aspects of insolvency, these reforms still shared some common features. For example, 27 economies passed new bankruptcy laws over the past 8 years. Many economies promoted reorganization proceedings by simplifying and accelerating procedures, defining the roles of the parties involved and introducing innovative instruments

such as out-of-court workouts. Shortening the time limits for different procedures was also a common feature of insolvency reforms. Other common features were regulating and refining standards for the profession of insolvency administrators and strengthening the rights of secured creditors.

The financial crisis prompted many economies to take immediate action to improve their insolvency regimes. *Doing Business 2012* reported a record number

of insolvency reforms globally: 29. *Doing Business 2006* recorded only 8. In the past year 4 regions had no insolvency reforms: East Asia and the Pacific, Latin America and the Caribbean, the Middle East and North Africa, and South Asia.

FIGURE 18.3  Poland improved the efficiency of insolvency proceedings in the past 6 years

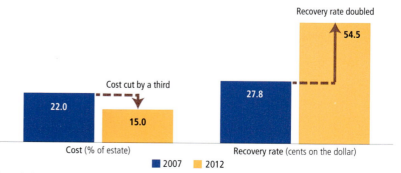

*Source: Doing Business* database.

How has the efficiency in resolving insolvency changed? No significant improvements were observed in low-income economies from 2005 to 2012: the average time to complete an insolvency proceeding remained at 3.9 years, and the average cost even increased from 23% to 24% of the value of the debtor's estate.[6] Globally over that period, the average time to complete an insolvency proceeding fell from 3 years to 2.8 years, the cost remained at about 20%, and the recovery rate rose from 31% to 35% (figure 18.2).

Poland is among those making the biggest improvements since 2005 in the efficiency of resolving insolvency as measured by *Doing Business* (table 18.4). Through extensive efforts to build a full-fledged insolvency regime, it reduced the cost to complete an insolvency proceeding by a third between 2007 and 2012—and doubled the recovery rate (figure 18.3). Among the highlights of Poland's insolvency reforms: specifying qualifications for insolvency administrators with the aim of improving the quality of professional services, reducing the cost by setting a maximum limit on pay for administrators, and introducing a pre-bankruptcy reorganization procedure. In the past year Poland continued its reform trajectory by strengthening the rights of secured creditors and making it easier to start bankruptcy proceedings.

## NOTES

This topic note was written by Valentina Saltane and Rong Chen.

1. Patrick Rizzo, "American Airlines Files for Bankruptcy Protection," *NBC News*, November 29, 2011, http://bottomline .nbcnews.com/; Kyle Peterson and Matt Daily, "American Airlines Files for Bankruptcy," *Reuters*, November 29, 2011, http://www.reuters.com/.

2. De Araujo, Xavier Ferreira and Funchal 2011.

3. Rodano, Serrano-Velarde and Tarantino 2011.

4. Benmelech and Bergman 2011.

5. Cirmizi, Klapper and Uttamchandani 2012.

6. To ensure an accurate comparison, only the 32 low-income economies included in the *Doing Business 2006* (2005) sample are included.

# Annex: employing workers

- Fourteen economies implemented changes in their labor regulations affecting the *Doing Business* indicators on employing workers in the past year; 72 did so in the past 8 years.

- In 107 economies there is no limit on how long fixed-term employment contracts may last. In the 78 economies that have set a limit, the average maximum duration of fixed-term contracts is 39.2 months.

- One hundred and seventy-four economies limit employees' workweek in manufacturing to 6 or fewer days, complying with International Labour Organization (ILO) Convention 14 on the length of the workweek.

- One hundred and fifty-four economies have set a minimum wage by law, and 48 of them have set a special minimum wage for apprentices.

- Redundancy dismissals are allowed in 183 of 185 economies.

- The average cost of redundancy dismissals in the 185 economies as measured by *Doing Business* is 17.2 weeks of salary.

*For more information on the methodology for the employing workers indicators, see the section on employing workers in the data notes.*

Employment laws are needed to protect workers from arbitrary or unfair treatment and to ensure efficient contracting between employers and workers. *Doing Business*, through its employing workers indicators, measures flexibility in the regulation of hiring, working hours and redundancy. These measures are consistent with the conventions of the International Labour Organization (ILO) but do not assess compliance with them. The indicators do not cover any of the ILO core labor standards, such as the right to collective bargaining, the elimination of forced labor, the abolition of child labor and equitable treatment in employment practices.

To make the data comparable across 185 economies, *Doing Business* uses a standardized case study that assumes, among other things, a company with 60 employees that operates in the manufacturing sector and an employee who is a nonexecutive, full-time worker.

## HIGHLIGHTS FROM THE EMPLOYING WORKERS DATA

*Doing Business* covers 28 different areas related to employing workers. This year's report highlights 2 of them—apprentice wages and the use of fixed-term contracts for permanent tasks, both likely to affect the employability of young workers. Future editions will analyze other areas.

### Apprentice wages

Young workers are especially likely to experience the negative effects of rigid employment regulation. They typically lack training and substantial experience, and burdensome regulation and high redundancy costs discourage potential employers. Apprentice wages are one way to address these issues and create new opportunities for young workers. They allow businesses to hire young, first-time employees for a portion—typically between 70% and 80%—of the mandatory minimum wage for a short period of time, typically 1 year. Data show that the average minimum wage ratio for apprentices around the world is 0.33.[1]

FIGURE 19.1   Apprentice wages are rare in the Middle East and North Africa

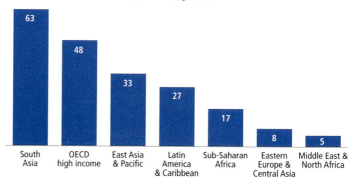

Share of economies with apprentice wages (%)

Source: *Doing Business* database.

FIGURE 19.2 Fixed-term contracts are more
widely allowed among high-
income economies

Share of economies allowing fixed-
term contracts by income group (%)

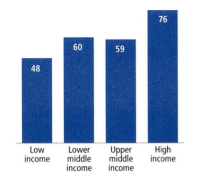

Source: *Doing Business* database.

| Feature | Economies | Some highlights |
|---|---|---|
| Strengthened fixed-term contracts | Czech Republic; Portugal; Slovak Republic; Spain | The Czech Republic and Slovak Republic increased the maximum duration of a single fixed-term contract from 24 months to 36. The Czech Republic also allows 2 renewals of the contract, for a total of up to 108 months. Portugal increased the maximum cumulative duration of fixed-term contracts from 36 months to 54. Spain temporarily allowed unlimited cumulative duration of fixed-term contracts. |
| Reduced redundancy costs | Czech Republic; Montenegro; Portugal; Slovak Republic | The Czech Republic made severance pay in cases of redundancy dismissal dependent on the employee's years of service. Montenegro reduced severance payments applicable in cases of redundancy dismissal, and the Slovak Republic eliminated them.[a] Portugal reduced the severance pay applicable to contracts signed after November 1, 2012, to 20 days. |
| Strengthened conditions on applicable hiring rules | Bhutan; Kosovo | Bhutan and Kosovo implemented a minimum wage in the private sector for the first time. |
| Streamlined process for redundancy dismissals | Latvia; Slovak Republic | Latvia and the Slovak Republic changed their restrictions on redundancy dismissals. An employer making 1 or more workers redundant no longer needs to notify the authorities beforehand. |

TABLE 19.1  Who made employing workers easier in 2011/12—and what did they do?

a. Montenegro also reduced the maximum duration of single and multiple fixed-term contracts from an unlimited period to 24 months, increased paid annual leave from 19 working days to 21 and increased the notice period applicable in cases of redundancy dismissal.

Source: *Doing Business* database.

Use of this practice is most common in South Asia, where 63% of economies have some kind of apprentice wages, and among OECD high-income economies, where 48% do. It is much less common in other regions: only 8% of economies in Eastern Europe and Central Asia have apprentice wages, and only 5% in the Middle East and North Africa do (figure 19.1). Economies without apprentice wages are missing an important opportunity to help young workers access the labor market. Apprenticeships can pay a "double dividend": securing the transition to permanent employment for young workers and providing lower labor costs (compensated by a training commitment) for the employer.[2]

## Fixed-term contracts for permanent tasks

Another measure that may encourage businesses to hire young workers is allowing the use of fixed-term contracts for permanent tasks. Such economies as Denmark and the United States allow this practice, and some, such as Italy and Lithuania, have reformed their labor regulations in recent years to allow it.

These contracts are used to screen workers for permanent positions, with on-the-job training providing a test of abilities. Both parties benefit: young fixed-term

workers are given the opportunity to acquire professional skills, and employers can optimize their labor costs while evaluating the workers' performance. And evidence suggests that fixed-term contracts maximize the chances of a temporary worker being promoted to a permanent position. Once a vacancy for a permanent position arises, employers would prefer to fill the vacancy with a worker who already has the skills required and who has performed adequately in previous months.[3]

Where restrictive regulations prohibiting these contracts are left in place, young workers therefore find it more difficult to access and transition to permanent employment. This is the case in more than half of low-income economies: 52% of such economies do not allow fixed-term contracts for permanent tasks. Use of such contracts increases with income level. Indeed, 38 of 50 high-income economies (76%) allow employers to use fixed-term contracts for permanent tasks (figure 19.2).

## WHO REFORMED IN EMPLOYING WORKERS IN 2011/12?

In 2011/12, 14 economies changed their labor regulations in ways that affect the *Doing Business* indicators on employing workers. Eight economies changed their laws to increase labor market flexibility; 6 economies did the opposite. Of those 8 economies, 3 are in Eastern Europe and Central Asia. Most of the legal changes increasing labor market flexibility focused on redundancy costs or procedures (table 19.1).

## WHAT HAVE WE LEARNED FROM 8 YEARS OF DATA?

In the past 8 years 72 economies around the world implemented 106 reforms affecting the employing workers indicators. OECD high-income economies had the most changes, with 37, followed by Eastern Europe and Central Asia with 26 and Sub-Saharan Africa with 16 (figure 19.3). The data also show differences in focus. Governments in Sub-Saharan Africa, for example, focused on reforming the regimes applicable to fixed-term contracts, generally allowing longer,

FIGURE 19.3 OECD high-income economies had the most legal and regulatory reforms in the past 8 years

Number of *Doing Business* reforms in employing workers by *Doing Business* report year

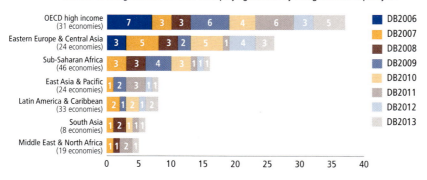

*Note:* An economy can be considered to have only 1 *Doing Business* reform per topic and year. The data sample for DB2006 (2005) includes 174 economies. The sample for DB2013 (2012) also includes The Bahamas, Bahrain, Barbados, Brunei Darussalam, Cyprus, Kosovo, Liberia, Luxembourg, Malta, Montenegro and Qatar, for a total of 185 economies.

*Source: Doing Business* database.

sometimes indefinite, duration. One such change was Rwanda's in 2010.

By contrast, governments in OECD high-income economies focused on reducing redundancy costs, addressing one of the main factors deterring employers from creating jobs in the formal sector.[4] Indeed, 15 labor regulation reforms introduced by OECD high-income economies in the past 8 years (including Portugal's reform of the past year) either shortened the required notice period for employees or reduced the severance pay applicable in cases of redundancy dismissal. Today the average severance payment in OECD high-income economies is 5.83 weeks of salary.[5]

Severance payments matter when it comes to labor regulation, since they are the prevalent form of insurance against unemployment, particularly in low-income economies that have not implemented unemployment protection schemes. They protect workers from abuses and provide a safety net in case of sudden job loss. But some economies adopt a very restrictive approach: the average severance payment in Sub-Saharan Africa is 15.81 weeks of salary,[6] almost 3 times the average in OECD high-income economies.

Economies in Eastern Europe and Central Asia focused on easing restrictions relating to redundancy dismissals. For example, in 2009 Estonia eliminated an employer's obligation to obtain prior approval from labor authorities when carrying out redundancy dismissals. And the Kyrgyz Republic, also in 2009, eliminated the priority rules mandating the dismissal of more junior workers first in cases of redundancy.

## NOTES

This annex was written by Fernando Dancausa Diaz, Raian Divanbeigi and Galina Rudenko.

1. Ratio of the apprentice minimum wage to the value added per worker.

2. Scarpetta, Sonnet and Manfredi 2010.

3. Varejão and Portugal 2007.

4. Bosch and Esteban-Pretel 2009.

5. Average for workers with 1, 5 and 10 years of tenure. Collective bargaining agreements in OECD high-income economies may establish severance payments that are more generous on average. See the data notes for more information on cases in which *Doing Business* considers collective bargaining agreements.

6. Average for workers with 1, 5 and 10 years of tenure.

# References

Aghion, Philippe, Robin Burgess, Stephen Redding and Fabrizio Zilibotti. 2008. "The Unequal Effects of Liberalization: Evidence from Dismantling the License Raj in India." *American Economic Review* 98 (4): 1397–412.

Ahlquist, John S., and Aseem Prakash. 2010. "FDI and the Costs of Contract Enforcement in Developing Countries." *Policy Sciences* 43 (2): 181–200.

Akerlof, George A. 1970. "The Market for Lemons: Quality Uncertainty and the Market Mechanism." *Quarterly Journal of Economics* 84 (3): 488–500.

Alesina, Alberto, Silvia Ardagna, Giuseppe Nicoletti and Fabio Schiantarelli. 2005. "Regulation and Investment." *Journal of the European Economic Association* 3 (4): 791–825.

Alvarez de la Campa, Alejandro, Santiago Croci Downes and Betina Tirelli Hennig. 2012. *Making Security Interests Public: Registration Mechanisms in 35 Jurisdictions.* Washington, DC: International Finance Corporation.

Amin, Mohammad. 2011. "Labor Productivity, Firm-Size and Gender: The Case of Informal Firms in Argentina and Peru." Enterprise Note 22, Enterprise Analysis Unit, World Bank Group, Washington, DC. http://www.enterprisesurveys.org/.

Antunes, Antonio, and Tiago Cavalcanti. 2007. "Start Up Costs, Limited Enforcement, and the Hidden Economy." *European Economic Review* 51 (1): 203–24.

APEC (Asia-Pacific Economic Cooperation). 2005. *A Mid-Term Stocktake of Progress towards the Bogor Goals: Busan Roadmap to Bogor Goals.* http://publications.apec.org/.

———. 2010a. *APEC at Glance, 2010.* APEC#210-SE-05.2. http://publications.apec.org/.

———. 2010b. *The Kyoto Report on Growth Strategy and Finance: 2010 APEC Finance Ministerial Meeting.* http://apec.org.

———. 2011a. *APEC New Strategy for Structural Reform: Economy Priorities and Progress Assessment Measures.* http://publications.apec.org/.

———. 2011b. *APEC's Ease of Doing Business: Interim Assessment.* http://publications.apec.org/.

———. 2012. "EoDB Starting a Business in Thailand." http://aimp.apec.org/.

Ardagna, Silvia, and Annamaria Lusardi. 2010. "Explaining International Differences in Entrepreneurship: The Role of Individual Characteristics and Regulatory Constraints." In *International Differences in Entrepreneurship,* ed. Josh Lerner and Antoinette Schoar, 17–62. Chicago: University of Chicago Press.

Arvis, Jean-François, Jean-François Marteau and Gaël Raballand. 2010. *The Cost of Being Landlocked: Logistics Costs and Supply Chain Reliability.* Washington, DC: World Bank.

Åslund, Anders. 2009. "How Latvia Can Escape from the Financial Crisis." Paper presented at the Annual Conference of the Bank of Latvia, Riga. Available at http://www.iie.com/.

Banerjee, Abhijit, and Esther Duflo. 2005. "Growth Theory through the Lens of Development Economics." In *Handbook of Development Economics,* ed. Philippe Aghion and Steven Durlauf, vol. 1A: 473–552. Amsterdam: Elsevier.

Barseghyan, Levon. 2008. "Entry Costs and Cross-Country Differences in Productivity and Output." *Journal of Economic Growth* 13 (2): 145–67.

Benmelech, Efraim, and Nittai K. Bergman. 2011. "Bankruptcy and the Collateral Channel." *Journal of Finance* 66 (2): 337–78.

Besley, Timothy, and Robin Burgess. 2002. "The Political Economy of Government Responsiveness: Theory and Evidence from India." *Quarterly Journal of Economics* 117 (4): 1415–51.

Blonigen, Bruce, and Jeremy Piger. 2011. "Determinants of Foreign Direct Investment." NBER Working Paper 16704, National Bureau of Economic Research, Cambridge, MA.

Bosch, Mariano, and Julen Esteban-Pretel. 2009. "Cyclical Informality and Unemployment." CIRJE Discussion Paper 613, Center for International Research on the Japanese Economy, Tokyo.

Botero, Juan Carlos, Simeon Djankov, Rafael La Porta, Florencio López-de-Silanes and Andrei Shleifer. 2004. "The Regulation of Labor." *Quarterly Journal of Economics* 119 (4): 1339–82.

Botero, Juan Carlos, Rafael La Porta, Florencio López-de-Silanes, Andrei Shleifer and Alexander Volokh. 2003. "Judicial Reform." *World Bank Research Observer* 18 (1): 67–88.

Branstetter, Lee G., Francisco Lima, Lowell J. Taylor and Ana Venâncio. 2010. "Do Entry Regulations Deter Entrepreneurship and Job Creation? Evidence from Recent Reforms in Portugal." NBER Working Paper 16473, National Bureau of Economic Research, Cambridge, MA.

Bruhn, Miriam. 2011. "License to Sell: The Effect of Business Registration Reform on Entrepreneurial Activity in Mexico." *Review of Economics and Statistics* 93 (1): 382–86.

___. 2012. "A Tale of Two Species: Revisiting the Effect of Registration Reform on Informal Business Owners in Mexico." Policy Research Working Paper 5971, World Bank, Washington, DC.

Busse, Matthias, and José Luis Groizard. 2008. "Foreign Direct Investment, Regulations, and Growth." *World Economy* 31 (7): 861–86.

Calderon, César, Alberto Chong and Gianmarco Leon. 2007. "Institutional Enforcement, Labor-Market Rigidities, and Economic Performance." *Emerging Markets Review* 8 (1): 38–49.

Calderon, César, and Luis Servén. 2003. "The Output Cost of Latin America's Infrastructure Gap." In *The Limits of Stabilization: Infrastructure, Public Deficits, and Growth in Latin America,* ed. William R. Easterly and Luis Servén. Washington, DC: World Bank.

Cardenas, Mauricio, and Sandra Rozo. 2009. "Firm Informality in Colombia: Problems and Solutions." *Desarrollo y Sociedad*, no. 63: 211–43.

Chang, Roberto, Linda Kaltani and Norman Loayza. 2009. "Openness Can Be Good for Growth: The Role of Policy Complementarities." *Journal of Development Economics* 90: 33–49.

Chari, Anusha. 2011. "Identifying the Aggregate Productivity Effects of Entry and Size Restrictions: An Empirical Analysis of License Reform in India."

*American Economic Journal: Economic Policy* 3: 66–96.

Ciccone, Antonio, and Elias Papaioannou. 2007. "Red Tape and Delayed Entry." *Journal of the European Economic Association* 5 (2–3): 444–58.

Cirmizi, Elena, Leora Klapper and Mahesh Uttamchandani. 2012. "The Challenges of Bankruptcy Reform." *World Bank Research Observer* 27 (2): 185–203.

Coolidge, Jacqueline, Lars Grava and Sanda Putnina. 2003. "Case Study: Inspectorate Reform in Latvia 1999–2003." Background paper prepared for World Bank, *World Development Report 2005.* Available at https://openknowledge .worldbank.org/.

Cuñat, Alejandro, and Marc J. Melitz. 2007. "Volatility, Labor Market Flexibility, and the Pattern of Comparative Advantage." NBER Working Paper 13062, National Bureau of Economic Research, Cambridge, MA.

de Araujo, Aloisio Pessoa, Rafael De Vasconcelos Xavier Ferreira and Bruno Funchal. 2011. "The Brazilian Bankruptcy Law Experiment." Working paper. Available at http://ssrn.com/ abstract=1853984.

Deininger, Klaus, and Paul Mpuga. 2005. "Does Greater Accountability Improve the Quality of Public Service Delivery? Evidence from Uganda." *World Development* 33 (1): 171–91.

Desai, Mihir, C. Fritz Foley and James Hines Jr. 2003. "Foreign Direct Investment in a World of Multiple Taxes." *Journal of Public Economics* 88: 2727–44.

de Soto, Hernando. 2000. *The Mystery of Capital: Why Capitalism Triumphs in the West and Fails Everywhere Else.* New York: Basic Books.

Dewaelheyns, Nico, and Cynthia Van Hulle. 2008. "Legal Reform and Aggregate Small and Micro Business Bankruptcy Rates: Evidence from the 1997 Belgian Bankruptcy Code." *Small Business Economics* 31 (4): 409–24.

Divanbeigi, Raian, and Rita Ramalho. 2012. "Smart Regulations and Growth." Draft paper, Doing Business Unit, World Bank Group, Washington, DC.

Djankov, Simeon. 2009. "The Regulation of Entry: A Survey." *World Bank Research Observer* 24 (2): 183–203.

Djankov, Simeon, Caroline Freund and Cong S. Pham. 2010. "Trading on Time." *Review of Economics and Statistics* 92 (1): 166–73.

Djankov, Simeon, Tim Ganser, Caralee McLiesh, Rita Ramalho and Andrei Shleifer. 2010. "The Effect of

Corporate Taxes on Investment and Entrepreneurship." *American Economic Journal: Macroeconomics* 2 (3): 31–64.

Djankov, Simeon, Oliver Hart, Caralee McLiesh and Andrei Shleifer. 2008. "Debt Enforcement around the World." *Journal of Political Economy* 116 (6): 1105–49.

Djankov, Simeon, Rafael La Porta, Florencio López-de-Silanes and Andrei Shleifer. 2002. "The Regulation of Entry." *Quarterly Journal of Economics* 117 (1): 1–37.

___. 2003. "Courts." *Quarterly Journal of Economics* 118 (2): 453–517.

___. 2008. "The Law and Economics of Self-Dealing." *Journal of Financial Economics* 88 (3): 430–65.

Djankov, Simeon, Darshini Manraj, Caralee McLiesh and Rita Ramalho. 2005. "Doing Business Indicators: Why Aggregate, and How to Do It." World Bank, Washington, DC.

Djankov, Simeon, Caralee McLiesh and Rita Ramalho. 2006. "Regulation and Growth." *Economics Letters* 92 (3): 395–401.

Djankov, Simeon, Caralee McLiesh and Andrei Shleifer. 2007. "Private Credit in 129 Countries." *Journal of Financial Economics* 84 (2): 299–329.

Dollar, David, Mary Hallward-Driemeier and Taye Mengistae. 2006. "Investment Climate and International Integration." *World Development* 34 (9): 1498–516.

Dulleck, Uwe, Paul Frijters and R. Winter-Ebmer. 2006. "Reducing Start-up Costs for New Firms: The Double Dividend on the Labor Market." *Scandinavian Journal of Economics* 108: 317–37.

EBRD (European Bank for Reconstruction and Development). 2011. "Strategy for Latvia." http://www.ebrd.com/.

Eifert, Benjamin. 2007. "Infrastructure and Market Structure in Least-Developed Countries." Department of Economics, University of California, Berkeley.

___. 2009. "Do Regulatory Reforms Stimulate Investment and Growth? Evidence from the Doing Business Data, 2003–07." Working Paper 159, Center for Global Development, Washington, DC.

Ferraz, Claudio, and Frederico Finan. 2011. "Electoral Accountability and Corruption: Evidence from the Audits of Local Governments." *American Economic Review* 101: 1274–311.

Fisman, Raymond, and Virginia Sarria-Allende. 2010. "Regulation of Entry and the Distortion of Industrial Organization."

*Journal of Applied Economics* 13 (1): 91–120.

Franks, Julian, Colin Mayer, Paolo Volpin and Hannes F. Wagner. 2011. "The Life Cycle of Family Ownership: International Evidence." *Review of Financial Studies* 25 (8): 1–38.

Freedom House. 2012. *Freedom in the World 2012.* Washington, DC: Freedom House.

Freund, Caroline, and Bineswaree Bolaky. 2008. "Trade, Regulations and Income." *Journal of Development Economics* 87: 309–21.

Freund, Caroline, and Nadia Rocha. 2011. "What Constrains Africa's Exports?" *World Bank Economic Review* 25 (3): 361–86.

Funchal, Bruno. 2008. "The Effects of the 2005 Bankruptcy Reform in Brazil." *Economics Letters* 101: 84–86.

Geginat, Carolin, Adrian Gonzalez and Valentina Saltane. 2012. "Cutting Out the Middle Man: Transparent Government and Business Regulation." Draft paper, Doing Business Unit, World Bank Group, Washington, DC.

Geginat, Carolin, and Rita Ramalho. 2010. "Connecting Businesses to the Electrical Grid in 140 Economies." Paper presented at the International Conference on Infrastructure Economics and Development, Toulouse, January 14–15.

Giné, Xavier, and Inessa Love. 2010. "Do Reorganization Costs Matter for Efficiency? Evidence from a Bankruptcy Reform in Colombia." *Journal of Law and Economics* 53 (4): 833–64.

Haidar, Jamal. 2012. "The Impact of Business Regulatory Reforms on Economic Growth." *Journal of the Japanese and International Economies.* Published online May 25. http://dx.doi.org/10.1016/j.jjie.2012.05.004.

Hallward-Driemeier, Mary, Gita Khun-Jush and Lant Pritchett. 2010. "Deals versus Rules: Policy Implementation Uncertainty and Why Firms Hate It." NBER Working Paper 16001, National Bureau of Economic Research, Cambridge, MA.

Hamdani, Assaf, and Yishay Yafeh. 2012. "Institutional Investors as Minority Shareholders." *Review of Finance.* Published online February 7. doi:10.1093/rof/rfr039.

Haselmann, Rainer, Katharina Pistor and Vikrant Vig. 2010. "How Law Affects Lending." *Review of Financial Studies* 23 (2): 549–80.

Helpman, Elhanan, Marc Melitz and Yona Rubinstein. 2008. "Estimating Trade Flows: Trading Partners and Trading Volumes." *Quarterly Journal of Economics* 123 (2): 441–87.

Hertveldt, Sabine. 2008. "Rwanda: Pragmatism Leads the Way in Setting Up Specialized Commercial Courts." World Bank Group, Washington, DC.

Hirschman, Albert O. 1970. *Exit, Voice, and Loyalty: Responses to Decline in Firms, Organizations, and States.* Cambridge, MA: Harvard University Press.

Hirshleifer, Jack. 1980. "Privacy: Its Origin, Function and Future." *Journal of Legal Studies* 9 (4): 649–64.

Hoekman, Bernard, and Alessandro Nicita. 2011. "Trade Policy, Trade Cost and Developing Country Trade." *World Development* 39 (12): 2069–79.

Hornberger, Kusi, Joseph Battat and Peter Kusek. 2011. "Attracting FDI: How Much Does Investment Climate Matter?" Viewpoint Note 327, World Bank Group, Washington, DC.

Houston, Joel, Chen Lin, Ping Lin and Yue Ma. 2010. "Creditor Rights, Information Sharing, and Bank Risk Taking." *Journal of Financial Economics* 96 (3): 485–512.

Iimi, Atsushi. 2011. "Effects of Improving Infrastructure Quality on Business Costs: Evidence from Firm-Level Data in Eastern Europe and Central Asia." *Developing Economies* 49 (2): 121–47.

Islam, Roumeen. 2006. "Does More Transparency Go Along with Better Governance?" *Economics and Politics* 18 (2): 121–67.

Iwanow, Thomasz, and Colin Kirkpatrick. 2009. "Trade Facilitation and Manufacturing Exports: Is Africa Different?" *World Development* 37 (6): 1039–50.

Jayasuriya, Dinuk. 2011. "Improvements in the World Bank's Ease of Doing Business Rankings: Do They Translate into Greater Foreign Direct Investment Inflows?" Policy Research Working Paper 5787, World Bank, Washington, DC.

Jensen, Nate, Quan Li and Aminur Rahman. 2010. "Understanding Corruption and Firm Responses in Cross-National Firm Level Surveys." *Journal of International Business Studies* 41: 1481–504.

Kaplan, David, Eduardo Piedra and Enrique Seira. 2007. "Entry Regulation and Business Start-Ups: Evidence from Mexico." Policy Research Working Paper 4322, World Bank, Washington, DC.

Karim, Tushabe. 2011. "Doing Business Reforms: Rwandan Experience." Presentation at U.S. Agency for International Development, Speed Program. http://www.speed-program.com/.

Kaufmann, Daniel. 2003. "Governance Redux: The Empirical Challenge." In World Economic Forum, *The Global Competitiveness Report 2003–2004.* New York: Oxford University Press.

Kaufmann, Daniel, Aart Kraay and Massimo Mastruzzi. 2010. "The Worldwide Governance Indicators: Methodology and Analytical Issues." Policy Research Working Paper 5430, World Bank, Washington, DC.

Klapper, Leora, Luc Laeven and Raghuram Rajan. 2006. "Entry Regulation as a Barrier to Entrepreneurship." *Journal of Financial Economics* 82 (3): 591–629.

Klapper, Leora, Anat Lewin and Juan Manuel Quesada Delgado. 2009. "The Impact of the Business Environment on the Business Creation Process." Policy Research Working Paper 4937, World Bank, Washington, DC.

Klapper, Leora, and Inessa Love. 2011a. "The Impact of Business Environment Reforms on New Firm Registration." Policy Research Working Paper 5493, World Bank, Washington, DC.

———. 2011b. "The Impact of the Financial Crisis on New Firm Registration." *Economics Letters* 113 (1): 1–4.

Kraay, Aart, and Norikazu Tawara. 2011. "Can Disaggregated Indicators Identify Governance Reform Priorities?" Policy Research Working Paper 5254, World Bank, Washington, DC.

Lagarde, Christine. 2012. "Latvia and the Baltics—a Story of Recovery." Speech as prepared for delivery in Riga, Latvia. http://www.imf.org/.

La Porta, Rafael, and Andrei Shleifer. 2008. "The Unofficial Economy and Economic Development." Tuck School of Business Working Paper 2009-57. Available at http://ssrn.com/abstract=1304760.

Latvia, Ministry of Economics. 2011. "National Reform Programme of Latvia for the Implementation of the 'Europe 2020' Strategy." Available at http://ec.europa.eu/europe2020/.

Liepina, Sanda, Jacqueline Coolidge and Lars Grava. 2008. "Improving the Business Environment in Latvia: The Impact of FIAS Assistance." Foreign Investment Advisory Service Occasional Paper 18, World Bank Group, Washington, DC.

Loayza, Norman, Ana Maria Oviedo and Luis Servén. 2005. "Regulation and Macroeconomic Performance." Policy Research Working Paper 3469, World Bank, Washington, DC.

Masatlioglu, Yusufcan, and Jamele Rigolini. 2008. "Informality Traps." *B.E. Journal of Economic Analysis & Policy* 8 (1).

Mclean, R. D., T. Zhang and M. Zhao. 2012. "Why Does the Law Matter? Investor Protection and Its Effects on Investment, Finance, and Growth." *Journal of Finance* 67: 313–50.

Micco, Alejandro, and Carmen Pagés. 2006. "The Economic Effects of Employment Protection: Evidence from International Industry-Level Data." IZA Discussion Paper 2433, Institute for the Study of Labor (IZA), Bonn.

Motta, Marialisa, Ana Maria Oviedo and Massimiliano Santini. 2010. "An Open Door for Firms: The Impact of Business Entry Reforms." Viewpoint Note 323, World Bank Group, Washington, DC.

Moullier, Thomas. 2009. "Reforming Building Permits: Why Is It Important and What Can IFC Really Do?" International Finance Corporation, Washington, DC.

Narayan, Deepa, Robert Chambers, Meer Kaul Shah and Patti Petesh. 2000. *Voices of the Poor: Crying Out for Change.* Washington, DC: World Bank.

Nunn, Nathan. 2007. "Relationship-Specificity, Incomplete Contracts, and the Pattern of Trade." *Quarterly Journal of Economics* 122 (2): 569–600.

OECD (Organisation for Economic Co-operation and Development). 2010. "Construction Industry." *OECD Journal of Competition Law and Policy* 10 (1).

Olken, Benjamin A. 2007. "Monitoring Corruption: Evidence from a Field Experiment in Indonesia." *Journal of Political Economy* 115 (2): 200–49.

Paul, Samuel. 1992. "Accountability in Public Services: Exit, Voice and Control." *World Development* 20 (7): 1047–60.

Perotti, Enrico, and Paolo Volpin. 2005. "The Political Economy of Entry: Lobbying and Financial Development." Paper presented at the American Finance Association 2005 Philadelphia Meetings.

Portugal-Perez, Alberto, and John Wilson. 2011. "Export Performance and Trade Facilitation Reform: Hard and Soft Infrastructure." *World Development* 40 (7): 1295–307.

Ramello, Giovanni, and Stephen Voigt. 2012. "The Economics of Efficiency and the Judicial System." *International Review of Law and Economics* 32: 1–2.

Rauch, James. 2010. "Development through Synergistic Reforms." *Journal of Development Economics* 93 (2): 153–61.

Reinikka, Ritva, and Jakob Svensson. 1999. "Confronting Competition: Investment Response and Constraints in Uganda." Policy Research Working Paper 2242, World Bank, Washington, DC.

___. 2005. "Fighting Corruption to Improve Schooling: Evidence from a Newspaper Campaign in Uganda." *Journal of the European Economic Association* 3 (2–3): 259–67.

Republic of Korea, Ministry of Justice. 2011. "Ease of Doing Business Enforcing Contracts of Indonesia and Peru." Available at http://aimp.apec.org.

Rocha, Roberto, Subika Farazi, Rania Khouri and Douglas Pearce. 2010. "The Status of Bank Lending to SMEs in the Middle East and North Africa Region: The Results of a Joint Survey of the Union of Arab Banks and the World Bank." World Bank, Washington, DC; and Union of Arab Banks, Beirut.

Rodano, Giacomo, Nicolas Andre Benigno Serrano-Velarde and Emanuele Tarantino. 2011. "The Causal Effect of Bankruptcy Law on the Cost of Finance." Available at http://ssrn.com/abstract=1967485.

Rwanda, Ministry of Finance and Economic Planning. 2000. *Rwanda Vision 2020.* Available at http://www.gesci.org/.

___. 2007. *Economic Development and Poverty Reduction Strategy, 2008–2012.* Available at http://planipolis.iiep.unesco.org/.

Safavian, Mehnaz, and Siddharth Sharma. 2007. "When Do Creditor Rights Work?" *Journal of Comparative Economics* 35 (3): 484–508.

Scarpetta, Stefano, Anne Sonnet and Thomas Manfredi. 2010. "Rising Youth Unemployment during the Crisis: How to Prevent Negative Long-Term Consequences on a Generation?" OECD Social, Employment and Migration Working Paper 106, Organisation for Economic Co-operation and Development, Paris.

Schneider, Friedrich. 2005. "The Informal Sector in 145 Countries." Department of Economics, University Linz, Austria.

Schneider, Friedrich, Andreas Buehn and Claudio E. Montenegro. 2010. "New Estimates for the Shadow Economies All Over the World." *International Economic Journal* 24 (4): 443–61.

Seker, Murat. 2011. "Trade Policies, Investment Climate, and Exports." Policy Research Working Paper 5654, World Bank, Washington, DC.

Sharma, Siddharth. 2009. "Entry Regulation, Labor Laws and Informality: Evidence from India." Enterprise Survey Working Paper, Enterprise Analysis Unit, World Bank Group, Washington, DC.

Sohn, Ira. 2008. "Back from the Brink: Economic and Financial Reform in Colombia." International Trade and Finance Association Working Paper, International Trade and Finance Association, Kingsville, TX.

Stampini, Marco, Ron Leung, Setou M. Diarra and Lauréline Pla. 2011. "How Large Is the Private Sector in Africa? Evidence from National Accounts and Labor Markets." IZA Discussion Paper 6267, Institute for the Study of Labor (IZA), Bonn.

Stigler, George J. 1961. "The Economics of Information." *Journal of Political Economy* 69 (3): 213–25.

___. 1971. "The Theory of Economic Regulation." *Bell Journal of Economics and Management Science* 2: 3–21.

Stiglitz, Joseph E. 2003. "Transparency of Government (Part 1): Breakthrough for Reforming the Shape of a Nation." *Economics Review* (Research Institute of Economy, Trade and Industry). http://www.rieti.go.jp/en/.

Stiglitz, Joseph E., and Andrew Weiss. 1981. "Credit Rationing in Markets with Imperfect Information." *American Economic Review* 71 (3): 393–410.

UNCITRAL (United Nations Commission on International Trade Law). 2004. *Legislative Guide on Insolvency Law.* New York: United Nations.

___. 2007. *Legislative Guide on Secured Transactions.* New York: United Nations.

USAID (U.S. Agency for International Development) and New Zealand Ministry of Foreign Affairs and Trade. 2010. "Making It Easier to Start a Business in Indonesia: Diagnostic Study." Available at http://aimp.apec.org.

Varejão, José, and Pedro Portugal. 2007. "Employment Dynamics and the Structure of Labor Adjustment Costs." *Journal of Labor Economics* 25: 137–65.

Visaria, Sujata. 2009. "Legal Reform and Loan Repayment: The Microeconomic Impact of Debt Recovery Tribunals in India." *American Economic Journal: Applied Economics* 1 (3): 59–81.

von Lilienfeld-Toal, Ulf, Dilip Mookherjee and Sujata Visaria. 2012. "The Distributive Impact of Reforms in Credit Enforcement: Evidence from Indian Debt Recovery Tribunals." *Econometrica* 80 (2): 497–558.

Waglé, Swarnim. 2011. "Investing across Borders with Heterogeneous Firms: Do FDI-Specific Regulations Matter?" Policy Research Working Paper 5914, World Bank, Washington, DC.

Walsh, James, and Jiangyan Yu. 2010. "Determinants of Foreign Direct Investment: A Sectoral and Institutional Approach." IMF Working Paper WP/10/87, International Monetary Fund, Washington, DC.

WEF (World Economic Forum). 2012. *The Global Competitiveness Report 2012–2013.* Geneva: WEF.

Wei, Shang-Jin. 2000. "How Taxing Is Corruption on International Investors?" *Review of Economics and Statistics* 82 (1): 1–11.

Williams, Andrew. 2009. "On the Release of Information by Governments: Causes and Consequences." *Journal of Development Economics* 89 (1): 124–38.

World Bank. 2001. "Latvia: Programmatic Structural Adjustment Loan Project." Report 22457, Europe and Central Asia Region, World Bank, Washington, DC.

___. 2003. *Doing Business in 2004: Understanding Regulation.* Washington, DC: World Bank Group.

___. 2004. *World Development Report 2004: Making Services Work for Poor People.* Washington, DC: World Bank.

___. 2005. *World Development Report 2005: A Better Investment Climate for Everyone.* Washington, DC: World Bank.

___. 2006. *Doing Business in 2007: How to Reform.* Washington, DC: World Bank Group.

___. 2007. *Doing Business in 2008.* Washington, DC: World Bank Group.

___. 2009a. *From Privilege to Competition: Unlocking Private-Led Growth in the Middle East and North Africa.* Washington, DC: World Bank.

___. 2009b. *How Many Stops in a One-Stop Shop?* Washington, DC: World Bank Group.

___. 2010a. *Doing Business 2011: Making a Difference for Entrepreneurs.* Washington, DC: World Bank Group.

___. 2010b. *Investing Across Borders 2010.* Washington, DC: World Bank Group.

___. 2011a. *Doing Business 2012: Doing Business in a More Transparent World.* Washington, DC: World Bank Group.

___. 2011b. "Principles for Effective Creditor Rights and Insolvency Systems." Revised draft, January 20. http://www.worldbank.org/ifa/rosc_icr.html.

___. 2012. *World Development Indicators 2012.* Washington, DC: World Bank.

World Bank Facility for Investment Climate Advisory Services. 2011. *Managing for Impact: FIAS Strategy for FY12–16.* Washington, DC: World Bank Group.

World Bank Independent Evaluation Group. 2008. *Doing Business: An Independent Evaluation—Taking the Measure of the World Bank–IFC Doing Business Indicators.* Washington, DC: World Bank.

Zoellick, Robert B., Ahmad M. Al-Madani, Donald Kaberuka, Haruhiko Kuroda, Thomas Mirow and Luis A. Moreno. 2012. "How to Make Trade Easier." Commentary, Project Syndicate. http://www.project-syndicate.org/.

# Data notes

The indicators presented and analyzed in *Doing Business* measure business regulation and the protection of property rights—and their effect on businesses, especially small and medium-size domestic firms. First, the indicators document the complexity of regulation, such as the number of procedures to start a business or to register and transfer commercial property. Second, they gauge the time and cost of achieving a regulatory goal or complying with regulation, such as the time and cost to enforce a contract, go through bankruptcy or trade across borders. Third, they measure the extent of legal protections of property, for example, the protections of investors against looting by company directors or the range of assets that can be used as collateral according to secured transactions laws. Fourth, a set of indicators documents the tax burden on businesses. Finally, a set of data covers different aspects of employment regulation. The 11 sets of indicators measured in *Doing Business* were added over time, and the sample of economies expanded (table 20.1).

The data for all sets of indicators in *Doing Business 2013* are for June 2012.[1]

## METHODOLOGY

The *Doing Business* data are collected in a standardized way. To start, the *Doing Business* team, with academic advisers, designs a questionnaire. The questionnaire uses a simple business case to ensure comparability across economies and over time—with assumptions about the legal form of the business, its size, its location and the nature of its operations. Questionnaires are administered through more than 9,600 local experts, including lawyers, business consultants, accountants, freight forwarders, government officials and other professionals routinely administering or advising on legal and regulatory requirements (table 20.2). These experts have several rounds of interaction with the *Doing Business* team, involving conference calls, written correspondence and visits by the team. For *Doing Business 2013* team

| TABLE 20.1 Topics and economies covered by each *Doing Business* report | | | | | | | | | | |
|---|---|---|---|---|---|---|---|---|---|---|
| Topic | DB 2004 | DB 2005 | DB 2006 | DB 2007 | DB 2008 | DB 2009 | DB 2010 | DB 2011 | DB 2012 | DB 2013 |
| Starting a business | | | | | | | | | | |
| Employing workers | | | | | | | | | | |
| Enforcing contracts | | | | | | | | | | |
| Resolving insolvency | | | | | | | | | | |
| Getting credit | | | | | | | | | | |
| Registering property | | | | | | | | | | |
| Protecting investors | | | | | | | | | | |
| Paying taxes | | | | | | | | | | |
| Trading across borders | | | | | | | | | | |
| Dealing with construction permits | | | | | | | | | | |
| Getting electricity | | | | | | | | | | |
| Number of economies | 133 | 145 | 155 | 175 | 178 | 181 | 183 | 183 | 183 | 185 |

*Note:* Data for the economies added to the sample each year are back-calculated to the previous year. The exception is Kosovo, which was added to the sample after it became a member of the World Bank Group.

| TABLE 20.2 How many experts does *Doing Business* consult? | |
|---|---|
| **Indicator set** | **Contributors** |
| Starting a business | 1,585 |
| Dealing with construction permits | 852 |
| Getting electricity | 830 |
| Registering property | 1,069 |
| Getting credit | 1,325 |
| Protecting investors | 1,083 |
| Paying taxes | 1,173 |
| Trading across borders | 933 |
| Enforcing contracts | 1,146 |
| Resolving insolvency | 1,085 |
| Employing workers | 1,052 |

members visited 24 economies to verify data and recruit respondents. The data from questionnaires are subjected to numerous rounds of verification, leading to revisions or expansions of the information collected.

The *Doing Business* methodology offers several advantages. It is transparent, using factual information about what laws and regulations say and allowing multiple interactions with local respondents to clarify potential misinterpretations of questions. Having representative samples of respondents is not an issue; *Doing Business* is not a statistical survey, and the texts of the relevant laws and regulations are collected and answers checked for accuracy. The methodology is inexpensive and easily replicable, so data can be collected in a large sample of economies. Because standard assumptions are used in the data collection, comparisons and benchmarks are valid across economies. Finally, the data not only highlight the extent of specific regulatory obstacles to business but also identify their source and point to what might be reformed.

## LIMITS TO WHAT IS MEASURED

The *Doing Business* methodology has 5 limitations that should be considered when interpreting the data. First, the collected data refer to businesses in the economy's largest business city (which in some economies differs from the capital) and may not be representative of regulation in other parts of the economy.

To address this limitation, subnational *Doing Business* indicators were created (box 20.1). Second, the data often focus on a specific business form—generally a limited liability company (or its legal equivalent) of a specified size—and may not be representative of the regulation on other businesses, for example, sole proprietorships. Third, transactions described in a standardized case scenario refer to a specific set of issues and may not represent the full set of issues a business encounters. Fourth, the measures of time involve an element of judgment by the expert respondents. When sources indicate different estimates, the time indicators reported in *Doing Business* represent the median values of several responses given under the assumptions of the standardized case.

Finally, the methodology assumes that a business has full information on what is required and does not waste time when completing procedures. In practice, completing a procedure may take longer if the business lacks information or is unable to follow up promptly. Alternatively, the business may choose to disregard some burdensome procedures. For both reasons the time delays reported in *Doing Business 2013* would differ from the recollection of entrepreneurs reported in the World Bank Enterprise Surveys or other perception surveys.

### BOX 20.1 SUBNATIONAL *DOING BUSINESS* INDICATORS

This year *Doing Business* completed subnational studies for Indonesia, Kenya, Mexico, Russia and the United Arab Emirates. Each of these countries had already asked to have subnational data in the past, and this year *Doing Business* updated the indicators, measured improvements over time and expanded geographic coverage to additional cities or added additional indicators. *Doing Business* also published regional studies for the Arab world, the East African Community and member states of the Organization for the Harmonization of Business Law in Africa (OHADA).

The subnational studies point to differences in business regulation and its implementation—as well as in the pace of regulatory reform—across cities in the same economy. For several economies subnational studies are now periodically updated to measure change over time or to expand geographic coverage to additional cities. This year that is the case for all the subnational studies published.

### ECONOMY CHARACTERISTICS

#### Gross national income per capita

*Doing Business 2013* reports 2011 income per capita as published in the World Bank's *World Development Indicators 2012*. Income is calculated using the Atlas method (current U.S. dollars). For cost indicators expressed as a percentage of income per capita, 2011 gross national income (GNI) in U.S. dollars is used as the denominator. GNI data were not available from the World Bank for Afghanistan, Australia, The Bahamas, Bahrain, Barbados, Brunei Darussalam, Cyprus, Djibouti, Guyana, the Islamic Republic of Iran, Kuwait, Malta, New Zealand, Oman, Puerto Rico (territory of the United States), Sudan, Suriname, the Syrian Arab Republic, Timor-Leste, West Bank and Gaza, and the Republic of Yemen. In these cases GDP or GNP per capita data and growth rates from the International Monetary Fund's World Economic Outlook database and the Economist Intelligence Unit were used.

#### Region and income group

*Doing Business* uses the World Bank regional and income group classifications, available at http://data.worldbank.org/about/country-classifications. The World Bank does not assign regional classifications to high-income economies. For the purpose of the *Doing Business* report, high-income OECD economies are assigned the "regional" classification *OECD high income*. Figures and tables presenting regional averages include economies from all income groups (low, lower middle, upper middle and high income).

#### Population

*Doing Business 2013* reports mid-year 2011 population statistics as published in *World Development Indicators 2012*.

## CHANGES IN WHAT IS MEASURED

The ranking methodology for paying taxes was updated this year. The threshold for the total tax rate introduced last year for the purpose of calculating the ranking on the ease of paying taxes was updated. All economies with a total tax rate below the threshold (which is calculated and adjusted on a yearly basis) receive the same ranking on the total tax rate indicator. The threshold is not based on any economic theory of an "optimal tax rate" that minimizes distortions or maximizes efficiency in the tax system of an economy overall. Instead, it is mainly empirical in nature, set at the lower end of the distribution of tax rates levied on medium-size enterprises in the manufacturing sector as observed through the paying taxes indicators. This reduces the bias in the indicators toward economies that do not need to levy significant taxes on companies like the *Doing Business* standardized case study company because they raise public revenue in other ways—for example, through taxes on foreign companies, through taxes on sectors other than manufacturing or from natural resources (all of which are outside the scope of the methodology). Giving the same ranking to all economies whose total tax rate is below the threshold avoids awarding economies in the scoring for having an unusually low total tax rate, often for reasons unrelated to government policies toward enterprises. For example, economies that are very small or that are rich in natural resources do not need to levy broad-based taxes.

## DATA CHALLENGES AND REVISIONS

Most laws and regulations underlying the *Doing Business* data are available on the *Doing Business* website at http://www.doingbusiness.org. All the sample questionnaires and the details underlying the indicators are also published on the website. Questions on the methodology and challenges to data can be submitted through the website's "Ask a Question" function at http://www.doingbusiness.org.

*Doing Business* publishes 9,620 indicators each year. To create these indicators, the team measures more than 57,000 data points, each of which is made available on the *Doing Business* website. Historical data for each indicator and economy are available on the website, beginning with the first year the indicator or economy was included in the report. To provide a comparable time series for research, the data set is back-calculated to adjust for changes in methodology and any revisions in data due to corrections. The website also makes available all original data sets used for background papers. The correction rate between *Doing Business 2012* and *Doing Business 2013* is 8.6%.[2]

## STARTING A BUSINESS

*Doing Business* records all procedures officially required, or commonly done in practice, for an entrepreneur to start up and formally operate an industrial or commercial business, as well as the time and cost to complete them and the paid-in minimum capital requirement (figure 20.1). These procedures include obtaining all necessary licenses and permits and completing any required notifications, verifications or inscriptions for the company and employees with relevant authorities. The ranking on the ease of starting a business is the simple average of the percentile rankings on its component indicators (figure 20.2).

After a study of laws, regulations and publicly available information on business entry, a detailed list of procedures is developed, along with the time and cost of complying with each procedure under normal circumstances and the paid-in minimum capital requirement. Subsequently, local incorporation lawyers, notaries and government officials complete and verify the data.

Information is also collected on the sequence in which procedures are to be completed and whether procedures may be carried out simultaneously. It is assumed that any required information is readily available and that the entrepreneur will pay no bribes. If answers by local experts differ, inquiries continue until the data are reconciled.

To make the data comparable across economies, several assumptions about the business and the procedures are used.

### Assumptions about the business

The business:

- Is a limited liability company (or its legal equivalent). If there is more than one type of limited liability company in the economy, the limited liability form most popular among domestic firms is chosen. Information on the most popular form is obtained from incorporation lawyers or the statistical office.

- Operates in the economy's largest business city.

---

FIGURE 20.1 **What are the time, cost, paid-in minimum capital and number of procedures to get a local limited liability company up and running?**

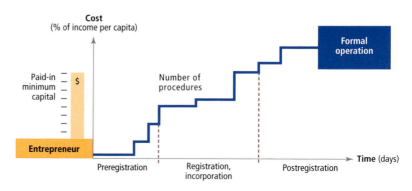

**FIGURE 20.2  Starting a business: getting a local limited liability company up and running**

Rankings are based on 4 indicators

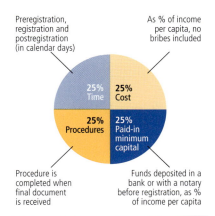

Preregistration, registration and postregistration (in calendar days)

As % of income per capita, no bribes included

25% Time

25% Cost

25% Procedures

25% Paid-in minimum capital

Procedure is completed when final document is received

Funds deposited in a bank or with a notary before registration, as % of income per capita

- Is 100% domestically owned and has 5 owners, none of whom is a legal entity.
- Has start-up capital of 10 times income per capita, paid in cash.
- Performs general industrial or commercial activities, such as the production or sale to the public of products or services. The business does not perform foreign trade activities and does not handle products subject to a special tax regime, for example, liquor or tobacco. It is not using heavily polluting production processes.
- Leases the commercial plant and offices and is not a proprietor of real estate.
- Does not qualify for investment incentives or any special benefits.
- Has at least 10 and up to 50 employees 1 month after the commencement of operations, all of them nationals.
- Has a turnover of at least 100 times income per capita.
- Has a company deed 10 pages long.

## Procedures

A procedure is defined as any interaction of the company founders with external parties (for example, government agencies, lawyers, auditors or notaries). Interactions between company founders or company officers and employees are not counted as procedures. Procedures that must be completed in the same building but in different

offices or at different counters are counted as separate procedures. If founders have to visit the same office several times for different sequential procedures, each is counted separately. The founders are assumed to complete all procedures themselves, without middlemen, facilitators, accountants or lawyers, unless the use of such a third party is mandated by law. If the services of professionals are required, procedures conducted by such professionals on behalf of the company are counted separately. Each electronic procedure is counted separately. If 2 procedures can be completed through the same website but require separate filings, they are counted as 2 procedures.

Both pre- and postincorporation procedures that are officially required for an entrepreneur to formally operate a business are recorded (table 20.3).

Procedures required for official correspondence or transactions with public agencies are also included. For example, if a company seal or stamp is required on official documents, such as tax declarations, obtaining the seal or stamp is

**TABLE 20.3  What do the starting a business indicators measure?**

**Procedures to legally start and operate a company** (number)

Preregistration (for example, name verification or reservation, notarization)

Registration in the economy's largest business city

Postregistration (for example, social security registration, company seal)

**Time required to complete each procedure** (calendar days)

Does not include time spent gathering information

Each procedure starts on a separate day

Procedure completed once final document is received

No prior contact with officials

**Cost required to complete each procedure** (% of income per capita)

Official costs only, no bribes

No professional fees unless services required by law

**Paid-in minimum capital** (% of income per capita)

Funds deposited in a bank or with a notary before registration (or within 3 months)

counted. Similarly, if a company must open a bank account before registering for sales tax or value added tax, this transaction is included as a procedure. Shortcuts are counted only if they fulfill 4 criteria: they are legal, they are available to the general public, they are used by the majority of companies, and avoiding them causes substantial delays.

Only procedures required of all businesses are covered. Industry-specific procedures are excluded. For example, procedures to comply with environmental regulations are included only when they apply to all businesses conducting general commercial or industrial activities. Procedures that the company undergoes to connect to electricity, water, gas and waste disposal services are not included.

### Time

Time is recorded in calendar days. The measure captures the median duration that incorporation lawyers indicate is necessary in practice to complete a procedure with minimum follow-up with government agencies and no extra payments. It is assumed that the minimum time required for each procedure is 1 day. Although procedures may take place simultaneously, they cannot start on the same day (that is, simultaneous procedures start on consecutive days). A procedure is considered completed once the company has received the final document, such as the company registration certificate or tax number. If a procedure can be accelerated for an additional cost, the fastest procedure is chosen if that option is more beneficial to the economy's ranking. It is assumed that the entrepreneur does not waste time and commits to completing each remaining procedure without delay. The time that the entrepreneur spends on gathering information is ignored. It is assumed that the entrepreneur is aware of all entry requirements and their sequence from the beginning but has had no prior contact with any of the officials.

## Cost

Cost is recorded as a percentage of the economy's income per capita. It includes all official fees and fees for legal or professional services if such services are required by law. Fees for purchasing and legalizing company books are included if these transactions are required by law. The company law, the commercial code and specific regulations and fee schedules are used as sources for calculating costs. In the absence of fee schedules, a government officer's estimate is taken as an official source. In the absence of a government officer's estimate, estimates of incorporation lawyers are used. If several incorporation lawyers provide different estimates, the median reported value is applied. In all cases the cost excludes bribes.

## Paid-in minimum capital

The paid-in minimum capital requirement reflects the amount that the entrepreneur needs to deposit in a bank or with a notary before registration and up to 3 months following incorporation and is recorded as a percentage of the economy's income per capita. The amount is typically specified in the commercial code or the company law. Many economies require minimum capital but allow businesses to pay only a part of it before registration, with the rest to be paid after the first year of operation. In Turkey in June 2012, for example, the minimum capital requirement was 5,000 Turkish liras, of which one-fourth needed to be paid before registration. The paid-in minimum capital recorded for Turkey is

therefore 1,250 Turkish liras, or 7.2% of income per capita.

*The data details on starting a business can be found for each economy at http://www.doingbusiness.org by selecting the economy in the drop-down list. This methodology was developed in Djankov and others (2002) and is adopted here with minor changes.*

## DEALING WITH CONSTRUCTION PERMITS

*Doing Business* records all procedures required for a business in the construction industry to build a warehouse (figure 20.3). These procedures include submitting all relevant project-specific documents (for example, building plans and site maps) to the authorities; obtaining all necessary clearances, licenses, permits and certificates; completing all required notifications; and receiving all necessary inspections. *Doing Business* also records procedures for obtaining connections for water, sewerage and a fixed landline.[3] Procedures necessary to register the property so that it can be used as collateral or transferred to another entity are also counted. The survey divides the process of building a warehouse into distinct procedures and calculates the time and cost of completing each procedure. The ranking on the ease of dealing with construction permits is the simple average of the percentile rankings on its component indicators (figure 20.4).

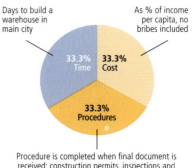

FIGURE 20.4  Dealing with construction permits: building a warehouse

**Rankings are based on 3 indicators**

Procedure is completed when final document is received; construction permits, inspections and utility connections included

Information is collected from experts in construction licensing, including architects, construction lawyers, construction firms, utility service providers and public officials who deal with building regulations, including approvals and inspections. To make the data comparable across economies, several assumptions about the business, the warehouse project and the utility connections are used.

## Assumptions about the construction company

The business (BuildCo):

- Is a limited liability company.
- Operates in the economy's largest business city.
- Is 100% domestically and privately owned.
- Has 5 owners, none of whom is a legal entity.
- Is fully licensed and insured to carry out construction projects, such as building warehouses.
- Has 60 builders and other employees, all of them nationals with the technical expertise and professional experience necessary to obtain construction permits and approvals.
- Has at least 1 employee who is a licensed architect and registered with the local association of architects.
- Has paid all taxes and taken out all necessary insurance applicable to its general business activity (for example,

FIGURE 20.3  What are the time, cost and number of procedures to comply with formalities to build a warehouse?

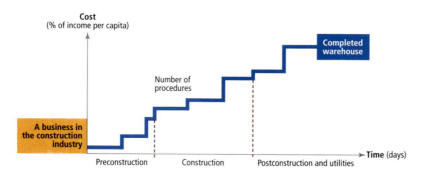

accidental insurance for construction workers and third-person liability).

- Owns the land on which the warehouse is built.

## Assumptions about the warehouse

The warehouse:

- Will be used for general storage activities, such as storage of books or stationery. The warehouse will not be used for any goods requiring special conditions, such as food, chemicals or pharmaceuticals.

- Has 2 stories, both above ground, with a total surface of approximately 1,300.6 square meters (14,000 square feet). Each floor is 3 meters (9 feet, 10 inches) high.

- Has road access and is located in the periurban area of the economy's largest business city (that is, on the fringes of the city but still within its official limits).

- Is not located in a special economic or industrial zone. The zoning requirements for warehouses are met by building in an area where similar warehouses can be found.

- Is located on a land plot of 929 square meters (10,000 square feet) that is 100% owned by BuildCo and is accurately registered in the cadastre and land registry.

- Is a new construction (there was no previous construction on the land).

- Has complete architectural and technical plans prepared by a licensed architect.

- Will include all technical equipment required to make the warehouse fully operational.

- Will take 30 weeks to construct (excluding all delays due to administrative and regulatory requirements).

## Assumptions about the utility connections

The water and sewerage connection:

- Is 10 meters (32 feet, 10 inches) from the existing water source and sewer tap.

- Does not require water for fire protection reasons; a fire extinguishing system (dry system) will be used instead. If a wet fire protection system is required by law, it is assumed that the water demand specified below also covers the water needed for fire protection.

- Has an average water use of 662 liters (175 gallons) a day and an average wastewater flow of 568 liters (150 gallons) a day.

- Has a peak water use of 1,325 liters (350 gallons) a day and a peak wastewater flow of 1,136 liters (300 gallons) a day.

- Will have a constant level of water demand and wastewater flow throughout the year.

The telephone connection:

- Is 10 meters (32 feet, 10 inches) from the main telephone network.

- Is a fixed telephone landline.

## Procedures

A procedure is any interaction of the company's employees or managers with external parties, including government agencies, notaries, the land registry, the cadastre, utility companies, public and private inspectors and technical experts apart from in-house architects and engineers. Interactions between company employees, such as development of the warehouse plans and inspections conducted by employees, are not counted as procedures. Procedures that the company undergoes to connect to water, sewerage and telephone services are included. All procedures that are legally or in practice required for building a warehouse are counted, even if they may be avoided in exceptional cases (table 20.4).

## Time

Time is recorded in calendar days. The measure captures the median duration that local experts indicate is necessary to complete a procedure in practice. It is assumed that the minimum time required for each procedure is 1 day. Although procedures may take place simultaneously, they cannot start on the same day

| TABLE 20.4  What do the dealing with construction permits indicators measure? |
| --- |
| **Procedures to legally build a warehouse** (number) |
| Submitting all relevant documents and obtaining all necessary clearances, licenses, permits and certificates |
| Completing all required notifications and receiving all necessary inspections |
| Obtaining utility connections for water, sewerage and a land telephone line |
| Registering the warehouse after its completion (if required for use as collateral or for transfer of the warehouse) |
| **Time required to complete each procedure** (calendar days) |
| Does not include time spent gathering information |
| Each procedure starts on a separate day |
| Procedure completed once final document is received |
| No prior contact with officials |
| **Cost required to complete each procedure** (% of income per capita) |
| Official costs only, no bribes |

(that is, simultaneous procedures start on consecutive days). If a procedure can be accelerated legally for an additional cost, the fastest procedure is chosen. It is assumed that BuildCo does not waste time and commits to completing each remaining procedure without delay. The time that BuildCo spends on gathering information is ignored. It is assumed that BuildCo is aware of all building requirements and their sequence from the beginning.

## Cost

Cost is recorded as a percentage of the economy's income per capita. Only official costs are recorded. All the fees associated with completing the procedures to legally build a warehouse are recorded, including those associated with obtaining land use approvals and preconstruction design clearances; receiving inspections before, during and after construction; getting utility connections; and registering the warehouse property. Nonrecurring taxes required for the completion of the warehouse project are also recorded. The building code, information from local experts and specific regulations and fee schedules are used as sources for costs. If several local partners provide different estimates, the median reported value is used.

*The data details on dealing with construction permits can be found for each economy at http://www.doingbusiness.org by selecting the economy in the drop-down list.*

## GETTING ELECTRICITY

*Doing Business* records all procedures required for a business to obtain a permanent electricity connection and supply for a standardized warehouse. These procedures include applications and contracts with electricity utilities, all necessary inspections and clearances from the utility and other agencies and the external and final connection works. The survey divides the process of getting an electricity connection into distinct procedures and calculates the time and cost of completing each procedure (figure 20.5). The ranking on the ease of getting electricity is the simple average of the percentile rankings on its component indicators (figure 20.6).

Data are collected from the electricity distribution utility, then completed and verified by electricity regulatory agencies and independent professionals such as electrical engineers, electrical contractors and construction companies. The electricity distribution utility surveyed is the one serving the area (or areas) where warehouses are located. If there is a choice of distribution utilities, the one serving the largest number of customers is selected.

To make the data comparable across economies, several assumptions about the warehouse and the electricity connection are used.

### Assumptions about the warehouse

The warehouse:

- Is owned by a local entrepreneur.
- Is located in the economy's largest business city.
- Is located within the city's official limits and in an area where other warehouses are located (a nonresidential area).

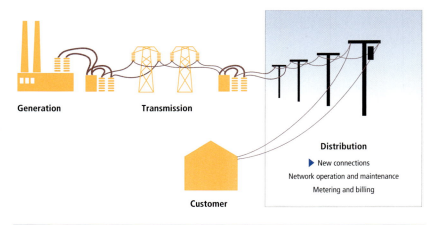

FIGURE 20.5  *Doing Business* measures the connection process at the level of distribution utilities

- Is not located in a special economic or investment zone; that is, the electricity connection is not eligible for subsidization or faster service under a special investment promotion regime. If several options for location are available, the warehouse is located where electricity is most easily available.

- Has road access. The connection works involve the crossing of a road (for excavation, overhead lines and the like), but they are all carried out on public land; that is, there is no crossing onto another owner's private property.

- Is located in an area with no physical constraints. For example, the property is not near a railway.

- Is used for storage of refrigerated goods.

- Is a new construction (that is, there was no previous construction on the land where it is located). It is being connected to electricity for the first time.

- Has 2 stories, both above ground, with a total surface area of approximately 1,300.6 square meters (14,000 square feet). The plot of land on which it is built is 929 square meters (10,000 square feet).

### Assumptions about the electricity connection

The electricity connection:

- Is a permanent one.

- Is a 3-phase, 4-wire Y, 140-kilovolt-ampere (kVA) (subscribed capacity) connection.

- Is 150 meters long. The connection is to either the low-voltage or the medium-voltage distribution network and either overhead or underground, whichever is more common in the economy and in the area where the warehouse is located. The length of any connection in the customer's private domain is negligible.

- Involves the installation of only one electricity meter. The monthly electricity consumption will be 0.07 gigawatt-hour (GWh). The internal electrical wiring has already been completed.

FIGURE 20.6  Getting electricity: obtaining an electricity connection

Rankings are based on 3 indicators

Steps to file an application, prepare a design, complete works, obtain approvals, go through inspections, install a meter and sign a supply contract

## Procedures

A procedure is defined as any interaction of the company's employees or its main electrician or electrical engineer (that is, the one who may have done the internal wiring) with external parties such as the electricity distribution utility, electricity supply utilities, government agencies, electrical contractors and electrical firms. Interactions between company employees and steps related to the internal electrical wiring, such as the design and execution of the internal electrical installation plans, are not counted as procedures. Procedures that must be completed with the same utility but with different departments are counted as separate procedures (table 20.5).

The company's employees are assumed to complete all procedures themselves unless the use of a third party is mandated (for example, if only an electrician registered with the utility is allowed to submit an application). If the company can, but is not required to, request the services of professionals (such as a private firm rather than the utility for the external works), these procedures are recorded if they are commonly done. For all procedures, only the most likely cases (for example, more

| TABLE 20.5 What do the getting electricity indicators measure? |
|---|
| **Procedures to obtain an electricity connection** (number) |
| Submitting all relevant documents and obtaining all necessary clearances and permits |
| Completing all required notifications and receiving all necessary inspections |
| Obtaining external installation works and possibly purchasing material for these works |
| Concluding any necessary supply contract and obtaining final supply |
| **Time required to complete each procedure** (calendar days) |
| Is at least 1 calendar day |
| Each procedure starts on a separate day |
| Does not include time spent gathering information |
| Reflects the time spent in practice, with little follow-up and no prior contact with officials |
| **Cost required to complete each procedure** (% of income per capita) |
| Official costs only, no bribes |
| Value added tax excluded |

than 50% of the time the utility has the material) and those followed in practice for connecting a warehouse to electricity are counted.

## Time

Time is recorded in calendar days. The measure captures the median duration that the electricity utility and experts indicate is necessary in practice, rather than required by law, to complete a procedure with minimum follow-up and no extra payments. It is also assumed that the minimum time required for each procedure is 1 day. Although procedures may take place simultaneously, they cannot start on the same day (that is, simultaneous procedures start on consecutive days). It is assumed that the company does not waste time and commits to completing each remaining procedure without delay. The time that the company spends on gathering information is ignored. It is assumed that the company is aware of all electricity connection requirements and their sequence from the beginning.

## Cost

Cost is recorded as a percentage of the economy's income per capita. Costs are recorded exclusive of value added tax. All the fees and costs associated with completing the procedures to connect a warehouse to electricity are recorded, including those related to obtaining clearances from government agencies, applying for the connection, receiving inspections of both the site and the internal wiring, purchasing material, getting the actual connection works and paying a security deposit. Information from local experts and specific regulations and fee schedules are used as sources for costs. If several local partners provide different estimates, the median reported value is used. In all cases the cost excludes bribes.

## Security deposit

Utilities require security deposits as a guarantee against the possible failure of customers to pay their consumption bills. For this reason the security deposit for a new customer is most often calculated

as a function of the customer's estimated consumption.

*Doing Business* does not record the full amount of the security deposit. If the deposit is based on the customer's actual consumption, this basis is the one assumed in the case study. Rather than the full amount of the security deposit, *Doing Business* records the present value of the losses in interest earnings experienced by the customer because the utility holds the security deposit over a prolonged period, in most cases until the end of the contract (assumed to be after 5 years). In cases where the security deposit is used to cover the first monthly consumption bills, it is not recorded. To calculate the present value of the lost interest earnings, the end-2011 lending rates from the International Monetary Fund's *International Financial Statistics* are used. In cases where the security deposit is returned with interest, the difference between the lending rate and the interest paid by the utility is used to calculate the present value.

In some economies the security deposit can be put up in the form of a bond: the company can obtain from a bank or an insurance company a guarantee issued on the assets it holds with that financial institution. In contrast to the scenario in which the customer pays the deposit in cash to the utility, in this scenario the company does not lose ownership control over the full amount and can continue using it. In return the company will pay the bank a commission for obtaining the bond. The commission charged may vary depending on the credit standing of the company. The best possible credit standing and thus the lowest possible commission are assumed. Where a bond can be put up, the value recorded for the deposit is the annual commission times the 5 years assumed to be the length of the contract. If both options exist, the cheaper alternative is recorded.

In Honduras in June 2012 a customer requesting a 140-kVA electricity connection would have had to put up a security deposit of 126,894 Honduran lempiras (L) in cash or check, and the deposit would have been returned only at the end of the contract. The customer could instead have invested this money at the prevailing lending rate of 18.56%. Over the 5 years of the contract this would imply a present value of lost interest earnings of L 72,719. In contrast, if the customer chose to settle the deposit with a bank guarantee at an annual rate of 2.5%, the amount lost over the 5 years would be just L 15,862.

*The data details on getting electricity can be found for each economy at http://www .doingbusiness.org.*

## REGISTERING PROPERTY

*Doing Business* records the full sequence of procedures necessary for a business (buyer) to purchase a property from another business (seller) and to transfer the property title to the buyer's name so that the buyer can use the property for expanding its business, use the property as collateral in taking new loans or, if necessary, sell the property to another business. The process starts with obtaining the necessary documents, such as a copy of the seller's title if necessary, and conducting due diligence if required. The transaction is considered complete when it is opposable to third parties and when the buyer can use the property, use it as collateral for a bank loan or resell it (figure 20.7). The ranking on the ease of registering property is the simple average of the

percentile rankings on its component indicators (figure 20.8).

Every procedure required by law or necessary in practice is included, whether it is the responsibility of the seller or the buyer or must be completed by a third party on their behalf. Local property lawyers, notaries and property registries provide information on procedures as well as the time and cost to complete each of them.

To make the data comparable across economies, several assumptions about the parties to the transaction, the property and the procedures are used.

### Assumptions about the parties

The parties (buyer and seller):

- Are limited liability companies.
- Are located in the periurban area of the economy's largest business city.
- Are 100% domestically and privately owned.
- Have 50 employees each, all of whom are nationals.
- Perform general commercial activities.

### Assumptions about the property

The property:

- Has a value of 50 times income per capita. The sale price equals the value.
- Is fully owned by the seller.
- Has no mortgages attached and has been under the same ownership for the past 10 years.

**FIGURE 20.8**   Registering property: transfer of property between 2 local companies

**Rankings are based on 3 indicators**

Days to transfer property in main city

As % of property value, no bribes included

Steps to check encumbrances, obtain clearance certificates, prepare deed and transfer title so that the property can be occupied, sold or used as collateral

- Is registered in the land registry or cadastre, or both, and is free of title disputes.
- Is located in a periurban commercial zone, and no rezoning is required.
- Consists of land and a building. The land area is 557.4 square meters (6,000 square feet). A 2-story warehouse of 929 square meters (10,000 square feet) is located on the land. The warehouse is 10 years old, is in good condition and complies with all safety standards, building codes and other legal requirements. The property of land and building will be transferred in its entirety.
- Will not be subject to renovations or additional building following the purchase.
- Has no trees, natural water sources, natural reserves or historical monuments of any kind.
- Will not be used for special purposes, and no special permits, such as for residential use, industrial plants, waste storage or certain types of agricultural activities, are required.
- Has no occupants (legal or illegal), and no other party holds a legal interest in it.

### Procedures

A procedure is defined as any interaction of the buyer or the seller, their agents (if

**FIGURE 20.7**   What are the time, cost and number of procedures required to transfer property between 2 local companies?

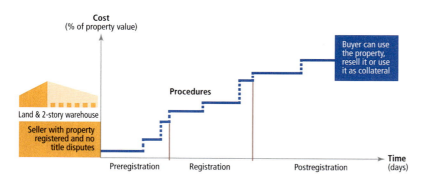

Cost
(% of property value)

Land & 2-story warehouse

Seller with property registered and no title disputes

Procedures

Buyer can use the property, resell it or use it as collateral

Preregistration       Registration       Postregistration

Time
(days)

| TABLE 20.6 | What do the registering property indicators measure? |
|---|---|
| **Procedures to legally transfer title on immovable property** (number) | |
| Preregistration procedures (for example, checking for liens, notarizing sales agreement, paying property transfer taxes) | |
| Registration procedures in the economy's largest business city | |
| Postregistration procedures (for example, filing title with municipality) | |
| **Time required to complete each procedure** (calendar days) | |
| Does not include time spent gathering information | |
| Each procedure starts on a separate day | |
| Procedure completed once final document is received | |
| No prior contact with officials | |
| **Cost required to complete each procedure** (% of of property value) | |
| Official costs only, no bribes | |
| No value added or capital gains taxes included | |

an agent is legally or in practice required) or the property with external parties, including government agencies, inspectors, notaries and lawyers. Interactions between company officers and employees are not considered. All procedures that are legally or in practice required for registering property are recorded, even if they may be avoided in exceptional cases (table 20.6). It is assumed that the buyer follows the fastest legal option available and used by the majority of property owners. Although the buyer may use lawyers or other professionals where necessary in the registration process, it is assumed that the buyer does not employ an outside facilitator in the registration process unless legally or in practice required to do so.

## Time

Time is recorded in calendar days. The measure captures the median duration that property lawyers, notaries or registry officials indicate is necessary to complete a procedure. It is assumed that the minimum time required for each procedure is 1 day. Although procedures may take place simultaneously, they cannot start on the same day. It is assumed that the buyer does not waste time and commits to completing each remaining procedure without delay. If a procedure can be accelerated for

an additional cost, the fastest legal procedure available and used by the majority of property owners is chosen. If procedures can be undertaken simultaneously, it is assumed that they are. It is assumed that the parties involved are aware of all requirements and their sequence from the beginning. Time spent on gathering information is not considered.

## Cost

Cost is recorded as a percentage of the property value, assumed to be equivalent to 50 times income per capita. Only official costs required by law are recorded, including fees, transfer taxes, stamp duties and any other payment to the property registry, notaries, public agencies or lawyers. Other taxes, such as capital gains tax or value added tax, are excluded from the cost measure. Both costs borne by the buyer and those borne by the seller are included. If cost estimates differ among sources, the median reported value is used.

*The data details on registering property can be found for each economy at http://www .doingbusiness.org by selecting the economy in the drop-down list.*

## GETTING CREDIT

*Doing Business* measures the legal rights of borrowers and lenders with respect to secured transactions through one set of indicators and the sharing of credit information through another. The first set of indicators measures whether certain

FIGURE 20.10 Getting credit: collateral rules and credit information

Rankings are based on 2 indicators

*Note:* Private bureau coverage and public registry coverage are measured but do not count for the rankings.

features that facilitate lending exist within the applicable collateral and bankruptcy laws. The second set measures the coverage, scope and accessibility of credit information available through public credit registries and private credit bureaus (figure 20.9). The ranking on the ease of getting credit is based on the percentile rankings on the sum of its component indicators: the depth of credit information index and the strength of legal rights index (figure 20.10).

## LEGAL RIGHTS

The data on the legal rights of borrowers and lenders are gathered through a survey of financial lawyers and verified through analysis of laws and regulations as well as public sources of information on collateral and bankruptcy laws. Survey responses are verified through several rounds of

FIGURE 20.9 Do lenders have credit information on entrepreneurs seeking credit? Is the law favorable to borrowers and lenders using movable assets as collateral?

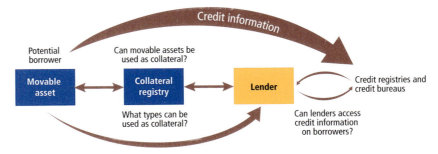

follow-up communication with respondents as well as by contacting third parties and consulting public sources. The survey data are confirmed through teleconference calls or on-site visits in all economies.

## Strength of legal rights index

The strength of legal rights index measures the degree to which collateral and bankruptcy laws protect the rights of borrowers and lenders and thus facilitate lending (table 20.7). Two case scenarios, case A and case B, are used to determine the scope of the secured transactions system. The case scenarios involve a secured borrower, the company ABC, and a secured lender, BizBank. In some economies the legal framework for secured transactions will allow only case A or case B to apply (not both). Both cases examine the same set of legal provisions relating to the use of movable collateral.

Several assumptions about the secured borrower and lender are used:

- ABC is a domestically incorporated, limited liability company.
- The company has up to 100 employees.
- ABC has its headquarters and only base of operations in the economy's largest business city.
- Both ABC and BizBank are 100% domestically owned.

**TABLE 20.7  What do the getting credit indicators measure?**

**Strength of legal rights index (0–10)**

Protection of rights of borrowers and lenders through collateral laws

Protection of secured creditors' rights through bankruptcy laws

**Depth of credit information index (0–6)**

Scope and accessibility of credit information distributed by public credit registries and private credit bureaus

**Public credit registry coverage (% of adults)**

Number of individuals and firms listed in a public credit registry as percentage of adult population

**Private credit bureau coverage (% of adults)**

Number of individuals and firms listed in largest private credit bureau as percentage of adult population

The case scenarios also involve assumptions. In case A, as collateral for the loan, ABC grants BizBank a nonpossessory security interest in one category of movable assets, for example, its machinery or its inventory. ABC wants to keep both possession and ownership of the collateral. In economies where the law does not allow nonpossessory security interests in movable property, ABC and BizBank use a fiduciary transfer-of-title arrangement (or a similar substitute for nonpossessory security interests). The strength of legal rights index does not cover functional equivalents to security over movable assets (for example, leasing or reservation of title).

In case B, ABC grants BizBank a business charge, enterprise charge, floating charge or any charge that gives BizBank a security interest over ABC's combined movable assets (or as much of ABC's movable assets as possible). ABC keeps ownership and possession of the assets.

The strength of legal rights index includes 8 aspects related to legal rights in collateral law and 2 aspects in bankruptcy law. A score of 1 is assigned for each of the following features of the laws:

- Any business may use movable assets as collateral while keeping possession of the assets, and any financial institution may accept such assets as collateral.
- The law allows a business to grant a nonpossessory security right in a single category of movable assets (such as accounts receivable or inventory), without requiring a specific description of the collateral.
- The law allows a business to grant a nonpossessory security right in substantially all its movable assets, without requiring a specific description of the collateral.
- A security right may extend to future or after-acquired assets and may extend automatically to the products, proceeds or replacements of the original assets.

- A general description of debts and obligations is permitted in the collateral agreement and in registration documents; all types of debts and obligations can be secured between the parties, and the collateral agreement can include a maximum amount for which the assets are encumbered.
- A collateral registry or registration institution for security interests over movable property is in operation, unified geographically and by asset type, with an electronic database indexed by debtors' names.
- Secured creditors are paid first (for example, before general tax claims and employee claims) when a debtor defaults outside an insolvency procedure.
- Secured creditors are paid first (for example, before general tax claims and employee claims) when a business is liquidated.
- Secured creditors either are not subject to an automatic stay or moratorium on enforcement procedures when a debtor enters a court-supervised reorganization procedure, or the law provides secured creditors with grounds for relief from an automatic stay or moratorium (for example, if the movable property is in danger) or sets a time limit for the automatic stay.
- The law allows parties to agree in a collateral agreement that the lender may enforce its security right out of court.

The index ranges from 0 to 10, with higher scores indicating that collateral and bankruptcy laws are better designed to expand access to credit.

## CREDIT INFORMATION

The data on credit information sharing are built in 2 stages. First, banking supervision authorities and public information sources are surveyed to confirm the presence of a public credit registry or private credit bureau. Second, when applicable, a detailed survey on the public credit registry's or private credit bureau's structure, laws and associated rules is administered to the entity itself. Survey responses are verified through several rounds of follow-up communication with respondents as well as by contacting third parties and consulting public sources. The survey data are confirmed through teleconference calls or on-site visits in all economies.

## Depth of credit information index

The depth of credit information index measures rules and practices affecting the coverage, scope and accessibility of credit information available through either a public credit registry or a private credit bureau. A score of 1 is assigned for each of the following 6 features of the public credit registry or private credit bureau (or both):

- Data on both firms and individuals are distributed.
- Both positive credit information (for example, outstanding loan amounts and pattern of on-time repayments) and negative information (for example, late payments, and number and amount of defaults and bankruptcies) are distributed.
- Data from retailers and utility companies as well as financial institutions are distributed.
- More than 2 years of historical data are distributed. Credit registries and bureaus that erase data on defaults as soon as they are repaid obtain a score of 0 for this indicator.
- Data on loan amounts below 1% of income per capita are distributed. Note that a credit registry or bureau must have a minimum coverage of 1% of the adult population to score a 1 on this indicator.
- By law, borrowers have the right to access their data in the largest credit registry or bureau in the economy.

The index ranges from 0 to 6, with higher values indicating the availability of more credit information, from either a public credit registry or a private credit bureau, to facilitate lending decisions. If the credit registry or bureau is not operational or has a coverage of less than 0.1% of the adult population, the score on the depth of credit information index is 0.

In Lithuania, for example, both a public credit registry and a private credit bureau operate. Both distribute positive and negative information (a score of 1). Both distribute data on firms and individuals (a score of 1). Both distribute more than 2 years of historical data (a score of 1). Although the public credit registry does not distribute data from retailers or utilities, the private credit bureau does do so (a score of 1). Although the public credit registry has a threshold of 1,000 litai, the private credit bureau distributes data on loans of any value (a score of 1). Borrowers have the right to access their data in both the public credit registry and the private credit bureau (a score of 1). Summing across the indicators gives Lithuania a total score of 6.

## Public credit registry coverage

The public credit registry coverage indicator reports the number of individuals and firms listed in a public credit registry with information on their borrowing history from the past 5 years. The number is expressed as a percentage of the adult population (the population age 15 and above in 2011 according to the World Bank's *World Development Indicators*). A public credit registry is defined as a database managed by the public sector, usually by the central bank or the superintendent of banks, that collects information on the creditworthiness of borrowers (individuals or firms) in the financial system and facilitates the exchange of credit information among banks and other regulated financial institutions. If no public registry operates, the coverage value is 0.

## Private credit bureau coverage

The private credit bureau coverage indicator reports the number of individuals and firms listed by a private credit bureau with information on their borrowing history from the past 5 years. The number is expressed as a percentage of the adult population (the population age 15 and above in 2011 according to the World Bank's *World Development Indicators*).

A private credit bureau is defined as a private firm or nonprofit organization that maintains a database on the creditworthiness of borrowers (individuals or firms) in the financial system and facilitates the exchange of credit information among creditors. Credit investigative bureaus and credit reporting firms that do not directly facilitate information exchange among banks and other financial institutions are not considered. If no private bureau operates, the coverage value is 0.

*The data details on getting credit can be found for each economy at http://www .doingbusiness.org by selecting the economy in the drop-down list. This methodology was developed in Djankov, McLiesh and Shleifer (2007) and is adopted here with minor changes.*

## PROTECTING INVESTORS

*Doing Business* measures the strength of minority shareholder protections against directors' misuse of corporate assets for personal gain. The indicators distinguish 3 dimensions of investor protections: transparency of related-party transactions (extent of disclosure index), liability for self-dealing (extent of director liability index) and shareholders' ability to sue officers and directors for misconduct (ease of shareholder suits index) (figure 20.11). The data come from a survey of corporate and securities lawyers and are based on securities regulations, company laws, civil procedure codes and court rules of evidence. The ranking on the strength of investor protection index is the simple average of the percentile rankings on its component indicators (figure 20.12).

To make the data comparable across economies, several assumptions about the business and the transaction are used.

### Assumptions about the business

The business (Buyer):

- Is a publicly traded corporation listed on the economy's most important stock exchange. If the number of publicly traded companies listed on that exchange is less than 10, or if there is

FIGURE 20.11  How well are minority shareholders protected against self-dealing in related-party transactions?

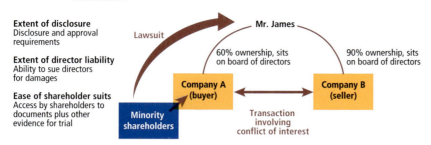

no stock exchange in the economy, it is assumed that Buyer is a large private company with multiple shareholders.

- Has a board of directors and a chief executive officer (CEO) who may legally act on behalf of Buyer where permitted, even if this is not specifically required by law.

- Has a supervisory board (applicable to economies with 2-tier board systems) of which 60% of the shareholder-elected members have been appointed by Mr. James.

- Is a manufacturing company.

- Has its own distribution network.

## Assumptions about the transaction

- Mr. James is Buyer's controlling shareholder and a member of Buyer's board of directors. He owns 60% of Buyer and elected 2 directors to Buyer's 5-member board.

FIGURE 20.12  Protecting investors: minority shareholder rights in related-party transactions

Rankings are based on 3 indicators

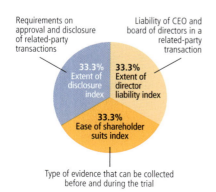

- Mr. James also owns 90% of Seller, a company that operates a chain of retail hardware stores. Seller recently closed a large number of its stores.

- Mr. James proposes that Buyer purchase Seller's unused fleet of trucks to expand Buyer's distribution of its products, a proposal to which Buyer agrees. The price is equal to 10% of Buyer's assets and is higher than the market value.

- The proposed transaction is part of the company's ordinary course of business and is not outside the authority of the company.

- Buyer enters into the transaction. All required approvals are obtained, and all required disclosures made (that is, the transaction is not fraudulent).

- The transaction causes damages to Buyer. Shareholders sue Mr. James and the other parties that approved the transaction.

## Extent of disclosure index

The extent of disclosure index has 5 components (table 20.8):

- Which corporate body can provide legally sufficient approval for the transaction. A score of 0 is assigned if it is the CEO or the managing director alone; 1 if the board of directors, the supervisory board or shareholders must vote and Mr. James is permitted to vote; 2 if the board of directors or the supervisory board must vote and Mr. James is not permitted to vote; 3 if shareholders must vote and Mr. James is not permitted to vote.

- Whether immediate disclosure of the transaction to the public, the regulator or the shareholders is required.[4] A score of 0 is assigned if no disclosure is required; 1 if disclosure on the terms of the transaction is required but not on Mr. James's conflict of interest; 2 if disclosure on both the terms and Mr. James's conflict of interest is required.

- Whether disclosure in the annual report is required. A score of 0 is assigned if no disclosure on the transaction is required; 1 if disclosure on the terms of the transaction is required but not on Mr. James's conflict of interest; 2 if disclosure on both the terms and Mr. James's conflict of interest is required.

- Whether disclosure by Mr. James to the board of directors or the supervisory board is required. A score of 0 is assigned if no disclosure is required; 1 if a general disclosure of the existence of a conflict of interest is required without any specifics; 2 if full disclosure of all material facts relating to Mr. James's interest in the Buyer-Seller transaction is required.

- Whether it is required that an external body, for example, an external auditor, review the transaction before it takes place. A score of 0 is assigned if no; 1 if yes.

The index ranges from 0 to 10, with higher values indicating greater disclosure. In Poland, for example, the board of directors must approve the transaction and Mr. James is not allowed to vote (a score of 2). Buyer is required to disclose immediately all information affecting the stock price, including the conflict of interest (a score of 2). In its annual report Buyer must also disclose the terms of the transaction and Mr. James's ownership in Buyer and Seller (a score of 2). Before the transaction Mr. James must disclose his conflict of interest to the other directors, but he is not required to provide specific information about it (a score of 1). Poland does not require an external body to review the transaction (a score of 0). Adding these numbers gives Poland a score of 7 on the extent of disclosure index.

| TABLE 20.8  What do the protecting investors indicators measure? |
|---|
| **Extent of disclosure index** (0–10) |
| Who can approve related-party transactions |
| Disclosure requirements in case of related-party transactions |
| **Extent of director liability index** (0–10) |
| Ability of shareholders to hold interested parties and members of the approving body liable in case of related-party transactions |
| Available legal remedies (damages, repayment of profits, fines and imprisonment) |
| Ability of shareholders to sue directly or derivatively |
| **Ease of shareholder suits index** (0–10) |
| Direct access to internal documents of the company and use of a government inspector without filing suit in court |
| Documents and information available during trial |
| **Strength of investor protection index** (0–10) |
| Simple average of the extent of disclosure, extent of director liability and ease of shareholder suits indices |

## Extent of director liability index

The extent of director liability index has 7 components:[5]

- Whether a shareholder plaintiff is able to hold Mr. James liable for the damage the Buyer-Seller transaction causes to the company. A score of 0 is assigned if Mr. James cannot be held liable or can be held liable only for fraud or bad faith; 1 if Mr. James can be held liable only if he influenced the approval of the transaction or was negligent; 2 if Mr. James can be held liable when the transaction is unfair or prejudicial to the other shareholders.

- Whether a shareholder plaintiff is able to hold the approving body (the CEO, the members of the board of directors, or members of the supervisory board) liable for the damage the transaction causes to the company. A score of 0 is assigned if the approving body cannot be held liable or can be held liable only for fraud or bad faith; 1 if the approving body can be held liable for negligence; 2 if the approving body can be held liable when the transaction is unfair or prejudicial to the other shareholders.

- Whether a court can void the transaction upon a successful claim by a shareholder plaintiff. A score of 0 is assigned if rescission is unavailable or is available only in case of fraud or bad faith; 1 if rescission is available when the transaction is oppressive or prejudicial to the other shareholders; 2 if rescission is available when the transaction is unfair or entails a conflict of interest.

- Whether Mr. James pays damages for the harm caused to the company upon a successful claim by the shareholder plaintiff. A score of 0 is assigned if no; 1 if yes.

- Whether Mr. James repays profits made from the transaction upon a successful claim by the shareholder plaintiff. A score of 0 is assigned if no; 1 if yes.

- Whether both fines and imprisonment can be applied against Mr. James. A score of 0 is assigned if no; 1 if yes.

- Whether shareholder plaintiffs are able to sue directly or derivatively for the damage the transaction causes to the company. A score of 0 is assigned if suits are unavailable or are available only for shareholders holding more than 10% of the company's share capital; 1 if direct or derivative suits are available for shareholders holding 10% or less of share capital.

The index ranges from 0 to 10, with higher values indicating greater liability of directors. Assuming that the prejudicial transaction was duly approved and disclosed, in order to hold Mr. James liable in Panama, for example, a plaintiff must prove that Mr. James influenced the approving body or acted negligently (a score of 1). To hold the other directors liable, a plaintiff must prove that they acted negligently (a score of 1). The prejudicial transaction cannot be voided (a score of 0). If Mr. James is found liable, he must pay damages (a score of 1) but he is not required to disgorge his profits (a score of 0). Mr. James cannot be fined and imprisoned (a score of 0). Direct or derivative suits are available for shareholders holding 10% or less of share capital (a score of 1). Adding these numbers gives Panama

a score of 4 on the extent of director liability index.

## Ease of shareholder suits index

The ease of shareholder suits index has 6 components:

- What range of documents is available to the shareholder plaintiff from the defendant and witnesses during trial. A score of 1 is assigned for each of the following types of documents available: information that the defendant has indicated he intends to rely on for his defense; information that directly proves specific facts in the plaintiff's claim; any information relevant to the subject matter of the claim; and any information that may lead to the discovery of relevant information.

- Whether the plaintiff can directly examine the defendant and witnesses during trial. A score of 0 is assigned if no; 1 if yes, with prior approval of the questions by the judge; 2 if yes, without prior approval.

- Whether the plaintiff can obtain categories of relevant documents from the defendant without identifying each document specifically. A score of 0 is assigned if no; 1 if yes.

- Whether shareholders owning 10% or less of the company's share capital can request that a government inspector investigate the Buyer-Seller transaction without filing suit in court. A score of 0 is assigned if no; 1 if yes.

- Whether shareholders owning 10% or less of the company's share capital have the right to inspect the transaction documents before filing suit. A score of 0 is assigned if no; 1 if yes.

- Whether the standard of proof for civil suits is lower than that for a criminal case. A score of 0 is assigned if no; 1 if yes.

The index ranges from 0 to 10, with higher values indicating greater powers of shareholders to challenge the transaction. In Greece, for example, the plaintiff can access documents that the defendant intends to rely on for his defense and that directly prove facts in the plaintiff's claim (a score of 2). The plaintiff can examine the defendant and witnesses during trial, though only with prior approval of the questions by the court (a score of 1). The plaintiff must specifically identify the documents being sought (for example, the Buyer-Seller purchase agreement of July 15, 2006) and cannot just request categories (for example, all documents related to the transaction) (a score of 0). A shareholder holding 5% of Buyer's shares can request that a government inspector review suspected mismanagement by Mr. James and the CEO without filing suit in court (a score of 1). Any shareholder can inspect the transaction documents before deciding whether to sue (a score of 1). The standard of proof for civil suits is the same as that for a criminal case (a score of 0). Adding these numbers gives Greece a score of 5 on the ease of shareholder suits index.

## Strength of investor protection index

The strength of investor protection index is the average of the extent of disclosure index, the extent of director liability index and the ease of shareholder suits index. The index ranges from 0 to 10, with higher values indicating more investor protection.

*The data details on protecting investors can be found for each economy at http://www .doingbusiness.org by selecting the economy in the drop-down list. This methodology was developed in Djankov, La Porta and others (2008).*

## PAYING TAXES

*Doing Business* records the taxes and mandatory contributions that a medium-size company must pay in a given year as well as measures of the administrative burden of paying taxes and contributions. The project was developed and implemented in cooperation with PwC.[6] Taxes and contributions measured include the profit or corporate income tax, social contributions and labor taxes paid by the employer, property taxes, property

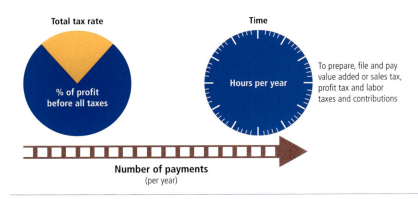

**FIGURE 20.13** What are the time, total tax rate and number of payments necessary for a local medium-size company to pay all taxes?

transfer taxes, dividend tax, capital gains tax, financial transactions tax, waste collection taxes, vehicle and road taxes, and any other small taxes or fees (figure 20.13).

The ranking on the ease of paying taxes is the simple average of the percentile rankings on its component indicators, with a threshold being applied to one of the component indicators, the total tax rate (figure 20.14). The threshold is defined as the highest total tax rate among the top 15% of economies in the ranking on the total tax rate. It is calculated and adjusted on a yearly basis. This year's threshold is 25.7%. All economies with a total tax rate below this threshold receive the same score as the economy at the threshold. The threshold is not based on any economic theory of an "optimal tax rate" that minimizes distortions or maximizes efficiency in the tax system of an economy overall. Instead, it is mainly empirical in nature, set at the lower end of the distribution of tax rates levied on medium-size enterprises in the manufacturing sector as observed through the paying taxes indicators. This reduces the bias in the indicators toward economies that do not need to levy significant taxes on companies like the *Doing Business* standardized case study company because they raise public revenue in other ways—for example, through taxes on foreign companies, through taxes on sectors other than manufacturing or from

natural resources (all of which are outside the scope of the methodology).

*Doing Business* measures all taxes and contributions that are government mandated (at any level—federal, state or local) and that apply to the standardized business and have an impact in its financial statements. In doing so, *Doing Business* goes beyond the traditional definition of a tax. As defined for the purposes of government national accounts, taxes include only compulsory, unrequited payments to general government. *Doing Business* departs from this definition because it measures imposed charges that affect business accounts, not government accounts. One main difference relates to labor contributions. The *Doing Business* measure includes government-mandated contributions paid by the employer to a

**FIGURE 20.14** Paying taxes: tax compliance for a local manufacturing company

Rankings are based on 3 indicators

Number of tax payments per year

requited private pension fund or workers' insurance fund. The indicator includes, for example, Australia's compulsory superannuation guarantee and workers' compensation insurance. For the purpose of calculating the total tax rate (defined below), only taxes borne are included. For example, value added taxes are generally excluded (provided they are not irrecoverable) because they do not affect the accounting profits of the business—that is, they are not reflected in the income statement. They are, however, included for the purpose of the compliance measures (time and payments), as they add to the burden of complying with the tax system.

*Doing Business* uses a case scenario to measure the taxes and contributions paid by a standardized business and the complexity of an economy's tax compliance system. This case scenario uses a set of financial statements and assumptions about transactions made over the course of the year. In each economy tax experts from a number of different firms (in many economies these include PwC) compute the taxes and mandatory contributions due in their jurisdiction based on the standardized case study facts. Information is also compiled on the frequency of filing and payments as well as time taken to comply with tax laws in an economy. To make the data comparable across economies, several assumptions about the business and the taxes and contributions are used.

The methodology for the paying taxes indicators has benefited from discussion with members of the International Tax Dialogue and other stakeholders, which led to a refinement of the survey questions on the time to pay taxes, the collection of additional data on the labor tax wedge for further research and the introduction of a threshold applied to the total tax rate for the purpose of calculating the ranking on the ease of paying taxes.

## Assumptions about the business

The business:

- Is a limited liability, taxable company. If there is more than one type of limited liability company in the economy, the limited liability form most common among domestic firms is chosen. The most common form is reported by incorporation lawyers or the statistical office.
- Started operations on January 1, 2010. At that time the company purchased all the assets shown in its balance sheet and hired all its workers.
- Operates in the economy's largest business city.
- Is 100% domestically owned and has 5 owners, all of whom are natural persons.
- At the end of 2010, has a start-up capital of 102 times income per capita.
- Performs general industrial or commercial activities. Specifically, it produces ceramic flowerpots and sells them at retail. It does not participate in foreign trade (no import or export) and does not handle products subject to a special tax regime, for example, liquor or tobacco.
- At the beginning of 2011, owns 2 plots of land, 1 building, machinery, office equipment, computers and 1 truck and leases 1 truck.
- Does not qualify for investment incentives or any benefits apart from those related to the age or size of the company.
- Has 60 employees—4 managers, 8 assistants and 48 workers. All are nationals, and 1 manager is also an owner. The company pays for additional medical insurance for employees (not mandated by any law) as an additional benefit. In addition, in some economies reimbursable business travel and client entertainment expenses are considered fringe benefits. When applicable, it is assumed that the company pays the fringe benefit tax on this expense or that the benefit becomes taxable income for the employee. The case study assumes no additional salary additions for meals, transportation, education or others. Therefore, even when such benefits are frequent, they are not added to or removed from the taxable gross salaries to arrive at the labor tax or contribution calculation.

- Has a turnover of 1,050 times income per capita.
- Makes a loss in the first year of operation.
- Has a gross margin (pretax) of 20% (that is, sales are 120% of the cost of goods sold).
- Distributes 50% of its net profits as dividends to the owners at the end of the second year.
- Sells one of its plots of land at a profit at the beginning of the second year.
- Has annual fuel costs for its trucks equal to twice income per capita.
- Is subject to a series of detailed assumptions on expenses and transactions to further standardize the case. All financial statement variables are proportional to 2005 income per capita. For example, the owner who is also a manager spends 10% of income per capita on traveling for the company (20% of this owner's expenses are purely private, 20% are for entertaining customers and 60% for business travel).

## Assumptions about the taxes and contributions

- All the taxes and contributions recorded are those paid in the second year of operation (calendar year 2011). A tax or contribution is considered distinct if it has a different name or is collected by a different agency. Taxes and contributions with the same name and agency, but charged at different rates depending on the business, are counted as the same tax or contribution.
- The number of times the company pays taxes and contributions in a year is the number of different taxes or contributions multiplied by the frequency of payment (or withholding) for each tax. The frequency of payment includes advance payments (or withholding) as well as regular payments (or withholding).

## Tax payments

The tax payments indicator reflects the total number of taxes and contributions paid, the method of payment, the

| TABLE 20.9  What do the paying taxes indicators measure? |
|---|
| **Tax payments for a manufacturing company in 2011** (number per year adjusted for electronic and joint filing and payment) |
| Total number of taxes and contributions paid, including consumption taxes (value added tax, sales tax or goods and service tax) |
| Method and frequency of filing and payment |
| **Time required to comply with 3 major taxes** (hours per year) |
| Collecting information and computing the tax payable |
| Completing tax return forms, filing with proper agencies |
| Arranging payment or withholding |
| Preparing separate mandatory tax accounting books, if required |
| **Total tax rate** (% of profit before all taxes) |
| Profit or corporate income tax |
| Social contributions and labor taxes paid by the employer |
| Property and property transfer taxes |
| Dividend, capital gains and financial transactions taxes |
| Waste collection, vehicle, road and other taxes |

frequency of payment, the frequency of filing and the number of agencies involved for this standardized case study company during the second year of operation (table 20.9). It includes taxes withheld by the company, such as sales tax, value added tax and employee-borne labor taxes. These taxes are traditionally collected by the company from the consumer or employee on behalf of the tax agencies. Although they do not affect the income statements of the company, they add to the administrative burden of complying with the tax system and so are included in the tax payments measure.

The number of payments takes into account electronic filing. Where full electronic filing and payment is allowed and it is used by the majority of medium-size businesses, the tax is counted as paid once a year even if filings and payments are more frequent. For payments made through third parties, such as tax on interest paid by a financial institution or fuel tax paid by a fuel distributor, only one payment is included even if payments are more frequent.

Where 2 or more taxes or contributions are filed for and paid jointly using the same form, each of these joint payments is counted once. For example, if mandatory health insurance contributions and mandatory pension contributions are filed for and paid together, only one of these contributions would be included in the number of payments.

## Time

Time is recorded in hours per year. The indicator measures the time taken to prepare, file and pay 3 major types of taxes and contributions: the corporate income tax, value added or sales tax, and labor taxes, including payroll taxes and social contributions. Preparation time includes the time to collect all information necessary to compute the tax payable and to calculate the amount payable. If separate accounting books must be kept for tax purposes—or separate calculations made—the time associated with these processes is included. This extra time is included only if the regular accounting work is not enough to fulfill the tax accounting requirements. Filing time includes the time to complete all necessary tax return forms and file the relevant returns at the tax authority. Payment time considers the hours needed to make the payment online or at the tax authorities. Where taxes and contributions are paid in person, the time includes delays while waiting.

## Total tax rate

The total tax rate measures the amount of taxes and mandatory contributions borne

by the business in the second year of operation, expressed as a share of commercial profit. Doing Business 2013 reports the total tax rate for calendar year 2011. The total amount of taxes borne is the sum of all the different taxes and contributions payable after accounting for allowable deductions and exemptions. The taxes withheld (such as personal income tax) or collected by the company and remitted to the tax authorities (such as value added tax, sales tax or goods and service tax) but not borne by the company are excluded. The taxes included can be divided into 5 categories: profit or corporate income tax, social contributions and labor taxes paid by the employer (in respect of which all mandatory contributions are included, even if paid to a private entity such as a requited pension fund), property taxes, turnover taxes and other taxes (such as municipal fees and vehicle and fuel taxes).

The total tax rate is designed to provide a comprehensive measure of the cost of all the taxes a business bears. It differs from the statutory tax rate, which merely provides the factor to be applied to the tax base. In computing the total tax rate, the actual tax payable is divided by commercial profit. Data for Norway illustrate (table 20.10).

Commercial profit is essentially net profit before all taxes borne. It differs from the conventional profit before tax, reported in financial statements. In computing profit before tax, many of the taxes borne by a

| TABLE 20.10  Computing the total tax rate for Norway | | | | | |
|---|---|---|---|---|---|
| Type of tax (tax base) | Statutory rate $r$ | Statutory tax base $b$ NKr | Actual tax payable $a = r \times b$ NKr | Commercial profit* $c$ NKr | Total tax rate $t = a/c$ |
| Corporate income tax (taxable income) | 28.0% | 20,612,719 | 5,771,561 | 23,651,183 | 24.4% |
| Social security contributions (taxable wages) | 14.1% | 26,684,645 | 3,762,535 | 23,651,183 | 15.9% |
| Fuel tax (fuel price) | NKr 4 per liter | 74,247 liters | 297,707 | 23,651,183 | 1.3% |
| Total | | | 9,831,803 | | 41.6% |

* Profit before all taxes borne.
Note: NKr is Norwegian kroner. Commercial profit is assumed to be 59.4 times income per capita.
Source: Doing Business database.

firm are deductible. In computing commercial profit, these taxes are not deductible. Commercial profit therefore presents a clear picture of the actual profit of a business before any of the taxes it bears in the course of the fiscal year.

Commercial profit is computed as sales minus cost of goods sold, minus gross salaries, minus administrative expenses, minus other expenses, minus provisions, plus capital gains (from the property sale) minus interest expense, plus interest income and minus commercial depreciation. To compute the commercial depreciation, a straight-line depreciation method is applied, with the following rates: 0% for the land, 5% for the building, 10% for the machinery, 33% for the computers, 20% for the office equipment, 20% for the truck and 10% for business development expenses. Commercial profit amounts to 59.4 times income per capita.

The methodology for calculating the total tax rate is broadly consistent with the Total Tax Contribution framework developed by PwC and the calculation within this framework for taxes borne. But while the work undertaken by PwC is usually based on data received from the largest companies in the economy, *Doing Business* focuses on a case study for a standardized medium-size company.

*The data details on paying taxes can be found for each economy at http://www .doingbusiness.org by selecting the economy in the drop-down list. This methodology was developed in Djankov, Ganser and others (2010).*

## TRADING ACROSS BORDERS

*Doing Business* measures the time and cost (excluding tariffs) associated with exporting and importing a standardized cargo of goods by sea transport. The time and cost necessary to complete every official procedure for exporting and importing the goods are recorded; however, the time and cost for sea transport are not included. All documents needed by the trader to export or import the goods

across the border are also recorded. For exporting goods, procedures range from packing the goods into the container at the warehouse to their departure from the port of exit. For importing goods, procedures range from the vessel's arrival at the port of entry to the cargo's delivery at the warehouse. For landlocked economies, these include procedures at the inland border post, since the port is located in the transit economy. Payment is made by letter of credit, and the time, cost and documents required for the issuance or advising of a letter of credit are taken into account (figure 20.15). The ranking on the ease of trading across borders is the simple average of the percentile rankings on its component indicators (figure 20.16).

Local freight forwarders, shipping lines, customs brokers, port officials and banks provide information on required documents and cost as well as the time to complete each procedure. To make the data comparable across economies, several assumptions about the business and the traded goods are used.

### Assumptions about the traded goods

The traded product travels in a dry-cargo, 20-foot, full container load. It weighs 10 tons and is valued at $20,000. The product:

• Is not hazardous nor does it include military items.

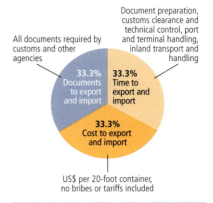

FIGURE 20.16  Trading across borders: exporting and importing by sea transport

Rankings are based on 3 indicators

• Does not require refrigeration or any other special environment.

• Does not require any special phytosanitary or environmental safety standards other than accepted international standards.

• Is one of the economy's leading export or import products.

### Assumptions about the business

The business:

• Has at least 60 employees.

• Is located in the economy's largest business city.

• Is a private, limited liability company. It does not operate in an export

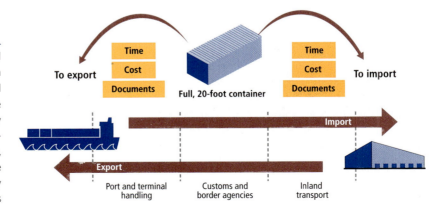

FIGURE 20.15  How much time, how many documents and what cost to export and import by sea transport?

| TABLE 20.11 What do the trading across borders indicators measure? |
| --- |
| **Documents required to export and import** (number) |
| Bank documents |
| Customs clearance documents |
| Port and terminal handling documents |
| Transport documents |
| **Time required to export and import** (days) |
| Obtaining, filling out and submitting all the documents |
| Inland transport and handling |
| Customs clearance and inspections |
| Port and terminal handling |
| Does not include sea transport time |
| **Cost required to export and import** (US$ per container) |
| All documentation |
| Inland transport and handling |
| Customs clearance and inspections |
| Port and terminal handling |
| Official costs only, no bribes |

processing zone or an industrial estate with special export or import privileges.

• Is 100% domestically owned.

• Exports more than 10% of its sales.

## Documents

All documents required per shipment to export and import the goods are recorded (table 20.11). It is assumed that a new contract is drafted per shipment and that the contract has already been agreed upon and executed by both parties. Documents required for clearance by relevant agencies—including government ministries, customs, port authorities and other control agencies—are taken into account. Since payment is by letter of credit, all documents required by banks for the issuance or securing of a letter of credit are also taken into account. Documents that are requested at the time of clearance but that are valid for a year or longer and do not require renewal per shipment (for example, an annual tax clearance certificate) are not included.

## Time

The time for exporting and importing is recorded in calendar days. The time calculation for a procedure starts from the moment it is initiated and runs until

it is completed. If a procedure can be accelerated for an additional cost and is available to all trading companies, the fastest legal procedure is chosen. Fast-track procedures applying only to firms located in an export processing zone, or only to certain accredited firms under authorized economic operator programs, are not taken into account because they are not available to all trading companies. Sea transport time is not included. It is assumed that neither the exporter nor the importer wastes time and that each commits to completing each remaining procedure without delay. Procedures that can be completed in parallel are measured as simultaneous. But it is assumed that document preparation, inland transport, customs and other clearance, and port and terminal handling require a minimum time of 1 day each and cannot take place simultaneously. The waiting time between procedures—for example, during unloading of the cargo—is included in the measure.

## Cost

Cost measures the fees levied on a 20-foot container in U.S. dollars. All the fees associated with completing the procedures to export or import the goods are taken into account. These include costs for documents, administrative fees for customs clearance and inspections, customs broker fees, port-related charges and inland transport costs. The cost does not include customs tariffs and duties or costs related to sea transport. Only official costs are recorded.

*The data details on trading across borders can be found for each economy at http://www .doingbusiness.org by selecting the economy in the drop-down list. This methodology was developed in Djankov, Freund and Pham (2010) and is adopted here with minor changes.*

## ENFORCING CONTRACTS

Indicators on enforcing contracts measure the efficiency of the judicial system in resolving a commercial dispute. The data are built by following the step-by-step

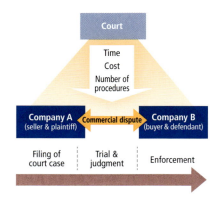

FIGURE 20.17 What are the time, cost and number of procedures to resolve a commercial dispute through the courts?

evolution of a commercial sale dispute before local courts. The data are collected through study of the codes of civil procedure and other court regulations as well as surveys completed by local litigation lawyers and by judges (figure 20.17). The ranking on the ease of enforcing contracts is the simple average of the percentile rankings on its component indicators (figure 20.18).

The name of the relevant court in each economy—the court in the largest business city with jurisdiction over commercial cases worth 200% of income per capita—is published at http://www .doingbusiness.org/ExploreTopics/ EnforcingContracts/.

FIGURE 20.18 Enforcing contracts: resolving a commercial dispute through the courts

Rankings are based on 3 indicators

## Assumptions about the case

- The value of the claim equals 200% of the economy's income per capita.

- The dispute concerns a lawful transaction between 2 businesses (Seller and Buyer), located in the economy's largest business city. Seller sells goods worth 200% of the economy's income per capita to Buyer. After Seller delivers the goods to Buyer, Buyer refuses to pay for the goods on the grounds that the delivered goods were not of adequate quality.

- Seller (the plaintiff) sues Buyer (the defendant) to recover the amount under the sales agreement (that is, 200% of the economy's income per capita). Buyer opposes Seller's claim, saying that the quality of the goods is not adequate. The claim is disputed on the merits. The court cannot decide the case on the basis of documentary evidence or legal title alone.

- A court in the economy's largest business city with jurisdiction over commercial cases worth 200% of income per capita decides the dispute.

- Seller attaches Buyer's movable assets (for example, office equipment and vehicles) before obtaining a judgment because Seller fears that Buyer may become insolvent.

- An expert opinion is given on the quality of the delivered goods. If it is standard practice in the economy for each party to call its own expert witness, the parties each call one expert witness. If it is standard practice for the judge to appoint an independent expert, the judge does so. In this case the judge does not allow opposing expert testimony.

- The judgment is 100% in favor of Seller: the judge decides that the goods are of adequate quality and that Buyer must pay the agreed price.

- Buyer does not appeal the judgment. Seller decides to start enforcing the judgment as soon as the time allocated by law for appeal expires.

- Seller takes all required steps for prompt enforcement of the judgment. The money is successfully collected through a public sale of Buyer's movable assets (for example, office equipment and vehicles).

## Procedures

The list of procedural steps compiled for each economy traces the chronology of a commercial dispute before the relevant court. A procedure is defined as any interaction, required by law or commonly used in practice, between the parties or between them and the judge or court officer. Other procedural steps, internal to the court or between the parties and their counsel, may be counted as well. Procedural steps include steps to file and serve the case, steps to assign the case to a judge, steps for trial and judgment and steps necessary to enforce the judgment (table 20.12).

The survey allows respondents to record procedures that exist in civil law but not common law jurisdictions and vice versa. For example, in civil law jurisdictions the judge can appoint an independent expert, while in common law jurisdictions each party submits a list of expert witnesses to the court. To indicate overall efficiency, 1 procedure is subtracted from the total number for economies that have specialized commercial courts, and 1 procedure for economies that allow electronic filing of the initial complaint in court cases. Some procedural steps that are part of others are not counted in the total number of procedures.

## Time

Time is recorded in calendar days, counted from the moment the plaintiff decides to file the lawsuit in court until payment. This includes both the days when actions take place and the waiting periods between. The average duration of different stages of dispute resolution is recorded: the completion of service of process (time to file and serve the case), the issuance of judgment (time for the trial and obtaining the judgment) and the moment of payment (time for enforcement of the judgment).

## Cost

Cost is recorded as a percentage of the claim, assumed to be equivalent to 200% of income per capita. No bribes are recorded. Three types of costs are recorded: court costs, enforcement costs and average attorney fees.

Court costs include all court costs that Seller (plaintiff) must advance to the court, regardless of the final cost to Seller. Enforcement costs are all costs that Seller (plaintiff) must advance to enforce the judgment through a public sale of Buyer's movable assets, regardless of the final cost to Seller. Average attorney fees are the fees that Seller (plaintiff) must advance to a local attorney to represent Seller in the standardized case.

*The data details on enforcing contracts can be found for each economy at http://www .doingbusiness.org by selecting the economy in the drop-down list. This methodology was developed in Djankov and others (2003) and is adopted here with minor changes.*

## RESOLVING INSOLVENCY

*Doing Business* studies the time, cost and outcome of insolvency proceedings

| TABLE 20.12  What do the enforcing contracts indicators measure? |
| --- |
| **Procedures to enforce a contract through the courts** (number) |
| Any interaction between the parties in a commercial dispute, or between them and the judge or court officer |
| Steps to file and serve the case |
| Steps for trial and judgment |
| Steps to enforce the judgment |
| **Time required to complete procedures** (calendar days) |
| Time to file and serve the case |
| Time for trial and obtaining judgment |
| Time to enforce the judgment |
| **Cost required to complete procedures** (% of claim) |
| No bribes |
| Average attorney fees |
| Court costs |
| Enforcement costs |

involving domestic entities. *The name of this indicator set was changed from closing a business to resolving insolvency to more accurately reflect the content of the indicators. The indicators did not change in content or scope.* The data are derived from questionnaire responses by local insolvency practitioners and verified through a study of laws and regulations as well as public information on bankruptcy systems (figure 20.19). The ranking on the ease of resolving insolvency is based on the recovery rate (figure 20.20).

To make the data comparable across economies, several assumptions about the business and the case are used.

## Assumptions about the business

The business:

- Is a limited liability company.
- Operates in the economy's largest business city.
- Is 100% domestically owned, with the founder, who is also the chairman of the supervisory board, owning 51% (no other shareholder holds more than 5% of shares).
- Has downtown real estate, where it runs a hotel, as its major asset. The hotel is valued at 100 times income per capita or $200,000, whichever is larger.
- Has a professional general manager.

---

**FIGURE 20.19** What are the time, cost and outcome of the insolvency proceedings against a local company?

**FIGURE 20.20** Resolving insolvency: time, cost and outcome of the insolvency proceedings against a local company

Rankings are based on 1 indicator

Recovery rate is a function of time, cost and other factors such as lending rate and the likelihood of the company continuing to operate

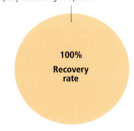

100% Recovery rate

*Note:* Time and cost do not count separately for the rankings.

---

- Has 201 employees and 50 suppliers, each of which is owed money for the last delivery.
- Has a 10-year loan agreement with a domestic bank secured by a universal business charge (for example, a floating charge) in economies where such collateral is recognized or by the hotel property. If the laws of the economy do not specifically provide for a universal business charge but contracts commonly use some other provision to that effect, this provision is specified in the loan agreement.
- Has observed the payment schedule and all other conditions of the loan up to now.
- Has a mortgage, with the value of the mortgage principal being exactly equal to the market value of the hotel.

## Assumptions about the case

The business is experiencing liquidity problems. The company's loss in 2011 reduced its net worth to a negative figure. It is January 1, 2012. There is no cash to pay the bank interest or principal in full, due the next day, January 2. The business will therefore default on its loan. Management believes that losses will be incurred in 2012 and 2013 as well.

The amount outstanding under the loan agreement is exactly equal to the market value of the hotel business and represents 74% of the company's total debt. The other 26% of its debt is held by unsecured creditors (suppliers, employees, tax authorities).

The company has too many creditors to negotiate an informal out-of-court workout. The following options are available: a judicial procedure aimed at the rehabilitation or reorganization of the company to permit its continued operation; a judicial procedure aimed at the liquidation or winding-up of the company; or a debt enforcement or foreclosure procedure against the company, enforced either in court (or through another government authority) or out of court (for example, by appointing a receiver).

## Assumptions about the parties

The bank wants to recover as much as possible of its loan, as quickly and cheaply as possible. The unsecured creditors will do everything permitted under the applicable laws to avoid a piecemeal sale of the assets. The majority shareholder wants to keep the company operating and under its control. Management wants to keep the company operating and preserve its employees' jobs. All the parties are local entities or citizens; no foreign parties are involved.

## Time

Time for creditors to recover their credit is recorded in calendar years (table 20.13). The period of time measured by *Doing Business* is from the company's default until the payment of some or all of the money owed to the bank. Potential delay tactics by the parties, such as the filing of dilatory appeals or requests for extension, are taken into consideration.

## Cost

The cost of the proceedings is recorded as a percentage of the value of the debtor's estate. The cost is calculated on the basis of questionnaire responses and includes court fees and government levies; fees of insolvency administrators, auctioneers, assessors and lawyers; and all other fees and costs.

| TABLE 20.13 What do the resolving insolvency indicators measure? |
|---|
| **Time required to recover debt (years)** |
| Measured in calendar years |
| Appeals and requests for extension are included |
| **Cost required to recover debt (% of debtor's estate)** |
| Measured as percentage of estate value |
| Court fees |
| Fees of insolvency administrators |
| Lawyers' fees |
| Assessors' and auctioneers' fees |
| Other related fees |
| **Recovery rate for creditors (cents on the dollar)** |
| Measures the cents on the dollar recovered by creditors |
| Present value of debt recovered |
| Official costs of the insolvency proceedings are deducted |
| Depreciation of furniture is taken into account |
| Outcome for the business (survival or not) affects the maximum value that can be recovered |

## Outcome

Recovery by creditors depends on whether the hotel business emerges from the proceedings as a going concern or the company's assets are sold piecemeal. If the business keeps operating, no value is lost and the bank can satisfy its claim in full, or recover 100 cents on the dollar. If the assets are sold piecemeal, the maximum amount that can be recovered will not exceed 70% of the bank's claim, which translates into 70 cents on the dollar.

## Recovery rate

The recovery rate is recorded as cents on the dollar recouped by creditors through reorganization, liquidation or debt enforcement (foreclosure) proceedings. The calculation takes into account the outcome: whether the business emerges from the proceedings as a going concern or the assets are sold piecemeal. Then the costs of the proceedings are deducted (1 cent for each percentage point of the value of the debtor's estate). Finally, the value lost as a result of the time the money remains tied up in insolvency proceedings is taken into account, including the loss of value due to depreciation of the hotel furniture. Consistent with international accounting practice, the annual depreciation rate for furniture is taken to be 20%. The furniture is assumed to account for a quarter of the total value of assets. The recovery rate is the present value of the remaining proceeds, based on end-2011 lending rates from the International Monetary Fund's *International Financial Statistics,* supplemented with data from central banks and the Economist Intelligence Unit.

## No practice

If an economy had zero cases a year over the past 5 years involving a judicial reorganization, judicial liquidation or debt enforcement procedure (foreclosure), the economy receives a "no practice" ranking. This means that creditors are unlikely to recover their money through a formal legal process (in or out of court). The recovery rate for "no practice" economies is zero.

*This methodology was developed in Djankov, Hart and others (2008) and is adopted here with minor changes.*

## EMPLOYING WORKERS

*Doing Business* measures flexibility in the regulation of employment, specifically as it affects the hiring and redundancy of workers and the rigidity of working hours. Over the period from 2007 to 2011 improvements were made to align the methodology for the employing workers indicators with the letter and spirit of the ILO conventions. Only 4 of the 188 ILO conventions cover areas measured by *Doing Business*: employee termination, weekend work, holiday with pay and night work. The *Doing Business* methodology is fully consistent with these 4 conventions. The ILO conventions covering areas related to the employing workers indicators do not include the ILO core labor standards—8 conventions covering the right to collective bargaining, the elimination of forced labor, the abolition of child labor and equitable treatment in employment practices.

Between 2009 and 2011 the World Bank Group worked with a consultative group—including labor lawyers, employer and employee representatives, and experts from the ILO, the OECD, civil society and the private sector—to review the employing workers methodology and explore future areas of research.[7] A full report with the conclusions of the consultative group is available at http://www.doingbusiness .org/methodology/employing-workers.

This year *Doing Business* continued research initiated last year, collecting additional data on regulations covering worker protection. The data will serve as a basis for developing a joint analysis of worker protection by the World Bank Group and the ILO and for developing new areas of research in the area of worker protection measures.

*Doing Business 2013* does not present rankings of economies on the employing workers indicators or include the topic in the aggregate ranking on the ease of doing business. The report does present the data on the employing workers indicators in an annex. Detailed data collected on labor regulations are available on the *Doing Business* website (http://www.doingbusiness.org).

The data on employing workers are based on a detailed survey of employment regulations that is completed by local lawyers and public officials. Employment laws and regulations as well as secondary sources are reviewed to ensure accuracy. To make the data comparable across economies, several assumptions about the worker and the business are used.

### Assumptions about the worker

The worker:

- Earns a salary plus benefits equal to the economy's average wage during the entire period of his employment.
- Has a pay period that is the most common for workers in the economy.
- Is a lawful citizen who belongs to the same race and religion as the majority of the economy's population.
- Resides in the economy's largest business city.

- Is not a member of a labor union, unless membership is mandatory.

## Assumptions about the business

The business:

- Is a limited liability company.
- Operates in the economy's largest business city.
- Is 100% domestically owned.
- Operates in the manufacturing sector.
- Has 60 employees.
- Is subject to collective bargaining agreements in economies where such agreements cover more than half the manufacturing sector and apply even to firms not party to them.
- Abides by every law and regulation but does not grant workers more benefits than mandated by law, regulation or (if applicable) collective bargaining agreement.

## Rigidity of employment index

The rigidity of employment index is the average of 3 subindices: the difficulty of hiring index, rigidity of hours index and difficulty of redundancy index. Data and scores for a particular country (country X) are provided as an example (table 20.14).

All the subindices have several components. And all take values between 0 and 100, with higher values indicating more rigid regulation.

The difficulty of hiring index measures (i) whether fixed-term contracts are prohibited for permanent tasks; (ii) the maximum cumulative duration of fixed-term contracts; and (iii) the ratio of the minimum wage for a trainee or first-time employee to the average value added per worker.[8] An economy is assigned a score of 1 if fixed-term contracts are prohibited for permanent tasks and a score of 0 if they can be used for any task. A score of 1 is assigned if the maximum cumulative duration of fixed-term contracts is less than 3 years; 0.5 if it is 3 years or more but less than 5 years; and 0 if fixed-term contracts can last 5 years or more. Finally, a score of 1 is assigned if the ratio of the minimum wage to the average value

| TABLE 20.14 What do the employing workers indicators measure? | | |
|---|---|---|
| | Data for country X | Score for country X |
| **Rigidity of employment index** (0–100) | | 45.33 |
| Simple average of the difficulty of hiring, rigidity of hours and difficulty of redundancy indices | | 56 + 10 + 70 |
| *Difficulty of hiring index (0–100)* | | 56 |
| Fixed-term contracts prohibited for permanent tasks? | Yes | 1 |
| Maximum duration of fixed-term contracts | 6 years | 0 |
| Ratio of minimum wage for trainee or first-time employee to value added per worker | 0.61 | 0.67 |
| *Rigidity of hours index (0–100)* | | 10 |
| Restrictions on night work and weekend work? | No | 0 |
| Allowed maximum length of the workweek in days and hours, including overtime | 5.5 days | 0 |
| Fifty-hour workweeks permitted for 2 months due to an increase in production? | Yes | 0 |
| Paid annual vacation days | 22 days | 0.5 |
| *Difficulty of redundancy index (0–100)* | | 70 |
| Redundancy allowed as grounds for termination? | Yes | 0 |
| Notification required for termination of a redundant worker or group of workers? | Yes | 2 |
| Approval required for termination of a redundant worker or group of workers? | Yes | 3 |
| Employer obligated to reassign or retrain and to follow priority rules for redundancy and reemployment? | Yes | 2 |
| **Redundancy cost** (weeks of salary) | | 23.9 |
| Notice requirements, severance payments and penalties due when terminating a redundant worker, expressed in weeks of salary | 8.66 weeks +15.22 weeks | 23.9 |

*Source: Doing Business database.*

added per worker is 0.75 or more; 0.67 for a ratio of 0.50 or more but less than 0.75; 0.33 for a ratio of 0.25 or more but less than 0.50; and 0 for a ratio of less than 0.25. A score of 0 is also assigned if the minimum wage is set by a collective bargaining agreement that applies to less than half the manufacturing sector or does not apply to firms not party to it, or if the minimum wage is set by law but does not apply to workers who are in their apprentice period. A ratio of 0.251 (and therefore a score of 0.33) is automatically assigned in 4 cases: if there is no minimum wage; if the law provides a regulatory mechanism for the minimum wage that is not enforced in practice; if there is no minimum wage set by law but there is a wage amount that is customarily used as a minimum; or if there is no minimum wage set by law in the private sector but there is one in the public sector.

In country X, for example, fixed-term contracts are prohibited for permanent tasks (a score of 1), and they can be used for a maximum of 6 years (a score of 0). The ratio of the mandated minimum wage to the value added per worker is 0.61 (a score of 0.67). Averaging the 3 values and scaling the index to 100 gives country X a score of 56.

The rigidity of hours index has 5 components: (i) whether there are restrictions on night work; (ii) whether there are restrictions on weekly holiday work; (iii) whether the workweek can consist of 5.5 days or is more than 6 days; (iv) whether the workweek can extend to 50 hours or more (including overtime) for 2 months a year to respond to a seasonal increase in production; and (v) whether the average paid annual leave for a worker with 1 year of tenure, a worker with 5 years and a worker with 10 years is more than 26 working days or fewer than 15 working days. For questions (i) and (ii), if restrictions other than premiums apply, a score of 1 is given. If the only restriction is a premium for night work or weekly holiday work, a score of 0, 0.33, 0.66 or 1 is given, depending on the quartile in which the economy's premium falls. If there are no restrictions, the economy receives a score of 0. For question (iii) a score of 1 is assigned if the legally permitted workweek is less than 5.5 days or more than 6 days; otherwise a score of 0 is assigned. For question (iv), if the answer is no, a score of 1 is assigned; otherwise a score of 0 is assigned. For question (v) a score of 0 is assigned if the average paid annual leave is between 15 and 21 working days, a score of 0.5 if it is more than 21 but less than 26 working days and a score of 1 if it is less than 15 or more than 26 working days.

For example, country X does not impose any restrictions either on night work (a score of 0) or on weekly holiday work (a score of 0), allows 5.5-day workweeks (a score of 0), permits 50-hour workweeks for 2 months (a score of 0) and requires average paid annual leave of 22 working days (a score of 0.5). Averaging the scores and scaling the result to 100 gives a final index of 10 for country X.

The difficulty of redundancy index has 8 components: (i) whether redundancy is disallowed as a basis for terminating workers; (ii) whether the employer needs to notify a third party (such as a government agency) to terminate 1 redundant worker; (iii) whether the employer needs to notify a third party to terminate a group of 9 redundant workers; (iv) whether the employer needs approval from a third party to terminate 1 redundant worker; (v) whether the employer needs approval from a third party to terminate a group of 9 redundant workers; (vi) whether the law requires the employer to reassign or retrain a worker before making the worker redundant; (vii) whether priority rules apply for redundancies; and (viii) whether priority rules apply for reemployment. For question (i) an answer of yes for workers of any income level gives a score of 10 and means that the rest of

the questions do not apply. An answer of yes to question (iv) gives a score of 2. For every other question, if the answer is yes, a score of 1 is assigned; otherwise a score of 0 is given. Questions (i) and (iv), as the most restrictive regulations, have greater weight in the construction of the index.

In country X, for example, redundancy is allowed as grounds for termination (a score of 0). An employer has to notify a third party to terminate a single redundant worker (a score of 1) as well as to terminate a group of 9 redundant workers (a score of 1), and the approval of a third party is also required in both these cases (a score of 3). The law does not mandate any retraining or alternative placement before termination (a score of 0). There are priority rules for termination (a score of 1) and reemployment (a score of 1). Adding the scores and scaling to 100 gives a final index of 70.

## Redundancy cost

The redundancy cost indicator measures the cost of advance notice requirements, severance payments and penalties due when terminating a redundant worker, expressed in weeks of salary. The average value of notice requirements and severance payments applicable to a worker with 1 year of tenure, a worker with 5 years and a worker with 10 years is used to assign the score. If the redundancy cost adds up to 8 or fewer weeks of salary and the workers can benefit from unemployment protection, a score of 0 is assigned, but the actual number of weeks is published. If the redundancy cost adds up to 8 or fewer weeks of salary and the workers cannot benefit from any type of unemployment protection, a score of 8.1 is assigned, although the actual number of weeks is published. If the cost adds up to more than 8 weeks of salary, the score is the number of weeks. One month is recorded as 4 and 1/3 weeks.

In country X, for example, an employer is required to give an average of 2 months' notice (8.66 weeks) before a redundancy termination, and the average severance pay for a worker with 1 year of service,

a worker with 5 years and a worker with 10 years equals 3.5 months of wages (15.22 weeks). No penalty is levied and the workers cannot benefit from any type of unemployment protection. Altogether, the employer pays the equivalent of 23.9 weeks of salary to dismiss a worker.

*The data details on employing workers can be found for each economy at http://www .doingbusiness.org. The* Doing Business *website provides historical data sets to allow comparison of data across years. The employing workers methodology was developed by Botero and others (2004).* Doing Business 2013 *does not present rankings of economies on the employing workers indicators.*

## NOTES

1.  The data for paying taxes refer to January–December 2011.
2.  This correction rate reflects changes that exceed 5% up or down.
3.  Following the inclusion of getting electricity indicators in the ease of doing business index in *Doing Business 2012,* additional procedures, time and cost related to obtaining an electricity connection in the preconstruction stage were removed from the dealing with construction permits indicators this year to avoid double counting.
4.  This question is usually regulated by stock exchange or securities laws. Points are awarded only to economies with more than 10 listed firms in their most important stock exchange.
5.  When evaluating the regime of liability for company directors for a prejudicial related-party transaction, *Doing Business* assumes that the transaction was duly disclosed and approved. *Doing Business* does not measure director liability in the event of fraud.
6.  *PwC* refers to the network of member firms of PricewaterhouseCoopers International Limited (PwCIL), or, as the context requires, individual member firms of the PwC network. Each member firm is a separate legal entity and does not act as agent of PwCIL or any other member firm. PwCIL does not provide any services to clients. PwCIL is not responsible or liable for the acts or omissions of any of its member firms nor can it control the exercise of their professional judgment or bind them in any way. No member firm is responsible or liable for the acts

or omissions of any other member firm
nor can it control the exercise of another
member firm's professional judgment or
bind another member firm or PwCIL in
any way.

7. For the terms of reference and com-
position of the consultative group, see
World Bank, "Doing Business Employing
Workers Indicator Consultative Group,"
http://www.doingbusiness.org.

8. The average value added per worker is the
ratio of an economy's GNI per capita to
the working-age population as a percentage of the total population.

# Ease of doing business and distance to frontier

This year's report presents results for 2 aggregate measures: the aggregate ranking on the ease of doing business and the distance to frontier measure. The ease of doing business ranking compares economies with one another, while the distance to frontier measure benchmarks economies to the frontier in regulatory practice, measuring the absolute distance to the best performance on each indicator. Both measures can be used for comparisons over time. When compared across years, the distance to frontier measure shows how much the regulatory environment for local entrepreneurs in each economy has changed over time in absolute terms, while the ease of doing business ranking can show only relative change.

## EASE OF DOING BUSINESS

The ease of doing business index ranks economies from 1 to 185. For each economy the ranking is calculated as the simple average of the percentile rankings on each of the 10 topics included in the index in *Doing Business 2013*: starting a business, dealing with construction permits, getting electricity, registering property, getting credit, protecting investors, paying taxes, trading across borders, enforcing contracts and resolving insolvency. The employing workers indicators are not included in this year's aggregate ease of doing business ranking. In addition to this year's ranking, *Doing Business* presents a comparable ranking for the previous year, adjusted for any changes in methodology as well as additions of economies or topics.[1]

## Construction of the ease of doing business index

Here is one example of how the ease of doing business index is constructed. In Finland it takes 3 procedures, 14 days and 4% of property value in fees to register a property. On these 3 indicators Finland ranks in the 6th, 16th and 39th percentiles. So on average Finland ranks in the 20th percentile on the ease of registering property. It ranks in the 30th percentile on starting a business, 28th percentile on getting credit, 24th percentile on paying taxes, 13th percentile on enforcing contracts, 5th percentile on trading across borders and so on. Higher rankings indicate simpler regulation and stronger protection of property rights. The simple average of Finland's percentile rankings on all topics is 21st. When all economies are ordered by their average percentile rankings, Finland stands at 11 in the aggregate ranking on the ease of doing business.

More complex aggregation methods— such as principal components and unobserved components—yield a ranking nearly identical to the simple average used by *Doing Business*.[2] Thus *Doing Business* uses the simplest method: weighting all topics equally and, within each topic, giving equal weight to each of the topic components.[3]

If an economy has no laws or regulations covering a specific area—for example, insolvency—it receives a "no practice" mark. Similarly, an economy receives a "no practice" or "not possible" mark if regulation exists but is never used in practice or if a competing regulation prohibits such practice. Either way, a "no practice" mark

| TABLE 21.1 Correlations between economy rankings on *Doing Business* topics | | | | | | | | | |
|---|---|---|---|---|---|---|---|---|---|
| | Dealing with construction permits | Registering property | Getting credit | Protecting investors | Paying taxes | Trading across borders | Enforcing contracts | Resolving insolvency | Getting electricity |
| Starting a business | 0.34 | 0.30 | 0.44 | 0.60 | 0.40 | 0.40 | 0.40 | 0.44 | 0.28 |
| Dealing with construction permits | | 0.24 | 0.19 | 0.21 | 0.41 | 0.49 | 0.23 | 0.36 | 0.49 |
| Registering property | | | 0.37 | 0.33 | 0.37 | 0.29 | 0.50 | 0.38 | 0.26 |
| Getting credit | | | | 0.49 | 0.26 | 0.38 | 0.43 | 0.49 | 0.22 |
| Protecting investors | | | | | 0.39 | 0.36 | 0.30 | 0.41 | 0.22 |
| Paying taxes | | | | | | 0.50 | 0.33 | 0.42 | 0.46 |
| Trading across borders | | | | | | | 0.36 | 0.55 | 0.58 |
| Enforcing contracts | | | | | | | | 0.46 | 0.24 |
| Resolving insolvency | | | | | | | | | 0.32 |

Source: *Doing Business* database.

puts the economy at the bottom of the ranking on the relevant indicator.

The ease of doing business index is limited in scope. It does not account for an economy's proximity to large markets, the quality of its infrastructure services (other than services related to trading across borders and getting electricity), the strength of its financial system, the security of property from theft and looting, macroeconomic conditions or the strength of underlying institutions.

## Variability of economies' rankings across topics

Each indicator set measures a different aspect of the business regulatory environment. The rankings of an economy can vary, sometimes significantly, across indicator sets. The average correlation coefficient between the 10 indicator sets included in the aggregate ranking is 0.37, and the coefficients between any 2 sets of indicators range from 0.19 (between dealing with construction permits and getting credit) to 0.60 (between starting a business and protecting investors). These correlations suggest that economies rarely score universally well or universally badly on the indicators (table 21.1).

Consider the example of Canada. It stands at 17 in the aggregate ranking on the ease of doing business. Its ranking is 3 on starting a business, and 4 on both resolving insolvency and protecting investors. But its ranking is only 62 on enforcing contracts, 69 on dealing with construction permits and 152 on getting electricity.

Figure 1.2 in the executive summary illustrates the degree of variability in each economy's performance across the different areas of business regulation covered by *Doing Business*. The figure draws attention to economies with a particularly uneven performance by showing the distance between the average of the highest 3 topic rankings and the average of the lowest 3 for each of 185 economies across the 10 topics included in this year's aggregate ranking. While a relatively small distance between these 2 averages suggests a broadly consistent approach across the areas of business regulation measured by *Doing Business*, a relatively large distance suggests a more uneven approach, with greater room for improvement in some areas than in others.

Variation in performance across the indicator sets is not at all unusual. It reflects differences in the degree of priority that government authorities give to particular

areas of business regulation reform and the ability of different government agencies to deliver tangible results in their area of responsibility.

## Economies that improved the most across 3 or more *Doing Business* topics in 2011/12

*Doing Business 2013* uses a simple method to calculate which economies improved the most in the ease of doing business. First, it selects the economies that in 2011/12 implemented regulatory reforms making it easier to do business in 3 or more of the 10 topics included in this year's ease of doing business ranking.[4] Twenty-three economies meet this criterion: Benin, Burundi, Costa Rica, the Czech Republic, Georgia, Greece, Guinea, Kazakhstan, Korea, Lao PDR, Liberia, Mongolia, the Netherlands, Panama, Poland, Portugal, Serbia, the Slovak Republic, Slovenia, Sri Lanka, Ukraine, the United Arab Emirates and Uzbekistan. Second, *Doing Business* ranks these economies on the increase in their ranking on the ease of doing business from the previous year using comparable rankings.

Selecting the economies that implemented regulatory reforms in at least 3 topics and improved the most in the aggregate ranking is intended to highlight economies with ongoing, broad-based reform programs.

## DISTANCE TO FRONTIER MEASURE

A drawback of the ease of doing business ranking is that it can measure the regulatory performance of economies only relative to the performance of others. It does not provide information on how the absolute quality of the regulatory environment is improving over time. Nor does it provide information on how large the gaps are between economies at a single point in time.

The distance to frontier measure is designed to address both shortcomings, complementing the ease of doing business ranking. This measure illustrates the distance of an economy to the "frontier," and the change in the measure over time shows the extent to which the economy has closed this gap. The frontier is a score derived from the most efficient practice or highest score achieved on each of the component indicators in 9 *Doing Business* indicator sets (excluding the employing workers and getting electricity indicators) by any economy since 2005. In starting a business, for example, New Zealand has achieved the highest performance on the time (1 day), Canada and New Zealand on the number of procedures required (1), Slovenia on the cost (0% of income per capita) and Australia and 90 other economies on the paid-in minimum capital requirement (0% of income per capita) (table 21.2).

Calculating the distance to frontier for each economy involves 2 main steps. First, individual indicator scores are normalized to a common unit: except for the total tax rate, each of the 28 component indicators $y$ is rescaled to (max − $y$)/(max − min), with the minimum value (min) representing the frontier—the highest performance on that indicator across all economies since 2005. For the total tax rate, consistent with the calculation of the rankings, the frontier is defined as the total tax rate corresponding to the 15th percentile based on the overall distribution of total tax rates for all years. Second, for each economy the scores obtained for individual indicators are aggregated through simple averaging into one distance to frontier score. An economy's distance to frontier is indicated on a scale from 0 to 100, where 0 represents the lowest performance and 100 the frontier.[5]

The difference between an economy's distance to frontier score in 2005 and its score in 2012 illustrates the extent to which the economy has closed the gap to the frontier over time. And in any given year the score measures how far an economy is from the highest performance at that time.

The maximum (max) and minimum (min) observed values are computed for the 174 economies included in the *Doing Business* sample since 2005 and for all years (from 2005 to 2012). The year 2005 was chosen as the baseline for the economy sample because it was the first year in which data were available for the majority of economies (a total of 174) and for all 9 indicator sets included in the measure. To mitigate the effects of extreme outliers in the distributions of the rescaled data (very few economies need 694 days to complete the procedures to start a business, but many need 9 days), the maximum (max) is defined as the 95th percentile of the pooled data for all economies and all years for each indicator. The exceptions are the getting credit, protecting investors and resolving insolvency indicators, whose construction precludes outliers.

Take Ghana, which has a score of 67 on the distance to frontier measure for 2012. This score indicates that the economy is 33 percentage points away from the frontier constructed from the best performances across all economies and all years. Ghana was further from the frontier in 2005, with a score of 54. The difference between the scores shows an improvement over time.

The distance to frontier measure can also be used for comparisons across

| TABLE 21.2  What is the frontier in regulatory practice? ||
|---|---|
| **Topic and indicator** | **Frontier** |
| **Starting a business** | |
| Procedures (number) | 1 |
| Time (days) | 1 |
| Cost (% of income per capita) | 0 |
| Minimum capital (% of income per capita) | 0 |
| **Dealing with construction permits** | |
| Procedures (number) | 6 |
| Time (days) | 25 |
| Cost (% of income per capita) | 0.2 |
| **Registering property** | |
| Procedures (number) | 1 |
| Time (days) | 1 |
| Cost (% of property value) | 0 |
| **Getting credit** | |
| Strength of legal rights index (0–10) | 10 |
| Depth of credit information index (0–6) | 6 |
| **Protecting investors** | |
| Extent of disclosure index (0–10) | 10 |
| Extent of director liability index (0–10) | 9 |
| Ease of shareholder suits index (0–10) | 10 |
| **Paying taxes** | |
| Payments (number per year) | 3 |
| Time (hours per year) | 0[a] |
| Total tax rate (% of profit) | 27.5[b] |
| **Trading across borders** | |
| Documents to export (number) | 2 |
| Time to export (days) | 5 |
| Cost to export (US$ per container) | 390 |
| Documents to import (number) | 2 |
| Time to import (days) | 4 |
| Cost to import (US$ per container) | 317 |
| **Enforcing contracts** | |
| Procedures (number) | 21 |
| Time (days) | 120 |
| Cost (% of claim) | 0.1 |
| **Resolving insolvency** | |
| Recovery rate (cents on the dollar) | 94.4 |

a. The time of 0 hours refers to Maldives, where the 3 major taxes covered by the paying taxes indicators did not exist until 2011.

b. The frontier total tax rate differs from the threshold set for the indicator this year. See the data notes for more details.

*Source: Doing Business* database.

economies in the same year, complementing the ease of doing business ranking. For example, Ghana stands at 64 this year in the ease of doing business ranking, while Peru, which is 29 percentage points from the frontier, stands at 43.

## NOTES

1. In case of revisions to the methodology or corrections to the underlying data, the data are back-calculated to provide a comparable time series since the year the relevant economy or topic was first included in the data set. The time series is available on the *Doing Business* website (http://www.doingbusiness.org). Six topics and more than 50 economies have been added since the inception of the project. Earlier rankings on the ease of doing business are therefore not comparable.

2. See Djankov and others (2005). Principal components and unobserved components methods yield a ranking nearly identical to that from the simple average method because both these methods assign roughly equal weights to the topics, since the pairwise correlations among indicators do not differ much. An alternative to the simple average method is to give different weights to the topics, depending on which are considered of more or less importance in the context of a specific economy.

3. A technical note on the different aggregation and weighting methods is available on the *Doing Business* website (http://www.doingbusiness.org).

4. *Doing Business* reforms making it more difficult to do business are subtracted from the total number of those making it easier to do business.

5. This represents a change from last year's report, where 100 represented the lowest performance and 0 the frontier.

# Summaries of *Doing Business* reforms in 2011/12

*Doing Business* reforms affecting all sets of indicators included in this year's report, implemented from June 2011 to June 2012.

- ✔ *Doing Business* reform making it easier to do business
- ✗ *Doing Business* reform making it more difficult to do business

## ALBANIA

**✔ Starting a business**

Albania made starting a business easier by making the notarization of incorporation documents optional.

**✔ Paying taxes**

Albania made paying taxes easier for companies by abolishing the vehicle tax and encouraging electronic filing for taxes.

## ALGERIA

**✔ Getting credit**

Algeria improved access to credit information by eliminating the minimum threshold for loans to be included in the database.

## ANGOLA

**✔ Getting electricity**

Angola made getting electricity easier by eliminating the requirement for customers applying for an electricity connection to obtain authorizations from the 2 utility companies.

## ANTIGUA AND BARBUDA

**✗ Trading across borders**

Antigua and Barbuda made trading across borders more difficult by increasing the number of documents required to import.

## ARGENTINA

**✗ Trading across borders**

Argentina increased the time, cost and number of documents needed to import

by expanding the list of products requiring nonautomatic licenses and introducing new preapproval procedures for all imports.

## ARMENIA

**✔ Getting electricity**

Armenia made getting electricity easier by streamlining procedures and reducing connection fees.

**✔ Protecting investors**

Armenia strengthened investor protections by introducing a requirement for shareholder approval of related-party transactions, requiring greater disclosure of such transactions in the annual report and making it easier to sue directors when such transactions are prejudicial.

## AUSTRALIA

**✔ Getting credit**

Australia strengthened its secured transactions system by adopting a new national legal regime governing the enforceability of security interests in personal property and implementing a unified collateral registry.

## BANGLADESH

**✗ Getting electricity**

Bangladesh made getting electricity more difficult by requiring all customers to meet 7% of their electricity needs through solar energy, making it necessary to install solar panels.

**✔ Getting credit**

Bangladesh improved access to credit information by establishing an online platform for sharing such information.

## BELARUS

**✗ Starting a business**

Belarus made starting a business more difficult by increasing the cost of business

---

Reforms affecting the employing workers indicators are included here but do not affect the ranking on the ease of doing business.

registration and the cost to obtain a company seal.

✔ **Paying taxes**

Belarus made paying taxes easier and less costly for companies by reducing the profit tax rate and encouraging the use of electronic filing and payment systems.

✔ **Resolving insolvency**

Belarus enhanced its insolvency process by exempting the previously state-owned property of a privatized company from the bankruptcy proceeding, requiring that immovable property not sold in the auction be offered to creditors for purchase and allowing immovable property to be sold without proof of state registration in a bankruptcy auction if there are no funds to pay for the registration.

## BELIZE

✔ **Trading across borders**

Belize reduced the time to export and import by implementing the ASYCUDA World electronic data interchange system.

## BENIN

✔ **Starting a business**

Benin made starting a business easier by appointing a representative of the commercial registry at the one-stop shop and reducing some fees.

✔ **Dealing with construction permits**

Benin reduced the time required to obtain a construction permit by speeding up the processing of applications.

✔ **Trading across borders**

Benin reduced the time required to trade across borders by implementing an electronic single-window system integrating customs, control agencies, port authorities and other service providers at the Cotonou port.

✔ **Enforcing contracts**

Benin made enforcing contracts easier by introducing a new code of civil, administrative and social procedures.

## BHUTAN

**Employing workers**

Bhutan introduced a minimum wage.

## BOSNIA AND HERZEGOVINA

✔ **Registering property**

Bosnia and Herzegovina made it easier to transfer property between companies by computerizing the commercial registry.

✘ **Getting credit**

Bosnia and Herzegovina made access to credit information more difficult by stopping the private credit bureau's collection of credit information on individuals.

✔ **Paying taxes**

Bosnia and Herzegovina eased the administrative burden of filing and paying social security contributions by implementing electronic filing and payment systems.

## BOTSWANA

✘ **Paying taxes**

Botswana made paying taxes more costly for companies by increasing the profit tax rate.

✔ **Trading across borders**

In Botswana exporting and importing became faster thanks to the introduction of a scanner by the country's customs authority and an upgrade of South Africa's customs declaration system, both at the Kopfontein–Tlokweng border post.

## BRAZIL

✘ **Registering property**

Brazil made transferring property more difficult by introducing a new certificate of good standing on labor debts, adding to the number of due diligence procedures.

✔ **Enforcing contracts**

Brazil made enforcing contracts easier by implementing an electronic system for filing initial complaints at the São Paulo civil district court.

**Employing workers**

Brazil increased the notice period applicable in cases of redundancy dismissal of employees.

## BRUNEI DARUSSALAM

✔ **Dealing with construction permits**

Brunei Darussalam made dealing with construction permits easier by creating a one-stop shop for preconstruction approvals.

✔ **Paying taxes**

Brunei Darussalam made paying taxes less costly for companies by reducing the profit tax rate.

## BULGARIA

✔ **Starting a business**

Bulgaria made starting a business easier by reducing the cost of registration.

## BURUNDI

✔ **Starting a business**

Burundi made starting a business easier by eliminating the requirements to have company documents notarized, to publish information on new companies in a journal and to register new companies with the Ministry of Trade and Industry.

✔ **Dealing with construction permits**

Burundi made obtaining a construction permit easier by eliminating the requirement for a clearance from the Ministry of Health and reducing the cost of the geotechnical study.

✔ **Registering property**

Burundi made property transfers faster by establishing a statutory time limit for processing property transfer requests at the land registry.

✔ **Trading across borders**

Burundi reduced the time to trade across borders by enhancing its use of electronic data interchange systems, introducing a more efficient system for monitoring goods going through transit countries and improving border coordination with neighboring transit countries.

## CAMBODIA

✔ **Getting credit**

Cambodia improved access to credit information by establishing its first private credit bureau.

✘ **Paying taxes**

Cambodia introduced a new tax on immovable property.

## CAMEROON

✔ **Enforcing contracts**

Cameroon made enforcing contracts easier by creating specialized commercial divisions within its courts of first instance.

## CANADA

✔ **Getting electricity**

Canada made getting an electricity connection easier by reducing the time needed for external connection works.

## CENTRAL AFRICAN REPUBLIC

✘ **Dealing with construction permits**

The Central African Republic made obtaining a construction permit more costly.

## CHAD

✔ **Starting a business**
Chad made starting a business easier by setting up a one-stop shop.

## CHINA

✔ **Starting a business**
China made starting a business less costly by exempting micro and small companies from paying several administrative fees from January 2012 to December 2014.

✔ **Dealing with construction permits**
China simplified the process of obtaining a construction permit by streamlining and centralizing preconstruction approvals.

## COLOMBIA

✔ **Starting a business**
Colombia made starting a business easier by eliminating the requirement to purchase and register accounting books at the time of incorporation.

## COMOROS

✔ **Starting a business**
The Comoros made starting a business easier and less costly by replacing the requirement for a copy of the founders' criminal records with one for a sworn declaration at the time of the company's registration and by reducing the fees to incorporate a company.

✔ **Registering property**
The Comoros made it easier to transfer property by reducing the property transfer tax.

## CONGO, DEM. REP.

✔ **Starting a business**
The Democratic Republic of Congo made starting a business easier by appointing additional public notaries.

## CONGO, REP.

✔ **Starting a business**
The Republic of Congo made starting a business easier by eliminating or reducing several administrative costs associated with incorporation.

✔ **Dealing with construction permits**
The Republic of Congo made dealing with construction permits less expensive by reducing the cost of registering a new building at the land registry.

## COSTA RICA

✔ **Starting a business**
Costa Rica made starting a business easier by streamlining the process of obtaining a sanitary permit for low-risk activities.

✔ **Dealing with construction permits**
Costa Rica streamlined the process for obtaining construction permits by implementing online approval systems.

✔ **Getting credit**
Costa Rica improved access to credit information by guaranteeing borrowers' right to inspect their personal data.

✔ **Paying taxes**
Costa Rica made paying taxes easier for companies by implementing electronic payment for municipal taxes—though it also introduced a registration flat tax.

## CROATIA

✔ **Paying taxes**
Croatia made paying taxes less costly for companies by reducing the health insurance contribution rate.

## CYPRUS

✔ **Registering property**
Cyprus made property transfers faster by computerizing its land registry.

✘ **Paying taxes**
Cyprus made paying taxes more costly for companies by increasing the special defense contribution rate on interest income and introducing a private sector special contribution and a fixed annual fee for companies registered in Cyprus. At the same time, it simplified tax compliance by introducing electronic filing for corporate income tax.

## CZECH REPUBLIC

✔ **Registering property**
The Czech Republic made registering property easier by allowing the cadastral office online access to the commercial registry's database and thus eliminating the need to obtain a paper certificate from the registry before applying for registration at the cadastre.

✔ **Paying taxes**
The Czech Republic made paying taxes faster for companies by promoting the use of electronic facilities.

✔ **Trading across borders**
The Czech Republic reduced the time to export and import by allowing electronic submission of customs declarations and other documents.

**Employing workers**
The Czech Republic increased the maximum duration of fixed-term contracts and reduced the severance pay applicable in cases of redundancy dismissal of employees with 1 year of service.

## DENMARK

✔ **Registering property**
Denmark made registering property easier by introducing electronic submission of property transfer applications at the land registry.

## DOMINICA

✔ **Trading across borders**
Dominica reduced the time to import by implementing the ASYCUDA World electronic data interchange system.

## DOMINICAN REPUBLIC

✘ **Paying taxes**
The Dominican Republic increased the corporate income tax rate.

## ECUADOR

✘ **Registering property**
In Ecuador property transfers became more time consuming as a result of implementation problems in transferring authority over property records to the municipality of Quito.

## EL SALVADOR

✔ **Getting credit**
El Salvador improved access to credit information through a new law regulating the management of personal credit information.

✘ **Paying taxes**
El Salvador introduced an alternative minimum tax.

## ETHIOPIA

✔ **Getting credit**
Ethiopia improved access to credit information by establishing an online platform for sharing such information and by guaranteeing borrowers' right to inspect their personal data.

✘ **Paying taxes**
Ethiopia introduced a social insurance contribution.

## FIJI

✘ **Starting a business**
Fiji made starting a business more difficult by requiring new companies applying for a business license to obtain a certificate from the national fire authority and a letter of compliance from the Ministry of Labor.

✘ **Dealing with construction permits**
Fiji made obtaining a construction permit more expensive by implementing a fee for the fire department clearance.

✘ **Registering property**
Fiji made transferring property more difficult by requiring parties to a property transaction to obtain a capital gains tax clearance certificate from the Fiji Revenue and Customs Authority.

✔ **Paying taxes**
Fiji made paying taxes less costly for companies by reducing the profit tax rate. At the same time, Fiji introduced a capital gains tax.

## GABON

✘ **Registering property**
In Gabon registering property became more difficult because of longer administrative delays at the land registry.

## GEORGIA

✔ **Getting electricity**
Georgia made getting electricity easier by simplifying the process of connecting new customers to the distribution network and reducing connection fees.

✔ **Getting credit**
Georgia strengthened its secured transactions system through an amendment to the civil code allowing a security interest to extend to the products, proceeds and replacements of collateral.

✔ **Paying taxes**
Georgia made paying taxes easier for companies by enhancing the use of electronic systems and providing more services to taxpayers.

✔ **Trading across borders**
Georgia reduced the time to export and import by creating customs clearance zones.

✔ **Enforcing contracts**
Georgia made enforcing contracts easier by simplifying and speeding up the proceedings for commercial disputes.

✔ **Resolving insolvency**
Georgia expedited the process of resolving insolvency by establishing or tightening time limits for all insolvency-related procedures, including auctions.

## GERMANY

✔ **Paying taxes**
Germany made paying taxes more convenient for companies by canceling ELENA procedures and implementing an electronic filing and payment system for most taxes.

✔ **Resolving insolvency**
Germany strengthened its insolvency process by adopting a new insolvency law that facilitates in-court restructurings of distressed companies and increases participation by creditors.

## GHANA

✘ **Trading across borders**
Ghana added to the time required to import by increasing its scanning of imports and changing its customs clearance system.

## GREECE

✔ **Dealing with construction permits**
Greece reduced the time required to obtain a construction permit by introducing strict time limits for processing permit applications at the municipality.

✔ **Protecting investors**
Greece strengthened investor protections by requiring greater immediate and annual disclosure of material related-party transactions.

✔ **Resolving insolvency**
Greece enhanced its insolvency process by abolishing the conciliation procedure and introducing a new rehabilitation proceeding.

## GRENADA

✔ **Trading across borders**
Grenada reduced the time to export and import by implementing the ASYCUDA World electronic data interchange system.

## GUATEMALA

✔ **Dealing with construction permits**
Guatemala made dealing with construction permits easier by introducing a risk-based approval system.

## GUINEA

✔ **Starting a business**
Guinea made starting a business easier by setting up a one-stop shop for company incorporation and by replacing the requirement for a copy of the founders' criminal records with one for a sworn declaration at the time of the company's registration.

✔ **Dealing with construction permits**
Guinea made obtaining a building permit less expensive by clarifying the method for calculating the cost.

✔ **Getting electricity**
Guinea made getting electricity easier by simplifying the process for connecting new customers to the distribution network.

## HUNGARY

✘ **Starting a business**
Hungary made starting a business more complex by increasing the registration fees for limited liability companies and adding a new tax registration at the time of incorporation.

✔ **Getting credit**
Hungary improved access to credit information by passing its first credit bureau law mandating the creation of a database with positive credit information on individuals.

✔ **Paying taxes**
Hungary made paying taxes easier for companies by abolishing the community tax. At the same time, Hungary increased health insurance contributions paid by the employer.

✔ **Trading across borders**
Hungary reduced the time to export and import by allowing electronic submission of customs declarations and other documents.

## ICELAND

✘ **Paying taxes**
Iceland increased the corporate income tax rate.

## INDIA

✔ **Dealing with construction permits**
India reduced the time required to obtain a building permit by establishing strict time limits for preconstruction approvals.

## INDONESIA

✔ **Getting electricity**

Indonesia made getting electricity easier by eliminating the requirement for new customers applying for an electricity connection to show a neighbor's electricity bill as a way to help determine their address.

## IRAN, ISLAMIC REP.

✘ **Starting a business**

The Islamic Republic of Iran made starting a business more difficult by requiring company founders to obtain a criminal record clearance to register a new company.

✔ **Protecting investors**

The Islamic Republic of Iran strengthened investor protections by requiring greater immediate disclosure of related-party transactions.

## IRELAND

✔ **Starting a business**

Ireland made starting a business easier by introducing a new online facility for business registration.

✔ **Registering property**

Ireland made property transfers less costly by introducing a single stamp duty rate for transfers of nonresidential property. It also extended compulsory registration to all property in Ireland.

## ISRAEL

✔ **Registering property**

Israel made transferring property easier by tightening time limits for tax authorities to process capital gains self-assessments on property transfers.

## ITALY

✔ **Getting electricity**

Italy made getting electricity easier and less costly by improving the efficiency of the utility Acea Distribuzione and reducing connection fees.

✔ **Registering property**

Italy made transferring property easier by digitizing cadastral maps of properties and making the maps available to notaries online.

## JAMAICA

✔ **Paying taxes**

Jamaica made paying taxes easier for companies by allowing joint filing and payment of all social security contributions.

✔ **Trading across borders**

Jamaica reduced the time to import by allowing customs entries to be lodged at night.

## JAPAN

✔ **Paying taxes**

Japan made paying taxes less costly for companies by reducing the corporate income tax rate—though it also introduced a restoration surtax for a 3-year period.

## KAZAKHSTAN

✔ **Starting a business**

Kazakhstan made starting a business easier by eliminating the requirement to pay in minimum capital within 3 months after incorporation.

✔ **Getting credit**

Kazakhstan strengthened secured creditor rights by introducing new grounds for relief from an automatic stay during rehabilitation proceedings.

✔ **Resolving insolvency**

Kazakhstan strengthened its insolvency process by introducing an accelerated rehabilitation proceeding, extending the period for rehabilitation, expanding the powers of and improving qualification requirements for insolvency administrators, changing requirements for bankruptcy filings, extending the rights of creditors, changing regulations related to the continuation of operations, introducing a time limit for adopting a rehabilitation plan and adding court supervision requirements.

## KENYA

✔ **Paying taxes**

Kenya made paying taxes faster for companies by enhancing electronic filing systems.

## KOREA, REP.

✔ **Getting electricity**

Korea made getting electricity less costly by introducing a new connection fee schedule and an installment payment system.

✔ **Protecting investors**

Korea strengthened investor protections by making it easier to sue directors in cases of prejudicial related-party transactions.

✔ **Paying taxes**

Korea made paying taxes less costly for companies by reducing the profit tax rate.

✔ **Resolving insolvency**

Korea expedited the insolvency process by implementing a fast track for company rehabilitation.

## KOSOVO

✔ **Starting a business**

Kosovo made starting a business easier by eliminating the minimum capital requirement and business registration fee and streamlining the business registration process.

✔ **Protecting investors**

Kosovo strengthened investor protections by introducing a requirement for shareholder approval of related-party transactions, requiring greater disclosure of such transactions in the annual report and making it easier to sue directors when such transactions are prejudicial.

**Employing workers**

Kosovo introduced a minimum wage.

## LAO PDR

✔ **Starting a business**

Lao PDR made starting a business easier by allowing entrepreneurs to apply for tax registration at the time of incorporation.

✔ **Paying taxes**

Lao PDR made paying taxes less costly for companies by reducing the corporate income tax rate.

✔ **Trading across borders**

Lao PDR reduced the time to export and import by implementing the ASYCUDA electronic data interchange system at the Thanaleng–Friendship Bridge border crossing.

## LATVIA

**Employing workers**

Latvia eliminated requirements for notification of third parties in cases of redundancy dismissal.

## LESOTHO

✔ **Starting a business**

Lesotho made starting a business easier by creating a one-stop shop for company incorporation and by eliminating the requirements for paid-in minimum capital and for notarization of the articles of association.

✔ **Protecting investors**

Lesotho strengthened investor protections by increasing the disclosure requirements for related-party transactions and improving the liability regime for company directors in cases of abusive related-party transactions.

## LIBERIA

✔ **Getting electricity**

In Liberia obtaining an electricity connection became easier thanks to the adoption of better procurement practices by the Liberia Electricity Corporation.

✔ **Paying taxes**

Liberia made paying taxes easier for companies by reducing the profit tax rate and abolishing the turnover tax.

✔ **Enforcing contracts**

Liberia made enforcing contracts easier by creating a specialized commercial court.

## LITHUANIA

✔ **Starting a business**

Lithuania made starting a business easier by introducing online registration for limited liability companies and eliminating the notarization requirement for incorporation documents.

✔ **Resolving insolvency**

Lithuania made resolving insolvency easier by establishing which cases against the company's property shall be taken to the bankruptcy court, tightening the time frame for decisions on appeals, abolishing the court's obligation to individually notify creditors and other stakeholders about restructuring proceedings and setting new time limits for creditors to file claims.

## MACEDONIA, FYR

✔ **Starting a business**

FYR Macedonia made starting a business easier by simplifying the process for obtaining a company seal.

## MADAGASCAR

✔ **Starting a business**

Madagascar made starting a business easier by allowing the one-stop shop to deal with the publication of the notice of incorporation.

## MALAWI

✘ **Dealing with construction permits**

Malawi made dealing with construction permits more expensive by increasing the cost to obtain the plan approval and to register the property.

✘ **Paying taxes**

Malawi introduced a mandatory pension contribution for companies.

✔ **Trading across borders**

Trading across borders became easier in Malawi thanks to improvements in customs clearance procedures and transport links between the port of Beira in Mozambique and Blantyre.

## MALAYSIA

✔ **Dealing with construction permits**

Malaysia made dealing with construction permits faster by improving the one-stop center for new buildings and by reducing the time to connect to telephone service.

✔ **Registering property**

Malaysia substantially reduced the number of days it takes to register property transfers.

## MALDIVES

✘ **Paying taxes**

Maldives introduced a goods and service tax, a business profit tax and additional social contributions.

## MALI

✔ **Paying taxes**

Mali made paying taxes less costly for companies by reducing the corporate income tax rate—though it also introduced a new tax on land. At the same time, Mali simplified the process of paying taxes by introducing a single form for joint filing and payment of several taxes.

## MAURITIUS

✔ **Registering property**

Mauritius made property transfers faster by implementing an electronic information management system at the Registrar-General's Department.

✔ **Getting credit**

Mauritius improved access to credit information by starting to collect and distribute payment information from retailers and beginning to distribute both positive and negative information.

## MEXICO

✔ **Starting a business**

Mexico made starting a business easier by eliminating the minimum capital requirement for limited liability companies.

✔ **Getting electricity**

In Mexico the distribution utility made getting electricity easier by streamlining procedures, offering training opportunities to private contractors, using a geographic information system (GIS) to map the electricity distribution network and increasing the stock of materials.

## MOLDOVA

✔ **Protecting investors**

Moldova strengthened investor protections by allowing the rescission of prejudicial related-party transactions.

✘ **Paying taxes**

Moldova made paying taxes more costly for companies by reintroducing the corporate income tax—but also made tax compliance easier by encouraging electronic filing and payment.

✘ **Enforcing contracts**

Moldova made enforcing contracts more difficult by abolishing the specialized economic courts.

✔ **Resolving insolvency**

Moldova strengthened its insolvency process by extending the duration of the reorganization proceeding and refining the qualification requirements for insolvency administrators.

## MONGOLIA

✔ **Starting a business**

Mongolia made starting a business easier by eliminating the minimum capital requirement for limited liability companies.

✔ **Getting credit**

Mongolia improved access to credit information by guaranteeing borrowers' right to inspect their personal data.

✔ **Protecting investors**

Mongolia strengthened investor protections by increasing the disclosure requirements for related-party transactions.

## MONTENEGRO

✔ **Dealing with construction permits**

Montenegro made dealing with construction permits less expensive by reducing the cost of pre- and postconstruction procedures.

✔ **Getting credit**

Montenegro improved access to credit information by guaranteeing borrowers' right to inspect their personal data.

**Employing workers**

Montenegro lowered redundancy costs—though it also reduced the maximum duration of fixed-term contracts and increased paid annual leave.

## MOROCCO

✔ **Starting a business**

Morocco made starting a business easier by eliminating the minimum capital requirement for limited liability companies.

✘ **Registering property**

Morocco made registering property more costly by increasing property registration fees.

## NAMIBIA

✔ **Getting electricity**

Namibia made getting electricity easier by reducing the time required to provide estimates and external connection works and by lowering the connection costs.

✘ **Registering property**

Namibia made transferring property more difficult by requiring conveyancers to obtain a building compliance certificate beforehand.

## NETHERLANDS

✔ **Starting a business**

The Netherlands made starting a business easier by eliminating the requirement for a declaration of nonobjection by the Ministry of Justice before incorporation.

✔ **Dealing with construction permits**

The Netherlands made dealing with construction permits simpler by merging several approvals and implementing an online application system.

✔ **Protecting investors**

The Netherlands strengthened investor protections through a new law regulating the approval of related-party transactions.

✔ **Trading across borders**

The Netherlands made importing easier by introducing a new web-based system for cargo release at the port terminals in Rotterdam.

## NEW ZEALAND

✔ **Getting credit**

New Zealand improved access to credit information by allowing credit bureaus to collect positive information on individuals.

## NIGER

✔ **Trading across borders**

Niger reduced the time to import by expanding and optimizing the use of an electronic data interchange system for customs clearance.

## NIGERIA

✘ **Paying taxes**

Nigeria introduced a new compulsory labor contribution paid by the employer.

## NORWAY

✔ **Starting a business**

Norway made starting a business easier by reducing the minimum capital requirement for private joint stock companies.

✔ **Dealing with construction permits**

Norway reduced the time required to obtain a building permit by implementing strict time limits for construction project approvals.

## OMAN

✔ **Getting credit**

Oman improved access to credit information by guaranteeing borrowers' right to inspect their personal data.

**Employing workers**

Oman reduced the maximum number of working days per week and increased the paid annual leave applicable for employees with 1 year of service.

## PANAMA

✔ **Dealing with construction permits**

Panama made dealing with construction permits easier by reducing the fees for a permit from the fire department's safety office and by accelerating the process at the building registry for obtaining a certificate of good standing and for registering the new building.

✔ **Registering property**

Panama made property transfers faster by increasing working hours at the registry and reorganizing the caseload of its staff.

✔ **Paying taxes**

Panama made paying taxes easier for companies by enhancing the electronic filing system for value added tax and simplifying tax return forms for corporate income tax—though it also began requiring companies to pay corporate income tax monthly rather than quarterly.

## PERU

✔ **Dealing with construction permits**

Peru made obtaining a construction permit easier by eliminating requirements for several preconstruction approvals.

✔ **Protecting investors**

Peru strengthened investor protections through a new law regulating the approval of related-party transactions and making it easier to sue directors when such transactions are prejudicial.

## POLAND

✔ **Registering property**

Poland made property registration faster by introducing a new caseload management system for the land and mortgage registries and by continuing to digitize the records of the registries.

✔ **Paying taxes**

Poland made paying taxes easier for companies by promoting the use of electronic filing and payment systems—though it also increased social security contributions.

✔ **Enforcing contracts**

Poland made enforcing contracts easier by amending the civil procedure code and appointing more judges to commercial courts.

✔ **Resolving insolvency**

Poland strengthened its insolvency process by updating guidelines on the information and documents that need to be included in the bankruptcy petition and by granting secured creditors the right to take over claims encumbered with financial pledges in case of liquidation.

## PORTUGAL

✔ **Dealing with construction permits**

Portugal made obtaining construction permits easier by implementing strict time limits to process urban projects and simplifying the associated procedures.

✔ **Trading across borders**

Portugal made trading across borders easier by implementing an electronic single window for port procedures.

✔ **Resolving insolvency**

Portugal made resolving insolvency easier by introducing a new insolvency law that expedites liquidation procedures and creates fast-track mechanisms both in and out of court.

**Employing workers**

Portugal increased the maximum duration of fixed-term contracts and reduced the severance pay applicable in cases of redundancy dismissal.

## PUERTO RICO (U.S.)

✔ **Paying taxes**

Puerto Rico (territory of the United States) made paying taxes easier and less costly for companies by introducing a new internal revenue code and tax codification and by reducing the effective corporate income tax rate.

## QATAR

✔ **Trading across borders**

Qatar reduced the time to export and import by introducing a new online portal allowing electronic submission of customs declarations for clearance at the Doha seaport.

## ROMANIA

✔ **Starting a business**

Romania made starting a business easier by reducing the time required to obtain a clearance certificate from the fiscal administration agency.

✔ **Getting credit**

Romania strengthened its legal framework for secured transactions by allowing the automatic extension of security interests to the products, proceeds and replacements of collateral.

## RUSSIAN FEDERATION

✔ **Dealing with construction permits**

Russia made obtaining a construction permit simpler by eliminating requirements for several preconstruction approvals.

✔ **Paying taxes**

Russia eased the administrative burden of taxes for firms by simplifying compliance procedures for value added tax and by promoting the use of tax accounting software and electronic services.

## RWANDA

✔ **Getting electricity**

Rwanda made getting electricity easier by reducing the cost of obtaining a new connection.

✔ **Enforcing contracts**

Rwanda made enforcing contracts easier by implementing an electronic filing system for initial complaints.

## SÃO TOMÉ AND PRÍNCIPE

✗ **Dealing with construction permits**

São Tomé and Príncipe made obtaining a construction permit more expensive by increasing the fees.

## SAUDI ARABIA

✗ **Getting electricity**

Saudi Arabia made getting electricity more expensive by increasing the connection fees.

✔ **Paying taxes**

Saudi Arabia made paying taxes easier for companies by introducing online filing and payment systems for social security contributions.

✔ **Enforcing contracts**

Saudi Arabia made enforcing contracts easier by expanding the computerization of its courts and introducing an electronic filing system.

## SERBIA

✔ **Starting a business**

Serbia made starting a business easier by eliminating the paid-in minimum capital requirement.

✔ **Enforcing contracts**

Serbia made enforcing contracts easier by introducing a private bailiff system.

✔ **Resolving insolvency**

Serbia strengthened its insolvency process by introducing private bailiffs, reducing the starting prices for the sale of assets, prohibiting appeals, expediting service of process and adopting an electronic registry for injunctions to make public all prohibitions on the disposal or pledge of movable or immovable property.

## SIERRA LEONE

✔ **Registering property**

Sierra Leone made registering property easier by computerizing the Ministry of Lands, Country Planning and the Environment.

✔ **Getting credit**

Sierra Leone improved access to credit information by establishing a public credit registry at its central bank and guaranteeing borrowers' right to inspect their personal data.

## SLOVAK REPUBLIC

✔ **Starting a business**

The Slovak Republic made starting a business easier by speeding up the processing of applications at the one-stop shop for trading licenses, income tax registration and health insurance registration.

✔ **Paying taxes**

The Slovak Republic made paying taxes easier for companies by implementing electronic filing and payment of social security and health insurance contributions.

✔ **Enforcing contracts**

The Slovak Republic made enforcing contracts easier by adopting several amendments to the code of civil procedure intended to simplify and speed up proceedings as well as to limit obstructive tactics by the parties to a case.

✔ **Resolving insolvency**

The Slovak Republic improved its insolvency process by redefining the roles and powers of creditors and trustees, strengthening the rights of secured creditors and redefining rules for the conversion of restructuring into a bankruptcy proceeding.

**Employing workers**

The Slovak Republic increased the maximum duration of fixed-term contracts, eliminated requirements for notification of third parties in cases of redundancy dismissal and reduced redundancy costs.

## SLOVENIA

✔ **Protecting investors**

Slovenia strengthened investor protections through a new law regulating the approval of related-party transactions.

✔ **Paying taxes**

Slovenia made paying taxes easier and less costly for companies by implementing electronic filing and payment of social security contributions and by reducing the corporate income tax rate.

✔ **Resolving insolvency**

Slovenia strengthened its insolvency process by requiring that the debtor offer creditors payment of at least 50% of the claims within 4 years; giving greater power to the creditors' committee in a bankruptcy proceeding; prohibiting insolvency administrators from allowing relatives to render services associated with the bankruptcy proceeding; and establishing fines for members of management that violate certain obligations or prohibitions.

## SOUTH AFRICA

✔ **Trading across borders**

South Africa reduced the time and documents required to export and import through its ongoing customs modernization program.

## SPAIN

✔ **Trading across borders**

Spain reduced the time to import by further expanding the use of electronic submission of customs declarations and improving the sharing of information among customs and other agencies.

✔ **Resolving insolvency**

Spain strengthened its insolvency process by making workouts easier, offering more protections for refinancing agreements, allowing conversion from reorganization into liquidation at any time, allowing reliefs of the stay under certain circumstances and permitting the judge to determine whether an asset of the insolvent company is necessary for its continued operation.

**Employing workers**

Spain temporarily allowed unlimited duration of fixed-term contracts.

## SRI LANKA

✔ **Starting a business**

Sri Lanka made starting a business easier by computerizing and expediting the process of obtaining a registration number for the Employees Provident Fund and Employees Trust Fund.

✔ **Registering property**

Sri Lanka made registering property faster by introducing an electronic system at the land registry in Colombo.

✔ **Getting credit**

Sri Lanka strengthened its secured transactions system by establishing an electronic, searchable collateral registry and issuing regulations for its operation.

✔ **Trading across borders**

Sri Lanka reduced the time to export by implementing the ASYCUDA World electronic data interchange system.

## ST. KITTS AND NEVIS

✘ **Trading across borders**

St. Kitts and Nevis made it more expensive to export by increasing the cost of operations at the port of Basseterre.

## SURINAME

✘ **Trading across borders**

Suriname increased the time to export by involving more customs departments in clearing exports.

## SWAZILAND

✔ **Paying taxes**

Swaziland introduced a value added tax.

## SWEDEN

✘ **Registering property**

In Sweden property transfers became more time consuming during implementation of a new information technology system at the land registry.

## SYRIAN ARAB REPUBLIC

✔ **Getting credit**

Syria improved access to credit information by establishing an online system for data exchange between all banks and microfinance institutions and the central bank's credit registry.

## TAIWAN, CHINA

✔ **Dealing with construction permits**

Taiwan, China, made dealing with construction permits easier by introducing a risk-based and self-regulatory inspection system and improving operational features of the one-stop shop for building permits.

✔ **Protecting investors**

Taiwan, China, strengthened investor protections by increasing disclosure requirements for related-party transactions and improving the liability regime for company directors in cases where such transactions are abusive.

## TAJIKISTAN

✔ **Protecting investors**

Tajikistan strengthened investor protections by making it easier to sue directors in cases of prejudicial related-party transactions.

## TANZANIA

✔ **Starting a business**

Tanzania made starting a business easier by eliminating the requirement for inspections by health, town and land officers as a prerequisite for a business license.

✘ **Dealing with construction permits**

Tanzania made dealing with construction permits more expensive by increasing the cost to obtain a building permit.

✘ **Trading across borders**

Tanzania made importing more difficult by introducing a requirement to obtain a certificate of conformity before the imported goods are shipped.

## THAILAND

✔ **Starting a business**

Thailand made starting a business easier by allowing the registrar at the Department of Business Development to receive the company's work regulations.

✔ **Paying taxes**

Thailand made paying taxes less costly for companies by reducing the profit tax rate.

## TIMOR-LESTE

**Employing workers**

Timor-Leste reduced the maximum duration of fixed-term contracts and also introduced a wage premium for night work.

## TOGO

✔ **Starting a business**

Togo made starting a business easier and less costly by reducing incorporation fees, improving the work flow at the one-stop shop for company registration and replacing the requirement for a copy of the founders' criminal records with one for a sworn declaration at the time of the company's registration.

**Employing workers**

Togo increased the wage premium for weekly holiday work and the severance payment in cases of redundancy dismissal.

## TRINIDAD AND TOBAGO

✔ **Registering property**

In Trinidad and Tobago property transfers became faster thanks to speedier issuance of clearance certificates by the Water and Sewerage Authority.

✔ **Trading across borders**

Trinidad and Tobago reduced the time to export and import by launching the ASYCUDA World electronic data interchange system and simplifying the process for obtaining a certificate of origin.

## TURKEY

✔ **Dealing with construction permits**

Turkey made dealing with construction permits easier by eliminating the requirement to build a shelter in nonresidential buildings with a total area of less than 1,500 square meters.

✔ **Enforcing contracts**

Turkey made enforcing contracts easier by introducing a new civil procedure law.

## UGANDA

✘ **Registering property**

Uganda made transferring property more difficult by introducing a requirement for property purchasers to obtain an income tax certificate before registration, resulting in delays at the Uganda Revenue Authority and the Ministry of Finance. At the same time, Uganda made it easier by digitizing records at the title registry, increasing efficiency at the assessor's office and making it possible for more banks to accept the stamp duty payment.

✔ **Resolving insolvency**

Uganda strengthened its insolvency process by clarifying rules on the creation of mortgages, establishing the duties of mortgagors and mortgagees, defining priority rules, providing remedies for mortgagors and mortgagees and establishing the powers of receivers.

## UKRAINE

✔ **Starting a business**

Ukraine made starting a business easier by eliminating the minimum capital requirement for company incorporation as well as the requirement to have incorporation documents notarized.

✔ **Registering property**

Ukraine made property transfers faster by introducing an effective time limit for processing transfer applications at the land cadastre in Kiev.

✔ **Paying taxes**

Ukraine made paying taxes easier by implementing electronic filing and payment for medium-size and large enterprises.

## UNITED ARAB EMIRATES

✔ **Starting a business**

The United Arab Emirates made starting a business easier by eliminating the requirement for a company to prepare a name board in English and Arabic after having received clearance on the use of office premises.

✔ **Getting electricity**

In the United Arab Emirates the Dubai Electricity and Water Authority made getting electricity easier by introducing an electronic "one window, one step" application process allowing customers to submit and track their applications online and reducing the time for processing the applications.

✔ **Paying taxes**

The United Arab Emirates made paying taxes easier for companies by establishing an online filing and payment system for social security contributions.

## UNITED KINGDOM

✔ **Paying taxes**

The United Kingdom made paying taxes less costly for companies by reducing the corporate income tax rate.

**Employing workers**

The United Kingdom increased the severance pay applicable in cases of redundancy dismissal.

## URUGUAY

✔ **Paying taxes**

Uruguay made paying taxes easier for small and medium-size companies by fully implementing an online filing and payment system for capital, value added and corporate income taxes and by improving the online facilities for social security contributions.

✔ **Trading across borders**

Uruguay reduced the time to import by improving port efficiency and introducing electronic payment and predeclaration systems for customs.

## UZBEKISTAN

✔ **Starting a business**

Uzbekistan made starting a business easier by introducing an online facility for name reservation and eliminating the fee to open a bank account for small businesses.

✔ **Getting credit**

Uzbekistan improved access to credit information by guaranteeing borrowers' right to inspect their personal data.

✔ **Trading across borders**

Uzbekistan reduced the time to export by introducing a single window for customs clearance and reduced the number of documents needed for each import transaction.

✔ **Resolving insolvency**

Uzbekistan strengthened its insolvency process by introducing new time limits for insolvency proceedings and new time limits and procedures for the second auction and by making it possible for businesses to continue operating throughout the liquidation proceeding.

## VANUATU

✘ **Dealing with construction permits**

Vanuatu made obtaining a construction permit more cumbersome by making a preliminary environmental assessment mandatory and made it more expensive by increasing the fees.

## VENEZUELA, RB

✘ **Starting a business**

República Bolivariana de Venezuela made starting a business more difficult by increasing the cost of company incorporation.

✘ **Paying taxes**

República Bolivariana de Venezuela made paying taxes more costly and difficult for companies by introducing a sports, physical activities and physical education tax.

**Employing workers**

República Bolivariana de Venezuela introduced a new labor code that prohibits redundancy dismissals.

## VIETNAM

✔ **Starting a business**

Vietnam made starting a business easier by allowing companies to use self-printed value added tax invoices.

## WEST BANK AND GAZA

✘ **Registering property**

West Bank and Gaza made transferring property more costly by increasing the property transfer fee.

✔ **Getting credit**

West Bank and Gaza improved access to credit information by guaranteeing borrowers' right to inspect their personal data.

## ZAMBIA

✔ **Resolving insolvency**

Zambia strengthened its insolvency process by introducing further qualification requirements for receivers and liquidators and by establishing specific duties and remuneration rules for them.

# Country tables

✔ Reform making it easier to do business  ✘ Reform making it more difficult to do business

| AFGHANISTAN | | South Asia | | GNI per capita (US$) | 585 |
|---|---|---|---|---|---|
| Ease of doing business (rank) | 168 | Low income | | Population (m) | 35.3 |
| **Starting a business** (rank) | 28 | **Registering property** (rank) | 174 | **Trading across borders** (rank) | 178 |
| Procedures (number) | 4 | Procedures (number) | 9 | Documents to export (number) | 10 |
| Time (days) | 7 | Time (days) | 250 | Time to export (days) | 74 |
| Cost (% of income per capita) | 22.5 | Cost (% of property value) | 5.0 | Cost to export (US$ per container) | 3,545 |
| Minimum capital (% of income per capita) | 0.0 | | | Documents to import (number) | 10 |
| | | **Getting credit** (rank) | 154 | Time to import (days) | 77 |
| **Dealing with construction permits** (rank) | 164 | Strength of legal rights index (0-10) | 6 | Cost to import (US$ per container) | 3,830 |
| Procedures (number) | 12 | Depth of credit information index (0-6) | 0 | | |
| Time (days) | 334 | Public registry coverage (% of adults) | 0.0 | **Enforcing contracts** (rank) | 164 |
| Cost (% of income per capita) | 4,308.6 | Private bureau coverage (% of adults) | 0.0 | Procedures (number) | 47 |
| | | | | Time (days) | 1,642 |
| **Getting electricity** (rank) | 110 | **Protecting investors** (rank) | 185 | Cost (% of claim) | 25.0 |
| Procedures (number) | 4 | Extent of disclosure index (0-10) | 1 | | |
| Time (days) | 109 | Extent of director liability index (0-10) | 1 | **Resolving insolvency** (rank) | 115 |
| Cost (% of income per capita) | 3,494.3 | Ease of shareholder suits index (0-10) | 1 | Time (years) | 2.0 |
| | | Strength of investor protection index (0-10) | 1.0 | Cost (% of estate) | 25 |
| | | | | Recovery rate (cents on the dollar) | 26.4 |
| | | **Paying taxes** (rank) | 94 | | |
| | | Payments (number per year) | 20 | | |
| | | Time (hours per year) | 275 | | |
| | | Total tax rate (% of profit) | 36.4 | | |

| ALBANIA | | Eastern Europe & Central Asia | | GNI per capita (US$) | 3,980 |
|---|---|---|---|---|---|
| Ease of doing business (rank) | 85 | Lower middle income | | Population (m) | 3.2 |
| ✔ **Starting a business** (rank) | 62 | **Registering property** (rank) | 121 | **Trading across borders** (rank) | 79 |
| Procedures (number) | 4 | Procedures (number) | 6 | Documents to export (number) | 7 |
| Time (days) | 4 | Time (days) | 33 | Time to export (days) | 19 |
| Cost (% of income per capita) | 22.1 | Cost (% of property value) | 11.4 | Cost to export (US$ per container) | 745 |
| Minimum capital (% of income per capita) | 0.0 | | | Documents to import (number) | 8 |
| | | **Getting credit** (rank) | 23 | Time to import (days) | 18 |
| **Dealing with construction permits** (rank) | 185 | Strength of legal rights index (0-10) | 9 | Cost to import (US$ per container) | 730 |
| Procedures (number) | NO PRACTICE | Depth of credit information index (0-6) | 4 | | |
| Time (days) | NO PRACTICE | Public registry coverage (% of adults) | 19.7 | **Enforcing contracts** (rank) | 85 |
| Cost (% of income per capita) | NO PRACTICE | Private bureau coverage (% of adults) | 0.0 | Procedures (number) | 39 |
| | | | | Time (days) | 390 |
| **Getting electricity** (rank) | 154 | **Protecting investors** (rank) | 17 | Cost (% of claim) | 35.7 |
| Procedures (number) | 6 | Extent of disclosure index (0-10) | 8 | | |
| Time (days) | 177 | Extent of director liability index (0-10) | 9 | **Resolving insolvency** (rank) | 66 |
| Cost (% of income per capita) | 573.7 | Ease of shareholder suits index (0-10) | 5 | Time (years) | 2.0 |
| | | Strength of investor protection index (0-10) | 7.3 | Cost (% of estate) | 10 |
| | | | | Recovery rate (cents on the dollar) | 39.6 |
| | | ✔ **Paying taxes** (rank) | 160 | | |
| | | Payments (number per year) | 44 | | |
| | | Time (hours per year) | 357 | | |
| | | Total tax rate (% of profit) | 38.7 | | |

*Note:* Most indicator sets refer to a case scenario in an economy's largest business city. For more details, see the data notes.

✔ Reform making it easier to do business  ✘ Reform making it more difficult to do business

## ALGERIA

| | | | | | | | |
|---|---|---|---|---|---|---|---|
| **Ease of doing business** (rank) | 152 | Middle East & North Africa<br>Upper middle income | | GNI per capita (US$)<br>Population (m) | | 4,470<br>36.0 | |

| | | | | | |
|---|---|---|---|---|---|
| **Starting a business** (rank) | 156 | **Registering property** (rank) | 172 | **Trading across borders** (rank) | 129 |
| Procedures (number) | 14 | Procedures (number) | 10 | Documents to export (number) | 8 |
| Time (days) | 25 | Time (days) | 63 | Time to export (days) | 17 |
| Cost (% of income per capita) | 12.1 | Cost (% of property value) | 7.1 | Cost to export (US$ per container) | 1,260 |
| Minimum capital (% of income per capita) | 27.2 | | | Documents to import (number) | 9 |
| | | ✔ **Getting credit** (rank) | 129 | Time to import (days) | 27 |
| **Dealing with construction permits** (rank) | 138 | Strength of legal rights index (0-10) | 3 | Cost to import (US$ per container) | 1,330 |
| Procedures (number) | 19 | Depth of credit information index (0-6) | 4 | | |
| Time (days) | 281 | Public registry coverage (% of adults) | 2.3 | **Enforcing contracts** (rank) | 126 |
| Cost (% of income per capita) | 54.6 | Private bureau coverage (% of adults) | 0.0 | Procedures (number) | 45 |
| | | | | Time (days) | 630 |
| **Getting electricity** (rank) | 165 | **Protecting investors** (rank) | 82 | Cost (% of claim) | 21.9 |
| Procedures (number) | 6 | Extent of disclosure index (0-10) | 6 | | |
| Time (days) | 159 | Extent of director liability index (0-10) | 6 | **Resolving insolvency** (rank) | 62 |
| Cost (% of income per capita) | 1,489.9 | Ease of shareholder suits index (0-10) | 4 | Time (years) | 2.5 |
| | | Strength of investor protection index (0-10) | 5.3 | Cost (% of estate) | 7 |
| | | | | Recovery rate (cents on the dollar) | 41.7 |
| | | **Paying taxes** (rank) | 170 | | |
| | | Payments (number per year) | 29 | | |
| | | Time (hours per year) | 451 | | |
| | | Total tax rate (% of profit) | 72.0 | | |

## ANGOLA

| | | | | | | | |
|---|---|---|---|---|---|---|---|
| **Ease of doing business** (rank) | 172 | Sub-Saharan Africa<br>Upper middle income | | GNI per capita (US$)<br>Population (m) | | 4,060<br>19.6 | |

| | | | | | |
|---|---|---|---|---|---|
| **Starting a business** (rank) | 171 | **Registering property** (rank) | 131 | **Trading across borders** (rank) | 164 |
| Procedures (number) | 8 | Procedures (number) | 7 | Documents to export (number) | 11 |
| Time (days) | 68 | Time (days) | 184 | Time to export (days) | 48 |
| Cost (% of income per capita) | 105.4 | Cost (% of property value) | 3.1 | Cost to export (US$ per container) | 1,850 |
| Minimum capital (% of income per capita) | 24.6 | | | Documents to import (number) | 8 |
| | | **Getting credit** (rank) | 129 | Time to import (days) | 45 |
| **Dealing with construction permits** (rank) | 124 | Strength of legal rights index (0-10) | 3 | Cost to import (US$ per container) | 2,690 |
| Procedures (number) | 12 | Depth of credit information index (0-6) | 4 | | |
| Time (days) | 348 | Public registry coverage (% of adults) | 1.8 | **Enforcing contracts** (rank) | 183 |
| Cost (% of income per capita) | 153.6 | Private bureau coverage (% of adults) | 0.0 | Procedures (number) | 46 |
| | | | | Time (days) | 1,011 |
| ✔ **Getting electricity** (rank) | 113 | **Protecting investors** (rank) | 70 | Cost (% of claim) | 44.4 |
| Procedures (number) | 7 | Extent of disclosure index (0-10) | 5 | | |
| Time (days) | 55 | Extent of director liability index (0-10) | 6 | **Resolving insolvency** (rank) | 162 |
| Cost (% of income per capita) | 754.9 | Ease of shareholder suits index (0-10) | 6 | Time (years) | 6.2 |
| | | Strength of investor protection index (0-10) | 5.7 | Cost (% of estate) | 22 |
| | | | | Recovery rate (cents on the dollar) | 8.0 |
| | | **Paying taxes** (rank) | 154 | | |
| | | Payments (number per year) | 31 | | |
| | | Time (hours per year) | 282 | | |
| | | Total tax rate (% of profit) | 53.2 | | |

## ANTIGUA AND BARBUDA

| | | | | | | | |
|---|---|---|---|---|---|---|---|
| **Ease of doing business** (rank) | 63 | Latin America & Caribbean<br>Upper middle income | | GNI per capita (US$)<br>Population (m) | | 12,060<br>0.1 | |

| | | | | | |
|---|---|---|---|---|---|
| **Starting a business** (rank) | 85 | **Registering property** (rank) | 125 | ✘ **Trading across borders** (rank) | 110 |
| Procedures (number) | 8 | Procedures (number) | 7 | Documents to export (number) | 5 |
| Time (days) | 21 | Time (days) | 26 | Time to export (days) | 16 |
| Cost (% of income per capita) | 10.9 | Cost (% of property value) | 10.9 | Cost to export (US$ per container) | 1,440 |
| Minimum capital (% of income per capita) | 0.0 | | | Documents to import (number) | 8 |
| | | **Getting credit** (rank) | 104 | Time to import (days) | 23 |
| **Dealing with construction permits** (rank) | 24 | Strength of legal rights index (0-10) | 8 | Cost to import (US$ per container) | 1,870 |
| Procedures (number) | 10 | Depth of credit information index (0-6) | 0 | | |
| Time (days) | 134 | Public registry coverage (% of adults) | 0.0 | **Enforcing contracts** (rank) | 72 |
| Cost (% of income per capita) | 23.4 | Private bureau coverage (% of adults) | 0.0 | Procedures (number) | 45 |
| | | | | Time (days) | 351 |
| **Getting electricity** (rank) | 18 | **Protecting investors** (rank) | 32 | Cost (% of claim) | 22.7 |
| Procedures (number) | 4 | Extent of disclosure index (0-10) | 4 | | |
| Time (days) | 42 | Extent of director liability index (0-10) | 8 | **Resolving insolvency** (rank) | 85 |
| Cost (% of income per capita) | 131.3 | Ease of shareholder suits index (0-10) | 7 | Time (years) | 3.0 |
| | | Strength of investor protection index (0-10) | 6.3 | Cost (% of estate) | 7 |
| | | | | Recovery rate (cents on the dollar) | 35.2 |
| | | **Paying taxes** (rank) | 142 | | |
| | | Payments (number per year) | 57 | | |
| | | Time (hours per year) | 207 | | |
| | | Total tax rate (% of profit) | 41.5 | | |

*Note:* Most indicator sets refer to a case scenario in an economy's largest business city. For more details, see the data notes.

✔ Reform making it easier to do business  ✘ Reform making it more difficult to do business

## ARGENTINA

| | | | | | | | |
|---|---|---|---|---|---|---|---|
| **Ease of doing business** (rank) | 124 | Latin America & Caribbean<br>Upper middle income | | GNI per capita (US$)<br>Population (m) | | 9,740<br>40.8 | |

| | | | | | |
|---|---|---|---|---|---|
| **Starting a business** (rank) | 154 | **Registering property** (rank) | 135 | ✘ **Trading across borders** (rank) | 139 |
| Procedures (number) | 14 | Procedures (number) | 7 | Documents to export (number) | 7 |
| Time (days) | 26 | Time (days) | 55 | Time to export (days) | 13 |
| Cost (% of income per capita) | 12.3 | Cost (% of property value) | 7.0 | Cost to export (US$ per container) | 1,650 |
| Minimum capital (% of income per capita) | 5.7 | | | Documents to import (number) | 10 |
| | | | | Time to import (days) | 30 |
| | | **Getting credit** (rank) | 70 | Cost to import (US$ per container) | 2,260 |
| **Dealing with construction permits** (rank) | 171 | Strength of legal rights index (0-10) | 4 | | |
| Procedures (number) | 24 | Depth of credit information index (0-6) | 6 | | |
| Time (days) | 365 | Public registry coverage (% of adults) | 37.0 | **Enforcing contracts** (rank) | 48 |
| Cost (% of income per capita) | 74.3 | Private bureau coverage (% of adults) | 100.0 | Procedures (number) | 36 |
| | | | | Time (days) | 590 |
| **Getting electricity** (rank) | 74 | **Protecting investors** (rank) | 117 | Cost (% of claim) | 16.5 |
| Procedures (number) | 6 | Extent of disclosure index (0-10) | 6 | | |
| Time (days) | 91 | Extent of director liability index (0-10) | 2 | **Resolving insolvency** (rank) | 94 |
| Cost (% of income per capita) | 36.0 | Ease of shareholder suits index (0-10) | 6 | Time (years) | 2.8 |
| | | Strength of investor protection index (0-10) | 4.7 | Cost (% of estate) | 12 |
| | | | | Recovery rate (cents on the dollar) | 30.8 |
| | | **Paying taxes** (rank) | 149 | | |
| | | Payments (number per year) | 9 | | |
| | | Time (hours per year) | 405 | | |
| | | Total tax rate (% of profit) | 108.3 | | |

## ARMENIA

| | | | | | | | |
|---|---|---|---|---|---|---|---|
| **Ease of doing business** (rank) | 32 | Eastern Europe & Central Asia<br>Lower middle income | | GNI per capita (US$)<br>Population (m) | | 3,360<br>3.1 | |

| | | | | | |
|---|---|---|---|---|---|
| **Starting a business** (rank) | 11 | **Registering property** (rank) | 4 | **Trading across borders** (rank) | 107 |
| Procedures (number) | 3 | Procedures (number) | 3 | Documents to export (number) | 5 |
| Time (days) | 8 | Time (days) | 7 | Time to export (days) | 13 |
| Cost (% of income per capita) | 2.5 | Cost (% of property value) | 0.2 | Cost to export (US$ per container) | 1,815 |
| Minimum capital (% of income per capita) | 0.0 | | | Documents to import (number) | 8 |
| | | **Getting credit** (rank) | 40 | Time to import (days) | 18 |
| Dealing with construction permits (rank) | 46 | Strength of legal rights index (0-10) | 6 | Cost to import (US$ per container) | 2,195 |
| Procedures (number) | 17 | Depth of credit information index (0-6) | 6 | | |
| Time (days) | 77 | Public registry coverage (% of adults) | 20.5 | **Enforcing contracts** (rank) | 91 |
| Cost (% of income per capita) | 50.1 | Private bureau coverage (% of adults) | 56.0 | Procedures (number) | 49 |
| | | | | Time (days) | 440 |
| ✔ **Getting electricity** (rank) | 101 | ✔ **Protecting investors** (rank) | 25 | Cost (% of claim) | 19.0 |
| Procedures (number) | 5 | Extent of disclosure index (0-10) | 6 | | |
| Time (days) | 242 | Extent of director liability index (0-10) | 6 | **Resolving insolvency** (rank) | 63 |
| Cost (% of income per capita) | 107.3 | Ease of shareholder suits index (0-10) | 8 | Time (years) | 1.9 |
| | | Strength of investor protection index (0-10) | 6.7 | Cost (% of estate) | 4 |
| | | | | Recovery rate (cents on the dollar) | 41.2 |
| | | **Paying taxes** (rank) | 108 | | |
| | | Payments (number per year) | 13 | | |
| | | Time (hours per year) | 380 | | |
| | | Total tax rate (% of profit) | 38.8 | | |

## AUSTRALIA

| | | | | | | | |
|---|---|---|---|---|---|---|---|
| **Ease of doing business** (rank) | 10 | OECD high income<br>High income | | GNI per capita (US$)<br>Population (m) | | 65,477<br>22.6 | |

| | | | | | |
|---|---|---|---|---|---|
| **Starting a business** (rank) | 2 | **Registering property** (rank) | 37 | **Trading across borders** (rank) | 44 |
| Procedures (number) | 2 | Procedures (number) | 5 | Documents to export (number) | 6 |
| Time (days) | 2 | Time (days) | 5 | Time to export (days) | 9 |
| Cost (% of income per capita) | 0.7 | Cost (% of property value) | 5.1 | Cost to export (US$ per container) | 1,100 |
| Minimum capital (% of income per capita) | 0.0 | | | Documents to import (number) | 7 |
| | | ✔ **Getting credit** (rank) | 4 | Time to import (days) | 8 |
| **Dealing with construction permits** (rank) | 11 | Strength of legal rights index (0-10) | 10 | Cost to import (US$ per container) | 1,120 |
| Procedures (number) | 11 | Depth of credit information index (0-6) | 5 | | |
| Time (days) | 112 | Public registry coverage (% of adults) | 0.0 | **Enforcing contracts** (rank) | 15 |
| Cost (% of income per capita) | 13.4 | Private bureau coverage (% of adults) | 100.0 | Procedures (number) | 28 |
| | | | | Time (days) | 395 |
| **Getting electricity** (rank) | 36 | **Protecting investors** (rank) | 70 | Cost (% of claim) | 21.8 |
| Procedures (number) | 5 | Extent of disclosure index (0-10) | 8 | | |
| Time (days) | 75 | Extent of director liability index (0-10) | 2 | **Resolving insolvency** (rank) | 18 |
| Cost (% of income per capita) | 8.7 | Ease of shareholder suits index (0-10) | 7 | Time (years) | 1.0 |
| | | Strength of investor protection index (0-10) | 5.7 | Cost (% of estate) | 8 |
| | | | | Recovery rate (cents on the dollar) | 80.8 |
| | | **Paying taxes** (rank) | 48 | | |
| | | Payments (number per year) | 11 | | |
| | | Time (hours per year) | 109 | | |
| | | Total tax rate (% of profit) | 47.5 | | |

*Note:* Most indicator sets refer to a case scenario in an economy's largest business city. For more details, see the data notes.

✔ Reform making it easier to do business  ✘ Reform making it more difficult to do business

## AUSTRIA

| | | | | | | |
|---|---|---|---|---|---|---|
| Ease of doing business (rank) | 29 | OECD high income / High income | | GNI per capita (US$) | 48,300 | |
| | | | | Population (m) | 8.4 | |

| | | | | | |
|---|---|---|---|---|---|
| **Starting a business** (rank) | 134 | **Registering property** (rank) | 34 | **Trading across borders** (rank) | 26 |
| Procedures (number) | 8 | Procedures (number) | 3 | Documents to export (number) | 4 |
| Time (days) | 25 | Time (days) | 21 | Time to export (days) | 8 |
| Cost (% of income per capita) | 4.9 | Cost (% of property value) | 4.6 | Cost to export (US$ per container) | 1,090 |
| Minimum capital (% of income per capita) | 49.1 | | | Documents to import (number) | 5 |
| | | **Getting credit** (rank) | 23 | Time to import (days) | 8 |
| | | Strength of legal rights index (0-10) | 7 | Cost to import (US$ per container) | 1,155 |
| **Dealing with construction permits** (rank) | 75 | Depth of credit information index (0-6) | 6 | | |
| Procedures (number) | 13 | Public registry coverage (% of adults) | 1.8 | **Enforcing contracts** (rank) | 7 |
| Time (days) | 194 | Private bureau coverage (% of adults) | 52.6 | Procedures (number) | 25 |
| Cost (% of income per capita) | 57.3 | | | Time (days) | 397 |
| | | **Protecting investors** (rank) | 100 | Cost (% of claim) | 18.0 |
| **Getting electricity** (rank) | 24 | Extent of disclosure index (0-10) | 5 | | |
| Procedures (number) | 5 | Extent of director liability index (0-10) | 5 | **Resolving insolvency** (rank) | 12 |
| Time (days) | 23 | Ease of shareholder suits index (0-10) | 5 | Time (years) | 1.1 |
| Cost (% of income per capita) | 104.5 | Strength of investor protection index (0-10) | 5.0 | Cost (% of estate) | 10 |
| | | | | Recovery rate (cents on the dollar) | 83.3 |
| | | **Paying taxes** (rank) | 77 | | |
| | | Payments (number per year) | 12 | | |
| | | Time (hours per year) | 170 | | |
| | | Total tax rate (% of profit) | 53.1 | | |

## AZERBAIJAN

| | | | | | | |
|---|---|---|---|---|---|---|
| Ease of doing business (rank) | 67 | Eastern Europe & Central Asia / Upper middle income | | GNI per capita (US$) | 5,290 | |
| | | | | Population (m) | 9.2 | |

| | | | | | |
|---|---|---|---|---|---|
| **Starting a business** (rank) | 18 | **Registering property** (rank) | 9 | **Trading across borders** (rank) | 169 |
| Procedures (number) | 6 | Procedures (number) | 4 | Documents to export (number) | 8 |
| Time (days) | 8 | Time (days) | 11 | Time to export (days) | 38 |
| Cost (% of income per capita) | 2.3 | Cost (% of property value) | 0.5 | Cost to export (US$ per container) | 3,430 |
| Minimum capital (% of income per capita) | 0.0 | | | Documents to import (number) | 10 |
| | | **Getting credit** (rank) | 53 | Time to import (days) | 38 |
| | | Strength of legal rights index (0-10) | 6 | Cost to import (US$ per container) | 3,490 |
| **Dealing with construction permits** (rank) | 177 | Depth of credit information index (0-6) | 5 | | |
| Procedures (number) | 28 | Public registry coverage (% of adults) | 17.7 | **Enforcing contracts** (rank) | 25 |
| Time (days) | 212 | Private bureau coverage (% of adults) | 0.0 | Procedures (number) | 39 |
| Cost (% of income per capita) | 292.4 | | | Time (days) | 237 |
| | | **Protecting investors** (rank) | 25 | Cost (% of claim) | 18.5 |
| **Getting electricity** (rank) | 175 | Extent of disclosure index (0-10) | 7 | | |
| Procedures (number) | 9 | Extent of director liability index (0-10) | 5 | **Resolving insolvency** (rank) | 95 |
| Time (days) | 241 | Ease of shareholder suits index (0-10) | 8 | Time (years) | 2.7 |
| Cost (% of income per capita) | 591.2 | Strength of investor protection index (0-10) | 6.7 | Cost (% of estate) | 8 |
| | | | | Recovery rate (cents on the dollar) | 30.6 |
| | | **Paying taxes** (rank) | 76 | | |
| | | Payments (number per year) | 18 | | |
| | | Time (hours per year) | 214 | | |
| | | Total tax rate (% of profit) | 40.0 | | |

## BAHAMAS, THE

| | | | | | | |
|---|---|---|---|---|---|---|
| Ease of doing business (rank) | 77 | Latin America & Caribbean / High income | | GNI per capita (US$) | 23,175 | |
| | | | | Population (m) | 0.3 | |

| | | | | | |
|---|---|---|---|---|---|
| **Starting a business** (rank) | 82 | **Registering property** (rank) | 179 | **Trading across borders** (rank) | 58 |
| Procedures (number) | 7 | Procedures (number) | 7 | Documents to export (number) | 5 |
| Time (days) | 31 | Time (days) | 122 | Time to export (days) | 19 |
| Cost (% of income per capita) | 10.3 | Cost (% of property value) | 13.5 | Cost to export (US$ per container) | 930 |
| Minimum capital (% of income per capita) | 0.0 | | | Documents to import (number) | 6 |
| | | **Getting credit** (rank) | 83 | Time to import (days) | 13 |
| | | Strength of legal rights index (0-10) | 9 | Cost to import (US$ per container) | 1,405 |
| **Dealing with construction permits** (rank) | 68 | Depth of credit information index (0-6) | 0 | | |
| Procedures (number) | 14 | Public registry coverage (% of adults) | 0.0 | **Enforcing contracts** (rank) | 123 |
| Time (days) | 178 | Private bureau coverage (% of adults) | 0.0 | Procedures (number) | 49 |
| Cost (% of income per capita) | 27.8 | | | Time (days) | 427 |
| | | **Protecting investors** (rank) | 117 | Cost (% of claim) | 28.9 |
| **Getting electricity** (rank) | 43 | Extent of disclosure index (0-10) | 2 | | |
| Procedures (number) | 5 | Extent of director liability index (0-10) | 5 | **Resolving insolvency** (rank) | 35 |
| Time (days) | 67 | Ease of shareholder suits index (0-10) | 7 | Time (years) | 5.0 |
| Cost (% of income per capita) | 103.0 | Strength of investor protection index (0-10) | 4.7 | Cost (% of estate) | 4 |
| | | | | Recovery rate (cents on the dollar) | 55.9 |
| | | **Paying taxes** (rank) | 51 | | |
| | | Payments (number per year) | 18 | | |
| | | Time (hours per year) | 58 | | |
| | | Total tax rate (% of profit) | 47.8 | | |

*Note:* Most indicator sets refer to a case scenario in an economy's largest business city. For more details, see the data notes.

✔ Reform making it easier to do business ✗ Reform making it more difficult to do business

## BAHRAIN

| | | | | | | | |
|---|---|---|---|---|---|---|---|
| Ease of doing business (rank) | **42** | Middle East & North Africa<br>High income | | GNI per capita (US$)<br>Population (m) | 23,132<br>1.3 | | |

| **Starting a business** (rank) | 88 | **Registering property** (rank) | 29 | **Trading across borders** (rank) | 54 |
|---|---|---|---|---|---|
| Procedures (number) | 7 | Procedures (number) | 2 | Documents to export (number) | 6 |
| Time (days) | 9 | Time (days) | 31 | Time to export (days) | 11 |
| Cost (% of income per capita) | 0.7 | Cost (% of property value) | 2.7 | Cost to export (US$ per container) | 955 |
| Minimum capital (% of income per capita) | 229.9 | | | Documents to import (number) | 7 |
| | | **Getting credit** (rank) | 129 | Time to import (days) | 15 |
| | | Strength of legal rights index (0-10) | 4 | Cost to import (US$ per container) | 995 |
| **Dealing with construction permits** (rank) | 7 | Depth of credit information index (0-6) | 3 | | |
| Procedures (number) | 12 | Public registry coverage (% of adults) | 0.0 | **Enforcing contracts** (rank) | 113 |
| Time (days) | 43 | Private bureau coverage (% of adults) | 23.5 | Procedures (number) | 48 |
| Cost (% of income per capita) | 9.5 | | | Time (days) | 635 |
| | | **Protecting investors** (rank) | 82 | Cost (% of claim) | 14.7 |
| **Getting electricity** (rank) | 48 | Extent of disclosure index (0-10) | 8 | | |
| Procedures (number) | 5 | Extent of director liability index (0-10) | 4 | **Resolving insolvency** (rank) | 27 |
| Time (days) | 90 | Ease of shareholder suits index (0-10) | 4 | Time (years) | 2.5 |
| Cost (% of income per capita) | 56.3 | Strength of investor protection index (0-10) | 5.3 | Cost (% of estate) | 10 |
| | | | | Recovery rate (cents on the dollar) | 66.2 |
| | | **Paying taxes** (rank) | 7 | | |
| | | Payments (number per year) | 13 | | |
| | | Time (hours per year) | 36 | | |
| | | Total tax rate (% of profit) | 13.9 | | |

## BANGLADESH

| | | | | | | | |
|---|---|---|---|---|---|---|---|
| Ease of doing business (rank) | **129** | South Asia<br>Low income | | GNI per capita (US$)<br>Population (m) | 770<br>150.5 | | |

| **Starting a business** (rank) | 95 | **Registering property** (rank) | 175 | **Trading across borders** (rank) | 119 |
|---|---|---|---|---|---|
| Procedures (number) | 7 | Procedures (number) | 8 | Documents to export (number) | 6 |
| Time (days) | 19 | Time (days) | 245 | Time to export (days) | 25 |
| Cost (% of income per capita) | 25.1 | Cost (% of property value) | 6.8 | Cost to export (US$ per container) | 1,025 |
| Minimum capital (% of income per capita) | 0.0 | | | Documents to import (number) | 8 |
| | | ✔ **Getting credit** (rank) | 83 | Time to import (days) | 34 |
| | | Strength of legal rights index (0-10) | 7 | Cost to import (US$ per container) | 1,430 |
| **Dealing with construction permits** (rank) | 83 | Depth of credit information index (0-6) | 2 | | |
| Procedures (number) | 11 | Public registry coverage (% of adults) | 0.8 | **Enforcing contracts** (rank) | 182 |
| Time (days) | 201 | Private bureau coverage (% of adults) | 0.0 | Procedures (number) | 41 |
| Cost (% of income per capita) | 126.5 | | | Time (days) | 1,442 |
| | | **Protecting investors** (rank) | 25 | Cost (% of claim) | 63.3 |
| ✗ **Getting electricity** (rank) | 185 | Extent of disclosure index (0-10) | 6 | | |
| Procedures (number) | 9 | Extent of director liability index (0-10) | 7 | **Resolving insolvency** (rank) | 119 |
| Time (days) | 404 | Ease of shareholder suits index (0-10) | 7 | Time (years) | 4.0 |
| Cost (% of income per capita) | 5,193.8 | Strength of investor protection index (0-10) | 6.7 | Cost (% of estate) | 8 |
| | | | | Recovery rate (cents on the dollar) | 25.5 |
| | | **Paying taxes** (rank) | 97 | | |
| | | Payments (number per year) | 20 | | |
| | | Time (hours per year) | 302 | | |
| | | Total tax rate (% of profit) | 35.0 | | |

## BARBADOS

| | | | | | | | |
|---|---|---|---|---|---|---|---|
| Ease of doing business (rank) | **88** | Latin America & Caribbean<br>High income | | GNI per capita (US$)<br>Population (m) | 16,149<br>0.3 | | |

| **Starting a business** (rank) | 70 | **Registering property** (rank) | 154 | **Trading across borders** (rank) | 31 |
|---|---|---|---|---|---|
| Procedures (number) | 8 | Procedures (number) | 6 | Documents to export (number) | 5 |
| Time (days) | 18 | Time (days) | 153 | Time to export (days) | 9 |
| Cost (% of income per capita) | 7.2 | Cost (% of property value) | 7.3 | Cost to export (US$ per container) | 810 |
| Minimum capital (% of income per capita) | 0.0 | | | Documents to import (number) | 6 |
| | | **Getting credit** (rank) | 83 | Time to import (days) | 8 |
| | | Strength of legal rights index (0-10) | 9 | Cost to import (US$ per container) | 1,615 |
| **Dealing with construction permits** (rank) | 53 | Depth of credit information index (0-6) | 0 | | |
| Procedures (number) | 10 | Public registry coverage (% of adults) | 0.0 | **Enforcing contracts** (rank) | 105 |
| Time (days) | 416 | Private bureau coverage (% of adults) | 0.0 | Procedures (number) | 38 |
| Cost (% of income per capita) | 8.3 | | | Time (days) | 1,340 |
| | | **Protecting investors** (rank) | 169 | Cost (% of claim) | 19.7 |
| **Getting electricity** (rank) | 81 | Extent of disclosure index (0-10) | 2 | | |
| Procedures (number) | 7 | Extent of director liability index (0-10) | 1 | **Resolving insolvency** (rank) | 28 |
| Time (days) | 65 | Ease of shareholder suits index (0-10) | 6 | Time (years) | 1.8 |
| Cost (% of income per capita) | 60.3 | Strength of investor protection index (0-10) | 3.0 | Cost (% of estate) | 15 |
| | | | | Recovery rate (cents on the dollar) | 65.1 |
| | | **Paying taxes** (rank) | 121 | | |
| | | Payments (number per year) | 28 | | |
| | | Time (hours per year) | 237 | | |
| | | Total tax rate (% of profit) | 45.4 | | |

*Note:* Most indicator sets refer to a case scenario in an economy's largest business city. For more details, see the data notes.

## BELARUS

| | | | | | | |
|---|---|---|---|---|---|---|
| Ease of doing business (rank) | **58** | Eastern Europe & Central Asia<br>Upper middle income | | GNI per capita (US$) | **5,830** | |
| | | | | Population (m) | **9.5** | |

| | | | | | |
|---|---|---|---|---|---|
| ✗ **Starting a business** (rank) | 9 | **Registering property** (rank) | 3 | **Trading across borders** (rank) | 151 |
| Procedures (number) | 5 | Procedures (number) | 2 | Documents to export (number) | 9 |
| Time (days) | 5 | Time (days) | 10 | Time to export (days) | 15 |
| Cost (% of income per capita) | 2.3 | Cost (% of property value) | 0.0 | Cost to export (US$ per container) | 1,510 |
| Minimum capital (% of income per capita) | 0.0 | | | Documents to import (number) | 10 |
| | | **Getting credit** (rank) | 104 | Time to import (days) | 30 |
| | | Strength of legal rights index (0-10) | 3 | Cost to import (US$ per container) | 2,315 |
| **Dealing with construction permits** (rank) | 30 | Depth of credit information index (0-6) | 5 | | |
| Procedures (number) | 12 | Public registry coverage (% of adults) | 56.2 | **Enforcing contracts** (rank) | 13 |
| Time (days) | 130 | Private bureau coverage (% of adults) | 0.0 | Procedures (number) | 29 |
| Cost (% of income per capita) | 24.8 | | | Time (days) | 275 |
| | | **Protecting investors** (rank) | 82 | Cost (% of claim) | 23.4 |
| **Getting electricity** (rank) | 171 | Extent of disclosure index (0-10) | 7 | | |
| Procedures (number) | 7 | Extent of director liability index (0-10) | 1 | ✔ **Resolving insolvency** (rank) | 56 |
| Time (days) | 179 | Ease of shareholder suits index (0-10) | 8 | Time (years) | 3.0 |
| Cost (% of income per capita) | 838.8 | Strength of investor protection index (0-10) | 5.3 | Cost (% of estate) | 22 |
| | | | | Recovery rate (cents on the dollar) | 43.0 |
| | | ✔ **Paying taxes** (rank) | 129 | | |
| | | Payments (number per year) | 10 | | |
| | | Time (hours per year) | 338 | | |
| | | Total tax rate (% of profit) | 60.7 | | |

## BELGIUM

| | | | | | | |
|---|---|---|---|---|---|---|
| Ease of doing business (rank) | **33** | OECD high income<br>High income | | GNI per capita (US$) | **46,160** | |
| | | | | Population (m) | **11.0** | |

| | | | | | |
|---|---|---|---|---|---|
| **Starting a business** (rank) | 44 | **Registering property** (rank) | 176 | **Trading across borders** (rank) | 29 |
| Procedures (number) | 3 | Procedures (number) | 8 | Documents to export (number) | 4 |
| Time (days) | 4 | Time (days) | 64 | Time to export (days) | 9 |
| Cost (% of income per capita) | 5.2 | Cost (% of property value) | 12.7 | Cost to export (US$ per container) | 1,230 |
| Minimum capital (% of income per capita) | 18.2 | | | Documents to import (number) | 5 |
| | | **Getting credit** (rank) | 70 | Time to import (days) | 9 |
| | | Strength of legal rights index (0-10) | 6 | Cost to import (US$ per container) | 1,400 |
| **Dealing with construction permits** (rank) | 57 | Depth of credit information index (0-6) | 4 | | |
| Procedures (number) | 11 | Public registry coverage (% of adults) | 89.0 | **Enforcing contracts** (rank) | 18 |
| Time (days) | 205 | Private bureau coverage (% of adults) | 0.0 | Procedures (number) | 26 |
| Cost (% of income per capita) | 54.2 | | | Time (days) | 505 |
| | | **Protecting investors** (rank) | 19 | Cost (% of claim) | 17.7 |
| **Getting electricity** (rank) | 82 | Extent of disclosure index (0-10) | 8 | | |
| Procedures (number) | 6 | Extent of director liability index (0-10) | 6 | **Resolving insolvency** (rank) | 7 |
| Time (days) | 88 | Ease of shareholder suits index (0-10) | 7 | Time (years) | 0.9 |
| Cost (% of income per capita) | 92.6 | Strength of investor protection index (0-10) | 7.0 | Cost (% of estate) | 4 |
| | | | | Recovery rate (cents on the dollar) | 88.7 |
| | | **Paying taxes** (rank) | 75 | | |
| | | Payments (number per year) | 11 | | |
| | | Time (hours per year) | 156 | | |
| | | Total tax rate (% of profit) | 57.7 | | |

## BELIZE

| | | | | | | |
|---|---|---|---|---|---|---|
| Ease of doing business (rank) | **105** | Latin America & Caribbean<br>Lower middle income | | GNI per capita (US$) | **3,690** | |
| | | | | Population (m) | **0.4** | |

| | | | | | |
|---|---|---|---|---|---|
| **Starting a business** (rank) | 158 | **Registering property** (rank) | 136 | ✔ **Trading across borders** (rank) | 102 |
| Procedures (number) | 9 | Procedures (number) | 8 | Documents to export (number) | 6 |
| Time (days) | 44 | Time (days) | 60 | Time to export (days) | 19 |
| Cost (% of income per capita) | 51.9 | Cost (% of property value) | 4.8 | Cost to export (US$ per container) | 1,355 |
| Minimum capital (% of income per capita) | 0.0 | | | Documents to import (number) | 7 |
| | | **Getting credit** (rank) | 129 | Time to import (days) | 20 |
| | | Strength of legal rights index (0-10) | 7 | Cost to import (US$ per container) | 1,600 |
| **Dealing with construction permits** (rank) | 21 | Depth of credit information index (0-6) | 0 | | |
| Procedures (number) | 8 | Public registry coverage (% of adults) | 0.0 | **Enforcing contracts** (rank) | 169 |
| Time (days) | 91 | Private bureau coverage (% of adults) | 0.0 | Procedures (number) | 51 |
| Cost (% of income per capita) | 97.9 | | | Time (days) | 892 |
| | | **Protecting investors** (rank) | 128 | Cost (% of claim) | 27.5 |
| **Getting electricity** (rank) | 58 | Extent of disclosure index (0-10) | 3 | | |
| Procedures (number) | 5 | Extent of director liability index (0-10) | 4 | **Resolving insolvency** (rank) | 30 |
| Time (days) | 66 | Ease of shareholder suits index (0-10) | 6 | Time (years) | 1.0 |
| Cost (% of income per capita) | 400.5 | Strength of investor protection index (0-10) | 4.3 | Cost (% of estate) | 23 |
| | | | | Recovery rate (cents on the dollar) | 64.0 |
| | | **Paying taxes** (rank) | 45 | | |
| | | Payments (number per year) | 29 | | |
| | | Time (hours per year) | 147 | | |
| | | Total tax rate (% of profit) | 33.2 | | |

*Note:* Most indicator sets refer to a case scenario in an economy's largest business city. For more details, see the data notes.

✔ Reform making it easier to do business  ✘ Reform making it more difficult to do business

## BENIN

| | | Sub-Saharan Africa | | GNI per capita (US$) | 780 |
|---|---|---|---|---|---|
| Ease of doing business (rank) | 175 | Low income | | Population (m) | 9.1 |

| | | | | | |
|---|---|---|---|---|---|
| ✔ **Starting a business** (rank) | 153 | **Registering property** (rank) | 133 | ✔ **Trading across borders** (rank) | 130 |
| Procedures (number) | 5 | Procedures (number) | 4 | Documents to export (number) | 7 |
| Time (days) | 26 | Time (days) | 120 | Time to export (days) | 29 |
| Cost (% of income per capita) | 126.8 | Cost (% of property value) | 11.8 | Cost to export (US$ per container) | 1,079 |
| Minimum capital (% of income per capita) | 264.5 | | | Documents to import (number) | 8 |
| | | **Getting credit** (rank) | 129 | Time to import (days) | 30 |
| ✔ **Dealing with construction permits** (rank) | 111 | Strength of legal rights index (0-10) | 6 | Cost to import (US$ per container) | 1,549 |
| Procedures (number) | 11 | Depth of credit information index (0-6) | 1 | | |
| Time (days) | 282 | Public registry coverage (% of adults) | 10.9 | ✔ **Enforcing contracts** (rank) | 178 |
| Cost (% of income per capita) | 167.4 | Private bureau coverage (% of adults) | 0.0 | Procedures (number) | 42 |
| | | | | Time (days) | 795 |
| **Getting electricity** (rank) | 141 | **Protecting investors** (rank) | 158 | Cost (% of claim) | 64.7 |
| Procedures (number) | 4 | Extent of disclosure index (0-10) | 6 | | |
| Time (days) | 158 | Extent of director liability index (0-10) | 1 | **Resolving insolvency** (rank) | 132 |
| Cost (% of income per capita) | 14,343.1 | Ease of shareholder suits index (0-10) | 3 | Time (years) | 4.0 |
| | | Strength of investor protection index (0-10) | 3.3 | Cost (% of estate) | 22 |
| | | | | Recovery rate (cents on the dollar) | 20.2 |
| | | **Paying taxes** (rank) | 173 | | |
| | | Payments (number per year) | 55 | | |
| | | Time (hours per year) | 270 | | |
| | | Total tax rate (% of profit) | 65.9 | | |

## BHUTAN

| | | South Asia | | GNI per capita (US$) | 2,070 |
|---|---|---|---|---|---|
| Ease of doing business (rank) | 148 | Lower middle income | | Population (m) | 0.7 |

| | | | | | |
|---|---|---|---|---|---|
| **Starting a business** (rank) | 94 | **Registering property** (rank) | 85 | **Trading across borders** (rank) | 172 |
| Procedures (number) | 8 | Procedures (number) | 3 | Documents to export (number) | 9 |
| Time (days) | 36 | Time (days) | 92 | Time to export (days) | 38 |
| Cost (% of income per capita) | 6.5 | Cost (% of property value) | 5.0 | Cost to export (US$ per container) | 2,230 |
| Minimum capital (% of income per capita) | 0.0 | | | Documents to import (number) | 12 |
| | | **Getting credit** (rank) | 129 | Time to import (days) | 38 |
| **Dealing with construction permits** (rank) | 124 | Strength of legal rights index (0-10) | 3 | Cost to import (US$ per container) | 2,330 |
| Procedures (number) | 22 | Depth of credit information index (0-6) | 4 | | |
| Time (days) | 150 | Public registry coverage (% of adults) | 13.5 | **Enforcing contracts** (rank) | 37 |
| Cost (% of income per capita) | 92.7 | Private bureau coverage (% of adults) | 0.0 | Procedures (number) | 47 |
| | | | | Time (days) | 225 |
| **Getting electricity** (rank) | 136 | **Protecting investors** (rank) | 150 | Cost (% of claim) | 0.1 |
| Procedures (number) | 6 | Extent of disclosure index (0-10) | 4 | | |
| Time (days) | 90 | Extent of director liability index (0-10) | 3 | **Resolving insolvency** (rank) | 185 |
| Cost (% of income per capita) | 1,149.6 | Ease of shareholder suits index (0-10) | 4 | Time (years) | NO PRACTICE |
| | | Strength of investor protection index (0-10) | 3.7 | Cost (% of estate) | NO PRACTICE |
| | | | | Recovery rate (cents on the dollar) | 0.0 |
| | | **Paying taxes** (rank) | 71 | | |
| | | Payments (number per year) | 8 | | |
| | | Time (hours per year) | 274 | | |
| | | Total tax rate (% of profit) | 40.8 | | |

## BOLIVIA

| | | Latin America & Caribbean | | GNI per capita (US$) | 2,040 |
|---|---|---|---|---|---|
| Ease of doing business (rank) | 155 | Lower middle income | | Population (m) | 10.1 |

| | | | | | |
|---|---|---|---|---|---|
| **Starting a business** (rank) | 174 | **Registering property** (rank) | 139 | **Trading across borders** (rank) | 125 |
| Procedures (number) | 15 | Procedures (number) | 7 | Documents to export (number) | 8 |
| Time (days) | 50 | Time (days) | 92 | Time to export (days) | 19 |
| Cost (% of income per capita) | 74.1 | Cost (% of property value) | 4.7 | Cost to export (US$ per container) | 1,425 |
| Minimum capital (% of income per capita) | 1.9 | | | Documents to import (number) | 7 |
| | | **Getting credit** (rank) | 129 | Time to import (days) | 23 |
| **Dealing with construction permits** (rank) | 114 | Strength of legal rights index (0-10) | 1 | Cost to import (US$ per container) | 1,747 |
| Procedures (number) | 14 | Depth of credit information index (0-6) | 6 | | |
| Time (days) | 249 | Public registry coverage (% of adults) | 14.8 | **Enforcing contracts** (rank) | 136 |
| Cost (% of income per capita) | 63.6 | Private bureau coverage (% of adults) | 34.7 | Procedures (number) | 40 |
| | | | | Time (days) | 591 |
| **Getting electricity** (rank) | 126 | **Protecting investors** (rank) | 139 | Cost (% of claim) | 33.2 |
| Procedures (number) | 8 | Extent of disclosure index (0-10) | 1 | | |
| Time (days) | 42 | Extent of director liability index (0-10) | 5 | **Resolving insolvency** (rank) | 68 |
| Cost (% of income per capita) | 1,036.1 | Ease of shareholder suits index (0-10) | 6 | Time (years) | 1.8 |
| | | Strength of investor protection index (0-10) | 4.0 | Cost (% of estate) | 15 |
| | | | | Recovery rate (cents on the dollar) | 39.0 |
| | | **Paying taxes** (rank) | 180 | | |
| | | Payments (number per year) | 42 | | |
| | | Time (hours per year) | 1,025 | | |
| | | Total tax rate (% of profit) | 83.4 | | |

*Note:* Most indicator sets refer to a case scenario in an economy's largest business city. For more details, see the data notes.

✔ Reform making it easier to do business ✘ Reform making it more difficult to do business

## BOSNIA AND HERZEGOVINA

| | | | | | | |
|---|---|---|---|---|---|---|
| Ease of doing business (rank) | 126 | Eastern Europe & Central Asia<br>Upper middle income | | GNI per capita (US$)<br>Population (m) | 4,780<br>3.8 |

| | | | | | |
|---|---|---|---|---|---|
| **Starting a business** (rank) | 162 | ✔ **Registering property** (rank) | 93 | **Trading across borders** (rank) | 103 |
| Procedures (number) | 11 | Procedures (number) | 7 | Documents to export (number) | 8 |
| Time (days) | 37 | Time (days) | 25 | Time to export (days) | 15 |
| Cost (% of income per capita) | 14.9 | Cost (% of property value) | 5.3 | Cost to export (US$ per container) | 1,240 |
| Minimum capital (% of income per capita) | 29.1 | | | Documents to import (number) | 9 |
| | | ✘ **Getting credit** (rank) | 70 | Time to import (days) | 13 |
| **Dealing with construction permits** (rank) | 163 | Strength of legal rights index (0-10) | 5 | Cost to import (US$ per container) | 1,200 |
| Procedures (number) | 17 | Depth of credit information index (0-6) | 5 | | |
| Time (days) | 180 | Public registry coverage (% of adults) | 36.2 | **Enforcing contracts** (rank) | 120 |
| Cost (% of income per capita) | 1,102.1 | Private bureau coverage (% of adults) | 4.8 | Procedures (number) | 37 |
| | | | | Time (days) | 595 |
| **Getting electricity** (rank) | 158 | **Protecting investors** (rank) | 100 | Cost (% of claim) | 34.0 |
| Procedures (number) | 8 | Extent of disclosure index (0-10) | 3 | | |
| Time (days) | 125 | Extent of director liability index (0-10) | 6 | **Resolving insolvency** (rank) | 83 |
| Cost (% of income per capita) | 493.3 | Ease of shareholder suits index (0-10) | 6 | Time (years) | 3.3 |
| | | Strength of investor protection index (0-10) | 5.0 | Cost (% of estate) | 9 |
| | | | | Recovery rate (cents on the dollar) | 35.4 |
| | | ✔ **Paying taxes** (rank) | 128 | | |
| | | Payments (number per year) | 44 | | |
| | | Time (hours per year) | 407 | | |
| | | Total tax rate (% of profit) | 24.1 | | |

## BOTSWANA

| | | | | | | |
|---|---|---|---|---|---|---|
| Ease of doing business (rank) | 59 | Sub-Saharan Africa<br>Upper middle income | | GNI per capita (US$)<br>Population (m) | 7,480<br>2.0 |

| | | | | | |
|---|---|---|---|---|---|
| **Starting a business** (rank) | 99 | **Registering property** (rank) | 51 | ✔ **Trading across borders** (rank) | 147 |
| Procedures (number) | 10 | Procedures (number) | 5 | Documents to export (number) | 6 |
| Time (days) | 61 | Time (days) | 16 | Time to export (days) | 27 |
| Cost (% of income per capita) | 1.6 | Cost (% of property value) | 5.1 | Cost to export (US$ per container) | 2,945 |
| Minimum capital (% of income per capita) | 0.0 | | | Documents to import (number) | 7 |
| | | **Getting credit** (rank) | 53 | Time to import (days) | 37 |
| **Dealing with construction permits** (rank) | 132 | Strength of legal rights index (0-10) | 7 | Cost to import (US$ per container) | 3,445 |
| Procedures (number) | 22 | Depth of credit information index (0-6) | 4 | | |
| Time (days) | 145 | Public registry coverage (% of adults) | 0.0 | **Enforcing contracts** (rank) | 68 |
| Cost (% of income per capita) | 172.7 | Private bureau coverage (% of adults) | 58.9 | Procedures (number) | 28 |
| | | | | Time (days) | 625 |
| **Getting electricity** (rank) | 90 | **Protecting investors** (rank) | 49 | Cost (% of claim) | 28.1 |
| Procedures (number) | 5 | Extent of disclosure index (0-10) | 7 | | |
| Time (days) | 121 | Extent of director liability index (0-10) | 8 | **Resolving insolvency** (rank) | 29 |
| Cost (% of income per capita) | 353.8 | Ease of shareholder suits index (0-10) | 3 | Time (years) | 1.7 |
| | | Strength of investor protection index (0-10) | 6.0 | Cost (% of estate) | 15 |
| | | | | Recovery rate (cents on the dollar) | 64.8 |
| | | ✘ **Paying taxes** (rank) | 39 | | |
| | | Payments (number per year) | 32 | | |
| | | Time (hours per year) | 152 | | |
| | | Total tax rate (% of profit) | 25.3 | | |

## BRAZIL

| | | | | | | |
|---|---|---|---|---|---|---|
| Ease of doing business (rank) | 130 | Latin America & Caribbean<br>Upper middle income | | GNI per capita (US$)<br>Population (m) | 10,720<br>196.7 |

| | | | | | |
|---|---|---|---|---|---|
| **Starting a business** (rank) | 121 | ✘ **Registering property** (rank) | 109 | **Trading across borders** (rank) | 123 |
| Procedures (number) | 13 | Procedures (number) | 14 | Documents to export (number) | 7 |
| Time (days) | 119 | Time (days) | 34 | Time to export (days) | 13 |
| Cost (% of income per capita) | 4.8 | Cost (% of property value) | 2.6 | Cost to export (US$ per container) | 2,215 |
| Minimum capital (% of income per capita) | 0.0 | | | Documents to import (number) | 8 |
| | | **Getting credit** (rank) | 104 | Time to import (days) | 17 |
| **Dealing with construction permits** (rank) | 131 | Strength of legal rights index (0-10) | 3 | Cost to import (US$ per container) | 2,275 |
| Procedures (number) | 17 | Depth of credit information index (0-6) | 5 | | |
| Time (days) | 469 | Public registry coverage (% of adults) | 46.8 | ✔ **Enforcing contracts** (rank) | 116 |
| Cost (% of income per capita) | 36.0 | Private bureau coverage (% of adults) | 62.2 | Procedures (number) | 44 |
| | | | | Time (days) | 731 |
| **Getting electricity** (rank) | 60 | **Protecting investors** (rank) | 82 | Cost (% of claim) | 16.5 |
| Procedures (number) | 6 | Extent of disclosure index (0-10) | 6 | | |
| Time (days) | 57 | Extent of director liability index (0-10) | 7 | **Resolving insolvency** (rank) | 143 |
| Cost (% of income per capita) | 116.7 | Ease of shareholder suits index (0-10) | 3 | Time (years) | 4.0 |
| | | Strength of investor protection index (0-10) | 5.3 | Cost (% of estate) | 12 |
| | | | | Recovery rate (cents on the dollar) | 15.9 |
| | | **Paying taxes** (rank) | 156 | | |
| | | Payments (number per year) | 9 | | |
| | | Time (hours per year) | 2,600 | | |
| | | Total tax rate (% of profit) | 69.3 | | |

*Note:* Most indicator sets refer to a case scenario in an economy's largest business city. For more details, see the data notes.

✔ Reform making it easier to do business  ✘ Reform making it more difficult to do business

## BRUNEI DARUSSALAM
| Ease of doing business (rank) | 79 |
|---|---|

East Asia & Pacific
High income

| GNI per capita (US$) | 36,584 |
|---|---|
| Population (m) | 0.4 |

| Starting a business (rank) | 135 |
|---|---|
| Procedures (number) | 15 |
| Time (days) | 101 |
| Cost (% of income per capita) | 10.7 |
| Minimum capital (% of income per capita) | 0.0 |

| Registering property (rank) | 115 |
|---|---|
| Procedures (number) | 7 |
| Time (days) | 298 |
| Cost (% of property value) | 0.6 |

| Trading across borders (rank) | 40 |
|---|---|
| Documents to export (number) | 6 |
| Time to export (days) | 19 |
| Cost to export (US$ per container) | 680 |
| Documents to import (number) | 6 |
| Time to import (days) | 15 |
| Cost to import (US$ per container) | 745 |

✔ **Dealing with construction permits** (rank) 43
Procedures (number) 22
Time (days) 95
Cost (% of income per capita) 4.0

| Getting credit (rank) | 129 |
|---|---|
| Strength of legal rights index (0-10) | 7 |
| Depth of credit information index (0-6) | 0 |
| Public registry coverage (% of adults) | 0.0 |
| Private bureau coverage (% of adults) | 0.0 |

| Enforcing contracts (rank) | 158 |
|---|---|
| Procedures (number) | 47 |
| Time (days) | 540 |
| Cost (% of claim) | 36.6 |

**Getting electricity** (rank) 29
Procedures (number) 5
Time (days) 56
Cost (% of income per capita) 40.6

| Protecting investors (rank) | 117 |
|---|---|
| Extent of disclosure index (0-10) | 4 |
| Extent of director liability index (0-10) | 2 |
| Ease of shareholder suits index (0-10) | 8 |
| Strength of investor protection index (0-10) | 4.7 |

| Resolving insolvency (rank) | 46 |
|---|---|
| Time (years) | 2.5 |
| Cost (% of estate) | 4 |
| Recovery rate (cents on the dollar) | 47.2 |

✔ **Paying taxes** (rank) 22
Payments (number per year) 27
Time (hours per year) 96
Total tax rate (% of profit) 16.8

## BULGARIA
| Ease of doing business (rank) | 66 |
|---|---|

Eastern Europe & Central Asia
Upper middle income

| GNI per capita (US$) | 6,550 |
|---|---|
| Population (m) | 7.5 |

✔ **Starting a business** (rank) 57
Procedures (number) 4
Time (days) 18
Cost (% of income per capita) 1.1
Minimum capital (% of income per capita) 0.0

| Registering property (rank) | 68 |
|---|---|
| Procedures (number) | 8 |
| Time (days) | 15 |
| Cost (% of property value) | 2.9 |

| Trading across borders (rank) | 93 |
|---|---|
| Documents to export (number) | 5 |
| Time to export (days) | 21 |
| Cost to export (US$ per container) | 1,551 |
| Documents to import (number) | 6 |
| Time to import (days) | 17 |
| Cost to import (US$ per container) | 1,626 |

**Dealing with construction permits** (rank) 123
Procedures (number) 21
Time (days) 107
Cost (% of income per capita) 293.5

| Getting credit (rank) | 40 |
|---|---|
| Strength of legal rights index (0-10) | 8 |
| Depth of credit information index (0-6) | 4 |
| Public registry coverage (% of adults) | 56.3 |
| Private bureau coverage (% of adults) | 0.0 |

| Enforcing contracts (rank) | 86 |
|---|---|
| Procedures (number) | 39 |
| Time (days) | 564 |
| Cost (% of claim) | 23.8 |

**Getting electricity** (rank) 128
Procedures (number) 6
Time (days) 130
Cost (% of income per capita) 340.7

| Protecting investors (rank) | 49 |
|---|---|
| Extent of disclosure index (0-10) | 10 |
| Extent of director liability index (0-10) | 1 |
| Ease of shareholder suits index (0-10) | 7 |
| Strength of investor protection index (0-10) | 6.0 |

| Resolving insolvency (rank) | 93 |
|---|---|
| Time (years) | 3.3 |
| Cost (% of estate) | 9 |
| Recovery rate (cents on the dollar) | 31.7 |

**Paying taxes** (rank) 91
Payments (number per year) 15
Time (hours per year) 454
Total tax rate (% of profit) 28.7

## BURKINA FASO
| Ease of doing business (rank) | 153 |
|---|---|

Sub-Saharan Africa
Low income

| GNI per capita (US$) | 570 |
|---|---|
| Population (m) | 17.0 |

| Starting a business (rank) | 120 |
|---|---|
| Procedures (number) | 3 |
| Time (days) | 13 |
| Cost (% of income per capita) | 46.8 |
| Minimum capital (% of income per capita) | 353.9 |

| Registering property (rank) | 113 |
|---|---|
| Procedures (number) | 4 |
| Time (days) | 59 |
| Cost (% of property value) | 12.6 |

| Trading across borders (rank) | 173 |
|---|---|
| Documents to export (number) | 10 |
| Time to export (days) | 41 |
| Cost to export (US$ per container) | 2,412 |
| Documents to import (number) | 10 |
| Time to import (days) | 47 |
| Cost to import (US$ per container) | 4,030 |

**Dealing with construction permits** (rank) 64
Procedures (number) 12
Time (days) 98
Cost (% of income per capita) 380.7

| Getting credit (rank) | 129 |
|---|---|
| Strength of legal rights index (0-10) | 6 |
| Depth of credit information index (0-6) | 1 |
| Public registry coverage (% of adults) | 1.7 |
| Private bureau coverage (% of adults) | 0.0 |

| Enforcing contracts (rank) | 109 |
|---|---|
| Procedures (number) | 37 |
| Time (days) | 446 |
| Cost (% of claim) | 81.7 |

**Getting electricity** (rank) 139
Procedures (number) 4
Time (days) 158
Cost (% of income per capita) 12,662.0

| Protecting investors (rank) | 150 |
|---|---|
| Extent of disclosure index (0-10) | 6 |
| Extent of director liability index (0-10) | 1 |
| Ease of shareholder suits index (0-10) | 4 |
| Strength of investor protection index (0-10) | 3.7 |

| Resolving insolvency (rank) | 113 |
|---|---|
| Time (years) | 4.0 |
| Cost (% of estate) | 9 |
| Recovery rate (cents on the dollar) | 27.3 |

**Paying taxes** (rank) 157
Payments (number per year) 46
Time (hours per year) 270
Total tax rate (% of profit) 43.6

*Note:* Most indicator sets refer to a case scenario in an economy's largest business city. For more details, see the data notes.

✔ Reform making it easier to do business  ✘ Reform making it more difficult to do business

## BURUNDI

| | | | | | | | |
|---|---|---|---|---|---|---|---|
| Ease of doing business (rank) | 159 | Sub-Saharan Africa<br>Low income | | GNI per capita (US$)<br>Population (m) | 250<br>8.6 |

| | | | | | |
|---|---|---|---|---|---|
| ✔ **Starting a business** (rank) | 28 | ✔ **Registering property** (rank) | 127 | ✔ **Trading across borders** (rank) | 177 |
| Procedures (number) | 4 | Procedures (number) | 8 | Documents to export (number) | 10 |
| Time (days) | 8 | Time (days) | 64 | Time to export (days) | 32 |
| Cost (% of income per capita) | 18.3 | Cost (% of property value) | 3.3 | Cost to export (US$ per container) | 2,965 |
| Minimum capital (% of income per capita) | 0.0 | | | Documents to import (number) | 11 |
| | | **Getting credit** (rank) | 167 | Time to import (days) | 46 |
| ✔ **Dealing with construction permits** (rank) | 141 | Strength of legal rights index (0-10) | 3 | Cost to import (US$ per container) | 5,005 |
| Procedures (number) | 21 | Depth of credit information index (0-6) | 1 | | |
| Time (days) | 99 | Public registry coverage (% of adults) | 0.3 | **Enforcing contracts** (rank) | 175 |
| Cost (% of income per capita) | 1,911.9 | Private bureau coverage (% of adults) | 0.0 | Procedures (number) | 44 |
| | | | | Time (days) | 832 |
| **Getting electricity** (rank) | 164 | **Protecting investors** (rank) | 49 | Cost (% of claim) | 38.6 |
| Procedures (number) | 5 | Extent of disclosure index (0-10) | 8 | | |
| Time (days) | 188 | Extent of director liability index (0-10) | 6 | **Resolving insolvency** (rank) | 161 |
| Cost (% of income per capita) | 21,481.7 | Ease of shareholder suits index (0-10) | 4 | Time (years) | 5.0 |
| | | Strength of investor protection index (0-10) | 6.0 | Cost (% of estate) | 30 |
| | | | | Recovery rate (cents on the dollar) | 8.0 |
| | | **Paying taxes** (rank) | 137 | | |
| | | Payments (number per year) | 25 | | |
| | | Time (hours per year) | 274 | | |
| | | Total tax rate (% of profit) | 53.0 | | |

## CAMBODIA

| | | | | | | | |
|---|---|---|---|---|---|---|---|
| Ease of doing business (rank) | 133 | East Asia & Pacific<br>Low income | | GNI per capita (US$)<br>Population (m) | 830<br>14.3 |

| | | | | | |
|---|---|---|---|---|---|
| **Starting a business** (rank) | 175 | **Registering property** (rank) | 115 | **Trading across borders** (rank) | 118 |
| Procedures (number) | 9 | Procedures (number) | 7 | Documents to export (number) | 9 |
| Time (days) | 85 | Time (days) | 56 | Time to export (days) | 22 |
| Cost (% of income per capita) | 100.5 | Cost (% of property value) | 4.3 | Cost to export (US$ per container) | 755 |
| Minimum capital (% of income per capita) | 28.5 | | | Documents to import (number) | 10 |
| | | ✔ **Getting credit** (rank) | 53 | Time to import (days) | 26 |
| **Dealing with construction permits** (rank) | 149 | Strength of legal rights index (0-10) | 8 | Cost to import (US$ per container) | 900 |
| Procedures (number) | 21 | Depth of credit information index (0-6) | 3 | | |
| Time (days) | 652 | Public registry coverage (% of adults) | 0.0 | **Enforcing contracts** (rank) | 142 |
| Cost (% of income per capita) | 36.9 | Private bureau coverage (% of adults) | 12.1 | Procedures (number) | 44 |
| | | | | Time (days) | 401 |
| **Getting electricity** (rank) | 132 | **Protecting investors** (rank) | 82 | Cost (% of claim) | 103.4 |
| Procedures (number) | 4 | Extent of disclosure index (0-10) | 5 | | |
| Time (days) | 183 | Extent of director liability index (0-10) | 9 | **Resolving insolvency** (rank) | 152 |
| Cost (% of income per capita) | 2,802.0 | Ease of shareholder suits index (0-10) | 2 | Time (years) | 6.0 |
| | | Strength of investor protection index (0-10) | 5.3 | Cost (% of estate) | 15 |
| | | | | Recovery rate (cents on the dollar) | 12.8 |
| | | ✘ **Paying taxes** (rank) | 66 | | |
| | | Payments (number per year) | 40 | | |
| | | Time (hours per year) | 173 | | |
| | | Total tax rate (% of profit) | 22.5 | | |

## CAMEROON

| | | | | | | | |
|---|---|---|---|---|---|---|---|
| Ease of doing business (rank) | 161 | Sub-Saharan Africa<br>Lower middle income | | GNI per capita (US$)<br>Population (m) | 1,210<br>20.0 |

| | | | | | |
|---|---|---|---|---|---|
| **Starting a business** (rank) | 125 | **Registering property** (rank) | 158 | **Trading across borders** (rank) | 157 |
| Procedures (number) | 5 | Procedures (number) | 5 | Documents to export (number) | 11 |
| Time (days) | 15 | Time (days) | 93 | Time to export (days) | 23 |
| Cost (% of income per capita) | 35.8 | Cost (% of property value) | 19.1 | Cost to export (US$ per container) | 1,379 |
| Minimum capital (% of income per capita) | 168.3 | | | Documents to import (number) | 12 |
| | | **Getting credit** (rank) | 104 | Time to import (days) | 25 |
| **Dealing with construction permits** (rank) | 95 | Strength of legal rights index (0-10) | 6 | Cost to import (US$ per container) | 2,167 |
| Procedures (number) | 11 | Depth of credit information index (0-6) | 2 | | |
| Time (days) | 147 | Public registry coverage (% of adults) | 9.1 | ✔ **Enforcing contracts** (rank) | 172 |
| Cost (% of income per capita) | 1,008.7 | Private bureau coverage (% of adults) | 0.0 | Procedures (number) | 42 |
| | | | | Time (days) | 800 |
| **Getting electricity** (rank) | 63 | **Protecting investors** (rank) | 128 | Cost (% of claim) | 46.6 |
| Procedures (number) | 4 | Extent of disclosure index (0-10) | 6 | | |
| Time (days) | 64 | Extent of director liability index (0-10) | 1 | **Resolving insolvency** (rank) | 150 |
| Cost (% of income per capita) | 1,772.8 | Ease of shareholder suits index (0-10) | 6 | Time (years) | 3.2 |
| | | Strength of investor protection index (0-10) | 4.3 | Cost (% of estate) | 34 |
| | | | | Recovery rate (cents on the dollar) | 13.6 |
| | | **Paying taxes** (rank) | 176 | | |
| | | Payments (number per year) | 44 | | |
| | | Time (hours per year) | 654 | | |
| | | Total tax rate (% of profit) | 49.1 | | |

*Note:* Most indicator sets refer to a case scenario in an economy's largest business city. For more details, see the data notes.

✔ Reform making it easier to do business ✘ Reform making it more difficult to do business

## CANADA

| | | OECD high income | | GNI per capita (US$) | 45,560 |
|---|---|---|---|---|---|
| Ease of doing business (rank) | 17 | High income | | Population (m) | 34.5 |

| | | | | | |
|---|---|---|---|---|---|
| **Starting a business** (rank) | 3 | **Registering property** (rank) | 54 | **Trading across borders** (rank) | 44 |
| Procedures (number) | 1 | Procedures (number) | 6 | Documents to export (number) | 3 |
| Time (days) | 5 | Time (days) | 17 | Time to export (days) | 7 |
| Cost (% of income per capita) | 0.4 | Cost (% of property value) | 3.4 | Cost to export (US$ per container) | 1,610 |
| Minimum capital (% of income per capita) | 0.0 | | | Documents to import (number) | 4 |
| | | **Getting credit** (rank) | 23 | Time to import (days) | 11 |
| **Dealing with construction permits** (rank) | 69 | Strength of legal rights index (0-10) | 7 | Cost to import (US$ per container) | 1,660 |
| Procedures (number) | 13 | Depth of credit information index (0-6) | 6 | | |
| Time (days) | 163 | Public registry coverage (% of adults) | 0.0 | **Enforcing contracts** (rank) | 62 |
| Cost (% of income per capita) | 64.1 | Private bureau coverage (% of adults) | 100.0 | Procedures (number) | 36 |
| | | | | Time (days) | 570 |
| ✔ **Getting electricity** (rank) | 152 | **Protecting investors** (rank) | 4 | Cost (% of claim) | 22.3 |
| Procedures (number) | 8 | Extent of disclosure index (0-10) | 8 | | |
| Time (days) | 142 | Extent of director liability index (0-10) | 9 | **Resolving insolvency** (rank) | 4 |
| Cost (% of income per capita) | 140.4 | Ease of shareholder suits index (0-10) | 9 | Time (years) | 0.8 |
| | | Strength of investor protection index (0-10) | 8.7 | Cost (% of estate) | 4 |
| | | | | Recovery rate (cents on the dollar) | 90.7 |
| | | **Paying taxes** (rank) | 8 | | |
| | | Payments (number per year) | 8 | | |
| | | Time (hours per year) | 131 | | |
| | | Total tax rate (% of profit) | 26.9 | | |

## CAPE VERDE

| | | Sub-Saharan Africa | | GNI per capita (US$) | 3,540 |
|---|---|---|---|---|---|
| Ease of doing business (rank) | 122 | Lower middle income | | Population (m) | 0.5 |

| | | | | | |
|---|---|---|---|---|---|
| **Starting a business** (rank) | 129 | **Registering property** (rank) | 69 | **Trading across borders** (rank) | 63 |
| Procedures (number) | 8 | Procedures (number) | 6 | Documents to export (number) | 5 |
| Time (days) | 11 | Time (days) | 31 | Time to export (days) | 19 |
| Cost (% of income per capita) | 14.9 | Cost (% of property value) | 3.7 | Cost to export (US$ per container) | 1,200 |
| Minimum capital (% of income per capita) | 34.2 | | | Documents to import (number) | 5 |
| | | **Getting credit** (rank) | 104 | Time to import (days) | 18 |
| **Dealing with construction permits** (rank) | 122 | Strength of legal rights index (0-10) | 3 | Cost to import (US$ per container) | 1,000 |
| Procedures (number) | 17 | Depth of credit information index (0-6) | 5 | | |
| Time (days) | 122 | Public registry coverage (% of adults) | 19.7 | **Enforcing contracts** (rank) | 38 |
| Cost (% of income per capita) | 459.4 | Private bureau coverage (% of adults) | 0.0 | Procedures (number) | 37 |
| | | | | Time (days) | 425 |
| **Getting electricity** (rank) | 106 | **Protecting investors** (rank) | 139 | Cost (% of claim) | 19.8 |
| Procedures (number) | 6 | Extent of disclosure index (0-10) | 1 | | |
| Time (days) | 58 | Extent of director liability index (0-10) | 5 | **Resolving insolvency** (rank) | 185 |
| Cost (% of income per capita) | 981.3 | Ease of shareholder suits index (0-10) | 6 | Time (years) | NO PRACTICE |
| | | Strength of investor protection index (0-10) | 4.0 | Cost (% of estate) | NO PRACTICE |
| | | | | Recovery rate (cents on the dollar) | 0.0 |
| | | **Paying taxes** (rank) | 102 | | |
| | | Payments (number per year) | 41 | | |
| | | Time (hours per year) | 186 | | |
| | | Total tax rate (% of profit) | 37.2 | | |

## CENTRAL AFRICAN REPUBLIC

| | | Sub-Saharan Africa | | GNI per capita (US$) | 470 |
|---|---|---|---|---|---|
| Ease of doing business (rank) | 185 | Low income | | Population (m) | 4.5 |

| | | | | | |
|---|---|---|---|---|---|
| **Starting a business** (rank) | 170 | **Registering property** (rank) | 132 | **Trading across borders** (rank) | 182 |
| Procedures (number) | 8 | Procedures (number) | 5 | Documents to export (number) | 9 |
| Time (days) | 22 | Time (days) | 75 | Time to export (days) | 54 |
| Cost (% of income per capita) | 172.6 | Cost (% of property value) | 11.0 | Cost to export (US$ per container) | 5,491 |
| Minimum capital (% of income per capita) | 444.1 | | | Documents to import (number) | 17 |
| | | **Getting credit** (rank) | 104 | Time to import (days) | 62 |
| ✘ **Dealing with construction permits** (rank) | 147 | Strength of legal rights index (0-10) | 6 | Cost to import (US$ per container) | 5,554 |
| Procedures (number) | 18 | Depth of credit information index (0-6) | 2 | | |
| Time (days) | 203 | Public registry coverage (% of adults) | 2.4 | **Enforcing contracts** (rank) | 177 |
| Cost (% of income per capita) | 194.0 | Private bureau coverage (% of adults) | 0.0 | Procedures (number) | 43 |
| | | | | Time (days) | 660 |
| **Getting electricity** (rank) | 173 | **Protecting investors** (rank) | 139 | Cost (% of claim) | 82.0 |
| Procedures (number) | 7 | Extent of disclosure index (0-10) | 6 | | |
| Time (days) | 102 | Extent of director liability index (0-10) | 1 | **Resolving insolvency** (rank) | 185 |
| Cost (% of income per capita) | 12,603.6 | Ease of shareholder suits index (0-10) | 5 | Time (years) | 4.8 |
| | | Strength of investor protection index (0-10) | 4.0 | Cost (% of estate) | 76 |
| | | | | Recovery rate (cents on the dollar) | 0.0 |
| | | **Paying taxes** (rank) | 181 | | |
| | | Payments (number per year) | 55 | | |
| | | Time (hours per year) | 504 | | |
| | | Total tax rate (% of profit) | 65.2 | | |

*Note:* Most indicator sets refer to a case scenario in an economy's largest business city. For more details, see the data notes.

## CHAD

| | | Sub-Saharan Africa | | GNI per capita (US$) | 690 |
|---|---|---|---|---|---|
| Ease of doing business (rank) | 184 | Low income | | Population (m) | 11.5 |

| | | | | | |
|---|---|---|---|---|---|
| ✔ Starting a business (rank) | 181 | Registering property (rank) | 140 | Trading across borders (rank) | 180 |
| Procedures (number) | 9 | Procedures (number) | 6 | Documents to export (number) | 8 |
| Time (days) | 62 | Time (days) | 44 | Time to export (days) | 75 |
| Cost (% of income per capita) | 202.0 | Cost (% of property value) | 17.9 | Cost to export (US$ per container) | 5,902 |
| Minimum capital (% of income per capita) | 289.4 | | | Documents to import (number) | 11 |
| | | Getting credit (rank) | 104 | Time to import (days) | 101 |
| Dealing with construction permits (rank) | 127 | Strength of legal rights index (0-10) | 6 | Cost to import (US$ per container) | 8,525 |
| Procedures (number) | 13 | Depth of credit information index (0-6) | 2 | | |
| Time (days) | 154 | Public registry coverage (% of adults) | 1.0 | Enforcing contracts (rank) | 167 |
| Cost (% of income per capita) | 5,106.8 | Private bureau coverage (% of adults) | 0.0 | Procedures (number) | 41 |
| | | | | Time (days) | 743 |
| Getting electricity (rank) | 149 | Protecting investors (rank) | 158 | Cost (% of claim) | 45.7 |
| Procedures (number) | 6 | Extent of disclosure index (0-10) | 6 | | |
| Time (days) | 67 | Extent of director liability index (0-10) | 1 | Resolving insolvency (rank) | 185 |
| Cost (% of income per capita) | 11,017.6 | Ease of shareholder suits index (0-10) | 3 | Time (years) | 4.0 |
| | | Strength of investor protection index (0-10) | 3.3 | Cost (% of estate) | 60 |
| | | | | Recovery rate (cents on the dollar) | 0.0 |
| | | Paying taxes (rank) | 184 | | |
| | | Payments (number per year) | 54 | | |
| | | Time (hours per year) | 732 | | |
| | | Total tax rate (% of profit) | 65.4 | | |

## CHILE

| | | Latin America & Caribbean | | GNI per capita (US$) | 12,280 |
|---|---|---|---|---|---|
| Ease of doing business (rank) | 37 | Upper middle income | | Population (m) | 17.3 |

| | | | | | |
|---|---|---|---|---|---|
| Starting a business (rank) | 32 | Registering property (rank) | 55 | Trading across borders (rank) | 48 |
| Procedures (number) | 7 | Procedures (number) | 6 | Documents to export (number) | 6 |
| Time (days) | 8 | Time (days) | 31 | Time to export (days) | 15 |
| Cost (% of income per capita) | 4.5 | Cost (% of property value) | 1.3 | Cost to export (US$ per container) | 980 |
| Minimum capital (% of income per capita) | 0.0 | | | Documents to import (number) | 6 |
| | | Getting credit (rank) | 53 | Time to import (days) | 12 |
| Dealing with construction permits (rank) | 84 | Strength of legal rights index (0-10) | 6 | Cost to import (US$ per container) | 965 |
| Procedures (number) | 15 | Depth of credit information index (0-6) | 5 | | |
| Time (days) | 155 | Public registry coverage (% of adults) | 37.4 | Enforcing contracts (rank) | 70 |
| Cost (% of income per capita) | 67.3 | Private bureau coverage (% of adults) | 3.5 | Procedures (number) | 36 |
| | | | | Time (days) | 480 |
| Getting electricity (rank) | 40 | Protecting investors (rank) | 32 | Cost (% of claim) | 28.6 |
| Procedures (number) | 6 | Extent of disclosure index (0-10) | 8 | | |
| Time (days) | 31 | Extent of director liability index (0-10) | 6 | Resolving insolvency (rank) | 98 |
| Cost (% of income per capita) | 67.6 | Ease of shareholder suits index (0-10) | 5 | Time (years) | 3.2 |
| | | Strength of investor protection index (0-10) | 6.3 | Cost (% of estate) | 15 |
| | | | | Recovery rate (cents on the dollar) | 30.0 |
| | | Paying taxes (rank) | 36 | | |
| | | Payments (number per year) | 6 | | |
| | | Time (hours per year) | 291 | | |
| | | Total tax rate (% of profit) | 28.1 | | |

## CHINA

| | | East Asia & Pacific | | GNI per capita (US$) | 4,930 |
|---|---|---|---|---|---|
| Ease of doing business (rank) | 91 | Upper middle income | | Population (m) | 1,344.1 |

| | | | | | |
|---|---|---|---|---|---|
| ✔ Starting a business (rank) | 151 | Registering property (rank) | 44 | Trading across borders (rank) | 68 |
| Procedures (number) | 13 | Procedures (number) | 4 | Documents to export (number) | 8 |
| Time (days) | 33 | Time (days) | 29 | Time to export (days) | 21 |
| Cost (% of income per capita) | 2.1 | Cost (% of property value) | 3.6 | Cost to export (US$ per container) | 580 |
| Minimum capital (% of income per capita) | 85.7 | | | Documents to import (number) | 5 |
| | | Getting credit (rank) | 70 | Time to import (days) | 24 |
| ✔ Dealing with construction permits (rank) | 181 | Strength of legal rights index (0-10) | 6 | Cost to import (US$ per container) | 615 |
| Procedures (number) | 28 | Depth of credit information index (0-6) | 4 | | |
| Time (days) | 270 | Public registry coverage (% of adults) | 27.7 | Enforcing contracts (rank) | 19 |
| Cost (% of income per capita) | 375.3 | Private bureau coverage (% of adults) | 0.0 | Procedures (number) | 37 |
| | | | | Time (days) | 406 |
| Getting electricity (rank) | 114 | Protecting investors (rank) | 100 | Cost (% of claim) | 11.1 |
| Procedures (number) | 5 | Extent of disclosure index (0-10) | 10 | | |
| Time (days) | 145 | Extent of director liability index (0-10) | 1 | Resolving insolvency (rank) | 82 |
| Cost (% of income per capita) | 547.0 | Ease of shareholder suits index (0-10) | 4 | Time (years) | 1.7 |
| | | Strength of investor protection index (0-10) | 5.0 | Cost (% of estate) | 22 |
| | | | | Recovery rate (cents on the dollar) | 35.7 |
| | | Paying taxes (rank) | 122 | | |
| | | Payments (number per year) | 7 | | |
| | | Time (hours per year) | 338 | | |
| | | Total tax rate (% of profit) | 63.7 | | |

*Note:* Most indicator sets refer to a case scenario in an economy's largest business city. For more details, see the data notes.

✔ Reform making it easier to do business ✘ Reform making it more difficult to do business

## COLOMBIA

| | | Latin America & Caribbean | | GNI per capita (US$) | 6,110 |
|---|---|---|---|---|---|
| Ease of doing business (rank) | 45 | Upper middle income | | Population (m) | 46.9 |

| | | | | | |
|---|---|---|---|---|---|
| ✔ **Starting a business** (rank) | 61 | **Registering property** (rank) | 52 | **Trading across borders** (rank) | 91 |
| Procedures (number) | 8 | Procedures (number) | 7 | Documents to export (number) | 5 |
| Time (days) | 13 | Time (days) | 15 | Time to export (days) | 14 |
| Cost (% of income per capita) | 7.3 | Cost (% of property value) | 2.0 | Cost to export (US$ per container) | 2,255 |
| Minimum capital (% of income per capita) | 0.0 | | | Documents to import (number) | 6 |
| | | **Getting credit** (rank) | 70 | Time to import (days) | 13 |
| **Dealing with construction permits** (rank) | 27 | Strength of legal rights index (0-10) | 5 | Cost to import (US$ per container) | 2,830 |
| Procedures (number) | 8 | Depth of credit information index (0-6) | 5 | | |
| Time (days) | 46 | Public registry coverage (% of adults) | 0.0 | **Enforcing contracts** (rank) | 154 |
| Cost (% of income per capita) | 312.0 | Private bureau coverage (% of adults) | 72.5 | Procedures (number) | 34 |
| | | | | Time (days) | 1,346 |
| **Getting electricity** (rank) | 134 | **Protecting investors** (rank) | 6 | Cost (% of claim) | 47.9 |
| Procedures (number) | 5 | Extent of disclosure index (0-10) | 8 | | |
| Time (days) | 165 | Extent of director liability index (0-10) | 8 | **Resolving insolvency** (rank) | 21 |
| Cost (% of income per capita) | 995.0 | Ease of shareholder suits index (0-10) | 9 | Time (years) | 1.3 |
| | | Strength of investor protection index (0-10) | 8.3 | Cost (% of estate) | 6 |
| | | | | Recovery rate (cents on the dollar) | 76.2 |
| | | **Paying taxes** (rank) | 99 | | |
| | | Payments (number per year) | 9 | | |
| | | Time (hours per year) | 203 | | |
| | | Total tax rate (% of profit) | 74.4 | | |

## COMOROS

| | | Sub-Saharan Africa | | GNI per capita (US$) | 770 |
|---|---|---|---|---|---|
| Ease of doing business (rank) | 158 | Low income | | Population (m) | 0.8 |

| | | | | | |
|---|---|---|---|---|---|
| ✔ **Starting a business** (rank) | 168 | ✔ **Registering property** (rank) | 77 | **Trading across borders** (rank) | 146 |
| Procedures (number) | 9 | Procedures (number) | 4 | Documents to export (number) | 9 |
| Time (days) | 20 | Time (days) | 30 | Time to export (days) | 31 |
| Cost (% of income per capita) | 150.0 | Cost (% of property value) | 10.5 | Cost to export (US$ per container) | 1,295 |
| Minimum capital (% of income per capita) | 261.9 | | | Documents to import (number) | 10 |
| | | **Getting credit** (rank) | 154 | Time to import (days) | 26 |
| **Dealing with construction permits** (rank) | 60 | Strength of legal rights index (0-10) | 6 | Cost to import (US$ per container) | 1,295 |
| Procedures (number) | 13 | Depth of credit information index (0-6) | 0 | | |
| Time (days) | 143 | Public registry coverage (% of adults) | 0.0 | **Enforcing contracts** (rank) | 159 |
| Cost (% of income per capita) | 74.5 | Private bureau coverage (% of adults) | 0.0 | Procedures (number) | 43 |
| | | | | Time (days) | 506 |
| **Getting electricity** (rank) | 104 | **Protecting investors** (rank) | 139 | Cost (% of claim) | 89.4 |
| Procedures (number) | 3 | Extent of disclosure index (0-10) | 6 | | |
| Time (days) | 120 | Extent of director liability index (0-10) | 1 | **Resolving insolvency** (rank) | 185 |
| Cost (% of income per capita) | 2,477.2 | Ease of shareholder suits index (0-10) | 5 | Time (years) | NO PRACTICE |
| | | Strength of investor protection index (0-10) | 4.0 | Cost (% of estate) | NO PRACTICE |
| | | | | Recovery rate (cents on the dollar) | 0.0 |
| | | **Paying taxes** (rank) | 114 | | |
| | | Payments (number per year) | 33 | | |
| | | Time (hours per year) | 100 | | |
| | | Total tax rate (% of profit) | 217.9 | | |

## CONGO, DEM. REP.

| | | Sub-Saharan Africa | | GNI per capita (US$) | 190 |
|---|---|---|---|---|---|
| Ease of doing business (rank) | 181 | Low income | | Population (m) | 67.8 |

| | | | | | |
|---|---|---|---|---|---|
| ✔ **Starting a business** (rank) | 149 | **Registering property** (rank) | 106 | **Trading across borders** (rank) | 170 |
| Procedures (number) | 10 | Procedures (number) | 6 | Documents to export (number) | 8 |
| Time (days) | 58 | Time (days) | 47 | Time to export (days) | 44 |
| Cost (% of income per capita) | 284.7 | Cost (% of property value) | 6.7 | Cost to export (US$ per container) | 3,155 |
| Minimum capital (% of income per capita) | 0.0 | | | Documents to import (number) | 9 |
| | | **Getting credit** (rank) | 176 | Time to import (days) | 63 |
| **Dealing with construction permits** (rank) | 81 | Strength of legal rights index (0-10) | 3 | Cost to import (US$ per container) | 3,435 |
| Procedures (number) | 11 | Depth of credit information index (0-6) | 0 | | |
| Time (days) | 117 | Public registry coverage (% of adults) | 0.0 | **Enforcing contracts** (rank) | 173 |
| Cost (% of income per capita) | 1,582.7 | Private bureau coverage (% of adults) | 0.0 | Procedures (number) | 43 |
| | | | | Time (days) | 610 |
| **Getting electricity** (rank) | 140 | **Protecting investors** (rank) | 158 | Cost (% of claim) | 147.6 |
| Procedures (number) | 6 | Extent of disclosure index (0-10) | 3 | | |
| Time (days) | 58 | Extent of director liability index (0-10) | 3 | **Resolving insolvency** (rank) | 168 |
| Cost (% of income per capita) | 27,211.6 | Ease of shareholder suits index (0-10) | 4 | Time (years) | 5.2 |
| | | Strength of investor protection index (0-10) | 3.3 | Cost (% of estate) | 29 |
| | | | | Recovery rate (cents on the dollar) | 1.6 |
| | | **Paying taxes** (rank) | 171 | | |
| | | Payments (number per year) | 32 | | |
| | | Time (hours per year) | 336 | | |
| | | Total tax rate (% of profit) | 339.7 | | |

*Note:* Most indicator sets refer to a case scenario in an economy's largest business city. For more details, see the data notes.

✔ Reform making it easier to do business  ✘ Reform making it more difficult to do business

## CONGO, REP.

| | | | | | | |
|---|---|---|---|---|---|---|
| Ease of doing business (rank) | 183 | Sub-Saharan Africa | | GNI per capita (US$) | 2,270 | |
| | | Lower middle income | | Population (m) | 4.1 | |

| | | | | | |
|---|---|---|---|---|---|
| ✔ **Starting a business** (rank) | 180 | **Registering property** (rank) | 156 | **Trading across borders** (rank) | 181 |
| Procedures (number) | 11 | Procedures (number) | 6 | Documents to export (number) | 11 |
| Time (days) | 161 | Time (days) | 55 | Time to export (days) | 50 |
| Cost (% of income per capita) | 55.3 | Cost (% of property value) | 21.3 | Cost to export (US$ per container) | 3,818 |
| Minimum capital (% of income per capita) | 80.5 | | | Documents to import (number) | 10 |
| | | **Getting credit** (rank) | 104 | Time to import (days) | 62 |
| ✔ **Dealing with construction permits** (rank) | 149 | Strength of legal rights index (0-10) | 6 | Cost to import (US$ per container) | 7,709 |
| Procedures (number) | 14 | Depth of credit information index (0-6) | 2 | | |
| Time (days) | 201 | Public registry coverage (% of adults) | 8.3 | **Enforcing contracts** (rank) | 162 |
| Cost (% of income per capita) | 1,151.4 | Private bureau coverage (% of adults) | 0.0 | Procedures (number) | 44 |
| | | | | Time (days) | 560 |
| **Getting electricity** (rank) | 170 | **Protecting investors** (rank) | 158 | Cost (% of claim) | 53.2 |
| Procedures (number) | 6 | Extent of disclosure index (0-10) | 6 | | |
| Time (days) | 135 | Extent of director liability index (0-10) | 1 | **Resolving insolvency** (rank) | 136 |
| Cost (% of income per capita) | 4,775.3 | Ease of shareholder suits index (0-10) | 3 | Time (years) | 3.3 |
| | | Strength of investor protection index (0-10) | 3.3 | Cost (% of estate) | 25 |
| | | | | Recovery rate (cents on the dollar) | 17.8 |
| | | **Paying taxes** (rank) | 182 | | |
| | | Payments (number per year) | 61 | | |
| | | Time (hours per year) | 606 | | |
| | | Total tax rate (% of profit) | 62.9 | | |

## COSTA RICA

| | | | | | |
|---|---|---|---|---|---|
| Ease of doing business (rank) | 110 | Latin America & Caribbean | | GNI per capita (US$) | 7,660 |
| | | Upper middle income | | Population (m) | 4.7 |

| | | | | | |
|---|---|---|---|---|---|
| ✔ **Starting a business** (rank) | 128 | **Registering property** (rank) | 46 | **Trading across borders** (rank) | 51 |
| Procedures (number) | 12 | Procedures (number) | 5 | Documents to export (number) | 6 |
| Time (days) | 60 | Time (days) | 20 | Time to export (days) | 13 |
| Cost (% of income per capita) | 11.4 | Cost (% of property value) | 3.4 | Cost to export (US$ per container) | 1,030 |
| Minimum capital (% of income per capita) | 0.0 | | | Documents to import (number) | 6 |
| | | ✔ **Getting credit** (rank) | 83 | Time to import (days) | 14 |
| ✔ **Dealing with construction permits** (rank) | 128 | Strength of legal rights index (0-10) | 3 | Cost to import (US$ per container) | 1,020 |
| Procedures (number) | 18 | Depth of credit information index (0-6) | 6 | | |
| Time (days) | 160 | Public registry coverage (% of adults) | 28.3 | **Enforcing contracts** (rank) | 128 |
| Cost (% of income per capita) | 154.7 | Private bureau coverage (% of adults) | 82.8 | Procedures (number) | 40 |
| | | | | Time (days) | 852 |
| **Getting electricity** (rank) | 45 | **Protecting investors** (rank) | 169 | Cost (% of claim) | 24.3 |
| Procedures (number) | 5 | Extent of disclosure index (0-10) | 2 | | |
| Time (days) | 62 | Extent of director liability index (0-10) | 5 | **Resolving insolvency** (rank) | 128 |
| Cost (% of income per capita) | 256.8 | Ease of shareholder suits index (0-10) | 2 | Time (years) | 3.5 |
| | | Strength of investor protection index (0-10) | 3.0 | Cost (% of estate) | 15 |
| | | | | Recovery rate (cents on the dollar) | 22.5 |
| | | ✔ **Paying taxes** (rank) | 125 | | |
| | | Payments (number per year) | 23 | | |
| | | Time (hours per year) | 226 | | |
| | | Total tax rate (% of profit) | 55.0 | | |

## CÔTE D'IVOIRE

| | | | | | |
|---|---|---|---|---|---|
| Ease of doing business (rank) | 177 | Sub-Saharan Africa | | GNI per capita (US$) | 1,100 |
| | | Lower middle income | | Population (m) | 20.2 |

| | | | | | |
|---|---|---|---|---|---|
| **Starting a business** (rank) | 176 | **Registering property** (rank) | 159 | **Trading across borders** (rank) | 163 |
| Procedures (number) | 10 | Procedures (number) | 6 | Documents to export (number) | 10 |
| Time (days) | 32 | Time (days) | 62 | Time to export (days) | 25 |
| Cost (% of income per capita) | 130.0 | Cost (% of property value) | 13.9 | Cost to export (US$ per container) | 1,999 |
| Minimum capital (% of income per capita) | 184.6 | | | Documents to import (number) | 10 |
| | | **Getting credit** (rank) | 129 | Time to import (days) | 34 |
| **Dealing with construction permits** (rank) | 169 | Strength of legal rights index (0-10) | 6 | Cost to import (US$ per container) | 2,710 |
| Procedures (number) | 17 | Depth of credit information index (0-6) | 1 | | |
| Time (days) | 475 | Public registry coverage (% of adults) | 2.9 | **Enforcing contracts** (rank) | 127 |
| Cost (% of income per capita) | 155.1 | Private bureau coverage (% of adults) | 0.0 | Procedures (number) | 33 |
| | | | | Time (days) | 770 |
| **Getting electricity** (rank) | 153 | **Protecting investors** (rank) | 158 | Cost (% of claim) | 41.7 |
| Procedures (number) | 8 | Extent of disclosure index (0-10) | 6 | | |
| Time (days) | 55 | Extent of director liability index (0-10) | 1 | **Resolving insolvency** (rank) | 76 |
| Cost (% of income per capita) | 3,685.7 | Ease of shareholder suits index (0-10) | 3 | Time (years) | 2.2 |
| | | Strength of investor protection index (0-10) | 3.3 | Cost (% of estate) | 18 |
| | | | | Recovery rate (cents on the dollar) | 37.6 |
| | | **Paying taxes** (rank) | 159 | | |
| | | Payments (number per year) | 62 | | |
| | | Time (hours per year) | 270 | | |
| | | Total tax rate (% of profit) | 39.5 | | |

*Note:* Most indicator sets refer to a case scenario in an economy's largest business city. For more details, see the data notes.

✔ Reform making it easier to do business   ✘ Reform making it more difficult to do business

## CROATIA

| | | | | | | |
|---|---|---|---|---|---|---|
| **Ease of doing business** (rank) | 84 | Eastern Europe & Central Asia<br>High income | | GNI per capita (US$)<br>Population (m) | | 13,850<br>4.4 |
| **Starting a business** (rank) | 80 | **Registering property** (rank) | 104 | **Trading across borders** (rank) | | 105 |
| Procedures (number) | 6 | Procedures (number) | 5 | Documents to export (number) | | 7 |
| Time (days) | 9 | Time (days) | 104 | Time to export (days) | | 20 |
| Cost (% of income per capita) | 7.3 | Cost (% of property value) | 5.0 | Cost to export (US$ per container) | | 1,300 |
| Minimum capital (% of income per capita) | 13.4 | | | Documents to import (number) | | 8 |
| | | **Getting credit** (rank) | 40 | Time to import (days) | | 16 |
| **Dealing with construction permits** (rank) | 143 | Strength of legal rights index (0-10) | 7 | Cost to import (US$ per container) | | 1,180 |
| Procedures (number) | 12 | Depth of credit information index (0-6) | 5 | | | |
| Time (days) | 317 | Public registry coverage (% of adults) | 0.0 | **Enforcing contracts** (rank) | | 52 |
| Cost (% of income per capita) | 573.3 | Private bureau coverage (% of adults) | 100.0 | Procedures (number) | | 38 |
| | | | | Time (days) | | 572 |
| **Getting electricity** (rank) | 56 | **Protecting investors** (rank) | 139 | Cost (% of claim) | | 13.8 |
| Procedures (number) | 5 | Extent of disclosure index (0-10) | 1 | | | |
| Time (days) | 70 | Extent of director liability index (0-10) | 5 | **Resolving insolvency** (rank) | | 97 |
| Cost (% of income per capita) | 318.7 | Ease of shareholder suits index (0-10) | 6 | Time (years) | | 3.1 |
| | | Strength of investor protection index (0-10) | 4.0 | Cost (% of estate) | | 15 |
| | | | | Recovery rate (cents on the dollar) | | 30.1 |
| | | ✔ **Paying taxes** (rank) | 42 | | | |
| | | Payments (number per year) | 18 | | | |
| | | Time (hours per year) | 196 | | | |
| | | Total tax rate (% of profit) | 32.8 | | | |

## CYPRUS

| | | | | | | |
|---|---|---|---|---|---|---|
| **Ease of doing business** (rank) | 36 | Eastern Europe & Central Asia<br>High income | | GNI per capita (US$)<br>Population (m) | | 30,571<br>1.1 |
| **Starting a business** (rank) | 37 | ✔ **Registering property** (rank) | 99 | **Trading across borders** (rank) | | 18 |
| Procedures (number) | 6 | Procedures (number) | 6 | Documents to export (number) | | 5 |
| Time (days) | 8 | Time (days) | 28 | Time to export (days) | | 7 |
| Cost (% of income per capita) | 12.4 | Cost (% of property value) | 9.7 | Cost to export (US$ per container) | | 790 |
| Minimum capital (% of income per capita) | 0.0 | | | Documents to import (number) | | 7 |
| | | **Getting credit** (rank) | 53 | Time to import (days) | | 5 |
| **Dealing with construction permits** (rank) | 80 | Strength of legal rights index (0-10) | 9 | Cost to import (US$ per container) | | 900 |
| Procedures (number) | 9 | Depth of credit information index (0-6) | 2 | | | |
| Time (days) | 677 | Public registry coverage (% of adults) | 0.0 | **Enforcing contracts** (rank) | | 108 |
| Cost (% of income per capita) | 51.1 | Private bureau coverage (% of adults) | 6.5 | Procedures (number) | | 43 |
| | | | | Time (days) | | 735 |
| **Getting electricity** (rank) | 98 | **Protecting investors** (rank) | 32 | Cost (% of claim) | | 16.4 |
| Procedures (number) | 5 | Extent of disclosure index (0-10) | 8 | | | |
| Time (days) | 247 | Extent of director liability index (0-10) | 4 | **Resolving insolvency** (rank) | | 25 |
| Cost (% of income per capita) | 86.5 | Ease of shareholder suits index (0-10) | 7 | Time (years) | | 1.5 |
| | | Strength of investor protection index (0-10) | 6.3 | Cost (% of estate) | | 15 |
| | | | | Recovery rate (cents on the dollar) | | 70.7 |
| | | ✘ **Paying taxes** (rank) | 31 | | | |
| | | Payments (number per year) | 28 | | | |
| | | Time (hours per year) | 147 | | | |
| | | Total tax rate (% of profit) | 23.0 | | | |

## CZECH REPUBLIC

| | | | | | | |
|---|---|---|---|---|---|---|
| **Ease of doing business** (rank) | 65 | OECD high income<br>High income | | GNI per capita (US$)<br>Population (m) | | 18,520<br>10.5 |
| **Starting a business** (rank) | 140 | ✔ **Registering property** (rank) | 27 | ✔ **Trading across borders** (rank) | | 68 |
| Procedures (number) | 9 | Procedures (number) | 3 | Documents to export (number) | | 4 |
| Time (days) | 20 | Time (days) | 24 | Time to export (days) | | 16 |
| Cost (% of income per capita) | 8.2 | Cost (% of property value) | 3.0 | Cost to export (US$ per container) | | 1,145 |
| Minimum capital (% of income per capita) | 29.7 | | | Documents to import (number) | | 7 |
| | | **Getting credit** (rank) | 53 | Time to import (days) | | 17 |
| **Dealing with construction permits** (rank) | 74 | Strength of legal rights index (0-10) | 6 | Cost to import (US$ per container) | | 1,180 |
| Procedures (number) | 33 | Depth of credit information index (0-6) | 5 | | | |
| Time (days) | 120 | Public registry coverage (% of adults) | 6.1 | **Enforcing contracts** (rank) | | 79 |
| Cost (% of income per capita) | 10.5 | Private bureau coverage (% of adults) | 98.7 | Procedures (number) | | 27 |
| | | | | Time (days) | | 611 |
| **Getting electricity** (rank) | 143 | **Protecting investors** (rank) | 100 | Cost (% of claim) | | 33.0 |
| Procedures (number) | 6 | Extent of disclosure index (0-10) | 2 | | | |
| Time (days) | 279 | Extent of director liability index (0-10) | 5 | **Resolving insolvency** (rank) | | 34 |
| Cost (% of income per capita) | 180.0 | Ease of shareholder suits index (0-10) | 8 | Time (years) | | 3.2 |
| | | Strength of investor protection index (0-10) | 5.0 | Cost (% of estate) | | 17 |
| | | | | Recovery rate (cents on the dollar) | | 56.3 |
| | | ✔ **Paying taxes** (rank) | 120 | | | |
| | | Payments (number per year) | 8 | | | |
| | | Time (hours per year) | 413 | | | |
| | | Total tax rate (% of profit) | 49.2 | | | |

*Note:* Most indicator sets refer to a case scenario in an economy's largest business city. For more details, see the data notes.

✔ Reform making it easier to do business ✘ Reform making it more difficult to do business

## DENMARK

| | | | | | | |
|---|---|---|---|---|---|---|
| Ease of doing business (rank) | 5 | OECD high income / High income | | GNI per capita (US$) | | 60,390 |
| | | | | Population (m) | | 5.6 |

| | | | | | |
|---|---|---|---|---|---|
| **Starting a business** (rank) | 33 | ✔ **Registering property** (rank) | 6 | **Trading across borders** (rank) | 4 |
| Procedures (number) | 4 | Procedures (number) | 3 | Documents to export (number) | 4 |
| Time (days) | 6 | Time (days) | 10 | Time to export (days) | 5 |
| Cost (% of income per capita) | 0.2 | Cost (% of property value) | 0.6 | Cost to export (US$ per container) | 744 |
| Minimum capital (% of income per capita) | 24.2 | | | Documents to import (number) | 3 |
| | | **Getting credit** (rank) | 23 | Time to import (days) | 5 |
| **Dealing with construction permits** (rank) | 8 | Strength of legal rights index (0-10) | 9 | Cost to import (US$ per container) | 744 |
| Procedures (number) | 8 | Depth of credit information index (0-6) | 4 | | |
| Time (days) | 68 | Public registry coverage (% of adults) | 0.0 | **Enforcing contracts** (rank) | 34 |
| Cost (% of income per capita) | 57.1 | Private bureau coverage (% of adults) | 7.3 | Procedures (number) | 35 |
| | | | | Time (days) | 410 |
| **Getting electricity** (rank) | 14 | **Protecting investors** (rank) | 32 | Cost (% of claim) | 23.3 |
| Procedures (number) | 4 | Extent of disclosure index (0-10) | 7 | | |
| Time (days) | 38 | Extent of director liability index (0-10) | 5 | **Resolving insolvency** (rank) | 10 |
| Cost (% of income per capita) | 119.7 | Ease of shareholder suits index (0-10) | 7 | Time (years) | 1.0 |
| | | Strength of investor protection index (0-10) | 6.3 | Cost (% of estate) | 4 |
| | | | | Recovery rate (cents on the dollar) | 87.1 |
| | | **Paying taxes** (rank) | 13 | | |
| | | Payments (number per year) | 10 | | |
| | | Time (hours per year) | 130 | | |
| | | Total tax rate (% of profit) | 27.7 | | |

## DJIBOUTI

| | | | | | | |
|---|---|---|---|---|---|---|
| Ease of doing business (rank) | 171 | Middle East & North Africa / Lower middle income | | GNI per capita (US$) | | 1,467 |
| | | | | Population (m) | | 0.9 |

| | | | | | |
|---|---|---|---|---|---|
| **Starting a business** (rank) | 185 | **Registering property** (rank) | 148 | **Trading across borders** (rank) | 41 |
| Procedures (number) | 11 | Procedures (number) | 7 | Documents to export (number) | 5 |
| Time (days) | 37 | Time (days) | 40 | Time to export (days) | 18 |
| Cost (% of income per capita) | 150.7 | Cost (% of property value) | 12.9 | Cost to export (US$ per container) | 836 |
| Minimum capital (% of income per capita) | 383.6 | | | Documents to import (number) | 5 |
| | | **Getting credit** (rank) | 180 | Time to import (days) | 18 |
| **Dealing with construction permits** (rank) | 145 | Strength of legal rights index (0-10) | 1 | Cost to import (US$ per container) | 911 |
| Procedures (number) | 15 | Depth of credit information index (0-6) | 1 | | |
| Time (days) | 172 | Public registry coverage (% of adults) | 0.2 | **Enforcing contracts** (rank) | 161 |
| Cost (% of income per capita) | 2,023.6 | Private bureau coverage (% of adults) | 0.0 | Procedures (number) | 40 |
| | | | | Time (days) | 1,225 |
| **Getting electricity** (rank) | 142 | **Protecting investors** (rank) | 181 | Cost (% of claim) | 34.0 |
| Procedures (number) | 4 | Extent of disclosure index (0-10) | 5 | | |
| Time (days) | 180 | Extent of director liability index (0-10) | 2 | **Resolving insolvency** (rank) | 142 |
| Cost (% of income per capita) | 7,776.4 | Ease of shareholder suits index (0-10) | 0 | Time (years) | 5.0 |
| | | Strength of investor protection index (0-10) | 2.3 | Cost (% of estate) | 18 |
| | | | | Recovery rate (cents on the dollar) | 16.5 |
| | | **Paying taxes** (rank) | 67 | | |
| | | Payments (number per year) | 35 | | |
| | | Time (hours per year) | 82 | | |
| | | Total tax rate (% of profit) | 38.7 | | |

## DOMINICA

| | | | | | | |
|---|---|---|---|---|---|---|
| Ease of doing business (rank) | 68 | Latin America & Caribbean / Upper middle income | | GNI per capita (US$) | | 7,090 |
| | | | | Population (m) | | 0.1 |

| | | | | | |
|---|---|---|---|---|---|
| **Starting a business** (rank) | 46 | **Registering property** (rank) | 119 | ✔ **Trading across borders** (rank) | 92 |
| Procedures (number) | 5 | Procedures (number) | 5 | Documents to export (number) | 7 |
| Time (days) | 13 | Time (days) | 42 | Time to export (days) | 13 |
| Cost (% of income per capita) | 15.4 | Cost (% of property value) | 13.2 | Cost to export (US$ per container) | 1,340 |
| Minimum capital (% of income per capita) | 0.0 | | | Documents to import (number) | 8 |
| | | **Getting credit** (rank) | 83 | Time to import (days) | 14 |
| **Dealing with construction permits** (rank) | 22 | Strength of legal rights index (0-10) | 9 | Cost to import (US$ per container) | 1,350 |
| Procedures (number) | 9 | Depth of credit information index (0-6) | 0 | | |
| Time (days) | 165 | Public registry coverage (% of adults) | 0.0 | **Enforcing contracts** (rank) | 170 |
| Cost (% of income per capita) | 7.6 | Private bureau coverage (% of adults) | 0.0 | Procedures (number) | 47 |
| | | | | Time (days) | 681 |
| **Getting electricity** (rank) | 61 | **Protecting investors** (rank) | 32 | Cost (% of claim) | 36.0 |
| Procedures (number) | 5 | Extent of disclosure index (0-10) | 4 | | |
| Time (days) | 61 | Extent of director liability index (0-10) | 8 | **Resolving insolvency** (rank) | 104 |
| Cost (% of income per capita) | 593.4 | Ease of shareholder suits index (0-10) | 7 | Time (years) | 4.0 |
| | | Strength of investor protection index (0-10) | 6.3 | Cost (% of estate) | 10 |
| | | | | Recovery rate (cents on the dollar) | 28.5 |
| | | **Paying taxes** (rank) | 74 | | |
| | | Payments (number per year) | 37 | | |
| | | Time (hours per year) | 120 | | |
| | | Total tax rate (% of profit) | 37.5 | | |

*Note:* Most indicator sets refer to a case scenario in an economy's largest business city. For more details, see the data notes.

✔ Reform making it easier to do business    ✘ Reform making it more difficult to do business

## DOMINICAN REPUBLIC

| | | | | | | |
|---|---|---|---|---|---|---|
| Ease of doing business (rank) | 116 | Latin America & Caribbean<br>Upper middle income | | GNI per capita (US$)<br>Population (m) | | 5,240<br>10.1 |

| | | | | | |
|---|---|---|---|---|---|
| **Starting a business** (rank) | 137 | **Registering property** (rank) | 110 | **Trading across borders** (rank) | 46 |
| Procedures (number) | 7 | Procedures (number) | 7 | Documents to export (number) | 6 |
| Time (days) | 19 | Time (days) | 60 | Time to export (days) | 8 |
| Cost (% of income per capita) | 17.3 | Cost (% of property value) | 3.7 | Cost to export (US$ per container) | 1,040 |
| Minimum capital (% of income per capita) | 49.3 | | | Documents to import (number) | 7 |
| | | **Getting credit** (rank) | 83 | Time to import (days) | 10 |
| **Dealing with construction permits** (rank) | 108 | Strength of legal rights index (0-10) | 3 | Cost to import (US$ per container) | 1,150 |
| Procedures (number) | 14 | Depth of credit information index (0-6) | 6 | | |
| Time (days) | 216 | Public registry coverage (% of adults) | 44.1 | **Enforcing contracts** (rank) | 84 |
| Cost (% of income per capita) | 72.7 | Private bureau coverage (% of adults) | 60.0 | Procedures (number) | 34 |
| | | | | Time (days) | 460 |
| **Getting electricity** (rank) | 122 | **Protecting investors** (rank) | 100 | Cost (% of claim) | 40.9 |
| Procedures (number) | 7 | Extent of disclosure index (0-10) | 5 | | |
| Time (days) | 87 | Extent of director liability index (0-10) | 4 | **Resolving insolvency** (rank) | 156 |
| Cost (% of income per capita) | 322.3 | Ease of shareholder suits index (0-10) | 6 | Time (years) | 3.5 |
| | | Strength of investor protection index (0-10) | 5.0 | Cost (% of estate) | 38 |
| | | | | Recovery rate (cents on the dollar) | 8.7 |
| | | ✘ **Paying taxes** (rank) | 98 | | |
| | | Payments (number per year) | 9 | | |
| | | Time (hours per year) | 324 | | |
| | | Total tax rate (% of profit) | 42.5 | | |

## ECUADOR

| | | | | | | |
|---|---|---|---|---|---|---|
| Ease of doing business (rank) | 139 | Latin America & Caribbean<br>Upper middle income | | GNI per capita (US$)<br>Population (m) | | 4,140<br>14.7 |

| | | | | | |
|---|---|---|---|---|---|
| **Starting a business** (rank) | 169 | ✘ **Registering property** (rank) | 101 | **Trading across borders** (rank) | 128 |
| Procedures (number) | 13 | Procedures (number) | 9 | Documents to export (number) | 8 |
| Time (days) | 56 | Time (days) | 39 | Time to export (days) | 20 |
| Cost (% of income per capita) | 29.9 | Cost (% of property value) | 2.1 | Cost to export (US$ per container) | 1,535 |
| Minimum capital (% of income per capita) | 4.5 | | | Documents to import (number) | 7 |
| | | **Getting credit** (rank) | 83 | Time to import (days) | 25 |
| **Dealing with construction permits** (rank) | 104 | Strength of legal rights index (0-10) | 3 | Cost to import (US$ per container) | 1,530 |
| Procedures (number) | 16 | Depth of credit information index (0-6) | 6 | | |
| Time (days) | 128 | Public registry coverage (% of adults) | 0.0 | **Enforcing contracts** (rank) | 99 |
| Cost (% of income per capita) | 208.5 | Private bureau coverage (% of adults) | 53.5 | Procedures (number) | 39 |
| | | | | Time (days) | 588 |
| **Getting electricity** (rank) | 146 | **Protecting investors** (rank) | 139 | Cost (% of claim) | 27.2 |
| Procedures (number) | 7 | Extent of disclosure index (0-10) | 1 | | |
| Time (days) | 89 | Extent of director liability index (0-10) | 5 | **Resolving insolvency** (rank) | 137 |
| Cost (% of income per capita) | 860.9 | Ease of shareholder suits index (0-10) | 6 | Time (years) | 5.3 |
| | | Strength of investor protection index (0-10) | 4.0 | Cost (% of estate) | 18 |
| | | | | Recovery rate (cents on the dollar) | 17.8 |
| | | **Paying taxes** (rank) | 84 | | |
| | | Payments (number per year) | 8 | | |
| | | Time (hours per year) | 654 | | |
| | | Total tax rate (% of profit) | 34.6 | | |

## EGYPT, ARAB REP.

| | | | | | | |
|---|---|---|---|---|---|---|
| Ease of doing business (rank) | 109 | Middle East & North Africa<br>Lower middle income | | GNI per capita (US$)<br>Population (m) | | 2,600<br>82.5 |

| | | | | | |
|---|---|---|---|---|---|
| **Starting a business** (rank) | 26 | **Registering property** (rank) | 95 | **Trading across borders** (rank) | 70 |
| Procedures (number) | 6 | Procedures (number) | 7 | Documents to export (number) | 8 |
| Time (days) | 7 | Time (days) | 72 | Time to export (days) | 12 |
| Cost (% of income per capita) | 10.2 | Cost (% of property value) | 0.7 | Cost to export (US$ per container) | 625 |
| Minimum capital (% of income per capita) | 0.0 | | | Documents to import (number) | 9 |
| | | **Getting credit** (rank) | 83 | Time to import (days) | 13 |
| **Dealing with construction permits** (rank) | 165 | Strength of legal rights index (0-10) | 3 | Cost to import (US$ per container) | 755 |
| Procedures (number) | 22 | Depth of credit information index (0-6) | 6 | | |
| Time (days) | 218 | Public registry coverage (% of adults) | 4.3 | **Enforcing contracts** (rank) | 152 |
| Cost (% of income per capita) | 135.0 | Private bureau coverage (% of adults) | 16.4 | Procedures (number) | 42 |
| | | | | Time (days) | 1,010 |
| **Getting electricity** (rank) | 99 | **Protecting investors** (rank) | 82 | Cost (% of claim) | 26.2 |
| Procedures (number) | 7 | Extent of disclosure index (0-10) | 8 | | |
| Time (days) | 54 | Extent of director liability index (0-10) | 3 | **Resolving insolvency** (rank) | 139 |
| Cost (% of income per capita) | 396.0 | Ease of shareholder suits index (0-10) | 5 | Time (years) | 4.2 |
| | | Strength of investor protection index (0-10) | 5.3 | Cost (% of estate) | 22 |
| | | | | Recovery rate (cents on the dollar) | 17.6 |
| | | **Paying taxes** (rank) | 145 | | |
| | | Payments (number per year) | 29 | | |
| | | Time (hours per year) | 392 | | |
| | | Total tax rate (% of profit) | 42.6 | | |

*Note:* Most indicator sets refer to a case scenario in an economy's largest business city. For more details, see the data notes.

✔ Reform making it easier to do business  ✘ Reform making it more difficult to do business

## EL SALVADOR

| | | | | | | |
|---|---|---|---|---|---|---|
| **Ease of doing business** (rank) | 113 | Latin America & Caribbean<br>Lower middle income | | GNI per capita (US$)<br>Population (m) | 3,480<br>6.2 |

| | | | | | |
|---|---|---|---|---|---|
| **Starting a business** (rank) | 139 | **Registering property** (rank) | 56 | **Trading across borders** (rank) | 80 |
| Procedures (number) | 8 | Procedures (number) | 5 | Documents to export (number) | 8 |
| Time (days) | 17 | Time (days) | 31 | Time to export (days) | 14 |
| Cost (% of income per capita) | 46.7 | Cost (% of property value) | 3.8 | Cost to export (US$ per container) | 980 |
| Minimum capital (% of income per capita) | 2.9 | | | Documents to import (number) | 8 |
| | | ✔ **Getting credit** (rank) | 53 | Time to import (days) | 10 |
| **Dealing with construction permits** (rank) | 146 | Strength of legal rights index (0-10) | 5 | Cost to import (US$ per container) | 980 |
| Procedures (number) | 33 | Depth of credit information index (0-6) | 6 | | |
| Time (days) | 157 | Public registry coverage (% of adults) | 26.5 | **Enforcing contracts** (rank) | 71 |
| Cost (% of income per capita) | 162.5 | Private bureau coverage (% of adults) | 83.7 | Procedures (number) | 34 |
| | | | | Time (days) | 786 |
| **Getting electricity** (rank) | 131 | **Protecting investors** (rank) | 169 | Cost (% of claim) | 19.2 |
| Procedures (number) | 7 | Extent of disclosure index (0-10) | 3 | | |
| Time (days) | 78 | Extent of director liability index (0-10) | 0 | **Resolving insolvency** (rank) | 89 |
| Cost (% of income per capita) | 554.8 | Ease of shareholder suits index (0-10) | 6 | Time (years) | 4.0 |
| | | Strength of investor protection index (0-10) | 3.0 | Cost (% of estate) | 9 |
| | | | | Recovery rate (cents on the dollar) | 32.2 |
| | | ✘ **Paying taxes** (rank) | 153 | | |
| | | Payments (number per year) | 53 | | |
| | | Time (hours per year) | 320 | | |
| | | Total tax rate (% of profit) | 35.0 | | |

## EQUATORIAL GUINEA

| | | | | | | |
|---|---|---|---|---|---|---|
| **Ease of doing business** (rank) | 162 | Sub-Saharan Africa<br>High income | | GNI per capita (US$)<br>Population (m) | 14,540<br>0.7 |

| | | | | | |
|---|---|---|---|---|---|
| **Starting a business** (rank) | 182 | **Registering property** (rank) | 103 | **Trading across borders** (rank) | 136 |
| Procedures (number) | 18 | Procedures (number) | 6 | Documents to export (number) | 7 |
| Time (days) | 135 | Time (days) | 23 | Time to export (days) | 29 |
| Cost (% of income per capita) | 98.2 | Cost (% of property value) | 12.5 | Cost to export (US$ per container) | 1,390 |
| Minimum capital (% of income per capita) | 11.7 | | | Documents to import (number) | 7 |
| | | **Getting credit** (rank) | 104 | Time to import (days) | 44 |
| **Dealing with construction permits** (rank) | 107 | Strength of legal rights index (0-10) | 6 | Cost to import (US$ per container) | 1,600 |
| Procedures (number) | 15 | Depth of credit information index (0-6) | 2 | | |
| Time (days) | 166 | Public registry coverage (% of adults) | 3.9 | **Enforcing contracts** (rank) | 61 |
| Cost (% of income per capita) | 120.4 | Private bureau coverage (% of adults) | 0.0 | Procedures (number) | 40 |
| | | | | Time (days) | 475 |
| **Getting electricity** (rank) | 86 | **Protecting investors** (rank) | 150 | Cost (% of claim) | 18.5 |
| Procedures (number) | 5 | Extent of disclosure index (0-10) | 6 | | |
| Time (days) | 106 | Extent of director liability index (0-10) | 1 | **Resolving insolvency** (rank) | 185 |
| Cost (% of income per capita) | 456.5 | Ease of shareholder suits index (0-10) | 4 | Time (years) | NO PRACTICE |
| | | Strength of investor protection index (0-10) | 3.7 | Cost (% of estate) | NO PRACTICE |
| | | | | Recovery rate (cents on the dollar) | 0.0 |
| | | **Paying taxes** (rank) | 173 | | |
| | | Payments (number per year) | 46 | | |
| | | Time (hours per year) | 492 | | |
| | | Total tax rate (% of profit) | 46.0 | | |

## ERITREA

| | | | | | | |
|---|---|---|---|---|---|---|
| **Ease of doing business** (rank) | 182 | Sub-Saharan Africa<br>Low income | | GNI per capita (US$)<br>Population (m) | 430<br>5.4 |

| | | | | | |
|---|---|---|---|---|---|
| **Starting a business** (rank) | 183 | **Registering property** (rank) | 181 | **Trading across borders** (rank) | 165 |
| Procedures (number) | 13 | Procedures (number) | 11 | Documents to export (number) | 10 |
| Time (days) | 84 | Time (days) | 78 | Time to export (days) | 50 |
| Cost (% of income per capita) | 52.3 | Cost (% of property value) | 9.1 | Cost to export (US$ per container) | 1,460 |
| Minimum capital (% of income per capita) | 203.1 | | | Documents to import (number) | 12 |
| | | **Getting credit** (rank) | 180 | Time to import (days) | 59 |
| **Dealing with construction permits** (rank) | 185 | Strength of legal rights index (0-10) | 2 | Cost to import (US$ per container) | 1,600 |
| Procedures (number) | NO PRACTICE | Depth of credit information index (0-6) | 0 | | |
| Time (days) | NO PRACTICE | Public registry coverage (% of adults) | 0.0 | **Enforcing contracts** (rank) | 51 |
| Cost (% of income per capita) | NO PRACTICE | Private bureau coverage (% of adults) | 0.0 | Procedures (number) | 39 |
| | | | | Time (days) | 405 |
| **Getting electricity** (rank) | 93 | **Protecting investors** (rank) | 117 | Cost (% of claim) | 22.6 |
| Procedures (number) | 5 | Extent of disclosure index (0-10) | 4 | | |
| Time (days) | 59 | Extent of director liability index (0-10) | 5 | **Resolving insolvency** (rank) | 185 |
| Cost (% of income per capita) | 3,508.0 | Ease of shareholder suits index (0-10) | 5 | Time (years) | NO PRACTICE |
| | | Strength of investor protection index (0-10) | 4.7 | Cost (% of estate) | NO PRACTICE |
| | | | | Recovery rate (cents on the dollar) | 0.0 |
| | | **Paying taxes** (rank) | 146 | | |
| | | Payments (number per year) | 30 | | |
| | | Time (hours per year) | 216 | | |
| | | Total tax rate (% of profit) | 84.5 | | |

*Note:* Most indicator sets refer to a case scenario in an economy's largest business city. For more details, see the data notes.

✔ Reform making it easier to do business ✘ Reform making it more difficult to do business

## ESTONIA

| | | | | | | |
|---|---|---|---|---|---|---|
| **Ease of doing business** (rank) | 21 | OECD high income / High income | | GNI per capita (US$) | 15,200 | |
| | | | | Population (m) | 1.3 | |

| | | | | | |
|---|---|---|---|---|---|
| **Starting a business** (rank) | 47 | **Registering property** (rank) | 14 | **Trading across borders** (rank) | 7 |
| Procedures (number) | 5 | Procedures (number) | 3 | Documents to export (number) | 3 |
| Time (days) | 7 | Time (days) | 18 | Time to export (days) | 5 |
| Cost (% of income per capita) | 1.6 | Cost (% of property value) | 0.4 | Cost to export (US$ per container) | 745 |
| Minimum capital (% of income per capita) | 22.1 | | | Documents to import (number) | 4 |
| | | **Getting credit** (rank) | 40 | Time to import (days) | 5 |
| **Dealing with construction permits** (rank) | 35 | Strength of legal rights index (0-10) | 7 | Cost to import (US$ per container) | 795 |
| Procedures (number) | 13 | Depth of credit information index (0-6) | 5 | | |
| Time (days) | 148 | Public registry coverage (% of adults) | 0.0 | **Enforcing contracts** (rank) | 31 |
| Cost (% of income per capita) | 16.1 | Private bureau coverage (% of adults) | 33.4 | Procedures (number) | 35 |
| | | | | Time (days) | 425 |
| **Getting electricity** (rank) | 52 | **Protecting investors** (rank) | 70 | Cost (% of claim) | 22.3 |
| Procedures (number) | 4 | Extent of disclosure index (0-10) | 8 | | |
| Time (days) | 111 | Extent of director liability index (0-10) | 3 | **Resolving insolvency** (rank) | 72 |
| Cost (% of income per capita) | 201.4 | Ease of shareholder suits index (0-10) | 6 | Time (years) | 3.0 |
| | | Strength of investor protection index (0-10) | 5.7 | Cost (% of estate) | 9 |
| | | | | Recovery rate (cents on the dollar) | 38.5 |
| | | **Paying taxes** (rank) | 50 | | |
| | | Payments (number per year) | 8 | | |
| | | Time (hours per year) | 85 | | |
| | | Total tax rate (% of profit) | 67.3 | | |

## ETHIOPIA

| | | | | | | |
|---|---|---|---|---|---|---|
| **Ease of doing business** (rank) | 127 | Sub-Saharan Africa / Low income | | GNI per capita (US$) | 400 | |
| | | | | Population (m) | 84.7 | |

| | | | | | |
|---|---|---|---|---|---|
| **Starting a business** (rank) | 163 | **Registering property** (rank) | 112 | **Trading across borders** (rank) | 161 |
| Procedures (number) | 9 | Procedures (number) | 10 | Documents to export (number) | 7 |
| Time (days) | 15 | Time (days) | 41 | Time to export (days) | 42 |
| Cost (% of income per capita) | 135.3 | Cost (% of property value) | 2.1 | Cost to export (US$ per container) | 2,160 |
| Minimum capital (% of income per capita) | 249.1 | | | Documents to import (number) | 9 |
| | | ✔ **Getting credit** (rank) | 104 | Time to import (days) | 44 |
| **Dealing with construction permits** (rank) | 53 | Strength of legal rights index (0-10) | 4 | Cost to import (US$ per container) | 2,660 |
| Procedures (number) | 9 | Depth of credit information index (0-6) | 4 | | |
| Time (days) | 128 | Public registry coverage (% of adults) | 0.1 | **Enforcing contracts** (rank) | 50 |
| Cost (% of income per capita) | 275.6 | Private bureau coverage (% of adults) | 0.0 | Procedures (number) | 38 |
| | | | | Time (days) | 530 |
| **Getting electricity** (rank) | 94 | **Protecting investors** (rank) | 128 | Cost (% of claim) | 15.2 |
| Procedures (number) | 4 | Extent of disclosure index (0-10) | 4 | | |
| Time (days) | 95 | Extent of director liability index (0-10) | 4 | **Resolving insolvency** (rank) | 117 |
| Cost (% of income per capita) | 2,544.3 | Ease of shareholder suits index (0-10) | 5 | Time (years) | 3.0 |
| | | Strength of investor protection index (0-10) | 4.3 | Cost (% of estate) | 15 |
| | | | | Recovery rate (cents on the dollar) | 25.9 |
| | | ✘ **Paying taxes** (rank) | 103 | | |
| | | Payments (number per year) | 31 | | |
| | | Time (hours per year) | 306 | | |
| | | Total tax rate (% of profit) | 33.3 | | |

## FIJI

| | | | | | | |
|---|---|---|---|---|---|---|
| **Ease of doing business** (rank) | 60 | East Asia & Pacific / Lower middle income | | GNI per capita (US$) | 3,680 | |
| | | | | Population (m) | 0.9 | |

| | | | | | |
|---|---|---|---|---|---|
| ✘ **Starting a business** (rank) | 138 | ✘ **Registering property** (rank) | 58 | **Trading across borders** (rank) | 111 |
| Procedures (number) | 11 | Procedures (number) | 4 | Documents to export (number) | 10 |
| Time (days) | 58 | Time (days) | 69 | Time to export (days) | 22 |
| Cost (% of income per capita) | 24.0 | Cost (% of property value) | 2.0 | Cost to export (US$ per container) | 655 |
| Minimum capital (% of income per capita) | 0.0 | | | Documents to import (number) | 10 |
| | | **Getting credit** (rank) | 70 | Time to import (days) | 23 |
| ✘ **Dealing with construction permits** (rank) | 82 | Strength of legal rights index (0-10) | 7 | Cost to import (US$ per container) | 635 |
| Procedures (number) | 17 | Depth of credit information index (0-6) | 3 | | |
| Time (days) | 148 | Public registry coverage (% of adults) | 0.0 | **Enforcing contracts** (rank) | 67 |
| Cost (% of income per capita) | 43.8 | Private bureau coverage (% of adults) | 69.5 | Procedures (number) | 34 |
| | | | | Time (days) | 397 |
| **Getting electricity** (rank) | 79 | **Protecting investors** (rank) | 49 | Cost (% of claim) | 38.9 |
| Procedures (number) | 4 | Extent of disclosure index (0-10) | 3 | | |
| Time (days) | 81 | Extent of director liability index (0-10) | 8 | **Resolving insolvency** (rank) | 48 |
| Cost (% of income per capita) | 1,904.7 | Ease of shareholder suits index (0-10) | 7 | Time (years) | 1.8 |
| | | Strength of investor protection index (0-10) | 6.0 | Cost (% of estate) | 10 |
| | | | | Recovery rate (cents on the dollar) | 45.2 |
| | | ✔ **Paying taxes** (rank) | 85 | | |
| | | Payments (number per year) | 34 | | |
| | | Time (hours per year) | 163 | | |
| | | Total tax rate (% of profit) | 37.6 | | |

*Note:* Most indicator sets refer to a case scenario in an economy's largest business city. For more details, see the data notes.

✔ Reform making it easier to do business ✘ Reform making it more difficult to do business

## FINLAND

| | | | | | | |
|---|---|---|---|---|---|---|
| Ease of doing business (rank) | 11 | OECD high income / High income | | GNI per capita (US$) | | 48,420 |
| | | | | Population (m) | | 5.4 |

| | | | | | | |
|---|---|---|---|---|---|---|
| **Starting a business** (rank) | 49 | **Registering property** (rank) | 24 | **Trading across borders** (rank) | | 6 |
| Procedures (number) | 3 | Procedures (number) | 3 | Documents to export (number) | | 4 |
| Time (days) | 14 | Time (days) | 14 | Time to export (days) | | 8 |
| Cost (% of income per capita) | 1.0 | Cost (% of property value) | 4.0 | Cost to export (US$ per container) | | 540 |
| Minimum capital (% of income per capita) | 7.0 | | | Documents to import (number) | | 5 |
| | | **Getting credit** (rank) | 40 | Time to import (days) | | 7 |
| **Dealing with construction permits** (rank) | 34 | Strength of legal rights index (0-10) | 8 | Cost to import (US$ per container) | | 620 |
| Procedures (number) | 16 | Depth of credit information index (0-6) | 4 | | | |
| Time (days) | 66 | Public registry coverage (% of adults) | 0.0 | **Enforcing contracts** (rank) | | 9 |
| Cost (% of income per capita) | 43.3 | Private bureau coverage (% of adults) | 18.9 | Procedures (number) | | 33 |
| | | | | Time (days) | | 375 |
| **Getting electricity** (rank) | 21 | **Protecting investors** (rank) | 70 | Cost (% of claim) | | 13.3 |
| Procedures (number) | 5 | Extent of disclosure index (0-10) | 6 | | | |
| Time (days) | 47 | Extent of director liability index (0-10) | 4 | **Resolving insolvency** (rank) | | 5 |
| Cost (% of income per capita) | 29.6 | Ease of shareholder suits index (0-10) | 7 | Time (years) | | 0.9 |
| | | Strength of investor protection index (0-10) | 5.7 | Cost (% of estate) | | 4 |
| | | | | Recovery rate (cents on the dollar) | | 89.7 |
| | | **Paying taxes** (rank) | 23 | | | |
| | | Payments (number per year) | 8 | | | |
| | | Time (hours per year) | 93 | | | |
| | | Total tax rate (% of profit) | 40.6 | | | |

## FRANCE

| | | | | | | |
|---|---|---|---|---|---|---|
| Ease of doing business (rank) | 34 | OECD high income / High income | | GNI per capita (US$) | | 42,420 |
| | | | | Population (m) | | 65.4 |

| | | | | | | |
|---|---|---|---|---|---|---|
| **Starting a business** (rank) | 27 | **Registering property** (rank) | 146 | **Trading across borders** (rank) | | 27 |
| Procedures (number) | 5 | Procedures (number) | 8 | Documents to export (number) | | 2 |
| Time (days) | 7 | Time (days) | 59 | Time to export (days) | | 9 |
| Cost (% of income per capita) | 0.9 | Cost (% of property value) | 6.1 | Cost to export (US$ per container) | | 1,078 |
| Minimum capital (% of income per capita) | 0.0 | | | Documents to import (number) | | 2 |
| | | **Getting credit** (rank) | 53 | Time to import (days) | | 11 |
| **Dealing with construction permits** (rank) | 52 | Strength of legal rights index (0-10) | 7 | Cost to import (US$ per container) | | 1,248 |
| Procedures (number) | 9 | Depth of credit information index (0-6) | 4 | | | |
| Time (days) | 184 | Public registry coverage (% of adults) | 42.4 | **Enforcing contracts** (rank) | | 8 |
| Cost (% of income per capita) | 68.0 | Private bureau coverage (% of adults) | 0.0 | Procedures (number) | | 29 |
| | | | | Time (days) | | 390 |
| **Getting electricity** (rank) | 42 | **Protecting investors** (rank) | 82 | Cost (% of claim) | | 17.4 |
| Procedures (number) | 5 | Extent of disclosure index (0-10) | 10 | | | |
| Time (days) | 79 | Extent of director liability index (0-10) | 1 | **Resolving insolvency** (rank) | | 43 |
| Cost (% of income per capita) | 43.9 | Ease of shareholder suits index (0-10) | 5 | Time (years) | | 1.9 |
| | | Strength of investor protection index (0-10) | 5.3 | Cost (% of estate) | | 9 |
| | | | | Recovery rate (cents on the dollar) | | 48.4 |
| | | **Paying taxes** (rank) | 53 | | | |
| | | Payments (number per year) | 7 | | | |
| | | Time (hours per year) | 132 | | | |
| | | Total tax rate (% of profit) | 65.7 | | | |

## GABON

| | | | | | | |
|---|---|---|---|---|---|---|
| Ease of doing business (rank) | 170 | Sub-Saharan Africa / Upper middle income | | GNI per capita (US$) | | 7,980 |
| | | | | Population (m) | | 1.5 |

| | | | | | | |
|---|---|---|---|---|---|---|
| **Starting a business** (rank) | 157 | ✘ **Registering property** (rank) | 170 | **Trading across borders** (rank) | | 135 |
| Procedures (number) | 9 | Procedures (number) | 7 | Documents to export (number) | | 7 |
| Time (days) | 58 | Time (days) | 104 | Time to export (days) | | 20 |
| Cost (% of income per capita) | 14.5 | Cost (% of property value) | 10.5 | Cost to export (US$ per container) | | 1,945 |
| Minimum capital (% of income per capita) | 22.3 | | | Documents to import (number) | | 8 |
| | | **Getting credit** (rank) | 104 | Time to import (days) | | 22 |
| **Dealing with construction permits** (rank) | 110 | Strength of legal rights index (0-10) | 6 | Cost to import (US$ per container) | | 1,955 |
| Procedures (number) | 13 | Depth of credit information index (0-6) | 2 | | | |
| Time (days) | 243 | Public registry coverage (% of adults) | 53.8 | **Enforcing contracts** (rank) | | 153 |
| Cost (% of income per capita) | 79.3 | Private bureau coverage (% of adults) | 0.0 | Procedures (number) | | 38 |
| | | | | Time (days) | | 1,070 |
| **Getting electricity** (rank) | 135 | **Protecting investors** (rank) | 158 | Cost (% of claim) | | 34.3 |
| Procedures (number) | 6 | Extent of disclosure index (0-10) | 6 | | | |
| Time (days) | 141 | Extent of director liability index (0-10) | 1 | **Resolving insolvency** (rank) | | 145 |
| Cost (% of income per capita) | 354.2 | Ease of shareholder suits index (0-10) | 3 | Time (years) | | 5.0 |
| | | Strength of investor protection index (0-10) | 3.3 | Cost (% of estate) | | 15 |
| | | | | Recovery rate (cents on the dollar) | | 15.2 |
| | | **Paying taxes** (rank) | 146 | | | |
| | | Payments (number per year) | 26 | | | |
| | | Time (hours per year) | 488 | | | |
| | | Total tax rate (% of profit) | 43.5 | | | |

*Note:* Most indicator sets refer to a case scenario in an economy's largest business city. For more details, see the data notes.

✔ Reform making it easier to do business  ✘ Reform making it more difficult to do business

## GAMBIA, THE

| | | | | | | |
|---|---|---|---|---|---|---|
| **Ease of doing business** (rank) | 147 | Sub-Saharan Africa<br>Low income | | GNI per capita (US$)<br>Population (m) | | 610<br>1.8 |

| | | | | | |
|---|---|---|---|---|---|
| **Starting a business** (rank) | 123 | **Registering property** (rank) | 120 | **Trading across borders** (rank) | 87 |
| Procedures (number) | 8 | Procedures (number) | 5 | Documents to export (number) | 6 |
| Time (days) | 27 | Time (days) | 66 | Time to export (days) | 23 |
| Cost (% of income per capita) | 158.7 | Cost (% of property value) | 7.6 | Cost to export (US$ per container) | 1,180 |
| Minimum capital (% of income per capita) | 0.0 | | | Documents to import (number) | 7 |
| | | **Getting credit** (rank) | 159 | Time to import (days) | 21 |
| **Dealing with construction permits** (rank) | 90 | Strength of legal rights index (0-10) | 5 | Cost to import (US$ per container) | 885 |
| Procedures (number) | 14 | Depth of credit information index (0-6) | 0 | | |
| Time (days) | 143 | Public registry coverage (% of adults) | 0.0 | **Enforcing contracts** (rank) | 65 |
| Cost (% of income per capita) | 124.7 | Private bureau coverage (% of adults) | 0.0 | Procedures (number) | 33 |
| | | | | Time (days) | 407 |
| **Getting electricity** (rank) | 119 | **Protecting investors** (rank) | 177 | Cost (% of claim) | 37.9 |
| Procedures (number) | 5 | Extent of disclosure index (0-10) | 2 | | |
| Time (days) | 78 | Extent of director liability index (0-10) | 1 | **Resolving insolvency** (rank) | 108 |
| Cost (% of income per capita) | 3,976.8 | Ease of shareholder suits index (0-10) | 5 | Time (years) | 2.0 |
| | | Strength of investor protection index (0-10) | 2.7 | Cost (% of estate) | 15 |
| | | | | Recovery rate (cents on the dollar) | 27.8 |
| | | **Paying taxes** (rank) | 179 | | |
| | | Payments (number per year) | 50 | | |
| | | Time (hours per year) | 376 | | |
| | | Total tax rate (% of profit) | 283.5 | | |

## GEORGIA

| | | | | | | |
|---|---|---|---|---|---|---|
| **Ease of doing business** (rank) | 9 | Eastern Europe & Central Asia<br>Lower middle income | | GNI per capita (US$)<br>Population (m) | | 2,860<br>4.5 |

| | | | | | |
|---|---|---|---|---|---|
| **Starting a business** (rank) | 7 | **Registering property** (rank) | 1 | ✔ **Trading across borders** (rank) | 38 |
| Procedures (number) | 2 | Procedures (number) | 1 | Documents to export (number) | 4 |
| Time (days) | 2 | Time (days) | 2 | Time to export (days) | 9 |
| Cost (% of income per capita) | 3.8 | Cost (% of property value) | 0.1 | Cost to export (US$ per container) | 1,355 |
| Minimum capital (% of income per capita) | 0.0 | | | Documents to import (number) | 4 |
| | | ✔ **Getting credit** (rank) | 4 | Time to import (days) | 10 |
| **Dealing with construction permits** (rank) | 3 | Strength of legal rights index (0-10) | 9 | Cost to import (US$ per container) | 1,595 |
| Procedures (number) | 9 | Depth of credit information index (0-6) | 6 | | |
| Time (days) | 74 | Public registry coverage (% of adults) | 0.0 | ✔ **Enforcing contracts** (rank) | 30 |
| Cost (% of income per capita) | 17.7 | Private bureau coverage (% of adults) | 35.5 | Procedures (number) | 33 |
| | | | | Time (days) | 285 |
| ✔ **Getting electricity** (rank) | 50 | **Protecting investors** (rank) | 19 | Cost (% of claim) | 29.9 |
| Procedures (number) | 4 | Extent of disclosure index (0-10) | 9 | | |
| Time (days) | 71 | Extent of director liability index (0-10) | 6 | ✔ **Resolving insolvency** (rank) | 81 |
| Cost (% of income per capita) | 561.8 | Ease of shareholder suits index (0-10) | 6 | Time (years) | 2.0 |
| | | Strength of investor protection index (0-10) | 7.0 | Cost (% of estate) | 4 |
| | | | | Recovery rate (cents on the dollar) | 35.7 |
| | | ✔ **Paying taxes** (rank) | 33 | | |
| | | Payments (number per year) | 5 | | |
| | | Time (hours per year) | 280 | | |
| | | Total tax rate (% of profit) | 16.5 | | |

## GERMANY

| | | | | | | |
|---|---|---|---|---|---|---|
| **Ease of doing business** (rank) | 20 | OECD high income<br>High income | | GNI per capita (US$)<br>Population (m) | | 43,980<br>81.7 |

| | | | | | |
|---|---|---|---|---|---|
| **Starting a business** (rank) | 106 | **Registering property** (rank) | 81 | **Trading across borders** (rank) | 13 |
| Procedures (number) | 9 | Procedures (number) | 5 | Documents to export (number) | 4 |
| Time (days) | 15 | Time (days) | 40 | Time to export (days) | 7 |
| Cost (% of income per capita) | 4.9 | Cost (% of property value) | 5.7 | Cost to export (US$ per container) | 872 |
| Minimum capital (% of income per capita) | 0.0 | | | Documents to import (number) | 5 |
| | | **Getting credit** (rank) | 23 | Time to import (days) | 7 |
| **Dealing with construction permits** (rank) | 14 | Strength of legal rights index (0-10) | 7 | Cost to import (US$ per container) | 937 |
| Procedures (number) | 9 | Depth of credit information index (0-6) | 6 | | |
| Time (days) | 97 | Public registry coverage (% of adults) | 1.3 | **Enforcing contracts** (rank) | 5 |
| Cost (% of income per capita) | 48.1 | Private bureau coverage (% of adults) | 100.0 | Procedures (number) | 30 |
| | | | | Time (days) | 394 |
| **Getting electricity** (rank) | 2 | **Protecting investors** (rank) | 100 | Cost (% of claim) | 14.4 |
| Procedures (number) | 3 | Extent of disclosure index (0-10) | 5 | | |
| Time (days) | 17 | Extent of director liability index (0-10) | 5 | ✔ **Resolving insolvency** (rank) | 19 |
| Cost (% of income per capita) | 48.3 | Ease of shareholder suits index (0-10) | 5 | Time (years) | 1.2 |
| | | Strength of investor protection index (0-10) | 5.0 | Cost (% of estate) | 8 |
| | | | | Recovery rate (cents on the dollar) | 78.1 |
| | | ✔ **Paying taxes** (rank) | 72 | | |
| | | Payments (number per year) | 9 | | |
| | | Time (hours per year) | 207 | | |
| | | Total tax rate (% of profit) | 46.8 | | |

*Note:* Most indicator sets refer to a case scenario in an economy's largest business city. For more details, see the data notes.

✔ Reform making it easier to do business ✘ Reform making it more difficult to do business

## GHANA

| | | | | | | | |
|---|---|---|---|---|---|---|---|
| Ease of doing business (rank) | 64 | Sub-Saharan Africa | | GNI per capita (US$) | 1,410 | | |
| | | Lower middle income | | Population (m) | 25.0 | | |

| | | | | | |
|---|---|---|---|---|---|
| **Starting a business** (rank) | 112 | **Registering property** (rank) | 45 | ✘ **Trading across borders** (rank) | 99 |
| Procedures (number) | 7 | Procedures (number) | 5 | Documents to export (number) | 7 |
| Time (days) | 12 | Time (days) | 34 | Time to export (days) | 19 |
| Cost (% of income per capita) | 18.5 | Cost (% of property value) | 1.2 | Cost to export (US$ per container) | 815 |
| Minimum capital (% of income per capita) | 4.3 | | | Documents to import (number) | 7 |
| | | **Getting credit** (rank) | 23 | Time to import (days) | 34 |
| **Dealing with construction permits** (rank) | 162 | Strength of legal rights index (0-10) | 8 | Cost to import (US$ per container) | 1,315 |
| Procedures (number) | 16 | Depth of credit information index (0-6) | 5 | | |
| Time (days) | 218 | Public registry coverage (% of adults) | 0.0 | **Enforcing contracts** (rank) | 48 |
| Cost (% of income per capita) | 481.2 | Private bureau coverage (% of adults) | 5.7 | Procedures (number) | 36 |
| | | | | Time (days) | 487 |
| **Getting electricity** (rank) | 63 | **Protecting investors** (rank) | 49 | Cost (% of claim) | 23.0 |
| Procedures (number) | 4 | Extent of disclosure index (0-10) | 7 | | |
| Time (days) | 78 | Extent of director liability index (0-10) | 5 | **Resolving insolvency** (rank) | 114 |
| Cost (% of income per capita) | 957.3 | Ease of shareholder suits index (0-10) | 6 | Time (years) | 1.9 |
| | | Strength of investor protection index (0-10) | 6.0 | Cost (% of estate) | 22 |
| | | | | Recovery rate (cents on the dollar) | 26.9 |
| | | **Paying taxes** (rank) | 89 | | |
| | | Payments (number per year) | 32 | | |
| | | Time (hours per year) | 224 | | |
| | | Total tax rate (% of profit) | 33.5 | | |

## GREECE

| | | | | | | | |
|---|---|---|---|---|---|---|---|
| Ease of doing business (rank) | 78 | OECD high income | | GNI per capita (US$) | 25,030 | | |
| | | High income | | Population (m) | 11.3 | | |

| | | | | | |
|---|---|---|---|---|---|
| **Starting a business** (rank) | 146 | **Registering property** (rank) | 150 | **Trading across borders** (rank) | 62 |
| Procedures (number) | 11 | Procedures (number) | 11 | Documents to export (number) | 5 |
| Time (days) | 11 | Time (days) | 18 | Time to export (days) | 19 |
| Cost (% of income per capita) | 20.5 | Cost (% of property value) | 11.8 | Cost to export (US$ per container) | 1,115 |
| Minimum capital (% of income per capita) | 24.4 | | | Documents to import (number) | 6 |
| | | **Getting credit** (rank) | 83 | Time to import (days) | 15 |
| ✔ **Dealing with construction permits** (rank) | 31 | Strength of legal rights index (0-10) | 4 | Cost to import (US$ per container) | 1,135 |
| Procedures (number) | 15 | Depth of credit information index (0-6) | 5 | | |
| Time (days) | 89 | Public registry coverage (% of adults) | 0.0 | **Enforcing contracts** (rank) | 87 |
| Cost (% of income per capita) | 27.5 | Private bureau coverage (% of adults) | 84.0 | Procedures (number) | 39 |
| | | | | Time (days) | 819 |
| **Getting electricity** (rank) | 59 | ✔ **Protecting investors** (rank) | 117 | Cost (% of claim) | 14.4 |
| Procedures (number) | 6 | Extent of disclosure index (0-10) | 5 | | |
| Time (days) | 62 | Extent of director liability index (0-10) | 4 | ✔ **Resolving insolvency** (rank) | 50 |
| Cost (% of income per capita) | 62.4 | Ease of shareholder suits index (0-10) | 5 | Time (years) | 2.0 |
| | | Strength of investor protection index (0-10) | 4.7 | Cost (% of estate) | 9 |
| | | | | Recovery rate (cents on the dollar) | 44.5 |
| | | **Paying taxes** (rank) | 56 | | |
| | | Payments (number per year) | 8 | | |
| | | Time (hours per year) | 202 | | |
| | | Total tax rate (% of profit) | 44.6 | | |

## GRENADA

| | | | | | | | |
|---|---|---|---|---|---|---|---|
| Ease of doing business (rank) | 100 | Latin America & Caribbean | | GNI per capita (US$) | 7,220 | | |
| | | Upper middle income | | Population (m) | 0.1 | | |

| | | | | | |
|---|---|---|---|---|---|
| **Starting a business** (rank) | 65 | **Registering property** (rank) | 151 | ✔ **Trading across borders** (rank) | 71 |
| Procedures (number) | 6 | Procedures (number) | 8 | Documents to export (number) | 5 |
| Time (days) | 15 | Time (days) | 47 | Time to export (days) | 9 |
| Cost (% of income per capita) | 19.1 | Cost (% of property value) | 7.4 | Cost to export (US$ per container) | 1,300 |
| Minimum capital (% of income per capita) | 0.0 | | | Documents to import (number) | 7 |
| | | **Getting credit** (rank) | 104 | Time to import (days) | 9 |
| **Dealing with construction permits** (rank) | 10 | Strength of legal rights index (0-10) | 8 | Cost to import (US$ per container) | 2,235 |
| Procedures (number) | 8 | Depth of credit information index (0-6) | 0 | | |
| Time (days) | 123 | Public registry coverage (% of adults) | 0.0 | **Enforcing contracts** (rank) | 165 |
| Cost (% of income per capita) | 17.9 | Private bureau coverage (% of adults) | 0.0 | Procedures (number) | 47 |
| | | | | Time (days) | 688 |
| **Getting electricity** (rank) | 66 | **Protecting investors** (rank) | 32 | Cost (% of claim) | 32.6 |
| Procedures (number) | 6 | Extent of disclosure index (0-10) | 4 | | |
| Time (days) | 49 | Extent of director liability index (0-10) | 8 | **Resolving insolvency** (rank) | 185 |
| Cost (% of income per capita) | 283.5 | Ease of shareholder suits index (0-10) | 7 | Time (years) | NO PRACTICE |
| | | Strength of investor protection index (0-10) | 6.3 | Cost (% of estate) | NO PRACTICE |
| | | | | Recovery rate (cents on the dollar) | 0.0 |
| | | **Paying taxes** (rank) | 85 | | |
| | | Payments (number per year) | 30 | | |
| | | Time (hours per year) | 140 | | |
| | | Total tax rate (% of profit) | 45.3 | | |

*Note:* Most indicator sets refer to a case scenario in an economy's largest business city. For more details, see the data notes.

✔ Reform making it easier to do business ✘ Reform making it more difficult to do business

## GUATEMALA

| | | | | | |
|---|---|---|---|---|---|
| **Ease of doing business** (rank) | 93 | Latin America & Caribbean<br>Lower middle income | | GNI per capita (US$)<br>Population (m) | 2,870<br>14.8 |

| | | | | | |
|---|---|---|---|---|---|
| **Starting a business** (rank) | 172 | **Registering property** (rank) | 20 | **Trading across borders** (rank) | 117 |
| Procedures (number) | 12 | Procedures (number) | 4 | Documents to export (number) | 9 |
| Time (days) | 40 | Time (days) | 23 | Time to export (days) | 17 |
| Cost (% of income per capita) | 48.1 | Cost (% of property value) | 0.8 | Cost to export (US$ per container) | 1,307 |
| Minimum capital (% of income per capita) | 20.9 | | | Documents to import (number) | 8 |
| | | **Getting credit** (rank) | 12 | Time to import (days) | 17 |
| ✔ **Dealing with construction permits** (rank) | 94 | Strength of legal rights index (0-10) | 8 | Cost to import (US$ per container) | 1,425 |
| Procedures (number) | 11 | Depth of credit information index (0-6) | 6 | | |
| Time (days) | 158 | Public registry coverage (% of adults) | 18.0 | **Enforcing contracts** (rank) | 96 |
| Cost (% of income per capita) | 500.4 | Private bureau coverage (% of adults) | 8.7 | Procedures (number) | 31 |
| | | | | Time (days) | 1,459 |
| **Getting electricity** (rank) | 34 | **Protecting investors** (rank) | 158 | Cost (% of claim) | 26.5 |
| Procedures (number) | 4 | Extent of disclosure index (0-10) | 3 | | |
| Time (days) | 39 | Extent of director liability index (0-10) | 2 | **Resolving insolvency** (rank) | 109 |
| Cost (% of income per capita) | 594.8 | Ease of shareholder suits index (0-10) | 5 | Time (years) | 3.0 |
| | | Strength of investor protection index (0-10) | 3.3 | Cost (% of estate) | 15 |
| | | | | Recovery rate (cents on the dollar) | 27.8 |
| | | **Paying taxes** (rank) | 124 | | |
| | | Payments (number per year) | 24 | | |
| | | Time (hours per year) | 332 | | |
| | | Total tax rate (% of profit) | 40.9 | | |

## GUINEA

| | | | | | |
|---|---|---|---|---|---|
| **Ease of doing business** (rank) | 178 | Sub-Saharan Africa<br>Low income | | GNI per capita (US$)<br>Population (m) | 440<br>10.2 |

| | | | | | |
|---|---|---|---|---|---|
| ✔ **Starting a business** (rank) | 158 | **Registering property** (rank) | 151 | **Trading across borders** (rank) | 133 |
| Procedures (number) | 6 | Procedures (number) | 6 | Documents to export (number) | 7 |
| Time (days) | 35 | Time (days) | 59 | Time to export (days) | 35 |
| Cost (% of income per capita) | 96.9 | Cost (% of property value) | 14.2 | Cost to export (US$ per container) | 855 |
| Minimum capital (% of income per capita) | 324.7 | | | Documents to import (number) | 9 |
| | | **Getting credit** (rank) | 154 | Time to import (days) | 32 |
| ✔ **Dealing with construction permits** (rank) | 152 | Strength of legal rights index (0-10) | 6 | Cost to import (US$ per container) | 1,391 |
| Procedures (number) | 29 | Depth of credit information index (0-6) | 0 | | |
| Time (days) | 197 | Public registry coverage (% of adults) | 0.0 | **Enforcing contracts** (rank) | 131 |
| Cost (% of income per capita) | 94.8 | Private bureau coverage (% of adults) | 0.0 | Procedures (number) | 49 |
| | | | | Time (days) | 276 |
| ✔ **Getting electricity** (rank) | 88 | **Protecting investors** (rank) | 177 | Cost (% of claim) | 45.0 |
| Procedures (number) | 4 | Extent of disclosure index (0-10) | 6 | | |
| Time (days) | 69 | Extent of director liability index (0-10) | 1 | **Resolving insolvency** (rank) | 141 |
| Cost (% of income per capita) | 8,377.7 | Ease of shareholder suits index (0-10) | 1 | Time (years) | 3.8 |
| | | Strength of investor protection index (0-10) | 2.7 | Cost (% of estate) | 8 |
| | | | | Recovery rate (cents on the dollar) | 17.1 |
| | | **Paying taxes** (rank) | 183 | | |
| | | Payments (number per year) | 58 | | |
| | | Time (hours per year) | 416 | | |
| | | Total tax rate (% of profit) | 73.2 | | |

## GUINEA-BISSAU

| | | | | | |
|---|---|---|---|---|---|
| **Ease of doing business** (rank) | 179 | Sub-Saharan Africa<br>Low income | | GNI per capita (US$)<br>Population (m) | 600<br>1.5 |

| | | | | | |
|---|---|---|---|---|---|
| **Starting a business** (rank) | 148 | **Registering property** (rank) | 180 | **Trading across borders** (rank) | 116 |
| Procedures (number) | 9 | Procedures (number) | 8 | Documents to export (number) | 6 |
| Time (days) | 9 | Time (days) | 210 | Time to export (days) | 23 |
| Cost (% of income per capita) | 42.2 | Cost (% of property value) | 10.5 | Cost to export (US$ per container) | 1,448 |
| Minimum capital (% of income per capita) | 338.0 | | | Documents to import (number) | 6 |
| | | **Getting credit** (rank) | 129 | Time to import (days) | 22 |
| **Dealing with construction permits** (rank) | 117 | Strength of legal rights index (0-10) | 6 | Cost to import (US$ per container) | 2,006 |
| Procedures (number) | 12 | Depth of credit information index (0-6) | 1 | | |
| Time (days) | 163 | Public registry coverage (% of adults) | 1.1 | **Enforcing contracts** (rank) | 142 |
| Cost (% of income per capita) | 785.2 | Private bureau coverage (% of adults) | 0.0 | Procedures (number) | 40 |
| | | | | Time (days) | 1,715 |
| **Getting electricity** (rank) | 182 | **Protecting investors** (rank) | 139 | Cost (% of claim) | 25.0 |
| Procedures (number) | 7 | Extent of disclosure index (0-10) | 6 | | |
| Time (days) | 455 | Extent of director liability index (0-10) | 1 | **Resolving insolvency** (rank) | 185 |
| Cost (% of income per capita) | 1,737.2 | Ease of shareholder suits index (0-10) | 5 | Time (years) | NO PRACTICE |
| | | Strength of investor protection index (0-10) | 4.0 | Cost (% of estate) | NO PRACTICE |
| | | | | Recovery rate (cents on the dollar) | 0.0 |
| | | **Paying taxes** (rank) | 146 | | |
| | | Payments (number per year) | 46 | | |
| | | Time (hours per year) | 208 | | |
| | | Total tax rate (% of profit) | 45.9 | | |

*Note:* Most indicator sets refer to a case scenario in an economy's largest business city. For more details, see the data notes.

✔ Reform making it easier to do business ✘ Reform making it more difficult to do business

## GUYANA

| | | | | | | |
|---|---|---|---|---|---|---|
| Ease of doing business (rank) | 114 | Latin America & Caribbean<br>Lower middle income | | GNI per capita (US$) | 3,202 | |
| | | | | Population (m) | 0.8 | |
| **Starting a business** (rank) | 89 | **Registering property** (rank) | 114 | **Trading across borders** (rank) | 84 | |
| Procedures (number) | 8 | Procedures (number) | 6 | Documents to export (number) | 7 | |
| Time (days) | 20 | Time (days) | 75 | Time to export (days) | 19 | |
| Cost (% of income per capita) | 13.9 | Cost (% of property value) | 4.6 | Cost to export (US$ per container) | 730 | |
| Minimum capital (% of income per capita) | 0.0 | | | Documents to import (number) | 8 | |
| | | **Getting credit** (rank) | 167 | Time to import (days) | 22 | |
| **Dealing with construction permits** (rank) | 29 | Strength of legal rights index (0-10) | 4 | Cost to import (US$ per container) | 745 | |
| Procedures (number) | 8 | Depth of credit information index (0-6) | 0 | | | |
| Time (days) | 195 | Public registry coverage (% of adults) | 0.0 | **Enforcing contracts** (rank) | 75 | |
| Cost (% of income per capita) | 18.3 | Private bureau coverage (% of adults) | 0.0 | Procedures (number) | 36 | |
| | | | | Time (days) | 581 | |
| **Getting electricity** (rank) | 148 | **Protecting investors** (rank) | 82 | Cost (% of claim) | 25.2 | |
| Procedures (number) | 7 | Extent of disclosure index (0-10) | 5 | | | |
| Time (days) | 109 | Extent of director liability index (0-10) | 5 | **Resolving insolvency** (rank) | 138 | |
| Cost (% of income per capita) | 542.9 | Ease of shareholder suits index (0-10) | 6 | Time (years) | 3.0 | |
| | | Strength of investor protection index (0-10) | 5.3 | Cost (% of estate) | 29 | |
| | | | | Recovery rate (cents on the dollar) | 17.6 | |
| | | **Paying taxes** (rank) | 118 | | | |
| | | Payments (number per year) | 35 | | | |
| | | Time (hours per year) | 263 | | | |
| | | Total tax rate (% of profit) | 36.1 | | | |

## HAITI

| | | | | | | |
|---|---|---|---|---|---|---|
| Ease of doing business (rank) | 174 | Latin America & Caribbean<br>Low income | | GNI per capita (US$) | 700 | |
| | | | | Population (m) | 10.1 | |
| **Starting a business** (rank) | 183 | **Registering property** (rank) | 130 | **Trading across borders** (rank) | 149 | |
| Procedures (number) | 12 | Procedures (number) | 5 | Documents to export (number) | 8 | |
| Time (days) | 105 | Time (days) | 301 | Time to export (days) | 33 | |
| Cost (% of income per capita) | 286.6 | Cost (% of property value) | 6.6 | Cost to export (US$ per container) | 1,185 | |
| Minimum capital (% of income per capita) | 21.0 | | | Documents to import (number) | 10 | |
| | | **Getting credit** (rank) | 159 | Time to import (days) | 31 | |
| **Dealing with construction permits** (rank) | 136 | Strength of legal rights index (0-10) | 3 | Cost to import (US$ per container) | 1,545 | |
| Procedures (number) | 9 | Depth of credit information index (0-6) | 2 | | | |
| Time (days) | 1,129 | Public registry coverage (% of adults) | 0.7 | **Enforcing contracts** (rank) | 97 | |
| Cost (% of income per capita) | 692.0 | Private bureau coverage (% of adults) | 0.0 | Procedures (number) | 35 | |
| | | | | Time (days) | 530 | |
| **Getting electricity** (rank) | 71 | **Protecting investors** (rank) | 169 | Cost (% of claim) | 42.6 | |
| Procedures (number) | 4 | Extent of disclosure index (0-10) | 2 | | | |
| Time (days) | 60 | Extent of director liability index (0-10) | 3 | **Resolving insolvency** (rank) | 160 | |
| Cost (% of income per capita) | 4,599.0 | Ease of shareholder suits index (0-10) | 4 | Time (years) | 5.7 | |
| | | Strength of investor protection index (0-10) | 3.0 | Cost (% of estate) | 30 | |
| | | | | Recovery rate (cents on the dollar) | 8.3 | |
| | | **Paying taxes** (rank) | 123 | | | |
| | | Payments (number per year) | 46 | | | |
| | | Time (hours per year) | 184 | | | |
| | | Total tax rate (% of profit) | 40.8 | | | |

## HONDURAS

| | | | | | | |
|---|---|---|---|---|---|---|
| Ease of doing business (rank) | 125 | Latin America & Caribbean<br>Lower middle income | | GNI per capita (US$) | 1,970 | |
| | | | | Population (m) | 7.8 | |
| **Starting a business** (rank) | 155 | **Registering property** (rank) | 92 | **Trading across borders** (rank) | 90 | |
| Procedures (number) | 13 | Procedures (number) | 7 | Documents to export (number) | 6 | |
| Time (days) | 14 | Time (days) | 23 | Time to export (days) | 12 | |
| Cost (% of income per capita) | 45.9 | Cost (% of property value) | 5.7 | Cost to export (US$ per container) | 1,342 | |
| Minimum capital (% of income per capita) | 15.7 | | | Documents to import (number) | 8 | |
| | | **Getting credit** (rank) | 12 | Time to import (days) | 16 | |
| **Dealing with construction permits** (rank) | 65 | Strength of legal rights index (0-10) | 8 | Cost to import (US$ per container) | 1,510 | |
| Procedures (number) | 13 | Depth of credit information index (0-6) | 6 | | | |
| Time (days) | 94 | Public registry coverage (% of adults) | 20.7 | **Enforcing contracts** (rank) | 179 | |
| Cost (% of income per capita) | 274.3 | Private bureau coverage (% of adults) | 32.9 | Procedures (number) | 47 | |
| | | | | Time (days) | 920 | |
| **Getting electricity** (rank) | 117 | **Protecting investors** (rank) | 169 | Cost (% of claim) | 35.2 | |
| Procedures (number) | 8 | Extent of disclosure index (0-10) | 0 | | | |
| Time (days) | 33 | Extent of director liability index (0-10) | 5 | **Resolving insolvency** (rank) | 133 | |
| Cost (% of income per capita) | 997.9 | Ease of shareholder suits index (0-10) | 4 | Time (years) | 3.8 | |
| | | Strength of investor protection index (0-10) | 3.0 | Cost (% of estate) | 15 | |
| | | | | Recovery rate (cents on the dollar) | 19.4 | |
| | | **Paying taxes** (rank) | 139 | | | |
| | | Payments (number per year) | 47 | | | |
| | | Time (hours per year) | 224 | | | |
| | | Total tax rate (% of profit) | 40.3 | | | |

*Note:* Most indicator sets refer to a case scenario in an economy's largest business city. For more details, see the data notes.

✔ Reform making it easier to do business ✘ Reform making it more difficult to do business

## HONG KONG SAR, CHINA

| | | | | | |
|---|---|---|---|---|---|
| Ease of doing business (rank) | 2 | East Asia & Pacific<br>High income | | GNI per capita (US$)<br>Population (m) | 35,160<br>7.1 |

| | | | | | |
|---|---|---|---|---|---|
| **Starting a business** (rank) | 6 | **Registering property** (rank) | 60 | **Trading across borders** (rank) | 2 |
| Procedures (number) | 3 | Procedures (number) | 5 | Documents to export (number) | 4 |
| Time (days) | 3 | Time (days) | 36 | Time to export (days) | 5 |
| Cost (% of income per capita) | 1.9 | Cost (% of property value) | 4.0 | Cost to export (US$ per container) | 575 |
| Minimum capital (% of income per capita) | 0.0 | | | Documents to import (number) | 4 |
| | | **Getting credit** (rank) | 4 | Time to import (days) | 5 |
| **Dealing with construction permits** (rank) | 1 | Strength of legal rights index (0-10) | 10 | Cost to import (US$ per container) | 565 |
| Procedures (number) | 6 | Depth of credit information index (0-6) | 5 | | |
| Time (days) | 67 | Public registry coverage (% of adults) | 0.0 | **Enforcing contracts** (rank) | 10 |
| Cost (% of income per capita) | 16.3 | Private bureau coverage (% of adults) | 89.4 | Procedures (number) | 27 |
| | | | | Time (days) | 360 |
| **Getting electricity** (rank) | 4 | **Protecting investors** (rank) | 3 | Cost (% of claim) | 21.2 |
| Procedures (number) | 4 | Extent of disclosure index (0-10) | 10 | | |
| Time (days) | 41 | Extent of director liability index (0-10) | 8 | **Resolving insolvency** (rank) | 17 |
| Cost (% of income per capita) | 1.6 | Ease of shareholder suits index (0-10) | 9 | Time (years) | 1.1 |
| | | Strength of investor protection index (0-10) | 9.0 | Cost (% of estate) | 9 |
| | | | | Recovery rate (cents on the dollar) | 81.2 |
| | | **Paying taxes** (rank) | 4 | | |
| | | Payments (number per year) | 3 | | |
| | | Time (hours per year) | 78 | | |
| | | Total tax rate (% of profit) | 23.0 | | |

## HUNGARY

| | | | | | |
|---|---|---|---|---|---|
| Ease of doing business (rank) | 54 | OECD high income<br>High income | | GNI per capita (US$)<br>Population (m) | 12,730<br>10.0 |

| | | | | | |
|---|---|---|---|---|---|
| ✘ **Starting a business** (rank) | 52 | **Registering property** (rank) | 43 | ✔ **Trading across borders** (rank) | 73 |
| Procedures (number) | 4 | Procedures (number) | 4 | Documents to export (number) | 6 |
| Time (days) | 5 | Time (days) | 17 | Time to export (days) | 17 |
| Cost (% of income per capita) | 8.9 | Cost (% of property value) | 5.0 | Cost to export (US$ per container) | 885 |
| Minimum capital (% of income per capita) | 9.4 | | | Documents to import (number) | 7 |
| | | ✔ **Getting credit** (rank) | 53 | Time to import (days) | 19 |
| **Dealing with construction permits** (rank) | 55 | Strength of legal rights index (0-10) | 7 | Cost to import (US$ per container) | 875 |
| Procedures (number) | 26 | Depth of credit information index (0-6) | 4 | | |
| Time (days) | 102 | Public registry coverage (% of adults) | 0.0 | **Enforcing contracts** (rank) | 16 |
| Cost (% of income per capita) | 5.7 | Private bureau coverage (% of adults) | 15.8 | Procedures (number) | 35 |
| | | | | Time (days) | 395 |
| **Getting electricity** (rank) | 109 | **Protecting investors** (rank) | 128 | Cost (% of claim) | 15.0 |
| Procedures (number) | 5 | Extent of disclosure index (0-10) | 2 | | |
| Time (days) | 252 | Extent of director liability index (0-10) | 4 | **Resolving insolvency** (rank) | 70 |
| Cost (% of income per capita) | 116.9 | Ease of shareholder suits index (0-10) | 7 | Time (years) | 2.0 |
| | | Strength of investor protection index (0-10) | 4.3 | Cost (% of estate) | 15 |
| | | | | Recovery rate (cents on the dollar) | 38.8 |
| | | ✔ **Paying taxes** (rank) | 118 | | |
| | | Payments (number per year) | 12 | | |
| | | Time (hours per year) | 277 | | |
| | | Total tax rate (% of profit) | 50.3 | | |

## ICELAND

| | | | | | |
|---|---|---|---|---|---|
| Ease of doing business (rank) | 14 | OECD high income<br>High income | | GNI per capita (US$)<br>Population (m) | 35,020<br>0.3 |

| | | | | | |
|---|---|---|---|---|---|
| **Starting a business** (rank) | 45 | **Registering property** (rank) | 9 | **Trading across borders** (rank) | 82 |
| Procedures (number) | 5 | Procedures (number) | 3 | Documents to export (number) | 5 |
| Time (days) | 5 | Time (days) | 4 | Time to export (days) | 19 |
| Cost (% of income per capita) | 3.0 | Cost (% of property value) | 2.4 | Cost to export (US$ per container) | 1,465 |
| Minimum capital (% of income per capita) | 11.5 | | | Documents to import (number) | 5 |
| | | **Getting credit** (rank) | 40 | Time to import (days) | 14 |
| **Dealing with construction permits** (rank) | 40 | Strength of legal rights index (0-10) | 7 | Cost to import (US$ per container) | 1,620 |
| Procedures (number) | 18 | Depth of credit information index (0-6) | 5 | | |
| Time (days) | 77 | Public registry coverage (% of adults) | 0.0 | **Enforcing contracts** (rank) | 3 |
| Cost (% of income per capita) | 27.4 | Private bureau coverage (% of adults) | 100.0 | Procedures (number) | 27 |
| | | | | Time (days) | 417 |
| **Getting electricity** (rank) | 1 | **Protecting investors** (rank) | 49 | Cost (% of claim) | 8.2 |
| Procedures (number) | 4 | Extent of disclosure index (0-10) | 7 | | |
| Time (days) | 22 | Extent of director liability index (0-10) | 5 | **Resolving insolvency** (rank) | 11 |
| Cost (% of income per capita) | 14.9 | Ease of shareholder suits index (0-10) | 6 | Time (years) | 1.0 |
| | | Strength of investor protection index (0-10) | 6.0 | Cost (% of estate) | 4 |
| | | | | Recovery rate (cents on the dollar) | 85.0 |
| | | ✘ **Paying taxes** (rank) | 41 | | |
| | | Payments (number per year) | 29 | | |
| | | Time (hours per year) | 140 | | |
| | | Total tax rate (% of profit) | 33.0 | | |

*Note:* Most indicator sets refer to a case scenario in an economy's largest business city. For more details, see the data notes.

✔ Reform making it easier to do business ✘ Reform making it more difficult to do business

## INDIA

| | | | | | | | |
|---|---|---|---|---|---|---|---|
| **Ease of doing business** (rank) | 132 | South Asia<br>Lower middle income | | | GNI per capita (US$)<br>Population (m) | | 1,420<br>1,241.5 |

| | | | | | | |
|---|---|---|---|---|---|---|
| **Starting a business** (rank) | 173 | **Registering property** (rank) | 94 | **Trading across borders** (rank) | | 127 |
| Procedures (number) | 12 | Procedures (number) | 5 | Documents to export (number) | | 9 |
| Time (days) | 27 | Time (days) | 44 | Time to export (days) | | 16 |
| Cost (% of income per capita) | 49.8 | Cost (% of property value) | 7.3 | Cost to export (US$ per container) | | 1,120 |
| Minimum capital (% of income per capita) | 140.1 | | | Documents to import (number) | | 11 |
| | | **Getting credit** (rank) | 23 | Time to import (days) | | 20 |
| ✔ **Dealing with construction permits** (rank) | 182 | Strength of legal rights index (0-10) | 8 | Cost to import (US$ per container) | | 1,200 |
| Procedures (number) | 34 | Depth of credit information index (0-6) | 5 | | | |
| Time (days) | 196 | Public registry coverage (% of adults) | 0.0 | **Enforcing contracts** (rank) | | 184 |
| Cost (% of income per capita) | 1,528.0 | Private bureau coverage (% of adults) | 14.9 | Procedures (number) | | 46 |
| | | | | Time (days) | | 1,420 |
| **Getting electricity** (rank) | 105 | **Protecting investors** (rank) | 49 | Cost (% of claim) | | 39.6 |
| Procedures (number) | 7 | Extent of disclosure index (0-10) | 7 | | | |
| Time (days) | 67 | Extent of director liability index (0-10) | 4 | **Resolving insolvency** (rank) | | 116 |
| Cost (% of income per capita) | 247.3 | Ease of shareholder suits index (0-10) | 7 | Time (years) | | 4.3 |
| | | Strength of investor protection index (0-10) | 6.0 | Cost (% of estate) | | 9 |
| | | | | Recovery rate (cents on the dollar) | | 26.0 |
| | | **Paying taxes** (rank) | 152 | | | |
| | | Payments (number per year) | 33 | | | |
| | | Time (hours per year) | 243 | | | |
| | | Total tax rate (% of profit) | 61.8 | | | |

## INDONESIA

| | | | | | | | |
|---|---|---|---|---|---|---|---|
| **Ease of doing business** (rank) | 128 | East Asia & Pacific<br>Lower middle income | | | GNI per capita (US$)<br>Population (m) | | 2,940<br>242.3 |

| | | | | | | |
|---|---|---|---|---|---|---|
| **Starting a business** (rank) | 166 | **Registering property** (rank) | 98 | **Trading across borders** (rank) | | 37 |
| Procedures (number) | 9 | Procedures (number) | 6 | Documents to export (number) | | 4 |
| Time (days) | 47 | Time (days) | 22 | Time to export (days) | | 17 |
| Cost (% of income per capita) | 22.7 | Cost (% of property value) | 10.8 | Cost to export (US$ per container) | | 644 |
| Minimum capital (% of income per capita) | 42.0 | | | Documents to import (number) | | 7 |
| | | **Getting credit** (rank) | 129 | Time to import (days) | | 23 |
| **Dealing with construction permits** (rank) | 75 | Strength of legal rights index (0-10) | 3 | Cost to import (US$ per container) | | 660 |
| Procedures (number) | 13 | Depth of credit information index (0-6) | 4 | | | |
| Time (days) | 158 | Public registry coverage (% of adults) | 36.0 | **Enforcing contracts** (rank) | | 144 |
| Cost (% of income per capita) | 95.0 | Private bureau coverage (% of adults) | 0.0 | Procedures (number) | | 40 |
| | | | | Time (days) | | 498 |
| ✔ **Getting electricity** (rank) | 147 | **Protecting investors** (rank) | 49 | Cost (% of claim) | | 139.4 |
| Procedures (number) | 6 | Extent of disclosure index (0-10) | 10 | | | |
| Time (days) | 108 | Extent of director liability index (0-10) | 5 | **Resolving insolvency** (rank) | | 148 |
| Cost (% of income per capita) | 1,243.7 | Ease of shareholder suits index (0-10) | 3 | Time (years) | | 5.5 |
| | | Strength of investor protection index (0-10) | 6.0 | Cost (% of estate) | | 18 |
| | | | | Recovery rate (cents on the dollar) | | 14.2 |
| | | **Paying taxes** (rank) | 131 | | | |
| | | Payments (number per year) | 51 | | | |
| | | Time (hours per year) | 259 | | | |
| | | Total tax rate (% of profit) | 34.5 | | | |

## IRAN, ISLAMIC REP.

| | | | | | | | |
|---|---|---|---|---|---|---|---|
| **Ease of doing business** (rank) | 145 | Middle East & North Africa<br>Upper middle income | | | GNI per capita (US$)<br>Population (m) | | 6,360<br>74.8 |

| | | | | | | |
|---|---|---|---|---|---|---|
| ✘ **Starting a business** (rank) | 87 | **Registering property** (rank) | 165 | **Trading across borders** (rank) | | 143 |
| Procedures (number) | 7 | Procedures (number) | 9 | Documents to export (number) | | 7 |
| Time (days) | 13 | Time (days) | 36 | Time to export (days) | | 25 |
| Cost (% of income per capita) | 3.3 | Cost (% of property value) | 10.5 | Cost to export (US$ per container) | | 1,470 |
| Minimum capital (% of income per capita) | 0.5 | | | Documents to import (number) | | 8 |
| | | **Getting credit** (rank) | 83 | Time to import (days) | | 32 |
| **Dealing with construction permits** (rank) | 166 | Strength of legal rights index (0-10) | 4 | Cost to import (US$ per container) | | 2,100 |
| Procedures (number) | 16 | Depth of credit information index (0-6) | 5 | | | |
| Time (days) | 320 | Public registry coverage (% of adults) | 25.9 | **Enforcing contracts** (rank) | | 53 |
| Cost (% of income per capita) | 262.3 | Private bureau coverage (% of adults) | 31.9 | Procedures (number) | | 39 |
| | | | | Time (days) | | 505 |
| **Getting electricity** (rank) | 163 | ✔ **Protecting investors** (rank) | 150 | Cost (% of claim) | | 17.0 |
| Procedures (number) | 7 | Extent of disclosure index (0-10) | 7 | | | |
| Time (days) | 140 | Extent of director liability index (0-10) | 4 | **Resolving insolvency** (rank) | | 126 |
| Cost (% of income per capita) | 788.4 | Ease of shareholder suits index (0-10) | 0 | Time (years) | | 4.5 |
| | | Strength of investor protection index (0-10) | 3.7 | Cost (% of estate) | | 9 |
| | | | | Recovery rate (cents on the dollar) | | 23.1 |
| | | **Paying taxes** (rank) | 129 | | | |
| | | Payments (number per year) | 20 | | | |
| | | Time (hours per year) | 344 | | | |
| | | Total tax rate (% of profit) | 44.1 | | | |

*Note:* Most indicator sets refer to a case scenario in an economy's largest business city. For more details, see the data notes.

✔ Reform making it easier to do business ✘ Reform making it more difficult to do business

## IRAQ

| | | Middle East & North Africa | | GNI per capita (US$) | 2,640 |
|---|---|---|---|---|---|
| Ease of doing business (rank) | 165 | Lower middle income | | Population (m) | 33.0 |

| | | | | | |
|---|---|---|---|---|---|
| **Starting a business** (rank) | 177 | **Registering property** (rank) | 100 | **Trading across borders** (rank) | 179 |
| Procedures (number) | 10 | Procedures (number) | 5 | Documents to export (number) | 10 |
| Time (days) | 74 | Time (days) | 51 | Time to export (days) | 80 |
| Cost (% of income per capita) | 81.1 | Cost (% of property value) | 7.5 | Cost to export (US$ per container) | 3,550 |
| Minimum capital (% of income per capita) | 25.2 | | | Documents to import (number) | 10 |
| | | **Getting credit** (rank) | 176 | Time to import (days) | 82 |
| **Dealing with construction permits** (rank) | 84 | Strength of legal rights index (0-10) | 3 | Cost to import (US$ per container) | 3,650 |
| Procedures (number) | 12 | Depth of credit information index (0-6) | 0 | | |
| Time (days) | 187 | Public registry coverage (% of adults) | 0.0 | **Enforcing contracts** (rank) | 141 |
| Cost (% of income per capita) | 109.8 | Private bureau coverage (% of adults) | 0.0 | Procedures (number) | 51 |
| | | | | Time (days) | 520 |
| **Getting electricity** (rank) | 46 | **Protecting investors** (rank) | 128 | Cost (% of claim) | 28.1 |
| Procedures (number) | 5 | Extent of disclosure index (0-10) | 4 | | |
| Time (days) | 47 | Extent of director liability index (0-10) | 5 | **Resolving insolvency** (rank) | 185 |
| Cost (% of income per capita) | 516.7 | Ease of shareholder suits index (0-10) | 4 | Time (years) | NO PRACTICE |
| | | Strength of investor protection index (0-10) | 4.3 | Cost (% of estate) | NO PRACTICE |
| | | | | Recovery rate (cents on the dollar) | 0.0 |
| | | **Paying taxes** (rank) | 65 | | |
| | | Payments (number per year) | 13 | | |
| | | Time (hours per year) | 312 | | |
| | | Total tax rate (% of profit) | 28.1 | | |

## IRELAND

| | | OECD high income | | GNI per capita (US$) | 38,580 |
|---|---|---|---|---|---|
| Ease of doing business (rank) | 15 | High income | | Population (m) | 4.5 |

| | | | | | |
|---|---|---|---|---|---|
| ✔ **Starting a business** (rank) | 10 | ✔ **Registering property** (rank) | 53 | **Trading across borders** (rank) | 28 |
| Procedures (number) | 4 | Procedures (number) | 5 | Documents to export (number) | 4 |
| Time (days) | 10 | Time (days) | 38 | Time to export (days) | 7 |
| Cost (% of income per capita) | 0.3 | Cost (% of property value) | 2.5 | Cost to export (US$ per container) | 1,135 |
| Minimum capital (% of income per capita) | 0.0 | | | Documents to import (number) | 4 |
| | | **Getting credit** (rank) | 12 | Time to import (days) | 12 |
| **Dealing with construction permits** (rank) | 106 | Strength of legal rights index (0-10) | 9 | Cost to import (US$ per container) | 1,121 |
| Procedures (number) | 12 | Depth of credit information index (0-6) | 5 | | |
| Time (days) | 156 | Public registry coverage (% of adults) | 0.0 | **Enforcing contracts** (rank) | 63 |
| Cost (% of income per capita) | 626.1 | Private bureau coverage (% of adults) | 100.0 | Procedures (number) | 21 |
| | | | | Time (days) | 650 |
| **Getting electricity** (rank) | 95 | **Protecting investors** (rank) | 6 | Cost (% of claim) | 26.9 |
| Procedures (number) | 5 | Extent of disclosure index (0-10) | 10 | | |
| Time (days) | 205 | Extent of director liability index (0-10) | 6 | **Resolving insolvency** (rank) | 9 |
| Cost (% of income per capita) | 94.2 | Ease of shareholder suits index (0-10) | 9 | Time (years) | 0.4 |
| | | Strength of investor protection index (0-10) | 8.3 | Cost (% of estate) | 9 |
| | | | | Recovery rate (cents on the dollar) | 87.5 |
| | | **Paying taxes** (rank) | 6 | | |
| | | Payments (number per year) | 8 | | |
| | | Time (hours per year) | 80 | | |
| | | Total tax rate (% of profit) | 26.4 | | |

## ISRAEL

| | | OECD high income | | GNI per capita (US$) | 28,930 |
|---|---|---|---|---|---|
| Ease of doing business (rank) | 38 | High income | | Population (m) | 7.8 |

| | | | | | |
|---|---|---|---|---|---|
| **Starting a business** (rank) | 41 | ✔ **Registering property** (rank) | 144 | **Trading across borders** (rank) | 10 |
| Procedures (number) | 5 | Procedures (number) | 6 | Documents to export (number) | 5 |
| Time (days) | 21 | Time (days) | 81 | Time to export (days) | 10 |
| Cost (% of income per capita) | 4.0 | Cost (% of property value) | 7.3 | Cost to export (US$ per container) | 620 |
| Minimum capital (% of income per capita) | 0.0 | | | Documents to import (number) | 4 |
| | | **Getting credit** (rank) | 12 | Time to import (days) | 10 |
| **Dealing with construction permits** (rank) | 139 | Strength of legal rights index (0-10) | 9 | Cost to import (US$ per container) | 565 |
| Procedures (number) | 19 | Depth of credit information index (0-6) | 5 | | |
| Time (days) | 212 | Public registry coverage (% of adults) | 0.0 | **Enforcing contracts** (rank) | 94 |
| Cost (% of income per capita) | 86.4 | Private bureau coverage (% of adults) | 100.0 | Procedures (number) | 35 |
| | | | | Time (days) | 890 |
| **Getting electricity** (rank) | 91 | **Protecting investors** (rank) | 6 | Cost (% of claim) | 25.3 |
| Procedures (number) | 6 | Extent of disclosure index (0-10) | 7 | | |
| Time (days) | 132 | Extent of director liability index (0-10) | 9 | **Resolving insolvency** (rank) | 47 |
| Cost (% of income per capita) | 13.8 | Ease of shareholder suits index (0-10) | 9 | Time (years) | 4.0 |
| | | Strength of investor protection index (0-10) | 8.3 | Cost (% of estate) | 23 |
| | | | | Recovery rate (cents on the dollar) | 45.9 |
| | | **Paying taxes** (rank) | 82 | | |
| | | Payments (number per year) | 33 | | |
| | | Time (hours per year) | 235 | | |
| | | Total tax rate (% of profit) | 30.5 | | |

*Note:* Most indicator sets refer to a case scenario in an economy's largest business city. For more details, see the data notes.

✔ Reform making it easier to do business ✘ Reform making it more difficult to do business

## ITALY

| | | | | | | | |
|---|---|---|---|---|---|---|---|
| Ease of doing business (rank) | 73 | OECD high income<br>High income | | GNI per capita (US$)<br>Population (m) | 35,330<br>60.8 | | |

| | | | | | | |
|---|---|---|---|---|---|---|
| **Starting a business** (rank) | 84 | ✔ **Registering property** (rank) | 39 | **Trading across borders** (rank) | 55 |
| Procedures (number) | 6 | Procedures (number) | 3 | Documents to export (number) | 4 |
| Time (days) | 6 | Time (days) | 24 | Time to export (days) | 19 |
| Cost (% of income per capita) | 16.5 | Cost (% of property value) | 4.5 | Cost to export (US$ per container) | 1,145 |
| Minimum capital (% of income per capita) | 9.7 | | | Documents to import (number) | 4 |
| | | **Getting credit** (rank) | 104 | Time to import (days) | 18 |
| **Dealing with construction permits** (rank) | 103 | Strength of legal rights index (0-10) | 3 | Cost to import (US$ per container) | 1,145 |
| Procedures (number) | 11 | Depth of credit information index (0-6) | 5 | | |
| Time (days) | 234 | Public registry coverage (% of adults) | 24.1 | **Enforcing contracts** (rank) | 160 |
| Cost (% of income per capita) | 184.2 | Private bureau coverage (% of adults) | 100.0 | Procedures (number) | 41 |
| | | | | Time (days) | 1,210 |
| ✔ **Getting electricity** (rank) | 107 | **Protecting investors** (rank) | 49 | Cost (% of claim) | 29.9 |
| Procedures (number) | 5 | Extent of disclosure index (0-10) | 7 | | |
| Time (days) | 155 | Extent of director liability index (0-10) | 4 | **Resolving insolvency** (rank) | 31 |
| Cost (% of income per capita) | 319.2 | Ease of shareholder suits index (0-10) | 7 | Time (years) | 1.8 |
| | | Strength of investor protection index (0-10) | 6.0 | Cost (% of estate) | 22 |
| | | | | Recovery rate (cents on the dollar) | 63.4 |
| | | **Paying taxes** (rank) | 131 | | |
| | | Payments (number per year) | 15 | | |
| | | Time (hours per year) | 269 | | |
| | | Total tax rate (% of profit) | 68.3 | | |

## JAMAICA

| | | | | | | | |
|---|---|---|---|---|---|---|---|
| Ease of doing business (rank) | 90 | Latin America & Caribbean<br>Upper middle income | | GNI per capita (US$)<br>Population (m) | 4,980<br>2.7 | | |

| | | | | | | |
|---|---|---|---|---|---|---|
| **Starting a business** (rank) | 21 | **Registering property** (rank) | 105 | ✔ **Trading across borders** (rank) | 106 |
| Procedures (number) | 6 | Procedures (number) | 6 | Documents to export (number) | 6 |
| Time (days) | 7 | Time (days) | 37 | Time to export (days) | 20 |
| Cost (% of income per capita) | 6.7 | Cost (% of property value) | 7.5 | Cost to export (US$ per container) | 1,500 |
| Minimum capital (% of income per capita) | 0.0 | | | Documents to import (number) | 7 |
| | | **Getting credit** (rank) | 104 | Time to import (days) | 17 |
| **Dealing with construction permits** (rank) | 50 | Strength of legal rights index (0-10) | 8 | Cost to import (US$ per container) | 1,560 |
| Procedures (number) | 8 | Depth of credit information index (0-6) | 0 | | |
| Time (days) | 145 | Public registry coverage (% of adults) | 0.0 | **Enforcing contracts** (rank) | 129 |
| Cost (% of income per capita) | 212.4 | Private bureau coverage (% of adults) | 0.0 | Procedures (number) | 35 |
| | | | | Time (days) | 655 |
| **Getting electricity** (rank) | 123 | **Protecting investors** (rank) | 82 | Cost (% of claim) | 45.6 |
| Procedures (number) | 6 | Extent of disclosure index (0-10) | 4 | | |
| Time (days) | 96 | Extent of director liability index (0-10) | 8 | **Resolving insolvency** (rank) | 32 |
| Cost (% of income per capita) | 557.0 | Ease of shareholder suits index (0-10) | 4 | Time (years) | 1.1 |
| | | Strength of investor protection index (0-10) | 5.3 | Cost (% of estate) | 18 |
| | | | | Recovery rate (cents on the dollar) | 63.1 |
| | | ✔ **Paying taxes** (rank) | 163 | | |
| | | Payments (number per year) | 36 | | |
| | | Time (hours per year) | 368 | | |
| | | Total tax rate (% of profit) | 45.6 | | |

## JAPAN

| | | | | | | | |
|---|---|---|---|---|---|---|---|
| Ease of doing business (rank) | 24 | OECD high income<br>High income | | GNI per capita (US$)<br>Population (m) | 45,180<br>127.8 | | |

| | | | | | | |
|---|---|---|---|---|---|---|
| **Starting a business** (rank) | 114 | **Registering property** (rank) | 64 | **Trading across borders** (rank) | 19 |
| Procedures (number) | 8 | Procedures (number) | 6 | Documents to export (number) | 3 |
| Time (days) | 23 | Time (days) | 14 | Time to export (days) | 10 |
| Cost (% of income per capita) | 7.5 | Cost (% of property value) | 5.8 | Cost to export (US$ per container) | 880 |
| Minimum capital (% of income per capita) | 0.0 | | | Documents to import (number) | 5 |
| | | **Getting credit** (rank) | 23 | Time to import (days) | 11 |
| **Dealing with construction permits** (rank) | 72 | Strength of legal rights index (0-10) | 7 | Cost to import (US$ per container) | 970 |
| Procedures (number) | 14 | Depth of credit information index (0-6) | 6 | | |
| Time (days) | 193 | Public registry coverage (% of adults) | 0.0 | **Enforcing contracts** (rank) | 35 |
| Cost (% of income per capita) | 28.5 | Private bureau coverage (% of adults) | 100.0 | Procedures (number) | 30 |
| | | | | Time (days) | 360 |
| **Getting electricity** (rank) | 27 | **Protecting investors** (rank) | 19 | Cost (% of claim) | 32.2 |
| Procedures (number) | 3 | Extent of disclosure index (0-10) | 7 | | |
| Time (days) | 105 | Extent of director liability index (0-10) | 6 | **Resolving insolvency** (rank) | 1 |
| Cost (% of income per capita) | 0.0 | Ease of shareholder suits index (0-10) | 8 | Time (years) | 0.6 |
| | | Strength of investor protection index (0-10) | 7.0 | Cost (% of estate) | 4 |
| | | | | Recovery rate (cents on the dollar) | 92.8 |
| | | ✔ **Paying taxes** (rank) | 127 | | |
| | | Payments (number per year) | 14 | | |
| | | Time (hours per year) | 330 | | |
| | | Total tax rate (% of profit) | 50.0 | | |

*Note:* Most indicator sets refer to a case scenario in an economy's largest business city. For more details, see the data notes.

✔ Reform making it easier to do business  ✘ Reform making it more difficult to do business

## JORDAN

| | | Middle East & North Africa | | GNI per capita (US$) | 4,380 |
|---|---|---|---|---|---|
| Ease of doing business (rank) | 106 | Upper middle income | | Population (m) | 6.2 |

| | | | | | |
|---|---|---|---|---|---|
| **Starting a business** (rank) | 103 | **Registering property** (rank) | 102 | **Trading across borders** (rank) | 52 |
| Procedures (number) | 7 | Procedures (number) | 7 | Documents to export (number) | 5 |
| Time (days) | 12 | Time (days) | 21 | Time to export (days) | 13 |
| Cost (% of income per capita) | 13.8 | Cost (% of property value) | 7.5 | Cost to export (US$ per container) | 825 |
| Minimum capital (% of income per capita) | 0.0 | | | Documents to import (number) | 7 |
| | | **Getting credit** (rank) | 167 | Time to import (days) | 15 |
| **Dealing with construction permits** (rank) | 102 | Strength of legal rights index (0-10) | 2 | Cost to import (US$ per container) | 1,335 |
| Procedures (number) | 17 | Depth of credit information index (0-6) | 2 | | |
| Time (days) | 70 | Public registry coverage (% of adults) | 1.9 | **Enforcing contracts** (rank) | 129 |
| Cost (% of income per capita) | 529.8 | Private bureau coverage (% of adults) | 0.0 | Procedures (number) | 38 |
| | | | | Time (days) | 689 |
| **Getting electricity** (rank) | 38 | **Protecting investors** (rank) | 128 | Cost (% of claim) | 31.2 |
| Procedures (number) | 5 | Extent of disclosure index (0-10) | 5 | | |
| Time (days) | 47 | Extent of director liability index (0-10) | 4 | **Resolving insolvency** (rank) | 112 |
| Cost (% of income per capita) | 292.3 | Ease of shareholder suits index (0-10) | 4 | Time (years) | 4.3 |
| | | Strength of investor protection index (0-10) | 4.3 | Cost (% of estate) | 9 |
| | | | | Recovery rate (cents on the dollar) | 27.4 |
| | | **Paying taxes** (rank) | 35 | | |
| | | Payments (number per year) | 25 | | |
| | | Time (hours per year) | 151 | | |
| | | Total tax rate (% of profit) | 28.1 | | |

## KAZAKHSTAN

| | | Eastern Europe & Central Asia | | GNI per capita (US$) | 8,220 |
|---|---|---|---|---|---|
| Ease of doing business (rank) | 49 | Upper middle income | | Population (m) | 16.6 |

| | | | | | |
|---|---|---|---|---|---|
| ✔ **Starting a business** (rank) | 25 | **Registering property** (rank) | 28 | **Trading across borders** (rank) | 182 |
| Procedures (number) | 6 | Procedures (number) | 4 | Documents to export (number) | 9 |
| Time (days) | 19 | Time (days) | 40 | Time to export (days) | 81 |
| Cost (% of income per capita) | 0.6 | Cost (% of property value) | 0.1 | Cost to export (US$ per container) | 4,685 |
| Minimum capital (% of income per capita) | 0.0 | | | Documents to import (number) | 12 |
| | | ✔ **Getting credit** (rank) | 83 | Time to import (days) | 69 |
| **Dealing with construction permits** (rank) | 155 | Strength of legal rights index (0-10) | 4 | Cost to import (US$ per container) | 4,665 |
| Procedures (number) | 32 | Depth of credit information index (0-6) | 5 | | |
| Time (days) | 189 | Public registry coverage (% of adults) | 0.0 | **Enforcing contracts** (rank) | 28 |
| Cost (% of income per capita) | 103.5 | Private bureau coverage (% of adults) | 39.3 | Procedures (number) | 37 |
| | | | | Time (days) | 370 |
| **Getting electricity** (rank) | 80 | **Protecting investors** (rank) | 10 | Cost (% of claim) | 22.0 |
| Procedures (number) | 6 | Extent of disclosure index (0-10) | 9 | | |
| Time (days) | 88 | Extent of director liability index (0-10) | 6 | ✔ **Resolving insolvency** (rank) | 55 |
| Cost (% of income per capita) | 71.1 | Ease of shareholder suits index (0-10) | 9 | Time (years) | 1.5 |
| | | Strength of investor protection index (0-10) | 8.0 | Cost (% of estate) | 15 |
| | | | | Recovery rate (cents on the dollar) | 43.1 |
| | | **Paying taxes** (rank) | 17 | | |
| | | Payments (number per year) | 7 | | |
| | | Time (hours per year) | 188 | | |
| | | Total tax rate (% of profit) | 28.6 | | |

## KENYA

| | | Sub-Saharan Africa | | GNI per capita (US$) | 820 |
|---|---|---|---|---|---|
| Ease of doing business (rank) | 121 | Low income | | Population (m) | 41.6 |

| | | | | | |
|---|---|---|---|---|---|
| **Starting a business** (rank) | 126 | **Registering property** (rank) | 161 | **Trading across borders** (rank) | 148 |
| Procedures (number) | 10 | Procedures (number) | 9 | Documents to export (number) | 8 |
| Time (days) | 32 | Time (days) | 73 | Time to export (days) | 26 |
| Cost (% of income per capita) | 40.4 | Cost (% of property value) | 4.3 | Cost to export (US$ per container) | 2,255 |
| Minimum capital (% of income per capita) | 0.0 | | | Documents to import (number) | 7 |
| | | **Getting credit** (rank) | 12 | Time to import (days) | 26 |
| **Dealing with construction permits** (rank) | 45 | Strength of legal rights index (0-10) | 10 | Cost to import (US$ per container) | 2,350 |
| Procedures (number) | 9 | Depth of credit information index (0-6) | 4 | | |
| Time (days) | 125 | Public registry coverage (% of adults) | 0.0 | **Enforcing contracts** (rank) | 149 |
| Cost (% of income per capita) | 211.9 | Private bureau coverage (% of adults) | 4.9 | Procedures (number) | 44 |
| | | | | Time (days) | 465 |
| **Getting electricity** (rank) | 162 | **Protecting investors** (rank) | 100 | Cost (% of claim) | 47.2 |
| Procedures (number) | 6 | Extent of disclosure index (0-10) | 3 | | |
| Time (days) | 146 | Extent of director liability index (0-10) | 2 | **Resolving insolvency** (rank) | 100 |
| Cost (% of income per capita) | 1,208.2 | Ease of shareholder suits index (0-10) | 10 | Time (years) | 4.5 |
| | | Strength of investor protection index (0-10) | 5.0 | Cost (% of estate) | 22 |
| | | | | Recovery rate (cents on the dollar) | 29.5 |
| | | ✔ **Paying taxes** (rank) | 164 | | |
| | | Payments (number per year) | 41 | | |
| | | Time (hours per year) | 340 | | |
| | | Total tax rate (% of profit) | 44.4 | | |

*Note:* Most indicator sets refer to a case scenario in an economy's largest business city. For more details, see the data notes.

✔ Reform making it easier to do business ✖ Reform making it more difficult to do business

## KIRIBATI

| | | | | | | |
|---|---|---|---|---|---|---|
| Ease of doing business (rank) | 117 | East Asia & Pacific<br>Lower middle income | | GNI per capita (US$)<br>Population (m) | 2,110<br>0.1 | |

| | | | | | |
|---|---|---|---|---|---|
| **Starting a business** (rank) | 145 | **Registering property** (rank) | 71 | **Trading across borders** (rank) | 88 |
| Procedures (number) | 7 | Procedures (number) | 5 | Documents to export (number) | 6 |
| Time (days) | 31 | Time (days) | 513 | Time to export (days) | 21 |
| Cost (% of income per capita) | 22.3 | Cost (% of property value) | 0.0 | Cost to export (US$ per container) | 1,120 |
| Minimum capital (% of income per capita) | 21.3 | | | Documents to import (number) | 7 |
| | | **Getting credit** (rank) | 159 | Time to import (days) | 21 |
| **Dealing with construction permits** (rank) | 120 | Strength of legal rights index (0-10) | 5 | Cost to import (US$ per container) | 1,120 |
| Procedures (number) | 16 | Depth of credit information index (0-6) | 0 | | |
| Time (days) | 170 | Public registry coverage (% of adults) | 0.0 | **Enforcing contracts** (rank) | 73 |
| Cost (% of income per capita) | 164.8 | Private bureau coverage (% of adults) | 0.0 | Procedures (number) | 32 |
| | | | | Time (days) | 660 |
| **Getting electricity** (rank) | 159 | **Protecting investors** (rank) | 49 | Cost (% of claim) | 25.8 |
| Procedures (number) | 6 | Extent of disclosure index (0-10) | 6 | | |
| Time (days) | 97 | Extent of director liability index (0-10) | 5 | **Resolving insolvency** (rank) | 185 |
| Cost (% of income per capita) | 5,199.7 | Ease of shareholder suits index (0-10) | 7 | Time (years) | NO PRACTICE |
| | | Strength of investor protection index (0-10) | 6.0 | Cost (% of estate) | NO PRACTICE |
| | | | | Recovery rate (cents on the dollar) | 0.0 |
| | | **Paying taxes** (rank) | 9 | | |
| | | Payments (number per year) | 7 | | |
| | | Time (hours per year) | 120 | | |
| | | Total tax rate (% of profit) | 31.8 | | |

## KOREA, REP.

| | | | | | | |
|---|---|---|---|---|---|---|
| Ease of doing business (rank) | 8 | OECD high income<br>High income | | GNI per capita (US$)<br>Population (m) | 20,870<br>49.8 | |

| | | | | | |
|---|---|---|---|---|---|
| **Starting a business** (rank) | 24 | **Registering property** (rank) | 75 | **Trading across borders** (rank) | 3 |
| Procedures (number) | 5 | Procedures (number) | 7 | Documents to export (number) | 3 |
| Time (days) | 7 | Time (days) | 11 | Time to export (days) | 7 |
| Cost (% of income per capita) | 14.6 | Cost (% of property value) | 5.1 | Cost to export (US$ per container) | 665 |
| Minimum capital (% of income per capita) | 0.0 | | | Documents to import (number) | 3 |
| | | **Getting credit** (rank) | 12 | Time to import (days) | 7 |
| **Dealing with construction permits** (rank) | 26 | Strength of legal rights index (0-10) | 8 | Cost to import (US$ per container) | 695 |
| Procedures (number) | 11 | Depth of credit information index (0-6) | 6 | | |
| Time (days) | 29 | Public registry coverage (% of adults) | 0.0 | **Enforcing contracts** (rank) | 2 |
| Cost (% of income per capita) | 127.2 | Private bureau coverage (% of adults) | 100.0 | Procedures (number) | 33 |
| | | | | Time (days) | 230 |
| ✔ **Getting electricity** (rank) | 3 | ✔ **Protecting investors** (rank) | 49 | Cost (% of claim) | 10.3 |
| Procedures (number) | 4 | Extent of disclosure index (0-10) | 7 | | |
| Time (days) | 28 | Extent of director liability index (0-10) | 4 | ✔ **Resolving insolvency** (rank) | 14 |
| Cost (% of income per capita) | 33.3 | Ease of shareholder suits index (0-10) | 7 | Time (years) | 1.5 |
| | | Strength of investor protection index (0-10) | 6.0 | Cost (% of estate) | 4 |
| | | | | Recovery rate (cents on the dollar) | 81.8 |
| | | ✔ **Paying taxes** (rank) | 30 | | |
| | | Payments (number per year) | 10 | | |
| | | Time (hours per year) | 207 | | |
| | | Total tax rate (% of profit) | 29.8 | | |

## KOSOVO

| | | | | | | |
|---|---|---|---|---|---|---|
| Ease of doing business (rank) | 98 | Eastern Europe & Central Asia<br>Lower middle income | | GNI per capita (US$)<br>Population (m) | 3,520<br>1.8 | |

| | | | | | |
|---|---|---|---|---|---|
| ✔ **Starting a business** (rank) | 126 | **Registering property** (rank) | 76 | **Trading across borders** (rank) | 124 |
| Procedures (number) | 9 | Procedures (number) | 8 | Documents to export (number) | 8 |
| Time (days) | 52 | Time (days) | 33 | Time to export (days) | 15 |
| Cost (% of income per capita) | 23.0 | Cost (% of property value) | 0.6 | Cost to export (US$ per container) | 1,775 |
| Minimum capital (% of income per capita) | 0.0 | | | Documents to import (number) | 8 |
| | | **Getting credit** (rank) | 23 | Time to import (days) | 15 |
| **Dealing with construction permits** (rank) | 144 | Strength of legal rights index (0-10) | 8 | Cost to import (US$ per container) | 1,810 |
| Procedures (number) | 16 | Depth of credit information index (0-6) | 5 | | |
| Time (days) | 156 | Public registry coverage (% of adults) | 22.2 | **Enforcing contracts** (rank) | 138 |
| Cost (% of income per capita) | 2,986.0 | Private bureau coverage (% of adults) | 0.0 | Procedures (number) | 53 |
| | | | | Time (days) | 420 |
| **Getting electricity** (rank) | 116 | ✔ **Protecting investors** (rank) | 100 | Cost (% of claim) | 33.0 |
| Procedures (number) | 7 | Extent of disclosure index (0-10) | 6 | | |
| Time (days) | 48 | Extent of director liability index (0-10) | 6 | **Resolving insolvency** (rank) | 87 |
| Cost (% of income per capita) | 915.4 | Ease of shareholder suits index (0-10) | 3 | Time (years) | 2.0 |
| | | Strength of investor protection index (0-10) | 5.0 | Cost (% of estate) | 15 |
| | | | | Recovery rate (cents on the dollar) | 34.7 |
| | | **Paying taxes** (rank) | 44 | | |
| | | Payments (number per year) | 33 | | |
| | | Time (hours per year) | 164 | | |
| | | Total tax rate (% of profit) | 15.4 | | |

*Note:* Most indicator sets refer to a case scenario in an economy's largest business city. For more details, see the data notes.

✔ Reform making it easier to do business ✘ Reform making it more difficult to do business

## KUWAIT

| | | Middle East & North Africa | | GNI per capita (US$) | 47,982 |
|---|---|---|---|---|---|
| Ease of doing business (rank) | 82 | High income | | Population (m) | 2.8 |

| | | | | | |
|---|---|---|---|---|---|
| **Starting a business** (rank) | 142 | **Registering property** (rank) | 89 | **Trading across borders** (rank) | 113 |
| Procedures (number) | 12 | Procedures (number) | 8 | Documents to export (number) | 7 |
| Time (days) | 32 | Time (days) | 47 | Time to export (days) | 16 |
| Cost (% of income per capita) | 1.1 | Cost (% of property value) | 0.5 | Cost to export (US$ per container) | 1,085 |
| Minimum capital (% of income per capita) | 56.7 | | | Documents to import (number) | 10 |
| | | **Getting credit** (rank) | 104 | Time to import (days) | 19 |
| **Dealing with construction permits** (rank) | 119 | Strength of legal rights index (0-10) | 4 | Cost to import (US$ per container) | 1,242 |
| Procedures (number) | 24 | Depth of credit information index (0-6) | 4 | | |
| Time (days) | 130 | Public registry coverage (% of adults) | 0.0 | **Enforcing contracts** (rank) | 117 |
| Cost (% of income per capita) | 96.1 | Private bureau coverage (% of adults) | 31.0 | Procedures (number) | 50 |
| | | | | Time (days) | 566 |
| **Getting electricity** (rank) | 55 | **Protecting investors** (rank) | 32 | Cost (% of claim) | 18.8 |
| Procedures (number) | 7 | Extent of disclosure index (0-10) | 7 | | |
| Time (days) | 42 | Extent of director liability index (0-10) | 7 | **Resolving insolvency** (rank) | 92 |
| Cost (% of income per capita) | 43.6 | Ease of shareholder suits index (0-10) | 5 | Time (years) | 4.2 |
| | | Strength of investor protection index (0-10) | 6.3 | Cost (% of estate) | 10 |
| | | | | Recovery rate (cents on the dollar) | 31.7 |
| | | **Paying taxes** (rank) | 11 | | |
| | | Payments (number per year) | 12 | | |
| | | Time (hours per year) | 98 | | |
| | | Total tax rate (% of profit) | 10.7 | | |

## KYRGYZ REPUBLIC

| | | Eastern Europe & Central Asia | | GNI per capita (US$) | 920 |
|---|---|---|---|---|---|
| Ease of doing business (rank) | 70 | Low income | | Population (m) | 5.5 |

| | | | | | |
|---|---|---|---|---|---|
| **Starting a business** (rank) | 15 | **Registering property** (rank) | 11 | **Trading across borders** (rank) | 174 |
| Procedures (number) | 2 | Procedures (number) | 4 | Documents to export (number) | 8 |
| Time (days) | 10 | Time (days) | 5 | Time to export (days) | 63 |
| Cost (% of income per capita) | 2.8 | Cost (% of property value) | 1.8 | Cost to export (US$ per container) | 4,160 |
| Minimum capital (% of income per capita) | 0.0 | | | Documents to import (number) | 10 |
| | | **Getting credit** (rank) | 12 | Time to import (days) | 75 |
| **Dealing with construction permits** (rank) | 67 | Strength of legal rights index (0-10) | 10 | Cost to import (US$ per container) | 4,700 |
| Procedures (number) | 12 | Depth of credit information index (0-6) | 4 | | |
| Time (days) | 142 | Public registry coverage (% of adults) | 0.0 | **Enforcing contracts** (rank) | 47 |
| Cost (% of income per capita) | 140.6 | Private bureau coverage (% of adults) | 24.6 | Procedures (number) | 38 |
| | | | | Time (days) | 260 |
| **Getting electricity** (rank) | 177 | **Protecting investors** (rank) | 13 | Cost (% of claim) | 29.0 |
| Procedures (number) | 7 | Extent of disclosure index (0-10) | 8 | | |
| Time (days) | 159 | Extent of director liability index (0-10) | 7 | **Resolving insolvency** (rank) | 155 |
| Cost (% of income per capita) | 2,428.6 | Ease of shareholder suits index (0-10) | 8 | Time (years) | 4.0 |
| | | Strength of investor protection index (0-10) | 7.7 | Cost (% of estate) | 15 |
| | | | | Recovery rate (cents on the dollar) | 9.1 |
| | | **Paying taxes** (rank) | 168 | | |
| | | Payments (number per year) | 51 | | |
| | | Time (hours per year) | 210 | | |
| | | Total tax rate (% of profit) | 68.9 | | |

## LAO PDR

| | | East Asia & Pacific | | GNI per capita (US$) | 1,130 |
|---|---|---|---|---|---|
| Ease of doing business (rank) | 163 | Lower middle income | | Population (m) | 6.3 |

| | | | | | |
|---|---|---|---|---|---|
| ✔ **Starting a business** (rank) | 81 | **Registering property** (rank) | 74 | ✔ **Trading across borders** (rank) | 160 |
| Procedures (number) | 6 | Procedures (number) | 5 | Documents to export (number) | 10 |
| Time (days) | 92 | Time (days) | 98 | Time to export (days) | 26 |
| Cost (% of income per capita) | 7.1 | Cost (% of property value) | 1.1 | Cost to export (US$ per container) | 2,140 |
| Minimum capital (% of income per capita) | 0.0 | | | Documents to import (number) | 10 |
| | | **Getting credit** (rank) | 167 | Time to import (days) | 26 |
| **Dealing with construction permits** (rank) | 87 | Strength of legal rights index (0-10) | 4 | Cost to import (US$ per container) | 2,125 |
| Procedures (number) | 23 | Depth of credit information index (0-6) | 0 | | |
| Time (days) | 108 | Public registry coverage (% of adults) | 0.0 | **Enforcing contracts** (rank) | 114 |
| Cost (% of income per capita) | 48.6 | Private bureau coverage (% of adults) | 0.0 | Procedures (number) | 42 |
| | | | | Time (days) | 443 |
| **Getting electricity** (rank) | 138 | **Protecting investors** (rank) | 184 | Cost (% of claim) | 31.6 |
| Procedures (number) | 5 | Extent of disclosure index (0-10) | 2 | | |
| Time (days) | 134 | Extent of director liability index (0-10) | 1 | **Resolving insolvency** (rank) | 185 |
| Cost (% of income per capita) | 2,130.5 | Ease of shareholder suits index (0-10) | 2 | Time (years) | NO PRACTICE |
| | | Strength of investor protection index (0-10) | 1.7 | Cost (% of estate) | NO PRACTICE |
| | | | | Recovery rate (cents on the dollar) | 0.0 |
| | | ✔ **Paying taxes** (rank) | 126 | | |
| | | Payments (number per year) | 34 | | |
| | | Time (hours per year) | 362 | | |
| | | Total tax rate (% of profit) | 33.3 | | |

*Note:* Most indicator sets refer to a case scenario in an economy's largest business city. For more details, see the data notes.

✔ Reform making it easier to do business ✘ Reform making it more difficult to do business

## LATVIA

| | | Eastern Europe & Central Asia | | GNI per capita (US$) | 12,350 |
|---|---|---|---|---|---|
| Ease of doing business (rank) | 25 | Upper middle income | | Population (m) | 2.2 |

| Starting a business (rank) | 59 | Registering property (rank) | 31 | Trading across borders (rank) | 16 |
|---|---|---|---|---|---|
| Procedures (number) | 4 | Procedures (number) | 5 | Documents to export (number) | 5 |
| Time (days) | 16 | Time (days) | 18 | Time to export (days) | 10 |
| Cost (% of income per capita) | 2.3 | Cost (% of property value) | 2.0 | Cost to export (US$ per container) | 600 |
| Minimum capital (% of income per capita) | 0.0 | | | Documents to import (number) | 6 |
| | | Getting credit (rank) | 4 | Time to import (days) | 11 |
| Dealing with construction permits (rank) | 113 | Strength of legal rights index (0-10) | 10 | Cost to import (US$ per container) | 801 |
| Procedures (number) | 21 | Depth of credit information index (0-6) | 5 | | |
| Time (days) | 203 | Public registry coverage (% of adults) | 63.8 | Enforcing contracts (rank) | 24 |
| Cost (% of income per capita) | 18.6 | Private bureau coverage (% of adults) | 0.0 | Procedures (number) | 27 |
| | | | | Time (days) | 469 |
| Getting electricity (rank) | 83 | Protecting investors (rank) | 70 | Cost (% of claim) | 23.1 |
| Procedures (number) | 5 | Extent of disclosure index (0-10) | 5 | | |
| Time (days) | 108 | Extent of director liability index (0-10) | 4 | Resolving insolvency (rank) | 33 |
| Cost (% of income per capita) | 389.1 | Ease of shareholder suits index (0-10) | 8 | Time (years) | 3.0 |
| | | Strength of investor protection index (0-10) | 5.7 | Cost (% of estate) | 13 |
| | | | | Recovery rate (cents on the dollar) | 59.8 |
| | | Paying taxes (rank) | 52 | | |
| | | Payments (number per year) | 7 | | |
| | | Time (hours per year) | 264 | | |
| | | Total tax rate (% of profit) | 36.6 | | |

## LEBANON

| | | Middle East & North Africa | | GNI per capita (US$) | 9,110 |
|---|---|---|---|---|---|
| Ease of doing business (rank) | 115 | Upper middle income | | Population (m) | 4.3 |

| Starting a business (rank) | 114 | Registering property (rank) | 108 | Trading across borders (rank) | 95 |
|---|---|---|---|---|---|
| Procedures (number) | 5 | Procedures (number) | 8 | Documents to export (number) | 5 |
| Time (days) | 9 | Time (days) | 25 | Time to export (days) | 22 |
| Cost (% of income per capita) | 67.0 | Cost (% of property value) | 5.8 | Cost to export (US$ per container) | 1,080 |
| Minimum capital (% of income per capita) | 35.2 | | | Documents to import (number) | 7 |
| | | Getting credit (rank) | 104 | Time to import (days) | 30 |
| Dealing with construction permits (rank) | 172 | Strength of legal rights index (0-10) | 3 | Cost to import (US$ per container) | 1,365 |
| Procedures (number) | 19 | Depth of credit information index (0-6) | 5 | | |
| Time (days) | 219 | Public registry coverage (% of adults) | 18.6 | Enforcing contracts (rank) | 121 |
| Cost (% of income per capita) | 301.8 | Private bureau coverage (% of adults) | 0.0 | Procedures (number) | 37 |
| | | | | Time (days) | 721 |
| Getting electricity (rank) | 47 | Protecting investors (rank) | 100 | Cost (% of claim) | 30.8 |
| Procedures (number) | 5 | Extent of disclosure index (0-10) | 9 | | |
| Time (days) | 75 | Extent of director liability index (0-10) | 1 | Resolving insolvency (rank) | 131 |
| Cost (% of income per capita) | 99.5 | Ease of shareholder suits index (0-10) | 5 | Time (years) | 4.0 |
| | | Strength of investor protection index (0-10) | 5.0 | Cost (% of estate) | 22 |
| | | | | Recovery rate (cents on the dollar) | 20.9 |
| | | Paying taxes (rank) | 37 | | |
| | | Payments (number per year) | 19 | | |
| | | Time (hours per year) | 180 | | |
| | | Total tax rate (% of profit) | 30.2 | | |

## LESOTHO

| | | Sub-Saharan Africa | | GNI per capita (US$) | 1,220 |
|---|---|---|---|---|---|
| Ease of doing business (rank) | 136 | Lower middle income | | Population (m) | 2.2 |

| ✔ Starting a business (rank) | 79 | Registering property (rank) | 157 | Trading across borders (rank) | 144 |
|---|---|---|---|---|---|
| Procedures (number) | 7 | Procedures (number) | 6 | Documents to export (number) | 7 |
| Time (days) | 24 | Time (days) | 101 | Time to export (days) | 31 |
| Cost (% of income per capita) | 13.0 | Cost (% of property value) | 7.9 | Cost to export (US$ per container) | 1,695 |
| Minimum capital (% of income per capita) | 0.0 | | | Documents to import (number) | 7 |
| | | Getting credit (rank) | 154 | Time to import (days) | 35 |
| Dealing with construction permits (rank) | 140 | Strength of legal rights index (0-10) | 6 | Cost to import (US$ per container) | 1,945 |
| Procedures (number) | 11 | Depth of credit information index (0-6) | 0 | | |
| Time (days) | 330 | Public registry coverage (% of adults) | 0.0 | Enforcing contracts (rank) | 139 |
| Cost (% of income per capita) | 950.4 | Private bureau coverage (% of adults) | 0.0 | Procedures (number) | 41 |
| | | | | Time (days) | 615 |
| Getting electricity (rank) | 133 | ✔ Protecting investors (rank) | 100 | Cost (% of claim) | 31.3 |
| Procedures (number) | 5 | Extent of disclosure index (0-10) | 3 | | |
| Time (days) | 125 | Extent of director liability index (0-10) | 4 | Resolving insolvency (rank) | 75 |
| Cost (% of income per capita) | 2,275.9 | Ease of shareholder suits index (0-10) | 8 | Time (years) | 2.6 |
| | | Strength of investor protection index (0-10) | 5.0 | Cost (% of estate) | 8 |
| | | | | Recovery rate (cents on the dollar) | 37.6 |
| | | Paying taxes (rank) | 95 | | |
| | | Payments (number per year) | 33 | | |
| | | Time (hours per year) | 324 | | |
| | | Total tax rate (% of profit) | 16.0 | | |

*Note:* Most indicator sets refer to a case scenario in an economy's largest business city. For more details, see the data notes.

✔ Reform making it easier to do business  ✘ Reform making it more difficult to do business

## LIBERIA

| Ease of doing business (rank) | 149 | Sub-Saharan Africa<br>Low income | | GNI per capita (US$)<br>Population (m) | 240<br>4.1 |
|---|---|---|---|---|---|

| | | | | | |
|---|---|---|---|---|---|
| **Starting a business** (rank) | 38 | **Registering property** (rank) | 178 | **Trading across borders** (rank) | 137 |
| Procedures (number) | 4 | Procedures (number) | 10 | Documents to export (number) | 10 |
| Time (days) | 6 | Time (days) | 50 | Time to export (days) | 15 |
| Cost (% of income per capita) | 52.7 | Cost (% of property value) | 13.1 | Cost to export (US$ per container) | 1,220 |
| Minimum capital (% of income per capita) | 0.0 | | | Documents to import (number) | 11 |
| | | **Getting credit** (rank) | 104 | Time to import (days) | 28 |
| **Dealing with construction permits** (rank) | 126 | Strength of legal rights index (0-10) | 7 | Cost to import (US$ per container) | 1,320 |
| Procedures (number) | 23 | Depth of credit information index (0-6) | 1 | | |
| Time (days) | 75 | Public registry coverage (% of adults) | 1.1 | ✔ **Enforcing contracts** (rank) | 163 |
| Cost (% of income per capita) | 559.7 | Private bureau coverage (% of adults) | 0.0 | Procedures (number) | 40 |
| | | | | Time (days) | 1,280 |
| ✔ **Getting electricity** (rank) | 145 | **Protecting investors** (rank) | 150 | Cost (% of claim) | 35.0 |
| Procedures (number) | 4 | Extent of disclosure index (0-10) | 4 | | |
| Time (days) | 465 | Extent of director liability index (0-10) | 1 | **Resolving insolvency** (rank) | 159 |
| Cost (% of income per capita) | 3,528.6 | Ease of shareholder suits index (0-10) | 6 | Time (years) | 3.0 |
| | | Strength of investor protection index (0-10) | 3.7 | Cost (% of estate) | 43 |
| | | | | Recovery rate (cents on the dollar) | 8.5 |
| | | ✔ **Paying taxes** (rank) | 45 | | |
| | | Payments (number per year) | 33 | | |
| | | Time (hours per year) | 158 | | |
| | | Total tax rate (% of profit) | 27.4 | | |

## LITHUANIA

| Ease of doing business (rank) | 27 | Eastern Europe & Central Asia<br>Upper middle income | | GNI per capita (US$)<br>Population (m) | 12,280<br>3.2 |
|---|---|---|---|---|---|

| | | | | | |
|---|---|---|---|---|---|
| ✔ **Starting a business** (rank) | 107 | **Registering property** (rank) | 5 | **Trading across borders** (rank) | 24 |
| Procedures (number) | 7 | Procedures (number) | 3 | Documents to export (number) | 5 |
| Time (days) | 20 | Time (days) | 3 | Time to export (days) | 9 |
| Cost (% of income per capita) | 1.1 | Cost (% of property value) | 0.8 | Cost to export (US$ per container) | 825 |
| Minimum capital (% of income per capita) | 31.3 | | | Documents to import (number) | 6 |
| | | **Getting credit** (rank) | 53 | Time to import (days) | 8 |
| **Dealing with construction permits** (rank) | 48 | Strength of legal rights index (0-10) | 5 | Cost to import (US$ per container) | 980 |
| Procedures (number) | 15 | Depth of credit information index (0-6) | 6 | | |
| Time (days) | 142 | Public registry coverage (% of adults) | 24.4 | **Enforcing contracts** (rank) | 14 |
| Cost (% of income per capita) | 22.3 | Private bureau coverage (% of adults) | 81.2 | Procedures (number) | 30 |
| | | | | Time (days) | 275 |
| **Getting electricity** (rank) | 75 | **Protecting investors** (rank) | 70 | Cost (% of claim) | 23.6 |
| Procedures (number) | 5 | Extent of disclosure index (0-10) | 7 | | |
| Time (days) | 148 | Extent of director liability index (0-10) | 4 | ✔ **Resolving insolvency** (rank) | 40 |
| Cost (% of income per capita) | 55.4 | Ease of shareholder suits index (0-10) | 6 | Time (years) | 1.5 |
| | | Strength of investor protection index (0-10) | 5.7 | Cost (% of estate) | 7 |
| | | | | Recovery rate (cents on the dollar) | 51.0 |
| | | **Paying taxes** (rank) | 60 | | |
| | | Payments (number per year) | 11 | | |
| | | Time (hours per year) | 175 | | |
| | | Total tax rate (% of profit) | 43.7 | | |

## LUXEMBOURG

| Ease of doing business (rank) | 56 | OECD high income<br>High income | | GNI per capita (US$)<br>Population (m) | 78,130<br>0.5 |
|---|---|---|---|---|---|

| | | | | | |
|---|---|---|---|---|---|
| **Starting a business** (rank) | 93 | **Registering property** (rank) | 134 | **Trading across borders** (rank) | 32 |
| Procedures (number) | 6 | Procedures (number) | 8 | Documents to export (number) | 5 |
| Time (days) | 19 | Time (days) | 29 | Time to export (days) | 7 |
| Cost (% of income per capita) | 1.9 | Cost (% of property value) | 10.1 | Cost to export (US$ per container) | 1,420 |
| Minimum capital (% of income per capita) | 20.9 | | | Documents to import (number) | 4 |
| | | **Getting credit** (rank) | 159 | Time to import (days) | 7 |
| **Dealing with construction permits** (rank) | 33 | Strength of legal rights index (0-10) | 5 | Cost to import (US$ per container) | 1,420 |
| Procedures (number) | 12 | Depth of credit information index (0-6) | 0 | | |
| Time (days) | 157 | Public registry coverage (% of adults) | 0.0 | **Enforcing contracts** (rank) | 1 |
| Cost (% of income per capita) | 19.2 | Private bureau coverage (% of adults) | 0.0 | Procedures (number) | 26 |
| | | | | Time (days) | 321 |
| **Getting electricity** (rank) | 63 | **Protecting investors** (rank) | 128 | Cost (% of claim) | 9.7 |
| Procedures (number) | 5 | Extent of disclosure index (0-10) | 6 | | |
| Time (days) | 120 | Extent of director liability index (0-10) | 4 | **Resolving insolvency** (rank) | 52 |
| Cost (% of income per capita) | 58.0 | Ease of shareholder suits index (0-10) | 3 | Time (years) | 2.0 |
| | | Strength of investor protection index (0-10) | 4.3 | Cost (% of estate) | 15 |
| | | | | Recovery rate (cents on the dollar) | 43.5 |
| | | **Paying taxes** (rank) | 14 | | |
| | | Payments (number per year) | 23 | | |
| | | Time (hours per year) | 59 | | |
| | | Total tax rate (% of profit) | 21.0 | | |

*Note:* Most indicator sets refer to a case scenario in an economy's largest business city. For more details, see the data notes.

✔ Reform making it easier to do business ✗ Reform making it more difficult to do business

## MACEDONIA, FYR

| | | Eastern Europe & Central Asia | | GNI per capita (US$) | 4,730 |
|---|---|---|---|---|---|
| Ease of doing business (rank) | 23 | Upper middle income | | Population (m) | 2.1 |

| | | | | | |
|---|---|---|---|---|---|
| ✔ **Starting a business** (rank) | 5 | **Registering property** (rank) | 50 | **Trading across borders** (rank) | 76 |
| Procedures (number) | 2 | Procedures (number) | 4 | Documents to export (number) | 6 |
| Time (days) | 2 | Time (days) | 40 | Time to export (days) | 12 |
| Cost (% of income per capita) | 1.9 | Cost (% of property value) | 3.2 | Cost to export (US$ per container) | 1,376 |
| Minimum capital (% of income per capita) | 0.0 | | | Documents to import (number) | 6 |
| | | **Getting credit** (rank) | 23 | Time to import (days) | 11 |
| **Dealing with construction permits** (rank) | 65 | Strength of legal rights index (0-10) | 7 | Cost to import (US$ per container) | 1,380 |
| Procedures (number) | 10 | Depth of credit information index (0-6) | 6 | | |
| Time (days) | 117 | Public registry coverage (% of adults) | 34.8 | **Enforcing contracts** (rank) | 59 |
| Cost (% of income per capita) | 517.8 | Private bureau coverage (% of adults) | 72.2 | Procedures (number) | 37 |
| | | | | Time (days) | 370 |
| **Getting electricity** (rank) | 101 | **Protecting investors** (rank) | 19 | Cost (% of claim) | 31.1 |
| Procedures (number) | 5 | Extent of disclosure index (0-10) | 9 | | |
| Time (days) | 151 | Extent of director liability index (0-10) | 7 | **Resolving insolvency** (rank) | 60 |
| Cost (% of income per capita) | 296.1 | Ease of shareholder suits index (0-10) | 5 | Time (years) | 2.0 |
| | | Strength of investor protection index (0-10) | 7.0 | Cost (% of estate) | 10 |
| | | | | Recovery rate (cents on the dollar) | 42.2 |
| | | **Paying taxes** (rank) | 24 | | |
| | | Payments (number per year) | 29 | | |
| | | Time (hours per year) | 119 | | |
| | | Total tax rate (% of profit) | 9.4 | | |

## MADAGASCAR

| | | Sub-Saharan Africa | | GNI per capita (US$) | 430 |
|---|---|---|---|---|---|
| Ease of doing business (rank) | 142 | Low income | | Population (m) | 21.3 |

| | | | | | |
|---|---|---|---|---|---|
| ✔ **Starting a business** (rank) | 17 | **Registering property** (rank) | 147 | **Trading across borders** (rank) | 112 |
| Procedures (number) | 2 | Procedures (number) | 6 | Documents to export (number) | 4 |
| Time (days) | 8 | Time (days) | 74 | Time to export (days) | 21 |
| Cost (% of income per capita) | 10.8 | Cost (% of property value) | 10.5 | Cost to export (US$ per container) | 1,197 |
| Minimum capital (% of income per capita) | 0.0 | | | Documents to import (number) | 9 |
| | | **Getting credit** (rank) | 180 | Time to import (days) | 24 |
| **Dealing with construction permits** (rank) | 148 | Strength of legal rights index (0-10) | 2 | Cost to import (US$ per container) | 1,555 |
| Procedures (number) | 16 | Depth of credit information index (0-6) | 0 | | |
| Time (days) | 172 | Public registry coverage (% of adults) | 0.1 | **Enforcing contracts** (rank) | 156 |
| Cost (% of income per capita) | 1,116.9 | Private bureau coverage (% of adults) | 0.0 | Procedures (number) | 38 |
| | | | | Time (days) | 871 |
| **Getting electricity** (rank) | 183 | **Protecting investors** (rank) | 70 | Cost (% of claim) | 42.4 |
| Procedures (number) | 6 | Extent of disclosure index (0-10) | 5 | | |
| Time (days) | 450 | Extent of director liability index (0-10) | 6 | **Resolving insolvency** (rank) | 151 |
| Cost (% of income per capita) | 9,056.7 | Ease of shareholder suits index (0-10) | 6 | Time (years) | 2.0 |
| | | Strength of investor protection index (0-10) | 5.7 | Cost (% of estate) | 30 |
| | | | | Recovery rate (cents on the dollar) | 12.9 |
| | | **Paying taxes** (rank) | 68 | | |
| | | Payments (number per year) | 23 | | |
| | | Time (hours per year) | 201 | | |
| | | Total tax rate (% of profit) | 36.0 | | |

## MALAWI

| | | Sub-Saharan Africa | | GNI per capita (US$) | 340 |
|---|---|---|---|---|---|
| Ease of doing business (rank) | 157 | Low income | | Population (m) | 15.4 |

| | | | | | |
|---|---|---|---|---|---|
| **Starting a business** (rank) | 141 | **Registering property** (rank) | 97 | ✔ **Trading across borders** (rank) | 168 |
| Procedures (number) | 10 | Procedures (number) | 6 | Documents to export (number) | 10 |
| Time (days) | 39 | Time (days) | 69 | Time to export (days) | 34 |
| Cost (% of income per capita) | 83.7 | Cost (% of property value) | 3.6 | Cost to export (US$ per container) | 2,175 |
| Minimum capital (% of income per capita) | 0.0 | | | Documents to import (number) | 9 |
| | | **Getting credit** (rank) | 129 | Time to import (days) | 43 |
| ✗ **Dealing with construction permits** (rank) | 175 | Strength of legal rights index (0-10) | 7 | Cost to import (US$ per container) | 2,870 |
| Procedures (number) | 18 | Depth of credit information index (0-6) | 0 | | |
| Time (days) | 200 | Public registry coverage (% of adults) | 0.0 | **Enforcing contracts** (rank) | 144 |
| Cost (% of income per capita) | 1,198.3 | Private bureau coverage (% of adults) | 0.0 | Procedures (number) | 42 |
| | | | | Time (days) | 432 |
| **Getting electricity** (rank) | 179 | **Protecting investors** (rank) | 82 | Cost (% of claim) | 94.1 |
| Procedures (number) | 6 | Extent of disclosure index (0-10) | 4 | | |
| Time (days) | 222 | Extent of director liability index (0-10) | 7 | **Resolving insolvency** (rank) | 134 |
| Cost (% of income per capita) | 8,854.9 | Ease of shareholder suits index (0-10) | 5 | Time (years) | 2.6 |
| | | Strength of investor protection index (0-10) | 5.3 | Cost (% of estate) | 25 |
| | | | | Recovery rate (cents on the dollar) | 18.5 |
| | | ✗ **Paying taxes** (rank) | 58 | | |
| | | Payments (number per year) | 26 | | |
| | | Time (hours per year) | 175 | | |
| | | Total tax rate (% of profit) | 34.7 | | |

*Note:* Most indicator sets refer to a case scenario in an economy's largest business city. For more details, see the data notes.

✔ Reform making it easier to do business ✘ Reform making it more difficult to do business

## MALAYSIA

| | | | | | | |
|---|---|---|---|---|---|
| **Ease of doing business** (rank) | 12 | East Asia & Pacific<br>Upper middle income | | GNI per capita (US$)<br>Population (m) | 8,420<br>28.9 |
| **Starting a business** (rank) | 54 | ✔ **Registering property** (rank) | 33 | **Trading across borders** (rank) | 11 |
| Procedures (number) | 3 | Procedures (number) | 5 | Documents to export (number) | 5 |
| Time (days) | 6 | Time (days) | 14 | Time to export (days) | 11 |
| Cost (% of income per capita) | 15.1 | Cost (% of property value) | 3.3 | Cost to export (US$ per container) | 435 |
| Minimum capital (% of income per capita) | 0.0 | | | Documents to import (number) | 6 |
| | | **Getting credit** (rank) | 1 | Time to import (days) | 8 |
| ✔ **Dealing with construction permits** (rank) | 96 | Strength of legal rights index (0-10) | 10 | Cost to import (US$ per container) | 420 |
| Procedures (number) | 37 | Depth of credit information index (0-6) | 6 | | |
| Time (days) | 140 | Public registry coverage (% of adults) | 56.1 | **Enforcing contracts** (rank) | 33 |
| Cost (% of income per capita) | 17.5 | Private bureau coverage (% of adults) | 81.8 | Procedures (number) | 29 |
| | | | | Time (days) | 425 |
| **Getting electricity** (rank) | 28 | **Protecting investors** (rank) | 4 | Cost (% of claim) | 27.5 |
| Procedures (number) | 5 | Extent of disclosure index (0-10) | 10 | | |
| Time (days) | 46 | Extent of director liability index (0-10) | 9 | **Resolving insolvency** (rank) | 49 |
| Cost (% of income per capita) | 53.9 | Ease of shareholder suits index (0-10) | 7 | Time (years) | 1.5 |
| | | Strength of investor protection index (0-10) | 8.7 | Cost (% of estate) | 15 |
| | | | | Recovery rate (cents on the dollar) | 44.7 |
| | | **Paying taxes** (rank) | 15 | | |
| | | Payments (number per year) | 13 | | |
| | | Time (hours per year) | 133 | | |
| | | Total tax rate (% of profit) | 24.5 | | |

## MALDIVES

| | | | | | | |
|---|---|---|---|---|---|
| **Ease of doing business** (rank) | 95 | South Asia<br>Upper middle income | | GNI per capita (US$)<br>Population (m) | 6,530<br>0.3 |
| **Starting a business** (rank) | 63 | **Registering property** (rank) | 151 | **Trading across borders** (rank) | 138 |
| Procedures (number) | 5 | Procedures (number) | 6 | Documents to export (number) | 8 |
| Time (days) | 9 | Time (days) | 57 | Time to export (days) | 21 |
| Cost (% of income per capita) | 6.7 | Cost (% of property value) | 16.1 | Cost to export (US$ per container) | 1,550 |
| Minimum capital (% of income per capita) | 2.2 | | | Documents to import (number) | 9 |
| | | **Getting credit** (rank) | 167 | Time to import (days) | 22 |
| **Dealing with construction permits** (rank) | 19 | Strength of legal rights index (0-10) | 4 | Cost to import (US$ per container) | 1,526 |
| Procedures (number) | 8 | Depth of credit information index (0-6) | 0 | | |
| Time (days) | 174 | Public registry coverage (% of adults) | 0.0 | **Enforcing contracts** (rank) | 92 |
| Cost (% of income per capita) | 8.2 | Private bureau coverage (% of adults) | 0.0 | Procedures (number) | 41 |
| | | | | Time (days) | 665 |
| **Getting electricity** (rank) | 120 | **Protecting investors** (rank) | 82 | Cost (% of claim) | 16.5 |
| Procedures (number) | 6 | Extent of disclosure index (0-10) | 0 | | |
| Time (days) | 108 | Extent of director liability index (0-10) | 8 | **Resolving insolvency** (rank) | 41 |
| Cost (% of income per capita) | 380.5 | Ease of shareholder suits index (0-10) | 8 | Time (years) | 1.5 |
| | | Strength of investor protection index (0-10) | 5.3 | Cost (% of estate) | 4 |
| | | | | Recovery rate (cents on the dollar) | 50.6 |
| | | ✘ **Paying taxes** (rank) | 57 | | |
| | | Payments (number per year) | 17 | | |
| | | Time (hours per year) | 252 | | |
| | | Total tax rate (% of profit) | 30.7 | | |

## MALI

| | | | | | | |
|---|---|---|---|---|---|
| **Ease of doing business** (rank) | 151 | Sub-Saharan Africa<br>Low income | | GNI per capita (US$)<br>Population (m) | 610<br>15.8 |
| **Starting a business** (rank) | 118 | **Registering property** (rank) | 91 | **Trading across borders** (rank) | 152 |
| Procedures (number) | 4 | Procedures (number) | 5 | Documents to export (number) | 6 |
| Time (days) | 8 | Time (days) | 29 | Time to export (days) | 26 |
| Cost (% of income per capita) | 86.2 | Cost (% of property value) | 12.0 | Cost to export (US$ per container) | 2,202 |
| Minimum capital (% of income per capita) | 331.9 | | | Documents to import (number) | 9 |
| | | **Getting credit** (rank) | 129 | Time to import (days) | 31 |
| **Dealing with construction permits** (rank) | 99 | Strength of legal rights index (0-10) | 6 | Cost to import (US$ per container) | 3,067 |
| Procedures (number) | 11 | Depth of credit information index (0-6) | 1 | | |
| Time (days) | 179 | Public registry coverage (% of adults) | 3.3 | **Enforcing contracts** (rank) | 133 |
| Cost (% of income per capita) | 418.6 | Private bureau coverage (% of adults) | 0.0 | Procedures (number) | 36 |
| | | | | Time (days) | 620 |
| **Getting electricity** (rank) | 115 | **Protecting investors** (rank) | 150 | Cost (% of claim) | 52.0 |
| Procedures (number) | 4 | Extent of disclosure index (0-10) | 6 | | |
| Time (days) | 120 | Extent of director liability index (0-10) | 1 | **Resolving insolvency** (rank) | 120 |
| Cost (% of income per capita) | 4,187.8 | Ease of shareholder suits index (0-10) | 4 | Time (years) | 3.6 |
| | | Strength of investor protection index (0-10) | 3.7 | Cost (% of estate) | 18 |
| | | | | Recovery rate (cents on the dollar) | 25.0 |
| | | ✔ **Paying taxes** (rank) | 166 | | |
| | | Payments (number per year) | 45 | | |
| | | Time (hours per year) | 270 | | |
| | | Total tax rate (% of profit) | 51.7 | | |

*Note:* Most indicator sets refer to a case scenario in an economy's largest business city. For more details, see the data notes.

✔ Reform making it easier to do business ✘ Reform making it more difficult to do business

## MALTA

| | | | | | | | |
|---|---|---|---|---|---|---|---|
| Ease of doing business (rank) | 102 | Middle East & North Africa<br>High income | | GNI per capita (US$)<br>Population (m) | 21,028<br>0.4 | | |

| | | | | | |
|---|---|---|---|---|---|
| **Starting a business** (rank) | 150 | **Registering property** (rank) | 80 | **Trading across borders** (rank) | 34 |
| Procedures (number) | 11 | Procedures (number) | 7 | Documents to export (number) | 6 |
| Time (days) | 40 | Time (days) | 15 | Time to export (days) | 11 |
| Cost (% of income per capita) | 8.9 | Cost (% of property value) | 5.2 | Cost to export (US$ per container) | 855 |
| Minimum capital (% of income per capita) | 1.5 | | | Documents to import (number) | 7 |
| | | **Getting credit** (rank) | 176 | Time to import (days) | 9 |
| **Dealing with construction permits** (rank) | 167 | Strength of legal rights index (0-10) | 3 | Cost to import (US$ per container) | 970 |
| Procedures (number) | 18 | Depth of credit information index (0-6) | 0 | | |
| Time (days) | 237 | Public registry coverage (% of adults) | 0.0 | **Enforcing contracts** (rank) | 121 |
| Cost (% of income per capita) | 243.9 | Private bureau coverage (% of adults) | 0.0 | Procedures (number) | 40 |
| | | | | Time (days) | 505 |
| **Getting electricity** (rank) | 111 | **Protecting investors** (rank) | 70 | Cost (% of claim) | 35.9 |
| Procedures (number) | 5 | Extent of disclosure index (0-10) | 3 | | |
| Time (days) | 136 | Extent of director liability index (0-10) | 6 | **Resolving insolvency** (rank) | 67 |
| Cost (% of income per capita) | 463.6 | Ease of shareholder suits index (0-10) | 8 | Time (years) | 3.0 |
| | | Strength of investor protection index (0-10) | 5.7 | Cost (% of estate) | 10 |
| | | | | Recovery rate (cents on the dollar) | 39.2 |
| | | **Paying taxes** (rank) | 27 | | |
| | | Payments (number per year) | 6 | | |
| | | Time (hours per year) | 139 | | |
| | | Total tax rate (% of profit) | 41.6 | | |

## MARSHALL ISLANDS

| | | | | | | | |
|---|---|---|---|---|---|---|---|
| Ease of doing business (rank) | 101 | East Asia & Pacific<br>Lower middle income | | GNI per capita (US$)<br>Population (m) | 3,910<br>0.1 | | |

| | | | | | |
|---|---|---|---|---|---|
| **Starting a business** (rank) | 48 | **Registering property** (rank) | 185 | **Trading across borders** (rank) | 65 |
| Procedures (number) | 5 | Procedures (number) | NO PRACTICE | Documents to export (number) | 5 |
| Time (days) | 17 | Time (days) | NO PRACTICE | Time to export (days) | 21 |
| Cost (% of income per capita) | 13.6 | Cost (% of property value) | NO PRACTICE | Cost to export (US$ per container) | 945 |
| Minimum capital (% of income per capita) | 0.0 | | | Documents to import (number) | 5 |
| | | **Getting credit** (rank) | 83 | Time to import (days) | 25 |
| **Dealing with construction permits** (rank) | 4 | Strength of legal rights index (0-10) | 9 | Cost to import (US$ per container) | 970 |
| Procedures (number) | 8 | Depth of credit information index (0-6) | 0 | | |
| Time (days) | 87 | Public registry coverage (% of adults) | 0.0 | **Enforcing contracts** (rank) | 66 |
| Cost (% of income per capita) | 22.3 | Private bureau coverage (% of adults) | 0.0 | Procedures (number) | 36 |
| | | | | Time (days) | 476 |
| **Getting electricity** (rank) | 73 | **Protecting investors** (rank) | 158 | Cost (% of claim) | 27.4 |
| Procedures (number) | 5 | Extent of disclosure index (0-10) | 2 | | |
| Time (days) | 67 | Extent of director liability index (0-10) | 0 | **Resolving insolvency** (rank) | 140 |
| Cost (% of income per capita) | 772.4 | Ease of shareholder suits index (0-10) | 8 | Time (years) | 2.0 |
| | | Strength of investor protection index (0-10) | 3.3 | Cost (% of estate) | 38 |
| | | | | Recovery rate (cents on the dollar) | 17.4 |
| | | **Paying taxes** (rank) | 92 | | |
| | | Payments (number per year) | 21 | | |
| | | Time (hours per year) | 128 | | |
| | | Total tax rate (% of profit) | 64.9 | | |

## MAURITANIA

| | | | | | | | |
|---|---|---|---|---|---|---|---|
| Ease of doing business (rank) | 167 | Sub-Saharan Africa<br>Low income | | GNI per capita (US$)<br>Population (m) | 1,000<br>3.5 | | |

| | | | | | |
|---|---|---|---|---|---|
| **Starting a business** (rank) | 160 | **Registering property** (rank) | 65 | **Trading across borders** (rank) | 150 |
| Procedures (number) | 9 | Procedures (number) | 4 | Documents to export (number) | 8 |
| Time (days) | 19 | Time (days) | 49 | Time to export (days) | 34 |
| Cost (% of income per capita) | 47.6 | Cost (% of property value) | 4.7 | Cost to export (US$ per container) | 1,520 |
| Minimum capital (% of income per capita) | 327.9 | | | Documents to import (number) | 8 |
| | | **Getting credit** (rank) | 167 | Time to import (days) | 38 |
| **Dealing with construction permits** (rank) | 115 | Strength of legal rights index (0-10) | 3 | Cost to import (US$ per container) | 1,523 |
| Procedures (number) | 16 | Depth of credit information index (0-6) | 1 | | |
| Time (days) | 82 | Public registry coverage (% of adults) | 0.5 | **Enforcing contracts** (rank) | 77 |
| Cost (% of income per capita) | 2,796.6 | Private bureau coverage (% of adults) | 0.0 | Procedures (number) | 46 |
| | | | | Time (days) | 370 |
| **Getting electricity** (rank) | 121 | **Protecting investors** (rank) | 150 | Cost (% of claim) | 23.2 |
| Procedures (number) | 5 | Extent of disclosure index (0-10) | 5 | | |
| Time (days) | 75 | Extent of director liability index (0-10) | 3 | **Resolving insolvency** (rank) | 153 |
| Cost (% of income per capita) | 7,516.9 | Ease of shareholder suits index (0-10) | 3 | Time (years) | 8.0 |
| | | Strength of investor protection index (0-10) | 3.7 | Cost (% of estate) | 9 |
| | | | | Recovery rate (cents on the dollar) | 10.3 |
| | | **Paying taxes** (rank) | 177 | | |
| | | Payments (number per year) | 37 | | |
| | | Time (hours per year) | 696 | | |
| | | Total tax rate (% of profit) | 68.2 | | |

*Note:* Most indicator sets refer to a case scenario in an economy's largest business city. For more details, see the data notes.

✔ Reform making it easier to do business ✘ Reform making it more difficult to do business

## MAURITIUS

| | | | | | | | |
|---|---|---|---|---|---|---|---|
| **Ease of doing business** (rank) | 19 | Sub-Saharan Africa | | GNI per capita (US$) | 8,240 | | |
| | | Upper middle income | | Population (m) | 1.3 | | |

| | | | | | | | |
|---|---|---|---|---|---|
| **Starting a business** (rank) | 14 | ✔ **Registering property** (rank) | 60 | **Trading across borders** (rank) | 15 |
| Procedures (number) | 5 | Procedures (number) | 4 | Documents to export (number) | 5 |
| Time (days) | 6 | Time (days) | 15 | Time to export (days) | 10 |
| Cost (% of income per capita) | 3.3 | Cost (% of property value) | 10.6 | Cost to export (US$ per container) | 660 |
| Minimum capital (% of income per capita) | 0.0 | | | Documents to import (number) | 6 |
| | | ✔ **Getting credit** (rank) | 53 | Time to import (days) | 10 |
| **Dealing with construction permits** (rank) | 62 | Strength of legal rights index (0-10) | 6 | Cost to import (US$ per container) | 695 |
| Procedures (number) | 16 | Depth of credit information index (0-6) | 5 | | |
| Time (days) | 143 | Public registry coverage (% of adults) | 56.3 | **Enforcing contracts** (rank) | 58 |
| Cost (% of income per capita) | 28.5 | Private bureau coverage (% of adults) | 0.0 | Procedures (number) | 36 |
| | | | | Time (days) | 645 |
| **Getting electricity** (rank) | 44 | **Protecting investors** (rank) | 13 | Cost (% of claim) | 16.3 |
| Procedures (number) | 4 | Extent of disclosure index (0-10) | 6 | | |
| Time (days) | 84 | Extent of director liability index (0-10) | 8 | **Resolving insolvency** (rank) | 64 |
| Cost (% of income per capita) | 295.1 | Ease of shareholder suits index (0-10) | 9 | Time (years) | 1.7 |
| | | Strength of investor protection index (0-10) | 7.7 | Cost (% of estate) | 15 |
| | | | | Recovery rate (cents on the dollar) | 40.9 |
| | | **Paying taxes** (rank) | 12 | | |
| | | Payments (number per year) | 7 | | |
| | | Time (hours per year) | 161 | | |
| | | Total tax rate (% of profit) | 28.5 | | |

## MEXICO

| | | | | | | | |
|---|---|---|---|---|---|---|---|
| **Ease of doing business** (rank) | 48 | Latin America & Caribbean | | GNI per capita (US$) | 9,240 | | |
| | | Upper middle income | | Population (m) | 114.8 | | |

| | | | | | | | |
|---|---|---|---|---|---|
| ✔ **Starting a business** (rank) | 36 | **Registering property** (rank) | 141 | **Trading across borders** (rank) | 61 |
| Procedures (number) | 6 | Procedures (number) | 7 | Documents to export (number) | 5 |
| Time (days) | 9 | Time (days) | 74 | Time to export (days) | 12 |
| Cost (% of income per capita) | 10.1 | Cost (% of property value) | 5.3 | Cost to export (US$ per container) | 1,450 |
| Minimum capital (% of income per capita) | 0.0 | | | Documents to import (number) | 4 |
| | | **Getting credit** (rank) | 40 | Time to import (days) | 12 |
| **Dealing with construction permits** (rank) | 36 | Strength of legal rights index (0-10) | 6 | Cost to import (US$ per container) | 1,780 |
| Procedures (number) | 10 | Depth of credit information index (0-6) | 6 | | |
| Time (days) | 69 | Public registry coverage (% of adults) | 0.0 | **Enforcing contracts** (rank) | 76 |
| Cost (% of income per capita) | 322.7 | Private bureau coverage (% of adults) | 99.2 | Procedures (number) | 38 |
| | | | | Time (days) | 415 |
| ✔ **Getting electricity** (rank) | 130 | **Protecting investors** (rank) | 49 | Cost (% of claim) | 31.0 |
| Procedures (number) | 7 | Extent of disclosure index (0-10) | 8 | | |
| Time (days) | 95 | Extent of director liability index (0-10) | 5 | **Resolving insolvency** (rank) | 26 |
| Cost (% of income per capita) | 382.8 | Ease of shareholder suits index (0-10) | 5 | Time (years) | 1.8 |
| | | Strength of investor protection index (0-10) | 6.0 | Cost (% of estate) | 18 |
| | | | | Recovery rate (cents on the dollar) | 67.3 |
| | | **Paying taxes** (rank) | 107 | | |
| | | Payments (number per year) | 6 | | |
| | | Time (hours per year) | 337 | | |
| | | Total tax rate (% of profit) | 52.5 | | |

## MICRONESIA, FED. STS.

| | | | | | | | |
|---|---|---|---|---|---|---|---|
| **Ease of doing business** (rank) | 150 | East Asia & Pacific | | GNI per capita (US$) | 2,900 | | |
| | | Lower middle income | | Population (m) | 0.1 | | |

| | | | | | | | |
|---|---|---|---|---|---|
| **Starting a business** (rank) | 104 | **Registering property** (rank) | 185 | **Trading across borders** (rank) | 100 |
| Procedures (number) | 7 | Procedures (number) | NO PRACTICE | Documents to export (number) | 5 |
| Time (days) | 16 | Time (days) | NO PRACTICE | Time to export (days) | 30 |
| Cost (% of income per capita) | 144.2 | Cost (% of property value) | NO PRACTICE | Cost to export (US$ per container) | 1,295 |
| Minimum capital (% of income per capita) | 0.0 | | | Documents to import (number) | 6 |
| | | **Getting credit** (rank) | 129 | Time to import (days) | 30 |
| **Dealing with construction permits** (rank) | 42 | Strength of legal rights index (0-10) | 7 | Cost to import (US$ per container) | 1,295 |
| Procedures (number) | 15 | Depth of credit information index (0-6) | 0 | | |
| Time (days) | 114 | Public registry coverage (% of adults) | 0.0 | **Enforcing contracts** (rank) | 149 |
| Cost (% of income per capita) | 32.7 | Private bureau coverage (% of adults) | 0.0 | Procedures (number) | 34 |
| | | | | Time (days) | 885 |
| **Getting electricity** (rank) | 53 | **Protecting investors** (rank) | 177 | Cost (% of claim) | 66.0 |
| Procedures (number) | 3 | Extent of disclosure index (0-10) | 0 | | |
| Time (days) | 105 | Extent of director liability index (0-10) | 0 | **Resolving insolvency** (rank) | 166 |
| Cost (% of income per capita) | 424.0 | Ease of shareholder suits index (0-10) | 8 | Time (years) | 5.3 |
| | | Strength of investor protection index (0-10) | 2.7 | Cost (% of estate) | 38 |
| | | | | Recovery rate (cents on the dollar) | 3.4 |
| | | **Paying taxes** (rank) | 85 | | |
| | | Payments (number per year) | 21 | | |
| | | Time (hours per year) | 128 | | |
| | | Total tax rate (% of profit) | 58.7 | | |

*Note:* Most indicator sets refer to a case scenario in an economy's largest business city. For more details, see the data notes.

✔ Reform making it easier to do business ✘ Reform making it more difficult to do business

## MOLDOVA

| | | Eastern Europe & Central Asia | | GNI per capita (US$) | 1,980 |
|---|---|---|---|---|---|
| Ease of doing business (rank) | 83 | Lower middle income | | Population (m) | 3.6 |

| | | | | | |
|---|---|---|---|---|---|
| **Starting a business** (rank) | 92 | **Registering property** (rank) | 16 | **Trading across borders** (rank) | 142 |
| Procedures (number) | 7 | Procedures (number) | 5 | Documents to export (number) | 7 |
| Time (days) | 9 | Time (days) | 5 | Time to export (days) | 32 |
| Cost (% of income per capita) | 5.7 | Cost (% of property value) | 0.9 | Cost to export (US$ per container) | 1,545 |
| Minimum capital (% of income per capita) | 8.7 | | | Documents to import (number) | 7 |
| | | **Getting credit** (rank) | 40 | Time to import (days) | 35 |
| **Dealing with construction permits** (rank) | 168 | Strength of legal rights index (0-10) | 8 | Cost to import (US$ per container) | 1,870 |
| Procedures (number) | 26 | Depth of credit information index (0-6) | 4 | | |
| Time (days) | 291 | Public registry coverage (% of adults) | 0.0 | ✘ **Enforcing contracts** (rank) | 26 |
| Cost (% of income per capita) | 69.3 | Private bureau coverage (% of adults) | 3.9 | Procedures (number) | 31 |
| | | | | Time (days) | 327 |
| **Getting electricity** (rank) | 161 | ✔ **Protecting investors** (rank) | 82 | Cost (% of claim) | 28.6 |
| Procedures (number) | 7 | Extent of disclosure index (0-10) | 7 | | |
| Time (days) | 140 | Extent of director liability index (0-10) | 3 | ✔ **Resolving insolvency** (rank) | 91 |
| Cost (% of income per capita) | 578.0 | Ease of shareholder suits index (0-10) | 6 | Time (years) | 2.8 |
| | | Strength of investor protection index (0-10) | 5.3 | Cost (% of estate) | 9 |
| | | | | Recovery rate (cents on the dollar) | 32.0 |
| | | ✘ **Paying taxes** (rank) | 109 | | |
| | | Payments (number per year) | 48 | | |
| | | Time (hours per year) | 220 | | |
| | | Total tax rate (% of profit) | 31.2 | | |

## MONGOLIA

| | | East Asia & Pacific | | GNI per capita (US$) | 2,320 |
|---|---|---|---|---|---|
| Ease of doing business (rank) | 76 | Lower middle income | | Population (m) | 2.8 |

| | | | | | |
|---|---|---|---|---|---|
| ✔ **Starting a business** (rank) | 39 | **Registering property** (rank) | 22 | **Trading across borders** (rank) | 175 |
| Procedures (number) | 7 | Procedures (number) | 5 | Documents to export (number) | 10 |
| Time (days) | 12 | Time (days) | 11 | Time to export (days) | 49 |
| Cost (% of income per capita) | 2.4 | Cost (% of property value) | 2.1 | Cost to export (US$ per container) | 2,555 |
| Minimum capital (% of income per capita) | 0.0 | | | Documents to import (number) | 11 |
| | | ✔ **Getting credit** (rank) | 53 | Time to import (days) | 50 |
| **Dealing with construction permits** (rank) | 121 | Strength of legal rights index (0-10) | 6 | Cost to import (US$ per container) | 2,710 |
| Procedures (number) | 19 | Depth of credit information index (0-6) | 5 | | |
| Time (days) | 208 | Public registry coverage (% of adults) | 58.9 | **Enforcing contracts** (rank) | 29 |
| Cost (% of income per capita) | 39.2 | Private bureau coverage (% of adults) | 0.0 | Procedures (number) | 32 |
| | | | | Time (days) | 314 |
| **Getting electricity** (rank) | 169 | ✔ **Protecting investors** (rank) | 25 | Cost (% of claim) | 30.6 |
| Procedures (number) | 8 | Extent of disclosure index (0-10) | 6 | | |
| Time (days) | 126 | Extent of director liability index (0-10) | 8 | **Resolving insolvency** (rank) | 127 |
| Cost (% of income per capita) | 1,012.6 | Ease of shareholder suits index (0-10) | 6 | Time (years) | 4.0 |
| | | Strength of investor protection index (0-10) | 6.7 | Cost (% of estate) | 8 |
| | | | | Recovery rate (cents on the dollar) | 22.7 |
| | | **Paying taxes** (rank) | 70 | | |
| | | Payments (number per year) | 41 | | |
| | | Time (hours per year) | 192 | | |
| | | Total tax rate (% of profit) | 24.6 | | |

## MONTENEGRO

| | | Eastern Europe & Central Asia | | GNI per capita (US$) | 7,060 |
|---|---|---|---|---|---|
| Ease of doing business (rank) | 51 | Upper middle income | | Population (m) | 0.6 |

| | | | | | |
|---|---|---|---|---|---|
| **Starting a business** (rank) | 58 | **Registering property** (rank) | 117 | **Trading across borders** (rank) | 42 |
| Procedures (number) | 6 | Procedures (number) | 7 | Documents to export (number) | 6 |
| Time (days) | 10 | Time (days) | 71 | Time to export (days) | 14 |
| Cost (% of income per capita) | 1.6 | Cost (% of property value) | 3.1 | Cost to export (US$ per container) | 855 |
| Minimum capital (% of income per capita) | 0.0 | | | Documents to import (number) | 6 |
| | | ✔ **Getting credit** (rank) | 4 | Time to import (days) | 14 |
| ✔ **Dealing with construction permits** (rank) | 176 | Strength of legal rights index (0-10) | 10 | Cost to import (US$ per container) | 915 |
| Procedures (number) | 16 | Depth of credit information index (0-6) | 5 | | |
| Time (days) | 267 | Public registry coverage (% of adults) | 25.2 | **Enforcing contracts** (rank) | 135 |
| Cost (% of income per capita) | 1,169.6 | Private bureau coverage (% of adults) | 0.0 | Procedures (number) | 49 |
| | | | | Time (days) | 545 |
| **Getting electricity** (rank) | 69 | **Protecting investors** (rank) | 32 | Cost (% of claim) | 25.7 |
| Procedures (number) | 5 | Extent of disclosure index (0-10) | 5 | | |
| Time (days) | 71 | Extent of director liability index (0-10) | 8 | **Resolving insolvency** (rank) | 44 |
| Cost (% of income per capita) | 490.3 | Ease of shareholder suits index (0-10) | 6 | Time (years) | 1.4 |
| | | Strength of investor protection index (0-10) | 6.3 | Cost (% of estate) | 8 |
| | | | | Recovery rate (cents on the dollar) | 48.3 |
| | | **Paying taxes** (rank) | 81 | | |
| | | Payments (number per year) | 29 | | |
| | | Time (hours per year) | 320 | | |
| | | Total tax rate (% of profit) | 22.3 | | |

*Note:* Most indicator sets refer to a case scenario in an economy's largest business city. For more details, see the data notes.

✔ Reform making it easier to do business ✘ Reform making it more difficult to do business

## MOROCCO

| | | | | | | |
|---|---|---|---|---|---|---|
| Ease of doing business (rank) | 97 | Middle East & North Africa / Lower middle income | | GNI per capita (US$) / Population (m) | | 2,970 / 32.3 |

| | | | | | | |
|---|---|---|---|---|---|---|
| ✔ **Starting a business** (rank) | 56 | ✘ **Registering property** (rank) | 163 | **Trading across borders** (rank) | 47 |
| Procedures (number) | 6 | Procedures (number) | 8 | Documents to export (number) | 6 |
| Time (days) | 12 | Time (days) | 75 | Time to export (days) | 11 |
| Cost (% of income per capita) | 15.5 | Cost (% of property value) | 5.9 | Cost to export (US$ per container) | 577 |
| Minimum capital (% of income per capita) | 0.0 | | | Documents to import (number) | 8 |
| | | **Getting credit** (rank) | 104 | Time to import (days) | 16 |
| **Dealing with construction permits** (rank) | 79 | Strength of legal rights index (0-10) | 3 | Cost to import (US$ per container) | 950 |
| Procedures (number) | 15 | Depth of credit information index (0-6) | 5 | | |
| Time (days) | 97 | Public registry coverage (% of adults) | 0.0 | **Enforcing contracts** (rank) | 88 |
| Cost (% of income per capita) | 220.2 | Private bureau coverage (% of adults) | 17.2 | Procedures (number) | 40 |
| | | | | Time (days) | 510 |
| **Getting electricity** (rank) | 92 | **Protecting investors** (rank) | 100 | Cost (% of claim) | 25.2 |
| Procedures (number) | 5 | Extent of disclosure index (0-10) | 7 | | |
| Time (days) | 62 | Extent of director liability index (0-10) | 2 | **Resolving insolvency** (rank) | 86 |
| Cost (% of income per capita) | 2,515.2 | Ease of shareholder suits index (0-10) | 6 | Time (years) | 1.8 |
| | | Strength of investor protection index (0-10) | 5.0 | Cost (% of estate) | 18 |
| | | | | Recovery rate (cents on the dollar) | 35.1 |
| | | **Paying taxes** (rank) | 110 | | |
| | | Payments (number per year) | 17 | | |
| | | Time (hours per year) | 238 | | |
| | | Total tax rate (% of profit) | 49.6 | | |

## MOZAMBIQUE

| | | | | | |
|---|---|---|---|---|---|
| Ease of doing business (rank) | 146 | Sub-Saharan Africa / Low income | | GNI per capita (US$) / Population (m) | 470 / 23.9 |

| | | | | | |
|---|---|---|---|---|---|
| **Starting a business** (rank) | 96 | **Registering property** (rank) | 155 | **Trading across borders** (rank) | 134 |
| Procedures (number) | 9 | Procedures (number) | 8 | Documents to export (number) | 7 |
| Time (days) | 13 | Time (days) | 42 | Time to export (days) | 23 |
| Cost (% of income per capita) | 19.7 | Cost (% of property value) | 8.0 | Cost to export (US$ per container) | 1,100 |
| Minimum capital (% of income per capita) | 0.0 | | | Documents to import (number) | 10 |
| | | **Getting credit** (rank) | 129 | Time to import (days) | 28 |
| **Dealing with construction permits** (rank) | 135 | Strength of legal rights index (0-10) | 3 | Cost to import (US$ per container) | 1,545 |
| Procedures (number) | 14 | Depth of credit information index (0-6) | 4 | | |
| Time (days) | 377 | Public registry coverage (% of adults) | 4.4 | **Enforcing contracts** (rank) | 132 |
| Cost (% of income per capita) | 113.3 | Private bureau coverage (% of adults) | 0.0 | Procedures (number) | 30 |
| | | | | Time (days) | 730 |
| **Getting electricity** (rank) | 174 | **Protecting investors** (rank) | 49 | Cost (% of claim) | 142.5 |
| Procedures (number) | 9 | Extent of disclosure index (0-10) | 5 | | |
| Time (days) | 117 | Extent of director liability index (0-10) | 4 | **Resolving insolvency** (rank) | 147 |
| Cost (% of income per capita) | 2,394.7 | Ease of shareholder suits index (0-10) | 9 | Time (years) | 5.0 |
| | | Strength of investor protection index (0-10) | 6.0 | Cost (% of estate) | 9 |
| | | | | Recovery rate (cents on the dollar) | 15.0 |
| | | **Paying taxes** (rank) | 105 | | |
| | | Payments (number per year) | 37 | | |
| | | Time (hours per year) | 230 | | |
| | | Total tax rate (% of profit) | 34.3 | | |

## NAMIBIA

| | | | | | |
|---|---|---|---|---|---|
| Ease of doing business (rank) | 87 | Sub-Saharan Africa / Upper middle income | | GNI per capita (US$) / Population (m) | 4,700 / 2.3 |

| | | | | | |
|---|---|---|---|---|---|
| **Starting a business** (rank) | 133 | ✘ **Registering property** (rank) | 169 | **Trading across borders** (rank) | 140 |
| Procedures (number) | 10 | Procedures (number) | 8 | Documents to export (number) | 9 |
| Time (days) | 66 | Time (days) | 46 | Time to export (days) | 25 |
| Cost (% of income per capita) | 18.5 | Cost (% of property value) | 13.8 | Cost to export (US$ per container) | 1,800 |
| Minimum capital (% of income per capita) | 0.0 | | | Documents to import (number) | 7 |
| | | **Getting credit** (rank) | 40 | Time to import (days) | 20 |
| **Dealing with construction permits** (rank) | 56 | Strength of legal rights index (0-10) | 8 | Cost to import (US$ per container) | 1,905 |
| Procedures (number) | 12 | Depth of credit information index (0-6) | 4 | | |
| Time (days) | 139 | Public registry coverage (% of adults) | 0.0 | **Enforcing contracts** (rank) | 41 |
| Cost (% of income per capita) | 110.9 | Private bureau coverage (% of adults) | 63.9 | Procedures (number) | 33 |
| | | | | Time (days) | 270 |
| ✔ **Getting electricity** (rank) | 87 | **Protecting investors** (rank) | 82 | Cost (% of claim) | 35.8 |
| Procedures (number) | 7 | Extent of disclosure index (0-10) | 5 | | |
| Time (days) | 38 | Extent of director liability index (0-10) | 5 | **Resolving insolvency** (rank) | 59 |
| Cost (% of income per capita) | 482.2 | Ease of shareholder suits index (0-10) | 6 | Time (years) | 1.5 |
| | | Strength of investor protection index (0-10) | 5.3 | Cost (% of estate) | 15 |
| | | | | Recovery rate (cents on the dollar) | 42.3 |
| | | **Paying taxes** (rank) | 112 | | |
| | | Payments (number per year) | 37 | | |
| | | Time (hours per year) | 350 | | |
| | | Total tax rate (% of profit) | 22.7 | | |

*Note:* Most indicator sets refer to a case scenario in an economy's largest business city. For more details, see the data notes.

✔ Reform making it easier to do business ✘ Reform making it more difficult to do business

## NEPAL

| | | | | | | |
|---|---|---|---|---|---|---|
| Ease of doing business (rank) | 108 | South Asia<br>Low income | | GNI per capita (US$)<br>Population (m) | | 540<br>30.5 |

| | | | | | | |
|---|---|---|---|---|---|---|
| **Starting a business** (rank) | 105 | **Registering property** (rank) | 21 | **Trading across borders** (rank) | | 171 |
| Procedures (number) | 7 | Procedures (number) | 3 | Documents to export (number) | | 11 |
| Time (days) | 29 | Time (days) | 5 | Time to export (days) | | 41 |
| Cost (% of income per capita) | 33.0 | Cost (% of property value) | 4.9 | Cost to export (US$ per container) | | 1,975 |
| Minimum capital (% of income per capita) | 0.0 | | | Documents to import (number) | | 11 |
| | | **Getting credit** (rank) | 70 | Time to import (days) | | 38 |
| **Dealing with construction permits** (rank) | 97 | Strength of legal rights index (0-10) | 7 | Cost to import (US$ per container) | | 2,095 |
| Procedures (number) | 13 | Depth of credit information index (0-6) | 3 | | | |
| Time (days) | 115 | Public registry coverage (% of adults) | 0.0 | **Enforcing contracts** (rank) | | 137 |
| Cost (% of income per capita) | 654.6 | Private bureau coverage (% of adults) | 0.5 | Procedures (number) | | 39 |
| | | | | Time (days) | | 910 |
| **Getting electricity** (rank) | 96 | **Protecting investors** (rank) | 82 | Cost (% of claim) | | 26.8 |
| Procedures (number) | 5 | Extent of disclosure index (0-10) | 6 | | | |
| Time (days) | 70 | Extent of director liability index (0-10) | 1 | **Resolving insolvency** (rank) | | 121 |
| Cost (% of income per capita) | 1,762.8 | Ease of shareholder suits index (0-10) | 9 | Time (years) | | 5.0 |
| | | Strength of investor protection index (0-10) | 5.3 | Cost (% of estate) | | 9 |
| | | | | Recovery rate (cents on the dollar) | | 24.5 |
| | | **Paying taxes** (rank) | 114 | | | |
| | | Payments (number per year) | 34 | | | |
| | | Time (hours per year) | 326 | | | |
| | | Total tax rate (% of profit) | 31.5 | | | |

## NETHERLANDS

| | | | | | | |
|---|---|---|---|---|---|---|
| Ease of doing business (rank) | 31 | OECD high income<br>High income | | GNI per capita (US$)<br>Population (m) | | 49,730<br>16.7 |

| | | | | | | |
|---|---|---|---|---|---|---|
| ✔ **Starting a business** (rank) | 67 | **Registering property** (rank) | 49 | ✔ **Trading across borders** (rank) | | 12 |
| Procedures (number) | 5 | Procedures (number) | 5 | Documents to export (number) | | 4 |
| Time (days) | 5 | Time (days) | 7 | Time to export (days) | | 6 |
| Cost (% of income per capita) | 5.1 | Cost (% of property value) | 6.1 | Cost to export (US$ per container) | | 895 |
| Minimum capital (% of income per capita) | 49.4 | | | Documents to import (number) | | 4 |
| | | **Getting credit** (rank) | 53 | Time to import (days) | | 6 |
| ✔ **Dealing with construction permits** (rank) | 89 | Strength of legal rights index (0-10) | 6 | Cost to import (US$ per container) | | 975 |
| Procedures (number) | 14 | Depth of credit information index (0-6) | 5 | | | |
| Time (days) | 159 | Public registry coverage (% of adults) | 0.0 | **Enforcing contracts** (rank) | | 32 |
| Cost (% of income per capita) | 78.9 | Private bureau coverage (% of adults) | 81.7 | Procedures (number) | | 26 |
| | | | | Time (days) | | 514 |
| **Getting electricity** (rank) | 67 | ✔ **Protecting investors** (rank) | 117 | Cost (% of claim) | | 23.9 |
| Procedures (number) | 5 | Extent of disclosure index (0-10) | 4 | | | |
| Time (days) | 143 | Extent of director liability index (0-10) | 4 | **Resolving insolvency** (rank) | | 6 |
| Cost (% of income per capita) | 33.5 | Ease of shareholder suits index (0-10) | 6 | Time (years) | | 1.1 |
| | | Strength of investor protection index (0-10) | 4.7 | Cost (% of estate) | | 4 |
| | | | | Recovery rate (cents on the dollar) | | 88.8 |
| | | **Paying taxes** (rank) | 29 | | | |
| | | Payments (number per year) | 9 | | | |
| | | Time (hours per year) | 127 | | | |
| | | Total tax rate (% of profit) | 40.1 | | | |

## NEW ZEALAND

| | | | | | | |
|---|---|---|---|---|---|---|
| Ease of doing business (rank) | 3 | OECD high income<br>High income | | GNI per capita (US$)<br>Population (m) | | 36,648<br>4.4 |

| | | | | | | |
|---|---|---|---|---|---|---|
| **Starting a business** (rank) | 1 | **Registering property** (rank) | 2 | **Trading across borders** (rank) | | 25 |
| Procedures (number) | 1 | Procedures (number) | 2 | Documents to export (number) | | 5 |
| Time (days) | 1 | Time (days) | 2 | Time to export (days) | | 10 |
| Cost (% of income per capita) | 0.4 | Cost (% of property value) | 0.1 | Cost to export (US$ per container) | | 870 |
| Minimum capital (% of income per capita) | 0.0 | | | Documents to import (number) | | 6 |
| | | ✔ **Getting credit** (rank) | 4 | Time to import (days) | | 9 |
| **Dealing with construction permits** (rank) | 6 | Strength of legal rights index (0-10) | 10 | Cost to import (US$ per container) | | 825 |
| Procedures (number) | 6 | Depth of credit information index (0-6) | 5 | | | |
| Time (days) | 89 | Public registry coverage (% of adults) | 0.0 | **Enforcing contracts** (rank) | | 17 |
| Cost (% of income per capita) | 29.8 | Private bureau coverage (% of adults) | 100.0 | Procedures (number) | | 30 |
| | | | | Time (days) | | 216 |
| **Getting electricity** (rank) | 32 | **Protecting investors** (rank) | 1 | Cost (% of claim) | | 27.2 |
| Procedures (number) | 5 | Extent of disclosure index (0-10) | 10 | | | |
| Time (days) | 50 | Extent of director liability index (0-10) | 9 | **Resolving insolvency** (rank) | | 13 |
| Cost (% of income per capita) | 76.1 | Ease of shareholder suits index (0-10) | 10 | Time (years) | | 1.3 |
| | | Strength of investor protection index (0-10) | 9.7 | Cost (% of estate) | | 4 |
| | | | | Recovery rate (cents on the dollar) | | 83.0 |
| | | **Paying taxes** (rank) | 21 | | | |
| | | Payments (number per year) | 8 | | | |
| | | Time (hours per year) | 152 | | | |
| | | Total tax rate (% of profit) | 33.5 | | | |

*Note:* Most indicator sets refer to a case scenario in an economy's largest business city. For more details, see the data notes.

✔ Reform making it easier to do business ✘ Reform making it more difficult to do business

## NICARAGUA

| | | Latin America & Caribbean | | GNI per capita (US$) | 1,170 |
|---|---|---|---|---|---|
| Ease of doing business (rank) | 119 | Lower middle income | | Population (m) | 5.9 |

| | | | | | |
|---|---|---|---|---|---|
| **Starting a business** (rank) | 131 | **Registering property** (rank) | 123 | **Trading across borders** (rank) | 81 |
| Procedures (number) | 8 | Procedures (number) | 8 | Documents to export (number) | 5 |
| Time (days) | 39 | Time (days) | 49 | Time to export (days) | 21 |
| Cost (% of income per capita) | 100.6 | Cost (% of property value) | 4.2 | Cost to export (US$ per container) | 1,140 |
| Minimum capital (% of income per capita) | 0.0 | | | Documents to import (number) | 6 |
| | | **Getting credit** (rank) | 104 | Time to import (days) | 20 |
| **Dealing with construction permits** (rank) | 154 | Strength of legal rights index (0-10) | 3 | Cost to import (US$ per container) | 1,245 |
| Procedures (number) | 16 | Depth of credit information index (0-6) | 5 | | |
| Time (days) | 218 | Public registry coverage (% of adults) | 10.8 | **Enforcing contracts** (rank) | 55 |
| Cost (% of income per capita) | 362.0 | Private bureau coverage (% of adults) | 29.5 | Procedures (number) | 37 |
| | | | | Time (days) | 409 |
| **Getting electricity** (rank) | 129 | **Protecting investors** (rank) | 100 | Cost (% of claim) | 26.8 |
| Procedures (number) | 6 | Extent of disclosure index (0-10) | 4 | | |
| Time (days) | 70 | Extent of director liability index (0-10) | 5 | **Resolving insolvency** (rank) | 80 |
| Cost (% of income per capita) | 1,526.6 | Ease of shareholder suits index (0-10) | 6 | Time (years) | 2.2 |
| | | Strength of investor protection index (0-10) | 5.0 | Cost (% of estate) | 15 |
| | | | | Recovery rate (cents on the dollar) | 36.0 |
| | | **Paying taxes** (rank) | 158 | | |
| | | Payments (number per year) | 42 | | |
| | | Time (hours per year) | 207 | | |
| | | Total tax rate (% of profit) | 65.0 | | |

## NIGER

| | | Sub-Saharan Africa | | GNI per capita (US$) | 360 |
|---|---|---|---|---|---|
| Ease of doing business (rank) | 176 | Low income | | Population (m) | 16.1 |

| | | | | | |
|---|---|---|---|---|---|
| **Starting a business** (rank) | 167 | **Registering property** (rank) | 87 | ✔ **Trading across borders** (rank) | 176 |
| Procedures (number) | 9 | Procedures (number) | 4 | Documents to export (number) | 8 |
| Time (days) | 17 | Time (days) | 35 | Time to export (days) | 59 |
| Cost (% of income per capita) | 112.8 | Cost (% of property value) | 11.0 | Cost to export (US$ per container) | 3,676 |
| Minimum capital (% of income per capita) | 572.8 | | | Documents to import (number) | 11 |
| | | **Getting credit** (rank) | 129 | Time to import (days) | 64 |
| **Dealing with construction permits** (rank) | 160 | Strength of legal rights index (0-10) | 6 | Cost to import (US$ per container) | 3,711 |
| Procedures (number) | 12 | Depth of credit information index (0-6) | 1 | | |
| Time (days) | 326 | Public registry coverage (% of adults) | 0.8 | **Enforcing contracts** (rank) | 140 |
| Cost (% of income per capita) | 1,612.8 | Private bureau coverage (% of adults) | 0.0 | Procedures (number) | 39 |
| | | | | Time (days) | 545 |
| **Getting electricity** (rank) | 118 | **Protecting investors** (rank) | 158 | Cost (% of claim) | 59.6 |
| Procedures (number) | 4 | Extent of disclosure index (0-10) | 6 | | |
| Time (days) | 115 | Extent of director liability index (0-10) | 1 | **Resolving insolvency** (rank) | 130 |
| Cost (% of income per capita) | 6,562.4 | Ease of shareholder suits index (0-10) | 3 | Time (years) | 5.0 |
| | | Strength of investor protection index (0-10) | 3.3 | Cost (% of estate) | 18 |
| | | | | Recovery rate (cents on the dollar) | 21.7 |
| | | **Paying taxes** (rank) | 151 | | |
| | | Payments (number per year) | 41 | | |
| | | Time (hours per year) | 270 | | |
| | | Total tax rate (% of profit) | 43.8 | | |

## NIGERIA

| | | Sub-Saharan Africa | | GNI per capita (US$) | 1,200 |
|---|---|---|---|---|---|
| Ease of doing business (rank) | 131 | Lower middle income | | Population (m) | 162.5 |

| | | | | | |
|---|---|---|---|---|---|
| **Starting a business** (rank) | 119 | **Registering property** (rank) | 182 | **Trading across borders** (rank) | 154 |
| Procedures (number) | 8 | Procedures (number) | 13 | Documents to export (number) | 10 |
| Time (days) | 34 | Time (days) | 86 | Time to export (days) | 24 |
| Cost (% of income per capita) | 60.4 | Cost (% of property value) | 20.8 | Cost to export (US$ per container) | 1,380 |
| Minimum capital (% of income per capita) | 0.0 | | | Documents to import (number) | 10 |
| | | **Getting credit** (rank) | 23 | Time to import (days) | 39 |
| **Dealing with construction permits** (rank) | 88 | Strength of legal rights index (0-10) | 9 | Cost to import (US$ per container) | 1,540 |
| Procedures (number) | 15 | Depth of credit information index (0-6) | 4 | | |
| Time (days) | 85 | Public registry coverage (% of adults) | 0.1 | **Enforcing contracts** (rank) | 98 |
| Cost (% of income per capita) | 417.7 | Private bureau coverage (% of adults) | 4.1 | Procedures (number) | 40 |
| | | | | Time (days) | 457 |
| **Getting electricity** (rank) | 178 | **Protecting investors** (rank) | 70 | Cost (% of claim) | 32.0 |
| Procedures (number) | 8 | Extent of disclosure index (0-10) | 5 | | |
| Time (days) | 260 | Extent of director liability index (0-10) | 7 | **Resolving insolvency** (rank) | 105 |
| Cost (% of income per capita) | 873.9 | Ease of shareholder suits index (0-10) | 5 | Time (years) | 2.0 |
| | | Strength of investor protection index (0-10) | 5.7 | Cost (% of estate) | 22 |
| | | | | Recovery rate (cents on the dollar) | 28.2 |
| | | ✘ **Paying taxes** (rank) | 155 | | |
| | | Payments (number per year) | 41 | | |
| | | Time (hours per year) | 956 | | |
| | | Total tax rate (% of profit) | 33.8 | | |

*Note:* Most indicator sets refer to a case scenario in an economy's largest business city. For more details, see the data notes.

✔ Reform making it easier to do business  ✗ Reform making it more difficult to do business

## NORWAY

| | | | | | | |
|---|---|---|---|---|---|---|
| **Ease of doing business** (rank) | 6 | OECD high income | | GNI per capita (US$) | 88,890 | |
| | | High income | | Population (m) | 5.0 | |

| | | | | | |
|---|---|---|---|---|---|
| ✔ **Starting a business** (rank) | 43 | **Registering property** (rank) | 7 | **Trading across borders** (rank) | 21 |
| Procedures (number) | 5 | Procedures (number) | 1 | Documents to export (number) | 4 |
| Time (days) | 7 | Time (days) | 3 | Time to export (days) | 7 |
| Cost (% of income per capita) | 1.7 | Cost (% of property value) | 2.5 | Cost to export (US$ per container) | 1,125 |
| Minimum capital (% of income per capita) | 5.4 | | | Documents to import (number) | 5 |
| | | **Getting credit** (rank) | 70 | Time to import (days) | 7 |
| ✔ **Dealing with construction permits** (rank) | 23 | Strength of legal rights index (0-10) | 6 | Cost to import (US$ per container) | 1,100 |
| Procedures (number) | 10 | Depth of credit information index (0-6) | 4 | | |
| Time (days) | 123 | Public registry coverage (% of adults) | 0.0 | **Enforcing contracts** (rank) | 4 |
| Cost (% of income per capita) | 30.2 | Private bureau coverage (% of adults) | 100.0 | Procedures (number) | 34 |
| | | | | Time (days) | 280 |
| **Getting electricity** (rank) | 14 | **Protecting investors** (rank) | 25 | Cost (% of claim) | 9.9 |
| Procedures (number) | 4 | Extent of disclosure index (0-10) | 7 | | |
| Time (days) | 66 | Extent of director liability index (0-10) | 6 | **Resolving insolvency** (rank) | 3 |
| Cost (% of income per capita) | 6.5 | Ease of shareholder suits index (0-10) | 7 | Time (years) | 0.9 |
| | | Strength of investor protection index (0-10) | 6.7 | Cost (% of estate) | 1 |
| | | | | Recovery rate (cents on the dollar) | 90.8 |
| | | **Paying taxes** (rank) | 19 | | |
| | | Payments (number per year) | 4 | | |
| | | Time (hours per year) | 87 | | |
| | | Total tax rate (% of profit) | 41.6 | | |

## OMAN

| | | | | | | |
|---|---|---|---|---|---|---|
| **Ease of doing business** (rank) | 47 | Middle East & North Africa | | GNI per capita (US$) | 23,315 | |
| | | High income | | Population (m) | 2.8 | |

| | | | | | |
|---|---|---|---|---|---|
| **Starting a business** (rank) | 73 | **Registering property** (rank) | 18 | **Trading across borders** (rank) | 49 |
| Procedures (number) | 5 | Procedures (number) | 2 | Documents to export (number) | 8 |
| Time (days) | 8 | Time (days) | 16 | Time to export (days) | 10 |
| Cost (% of income per capita) | 2.6 | Cost (% of property value) | 3.0 | Cost to export (US$ per container) | 745 |
| Minimum capital (% of income per capita) | 223.1 | | | Documents to import (number) | 8 |
| | | ✔ **Getting credit** (rank) | 83 | Time to import (days) | 9 |
| **Dealing with construction permits** (rank) | 59 | Strength of legal rights index (0-10) | 4 | Cost to import (US$ per container) | 680 |
| Procedures (number) | 13 | Depth of credit information index (0-6) | 5 | | |
| Time (days) | 174 | Public registry coverage (% of adults) | 37.3 | **Enforcing contracts** (rank) | 107 |
| Cost (% of income per capita) | 37.6 | Private bureau coverage (% of adults) | 0.0 | Procedures (number) | 51 |
| | | | | Time (days) | 598 |
| **Getting electricity** (rank) | 54 | **Protecting investors** (rank) | 100 | Cost (% of claim) | 13.5 |
| Procedures (number) | 6 | Extent of disclosure index (0-10) | 8 | | |
| Time (days) | 62 | Extent of director liability index (0-10) | 5 | **Resolving insolvency** (rank) | 77 |
| Cost (% of income per capita) | 51.3 | Ease of shareholder suits index (0-10) | 2 | Time (years) | 4.0 |
| | | Strength of investor protection index (0-10) | 5.0 | Cost (% of estate) | 4 |
| | | | | Recovery rate (cents on the dollar) | 36.6 |
| | | **Paying taxes** (rank) | 10 | | |
| | | Payments (number per year) | 14 | | |
| | | Time (hours per year) | 62 | | |
| | | Total tax rate (% of profit) | 22.0 | | |

## PAKISTAN

| | | | | | | |
|---|---|---|---|---|---|---|
| **Ease of doing business** (rank) | 107 | South Asia | | GNI per capita (US$) | 1,120 | |
| | | Lower middle income | | Population (m) | 176.7 | |

| | | | | | |
|---|---|---|---|---|---|
| **Starting a business** (rank) | 98 | **Registering property** (rank) | 126 | **Trading across borders** (rank) | 85 |
| Procedures (number) | 10 | Procedures (number) | 6 | Documents to export (number) | 8 |
| Time (days) | 21 | Time (days) | 50 | Time to export (days) | 21 |
| Cost (% of income per capita) | 9.9 | Cost (% of property value) | 7.8 | Cost to export (US$ per container) | 660 |
| Minimum capital (% of income per capita) | 0.0 | | | Documents to import (number) | 8 |
| | | **Getting credit** (rank) | 70 | Time to import (days) | 18 |
| **Dealing with construction permits** (rank) | 105 | Strength of legal rights index (0-10) | 6 | Cost to import (US$ per container) | 705 |
| Procedures (number) | 11 | Depth of credit information index (0-6) | 4 | | |
| Time (days) | 222 | Public registry coverage (% of adults) | 7.2 | **Enforcing contracts** (rank) | 155 |
| Cost (% of income per capita) | 216.0 | Private bureau coverage (% of adults) | 2.0 | Procedures (number) | 46 |
| | | | | Time (days) | 976 |
| **Getting electricity** (rank) | 171 | **Protecting investors** (rank) | 32 | Cost (% of claim) | 23.8 |
| Procedures (number) | 6 | Extent of disclosure index (0-10) | 6 | | |
| Time (days) | 206 | Extent of director liability index (0-10) | 6 | **Resolving insolvency** (rank) | 78 |
| Cost (% of income per capita) | 1,673.7 | Ease of shareholder suits index (0-10) | 7 | Time (years) | 2.8 |
| | | Strength of investor protection index (0-10) | 6.3 | Cost (% of estate) | 4 |
| | | | | Recovery rate (cents on the dollar) | 36.2 |
| | | **Paying taxes** (rank) | 162 | | |
| | | Payments (number per year) | 47 | | |
| | | Time (hours per year) | 560 | | |
| | | Total tax rate (% of profit) | 35.3 | | |

*Note:* Most indicator sets refer to a case scenario in an economy's largest business city. For more details, see the data notes.

✔ Reform making it easier to do business  ✘ Reform making it more difficult to do business

## PALAU

| | | East Asia & Pacific | | GNI per capita (US$) | 7,250 |
|---|---|---|---|---|---|
| Ease of doing business (rank) | 111 | Upper middle income | | Population (m) | 0.0 |

| | | | | | |
|---|---|---|---|---|---|
| **Starting a business** (rank) | 130 | **Registering property** (rank) | 17 | **Trading across borders** (rank) | 108 |
| Procedures (number) | 8 | Procedures (number) | 5 | Documents to export (number) | 5 |
| Time (days) | 28 | Time (days) | 14 | Time to export (days) | 29 |
| Cost (% of income per capita) | 5.2 | Cost (% of property value) | 0.4 | Cost to export (US$ per container) | 970 |
| Minimum capital (% of income per capita) | 13.8 | | | Documents to import (number) | 9 |
| | | **Getting credit** (rank) | 185 | Time to import (days) | 33 |
| | | Strength of legal rights index (0-10) | 1 | Cost to import (US$ per container) | 930 |
| **Dealing with construction permits** (rank) | 44 | Depth of credit information index (0-6) | 0 | | |
| Procedures (number) | 22 | Public registry coverage (% of adults) | 0.0 | **Enforcing contracts** (rank) | 146 |
| Time (days) | 93 | Private bureau coverage (% of adults) | 0.0 | Procedures (number) | 38 |
| Cost (% of income per capita) | 7.6 | | | Time (days) | 810 |
| | | **Protecting investors** (rank) | 177 | Cost (% of claim) | 35.3 |
| **Getting electricity** (rank) | 78 | Extent of disclosure index (0-10) | 0 | | |
| Procedures (number) | 5 | Extent of director liability index (0-10) | 0 | **Resolving insolvency** (rank) | 71 |
| Time (days) | 125 | Ease of shareholder suits index (0-10) | 8 | Time (years) | 1.0 |
| Cost (% of income per capita) | 173.8 | Strength of investor protection index (0-10) | 2.7 | Cost (% of estate) | 23 |
| | | | | Recovery rate (cents on the dollar) | 38.6 |
| | | **Paying taxes** (rank) | 83 | | |
| | | Payments (number per year) | 11 | | |
| | | Time (hours per year) | 142 | | |
| | | Total tax rate (% of profit) | 75.7 | | |

## PANAMA

| | | Latin America & Caribbean | | GNI per capita (US$) | 7,910 |
|---|---|---|---|---|---|
| Ease of doing business (rank) | 61 | Upper middle income | | Population (m) | 3.6 |

| | | | | | |
|---|---|---|---|---|---|
| **Starting a business** (rank) | 23 | ✔ **Registering property** (rank) | 107 | **Trading across borders** (rank) | 9 |
| Procedures (number) | 6 | Procedures (number) | 8 | Documents to export (number) | 3 |
| Time (days) | 7 | Time (days) | 28 | Time to export (days) | 9 |
| Cost (% of income per capita) | 8.8 | Cost (% of property value) | 5.3 | Cost to export (US$ per container) | 615 |
| Minimum capital (% of income per capita) | 0.0 | | | Documents to import (number) | 3 |
| | | **Getting credit** (rank) | 53 | Time to import (days) | 9 |
| | | Strength of legal rights index (0-10) | 5 | Cost to import (US$ per container) | 965 |
| ✔ **Dealing with construction permits** (rank) | 73 | Depth of credit information index (0-6) | 6 | | |
| Procedures (number) | 17 | Public registry coverage (% of adults) | 0.0 | **Enforcing contracts** (rank) | 125 |
| Time (days) | 101 | Private bureau coverage (% of adults) | 57.9 | Procedures (number) | 32 |
| Cost (% of income per capita) | 83.7 | | | Time (days) | 686 |
| | | **Protecting investors** (rank) | 82 | Cost (% of claim) | 50.0 |
| **Getting electricity** (rank) | 16 | Extent of disclosure index (0-10) | 3 | | |
| Procedures (number) | 5 | Extent of director liability index (0-10) | 4 | **Resolving insolvency** (rank) | 110 |
| Time (days) | 35 | Ease of shareholder suits index (0-10) | 9 | Time (years) | 2.5 |
| Cost (% of income per capita) | 13.6 | Strength of investor protection index (0-10) | 5.3 | Cost (% of estate) | 25 |
| | | | | Recovery rate (cents on the dollar) | 27.5 |
| | | ✔ **Paying taxes** (rank) | 172 | | |
| | | Payments (number per year) | 60 | | |
| | | Time (hours per year) | 431 | | |
| | | Total tax rate (% of profit) | 42.0 | | |

## PAPUA NEW GUINEA

| | | East Asia & Pacific | | GNI per capita (US$) | 1,480 |
|---|---|---|---|---|---|
| Ease of doing business (rank) | 104 | Lower middle income | | Population (m) | 7.0 |

| | | | | | |
|---|---|---|---|---|---|
| **Starting a business** (rank) | 91 | **Registering property** (rank) | 88 | **Trading across borders** (rank) | 120 |
| Procedures (number) | 6 | Procedures (number) | 4 | Documents to export (number) | 7 |
| Time (days) | 51 | Time (days) | 72 | Time to export (days) | 23 |
| Cost (% of income per capita) | 13.6 | Cost (% of property value) | 5.1 | Cost to export (US$ per container) | 949 |
| Minimum capital (% of income per capita) | 0.0 | | | Documents to import (number) | 9 |
| | | **Getting credit** (rank) | 83 | Time to import (days) | 32 |
| | | Strength of legal rights index (0-10) | 5 | Cost to import (US$ per container) | 1,130 |
| **Dealing with construction permits** (rank) | 159 | Depth of credit information index (0-6) | 4 | | |
| Procedures (number) | 21 | Public registry coverage (% of adults) | 0.0 | **Enforcing contracts** (rank) | 166 |
| Time (days) | 219 | Private bureau coverage (% of adults) | 2.9 | Procedures (number) | 42 |
| Cost (% of income per capita) | 114.7 | | | Time (days) | 591 |
| | | **Protecting investors** (rank) | 49 | Cost (% of claim) | 110.3 |
| **Getting electricity** (rank) | 23 | Extent of disclosure index (0-10) | 5 | | |
| Procedures (number) | 4 | Extent of director liability index (0-10) | 5 | **Resolving insolvency** (rank) | 125 |
| Time (days) | 66 | Ease of shareholder suits index (0-10) | 8 | Time (years) | 3.0 |
| Cost (% of income per capita) | 59.9 | Strength of investor protection index (0-10) | 6.0 | Cost (% of estate) | 23 |
| | | | | Recovery rate (cents on the dollar) | 23.5 |
| | | **Paying taxes** (rank) | 106 | | |
| | | Payments (number per year) | 33 | | |
| | | Time (hours per year) | 207 | | |
| | | Total tax rate (% of profit) | 42.2 | | |

*Note:* Most indicator sets refer to a case scenario in an economy's largest business city. For more details, see the data notes.

✔ Reform making it easier to do business ✘ Reform making it more difficult to do business

## PARAGUAY

| Ease of doing business (rank) | 103 | Latin America & Caribbean — Lower middle income | | GNI per capita (US$) | 2,970 |
| | | | | Population (m) | 6.6 |

| Starting a business (rank) | 111 | Registering property (rank) | 67 | Trading across borders (rank) | 155 |
| Procedures (number) | 7 | Procedures (number) | 6 | Documents to export (number) | 8 |
| Time (days) | 35 | Time (days) | 46 | Time to export (days) | 33 |
| Cost (% of income per capita) | 46.8 | Cost (% of property value) | 1.9 | Cost to export (US$ per container) | 1,440 |
| Minimum capital (% of income per capita) | 0.0 | | | Documents to import (number) | 10 |
| | | Getting credit (rank) | 83 | Time to import (days) | 33 |
| | | Strength of legal rights index (0-10) | 3 | Cost to import (US$ per container) | 1,750 |
| Dealing with construction permits (rank) | 71 | Depth of credit information index (0-6) | 6 | | |
| Procedures (number) | 12 | Public registry coverage (% of adults) | 16.7 | Enforcing contracts (rank) | 106 |
| Time (days) | 137 | Private bureau coverage (% of adults) | 47.5 | Procedures (number) | 38 |
| Cost (% of income per capita) | 223.6 | | | Time (days) | 591 |
| | | Protecting investors (rank) | 70 | Cost (% of claim) | 30.0 |
| Getting electricity (rank) | 26 | Extent of disclosure index (0-10) | 6 | | |
| Procedures (number) | 4 | Extent of director liability index (0-10) | 5 | Resolving insolvency (rank) | 144 |
| Time (days) | 53 | Ease of shareholder suits index (0-10) | 6 | Time (years) | 3.9 |
| Cost (% of income per capita) | 221.7 | Strength of investor protection index (0-10) | 5.7 | Cost (% of estate) | 9 |
| | | | | Recovery rate (cents on the dollar) | 15.3 |
| | | Paying taxes (rank) | 141 | | |
| | | Payments (number per year) | 35 | | |
| | | Time (hours per year) | 387 | | |
| | | Total tax rate (% of profit) | 35.0 | | |

## PERU

| Ease of doing business (rank) | 43 | Latin America & Caribbean — Upper middle income | | GNI per capita (US$) | 5,500 |
| | | | | Population (m) | 29.4 |

| Starting a business (rank) | 60 | Registering property (rank) | 19 | Trading across borders (rank) | 60 |
| Procedures (number) | 5 | Procedures (number) | 4 | Documents to export (number) | 6 |
| Time (days) | 26 | Time (days) | 7 | Time to export (days) | 12 |
| Cost (% of income per capita) | 10.6 | Cost (% of property value) | 3.3 | Cost to export (US$ per container) | 890 |
| Minimum capital (% of income per capita) | 0.0 | | | Documents to import (number) | 8 |
| | | Getting credit (rank) | 23 | Time to import (days) | 17 |
| | | Strength of legal rights index (0-10) | 7 | Cost to import (US$ per container) | 880 |
| ✔ Dealing with construction permits (rank) | 86 | Depth of credit information index (0-6) | 6 | | |
| Procedures (number) | 14 | Public registry coverage (% of adults) | 31.2 | Enforcing contracts (rank) | 115 |
| Time (days) | 173 | Private bureau coverage (% of adults) | 42.5 | Procedures (number) | 41 |
| Cost (% of income per capita) | 62.8 | | | Time (days) | 428 |
| | | ✔ Protecting investors (rank) | 13 | Cost (% of claim) | 35.7 |
| Getting electricity (rank) | 77 | Extent of disclosure index (0-10) | 9 | | |
| Procedures (number) | 5 | Extent of director liability index (0-10) | 6 | Resolving insolvency (rank) | 106 |
| Time (days) | 100 | Ease of shareholder suits index (0-10) | 8 | Time (years) | 3.1 |
| Cost (% of income per capita) | 378.2 | Strength of investor protection index (0-10) | 7.7 | Cost (% of estate) | 7 |
| | | | | Recovery rate (cents on the dollar) | 28.1 |
| | | Paying taxes (rank) | 85 | | |
| | | Payments (number per year) | 9 | | |
| | | Time (hours per year) | 293 | | |
| | | Total tax rate (% of profit) | 40.5 | | |

## PHILIPPINES

| Ease of doing business (rank) | 138 | East Asia & Pacific — Lower middle income | | GNI per capita (US$) | 2,210 |
| | | | | Population (m) | 94.9 |

| Starting a business (rank) | 161 | Registering property (rank) | 122 | Trading across borders (rank) | 53 |
| Procedures (number) | 16 | Procedures (number) | 8 | Documents to export (number) | 7 |
| Time (days) | 36 | Time (days) | 39 | Time to export (days) | 15 |
| Cost (% of income per capita) | 18.1 | Cost (% of property value) | 4.8 | Cost to export (US$ per container) | 585 |
| Minimum capital (% of income per capita) | 4.8 | | | Documents to import (number) | 8 |
| | | Getting credit (rank) | 129 | Time to import (days) | 14 |
| | | Strength of legal rights index (0-10) | 4 | Cost to import (US$ per container) | 660 |
| Dealing with construction permits (rank) | 100 | Depth of credit information index (0-6) | 3 | | |
| Procedures (number) | 29 | Public registry coverage (% of adults) | 0.0 | Enforcing contracts (rank) | 111 |
| Time (days) | 84 | Private bureau coverage (% of adults) | 9.0 | Procedures (number) | 37 |
| Cost (% of income per capita) | 103.0 | | | Time (days) | 842 |
| | | Protecting investors (rank) | 128 | Cost (% of claim) | 26.0 |
| Getting electricity (rank) | 57 | Extent of disclosure index (0-10) | 2 | | |
| Procedures (number) | 5 | Extent of director liability index (0-10) | 3 | Resolving insolvency (rank) | 165 |
| Time (days) | 50 | Ease of shareholder suits index (0-10) | 8 | Time (years) | 5.7 |
| Cost (% of income per capita) | 833.3 | Strength of investor protection index (0-10) | 4.3 | Cost (% of estate) | 38 |
| | | | | Recovery rate (cents on the dollar) | 4.9 |
| | | Paying taxes (rank) | 143 | | |
| | | Payments (number per year) | 47 | | |
| | | Time (hours per year) | 193 | | |
| | | Total tax rate (% of profit) | 46.6 | | |

*Note:* Most indicator sets refer to a case scenario in an economy's largest business city. For more details, see the data notes.

✔ Reform making it easier to do business  ✘ Reform making it more difficult to do business

## POLAND

| | | | | | | |
|---|---|---|---|---|---|---|
| **Ease of doing business** (rank) | 55 | OECD high income<br>High income | | GNI per capita (US$)<br>Population (m) | 12,480<br>38.2 |

| | | | | | |
|---|---|---|---|---|---|
| **Starting a business** (rank) | 124 | ✔ **Registering property** (rank) | 62 | **Trading across borders** (rank) | 50 |
| Procedures (number) | 6 | Procedures (number) | 6 | Documents to export (number) | 5 |
| Time (days) | 32 | Time (days) | 54 | Time to export (days) | 17 |
| Cost (% of income per capita) | 14.4 | Cost (% of property value) | 0.4 | Cost to export (US$ per container) | 1,050 |
| Minimum capital (% of income per capita) | 13.0 | | | Documents to import (number) | 5 |
| | | **Getting credit** (rank) | 4 | Time to import (days) | 16 |
| **Dealing with construction permits** (rank) | 161 | Strength of legal rights index (0-10) | 9 | Cost to import (US$ per container) | 1,025 |
| Procedures (number) | 29 | Depth of credit information index (0-6) | 6 | | |
| Time (days) | 301 | Public registry coverage (% of adults) | 0.0 | ✔ **Enforcing contracts** (rank) | 56 |
| Cost (% of income per capita) | 49.4 | Private bureau coverage (% of adults) | 76.9 | Procedures (number) | 33 |
| | | | | Time (days) | 685 |
| **Getting electricity** (rank) | 137 | **Protecting investors** (rank) | 49 | Cost (% of claim) | 19.0 |
| Procedures (number) | 6 | Extent of disclosure index (0-10) | 7 | | |
| Time (days) | 186 | Extent of director liability index (0-10) | 2 | ✔ **Resolving insolvency** (rank) | 37 |
| Cost (% of income per capita) | 208.3 | Ease of shareholder suits index (0-10) | 9 | Time (years) | 3.0 |
| | | Strength of investor protection index (0-10) | 6.0 | Cost (% of estate) | 15 |
| | | | | Recovery rate (cents on the dollar) | 54.5 |
| | | ✔ **Paying taxes** (rank) | 114 | | |
| | | Payments (number per year) | 18 | | |
| | | Time (hours per year) | 286 | | |
| | | Total tax rate (% of profit) | 43.8 | | |

## PORTUGAL

| | | | | | | |
|---|---|---|---|---|---|---|
| **Ease of doing business** (rank) | 30 | OECD high income<br>High income | | GNI per capita (US$)<br>Population (m) | 21,250<br>10.6 |

| | | | | | |
|---|---|---|---|---|---|
| **Starting a business** (rank) | 31 | **Registering property** (rank) | 30 | ✔ **Trading across borders** (rank) | 17 |
| Procedures (number) | 5 | Procedures (number) | 1 | Documents to export (number) | 4 |
| Time (days) | 5 | Time (days) | 1 | Time to export (days) | 13 |
| Cost (% of income per capita) | 2.3 | Cost (% of property value) | 7.3 | Cost to export (US$ per container) | 685 |
| Minimum capital (% of income per capita) | 0.0 | | | Documents to import (number) | 5 |
| | | **Getting credit** (rank) | 104 | Time to import (days) | 12 |
| ✔ **Dealing with construction permits** (rank) | 78 | Strength of legal rights index (0-10) | 3 | Cost to import (US$ per container) | 899 |
| Procedures (number) | 13 | Depth of credit information index (0-6) | 5 | | |
| Time (days) | 108 | Public registry coverage (% of adults) | 90.7 | **Enforcing contracts** (rank) | 22 |
| Cost (% of income per capita) | 370.0 | Private bureau coverage (% of adults) | 22.9 | Procedures (number) | 32 |
| | | | | Time (days) | 547 |
| **Getting electricity** (rank) | 35 | **Protecting investors** (rank) | 49 | Cost (% of claim) | 13.0 |
| Procedures (number) | 5 | Extent of disclosure index (0-10) | 6 | | |
| Time (days) | 64 | Extent of director liability index (0-10) | 5 | ✔ **Resolving insolvency** (rank) | 23 |
| Cost (% of income per capita) | 52.7 | Ease of shareholder suits index (0-10) | 7 | Time (years) | 2.0 |
| | | Strength of investor protection index (0-10) | 6.0 | Cost (% of estate) | 9 |
| | | | | Recovery rate (cents on the dollar) | 74.6 |
| | | **Paying taxes** (rank) | 77 | | |
| | | Payments (number per year) | 8 | | |
| | | Time (hours per year) | 275 | | |
| | | Total tax rate (% of profit) | 42.6 | | |

## PUERTO RICO (U.S.)

| | | | | | | |
|---|---|---|---|---|---|---|
| **Ease of doing business** (rank) | 41 | Latin America & Caribbean<br>High income | | GNI per capita (US$)<br>Population (m) | 17,655<br>3.7 |

| | | | | | |
|---|---|---|---|---|---|
| **Starting a business** (rank) | 12 | **Registering property** (rank) | 128 | **Trading across borders** (rank) | 96 |
| Procedures (number) | 6 | Procedures (number) | 8 | Documents to export (number) | 6 |
| Time (days) | 6 | Time (days) | 194 | Time to export (days) | 15 |
| Cost (% of income per capita) | 0.9 | Cost (% of property value) | 0.9 | Cost to export (US$ per container) | 1,300 |
| Minimum capital (% of income per capita) | 0.0 | | | Documents to import (number) | 9 |
| | | **Getting credit** (rank) | 12 | Time to import (days) | 15 |
| **Dealing with construction permits** (rank) | 156 | Strength of legal rights index (0-10) | 9 | Cost to import (US$ per container) | 1,350 |
| Procedures (number) | 18 | Depth of credit information index (0-6) | 5 | | |
| Time (days) | 189 | Public registry coverage (% of adults) | 0.0 | **Enforcing contracts** (rank) | 101 |
| Cost (% of income per capita) | 361.3 | Private bureau coverage (% of adults) | 81.5 | Procedures (number) | 39 |
| | | | | Time (days) | 620 |
| **Getting electricity** (rank) | 37 | **Protecting investors** (rank) | 19 | Cost (% of claim) | 25.6 |
| Procedures (number) | 5 | Extent of disclosure index (0-10) | 7 | | |
| Time (days) | 32 | Extent of director liability index (0-10) | 6 | **Resolving insolvency** (rank) | 24 |
| Cost (% of income per capita) | 384.0 | Ease of shareholder suits index (0-10) | 8 | Time (years) | 2.5 |
| | | Strength of investor protection index (0-10) | 7.0 | Cost (% of estate) | 8 |
| | | | | Recovery rate (cents on the dollar) | 73.4 |
| | | ✔ **Paying taxes** (rank) | 104 | | |
| | | Payments (number per year) | 16 | | |
| | | Time (hours per year) | 218 | | |
| | | Total tax rate (% of profit) | 50.7 | | |

*Note:* Most indicator sets refer to a case scenario in an economy's largest business city. For more details, see the data notes.

✔ Reform making it easier to do business ✘ Reform making it more difficult to do business

## QATAR

| | | | | | | |
|---|---|---|---|---|---|---|
| **Ease of doing business** (rank) | 40 | Middle East & North Africa<br>High income | | GNI per capita (US$)<br>Population (m) | | 80,440<br>1.9 |

| | | | | | |
|---|---|---|---|---|---|
| **Starting a business** (rank) | 109 | **Registering property** (rank) | 40 | ✔ **Trading across borders** (rank) | 58 |
| Procedures (number) | 8 | Procedures (number) | 7 | Documents to export (number) | 5 |
| Time (days) | 9 | Time (days) | 13 | Time to export (days) | 17 |
| Cost (% of income per capita) | 4.9 | Cost (% of property value) | 0.3 | Cost to export (US$ per container) | 885 |
| Minimum capital (% of income per capita) | 60.7 | | | Documents to import (number) | 7 |
| | | **Getting credit** (rank) | 104 | Time to import (days) | 17 |
| **Dealing with construction permits** (rank) | 18 | Strength of legal rights index (0-10) | 4 | Cost to import (US$ per container) | 1,033 |
| Procedures (number) | 16 | Depth of credit information index (0-6) | 4 | | |
| Time (days) | 62 | Public registry coverage (% of adults) | 25.2 | **Enforcing contracts** (rank) | 95 |
| Cost (% of income per capita) | 1.1 | Private bureau coverage (% of adults) | 0.0 | Procedures (number) | 43 |
| | | | | Time (days) | 570 |
| **Getting electricity** (rank) | 25 | **Protecting investors** (rank) | 100 | Cost (% of claim) | 21.6 |
| Procedures (number) | 4 | Extent of disclosure index (0-10) | 5 | | |
| Time (days) | 90 | Extent of director liability index (0-10) | 6 | **Resolving insolvency** (rank) | 36 |
| Cost (% of income per capita) | 3.9 | Ease of shareholder suits index (0-10) | 4 | Time (years) | 2.8 |
| | | Strength of investor protection index (0-10) | 5.0 | Cost (% of estate) | 22 |
| | | | | Recovery rate (cents on the dollar) | 55.5 |
| | | **Paying taxes** (rank) | 2 | | |
| | | Payments (number per year) | 4 | | |
| | | Time (hours per year) | 48 | | |
| | | Total tax rate (% of profit) | 11.3 | | |

## ROMANIA

| | | | | | | |
|---|---|---|---|---|---|---|
| **Ease of doing business** (rank) | 72 | Eastern Europe & Central Asia<br>Upper middle income | | GNI per capita (US$)<br>Population (m) | | 7,910<br>21.4 |

| | | | | | |
|---|---|---|---|---|---|
| ✔ **Starting a business** (rank) | 68 | **Registering property** (rank) | 72 | **Trading across borders** (rank) | 72 |
| Procedures (number) | 6 | Procedures (number) | 8 | Documents to export (number) | 5 |
| Time (days) | 10 | Time (days) | 26 | Time to export (days) | 12 |
| Cost (% of income per capita) | 2.8 | Cost (% of property value) | 1.2 | Cost to export (US$ per container) | 1,485 |
| Minimum capital (% of income per capita) | 0.8 | | | Documents to import (number) | 6 |
| | | ✔ **Getting credit** (rank) | 12 | Time to import (days) | 13 |
| **Dealing with construction permits** (rank) | 129 | Strength of legal rights index (0-10) | 9 | Cost to import (US$ per container) | 1,495 |
| Procedures (number) | 15 | Depth of credit information index (0-6) | 5 | | |
| Time (days) | 287 | Public registry coverage (% of adults) | 14.0 | **Enforcing contracts** (rank) | 60 |
| Cost (% of income per capita) | 79.1 | Private bureau coverage (% of adults) | 44.9 | Procedures (number) | 32 |
| | | | | Time (days) | 512 |
| **Getting electricity** (rank) | 168 | **Protecting investors** (rank) | 49 | Cost (% of claim) | 28.9 |
| Procedures (number) | 7 | Extent of disclosure index (0-10) | 9 | | |
| Time (days) | 223 | Extent of director liability index (0-10) | 5 | **Resolving insolvency** (rank) | 102 |
| Cost (% of income per capita) | 584.2 | Ease of shareholder suits index (0-10) | 4 | Time (years) | 3.3 |
| | | Strength of investor protection index (0-10) | 6.0 | Cost (% of estate) | 11 |
| | | | | Recovery rate (cents on the dollar) | 29.2 |
| | | **Paying taxes** (rank) | 136 | | |
| | | Payments (number per year) | 41 | | |
| | | Time (hours per year) | 216 | | |
| | | Total tax rate (% of profit) | 44.2 | | |

## RUSSIAN FEDERATION

| | | | | | | |
|---|---|---|---|---|---|---|
| **Ease of doing business** (rank) | 112 | Eastern Europe & Central Asia<br>Upper middle income | | GNI per capita (US$)<br>Population (m) | | 10,400<br>141.9 |

| | | | | | |
|---|---|---|---|---|---|
| **Starting a business** (rank) | 101 | **Registering property** (rank) | 46 | **Trading across borders** (rank) | 162 |
| Procedures (number) | 8 | Procedures (number) | 5 | Documents to export (number) | 8 |
| Time (days) | 18 | Time (days) | 44 | Time to export (days) | 21 |
| Cost (% of income per capita) | 2.0 | Cost (% of property value) | 0.2 | Cost to export (US$ per container) | 2,820 |
| Minimum capital (% of income per capita) | 1.4 | | | Documents to import (number) | 11 |
| | | **Getting credit** (rank) | 104 | Time to import (days) | 36 |
| ✔ **Dealing with construction permits** (rank) | 178 | Strength of legal rights index (0-10) | 3 | Cost to import (US$ per container) | 2,920 |
| Procedures (number) | 42 | Depth of credit information index (0-6) | 5 | | |
| Time (days) | 344 | Public registry coverage (% of adults) | 0.0 | **Enforcing contracts** (rank) | 11 |
| Cost (% of income per capita) | 129.2 | Private bureau coverage (% of adults) | 45.4 | Procedures (number) | 36 |
| | | | | Time (days) | 270 |
| **Getting electricity** (rank) | 184 | **Protecting investors** (rank) | 117 | Cost (% of claim) | 13.4 |
| Procedures (number) | 10 | Extent of disclosure index (0-10) | 6 | | |
| Time (days) | 281 | Extent of director liability index (0-10) | 2 | **Resolving insolvency** (rank) | 53 |
| Cost (% of income per capita) | 1,573.7 | Ease of shareholder suits index (0-10) | 6 | Time (years) | 2.0 |
| | | Strength of investor protection index (0-10) | 4.7 | Cost (% of estate) | 9 |
| | | | | Recovery rate (cents on the dollar) | 43.4 |
| | | ✔ **Paying taxes** (rank) | 64 | | |
| | | Payments (number per year) | 7 | | |
| | | Time (hours per year) | 177 | | |
| | | Total tax rate (% of profit) | 54.1 | | |

*Note:* Most indicator sets refer to a case scenario in an economy's largest business city. For more details, see the data notes.

✔ Reform making it easier to do business ✘ Reform making it more difficult to do business

## RWANDA

| | | Sub-Saharan Africa | | GNI per capita (US$) | 570 |
|---|---|---|---|---|---|
| **Ease of doing business** (rank) | 52 | Low income | | Population (m) | 10.9 |

| | | | | | |
|---|---|---|---|---|---|
| **Starting a business** (rank) | 8 | **Registering property** (rank) | 63 | **Trading across borders** (rank) | 158 |
| Procedures (number) | 2 | Procedures (number) | 5 | Documents to export (number) | 8 |
| Time (days) | 3 | Time (days) | 25 | Time to export (days) | 29 |
| Cost (% of income per capita) | 4.3 | Cost (% of property value) | 5.6 | Cost to export (US$ per container) | 3,245 |
| Minimum capital (% of income per capita) | 0.0 | | | Documents to import (number) | 8 |
| | | **Getting credit** (rank) | 23 | Time to import (days) | 31 |
| **Dealing with construction permits** (rank) | 98 | Strength of legal rights index (0-10) | 7 | Cost to import (US$ per container) | 4,990 |
| Procedures (number) | 12 | Depth of credit information index (0-6) | 6 | | |
| Time (days) | 164 | Public registry coverage (% of adults) | 0.0 | ✔ **Enforcing contracts** (rank) | 39 |
| Cost (% of income per capita) | 278.4 | Private bureau coverage (% of adults) | 7.1 | Procedures (number) | 23 |
| | | | | Time (days) | 230 |
| ✔ **Getting electricity** (rank) | 49 | **Protecting investors** (rank) | 32 | Cost (% of claim) | 78.7 |
| Procedures (number) | 4 | Extent of disclosure index (0-10) | 7 | | |
| Time (days) | 30 | Extent of director liability index (0-10) | 9 | **Resolving insolvency** (rank) | 167 |
| Cost (% of income per capita) | 3,948.1 | Ease of shareholder suits index (0-10) | 3 | Time (years) | 3.0 |
| | | Strength of investor protection index (0-10) | 6.3 | Cost (% of estate) | 50 |
| | | | | Recovery rate (cents on the dollar) | 3.1 |
| | | **Paying taxes** (rank) | 25 | | |
| | | Payments (number per year) | 17 | | |
| | | Time (hours per year) | 134 | | |
| | | Total tax rate (% of profit) | 31.3 | | |

## SAMOA

| | | East Asia & Pacific | | GNI per capita (US$) | 3,190 |
|---|---|---|---|---|---|
| **Ease of doing business** (rank) | 57 | Lower middle income | | Population (m) | 0.2 |

| | | | | | |
|---|---|---|---|---|---|
| **Starting a business** (rank) | 20 | **Registering property** (rank) | 23 | **Trading across borders** (rank) | 66 |
| Procedures (number) | 4 | Procedures (number) | 5 | Documents to export (number) | 5 |
| Time (days) | 9 | Time (days) | 15 | Time to export (days) | 25 |
| Cost (% of income per capita) | 9.5 | Cost (% of property value) | 1.6 | Cost to export (US$ per container) | 690 |
| Minimum capital (% of income per capita) | 0.0 | | | Documents to import (number) | 6 |
| | | **Getting credit** (rank) | 129 | Time to import (days) | 28 |
| **Dealing with construction permits** (rank) | 70 | Strength of legal rights index (0-10) | 7 | Cost to import (US$ per container) | 775 |
| Procedures (number) | 21 | Depth of credit information index (0-6) | 0 | | |
| Time (days) | 87 | Public registry coverage (% of adults) | 0.0 | **Enforcing contracts** (rank) | 81 |
| Cost (% of income per capita) | 57.7 | Private bureau coverage (% of adults) | 0.0 | Procedures (number) | 44 |
| | | | | Time (days) | 455 |
| **Getting electricity** (rank) | 33 | **Protecting investors** (rank) | 32 | Cost (% of claim) | 19.7 |
| Procedures (number) | 4 | Extent of disclosure index (0-10) | 5 | | |
| Time (days) | 34 | Extent of director liability index (0-10) | 6 | **Resolving insolvency** (rank) | 146 |
| Cost (% of income per capita) | 790.8 | Ease of shareholder suits index (0-10) | 8 | Time (years) | 2.5 |
| | | Strength of investor protection index (0-10) | 6.3 | Cost (% of estate) | 38 |
| | | | | Recovery rate (cents on the dollar) | 15.2 |
| | | **Paying taxes** (rank) | 79 | | |
| | | Payments (number per year) | 37 | | |
| | | Time (hours per year) | 224 | | |
| | | Total tax rate (% of profit) | 18.9 | | |

## SÃO TOMÉ AND PRÍNCIPE

| | | Sub-Saharan Africa | | GNI per capita (US$) | 1,360 |
|---|---|---|---|---|---|
| **Ease of doing business** (rank) | 160 | Lower middle income | | Population (m) | 0.2 |

| | | | | | |
|---|---|---|---|---|---|
| **Starting a business** (rank) | 100 | **Registering property** (rank) | 161 | **Trading across borders** (rank) | 89 |
| Procedures (number) | 4 | Procedures (number) | 7 | Documents to export (number) | 8 |
| Time (days) | 7 | Time (days) | 62 | Time to export (days) | 26 |
| Cost (% of income per capita) | 19.1 | Cost (% of property value) | 9.0 | Cost to export (US$ per container) | 690 |
| Minimum capital (% of income per capita) | 285.8 | | | Documents to import (number) | 7 |
| | | **Getting credit** (rank) | 180 | Time to import (days) | 28 |
| ✘ **Dealing with construction permits** (rank) | 91 | Strength of legal rights index (0-10) | 2 | Cost to import (US$ per container) | 577 |
| Procedures (number) | 13 | Depth of credit information index (0-6) | 0 | | |
| Time (days) | 118 | Public registry coverage (% of adults) | 0.0 | **Enforcing contracts** (rank) | 181 |
| Cost (% of income per capita) | 386.7 | Private bureau coverage (% of adults) | 0.0 | Procedures (number) | 43 |
| | | | | Time (days) | 1,185 |
| **Getting electricity** (rank) | 72 | **Protecting investors** (rank) | 158 | Cost (% of claim) | 50.5 |
| Procedures (number) | 4 | Extent of disclosure index (0-10) | 3 | | |
| Time (days) | 89 | Extent of director liability index (0-10) | 1 | **Resolving insolvency** (rank) | 164 |
| Cost (% of income per capita) | 1,066.6 | Ease of shareholder suits index (0-10) | 6 | Time (years) | 6.2 |
| | | Strength of investor protection index (0-10) | 3.3 | Cost (% of estate) | 22 |
| | | | | Recovery rate (cents on the dollar) | 5.2 |
| | | **Paying taxes** (rank) | 144 | | |
| | | Payments (number per year) | 42 | | |
| | | Time (hours per year) | 424 | | |
| | | Total tax rate (% of profit) | 32.5 | | |

*Note:* Most indicator sets refer to a case scenario in an economy's largest business city. For more details, see the data notes.

✔ Reform making it easier to do business ✘ Reform making it more difficult to do business

## SAUDI ARABIA

| | | | | | | |
|---|---|---|---|---|---|---|
| Ease of doing business (rank) | 22 | Middle East & North Africa | | GNI per capita (US$) | 17,820 | |
| | | High income | | Population (m) | 28.1 | |

| | | | | | |
|---|---|---|---|---|---|
| **Starting a business** (rank) | 78 | **Registering property** (rank) | 12 | **Trading across borders** (rank) | 36 |
| Procedures (number) | 9 | Procedures (number) | 5 | Documents to export (number) | 5 |
| Time (days) | 21 | Time (days) | 8 | Time to export (days) | 13 |
| Cost (% of income per capita) | 5.0 | Cost (% of property value) | 0.0 | Cost to export (US$ per container) | 935 |
| Minimum capital (% of income per capita) | 0.0 | | | Documents to import (number) | 5 |
| | | **Getting credit** (rank) | 53 | Time to import (days) | 17 |
| **Dealing with construction permits** (rank) | 32 | Strength of legal rights index (0-10) | 5 | Cost to import (US$ per container) | 1,054 |
| Procedures (number) | 14 | Depth of credit information index (0-6) | 6 | | |
| Time (days) | 103 | Public registry coverage (% of adults) | 0.0 | ✔ **Enforcing contracts** (rank) | 124 |
| Cost (% of income per capita) | 24.7 | Private bureau coverage (% of adults) | 33.3 | Procedures (number) | 40 |
| | | | | Time (days) | 635 |
| ✘ **Getting electricity** (rank) | 12 | **Protecting investors** (rank) | 19 | Cost (% of claim) | 27.5 |
| Procedures (number) | 4 | Extent of disclosure index (0-10) | 9 | | |
| Time (days) | 61 | Extent of director liability index (0-10) | 8 | **Resolving insolvency** (rank) | 107 |
| Cost (% of income per capita) | 31.5 | Ease of shareholder suits index (0-10) | 4 | Time (years) | 2.8 |
| | | Strength of investor protection index (0-10) | 7.0 | Cost (% of estate) | 22 |
| | | | | Recovery rate (cents on the dollar) | 28.0 |
| | | ✔ **Paying taxes** (rank) | 3 | | |
| | | Payments (number per year) | 3 | | |
| | | Time (hours per year) | 72 | | |
| | | Total tax rate (% of profit) | 14.5 | | |

## SENEGAL

| | | | | | | |
|---|---|---|---|---|---|---|
| Ease of doing business (rank) | 166 | Sub-Saharan Africa | | GNI per capita (US$) | 1,070 | |
| | | Lower middle income | | Population (m) | 12.8 | |

| | | | | | |
|---|---|---|---|---|---|
| **Starting a business** (rank) | 102 | **Registering property** (rank) | 173 | **Trading across borders** (rank) | 67 |
| Procedures (number) | 3 | Procedures (number) | 6 | Documents to export (number) | 6 |
| Time (days) | 5 | Time (days) | 122 | Time to export (days) | 11 |
| Cost (% of income per capita) | 64.4 | Cost (% of property value) | 20.2 | Cost to export (US$ per container) | 1,098 |
| Minimum capital (% of income per capita) | 192.3 | | | Documents to import (number) | 5 |
| | | **Getting credit** (rank) | 129 | Time to import (days) | 14 |
| **Dealing with construction permits** (rank) | 133 | Strength of legal rights index (0-10) | 6 | Cost to import (US$ per container) | 1,740 |
| Procedures (number) | 13 | Depth of credit information index (0-6) | 1 | | |
| Time (days) | 210 | Public registry coverage (% of adults) | 4.6 | **Enforcing contracts** (rank) | 148 |
| Cost (% of income per capita) | 529.1 | Private bureau coverage (% of adults) | 0.0 | Procedures (number) | 43 |
| | | | | Time (days) | 780 |
| **Getting electricity** (rank) | 180 | **Protecting investors** (rank) | 169 | Cost (% of claim) | 26.5 |
| Procedures (number) | 8 | Extent of disclosure index (0-10) | 6 | | |
| Time (days) | 125 | Extent of director liability index (0-10) | 1 | **Resolving insolvency** (rank) | 90 |
| Cost (% of income per capita) | 5,624.9 | Ease of shareholder suits index (0-10) | 2 | Time (years) | 3.0 |
| | | Strength of investor protection index (0-10) | 3.0 | Cost (% of estate) | 7 |
| | | | | Recovery rate (cents on the dollar) | 32.0 |
| | | **Paying taxes** (rank) | 178 | | |
| | | Payments (number per year) | 59 | | |
| | | Time (hours per year) | 666 | | |
| | | Total tax rate (% of profit) | 46.0 | | |

## SERBIA

| | | | | | | |
|---|---|---|---|---|---|---|
| Ease of doing business (rank) | 86 | Eastern Europe & Central Asia | | GNI per capita (US$) | 5,680 | |
| | | Upper middle income | | Population (m) | 7.3 | |

| | | | | | |
|---|---|---|---|---|---|
| ✔ **Starting a business** (rank) | 42 | **Registering property** (rank) | 41 | **Trading across borders** (rank) | 94 |
| Procedures (number) | 6 | Procedures (number) | 6 | Documents to export (number) | 7 |
| Time (days) | 12 | Time (days) | 11 | Time to export (days) | 12 |
| Cost (% of income per capita) | 7.7 | Cost (% of property value) | 2.8 | Cost to export (US$ per container) | 1,455 |
| Minimum capital (% of income per capita) | 0.0 | | | Documents to import (number) | 7 |
| | | **Getting credit** (rank) | 40 | Time to import (days) | 14 |
| **Dealing with construction permits** (rank) | 179 | Strength of legal rights index (0-10) | 7 | Cost to import (US$ per container) | 1,660 |
| Procedures (number) | 18 | Depth of credit information index (0-6) | 5 | | |
| Time (days) | 269 | Public registry coverage (% of adults) | 0.0 | ✔ **Enforcing contracts** (rank) | 103 |
| Cost (% of income per capita) | 1,427.2 | Private bureau coverage (% of adults) | 100.0 | Procedures (number) | 36 |
| | | | | Time (days) | 635 |
| **Getting electricity** (rank) | 76 | **Protecting investors** (rank) | 82 | Cost (% of claim) | 31.3 |
| Procedures (number) | 4 | Extent of disclosure index (0-10) | 7 | | |
| Time (days) | 131 | Extent of director liability index (0-10) | 6 | ✔ **Resolving insolvency** (rank) | 103 |
| Cost (% of income per capita) | 502.6 | Ease of shareholder suits index (0-10) | 3 | Time (years) | 2.0 |
| | | Strength of investor protection index (0-10) | 5.3 | Cost (% of estate) | 20 |
| | | | | Recovery rate (cents on the dollar) | 29.1 |
| | | **Paying taxes** (rank) | 149 | | |
| | | Payments (number per year) | 66 | | |
| | | Time (hours per year) | 279 | | |
| | | Total tax rate (% of profit) | 34.0 | | |

*Note:* Most indicator sets refer to a case scenario in an economy's largest business city. For more details, see the data notes.

✔ Reform making it easier to do business  ✘ Reform making it more difficult to do business

## SEYCHELLES

| | | | | | | |
|---|---|---|---|---|---|---|
| Sub-Saharan Africa | | | GNI per capita (US$) | | | 11,130 |
| **Ease of doing business** (rank) | 74 | Upper middle income | | Population (m) | | 0.1 |

| | | | | | |
|---|---|---|---|---|---|
| **Starting a business** (rank) | 117 | **Registering property** (rank) | 66 | **Trading across borders** (rank) | 33 |
| Procedures (number) | 10 | Procedures (number) | 4 | Documents to export (number) | 5 |
| Time (days) | 39 | Time (days) | 33 | Time to export (days) | 16 |
| Cost (% of income per capita) | 14.3 | Cost (% of property value) | 7.0 | Cost to export (US$ per container) | 876 |
| Minimum capital (% of income per capita) | 0.0 | | | Documents to import (number) | 5 |
| | | **Getting credit** (rank) | 167 | Time to import (days) | 17 |
| **Dealing with construction permits** (rank) | 57 | Strength of legal rights index (0-10) | 4 | Cost to import (US$ per container) | 876 |
| Procedures (number) | 17 | Depth of credit information index (0-6) | 0 | | |
| Time (days) | 126 | Public registry coverage (% of adults) | 0.0 | **Enforcing contracts** (rank) | 83 |
| Cost (% of income per capita) | 25.3 | Private bureau coverage (% of adults) | 0.0 | Procedures (number) | 37 |
| | | | | Time (days) | 915 |
| **Getting electricity** (rank) | 144 | **Protecting investors** (rank) | 70 | Cost (% of claim) | 15.4 |
| Procedures (number) | 6 | Extent of disclosure index (0-10) | 4 | | |
| Time (days) | 147 | Extent of director liability index (0-10) | 8 | **Resolving insolvency** (rank) | 65 |
| Cost (% of income per capita) | 429.8 | Ease of shareholder suits index (0-10) | 5 | Time (years) | 2.0 |
| | | Strength of investor protection index (0-10) | 5.7 | Cost (% of estate) | 11 |
| | | | | Recovery rate (cents on the dollar) | 39.6 |
| | | **Paying taxes** (rank) | 20 | | |
| | | Payments (number per year) | 27 | | |
| | | Time (hours per year) | 76 | | |
| | | Total tax rate (% of profit) | 25.7 | | |

## SIERRA LEONE

| | | | | | | |
|---|---|---|---|---|---|---|
| Sub-Saharan Africa | | | GNI per capita (US$) | | | 340 |
| **Ease of doing business** (rank) | 140 | Low income | | Population (m) | | 6.0 |

| | | | | | |
|---|---|---|---|---|---|
| **Starting a business** (rank) | 76 | ✔ **Registering property** (rank) | 167 | **Trading across borders** (rank) | 131 |
| Procedures (number) | 6 | Procedures (number) | 7 | Documents to export (number) | 7 |
| Time (days) | 12 | Time (days) | 67 | Time to export (days) | 24 |
| Cost (% of income per capita) | 80.4 | Cost (% of property value) | 11.6 | Cost to export (US$ per container) | 1,385 |
| Minimum capital (% of income per capita) | 0.0 | | | Documents to import (number) | 7 |
| | | ✔ **Getting credit** (rank) | 83 | Time to import (days) | 27 |
| **Dealing with construction permits** (rank) | 173 | Strength of legal rights index (0-10) | 7 | Cost to import (US$ per container) | 1,780 |
| Procedures (number) | 20 | Depth of credit information index (0-6) | 2 | | |
| Time (days) | 238 | Public registry coverage (% of adults) | 0.7 | **Enforcing contracts** (rank) | 147 |
| Cost (% of income per capita) | 265.9 | Private bureau coverage (% of adults) | 0.0 | Procedures (number) | 39 |
| | | | | Time (days) | 515 |
| **Getting electricity** (rank) | 176 | **Protecting investors** (rank) | 32 | Cost (% of claim) | 149.5 |
| Procedures (number) | 8 | Extent of disclosure index (0-10) | 6 | | |
| Time (days) | 137 | Extent of director liability index (0-10) | 7 | **Resolving insolvency** (rank) | 154 |
| Cost (% of income per capita) | 2,124.4 | Ease of shareholder suits index (0-10) | 6 | Time (years) | 2.6 |
| | | Strength of investor protection index (0-10) | 6.3 | Cost (% of estate) | 42 |
| | | | | Recovery rate (cents on the dollar) | 9.2 |
| | | **Paying taxes** (rank) | 117 | | |
| | | Payments (number per year) | 33 | | |
| | | Time (hours per year) | 357 | | |
| | | Total tax rate (% of profit) | 32.1 | | |

## SINGAPORE

| | | | | | | |
|---|---|---|---|---|---|---|
| East Asia & Pacific | | | GNI per capita (US$) | | | 42,930 |
| **Ease of doing business** (rank) | 1 | High income | | Population (m) | | 5.2 |

| | | | | | |
|---|---|---|---|---|---|
| **Starting a business** (rank) | 4 | **Registering property** (rank) | 36 | **Trading across borders** (rank) | 1 |
| Procedures (number) | 3 | Procedures (number) | 5 | Documents to export (number) | 4 |
| Time (days) | 3 | Time (days) | 21 | Time to export (days) | 5 |
| Cost (% of income per capita) | 0.6 | Cost (% of property value) | 2.9 | Cost to export (US$ per container) | 456 |
| Minimum capital (% of income per capita) | 0.0 | | | Documents to import (number) | 4 |
| | | **Getting credit** (rank) | 12 | Time to import (days) | 4 |
| **Dealing with construction permits** (rank) | 2 | Strength of legal rights index (0-10) | 10 | Cost to import (US$ per container) | 439 |
| Procedures (number) | 11 | Depth of credit information index (0-6) | 4 | | |
| Time (days) | 26 | Public registry coverage (% of adults) | 0.0 | **Enforcing contracts** (rank) | 12 |
| Cost (% of income per capita) | 16.7 | Private bureau coverage (% of adults) | 58.3 | Procedures (number) | 21 |
| | | | | Time (days) | 150 |
| **Getting electricity** (rank) | 5 | **Protecting investors** (rank) | 2 | Cost (% of claim) | 25.8 |
| Procedures (number) | 4 | Extent of disclosure index (0-10) | 10 | | |
| Time (days) | 36 | Extent of director liability index (0-10) | 9 | **Resolving insolvency** (rank) | 2 |
| Cost (% of income per capita) | 28.6 | Ease of shareholder suits index (0-10) | 9 | Time (years) | 0.8 |
| | | Strength of investor protection index (0-10) | 9.3 | Cost (% of estate) | 1 |
| | | | | Recovery rate (cents on the dollar) | 91.3 |
| | | **Paying taxes** (rank) | 5 | | |
| | | Payments (number per year) | 5 | | |
| | | Time (hours per year) | 82 | | |
| | | Total tax rate (% of profit) | 27.6 | | |

*Note:* Most indicator sets refer to a case scenario in an economy's largest business city. For more details, see the data notes.

✔ Reform making it easier to do business  ✘ Reform making it more difficult to do business

## SLOVAK REPUBLIC

| | | | | | | |
|---|---|---|---|---|---|---|
| Ease of doing business (rank) | 46 | OECD high income<br>High income | | GNI per capita (US$)<br>Population (m) | 16,070<br>5.4 | |

| | | | | | |
|---|---|---|---|---|---|
| ✔ **Starting a business** (rank) | 83 | **Registering property** (rank) | 8 | **Trading across borders** (rank) | 98 |
| Procedures (number) | 6 | Procedures (number) | 3 | Documents to export (number) | 6 |
| Time (days) | 16 | Time (days) | 17 | Time to export (days) | 17 |
| Cost (% of income per capita) | 1.8 | Cost (% of property value) | 0.0 | Cost to export (US$ per container) | 1,560 |
| Minimum capital (% of income per capita) | 21.3 | | | Documents to import (number) | 7 |
| | | **Getting credit** (rank) | 23 | Time to import (days) | 17 |
| **Dealing with construction permits** (rank) | 46 | Strength of legal rights index (0-10) | 9 | Cost to import (US$ per container) | 1,540 |
| Procedures (number) | 11 | Depth of credit information index (0-6) | 4 | | |
| Time (days) | 286 | Public registry coverage (% of adults) | 2.7 | ✔ **Enforcing contracts** (rank) | 69 |
| Cost (% of income per capita) | 7.3 | Private bureau coverage (% of adults) | 58.5 | Procedures (number) | 32 |
| | | | | Time (days) | 545 |
| **Getting electricity** (rank) | 100 | **Protecting investors** (rank) | 117 | Cost (% of claim) | 30.0 |
| Procedures (number) | 5 | Extent of disclosure index (0-10) | 3 | | |
| Time (days) | 158 | Extent of director liability index (0-10) | 4 | ✔ **Resolving insolvency** (rank) | 38 |
| Cost (% of income per capita) | 249.1 | Ease of shareholder suits index (0-10) | 7 | Time (years) | 4.0 |
| | | Strength of investor protection index (0-10) | 4.7 | Cost (% of estate) | 18 |
| | | | | Recovery rate (cents on the dollar) | 53.6 |
| | | ✔ **Paying taxes** (rank) | 100 | | |
| | | Payments (number per year) | 20 | | |
| | | Time (hours per year) | 207 | | |
| | | Total tax rate (% of profit) | 47.9 | | |

## SLOVENIA

| | | | | | | |
|---|---|---|---|---|---|---|
| Ease of doing business (rank) | 35 | OECD high income<br>High income | | GNI per capita (US$)<br>Population (m) | 23,610<br>2.1 | |

| | | | | | |
|---|---|---|---|---|---|
| **Starting a business** (rank) | 30 | **Registering property** (rank) | 83 | **Trading across borders** (rank) | 57 |
| Procedures (number) | 2 | Procedures (number) | 5 | Documents to export (number) | 6 |
| Time (days) | 6 | Time (days) | 110 | Time to export (days) | 16 |
| Cost (% of income per capita) | 0.0 | Cost (% of property value) | 2.0 | Cost to export (US$ per container) | 745 |
| Minimum capital (% of income per capita) | 43.9 | | | Documents to import (number) | 8 |
| | | **Getting credit** (rank) | 104 | Time to import (days) | 14 |
| **Dealing with construction permits** (rank) | 61 | Strength of legal rights index (0-10) | 4 | Cost to import (US$ per container) | 830 |
| Procedures (number) | 11 | Depth of credit information index (0-6) | 4 | | |
| Time (days) | 197 | Public registry coverage (% of adults) | 3.4 | **Enforcing contracts** (rank) | 56 |
| Cost (% of income per capita) | 65.3 | Private bureau coverage (% of adults) | 98.9 | Procedures (number) | 32 |
| | | | | Time (days) | 1,290 |
| **Getting electricity** (rank) | 31 | ✔ **Protecting investors** (rank) | 17 | Cost (% of claim) | 12.7 |
| Procedures (number) | 5 | Extent of disclosure index (0-10) | 5 | | |
| Time (days) | 38 | Extent of director liability index (0-10) | 9 | ✔ **Resolving insolvency** (rank) | 42 |
| Cost (% of income per capita) | 119.9 | Ease of shareholder suits index (0-10) | 8 | Time (years) | 2.0 |
| | | Strength of investor protection index (0-10) | 7.3 | Cost (% of estate) | 4 |
| | | | | Recovery rate (cents on the dollar) | 49.8 |
| | | ✔ **Paying taxes** (rank) | 63 | | |
| | | Payments (number per year) | 11 | | |
| | | Time (hours per year) | 260 | | |
| | | Total tax rate (% of profit) | 34.7 | | |

## SOLOMON ISLANDS

| | | | | | | |
|---|---|---|---|---|---|---|
| Ease of doing business (rank) | 92 | East Asia & Pacific<br>Lower middle income | | GNI per capita (US$)<br>Population (m) | 1,110<br>0.6 | |

| | | | | | |
|---|---|---|---|---|---|
| **Starting a business** (rank) | 75 | **Registering property** (rank) | 168 | **Trading across borders** (rank) | 86 |
| Procedures (number) | 7 | Procedures (number) | 10 | Documents to export (number) | 7 |
| Time (days) | 9 | Time (days) | 87 | Time to export (days) | 24 |
| Cost (% of income per capita) | 47.9 | Cost (% of property value) | 4.8 | Cost to export (US$ per container) | 1,070 |
| Minimum capital (% of income per capita) | 0.0 | | | Documents to import (number) | 5 |
| | | **Getting credit** (rank) | 83 | Time to import (days) | 20 |
| **Dealing with construction permits** (rank) | 77 | Strength of legal rights index (0-10) | 9 | Cost to import (US$ per container) | 1,037 |
| Procedures (number) | 15 | Depth of credit information index (0-6) | 0 | | |
| Time (days) | 92 | Public registry coverage (% of adults) | 0.0 | **Enforcing contracts** (rank) | 109 |
| Cost (% of income per capita) | 248.5 | Private bureau coverage (% of adults) | 0.0 | Procedures (number) | 37 |
| | | | | Time (days) | 455 |
| **Getting electricity** (rank) | 125 | **Protecting investors** (rank) | 49 | Cost (% of claim) | 78.9 |
| Procedures (number) | 4 | Extent of disclosure index (0-10) | 3 | | |
| Time (days) | 160 | Extent of director liability index (0-10) | 7 | **Resolving insolvency** (rank) | 123 |
| Cost (% of income per capita) | 2,044.4 | Ease of shareholder suits index (0-10) | 8 | Time (years) | 1.0 |
| | | Strength of investor protection index (0-10) | 6.0 | Cost (% of estate) | 38 |
| | | | | Recovery rate (cents on the dollar) | 23.9 |
| | | **Paying taxes** (rank) | 26 | | |
| | | Payments (number per year) | 33 | | |
| | | Time (hours per year) | 80 | | |
| | | Total tax rate (% of profit) | 25.3 | | |

*Note:* Most indicator sets refer to a case scenario in an economy's largest business city. For more details, see the data notes.

✔ Reform making it easier to do business  ✘ Reform making it more difficult to do business

## SOUTH AFRICA

| Ease of doing business (rank) | 39 | Sub-Saharan Africa | | GNI per capita (US$) | 6,960 |
| | | Upper middle income | | Population (m) | 50.6 |

| Starting a business (rank) | 53 | Registering property (rank) | 79 | ✔ Trading across borders (rank) | 115 |
| Procedures (number) | 5 | Procedures (number) | 6 | Documents to export (number) | 6 |
| Time (days) | 19 | Time (days) | 23 | Time to export (days) | 16 |
| Cost (% of income per capita) | 0.3 | Cost (% of property value) | 5.9 | Cost to export (US$ per container) | 1,620 |
| Minimum capital (% of income per capita) | 0.0 | | | Documents to import (number) | 7 |
| | | Getting credit (rank) | 1 | Time to import (days) | 23 |
| Dealing with construction permits (rank) | 39 | Strength of legal rights index (0-10) | 10 | Cost to import (US$ per container) | 1,940 |
| Procedures (number) | 13 | Depth of credit information index (0-6) | 6 | | |
| Time (days) | 127 | Public registry coverage (% of adults) | 0.0 | Enforcing contracts (rank) | 82 |
| Cost (% of income per capita) | 33.4 | Private bureau coverage (% of adults) | 54.0 | Procedures (number) | 29 |
| | | | | Time (days) | 600 |
| Getting electricity (rank) | 150 | Protecting investors (rank) | 10 | Cost (% of claim) | 33.2 |
| Procedures (number) | 5 | Extent of disclosure index (0-10) | 8 | | |
| Time (days) | 226 | Extent of director liability index (0-10) | 8 | Resolving insolvency (rank) | 84 |
| Cost (% of income per capita) | 1,505.8 | Ease of shareholder suits index (0-10) | 8 | Time (years) | 2.0 |
| | | Strength of investor protection index (0-10) | 8.0 | Cost (% of estate) | 18 |
| | | | | Recovery rate (cents on the dollar) | 35.4 |
| | | Paying taxes (rank) | 32 | | |
| | | Payments (number per year) | 9 | | |
| | | Time (hours per year) | 200 | | |
| | | Total tax rate (% of profit) | 33.3 | | |

## SPAIN

| Ease of doing business (rank) | 44 | OECD high income | | GNI per capita (US$) | 30,990 |
| | | High income | | Population (m) | 46.2 |

| Starting a business (rank) | 136 | Registering property (rank) | 57 | ✔ Trading across borders (rank) | 39 |
| Procedures (number) | 10 | Procedures (number) | 5 | Documents to export (number) | 5 |
| Time (days) | 28 | Time (days) | 13 | Time to export (days) | 9 |
| Cost (% of income per capita) | 4.7 | Cost (% of property value) | 7.1 | Cost to export (US$ per container) | 1,260 |
| Minimum capital (% of income per capita) | 13.2 | | | Documents to import (number) | 6 |
| | | Getting credit (rank) | 53 | Time to import (days) | 9 |
| Dealing with construction permits (rank) | 38 | Strength of legal rights index (0-10) | 6 | Cost to import (US$ per container) | 1,350 |
| Procedures (number) | 8 | Depth of credit information index (0-6) | 5 | | |
| Time (days) | 182 | Public registry coverage (% of adults) | 53.3 | Enforcing contracts (rank) | 64 |
| Cost (% of income per capita) | 51.8 | Private bureau coverage (% of adults) | 13.2 | Procedures (number) | 40 |
| | | | | Time (days) | 510 |
| Getting electricity (rank) | 70 | Protecting investors (rank) | 100 | Cost (% of claim) | 17.2 |
| Procedures (number) | 5 | Extent of disclosure index (0-10) | 5 | | |
| Time (days) | 101 | Extent of director liability index (0-10) | 6 | ✔ Resolving insolvency (rank) | 20 |
| Cost (% of income per capita) | 232.0 | Ease of shareholder suits index (0-10) | 4 | Time (years) | 1.5 |
| | | Strength of investor protection index (0-10) | 5.0 | Cost (% of estate) | 11 |
| | | | | Recovery rate (cents on the dollar) | 76.5 |
| | | Paying taxes (rank) | 34 | | |
| | | Payments (number per year) | 8 | | |
| | | Time (hours per year) | 167 | | |
| | | Total tax rate (% of profit) | 38.7 | | |

## SRI LANKA

| Ease of doing business (rank) | 81 | South Asia | | GNI per capita (US$) | 2,580 |
| | | Lower middle income | | Population (m) | 20.9 |

| ✔ Starting a business (rank) | 33 | ✔ Registering property (rank) | 143 | ✔ Trading across borders (rank) | 56 |
| Procedures (number) | 5 | Procedures (number) | 8 | Documents to export (number) | 6 |
| Time (days) | 7 | Time (days) | 60 | Time to export (days) | 20 |
| Cost (% of income per capita) | 19.1 | Cost (% of property value) | 5.1 | Cost to export (US$ per container) | 720 |
| Minimum capital (% of income per capita) | 0.0 | | | Documents to import (number) | 6 |
| | | ✔ Getting credit (rank) | 70 | Time to import (days) | 19 |
| Dealing with construction permits (rank) | 112 | Strength of legal rights index (0-10) | 5 | Cost to import (US$ per container) | 775 |
| Procedures (number) | 17 | Depth of credit information index (0-6) | 5 | | |
| Time (days) | 216 | Public registry coverage (% of adults) | 0.0 | Enforcing contracts (rank) | 133 |
| Cost (% of income per capita) | 35.4 | Private bureau coverage (% of adults) | 33.6 | Procedures (number) | 40 |
| | | | | Time (days) | 1,318 |
| Getting electricity (rank) | 103 | Protecting investors (rank) | 49 | Cost (% of claim) | 22.8 |
| Procedures (number) | 4 | Extent of disclosure index (0-10) | 6 | | |
| Time (days) | 132 | Extent of director liability index (0-10) | 5 | Resolving insolvency (rank) | 51 |
| Cost (% of income per capita) | 1,257.5 | Ease of shareholder suits index (0-10) | 7 | Time (years) | 1.7 |
| | | Strength of investor protection index (0-10) | 6.0 | Cost (% of estate) | 10 |
| | | | | Recovery rate (cents on the dollar) | 43.9 |
| | | Paying taxes (rank) | 169 | | |
| | | Payments (number per year) | 61 | | |
| | | Time (hours per year) | 254 | | |
| | | Total tax rate (% of profit) | 50.1 | | |

*Note:* Most indicator sets refer to a case scenario in an economy's largest business city. For more details, see the data notes.

✔ Reform making it easier to do business  ✘ Reform making it more difficult to do business

## ST. KITTS AND NEVIS

| | | | | | | |
|---|---|---|---|---|---|---|
| Ease of doing business (rank) | 96 | Latin America & Caribbean<br>High income | | GNI per capita (US$)<br>Population (m) | | 12,480<br>0.1 |

| | | | | | |
|---|---|---|---|---|---|
| **Starting a business** (rank) | 69 | **Registering property** (rank) | 166 | ✘ **Trading across borders** (rank) | 64 |
| Procedures (number) | 7 | Procedures (number) | 6 | Documents to export (number) | 5 |
| Time (days) | 19 | Time (days) | 81 | Time to export (days) | 13 |
| Cost (% of income per capita) | 9.1 | Cost (% of property value) | 13.3 | Cost to export (US$ per container) | 805 |
| Minimum capital (% of income per capita) | 0.0 | | | Documents to import (number) | 7 |
| | | **Getting credit** (rank) | 129 | Time to import (days) | 12 |
| **Dealing with construction permits** (rank) | 15 | Strength of legal rights index (0-10) | 7 | Cost to import (US$ per container) | 2,635 |
| Procedures (number) | 11 | Depth of credit information index (0-6) | 0 | | |
| Time (days) | 139 | Public registry coverage (% of adults) | 0.0 | **Enforcing contracts** (rank) | 119 |
| Cost (% of income per capita) | 5.4 | Private bureau coverage (% of adults) | 0.0 | Procedures (number) | 47 |
| | | | | Time (days) | 578 |
| **Getting electricity** (rank) | 17 | **Protecting investors** (rank) | 32 | Cost (% of claim) | 20.5 |
| Procedures (number) | 4 | Extent of disclosure index (0-10) | 4 | | |
| Time (days) | 18 | Extent of director liability index (0-10) | 8 | **Resolving insolvency** (rank) | 185 |
| Cost (% of income per capita) | 304.3 | Ease of shareholder suits index (0-10) | 7 | Time (years) | NO PRACTICE |
| | | Strength of investor protection index (0-10) | 6.3 | Cost (% of estate) | NO PRACTICE |
| | | | | Recovery rate (cents on the dollar) | 0.0 |
| | | **Paying taxes** (rank) | 135 | | |
| | | Payments (number per year) | 36 | | |
| | | Time (hours per year) | 203 | | |
| | | Total tax rate (% of profit) | 52.1 | | |

## ST. LUCIA

| | | | | | | |
|---|---|---|---|---|---|---|
| Ease of doing business (rank) | 53 | Latin America & Caribbean<br>Upper middle income | | GNI per capita (US$)<br>Population (m) | | 6,680<br>0.2 |

| | | | | | |
|---|---|---|---|---|---|
| **Starting a business** (rank) | 51 | **Registering property** (rank) | 117 | **Trading across borders** (rank) | 109 |
| Procedures (number) | 5 | Procedures (number) | 8 | Documents to export (number) | 5 |
| Time (days) | 15 | Time (days) | 17 | Time to export (days) | 14 |
| Cost (% of income per capita) | 17.8 | Cost (% of property value) | 7.6 | Cost to export (US$ per container) | 1,375 |
| Minimum capital (% of income per capita) | 0.0 | | | Documents to import (number) | 9 |
| | | **Getting credit** (rank) | 104 | Time to import (days) | 17 |
| **Dealing with construction permits** (rank) | 11 | Strength of legal rights index (0-10) | 8 | Cost to import (US$ per container) | 2,675 |
| Procedures (number) | 7 | Depth of credit information index (0-6) | 0 | | |
| Time (days) | 125 | Public registry coverage (% of adults) | 0.0 | **Enforcing contracts** (rank) | 168 |
| Cost (% of income per capita) | 23.0 | Private bureau coverage (% of adults) | 0.0 | Procedures (number) | 47 |
| | | | | Time (days) | 635 |
| **Getting electricity** (rank) | 12 | **Protecting investors** (rank) | 32 | Cost (% of claim) | 37.3 |
| Procedures (number) | 4 | Extent of disclosure index (0-10) | 4 | | |
| Time (days) | 25 | Extent of director liability index (0-10) | 8 | **Resolving insolvency** (rank) | 61 |
| Cost (% of income per capita) | 202.8 | Ease of shareholder suits index (0-10) | 7 | Time (years) | 2.0 |
| | | Strength of investor protection index (0-10) | 6.3 | Cost (% of estate) | 9 |
| | | | | Recovery rate (cents on the dollar) | 42.0 |
| | | **Paying taxes** (rank) | 43 | | |
| | | Payments (number per year) | 32 | | |
| | | Time (hours per year) | 92 | | |
| | | Total tax rate (% of profit) | 34.6 | | |

## ST. VINCENT AND THE GRENADINES

| | | | | | | |
|---|---|---|---|---|---|---|
| Ease of doing business (rank) | 75 | Latin America & Caribbean<br>Upper middle income | | GNI per capita (US$)<br>Population (m) | | 6,100<br>0.1 |

| | | | | | |
|---|---|---|---|---|---|
| **Starting a business** (rank) | 64 | **Registering property** (rank) | 145 | **Trading across borders** (rank) | 43 |
| Procedures (number) | 7 | Procedures (number) | 7 | Documents to export (number) | 5 |
| Time (days) | 10 | Time (days) | 38 | Time to export (days) | 12 |
| Cost (% of income per capita) | 17.9 | Cost (% of property value) | 11.9 | Cost to export (US$ per container) | 935 |
| Minimum capital (% of income per capita) | 0.0 | | | Documents to import (number) | 5 |
| | | **Getting credit** (rank) | 129 | Time to import (days) | 13 |
| **Dealing with construction permits** (rank) | 5 | Strength of legal rights index (0-10) | 7 | Cost to import (US$ per container) | 1,575 |
| Procedures (number) | 8 | Depth of credit information index (0-6) | 0 | | |
| Time (days) | 112 | Public registry coverage (% of adults) | 0.0 | **Enforcing contracts** (rank) | 99 |
| Cost (% of income per capita) | 9.8 | Private bureau coverage (% of adults) | 0.0 | Procedures (number) | 45 |
| | | | | Time (days) | 394 |
| **Getting electricity** (rank) | 22 | **Protecting investors** (rank) | 32 | Cost (% of claim) | 30.3 |
| Procedures (number) | 3 | Extent of disclosure index (0-10) | 4 | | |
| Time (days) | 52 | Extent of director liability index (0-10) | 8 | **Resolving insolvency** (rank) | 185 |
| Cost (% of income per capita) | 246.7 | Ease of shareholder suits index (0-10) | 7 | Time (years) | NO PRACTICE |
| | | Strength of investor protection index (0-10) | 6.3 | Cost (% of estate) | NO PRACTICE |
| | | | | Recovery rate (cents on the dollar) | 0.0 |
| | | **Paying taxes** (rank) | 72 | | |
| | | Payments (number per year) | 36 | | |
| | | Time (hours per year) | 111 | | |
| | | Total tax rate (% of profit) | 38.7 | | |

*Note:* Most indicator sets refer to a case scenario in an economy's largest business city. For more details, see the data notes.

✔ Reform making it easier to do business   ✘ Reform making it more difficult to do business

## SUDAN

| | | Sub-Saharan Africa | | GNI per capita (US$) | 1,982 |
|---|---|---|---|---|---|
| Ease of doing business (rank) | 143 | Lower middle income | | Population (m) | 34.3 |

| | | | | | |
|---|---|---|---|---|---|
| **Starting a business** (rank) | 122 | **Registering property** (rank) | 37 | **Trading across borders** (rank) | 153 |
| Procedures (number) | 10 | Procedures (number) | 6 | Documents to export (number) | 7 |
| Time (days) | 36 | Time (days) | 9 | Time to export (days) | 32 |
| Cost (% of income per capita) | 20.0 | Cost (% of property value) | 2.8 | Cost to export (US$ per container) | 2,050 |
| Minimum capital (% of income per capita) | 0.0 | | | Documents to import (number) | 7 |
| | | **Getting credit** (rank) | 167 | Time to import (days) | 46 |
| **Dealing with construction permits** (rank) | 156 | Strength of legal rights index (0-10) | 4 | Cost to import (US$ per container) | 2,900 |
| Procedures (number) | 16 | Depth of credit information index (0-6) | 0 | | |
| Time (days) | 270 | Public registry coverage (% of adults) | 0.0 | **Enforcing contracts** (rank) | 151 |
| Cost (% of income per capita) | 240.3 | Private bureau coverage (% of adults) | 0.0 | Procedures (number) | 53 |
| | | | | Time (days) | 810 |
| **Getting electricity** (rank) | 108 | **Protecting investors** (rank) | 158 | Cost (% of claim) | 19.8 |
| Procedures (number) | 5 | Extent of disclosure index (0-10) | 0 | | |
| Time (days) | 70 | Extent of director liability index (0-10) | 6 | **Resolving insolvency** (rank) | 88 |
| Cost (% of income per capita) | 2,527.3 | Ease of shareholder suits index (0-10) | 4 | Time (years) | 2.0 |
| | | Strength of investor protection index (0-10) | 3.3 | Cost (% of estate) | 20 |
| | | | | Recovery rate (cents on the dollar) | 33.2 |
| | | **Paying taxes** (rank) | 101 | | |
| | | Payments (number per year) | 42 | | |
| | | Time (hours per year) | 180 | | |
| | | Total tax rate (% of profit) | 36.1 | | |

## SURINAME

| | | Latin America & Caribbean | | GNI per capita (US$) | 7,096 |
|---|---|---|---|---|---|
| Ease of doing business (rank) | 164 | Upper middle income | | Population (m) | 0.5 |

| | | | | | |
|---|---|---|---|---|---|
| **Starting a business** (rank) | 178 | **Registering property** (rank) | 171 | ✘ **Trading across borders** (rank) | 97 |
| Procedures (number) | 13 | Procedures (number) | 6 | Documents to export (number) | 8 |
| Time (days) | 694 | Time (days) | 197 | Time to export (days) | 23 |
| Cost (% of income per capita) | 110.9 | Cost (% of property value) | 13.7 | Cost to export (US$ per container) | 1,000 |
| Minimum capital (% of income per capita) | 0.4 | | | Documents to import (number) | 6 |
| | | **Getting credit** (rank) | 159 | Time to import (days) | 21 |
| **Dealing with construction permits** (rank) | 92 | Strength of legal rights index (0-10) | 5 | Cost to import (US$ per container) | 1,165 |
| Procedures (number) | 11 | Depth of credit information index (0-6) | 0 | | |
| Time (days) | 461 | Public registry coverage (% of adults) | 0.0 | **Enforcing contracts** (rank) | 180 |
| Cost (% of income per capita) | 60.4 | Private bureau coverage (% of adults) | 0.0 | Procedures (number) | 44 |
| | | | | Time (days) | 1,715 |
| **Getting electricity** (rank) | 39 | **Protecting investors** (rank) | 183 | Cost (% of claim) | 37.1 |
| Procedures (number) | 4 | Extent of disclosure index (0-10) | 1 | | |
| Time (days) | 58 | Extent of director liability index (0-10) | 0 | **Resolving insolvency** (rank) | 158 |
| Cost (% of income per capita) | 634.4 | Ease of shareholder suits index (0-10) | 5 | Time (years) | 5.0 |
| | | Strength of investor protection index (0-10) | 2.0 | Cost (% of estate) | 30 |
| | | | | Recovery rate (cents on the dollar) | 8.6 |
| | | **Paying taxes** (rank) | 49 | | |
| | | Payments (number per year) | 29 | | |
| | | Time (hours per year) | 199 | | |
| | | Total tax rate (% of profit) | 27.9 | | |

## SWAZILAND

| | | Sub-Saharan Africa | | GNI per capita (US$) | 3,300 |
|---|---|---|---|---|---|
| Ease of doing business (rank) | 123 | Lower middle income | | Population (m) | 1.1 |

| | | | | | |
|---|---|---|---|---|---|
| **Starting a business** (rank) | 165 | **Registering property** (rank) | 129 | **Trading across borders** (rank) | 141 |
| Procedures (number) | 12 | Procedures (number) | 9 | Documents to export (number) | 8 |
| Time (days) | 56 | Time (days) | 21 | Time to export (days) | 18 |
| Cost (% of income per capita) | 24.1 | Cost (% of property value) | 7.1 | Cost to export (US$ per container) | 1,880 |
| Minimum capital (% of income per capita) | 0.4 | | | Documents to import (number) | 8 |
| | | **Getting credit** (rank) | 53 | Time to import (days) | 27 |
| **Dealing with construction permits** (rank) | 41 | Strength of legal rights index (0-10) | 6 | Cost to import (US$ per container) | 2,085 |
| Procedures (number) | 13 | Depth of credit information index (0-6) | 5 | | |
| Time (days) | 95 | Public registry coverage (% of adults) | 0.0 | **Enforcing contracts** (rank) | 174 |
| Cost (% of income per capita) | 94.9 | Private bureau coverage (% of adults) | 47.8 | Procedures (number) | 40 |
| | | | | Time (days) | 956 |
| **Getting electricity** (rank) | 156 | **Protecting investors** (rank) | 128 | Cost (% of claim) | 56.1 |
| Procedures (number) | 6 | Extent of disclosure index (0-10) | 2 | | |
| Time (days) | 137 | Extent of director liability index (0-10) | 5 | **Resolving insolvency** (rank) | 74 |
| Cost (% of income per capita) | 1,071.8 | Ease of shareholder suits index (0-10) | 6 | Time (years) | 2.0 |
| | | Strength of investor protection index (0-10) | 4.3 | Cost (% of estate) | 15 |
| | | | | Recovery rate (cents on the dollar) | 38.3 |
| | | ✔ **Paying taxes** (rank) | 58 | | |
| | | Payments (number per year) | 33 | | |
| | | Time (hours per year) | 104 | | |
| | | Total tax rate (% of profit) | 36.8 | | |

*Note:* Most indicator sets refer to a case scenario in an economy's largest business city. For more details, see the data notes.

✔ Reform making it easier to do business  ✗ Reform making it more difficult to do business

## SWEDEN

| | | | | | | |
|---|---|---|---|---|---|---|
| **Ease of doing business** (rank) | 13 | OECD high income | | GNI per capita (US$) | 53,230 | |
| | | High income | | Population (m) | 9.5 | |

| | | | | | | |
|---|---|---|---|---|---|---|
| **Starting a business** (rank) | 54 | ✗ **Registering property** (rank) | 35 | **Trading across borders** (rank) | 8 | |
| Procedures (number) | 3 | Procedures (number) | 1 | Documents to export (number) | 3 | |
| Time (days) | 16 | Time (days) | 30 | Time to export (days) | 8 | |
| Cost (% of income per capita) | 0.5 | Cost (% of property value) | 4.3 | Cost to export (US$ per container) | 705 | |
| Minimum capital (% of income per capita) | 13.2 | | | Documents to import (number) | 3 | |
| | | **Getting credit** (rank) | 40 | Time to import (days) | 6 | |
| **Dealing with construction permits** (rank) | 25 | Strength of legal rights index (0-10) | 8 | Cost to import (US$ per container) | 735 | |
| Procedures (number) | 7 | Depth of credit information index (0-6) | 4 | | | |
| Time (days) | 116 | Public registry coverage (% of adults) | 0.0 | **Enforcing contracts** (rank) | 27 | |
| Cost (% of income per capita) | 77.3 | Private bureau coverage (% of adults) | 100.0 | Procedures (number) | 30 | |
| | | | | Time (days) | 314 | |
| **Getting electricity** (rank) | 9 | **Protecting investors** (rank) | 32 | Cost (% of claim) | 31.2 | |
| Procedures (number) | 3 | Extent of disclosure index (0-10) | 8 | | | |
| Time (days) | 52 | Extent of director liability index (0-10) | 4 | **Resolving insolvency** (rank) | 22 | |
| Cost (% of income per capita) | 37.1 | Ease of shareholder suits index (0-10) | 7 | Time (years) | 2.0 | |
| | | Strength of investor protection index (0-10) | 6.3 | Cost (% of estate) | 9 | |
| | | | | Recovery rate (cents on the dollar) | 74.7 | |
| | | **Paying taxes** (rank) | 38 | | | |
| | | Payments (number per year) | 4 | | | |
| | | Time (hours per year) | 122 | | | |
| | | Total tax rate (% of profit) | 53.0 | | | |

## SWITZERLAND

| | | | | | | |
|---|---|---|---|---|---|---|
| **Ease of doing business** (rank) | 28 | OECD high income | | GNI per capita (US$) | 76,380 | |
| | | High income | | Population (m) | 7.9 | |

| | | | | | | |
|---|---|---|---|---|---|---|
| **Starting a business** (rank) | 97 | **Registering property** (rank) | 15 | **Trading across borders** (rank) | 35 | |
| Procedures (number) | 6 | Procedures (number) | 4 | Documents to export (number) | 4 | |
| Time (days) | 18 | Time (days) | 16 | Time to export (days) | 8 | |
| Cost (% of income per capita) | 2.1 | Cost (% of property value) | 0.4 | Cost to export (US$ per container) | 1,435 | |
| Minimum capital (% of income per capita) | 26.3 | | | Documents to import (number) | 5 | |
| | | **Getting credit** (rank) | 23 | Time to import (days) | 9 | |
| **Dealing with construction permits** (rank) | 50 | Strength of legal rights index (0-10) | 8 | Cost to import (US$ per container) | 1,440 | |
| Procedures (number) | 13 | Depth of credit information index (0-6) | 5 | | | |
| Time (days) | 154 | Public registry coverage (% of adults) | 0.0 | **Enforcing contracts** (rank) | 20 | |
| Cost (% of income per capita) | 39.1 | Private bureau coverage (% of adults) | 26.8 | Procedures (number) | 32 | |
| | | | | Time (days) | 390 | |
| **Getting electricity** (rank) | 8 | **Protecting investors** (rank) | 169 | Cost (% of claim) | 24.0 | |
| Procedures (number) | 3 | Extent of disclosure index (0-10) | 0 | | | |
| Time (days) | 39 | Extent of director liability index (0-10) | 5 | **Resolving insolvency** (rank) | 45 | |
| Cost (% of income per capita) | 61.1 | Ease of shareholder suits index (0-10) | 4 | Time (years) | 3.0 | |
| | | Strength of investor protection index (0-10) | 3.0 | Cost (% of estate) | 4 | |
| | | | | Recovery rate (cents on the dollar) | 47.5 | |
| | | **Paying taxes** (rank) | 18 | | | |
| | | Payments (number per year) | 19 | | | |
| | | Time (hours per year) | 63 | | | |
| | | Total tax rate (% of profit) | 30.2 | | | |

## SYRIAN ARAB REPUBLIC

| | | | | | | |
|---|---|---|---|---|---|---|
| **Ease of doing business** (rank) | 144 | Middle East & North Africa | | GNI per capita (US$) | 2,803 | |
| | | Lower middle income | | Population (m) | 20.8 | |

| | | | | | | |
|---|---|---|---|---|---|---|
| **Starting a business** (rank) | 132 | **Registering property** (rank) | 84 | **Trading across borders** (rank) | 125 | |
| Procedures (number) | 7 | Procedures (number) | 4 | Documents to export (number) | 8 | |
| Time (days) | 13 | Time (days) | 19 | Time to export (days) | 15 | |
| Cost (% of income per capita) | 15.6 | Cost (% of property value) | 27.8 | Cost to export (US$ per container) | 1,190 | |
| Minimum capital (% of income per capita) | 122.6 | | | Documents to import (number) | 9 | |
| | | ✔ **Getting credit** (rank) | 176 | Time to import (days) | 21 | |
| **Dealing with construction permits** (rank) | 134 | Strength of legal rights index (0-10) | 1 | Cost to import (US$ per container) | 1,625 | |
| Procedures (number) | 23 | Depth of credit information index (0-6) | 2 | | | |
| Time (days) | 104 | Public registry coverage (% of adults) | 4.9 | **Enforcing contracts** (rank) | 176 | |
| Cost (% of income per capita) | 483.9 | Private bureau coverage (% of adults) | 0.0 | Procedures (number) | 55 | |
| | | | | Time (days) | 872 | |
| **Getting electricity** (rank) | 84 | **Protecting investors** (rank) | 117 | Cost (% of claim) | 29.3 | |
| Procedures (number) | 5 | Extent of disclosure index (0-10) | 7 | | | |
| Time (days) | 71 | Extent of director liability index (0-10) | 5 | **Resolving insolvency** (rank) | 111 | |
| Cost (% of income per capita) | 902.9 | Ease of shareholder suits index (0-10) | 2 | Time (years) | 4.1 | |
| | | Strength of investor protection index (0-10) | 4.7 | Cost (% of estate) | 9 | |
| | | | | Recovery rate (cents on the dollar) | 27.5 | |
| | | **Paying taxes** (rank) | 111 | | | |
| | | Payments (number per year) | 19 | | | |
| | | Time (hours per year) | 336 | | | |
| | | Total tax rate (% of profit) | 39.7 | | | |

*Note:* Most indicator sets refer to a case scenario in an economy's largest business city. For more details, see the data notes.

✔ Reform making it easier to do business  ✘ Reform making it more difficult to do business

## TAIWAN, CHINA

| | | | | | | |
|---|---|---|---|---|---|---|
| **Ease of doing business** (rank) | 16 | East Asia & Pacific | | GNI per capita (US$) | 20,200 | |
| | | High income | | Population (m) | 23.2 | |

| | | | | | |
|---|---|---|---|---|---|
| **Starting a business** (rank) | 16 | **Registering property** (rank) | 32 | **Trading across borders** (rank) | 23 |
| Procedures (number) | 3 | Procedures (number) | 3 | Documents to export (number) | 6 |
| Time (days) | 10 | Time (days) | 5 | Time to export (days) | 10 |
| Cost (% of income per capita) | 2.4 | Cost (% of property value) | 6.2 | Cost to export (US$ per container) | 655 |
| Minimum capital (% of income per capita) | 0.0 | | | Documents to import (number) | 6 |
| | | **Getting credit** (rank) | 70 | Time to import (days) | 10 |
| ✔ **Dealing with construction permits** (rank) | 9 | Strength of legal rights index (0-10) | 5 | Cost to import (US$ per container) | 720 |
| Procedures (number) | 11 | Depth of credit information index (0-6) | 5 | | |
| Time (days) | 94 | Public registry coverage (% of adults) | 0.0 | **Enforcing contracts** (rank) | 90 |
| Cost (% of income per capita) | 16.3 | Private bureau coverage (% of adults) | 94.1 | Procedures (number) | 45 |
| | | | | Time (days) | 510 |
| **Getting electricity** (rank) | 6 | ✔ **Protecting investors** (rank) | 32 | Cost (% of claim) | 17.7 |
| Procedures (number) | 4 | Extent of disclosure index (0-10) | 9 | | |
| Time (days) | 24 | Extent of director liability index (0-10) | 5 | **Resolving insolvency** (rank) | 15 |
| Cost (% of income per capita) | 50.4 | Ease of shareholder suits index (0-10) | 5 | Time (years) | 1.9 |
| | | Strength of investor protection index (0-10) | 6.3 | Cost (% of estate) | 4 |
| | | | | Recovery rate (cents on the dollar) | 81.8 |
| | | **Paying taxes** (rank) | 54 | | |
| | | Payments (number per year) | 12 | | |
| | | Time (hours per year) | 221 | | |
| | | Total tax rate (% of profit) | 34.8 | | |

## TAJIKISTAN

| | | | | | |
|---|---|---|---|---|---|
| **Ease of doing business** (rank) | 141 | Eastern Europe & Central Asia | | GNI per capita (US$) | 870 |
| | | Low income | | Population (m) | 7.0 |

| | | | | | |
|---|---|---|---|---|---|
| **Starting a business** (rank) | 77 | **Registering property** (rank) | 82 | **Trading across borders** (rank) | 184 |
| Procedures (number) | 5 | Procedures (number) | 6 | Documents to export (number) | 11 |
| Time (days) | 24 | Time (days) | 37 | Time to export (days) | 71 |
| Cost (% of income per capita) | 27.1 | Cost (% of property value) | 4.3 | Cost to export (US$ per container) | 8,450 |
| Minimum capital (% of income per capita) | 0.0 | | | Documents to import (number) | 11 |
| | | **Getting credit** (rank) | 180 | Time to import (days) | 72 |
| **Dealing with construction permits** (rank) | 180 | Strength of legal rights index (0-10) | 2 | Cost to import (US$ per container) | 9,800 |
| Procedures (number) | 24 | Depth of credit information index (0-6) | 0 | | |
| Time (days) | 228 | Public registry coverage (% of adults) | 0.0 | **Enforcing contracts** (rank) | 43 |
| Cost (% of income per capita) | 638.5 | Private bureau coverage (% of adults) | 0.0 | Procedures (number) | 35 |
| | | | | Time (days) | 430 |
| **Getting electricity** (rank) | 181 | ✔ **Protecting investors** (rank) | 25 | Cost (% of claim) | 25.5 |
| Procedures (number) | 9 | Extent of disclosure index (0-10) | 8 | | |
| Time (days) | 185 | Extent of director liability index (0-10) | 6 | **Resolving insolvency** (rank) | 79 |
| Cost (% of income per capita) | 1,140.6 | Ease of shareholder suits index (0-10) | 6 | Time (years) | 1.7 |
| | | Strength of investor protection index (0-10) | 6.7 | Cost (% of estate) | 9 |
| | | | | Recovery rate (cents on the dollar) | 36.0 |
| | | **Paying taxes** (rank) | 175 | | |
| | | Payments (number per year) | 69 | | |
| | | Time (hours per year) | 224 | | |
| | | Total tax rate (% of profit) | 84.5 | | |

## TANZANIA

| | | | | | |
|---|---|---|---|---|---|
| **Ease of doing business** (rank) | 134 | Sub-Saharan Africa | | GNI per capita (US$) | 540 |
| | | Low income | | Population (m) | 46.2 |

| | | | | | |
|---|---|---|---|---|---|
| ✔ **Starting a business** (rank) | 113 | **Registering property** (rank) | 137 | ✘ **Trading across borders** (rank) | 122 |
| Procedures (number) | 9 | Procedures (number) | 8 | Documents to export (number) | 6 |
| Time (days) | 26 | Time (days) | 68 | Time to export (days) | 18 |
| Cost (% of income per capita) | 28.2 | Cost (% of property value) | 4.4 | Cost to export (US$ per container) | 1,040 |
| Minimum capital (% of income per capita) | 0.0 | | | Documents to import (number) | 10 |
| | | **Getting credit** (rank) | 129 | Time to import (days) | 31 |
| ✘ **Dealing with construction permits** (rank) | 174 | Strength of legal rights index (0-10) | 7 | Cost to import (US$ per container) | 1,565 |
| Procedures (number) | 19 | Depth of credit information index (0-6) | 0 | | |
| Time (days) | 206 | Public registry coverage (% of adults) | 0.0 | **Enforcing contracts** (rank) | 36 |
| Cost (% of income per capita) | 564.6 | Private bureau coverage (% of adults) | 0.0 | Procedures (number) | 38 |
| | | | | Time (days) | 462 |
| **Getting electricity** (rank) | 96 | **Protecting investors** (rank) | 100 | Cost (% of claim) | 14.3 |
| Procedures (number) | 4 | Extent of disclosure index (0-10) | 3 | | |
| Time (days) | 109 | Extent of director liability index (0-10) | 4 | **Resolving insolvency** (rank) | 129 |
| Cost (% of income per capita) | 1,944.1 | Ease of shareholder suits index (0-10) | 8 | Time (years) | 3.0 |
| | | Strength of investor protection index (0-10) | 5.0 | Cost (% of estate) | 22 |
| | | | | Recovery rate (cents on the dollar) | 21.7 |
| | | **Paying taxes** (rank) | 133 | | |
| | | Payments (number per year) | 48 | | |
| | | Time (hours per year) | 172 | | |
| | | Total tax rate (% of profit) | 45.3 | | |

*Note:* Most indicator sets refer to a case scenario in an economy's largest business city. For more details, see the data notes.

✔ Reform making it easier to do business  ✘ Reform making it more difficult to do business

## THAILAND

| | | | | | | |
|---|---|---|---|---|---|---|
| Ease of doing business (rank) | 18 | East Asia & Pacific Upper middle income | | GNI per capita (US$) Population (m) | 4,420 69.5 |

| | | | | | |
|---|---|---|---|---|---|
| ✔ **Starting a business** (rank) | 85 | **Registering property** (rank) | 26 | **Trading across borders** (rank) | 20 |
| Procedures (number) | 4 | Procedures (number) | 2 | Documents to export (number) | 5 |
| Time (days) | 29 | Time (days) | 2 | Time to export (days) | 14 |
| Cost (% of income per capita) | 6.7 | Cost (% of property value) | 6.3 | Cost to export (US$ per container) | 585 |
| Minimum capital (% of income per capita) | 0.0 | | | Documents to import (number) | 5 |
| | | **Getting credit** (rank) | 70 | Time to import (days) | 13 |
| **Dealing with construction permits** (rank) | 16 | Strength of legal rights index (0-10) | 5 | Cost to import (US$ per container) | 750 |
| Procedures (number) | 8 | Depth of credit information index (0-6) | 5 | | |
| Time (days) | 157 | Public registry coverage (% of adults) | 0.0 | **Enforcing contracts** (rank) | 23 |
| Cost (% of income per capita) | 9.2 | Private bureau coverage (% of adults) | 44.1 | Procedures (number) | 36 |
| | | | | Time (days) | 440 |
| **Getting electricity** (rank) | 10 | **Protecting investors** (rank) | 13 | Cost (% of claim) | 15.0 |
| Procedures (number) | 4 | Extent of disclosure index (0-10) | 10 | | |
| Time (days) | 35 | Extent of director liability index (0-10) | 7 | **Resolving insolvency** (rank) | 58 |
| Cost (% of income per capita) | 75.3 | Ease of shareholder suits index (0-10) | 6 | Time (years) | 2.7 |
| | | Strength of investor protection index (0-10) | 7.7 | Cost (% of estate) | 36 |
| | | | | Recovery rate (cents on the dollar) | 42.4 |
| | | ✔ **Paying taxes** (rank) | 96 | | |
| | | Payments (number per year) | 22 | | |
| | | Time (hours per year) | 264 | | |
| | | Total tax rate (% of profit) | 37.6 | | |

## TIMOR-LESTE

| | | | | | | |
|---|---|---|---|---|---|---|
| Ease of doing business (rank) | 169 | East Asia & Pacific Lower middle income | | GNI per capita (US$) Population (m) | 3,949 1.2 |

| | | | | | |
|---|---|---|---|---|---|
| **Starting a business** (rank) | 147 | **Registering property** (rank) | 185 | **Trading across borders** (rank) | 83 |
| Procedures (number) | 8 | Procedures (number) | NO PRACTICE | Documents to export (number) | 6 |
| Time (days) | 94 | Time (days) | NO PRACTICE | Time to export (days) | 25 |
| Cost (% of income per capita) | 2.9 | Cost (% of property value) | NO PRACTICE | Cost to export (US$ per container) | 750 |
| Minimum capital (% of income per capita) | 126.6 | | | Documents to import (number) | 7 |
| | | **Getting credit** (rank) | 159 | Time to import (days) | 26 |
| **Dealing with construction permits** (rank) | 116 | Strength of legal rights index (0-10) | 2 | Cost to import (US$ per container) | 755 |
| Procedures (number) | 19 | Depth of credit information index (0-6) | 3 | | |
| Time (days) | 238 | Public registry coverage (% of adults) | 2.0 | **Enforcing contracts** (rank) | 185 |
| Cost (% of income per capita) | 13.9 | Private bureau coverage (% of adults) | 0.0 | Procedures (number) | 51 |
| | | | | Time (days) | 1,285 |
| **Getting electricity** (rank) | 40 | **Protecting investors** (rank) | 139 | Cost (% of claim) | 163.2 |
| Procedures (number) | 3 | Extent of disclosure index (0-10) | 3 | | |
| Time (days) | 63 | Extent of director liability index (0-10) | 4 | **Resolving insolvency** (rank) | 185 |
| Cost (% of income per capita) | 593.0 | Ease of shareholder suits index (0-10) | 5 | Time (years) | NO PRACTICE |
| | | Strength of investor protection index (0-10) | 4.0 | Cost (% of estate) | NO PRACTICE |
| | | | | Recovery rate (cents on the dollar) | 0.0 |
| | | **Paying taxes** (rank) | 61 | | |
| | | Payments (number per year) | 18 | | |
| | | Time (hours per year) | 276 | | |
| | | Total tax rate (% of profit) | 15.1 | | |

## TOGO

| | | | | | | |
|---|---|---|---|---|---|---|
| Ease of doing business (rank) | 156 | Sub-Saharan Africa Low income | | GNI per capita (US$) Population (m) | 560 6.2 |

| | | | | | |
|---|---|---|---|---|---|
| ✔ **Starting a business** (rank) | 164 | **Registering property** (rank) | 160 | **Trading across borders** (rank) | 101 |
| Procedures (number) | 6 | Procedures (number) | 5 | Documents to export (number) | 6 |
| Time (days) | 38 | Time (days) | 295 | Time to export (days) | 24 |
| Cost (% of income per capita) | 119.4 | Cost (% of property value) | 12.5 | Cost to export (US$ per container) | 940 |
| Minimum capital (% of income per capita) | 365.6 | | | Documents to import (number) | 8 |
| | | **Getting credit** (rank) | 129 | Time to import (days) | 28 |
| **Dealing with construction permits** (rank) | 137 | Strength of legal rights index (0-10) | 6 | Cost to import (US$ per container) | 1,109 |
| Procedures (number) | 12 | Depth of credit information index (0-6) | 1 | | |
| Time (days) | 309 | Public registry coverage (% of adults) | 2.8 | **Enforcing contracts** (rank) | 157 |
| Cost (% of income per capita) | 431.5 | Private bureau coverage (% of adults) | 0.0 | Procedures (number) | 41 |
| | | | | Time (days) | 588 |
| **Getting electricity** (rank) | 89 | **Protecting investors** (rank) | 150 | Cost (% of claim) | 47.5 |
| Procedures (number) | 4 | Extent of disclosure index (0-10) | 6 | | |
| Time (days) | 74 | Extent of director liability index (0-10) | 1 | **Resolving insolvency** (rank) | 96 |
| Cost (% of income per capita) | 4,732.5 | Ease of shareholder suits index (0-10) | 4 | Time (years) | 3.0 |
| | | Strength of investor protection index (0-10) | 3.7 | Cost (% of estate) | 15 |
| | | | | Recovery rate (cents on the dollar) | 30.5 |
| | | **Paying taxes** (rank) | 167 | | |
| | | Payments (number per year) | 53 | | |
| | | Time (hours per year) | 270 | | |
| | | Total tax rate (% of profit) | 49.5 | | |

*Note:* Most indicator sets refer to a case scenario in an economy's largest business city. For more details, see the data notes.

✔ Reform making it easier to do business ✘ Reform making it more difficult to do business

## TONGA

| | | | | | | |
|---|---|---|---|---|---|---|
| Ease of doing business (rank) | 62 | East Asia & Pacific<br>Lower middle income | | GNI per capita (US$)<br>Population (m) | 3,580<br>0.1 | |

| | | | | | |
|---|---|---|---|---|---|
| **Starting a business** (rank) | 35 | **Registering property** (rank) | 142 | **Trading across borders** (rank) | 77 |
| Procedures (number) | 4 | Procedures (number) | 4 | Documents to export (number) | 6 |
| Time (days) | 16 | Time (days) | 112 | Time to export (days) | 22 |
| Cost (% of income per capita) | 8.3 | Cost (% of property value) | 15.1 | Cost to export (US$ per container) | 755 |
| Minimum capital (% of income per capita) | 0.0 | | | Documents to import (number) | 6 |
| | | **Getting credit** (rank) | 83 | Time to import (days) | 26 |
| **Dealing with construction permits** (rank) | 37 | Strength of legal rights index (0-10) | 9 | Cost to import (US$ per container) | 740 |
| Procedures (number) | 13 | Depth of credit information index (0-6) | 0 | | |
| Time (days) | 69 | Public registry coverage (% of adults) | 0.0 | **Enforcing contracts** (rank) | 54 |
| Cost (% of income per capita) | 103.4 | Private bureau coverage (% of adults) | 0.0 | Procedures (number) | 37 |
| | | | | Time (days) | 350 |
| **Getting electricity** (rank) | 30 | **Protecting investors** (rank) | 117 | Cost (% of claim) | 30.5 |
| Procedures (number) | 5 | Extent of disclosure index (0-10) | 3 | | |
| Time (days) | 42 | Extent of director liability index (0-10) | 3 | **Resolving insolvency** (rank) | 118 |
| Cost (% of income per capita) | 101.5 | Ease of shareholder suits index (0-10) | 8 | Time (years) | 2.7 |
| | | Strength of investor protection index (0-10) | 4.7 | Cost (% of estate) | 22 |
| | | | | Recovery rate (cents on the dollar) | 25.7 |
| | | **Paying taxes** (rank) | 40 | | |
| | | Payments (number per year) | 31 | | |
| | | Time (hours per year) | 164 | | |
| | | Total tax rate (% of profit) | 25.7 | | |

## TRINIDAD AND TOBAGO

| | | | | | | |
|---|---|---|---|---|---|---|
| Ease of doing business (rank) | 69 | Latin America & Caribbean<br>High income | | GNI per capita (US$)<br>Population (m) | 15,040<br>1.3 | |

| | | | | | |
|---|---|---|---|---|---|
| **Starting a business** (rank) | 71 | ✔ **Registering property** (rank) | 176 | ✔ **Trading across borders** (rank) | 75 |
| Procedures (number) | 8 | Procedures (number) | 9 | Documents to export (number) | 5 |
| Time (days) | 41 | Time (days) | 78 | Time to export (days) | 11 |
| Cost (% of income per capita) | 0.7 | Cost (% of property value) | 7.0 | Cost to export (US$ per container) | 843 |
| Minimum capital (% of income per capita) | 0.0 | | | Documents to import (number) | 10 |
| | | **Getting credit** (rank) | 23 | Time to import (days) | 14 |
| **Dealing with construction permits** (rank) | 101 | Strength of legal rights index (0-10) | 9 | Cost to import (US$ per container) | 1,260 |
| Procedures (number) | 17 | Depth of credit information index (0-6) | 4 | | |
| Time (days) | 297 | Public registry coverage (% of adults) | 0.0 | **Enforcing contracts** (rank) | 170 |
| Cost (% of income per capita) | 5.3 | Private bureau coverage (% of adults) | 46.0 | Procedures (number) | 42 |
| | | | | Time (days) | 1,340 |
| **Getting electricity** (rank) | 11 | **Protecting investors** (rank) | 25 | Cost (% of claim) | 33.5 |
| Procedures (number) | 4 | Extent of disclosure index (0-10) | 4 | | |
| Time (days) | 61 | Extent of director liability index (0-10) | 9 | **Resolving insolvency** (rank) | 135 |
| Cost (% of income per capita) | 6.6 | Ease of shareholder suits index (0-10) | 7 | Time (years) | 4.0 |
| | | Strength of investor protection index (0-10) | 6.7 | Cost (% of estate) | 25 |
| | | | | Recovery rate (cents on the dollar) | 18.4 |
| | | **Paying taxes** (rank) | 90 | | |
| | | Payments (number per year) | 39 | | |
| | | Time (hours per year) | 210 | | |
| | | Total tax rate (% of profit) | 29.1 | | |

## TUNISIA

| | | | | | | |
|---|---|---|---|---|---|---|
| Ease of doing business (rank) | 50 | Middle East & North Africa<br>Upper middle income | | GNI per capita (US$)<br>Population (m) | 4,070<br>10.7 | |

| | | | | | |
|---|---|---|---|---|---|
| **Starting a business** (rank) | 66 | **Registering property** (rank) | 70 | **Trading across borders** (rank) | 30 |
| Procedures (number) | 10 | Procedures (number) | 4 | Documents to export (number) | 4 |
| Time (days) | 11 | Time (days) | 39 | Time to export (days) | 13 |
| Cost (% of income per capita) | 4.1 | Cost (% of property value) | 6.1 | Cost to export (US$ per container) | 773 |
| Minimum capital (% of income per capita) | 0.0 | | | Documents to import (number) | 7 |
| | | **Getting credit** (rank) | 104 | Time to import (days) | 17 |
| **Dealing with construction permits** (rank) | 93 | Strength of legal rights index (0-10) | 3 | Cost to import (US$ per container) | 858 |
| Procedures (number) | 17 | Depth of credit information index (0-6) | 5 | | |
| Time (days) | 88 | Public registry coverage (% of adults) | 27.8 | **Enforcing contracts** (rank) | 78 |
| Cost (% of income per capita) | 256.0 | Private bureau coverage (% of adults) | 0.0 | Procedures (number) | 39 |
| | | | | Time (days) | 565 |
| **Getting electricity** (rank) | 51 | **Protecting investors** (rank) | 49 | Cost (% of claim) | 21.8 |
| Procedures (number) | 4 | Extent of disclosure index (0-10) | 5 | | |
| Time (days) | 65 | Extent of director liability index (0-10) | 7 | **Resolving insolvency** (rank) | 39 |
| Cost (% of income per capita) | 878.5 | Ease of shareholder suits index (0-10) | 6 | Time (years) | 1.3 |
| | | Strength of investor protection index (0-10) | 6.0 | Cost (% of estate) | 7 |
| | | | | Recovery rate (cents on the dollar) | 52.0 |
| | | **Paying taxes** (rank) | 62 | | |
| | | Payments (number per year) | 8 | | |
| | | Time (hours per year) | 144 | | |
| | | Total tax rate (% of profit) | 62.9 | | |

*Note:* Most indicator sets refer to a case scenario in an economy's largest business city. For more details, see the data notes.

✔ Reform making it easier to do business    ✘ Reform making it more difficult to do business

## TURKEY

| | | | | | | | |
|---|---|---|---|---|---|---|---|
| Ease of doing business (rank) | 71 | Eastern Europe & Central Asia<br>Upper middle income | | GNI per capita (US$)<br>Population (m) | 10,410<br>73.6 | | |

| | | | | | | |
|---|---|---|---|---|---|
| **Starting a business** (rank) | 72 | **Registering property** (rank) | 42 | **Trading across borders** (rank) | 78 |
| Procedures (number) | 6 | Procedures (number) | 6 | Documents to export (number) | 7 |
| Time (days) | 6 | Time (days) | 6 | Time to export (days) | 13 |
| Cost (% of income per capita) | 10.5 | Cost (% of property value) | 3.3 | Cost to export (US$ per container) | 990 |
| Minimum capital (% of income per capita) | 7.2 | | | Documents to import (number) | 7 |
| | | **Getting credit** (rank) | 83 | Time to import (days) | 14 |
| | | Strength of legal rights index (0-10) | 4 | Cost to import (US$ per container) | 1,235 |
| ✔ **Dealing with construction permits** (rank) | 142 | Depth of credit information index (0-6) | 5 | | |
| Procedures (number) | 20 | Public registry coverage (% of adults) | 23.5 | ✔ **Enforcing contracts** (rank) | 40 |
| Time (days) | 180 | Private bureau coverage (% of adults) | 63.0 | Procedures (number) | 36 |
| Cost (% of income per capita) | 164.3 | | | Time (days) | 420 |
| | | **Protecting investors** (rank) | 70 | Cost (% of claim) | 24.9 |
| **Getting electricity** (rank) | 68 | Extent of disclosure index (0-10) | 9 | | |
| Procedures (number) | 5 | Extent of director liability index (0-10) | 4 | **Resolving insolvency** (rank) | 124 |
| Time (days) | 70 | Ease of shareholder suits index (0-10) | 4 | Time (years) | 3.3 |
| Cost (% of income per capita) | 517.9 | Strength of investor protection index (0-10) | 5.7 | Cost (% of estate) | 15 |
| | | | | Recovery rate (cents on the dollar) | 23.6 |
| | | **Paying taxes** (rank) | 80 | | |
| | | Payments (number per year) | 15 | | |
| | | Time (hours per year) | 223 | | |
| | | Total tax rate (% of profit) | 41.2 | | |

## UGANDA

| | | | | | | | |
|---|---|---|---|---|---|---|---|
| Ease of doing business (rank) | 120 | Sub-Saharan Africa<br>Low income | | GNI per capita (US$)<br>Population (m) | 510<br>34.5 | | |

| | | | | | | |
|---|---|---|---|---|---|
| **Starting a business** (rank) | 144 | ✘ **Registering property** (rank) | 124 | **Trading across borders** (rank) | 159 |
| Procedures (number) | 15 | Procedures (number) | 12 | Documents to export (number) | 7 |
| Time (days) | 33 | Time (days) | 52 | Time to export (days) | 33 |
| Cost (% of income per capita) | 76.7 | Cost (% of property value) | 1.9 | Cost to export (US$ per container) | 3,050 |
| Minimum capital (% of income per capita) | 0.0 | | | Documents to import (number) | 9 |
| | | **Getting credit** (rank) | 40 | Time to import (days) | 33 |
| | | Strength of legal rights index (0-10) | 7 | Cost to import (US$ per container) | 3,215 |
| **Dealing with construction permits** (rank) | 118 | Depth of credit information index (0-6) | 5 | | |
| Procedures (number) | 15 | Public registry coverage (% of adults) | 0.0 | **Enforcing contracts** (rank) | 117 |
| Time (days) | 125 | Private bureau coverage (% of adults) | 3.7 | Procedures (number) | 38 |
| Cost (% of income per capita) | 853.1 | | | Time (days) | 490 |
| | | **Protecting investors** (rank) | 139 | Cost (% of claim) | 44.9 |
| **Getting electricity** (rank) | 127 | Extent of disclosure index (0-10) | 2 | | |
| Procedures (number) | 5 | Extent of director liability index (0-10) | 5 | ✔ **Resolving insolvency** (rank) | 69 |
| Time (days) | 91 | Ease of shareholder suits index (0-10) | 5 | Time (years) | 2.2 |
| Cost (% of income per capita) | 4,622.9 | Strength of investor protection index (0-10) | 4.0 | Cost (% of estate) | 30 |
| | | | | Recovery rate (cents on the dollar) | 38.9 |
| | | **Paying taxes** (rank) | 93 | | |
| | | Payments (number per year) | 31 | | |
| | | Time (hours per year) | 213 | | |
| | | Total tax rate (% of profit) | 37.1 | | |

## UKRAINE

| | | | | | | | |
|---|---|---|---|---|---|---|---|
| Ease of doing business (rank) | 137 | Eastern Europe & Central Asia<br>Lower middle income | | GNI per capita (US$)<br>Population (m) | 3,120<br>45.7 | | |

| | | | | | | |
|---|---|---|---|---|---|
| ✔ **Starting a business** (rank) | 50 | ✔ **Registering property** (rank) | 149 | **Trading across borders** (rank) | 145 |
| Procedures (number) | 7 | Procedures (number) | 10 | Documents to export (number) | 6 |
| Time (days) | 22 | Time (days) | 69 | Time to export (days) | 30 |
| Cost (% of income per capita) | 1.5 | Cost (% of property value) | 3.7 | Cost to export (US$ per container) | 1,865 |
| Minimum capital (% of income per capita) | 0.0 | | | Documents to import (number) | 8 |
| | | **Getting credit** (rank) | 23 | Time to import (days) | 33 |
| | | Strength of legal rights index (0-10) | 9 | Cost to import (US$ per container) | 2,155 |
| **Dealing with construction permits** (rank) | 183 | Depth of credit information index (0-6) | 4 | | |
| Procedures (number) | 20 | Public registry coverage (% of adults) | 0.0 | **Enforcing contracts** (rank) | 42 |
| Time (days) | 375 | Private bureau coverage (% of adults) | 23.3 | Procedures (number) | 30 |
| Cost (% of income per capita) | 1,262.6 | | | Time (days) | 343 |
| | | **Protecting investors** (rank) | 117 | Cost (% of claim) | 41.5 |
| **Getting electricity** (rank) | 166 | Extent of disclosure index (0-10) | 5 | | |
| Procedures (number) | 11 | Extent of director liability index (0-10) | 2 | **Resolving insolvency** (rank) | 157 |
| Time (days) | 285 | Ease of shareholder suits index (0-10) | 7 | Time (years) | 2.9 |
| Cost (% of income per capita) | 192.3 | Strength of investor protection index (0-10) | 4.7 | Cost (% of estate) | 42 |
| | | | | Recovery rate (cents on the dollar) | 8.7 |
| | | ✔ **Paying taxes** (rank) | 165 | | |
| | | Payments (number per year) | 28 | | |
| | | Time (hours per year) | 491 | | |
| | | Total tax rate (% of profit) | 55.4 | | |

*Note:* Most indicator sets refer to a case scenario in an economy's largest business city. For more details, see the data notes.

✔ Reform making it easier to do business ✗ Reform making it more difficult to do business

## UNITED ARAB EMIRATES

| | | | | | | |
|---|---|---|---|---|---|---|
| Ease of doing business (rank) | 26 | Middle East & North Africa<br>High income | | GNI per capita (US$)<br>Population (m) | 40,760<br>7.9 |

| | | | | | |
|---|---|---|---|---|---|
| ✔ **Starting a business** (rank) | 22 | **Registering property** (rank) | 12 | **Trading across borders** (rank) | 5 |
| Procedures (number) | 6 | Procedures (number) | 2 | Documents to export (number) | 4 |
| Time (days) | 8 | Time (days) | 10 | Time to export (days) | 7 |
| Cost (% of income per capita) | 6.0 | Cost (% of property value) | 2.3 | Cost to export (US$ per container) | 630 |
| Minimum capital (% of income per capita) | 0.0 | | | Documents to import (number) | 5 |
| | | **Getting credit** (rank) | 83 | Time to import (days) | 7 |
| **Dealing with construction permits** (rank) | 13 | Strength of legal rights index (0-10) | 4 | Cost to import (US$ per container) | 590 |
| Procedures (number) | 14 | Depth of credit information index (0-6) | 5 | | |
| Time (days) | 46 | Public registry coverage (% of adults) | 5.9 | **Enforcing contracts** (rank) | 104 |
| Cost (% of income per capita) | 9.2 | Private bureau coverage (% of adults) | 31.7 | Procedures (number) | 49 |
| | | | | Time (days) | 524 |
| ✔ **Getting electricity** (rank) | 7 | **Protecting investors** (rank) | 128 | Cost (% of claim) | 19.5 |
| Procedures (number) | 4 | Extent of disclosure index (0-10) | 4 | | |
| Time (days) | 40 | Extent of director liability index (0-10) | 7 | **Resolving insolvency** (rank) | 101 |
| Cost (% of income per capita) | 19.3 | Ease of shareholder suits index (0-10) | 2 | Time (years) | 3.2 |
| | | Strength of investor protection index (0-10) | 4.3 | Cost (% of estate) | 20 |
| | | | | Recovery rate (cents on the dollar) | 29.4 |
| | | ✔ **Paying taxes** (rank) | 1 | | |
| | | Payments (number per year) | 4 | | |
| | | Time (hours per year) | 12 | | |
| | | Total tax rate (% of profit) | 14.9 | | |

## UNITED KINGDOM

| | | | | | | |
|---|---|---|---|---|---|---|
| Ease of doing business (rank) | 7 | OECD high income<br>High income | | GNI per capita (US$)<br>Population (m) | 37,780<br>62.6 |

| | | | | | |
|---|---|---|---|---|---|
| **Starting a business** (rank) | 19 | **Registering property** (rank) | 73 | **Trading across borders** (rank) | 14 |
| Procedures (number) | 6 | Procedures (number) | 6 | Documents to export (number) | 4 |
| Time (days) | 13 | Time (days) | 29 | Time to export (days) | 7 |
| Cost (% of income per capita) | 0.7 | Cost (% of property value) | 4.7 | Cost to export (US$ per container) | 950 |
| Minimum capital (% of income per capita) | 0.0 | | | Documents to import (number) | 4 |
| | | **Getting credit** (rank) | 1 | Time to import (days) | 6 |
| **Dealing with construction permits** (rank) | 20 | Strength of legal rights index (0-10) | 10 | Cost to import (US$ per container) | 1,045 |
| Procedures (number) | 9 | Depth of credit information index (0-6) | 6 | | |
| Time (days) | 99 | Public registry coverage (% of adults) | 0.0 | **Enforcing contracts** (rank) | 21 |
| Cost (% of income per capita) | 62.4 | Private bureau coverage (% of adults) | 100.0 | Procedures (number) | 28 |
| | | | | Time (days) | 399 |
| **Getting electricity** (rank) | 62 | **Protecting investors** (rank) | 10 | Cost (% of claim) | 25.9 |
| Procedures (number) | 5 | Extent of disclosure index (0-10) | 10 | | |
| Time (days) | 105 | Extent of director liability index (0-10) | 7 | **Resolving insolvency** (rank) | 8 |
| Cost (% of income per capita) | 108.9 | Ease of shareholder suits index (0-10) | 7 | Time (years) | 1.0 |
| | | Strength of investor protection index (0-10) | 8.0 | Cost (% of estate) | 6 |
| | | | | Recovery rate (cents on the dollar) | 88.6 |
| | | ✔ **Paying taxes** (rank) | 16 | | |
| | | Payments (number per year) | 8 | | |
| | | Time (hours per year) | 110 | | |
| | | Total tax rate (% of profit) | 35.5 | | |

## UNITED STATES

| | | | | | | |
|---|---|---|---|---|---|---|
| Ease of doing business (rank) | 4 | OECD high income<br>High income | | GNI per capita (US$)<br>Population (m) | 48,450<br>311.6 |

| | | | | | |
|---|---|---|---|---|---|
| **Starting a business** (rank) | 13 | **Registering property** (rank) | 25 | **Trading across borders** (rank) | 22 |
| Procedures (number) | 6 | Procedures (number) | 4 | Documents to export (number) | 4 |
| Time (days) | 6 | Time (days) | 12 | Time to export (days) | 6 |
| Cost (% of income per capita) | 1.4 | Cost (% of property value) | 3.5 | Cost to export (US$ per container) | 1,090 |
| Minimum capital (% of income per capita) | 0.0 | | | Documents to import (number) | 5 |
| | | **Getting credit** (rank) | 4 | Time to import (days) | 5 |
| **Dealing with construction permits** (rank) | 17 | Strength of legal rights index (0-10) | 9 | Cost to import (US$ per container) | 1,315 |
| Procedures (number) | 15 | Depth of credit information index (0-6) | 6 | | |
| Time (days) | 27 | Public registry coverage (% of adults) | 0.0 | **Enforcing contracts** (rank) | 6 |
| Cost (% of income per capita) | 14.4 | Private bureau coverage (% of adults) | 100.0 | Procedures (number) | 32 |
| | | | | Time (days) | 370 |
| **Getting electricity** (rank) | 19 | **Protecting investors** (rank) | 6 | Cost (% of claim) | 14.4 |
| Procedures (number) | 4 | Extent of disclosure index (0-10) | 7 | | |
| Time (days) | 68 | Extent of director liability index (0-10) | 9 | **Resolving insolvency** (rank) | 16 |
| Cost (% of income per capita) | 16.1 | Ease of shareholder suits index (0-10) | 9 | Time (years) | 1.5 |
| | | Strength of investor protection index (0-10) | 8.3 | Cost (% of estate) | 7 |
| | | | | Recovery rate (cents on the dollar) | 81.5 |
| | | **Paying taxes** (rank) | 69 | | |
| | | Payments (number per year) | 11 | | |
| | | Time (hours per year) | 175 | | |
| | | Total tax rate (% of profit) | 46.7 | | |

*Note:* Most indicator sets refer to a case scenario in an economy's largest business city. For more details, see the data notes.

## URUGUAY

| | | | | | | |
|---|---|---|---|---|---|---|
| Ease of doing business (rank) | 89 | Latin America & Caribbean<br>Upper middle income | | GNI per capita (US$)<br>Population (m) | | 11,860<br>3.4 |
| **Starting a business** (rank) | 39 | **Registering property** (rank) | 164 | ✔ **Trading across borders** (rank) | | 104 |
| Procedures (number) | 5 | Procedures (number) | 8 | Documents to export (number) | | 7 |
| Time (days) | 7 | Time (days) | 66 | Time to export (days) | | 16 |
| Cost (% of income per capita) | 24.3 | Cost (% of property value) | 7.1 | Cost to export (US$ per container) | | 1,125 |
| Minimum capital (% of income per capita) | 0.0 | | | Documents to import (number) | | 8 |
| | | **Getting credit** (rank) | 70 | Time to import (days) | | 18 |
| **Dealing with construction permits** (rank) | 158 | Strength of legal rights index (0-10) | 4 | Cost to import (US$ per container) | | 1,440 |
| Procedures (number) | 27 | Depth of credit information index (0-6) | 6 | | | |
| Time (days) | 234 | Public registry coverage (% of adults) | 32.9 | **Enforcing contracts** (rank) | | 102 |
| Cost (% of income per capita) | 67.0 | Private bureau coverage (% of adults) | 100.0 | Procedures (number) | | 41 |
| | | | | Time (days) | | 725 |
| **Getting electricity** (rank) | 20 | **Protecting investors** (rank) | 100 | Cost (% of claim) | | 19.0 |
| Procedures (number) | 5 | Extent of disclosure index (0-10) | 3 | | | |
| Time (days) | 48 | Extent of director liability index (0-10) | 4 | **Resolving insolvency** (rank) | | 54 |
| Cost (% of income per capita) | 14.3 | Ease of shareholder suits index (0-10) | 8 | Time (years) | | 2.1 |
| | | Strength of investor protection index (0-10) | 5.0 | Cost (% of estate) | | 7 |
| | | | | Recovery rate (cents on the dollar) | | 43.3 |
| | | ✔ **Paying taxes** (rank) | 140 | | | |
| | | Payments (number per year) | 33 | | | |
| | | Time (hours per year) | 310 | | | |
| | | Total tax rate (% of profit) | 42.0 | | | |

## UZBEKISTAN

| | | | | | | |
|---|---|---|---|---|---|---|
| Ease of doing business (rank) | 154 | Eastern Europe & Central Asia<br>Lower middle income | | GNI per capita (US$)<br>Population (m) | | 1,510<br>29.3 |
| ✔ **Starting a business** (rank) | 90 | **Registering property** (rank) | 138 | ✔ **Trading across borders** (rank) | | 185 |
| Procedures (number) | 6 | Procedures (number) | 15 | Documents to export (number) | | 13 |
| Time (days) | 12 | Time (days) | 78 | Time to export (days) | | 80 |
| Cost (% of income per capita) | 3.8 | Cost (% of property value) | 1.0 | Cost to export (US$ per container) | | 4,585 |
| Minimum capital (% of income per capita) | 27.4 | | | Documents to import (number) | | 14 |
| | | ✔ **Getting credit** (rank) | 154 | Time to import (days) | | 99 |
| **Dealing with construction permits** (rank) | 152 | Strength of legal rights index (0-10) | 2 | Cost to import (US$ per container) | | 4,750 |
| Procedures (number) | 25 | Depth of credit information index (0-6) | 4 | | | |
| Time (days) | 243 | Public registry coverage (% of adults) | 0.0 | **Enforcing contracts** (rank) | | 46 |
| Cost (% of income per capita) | 60.7 | Private bureau coverage (% of adults) | 15.7 | Procedures (number) | | 42 |
| | | | | Time (days) | | 195 |
| **Getting electricity** (rank) | 167 | **Protecting investors** (rank) | 139 | Cost (% of claim) | | 22.2 |
| Procedures (number) | 9 | Extent of disclosure index (0-10) | 4 | | | |
| Time (days) | 108 | Extent of director liability index (0-10) | 1 | ✔ **Resolving insolvency** (rank) | | 73 |
| Cost (% of income per capita) | 1,420.3 | Ease of shareholder suits index (0-10) | 7 | Time (years) | | 2.0 |
| | | Strength of investor protection index (0-10) | 4.0 | Cost (% of estate) | | 10 |
| | | | | Recovery rate (cents on the dollar) | | 38.5 |
| | | **Paying taxes** (rank) | 161 | | | |
| | | Payments (number per year) | 41 | | | |
| | | Time (hours per year) | 205 | | | |
| | | Total tax rate (% of profit) | 98.5 | | | |

## VANUATU

| | | | | | | |
|---|---|---|---|---|---|---|
| Ease of doing business (rank) | 80 | East Asia & Pacific<br>Lower middle income | | GNI per capita (US$)<br>Population (m) | | 2,870<br>0.2 |
| **Starting a business** (rank) | 116 | **Registering property** (rank) | 110 | **Trading across borders** (rank) | | 132 |
| Procedures (number) | 8 | Procedures (number) | 4 | Documents to export (number) | | 7 |
| Time (days) | 35 | Time (days) | 118 | Time to export (days) | | 21 |
| Cost (% of income per capita) | 47.2 | Cost (% of property value) | 7.0 | Cost to export (US$ per container) | | 1,690 |
| Minimum capital (% of income per capita) | 0.0 | | | Documents to import (number) | | 8 |
| | | **Getting credit** (rank) | 83 | Time to import (days) | | 20 |
| ✘ **Dealing with construction permits** (rank) | 48 | Strength of legal rights index (0-10) | 9 | Cost to import (US$ per container) | | 1,690 |
| Procedures (number) | 12 | Depth of credit information index (0-6) | 0 | | | |
| Time (days) | 54 | Public registry coverage (% of adults) | 0.0 | **Enforcing contracts** (rank) | | 74 |
| Cost (% of income per capita) | 431.2 | Private bureau coverage (% of adults) | 0.0 | Procedures (number) | | 30 |
| | | | | Time (days) | | 430 |
| **Getting electricity** (rank) | 124 | **Protecting investors** (rank) | 82 | Cost (% of claim) | | 56.0 |
| Procedures (number) | 5 | Extent of disclosure index (0-10) | 5 | | | |
| Time (days) | 122 | Extent of director liability index (0-10) | 6 | **Resolving insolvency** (rank) | | 57 |
| Cost (% of income per capita) | 1,248.1 | Ease of shareholder suits index (0-10) | 5 | Time (years) | | 2.6 |
| | | Strength of investor protection index (0-10) | 5.3 | Cost (% of estate) | | 38 |
| | | | | Recovery rate (cents on the dollar) | | 42.7 |
| | | **Paying taxes** (rank) | 28 | | | |
| | | Payments (number per year) | 31 | | | |
| | | Time (hours per year) | 120 | | | |
| | | Total tax rate (% of profit) | 8.4 | | | |

*Note:* Most indicator sets refer to a case scenario in an economy's largest business city. For more details, see the data notes.

✔ Reform making it easier to do business  ✗ Reform making it more difficult to do business

## VENEZUELA, RB

| | | | | | | |
|---|---|---|---|---|---|
| Ease of doing business (rank) | 180 | Latin America & Caribbean<br>Upper middle income | | GNI per capita (US$)<br>Population (m) | 11,920<br>29.3 |

| | | | | | |
|---|---|---|---|---|---|
| ✗ **Starting a business** (rank) | 152 | **Registering property** (rank) | 90 | **Trading across borders** (rank) | 166 |
| Procedures (number) | 17 | Procedures (number) | 8 | Documents to export (number) | 8 |
| Time (days) | 144 | Time (days) | 38 | Time to export (days) | 49 |
| Cost (% of income per capita) | 27.7 | Cost (% of property value) | 2.5 | Cost to export (US$ per container) | 2,590 |
| Minimum capital (% of income per capita) | 0.0 | | | Documents to import (number) | 9 |
| | | **Getting credit** (rank) | 159 | Time to import (days) | 71 |
| **Dealing with construction permits** (rank) | 109 | Strength of legal rights index (0-10) | 1 | Cost to import (US$ per container) | 2,868 |
| Procedures (number) | 10 | Depth of credit information index (0-6) | 4 | | |
| Time (days) | 381 | Public registry coverage (% of adults) | 0.0 | **Enforcing contracts** (rank) | 80 |
| Cost (% of income per capita) | 123.5 | Private bureau coverage (% of adults) | 15.7 | Procedures (number) | 30 |
| | | | | Time (days) | 510 |
| **Getting electricity** (rank) | 160 | **Protecting investors** (rank) | 181 | Cost (% of claim) | 43.7 |
| Procedures (number) | 6 | Extent of disclosure index (0-10) | 3 | | |
| Time (days) | 158 | Extent of director liability index (0-10) | 2 | **Resolving insolvency** (rank) | 163 |
| Cost (% of income per capita) | 1,022.6 | Ease of shareholder suits index (0-10) | 2 | Time (years) | 4.0 |
| | | Strength of investor protection index (0-10) | 2.3 | Cost (% of estate) | 38 |
| | | | | Recovery rate (cents on the dollar) | 6.4 |
| | | ✗ **Paying taxes** (rank) | 185 | | |
| | | Payments (number per year) | 71 | | |
| | | Time (hours per year) | 792 | | |
| | | Total tax rate (% of profit) | 62.7 | | |

## VIETNAM

| | | | | | | |
|---|---|---|---|---|---|
| Ease of doing business (rank) | 99 | East Asia & Pacific<br>Lower middle income | | GNI per capita (US$)<br>Population (m) | 1,260<br>87.8 |

| | | | | | |
|---|---|---|---|---|---|
| ✔ **Starting a business** (rank) | 108 | **Registering property** (rank) | 48 | **Trading across borders** (rank) | 74 |
| Procedures (number) | 10 | Procedures (number) | 4 | Documents to export (number) | 6 |
| Time (days) | 34 | Time (days) | 57 | Time to export (days) | 21 |
| Cost (% of income per capita) | 8.7 | Cost (% of property value) | 0.6 | Cost to export (US$ per container) | 610 |
| Minimum capital (% of income per capita) | 0.0 | | | Documents to import (number) | 8 |
| | | **Getting credit** (rank) | 40 | Time to import (days) | 21 |
| **Dealing with construction permits** (rank) | 28 | Strength of legal rights index (0-10) | 8 | Cost to import (US$ per container) | 600 |
| Procedures (number) | 11 | Depth of credit information index (0-6) | 4 | | |
| Time (days) | 110 | Public registry coverage (% of adults) | 37.8 | **Enforcing contracts** (rank) | 44 |
| Cost (% of income per capita) | 67.3 | Private bureau coverage (% of adults) | 0.0 | Procedures (number) | 34 |
| | | | | Time (days) | 400 |
| **Getting electricity** (rank) | 155 | **Protecting investors** (rank) | 169 | Cost (% of claim) | 29.0 |
| Procedures (number) | 6 | Extent of disclosure index (0-10) | 6 | | |
| Time (days) | 115 | Extent of director liability index (0-10) | 1 | **Resolving insolvency** (rank) | 149 |
| Cost (% of income per capita) | 1,988.3 | Ease of shareholder suits index (0-10) | 2 | Time (years) | 5.0 |
| | | Strength of investor protection index (0-10) | 3.0 | Cost (% of estate) | 15 |
| | | | | Recovery rate (cents on the dollar) | 13.9 |
| | | **Paying taxes** (rank) | 138 | | |
| | | Payments (number per year) | 32 | | |
| | | Time (hours per year) | 872 | | |
| | | Total tax rate (% of profit) | 34.5 | | |

## WEST BANK AND GAZA

| | | | | | | |
|---|---|---|---|---|---|
| Ease of doing business (rank) | 135 | Middle East & North Africa<br>Lower middle income | | GNI per capita (US$)<br>Population (m) | 1,610<br>4.0 |

| | | | | | |
|---|---|---|---|---|---|
| **Starting a business** (rank) | 179 | ✗ **Registering property** (rank) | 78 | **Trading across borders** (rank) | 114 |
| Procedures (number) | 11 | Procedures (number) | 7 | Documents to export (number) | 6 |
| Time (days) | 48 | Time (days) | 30 | Time to export (days) | 23 |
| Cost (% of income per capita) | 91.0 | Cost (% of property value) | 3.0 | Cost to export (US$ per container) | 1,310 |
| Minimum capital (% of income per capita) | 206.7 | | | Documents to import (number) | 6 |
| | | ✔ **Getting credit** (rank) | 159 | Time to import (days) | 38 |
| **Dealing with construction permits** (rank) | 130 | Strength of legal rights index (0-10) | 1 | Cost to import (US$ per container) | 1,295 |
| Procedures (number) | 17 | Depth of credit information index (0-6) | 4 | | |
| Time (days) | 119 | Public registry coverage (% of adults) | 8.1 | **Enforcing contracts** (rank) | 93 |
| Cost (% of income per capita) | 948.1 | Private bureau coverage (% of adults) | 0.0 | Procedures (number) | 44 |
| | | | | Time (days) | 540 |
| **Getting electricity** (rank) | 85 | **Protecting investors** (rank) | 49 | Cost (% of claim) | 21.2 |
| Procedures (number) | 5 | Extent of disclosure index (0-10) | 6 | | |
| Time (days) | 63 | Extent of director liability index (0-10) | 5 | **Resolving insolvency** (rank) | 185 |
| Cost (% of income per capita) | 1,549.1 | Ease of shareholder suits index (0-10) | 7 | Time (years) | NO PRACTICE |
| | | Strength of investor protection index (0-10) | 6.0 | Cost (% of estate) | NO PRACTICE |
| | | | | Recovery rate (cents on the dollar) | 0.0 |
| | | **Paying taxes** (rank) | 55 | | |
| | | Payments (number per year) | 39 | | |
| | | Time (hours per year) | 154 | | |
| | | Total tax rate (% of profit) | 16.8 | | |

*Note:* Most indicator sets refer to a case scenario in an economy's largest business city. For more details, see the data notes.

✔ Reform making it easier to do business  ✘ Reform making it more difficult to do business

## YEMEN, REP.

| | | Middle East & North Africa | | GNI per capita (US$) | 1,070 |
|---|---|---|---|---|---|
| Ease of doing business (rank) | 118 | Lower middle income | | Population (m) | 24.8 |

| | | | | | |
|---|---|---|---|---|---|
| **Starting a business** (rank) | 110 | **Registering property** (rank) | 59 | **Trading across borders** (rank) | 121 |
| Procedures (number) | 6 | Procedures (number) | 6 | Documents to export (number) | 6 |
| Time (days) | 40 | Time (days) | 19 | Time to export (days) | 29 |
| Cost (% of income per capita) | 71.9 | Cost (% of property value) | 3.8 | Cost to export (US$ per container) | 995 |
| Minimum capital (% of income per capita) | 0.0 | | | Documents to import (number) | 9 |
| | | **Getting credit** (rank) | 167 | Time to import (days) | 25 |
| **Dealing with construction permits** (rank) | 62 | Strength of legal rights index (0-10) | 2 | Cost to import (US$ per container) | 1,490 |
| Procedures (number) | 12 | Depth of credit information index (0-6) | 2 | | |
| Time (days) | 191 | Public registry coverage (% of adults) | 0.9 | **Enforcing contracts** (rank) | 45 |
| Cost (% of income per capita) | 52.4 | Private bureau coverage (% of adults) | 0.0 | Procedures (number) | 36 |
| | | | | Time (days) | 569 |
| **Getting electricity** (rank) | 112 | **Protecting investors** (rank) | 139 | Cost (% of claim) | 16.5 |
| Procedures (number) | 4 | Extent of disclosure index (0-10) | 6 | | |
| Time (days) | 110 | Extent of director liability index (0-10) | 4 | **Resolving insolvency** (rank) | 122 |
| Cost (% of income per capita) | 3,921.2 | Ease of shareholder suits index (0-10) | 2 | Time (years) | 3.0 |
| | | Strength of investor protection index (0-10) | 4.0 | Cost (% of estate) | 8 |
| | | | | Recovery rate (cents on the dollar) | 24.1 |
| | | **Paying taxes** (rank) | 113 | | |
| | | Payments (number per year) | 44 | | |
| | | Time (hours per year) | 248 | | |
| | | Total tax rate (% of profit) | 32.9 | | |

## ZAMBIA

| | | Sub-Saharan Africa | | GNI per capita (US$) | 1,160 |
|---|---|---|---|---|---|
| Ease of doing business (rank) | 94 | Lower middle income | | Population (m) | 13.5 |

| | | | | | |
|---|---|---|---|---|---|
| **Starting a business** (rank) | 74 | **Registering property** (rank) | 96 | **Trading across borders** (rank) | 156 |
| Procedures (number) | 6 | Procedures (number) | 5 | Documents to export (number) | 6 |
| Time (days) | 17 | Time (days) | 40 | Time to export (days) | 44 |
| Cost (% of income per capita) | 26.6 | Cost (% of property value) | 8.2 | Cost to export (US$ per container) | 2,765 |
| Minimum capital (% of income per capita) | 0.0 | | | Documents to import (number) | 8 |
| | | **Getting credit** (rank) | 12 | Time to import (days) | 56 |
| **Dealing with construction permits** (rank) | 151 | Strength of legal rights index (0-10) | 9 | Cost to import (US$ per container) | 3,560 |
| Procedures (number) | 14 | Depth of credit information index (0-6) | 5 | | |
| Time (days) | 196 | Public registry coverage (% of adults) | 0.0 | **Enforcing contracts** (rank) | 89 |
| Cost (% of income per capita) | 1,679.1 | Private bureau coverage (% of adults) | 5.4 | Procedures (number) | 35 |
| | | | | Time (days) | 471 |
| **Getting electricity** (rank) | 151 | **Protecting investors** (rank) | 82 | Cost (% of claim) | 38.7 |
| Procedures (number) | 6 | Extent of disclosure index (0-10) | 3 | | |
| Time (days) | 117 | Extent of director liability index (0-10) | 6 | ✔ **Resolving insolvency** (rank) | 99 |
| Cost (% of income per capita) | 1,109.5 | Ease of shareholder suits index (0-10) | 7 | Time (years) | 2.7 |
| | | Strength of investor protection index (0-10) | 5.3 | Cost (% of estate) | 9 |
| | | | | Recovery rate (cents on the dollar) | 29.8 |
| | | **Paying taxes** (rank) | 47 | | |
| | | Payments (number per year) | 37 | | |
| | | Time (hours per year) | 132 | | |
| | | Total tax rate (% of profit) | 15.2 | | |

## ZIMBABWE

| | | Sub-Saharan Africa | | GNI per capita (US$) | 640 |
|---|---|---|---|---|---|
| Ease of doing business (rank) | 172 | Low income | | Population (m) | 12.8 |

| | | | | | |
|---|---|---|---|---|---|
| **Starting a business** (rank) | 143 | **Registering property** (rank) | 85 | **Trading across borders** (rank) | 167 |
| Procedures (number) | 9 | Procedures (number) | 5 | Documents to export (number) | 8 |
| Time (days) | 90 | Time (days) | 31 | Time to export (days) | 53 |
| Cost (% of income per capita) | 107.0 | Cost (% of property value) | 7.8 | Cost to export (US$ per container) | 3,280 |
| Minimum capital (% of income per capita) | 0.0 | | | Documents to import (number) | 8 |
| | | **Getting credit** (rank) | 129 | Time to import (days) | 73 |
| **Dealing with construction permits** (rank) | 170 | Strength of legal rights index (0-10) | 7 | Cost to import (US$ per container) | 5,200 |
| Procedures (number) | 12 | Depth of credit information index (0-6) | 0 | | |
| Time (days) | 614 | Public registry coverage (% of adults) | 0.0 | **Enforcing contracts** (rank) | 111 |
| Cost (% of income per capita) | 4,423.4 | Private bureau coverage (% of adults) | 0.0 | Procedures (number) | 38 |
| | | | | Time (days) | 410 |
| **Getting electricity** (rank) | 157 | **Protecting investors** (rank) | 128 | Cost (% of claim) | 113.1 |
| Procedures (number) | 6 | Extent of disclosure index (0-10) | 8 | | |
| Time (days) | 106 | Extent of director liability index (0-10) | 1 | **Resolving insolvency** (rank) | 169 |
| Cost (% of income per capita) | 3,917.2 | Ease of shareholder suits index (0-10) | 4 | Time (years) | 3.3 |
| | | Strength of investor protection index (0-10) | 4.3 | Cost (% of estate) | 22 |
| | | | | Recovery rate (cents on the dollar) | 0.1 |
| | | **Paying taxes** (rank) | 134 | | |
| | | Payments (number per year) | 49 | | |
| | | Time (hours per year) | 242 | | |
| | | Total tax rate (% of profit) | 35.8 | | |

*Note:* Most indicator sets refer to a case scenario in an economy's largest business city. For more details, see the data notes.

# Employing
# workers data

## Employing workers data

| Country | Fixed-term contracts prohibited for permanent tasks? | Maximum length of fixed-term contracts (months)[a] | Minimum wage for a 19-year-old worker or an apprentice (US$/month)[b] | Ratio of minimum wage to value added per worker | 50-hour workweek allowed?[c] | Maximum working days per week | Premium for night work (% of hourly pay)[d] | Premium for work on weekly rest day (% of hourly pay)[d] | Major restrictions on night work?[d] | Major restrictions on weekly holiday work?[d] | Paid annual leave (working days)[e] | Dismissal due to redundancy allowed by law? | Third-party notification if 1 worker is dismissed? | Third-party approval if 1 worker is dismissed? | Third-party notification if 9 workers are dismissed? | Third-party approval if 9 workers are dismissed? | Retraining or reassignment?[f] | Priority rules for redundancies? | Priority rules for reemployment? | Notice period for redundancy dismissal (weeks of salary)[e] | Severance pay for redundancy dismissal (weeks of salary)[e] |
|---|---|---|---|---|---|---|---|---|---|---|---|---|---|---|---|---|---|---|---|---|---|
| | **Difficulty of hiring index** | | | | **Rigidity of hours index** | | | | | | | **Difficulty of redundancy index** | | | | | | | | **Redundancy cost** | |
| Afghanistan | No | No limit | 0.0 | 0.00 | Yes | 6 | 25 | 50 | No | No | 20.0 | Yes | Yes | No | Yes | Yes | No | No | No | 4.3 | 17.3 |
| Albania | Yes | No limit | 196.6 | 0.40 | Yes | 6 | 50 | 25 | Yes | No | 20.0 | Yes | No | No | No | No | Yes | Yes | Yes | 10.1 | 10.7 |
| Algeria | Yes | No limit | 219.1 | 0.40 | No | 6 | 0 | 0 | Yes | No | 22.0 | Yes | No | No | Yes | No | Yes | No | No | 4.3 | 13.0 |
| Angola | Yes | 12 | 110.6 | 0.17 | Yes | 6 | 0 | 0 | No | No | 22.0 | Yes | No | No | No | No | Yes | Yes | No | 13.0 | 26.7 |
| Antigua and Barbuda | No | No limit | 569.2 | 0.36 | Yes | 6 | 25 | 100 | No | No | 12.0 | Yes | No | No | No | No | No | No | No | 3.4 | 12.8 |
| Argentina | Yes | 60 | 508.1 | 0.40 | Yes | 6 | 0 | 0 | No | No | 18.0 | Yes | No | No | No | No | No | No | No | 7.2 | 23.1 |
| Armenia | Yes | No limit | 84.1 | 0.21 | Yes | 6 | 30 | 50 | No | No | 20.0 | Yes | No | No | Yes | No | Yes | No | Yes | 6.0 | 5.0 |
| Australia | No | No limit | 1,845.9 | 0.23 | Yes | 7 | 13 | 0 | No | Yes | 25.0 | Yes | No | No | Yes | No | Yes | No | No | 4.3 | 0.0 |
| Austria | No | No limit | 723.0 | 0.12 | Yes | 5.5 | 0 | 100 | No | No | 25.0 | Yes | Yes | No | Yes | No | No | Yes | No | 2.7 | 8.7 |
| Azerbaijan | No | 60 | 101.9 | 0.17 | Yes | 6 | 40 | 150 | Yes | No | 17.0 | Yes | No | No | No | No | No | Yes | Yes | 8.7 | 13.0 |
| Bahamas, The | No | No limit | 693.3 | 0.25 | Yes | 5.5 | 0 | 0 | No | No | 11.7 | Yes | No | No | No | No | No | No | No | 2.0 | 10.7 |
| Bahrain | No | No limit | 0.0 | 0.00 | Yes | 6 | 0 | 50 | No | No | 18.3 | Yes | No | No | Yes | No | No | No | No | 4.3 | 26.7 |
| Bangladesh | Yes | No limit | 41.0 | 0.41 | Yes | 6 | 50 | 100 | No | Yes | 17.0 | Yes | No | No | No | No | No | Yes | Yes | 4.3 | 13.3 |
| Barbados | No | No limit | 0.0 | 0.00 | Yes | 7 | 0 | 0 | No | No | 20.3 | Yes | No | No | No | No | No | Yes | No | 2.7 | 13.0 |
| Belarus | No | No limit | 208.1 | 0.31 | Yes | 6 | 20 | 100 | No | No | 18.0 | Yes | Yes | No | Yes | No | Yes | Yes | Yes | 8.7 | 0.0 |
| Belgium | No | No limit | 1,757.4 | 0.30 | Yes | 6 | 4 | 100 | No | No | 20.0 | Yes | No | No | Yes | No | No | No | No | 7.2 | 0.0 |
| Belize | No | No limit | 381.9 | 0.77 | Yes | 6 | 0 | 0 | No | No | 10.0 | Yes | Yes | No | Yes | No | No | No | No | 3.3 | 5.0 |
| Benin | No | 48 | 65.2 | 0.54 | Yes | 6 | 30 | 0 | No | No | 24.0 | Yes | Yes | No | Yes | No | No | Yes | Yes | 4.3 | 7.3 |
| Bhutan | No | No limit | 0.0 | 0.00 | Yes | 6 | 0 | 0 | No | No | 15.0 | Yes | No | No | No | No | No | No | No | 8.3 | 13.0 |
| Bolivia[g] | Yes | 24 | 103.0 | 0.36 | Yes | 6 | 30 | 100 | No | No | 21.7 | No | n.a. | n.a. | n.a. | n.a. | n.a. | n.a. | n.a. | n.a. | n.a. |
| Bosnia and Herzegovina | No | 24 | 393.6 | 0.70 | Yes | 6 | 0 | 20 | No | No | 18.0 | Yes | No | No | Yes | No | Yes | No | Yes | 2.0 | 7.2 |
| Botswana | No | No limit | 92.5 | 0.09 | Yes | 6 | 0 | 100 | Yes | No | 15.0 | Yes | Yes | No | Yes | No | No | Yes | Yes | 4.9 | 16.8 |
| Brazil | Yes | 24 | 349.4 | 0.27 | Yes | 6 | 20 | 100 | No | No | 26.0 | Yes | No | No | No | No | No | No | No | 6.6 | 8.9 |
| Brunei Darussalam | No | No limit | 0.0 | 0.00 | Yes | 6 | 0 | 50 | No | No | 13.3 | Yes | No | No | No | No | No | No | No | 3.0 | 0.0 |

Employing workers data

| | Difficulty of hiring index | | | | Rigidity of hours index | | | | | | | Difficulty of redundancy index | | | | | | | | Redundancy cost | |
|---|---|---|---|---|---|---|---|---|---|---|---|---|---|---|---|---|---|---|---|---|---|
| | Fixed-term contracts prohibited for permanent tasks? | Maximum length of fixed-term contracts (months)[a] | Minimum wage for a 19-year-old worker or an apprentice (US$/month)[b] | Ratio of minimum wage to value added per worker | 50-hour workweek allowed?[c] | Maximum working days per week | Premium for night work (% of hourly pay)[d] | Premium for work on weekly rest day (% of hourly pay)[d] | Major restrictions on night work?[d] | Major restrictions on weekly holiday work?[d] | Paid annual leave (working days)[e] | Dismissal due to redundancy allowed by law? | Third-party notification if 1 worker is dismissed? | Third-party approval if 1 worker is dismissed? | Third-party notification if 9 workers are dismissed? | Third-party approval if 9 workers are dismissed? | Retraining or reassignment?[f] | Priority rules for redundancies? | Priority rules for reemployment? | Notice period for redundancy dismissal (weeks of salary)[e] | Severance pay for redundancy dismissal (weeks of salary)[e] |
| Bulgaria | No | 36 | 197.0 | 0.25 | Yes | 6 | 10 | 0 | Yes | No | 20.0 | Yes | No | No | No | No | No | No | No | 4.3 | 3.2 |
| Burkina Faso | No | No limit | 66.8 | 0.74 | Yes | 6 | 0 | 0 | No | No | 22.0 | Yes | No | No | Yes | No | No | Yes | Yes | 4.3 | 6.1 |
| Burundi | No | No limit | 2.9 | 0.08 | Yes | 6 | 35 | 100 | No | No | 21.0 | Yes | No | No | No | No | No | Yes | Yes | 8.7 | 7.2 |
| Cambodia | No | 24 | 43.0 | 0.40 | Yes | 6 | 30 | 100 | No | No | 19.3 | Yes | No | No | No | No | No | Yes | Yes | 7.9 | 11.4 |
| Cameroon | No | 48 | 57.5 | 0.32 | Yes | 6 | 50 | 0 | No | No | 19.0 | Yes | No | No | Yes | No | Yes | Yes | Yes | 7.2 | 8.1 |
| Canada | No | No limit | 1,652.9 | 0.30 | Yes | 6 | 0 | 0 | No | No | 10.0 | Yes | No | No | No | No | No | No | No | 5.0 | 5.0 |
| Cape Verde | Yes | 60 | 0.0 | 0.00 | Yes | 6 | 25 | 0 | No | No | 22.0 | Yes | No | Yes | Yes | Yes | No | Yes | No | 6.4 | 23.1 |
| Central African Republic | Yes | 48 | 39.3 | 0.56 | Yes | 5 | 0 | 50 | No | Yes | 25.3 | Yes | No | Yes | Yes | Yes | Yes | Yes | Yes | 4.3 | 17.3 |
| Chad | No | 48 | 119.8 | 1.08 | Yes | 6 | 0 | 100 | No | No | 24.7 | Yes | No | No | Yes | No | No | Yes | Yes | 7.2 | 5.8 |
| Chile | No | 24 | 0.0 | 0.00 | Yes | 6 | 0 | 0 | No | No | 15.0 | Yes | No | No | No | No | No | No | No | 4.3 | 23.1 |
| China | No | No limit | 204.2 | 0.36 | Yes | 6 | 39 | 100 | No | No | 6.7 | Yes | Yes | No | Yes | No | Yes | No | Yes | 4.3 | 23.1 |
| Colombia | No | No limit | 277.8 | 0.36 | Yes | 6 | 35 | 75 | No | No | 15.0 | Yes | No | No | No | No | No | No | Yes | 0.0 | 16.7 |
| Comoros | No | 36 | 0.0 | 0.00 | Yes | 6 | 0 | 0 | No | No | 22.0 | Yes | No | No | Yes | No | No | Yes | Yes | 13.0 | 23.1 |
| Congo, Dem. Rep. | Yes | 48 | 65.0 | 2.11 | Yes | 6 | 25 | 0 | No | No | 13.0 | Yes | No | Yes | Yes | Yes | No | Yes | Yes | 10.3 | 0.0 |
| Congo, Rep. | Yes | 24 | 92.1 | 0.27 | Yes | 6 | 0 | 50 | No | Yes | 29.0 | Yes | No | Yes | Yes | Yes | No | Yes | Yes | 4.3 | 6.5 |
| Costa Rica | Yes | 12 | 420.4 | 0.45 | Yes | 6 | 0 | 100 | Yes | No | 12.0 | Yes | No | No | No | No | No | No | No | 4.3 | 14.4 |
| Côte d'Ivoire | No | 24 | 0.0 | 0.00 | No | 6 | 38 | 0 | No | No | 27.4 | Yes | No | No | Yes | No | No | No | No | 5.8 | 7.3 |
| Croatia | Yes | 36 | 521.5 | 0.31 | Yes | 6 | 10 | 35 | No | Yes | 20.0 | Yes | Yes | No | Yes | No | Yes | Yes | Yes | 7.9 | 7.2 |
| Cyprus | No | 30 | 0.0 | 0.00 | Yes | 6 | 0 | 0 | No | No | 20.0 | Yes | Yes | No | Yes | No | No | Yes | Yes | 5.7 | 0.0 |
| Czech Republic | No | 108 | 440.1 | 0.20 | Yes | 6 | 10 | 10 | No | No | 20.0 | Yes | Yes | No | Yes | Yes | Yes | No | No | 8.7 | 11.6 |
| Denmark | No | No limit | 0.0 | 0.00 | Yes | 6 | 0 | 0 | No | No | 25.0 | Yes | No | No | No | No | No | No | No | 0.0 | 0.0 |
| Djibouti | Yes | 24 | 0.0 | 0.00 | Yes | 6 | 0 | 0 | No | No | 30.0 | Yes | Yes | No | Yes | No | No | No | Yes | 4.3 | 0.0 |
| Dominica | No | No limit | 234.1 | 0.25 | Yes | 6 | 0 | 0 | No | No | 13.3 | Yes | No | No | Yes | No | No | Yes | Yes | 5.8 | 9.3 |
| Dominican Republic | Yes | No limit | 277.2 | 0.40 | Yes | 6 | 0 | 100 | No | Yes | 14.0 | Yes | No | No | No | No | No | No | No | 4.0 | 22.2 |

## Employing workers data

| | Difficulty of hiring index | | | | Rigidity of hours index | | | | | | | Difficulty of redundancy index | | | | | | | | Redundancy cost | |
|---|---|---|---|---|---|---|---|---|---|---|---|---|---|---|---|---|---|---|---|---|---|
| | Fixed-term contracts prohibited for permanent tasks? | Maximum length of fixed-term contracts (months)[a] | Minimum wage for a 19-year-old worker or an apprentice (US$/month)[b] | Ratio of minimum wage to value added per worker | 50-hour workweek allowed?[c] | Maximum working days per week | Premium for night work (% of hourly pay)[d] | Premium for work on weekly rest day (% of hourly pay)[d] | Major restrictions on night work?[d] | Major restrictions on weekly holiday work?[d] | Paid annual leave (working days)[e] | Dismissal due to redundancy allowed by law? | Third-party notification if 1 worker is dismissed? | Third-party approval if 1 worker is dismissed? | Third-party notification if 9 workers are dismissed? | Third-party approval if 9 workers are dismissed? | Retraining or reassignment?[f] | Priority rules for redundancies? | Priority rules for reemployment? | Notice period for redundancy dismissal (weeks of salary)[e] | Severance pay for redundancy dismissal (weeks of salary)[e] |
| Ecuador | No | 24 | 251.9 | 0.47 | Yes | 5 | 25 | 100 | No | No | 12.0 | Yes | No | No | No | No | No | No | No | 0.0 | 31.8 |
| Egypt, Arab Rep. | No | No limit | 113.0 | 0.33 | Yes | 6 | 0 | 0 | No | No | 24.0 | Yes | Yes | No | Yes | No | No | No | No | 10.1 | 26.7 |
| El Salvador | Yes | No limit | 91.7 | 0.20 | Yes | 6 | 25 | 100 | No | No | 11.0 | Yes | Yes | Yes | Yes | Yes | No | No | No | 0.0 | 22.9 |
| Equatorial Guinea | Yes | 24 | 279.0 | 0.13 | Yes | 6 | 25 | 50 | Yes | Yes | 22.0 | Yes | Yes | Yes | Yes | Yes | Yes | No | Yes | 4.3 | 34.3 |
| Eritrea | Yes | No limit | 0.0 | 0.00 | Yes | 6 | 0 | 0 | No | No | 19.0 | Yes | No | No | No | No | No | No | No | 3.1 | 12.3 |
| Estonia | Yes | 120 | 389.5 | 0.21 | Yes | 5 | 25 | 0 | No | No | 24.0 | Yes | No | No | Yes | No | No | Yes | No | 8.6 | 4.3 |
| Ethiopia | Yes | No limit | 0.0 | 0.00 | Yes | 6 | 0 | 0 | No | No | 18.3 | Yes | No | No | No | No | Yes | Yes | No | 8.7 | 10.5 |
| Fiji | No | No limit | 304.2 | 0.66 | Yes | 6 | 3 | 100 | No | No | 10.0 | Yes | No | No | No | No | No | No | No | 4.3 | 5.3 |
| Finland | Yes | 60 | 1,983.8 | 0.32 | Yes | 6 | 8 | 100 | No | No | 30.0 | Yes | Yes | No | Yes | No | Yes | Yes | Yes | 10.1 | 0.0 |
| France | Yes | 18 | 782.3 | 0.14 | No | 5 | 0 | 0 | No | Yes | 30.0 | Yes | No | No | Yes | No | Yes | Yes | Yes | 7.2 | 4.6 |
| Gabon | No | 48 | 66.7 | 0.06 | Yes | 6 | 50 | 0 | No | No | 24.0 | Yes | No | No | No | No | No | Yes | Yes | 4.3 | 4.3 |
| Gambia, The | No | No limit | 0.0 | 0.00 | Yes | 5 | 0 | 100 | No | No | 21.0 | Yes | No | No | No | No | No | No | No | 26.0 | 0.0 |
| Georgia | No | No limit | 21.7 | 0.06 | Yes | 7 | 0 | 0 | No | No | 24.0 | Yes | No | No | No | No | No | No | No | 0.0 | 4.3 |
| Germany | No | 24 | 1,126.1 | 0.20 | Yes | 6 | 13 | 0 | No | No | 24.0 | Yes | Yes | No | Yes | No | Yes | Yes | No | 10.0 | 0.0 |
| Ghana | No | No limit | 29.7 | 0.15 | Yes | 5 | 0 | 0 | No | No | 15.0 | Yes | Yes | No | Yes | No | No | No | No | 3.6 | 46.2 |
| Greece | Yes | No limit | 672.2 | 0.21 | Yes | 5 | 25 | 75 | No | Yes | 22.3 | Yes | Yes | No | Yes | No | Yes | Yes | Yes | 10.4 | 15.9 |
| Grenada | Yes | No limit | 355.9 | 0.39 | Yes | 6 | 0 | 50 | No | No | 13.3 | Yes | No | No | No | No | No | Yes | No | 7.2 | 5.3 |
| Guatemala | Yes | No limit | 325.3 | 0.74 | Yes | 6 | 20 | 50 | Yes | Yes | 15.0 | Yes | No | No | No | No | No | No | No | 0.0 | 27.0 |
| Guinea | No | 24 | 0.0 | 0.00 | Yes | 6 | 20 | 45 | No | No | 30.0 | Yes | Yes | No | Yes | No | Yes | Yes | No | 2.1 | 5.8 |
| Guinea-Bissau | Yes | 12 | 0.0 | 0.00 | Yes | 6 | 25 | 50 | No | No | 21.0 | Yes | Yes | Yes | Yes | Yes | No | Yes | Yes | 0.0 | 26.0 |
| Guyana | No | No limit | 0.0 | 0.00 | Yes | 7 | 0 | 100 | No | No | 12.0 | Yes | Yes | No | Yes | No | No | No | No | 4.3 | 12.3 |
| Haiti | No | No limit | 122.5 | 1.26 | Yes | 6 | 50 | 50 | No | No | 13.0 | Yes | No | No | No | No | No | No | No | 10.1 | 0.0 |
| Honduras | Yes | 24 | 396.9 | 1.44 | Yes | 6 | 25 | 100 | Yes | No | 16.7 | Yes | Yes | Yes | Yes | Yes | No | Yes | No | 7.2 | 23.1 |
| Hong Kong SAR, China | No | No limit | 0.0 | 0.00 | Yes | 6 | 0 | 0 | No | No | 10.3 | Yes | No | No | No | No | No | No | No | 4.3 | 1.5 |

**Employing workers data**

| | Fixed-term contracts prohibited for permanent tasks? | Maximum length of fixed-term contracts (months)[a] | Minimum wage for a 19-year-old worker or an apprentice (US$/month)[b] | Ratio of minimum wage to value added per worker | 50-hour workweek allowed?[c] | Maximum working days per week | Premium for night work (% of hourly pay)[d] | Premium for work on weekly rest day (% of hourly pay)[d] | Major restrictions on night work?[d] | Major restrictions on weekly holiday work?[d] | Paid annual leave (working days)[e] | Dismissal due to redundancy allowed by law? | Third-party notification if 1 worker is dismissed? | Third-party approval if 1 worker is dismissed? | Third-party notification if 9 workers are dismissed? | Third-party approval if 9 workers are dismissed? | Retraining or reassignment?[f] | Priority rules for redundancies? | Priority rules for reemployment? | Notice period for redundancy dismissal (weeks of salary)[e] | Severance pay for redundancy dismissal (weeks of salary)[e] |
|---|---|---|---|---|---|---|---|---|---|---|---|---|---|---|---|---|---|---|---|---|---|
| | *Difficulty of hiring index* | | | | *Rigidity of hours index* | | | | | | | *Difficulty of redundancy index* | | | | | | | | *Redundancy cost* | |
| Hungary | No | 60 | 447.1 | 0.29 | No | 5 | 40 | 100 | No | No | 21.3 | Yes | No | No | No | No | No | No | No | 6.2 | 7.2 |
| Iceland | No | 24 | 1,527.3 | 0.35 | Yes | 6 | 80 | 80 | No | No | 24.0 | Yes | No | No | No | No | No | No | No | 10.1 | 0.0 |
| India | No | No limit | 29.7 | 0.16 | Yes | 6 | 0 | 0 | No | No | 15.0 | Yes | Yes | No | Yes | No | No | Yes | Yes | 4.3 | 11.4 |
| Indonesia | Yes | 36 | 151.0 | 0.42 | Yes | 6 | 0 | 0 | No | No | 12.0 | Yes | Yes | Yes | Yes | Yes | Yes | No | No | 0.0 | 57.8 |
| Iran, Islamic Rep. | No | No limit | 344.6 | 0.47 | Yes | 6 | 23 | 40 | No | No | 24.0 | Yes | No | Yes | No | Yes | No | No | No | 0.0 | 23.1 |
| Iraq | Yes | No limit | 79.7 | 0.20 | Yes | 6 | 0 | 50 | No | No | 22.0 | Yes | No | No | No | No | Yes | No | No | 0.0 | 0.0 |
| Ireland | No | No limit | 1,659.3 | 0.34 | Yes | 6 | 0 | 0 | No | No | 20.0 | Yes | No | No | Yes | No | No | No | No | 4.0 | 2.8 |
| Israel | No | No limit | 1,087.8 | 0.28 | Yes | 5.5 | 14 | 50 | No | No | 18.0 | Yes | No | No | No | No | No | No | No | 4.3 | 23.1 |
| Italy | No | 44 | 1,787.3 | 0.40 | Yes | 6 | 15 | 50 | Yes | No | 20.3 | Yes | No | No | Yes | No | No | Yes | Yes | 7.2 | 0.0 |
| Jamaica | No | No limit | 210.5 | 0.32 | Yes | 6 | 0 | 100 | No | No | 11.7 | Yes | No | No | No | No | No | No | No | 4.0 | 10.0 |
| Japan | No | No limit | 1,726.9 | 0.29 | Yes | 6 | 25 | 35 | No | No | 15.3 | Yes | Yes | No | Yes | No | Yes | No | No | 4.3 | 0.0 |
| Jordan | No | No limit | 199.6 | 0.32 | Yes | 6 | 0 | 150 | No | No | 18.7 | Yes | Yes | No | Yes | No | No | No | No | 4.3 | 0.0 |
| Kazakhstan | No | No limit | 0.1 | 0.00 | Yes | 6 | 50 | 100 | No | No | 18.0 | Yes | No | No | No | No | No | No | No | 4.3 | 4.3 |
| Kenya | No | No limit | 111.1 | 0.89 | Yes | 6 | 0 | 0 | No | No | 21.0 | Yes | Yes | Yes | Yes | Yes | No | Yes | Yes | 4.3 | 11.4 |
| Kiribati | No | No limit | 0.0 | 0.00 | Yes | 7 | 0 | 0 | No | No | 0.0 | Yes | No | No | No | No | No | No | No | 4.3 | 0.0 |
| Korea, Rep. | No | 24 | 648.3 | 0.27 | Yes | 6 | 50 | 50 | No | No | 17.0 | Yes | No | No | Yes | No | No | No | No | 4.3 | 23.1 |
| Kosovo | No | No limit | 172.4 | 0.16 | No | 6 | 30 | 0 | No | No | 21.0 | Yes | No | No | No | No | No | No | No | 4.3 | 7.2 |
| Kuwait | No | No limit | 217.5 | 0.04 | Yes | 6 | 0 | 50 | No | No | 30.0 | Yes | No | No | No | No | No | No | No | 13.0 | 15.1 |
| Kyrgyz Republic | Yes | 60 | 15.0 | 0.13 | Yes | 6 | 50 | 100 | Yes | No | 20.0 | Yes | No | Yes | No | Yes | Yes | Yes | No | 4.3 | 13.0 |
| Lao PDR | No | No limit | 72.0 | 0.48 | Yes | 6 | 15 | 150 | Yes | No | 15.0 | Yes | No | No | No | No | No | No | No | 4.3 | 13.0 |
| Latvia | Yes | 36 | 384.5 | 0.25 | Yes | 5.5 | 50 | 0 | No | No | 20.0 | Yes | Yes | No | Yes | No | No | No | No | 1.0 | 8.7 |
| Lebanon | No | 24 | 432.6 | 0.39 | Yes | 6 | 0 | 50 | No | No | 15.0 | Yes | No | No | Yes | No | No | Yes | Yes | 8.7 | 0.0 |
| Lesotho | No | No limit | 105.1 | 0.61 | Yes | 6 | 0 | 100 | Yes | No | 12.0 | Yes | No | No | No | No | No | No | No | 4.3 | 10.7 |
| Liberia | No | No limit | 52.0 | 1.40 | Yes | 6 | 0 | 50 | No | No | 16.0 | Yes | Yes | No | Yes | No | No | Yes | Yes | 4.3 | 21.3 |

**Employing workers data**

| Economy | Fixed-term contracts prohibited for permanent tasks? | Maximum length of fixed-term contracts (months)[a] | Minimum wage for a 19-year-old worker or an apprentice (US$/month)[b] | Ratio of minimum wage to value added per worker | 50-hour workweek allowed?[c] | Maximum working days per week | Premium for night work (% of hourly pay)[d] | Premium for work on weekly rest day (% of hourly pay)[d] | Major restrictions on night work?[d] | Major restrictions on weekly holiday work?[d] | Paid annual leave (working days)[e] | Dismissal due to redundancy allowed by law? | Third-party notification if 1 worker is dismissed? | Third-party approval if 1 worker is dismissed? | Third-party notification if 9 workers are dismissed? | Third-party approval if 9 workers are dismissed? | Retraining or reassignment?[f] | Priority rules for redundancies? | Priority rules for reemployment? | Notice period for redundancy dismissal (weeks of salary)[e] | Severance pay for redundancy dismissal (weeks of salary)[e] |
|---|---|---|---|---|---|---|---|---|---|---|---|---|---|---|---|---|---|---|---|---|---|
| Lithuania | No | 60 | 307.0 | 0.21 | No | 5.5 | 50 | 100 | No | No | 20.7 | Yes | No | No | Yes | No | Yes | Yes | No | 8.7 | 15.9 |
| Luxembourg | Yes | 24 | 2,374.4 | 0.25 | No | 5.5 | 15 | 70 | No | Yes | 25.0 | Yes | Yes | No | Yes | No | No | No | Yes | 17.3 | 4.3 |
| Macedonia, FYR | No | 60 | 168.4 | 0.30 | Yes | 6 | 35 | 50 | No | No | 20.0 | Yes | No | No | Yes | No | No | No | No | 4.3 | 8.7 |
| Madagascar | Yes | 24 | 41.4 | 0.63 | Yes | 6 | 30 | 40 | Yes | No | 24.0 | Yes | Yes | No | Yes | No | Yes | Yes | Yes | 3.4 | 8.9 |
| Malawi | Yes | No limit | 28.6 | 0.52 | Yes | 6 | 0 | 100 | No | No | 18.0 | Yes | Yes | Yes | Yes | Yes | No | No | No | 4.3 | 12.3 |
| Malaysia | No | No limit | 0.0 | 0.00 | Yes | 6 | 0 | 0 | No | No | 13.3 | Yes | No | No | Yes | No | No | No | No | 6.7 | 17.2 |
| Maldives | No | 24 | 0.0 | 0.00 | Yes | 6 | 0 | 50 | No | No | 30.0 | Yes | No | No | No | No | No | No | No | 5.8 | 0.0 |
| Mali | Yes | 72 | 14.4 | 0.14 | Yes | 6 | 0 | 0 | No | No | 22.0 | Yes | Yes | No | Yes | No | No | Yes | Yes | 4.3 | 9.3 |
| Malta | No | 48 | 953.3 | 0.39 | No | 6 | 0 | 0 | No | No | 24.0 | Yes | No | No | Yes | No | No | No | No | 7.3 | 0.0 |
| Marshall Islands | No | No limit | 0.0 | 0.00 | Yes | 7 | 100 | 50 | No | No | 0.0 | Yes | No | No | No | No | No | No | No | 0.0 | 0.0 |
| Mauritania | No | 24 | 68.9 | 0.48 | Yes | 6 | 0 | 100 | No | No | 18.0 | Yes | No | No | Yes | No | No | Yes | Yes | 4.3 | 6.1 |
| Mauritius | Yes | No limit | 166.3 | 0.17 | Yes | 6 | 0 | 25 | Yes | No | 22.0 | Yes | Yes | No | Yes | Yes | No | Yes | Yes | 4.3 | 6.3 |
| Mexico | No | No limit | 121.4 | 0.10 | Yes | 6 | 0 | 0 | No | No | 12.0 | Yes | Yes | Yes | Yes | Yes | No | Yes | No | 0.0 | 22.0 |
| Micronesia, Fed. Sts. | No | No limit | 271.7 | 0.68 | Yes | 7 | 50 | 0 | No | No | 0.0 | Yes | No | No | No | No | No | No | No | 0.0 | 0.0 |
| Moldova | Yes | No limit | 87.4 | 0.38 | Yes | 6 | 50 | 100 | Yes | Yes | 20.0 | Yes | No | No | Yes | No | Yes | Yes | Yes | 4.3 | 4.3 |
| Mongolia | No | No limit | 91.9 | 0.32 | Yes | 5 | 40 | 50 | No | No | 16.0 | Yes | No | No | Yes | No | Yes | No | No | 8.7 | 13.9 |
| Montenegro | No | 24 | 294.8 | 0.34 | Yes | 6 | 0 | 0 | No | No | 21.0 | Yes | No | No | Yes | No | No | Yes | Yes | 4.3 | 6.9 |
| Morocco | Yes | 12 | 272.7 | 0.74 | Yes | 6 | 0 | 0 | No | Yes | 19.5 | Yes | No | No | Yes | No | No | No | No | 7.2 | 13.5 |
| Mozambique | Yes | 72 | 108.6 | 1.46 | Yes | 6 | 0 | 100 | No | No | 24.0 | Yes | Yes | Yes | Yes | Yes | No | No | Yes | 4.3 | 33.2 |
| Namibia | No | No limit | 0.0 | 0.00 | Yes | 6 | 6 | 100 | No | Yes | 20.0 | Yes | Yes | Yes | Yes | No | No | No | No | 4.3 | 5.3 |
| Nepal | Yes | No limit | 74.7 | 1.00 | Yes | 6 | 0 | 50 | Yes | No | 18.0 | Yes | Yes | Yes | Yes | Yes | No | Yes | Yes | 4.3 | 22.9 |
| Netherlands | No | 36 | 1,036.8 | 0.17 | Yes | 5.5 | 0 | 0 | No | No | 20.0 | Yes | Yes | Yes | Yes | Yes | Yes | No | No | 8.7 | 0.0 |
| New Zealand | No | No limit | 1,851.3 | 0.40 | Yes | 7 | 0 | 0 | No | No | 20.0 | Yes | No | No | No | No | Yes | No | Yes | 0.0 | 0.0 |
| Nicaragua | No | No limit | 137.2 | 0.86 | Yes | 6 | 0 | 100 | Yes | Yes | 30.0 | Yes | No | No | No | No | No | No | No | 0.0 | 14.9 |

Column groups: *Difficulty of hiring index* (Fixed-term contracts prohibited … Ratio of minimum wage to value added per worker); *Rigidity of hours index* (50-hour workweek allowed … Paid annual leave); *Difficulty of redundancy index* (Dismissal due to redundancy allowed … Priority rules for reemployment); *Redundancy cost* (Notice period … Severance pay).

**Employing workers data**

| Economy | Difficulty of hiring index | | | | Rigidity of hours index | | | | | | | Difficulty of redundancy index | | | | | | | | Redundancy cost | |
|---|---|---|---|---|---|---|---|---|---|---|---|---|---|---|---|---|---|---|---|---|---|
| | Fixed-term contracts prohibited for permanent tasks? | Maximum length of fixed-term contracts (months)[a] | Minimum wage for a 19-year-old worker or an apprentice (US$/month)[b] | Ratio of minimum wage to value added per worker | 50-hour workweek allowed?[c] | Maximum working days per week | Premium for night work (% of hourly pay)[d] | Premium for work on weekly rest day (% of hourly pay)[d] | Major restrictions on night work?[d] | Major restrictions on weekly holiday work?[d] | Paid annual leave (working days)[e] | Dismissal due to redundancy allowed by law? | Third-party notification if 1 worker is dismissed? | Third-party approval if 1 worker is dismissed? | Third-party notification if 9 workers are dismissed? | Third-party approval if 9 workers are dismissed? | Retraining or reassignment?[f] | Priority rules for redundancies? | Priority rules for reemployment? | Notice period for redundancy dismissal (weeks of salary)[e] | Severance pay for redundancy dismissal (weeks of salary)[e] |
| Niger | Yes | 24 | 58.5 | 0.95 | No | 6 | 38 | 0 | No | No | 22.0 | Yes | Yes | No | Yes | No | Yes | Yes | Yes | 5.8 | 5.8 |
| Nigeria | No | No limit | 106.5 | 0.57 | Yes | 6 | 0 | 0 | No | No | 20.0 | Yes | No | No | No | No | Yes | No | No | 4.0 | 12.2 |
| Norway | Yes | 48 | 3,893.4 | 0.35 | Yes | 6 | 0 | 0 | No | Yes | 21.0 | Yes | Yes | No | Yes | No | No | Yes | Yes | 8.7 | 0.0 |
| Oman | No | No limit | 520.1 | 0.19 | Yes | 5 | 50 | 100 | Yes | No | 22.0 | Yes | No | No | No | No | Yes | No | No | 4.3 | 0.0 |
| Pakistan | Yes | 9 | 36.7 | 0.24 | Yes | 6 | 0 | 100 | No | Yes | 14.0 | Yes | No | No | Yes | Yes | No | Yes | Yes | 4.3 | 22.9 |
| Palau | No | No limit | 525.9 | 0.55 | Yes | 7 | 0 | 0 | No | No | 0.0 | Yes | No | No | No | No | Yes | No | No | 0.0 | 0.0 |
| Panama | Yes | 12 | 438.6 | 0.43 | Yes | 6 | 0 | 0 | Yes | Yes | 22.0 | Yes | No | No | Yes | Yes | No | Yes | Yes | 0.0 | 18.1 |
| Papua New Guinea | No | No limit | 115.4 | 0.55 | Yes | 6 | 0 | 50 | No | No | 11.0 | Yes | No | No | No | No | Yes | No | No | 3.3 | 9.2 |
| Paraguay | Yes | No limit | 198.7 | 0.50 | Yes | 6 | 30 | 0 | Yes | Yes | 20.0 | Yes | No | No | No | No | No | No | Yes | 7.5 | 18.6 |
| Peru | Yes | 60 | 253.2 | 0.35 | Yes | 6 | 35 | 100 | No | No | 13.0 | Yes | No | Yes | Yes | Yes | No | Yes | No | 0.0 | 11.4 |
| Philippines | Yes | No limit | 192.5 | 0.64 | Yes | 6 | 10 | 30 | No | No | 5.0 | Yes | Yes | Yes | Yes | Yes | No | Yes | Yes | 4.3 | 23.1 |
| Poland | No | No limit | 390.7 | 0.27 | Yes | 6 | 20 | 100 | No | No | 22.0 | Yes | No | No | Yes | No | No | Yes | Yes | 10.1 | 8.7 |
| Portugal | Yes | 54 | 775.5 | 0.29 | Yes | 6 | 25 | 100 | No | No | 22.0 | Yes | Yes | No | Yes | No | Yes | Yes | Yes | 7.9 | 26.0 |
| Puerto Rico (U.S.) | No | No limit | 1,256.7 | 0.57 | Yes | 7 | 0 | 100 | No | No | 15.0 | Yes | No | No | No | No | No | No | No | 0.0 | 0.0 |
| Qatar | No | No limit | 0.0 | 0.00 | Yes | 6 | 0 | 0 | No | No | 22.0 | Yes | No | No | No | No | Yes | No | No | 7.2 | 16.0 |
| Romania | Yes | 36 | 216.4 | 0.23 | Yes | 5 | 25 | 100 | No | No | 20.0 | Yes | No | No | Yes | No | No | Yes | No | 4.0 | 0.0 |
| Russian Federation | Yes | 60 | 325.6 | 0.27 | Yes | 6 | 20 | 100 | No | No | 22.0 | Yes | No | No | No | No | No | Yes | No | 8.7 | 8.7 |
| Rwanda | No | No limit | 0.0 | 0.00 | Yes | 6 | 0 | 0 | No | No | 19.3 | Yes | Yes | No | Yes | No | Yes | Yes | Yes | 4.3 | 8.7 |
| Samoa | No | No limit | 167.5 | 0.36 | Yes | 6 | 0 | 100 | No | No | 10.0 | Yes | No | No | No | No | No | No | No | 5.8 | 0.0 |
| São Tomé and Principe | Yes | 36 | 0.0 | 0.00 | No | 6 | 25 | 26 | No | Yes | 26.0 | Yes | Yes | Yes | Yes | Yes | No | No | Yes | 4.3 | 26.0 |
| Saudi Arabia | No | No limit | 0.0 | 0.00 | Yes | 6 | 0 | 50 | No | No | 20.7 | Yes | No | No | No | No | No | No | No | 4.3 | 15.2 |
| Senegal | Yes | 24 | 74.6 | 0.45 | Yes | 6 | 38 | 0 | No | Yes | 24.3 | Yes | Yes | No | Yes | No | Yes | Yes | Yes | 3.2 | 10.5 |
| Serbia | Yes | 12 | 203.8 | 0.29 | Yes | 6 | 26 | 26 | No | No | 20.0 | Yes | No | No | No | No | Yes | No | Yes | 0.0 | 7.7 |
| Seychelles | Yes | No limit | 349.8 | 0.24 | Yes | 6 | 0 | 100 | No | No | 21.0 | Yes | Yes | Yes | Yes | Yes | No | No | No | 4.3 | 9.1 |

## Employing workers data

| Economy | Fixed-term contracts prohibited for permanent tasks? | Maximum length of fixed-term contracts (months)[a] | Minimum wage for a 19-year-old worker or an apprentice (US$/month)[b] | Ratio of minimum wage to value added per worker | 50-hour workweek allowed?[c] | Maximum working days per week | Premium for night work (% of hourly pay)[d] | Premium for work on weekly rest day (% of hourly pay)[d] | Major restrictions on night work?[d] | Major restrictions on weekly holiday work?[d] | Paid annual leave (working days)[e] | Dismissal due to redundancy allowed by law? | Third-party notification if 1 worker is dismissed? | Third-party approval if 1 worker is dismissed? | Third-party notification if 9 workers are dismissed? | Third-party approval if 9 workers are dismissed? | Retraining or reassignment?[f] | Priority rules for redundancies? | Priority rules for reemployment? | Notice period for redundancy dismissal (weeks of salary)[e] | Severance pay for redundancy dismissal (weeks of salary)[e] |
|---|---|---|---|---|---|---|---|---|---|---|---|---|---|---|---|---|---|---|---|---|---|
| | **Difficulty of hiring index** | | | | **Rigidity of hours index** | | | | | | | **Difficulty of redundancy index** | | | | | | | | **Redundancy cost** | |
| Sierra Leone | Yes | No limit | 37.3 | 0.73 | Yes | 5 | 15 | 100 | No | No | 21.3 | Yes | Yes | No | Yes | No | Yes | Yes | Yes | 8.7 | 69.6 |
| Singapore | No | No limit | 0.0 | 0.00 | Yes | 6 | 0 | 100 | No | No | 10.7 | Yes | No | No | No | No | No | No | No | 3.0 | 0.0 |
| Slovak Republic | No | 36 | 447.5 | 0.24 | Yes | 6 | 20 | 50 | No | No | 25.0 | Yes | No | No | No | No | No | No | No | 11.6 | 0.0 |
| Slovenia | Yes | 24 | 1,054.8 | 0.37 | Yes | 6 | 50 | 50 | No | No | 21.0 | Yes | Yes | No | Yes | No | Yes | Yes | No | 5.7 | 5.7 |
| Solomon Islands | No | No limit | 111.9 | 0.69 | Yes | 6 | 0 | 0 | No | No | 15.0 | Yes | No | No | No | No | No | No | Yes | 4.3 | 10.7 |
| South Africa | Yes | No limit | 621.6 | 0.70 | Yes | 6 | 25 | 100 | No | No | 15.0 | Yes | No | No | Yes | No | Yes | No | No | 4.0 | 5.3 |
| Spain | Yes | No limit | 1,022.9 | 0.27 | Yes | 5.5 | 0 | 0 | Yes | No | 22.0 | Yes | No | No | Yes | No | No | No | No | 2.1 | 15.2 |
| Sri Lanka | No | No limit | 40.2 | 0.12 | Yes | 5.5 | 0 | 50 | No | No | 14.0 | Yes | No | Yes | No | Yes | Yes | Yes | Yes | 4.3 | 54.2 |
| St. Kitts and Nevis | No | No limit | 501.5 | 0.31 | Yes | 7 | 0 | 0 | No | No | 14.0 | Yes | No | Yes | No | No | No | No | No | 8.7 | 0.0 |
| St. Lucia | No | No limit | 0.0 | 0.00 | Yes | 6 | 0 | 150 | No | No | 21.0 | Yes | No | No | Yes | Yes | No | Yes | Yes | 3.7 | 9.3 |
| St. Vincent and the Grenadines | No | No limit | 191.2 | 0.25 | Yes | 6 | 0 | 0 | No | Yes | 19.3 | Yes | No | No | No | No | No | No | No | 4.0 | 10.0 |
| Sudan | No | 48 | 75.0 | 0.26 | Yes | 6 | 0 | 0 | No | No | 23.3 | Yes | Yes | Yes | Yes | Yes | No | No | No | 4.3 | 0.0 |
| Suriname | No | No limit | 0.0 | 0.00 | Yes | 6 | 0 | 100 | No | No | 16.0 | Yes | Yes | Yes | Yes | Yes | No | No | No | 0.0 | 8.8 |
| Swaziland | No | No limit | 96.3 | 0.21 | Yes | 5.5 | 0 | 0 | No | No | 11.0 | Yes | No | Yes | Yes | Yes | No | No | No | 5.9 | 8.7 |
| Sweden | No | 24 | 0.0 | 0.00 | Yes | 5.5 | 0 | 0 | No | No | 25.0 | Yes | No | No | Yes | No | Yes | Yes | Yes | 14.4 | 0.0 |
| Switzerland | No | 120 | 0.0 | 0.00 | Yes | 6 | 0 | 0 | No | Yes | 20.0 | Yes | No | No | Yes | No | No | No | No | 10.1 | 0.0 |
| Syrian Arab Republic | No | 60 | 209.7 | 0.54 | Yes | 6 | 0 | 100 | No | No | 21.7 | Yes | Yes | Yes | Yes | Yes | No | No | Yes | 8.7 | 21.7 |
| Taiwan, China | Yes | 12 | 621.5 | 0.26 | No | 6 | 0 | 100 | No | No | 12.0 | Yes | Yes | No | Yes | No | Yes | No | No | 3.8 | 18.8 |
| Tajikistan | Yes | No limit | 16.4 | 0.14 | Yes | 6 | 50 | 100 | Yes | No | 23.3 | Yes | Yes | No | Yes | No | Yes | No | No | 8.7 | 18.8 |
| Tanzania | Yes | No limit | 52.5 | 0.61 | Yes | 6 | 5 | 100 | No | No | 20.0 | Yes | Yes | Yes | Yes | Yes | Yes | Yes | No | 4.0 | 5.3 |
| Thailand | Yes | No limit | 117.9 | 0.23 | Yes | 6 | 0 | 100 | No | No | 6.0 | Yes | No | No | Yes | No | No | No | No | 4.3 | 31.7 |
| Timor-Leste | Yes | 36 | 0.0 | 0.00 | Yes | 6 | 25 | 100 | No | No | 12.0 | Yes | Yes | No | Yes | No | No | No | No | 4.3 | 0.0 |
| Togo | Yes | 48 | 71.7 | 0.88 | Yes | 6 | 200 | 65 | No | No | 30.0 | Yes | Yes | No | Yes | No | Yes | Yes | Yes | 4.3 | 8.8 |
| Tonga | No | No limit | 0.0 | 0.00 | Yes | 6 | 0 | 0 | No | Yes | 0.0 | Yes | No | No | No | No | No | No | No | 0.0 | 0.0 |

## Employing workers data

| | Difficulty of hiring index | | | | Rigidity of hours index | | | | | | | Difficulty of redundancy index | | | | | | | | Redundancy cost | |
|---|---|---|---|---|---|---|---|---|---|---|---|---|---|---|---|---|---|---|---|---|---|
| | Fixed-term contracts prohibited for permanent tasks? | Maximum length of fixed-term contracts (months)[a] | Minimum wage for a 19-year-old worker or an apprentice (US$/month)[b] | Ratio of minimum wage to value added per worker | 50-hour workweek allowed?[c] | Maximum working days per week | Premium for night work (% of hourly pay)[d] | Premium for work on weekly rest day (% of hourly pay)[d] | Major restrictions on night work?[d] | Major restrictions on weekly holiday work?[d] | Paid annual leave (working days)[e] | Dismissal due to redundancy allowed by law? | Third-party notification if 1 worker is dismissed? | Third-party approval if 1 worker is dismissed? | Third-party notification if 9 workers are dismissed? | Third-party approval if 9 workers are dismissed? | Retraining or reassignment?[f] | Priority rules for redundancies? | Priority rules for reemployment? | Notice period for redundancy dismissal (weeks of salary)[e] | Severance pay for redundancy dismissal (weeks of salary)[e] |
| Trinidad and Tobago | No | No limit | 0.0 | 0.00 | Yes | 6 | 0 | 100 | No | No | 10.0 | Yes | No | No | Yes | No | No | No | No | 6.4 | 14.1 |
| Tunisia | No | 48 | 119.6 | 0.25 | Yes | 6 | 0 | 100 | No | No | 13.0 | Yes | Yes | Yes | Yes | Yes | Yes | Yes | Yes | 4.3 | 7.8 |
| Turkey | Yes | No limit | 529.7 | 0.41 | Yes | 6 | 0 | 100 | No | No | 18.0 | Yes | No | No | Yes | No | Yes | No | Yes | 6.7 | 23.1 |
| Uganda | No | No limit | 2.7 | 0.03 | Yes | 6 | 0 | 0 | No | No | 21.0 | Yes | No | No | No | No | No | No | No | 8.7 | 0.0 |
| Ukraine | Yes | No limit | 119.1 | 0.32 | No | 5.5 | 20 | 100 | No | No | 18.0 | Yes | Yes | No | Yes | No | Yes | Yes | Yes | 8.7 | 4.3 |
| United Arab Emirates | No | No limit | 0.0 | 0.00 | Yes | 6 | 0 | 50 | No | No | 26.0 | Yes | No | No | No | No | No | No | No | 4.3 | 0.0 |
| United Kingdom | No | No limit | 1,338.2 | 0.28 | Yes | 6 | 0 | 0 | No | No | 28.0 | Yes | No | No | No | No | No | No | No | 5.3 | 3.0 |
| United States | No | No limit | 1,245.5 | 0.21 | Yes | 6 | 0 | 0 | No | No | 0.0 | Yes | No | No | No | No | No | No | No | 0.0 | 0.0 |
| Uruguay | Yes | No limit | 355.9 | 0.23 | Yes | 6 | 0 | 100 | No | No | 21.0 | Yes | No | No | Yes | No | No | No | No | 0.0 | 20.8 |
| Uzbekistan | Yes | 60 | 34.4 | 0.18 | Yes | 6 | 50 | 100 | No | No | 15.0 | Yes | No | No | Yes | No | Yes | Yes | No | 8.7 | 8.7 |
| Vanuatu | No | No limit | 264.8 | 0.65 | Yes | 6 | 75 | 50 | No | No | 15.0 | Yes | No | No | No | No | No | No | No | 9.3 | 23.1 |
| Venezuela, RB[g] | Yes | 24 | 301.1 | 0.20 | Yes | 6 | 30 | 50 | Yes | No | 19.3 | No | n.a. | n.a. | n.a. | n.a. | n.a. | n.a. | n.a. | n.a. | n.a. |
| Vietnam | No | 72 | 64.5 | 0.43 | Yes | 6 | 30 | 100 | No | No | 13.0 | Yes | No | No | Yes | Yes | Yes | Yes | No | 0.0 | 24.6 |
| West Bank and Gaza | No | 24 | 0.0 | 0.00 | Yes | 6 | 0 | 150 | No | Yes | 18.0 | Yes | No | No | Yes | No | No | No | No | 4.3 | 23.1 |
| Yemen, Rep. | No | No limit | 78.9 | 0.47 | Yes | 6 | 15 | 100 | No | No | 30.0 | Yes | Yes | No | Yes | No | Yes | No | Yes | 4.3 | 23.1 |
| Zambia | No | No limit | 75.8 | 0.40 | Yes | 5.5 | 4 | 100 | No | No | 24.0 | Yes | Yes | No | Yes | No | No | No | Yes | 4.3 | 46.2 |
| Zimbabwe | No | No limit | 167.4 | 1.80 | Yes | 6 | 15 | 100 | Yes | No | 22.0 | Yes | Yes | Yes | Yes | Yes | Yes | No | No | 13.0 | 69.3 |

a. Including renewals.

b. Economies for which 0.0 is shown have no minimum wage.

c. For 2 months a year in case of a seasonal increase in production.

d. In case of continuous operations.

e. Average for workers with 1, 5 and 10 years of tenure.

f. Whether compulsory before redundancy.

g. Some answers are not applicable ("n.a.") for economies where dismissal due to redundancy is disallowed.

*Source: Doing Business database.*

# Acknowledgments

*Doing Business* would not be possible without the expertise and generous input of a network of more than 9,600 local partners, including legal experts, business consultants, accountants, freight forwarders, government officials and other professionals routinely administering or advising on the relevant legal and regulatory requirements in the 185 economies covered. Contact details for local partners are available on the *Doing Business* website at http://www.doingbusiness.org.

The online service of the *Doing Business* database is managed by Andres Baquero Franco, Varun Doiphode, Graeme Littler, Kunal Patel, Mohan Pathapati, Vinod Thottikkatu and Hashim Zia under the direction of Preeti Endlaw. The *Doing Business 2013* report media and marketing strategy is managed by Nadine Ghannam. The events and road-show strategy is managed by Sushmitha Malini Narsiah.

The team is grateful for valuable comments provided by colleagues across the World Bank Group and for the guidance of World Bank Group Executive Directors. It would especially like to acknowledge the comments and guidance of Aart C. Kraay. Comments were also received from Ali Abukumail, Hormoz Aghdaey, Pedro Alba, Alejandro Alvarez de la Campa, Inger Anderson, Nabila Assaf, Simon Bell, Najy Benhassine, Alexander Berg, Tony Bigio, Christopher Bleakley, Frank Fulgence K. Byamugisha, Otaviano Canuto, Kevin Carey, Guang Zhe Chen, Pamela Cox, Boris Divjak, Grahame Dixie, Delores Elliot, Fabrizio Fraboni, Jose Maria Garrido, Frederico Gil Sander, Indermit S. Gill, Eva M. Gutierrez, Mary Hallward-Driemeier, Marek Hanusch, Caroline Heider, Vijay Iyer, Karina Izaguirre, Melissa Johns, Lisa Kaestner, Arvo Kuddo, Sumir Lal, Giuseppe Larossi, Anne-Marie Leroy, Oscar Madeddu, Marie Francoise Marie-Nelly, Andres Federico Martinez, Philippe De Meneval, Riz Mokal, Marcin Piatkowski, Mohammad Zia M. Qureshi, Fanja Sahondraniaina Ravoavy, Susan Razzaz, Maria Camila Roberts, Michal Rutkowski, Shalini Sankaranarayanan, Massimiliano Santini, Jordan Schwartz, Peter Sheerin, Victoria Stanley, Rodrigo de Jesus Suescun, Mark Sundberg, Stoyan Tenev, Axel van Trotsenburg, Mahesh Uttamchandani, Tunc Uyanic, Jan Walliser, Wendy Jo Werner and Grace M. Yabrudy.

The paying taxes project was conducted in collaboration with PwC, led by John Preston. The development of the getting electricity indicators was financed by the Norwegian Trust Fund. The APEC Secretariat commented on the APEC case study. Jonathan Bailey, Omowunmi Ladipo and César Chaparro Yedro commented on the Rwanda case study. Aart C. Kraay and Alejandro Ponce commented on the case study on the transparency of business regulation.

Alison Strong copyedited the manuscript. Corporate Visions, Inc. designed the report and the graphs.

Quotations in this report are from *Doing Business* local partners unless otherwise indicated. The names of those wishing to be acknowledged individually are listed below. The global and regional contributors listed are firms that have completed multiple surveys in their various offices around the world.

## GLOBAL CONTRIBUTORS

*Advocates for International Development*

*Allen & Overy LLP*

*American Bar Association, Section of International Law*

*Baker & McKenzie*

*Cleary Gottlieb Steen & Hamilton LLP*

*Ernst & Young*

*Ius Laboris, Alliance of Labor, Employment, Benefits and Pensions Law Firms*

*KPMG*

*Law Society of England and Wales*

*Lex Mundi, Association of Independent Law Firms*

*Panalpina*

*PwC*[1]

*Raposo Bernardo & Associados*

*Russell Bedford International*

*SDV International Logistics*

*Security Cargo Network*

## REGIONAL CONTRIBUTORS

*A.P. Moller-Maersk Group*

*Association of Consumer Credit Information Suppliers (ACCIS)*

*Cabinet John W. Ffooks & Co.*

*Globalink Transportation & Logistics Worldwide LLP*

*Grata Law Firm*

*Jones Lang LaSalle*

*Salans International Law Firm*

*Talal Abu Ghazaleh Legal (TAG-Legal)*

*TransUnion International*

## AFGHANISTAN

Mirza Taqi Ud Din Ahmad
*A.F. Ferguson & Co., Chartered Accountants, a member firm of PwC network*

Naseem Akbar
*Afghanistan Investment Support Agency*

Mirwais Alami
*Da Afghanistan Breshna Sherkat*

Zabiullah Amin
*PSD Cluster*

Ziaullah Astana
*Afghan Land Consulting Organization (ALCO)*

Nadia Bazidwal
*Ministry of Commerce and Industry*

Abdullah Dowrani
*Financial Disputes Resolution Commission (FDRC)*

Suleman Fatimie
*Afghanistan Financial Services, LLC*

Amanda Galton
*Orrick, Herrington & Sutcliffe LLP*

Abdul Hanan
*Afghan Land Consulting Organization (ALCO)*

Rashid Ibrahim
*A.F. Ferguson & Co., Chartered Accountants, a member firm of PwC network*

Omar Joya
*Afghanistan Investment Support Agency*

Sanzar Kakar
*Afghanistan Financial Services, LLC*

Mohammed Masood Khwaja
*Da Afghanistan Breshna Sherkat*

Gaurav Lekh Raj Kukreja
*Afghan Container Transport Company*

Ghulam Rabani Mansoori
*Afghanistan Investment Support Agency*

Tali Mohammed
*Afghanistan Investment Support Agency*

Shekeeb Nessar
*Da Afghanistan Breshna Sherkat*

Ateequlah Nosher
*Da Afghanistan Bank*

Gul Pacha
*Afghanistan Investment Support Agency*

Tamsil Rashid
*Afghanistan International Bank*

Abdul Rahim Saeedi
*Ministry of Commerce and Industry*

Khalil Sediq
*Afghanistan International Bank*

Sharifullah Shirzad
*Da Afghanistan Bank*

Najibullah Wardak
*LARA*

Mohammadi Khan Yaqoobi
*Da Afghanistan Bank*

## ALBANIA

*Dyrrahsped SHPK*

Eduart Ahmeti
*Boga & Associates Tirana*

Artur Asllani
*Tonucci & Partners*

Sabina Baboci
*Kalo & Associates*

Redjan Basha
*A&B Business Consulting*

Ledia Beçi
*Hoxha, Memi & Hoxha*

Alban Bello
*KPMG Albania shpk*

Jona Bica
*Kalo & Associates*

Artan Bozo
*Bozo & Associates Law Firm*

Jonida Braja Melani
*Wolf Theiss*

Alban Caushi
*Kalo & Associates*

Sajmir Dautaj
*Tonucci & Partners*

Eniana Dupi
*AECO Consulting*

Erinda Duraj
*Bozo & Associates Law Firm*

Sokol Elmazaj
*Boga & Associates Tirana*

Alba Fagu
*Bank of Albania*

Lavdimir Fusha
*Alb BB Auditing SHPK - correspondent of Russell Bedford International*

Lisjana Fusha
*Alb BB Auditing SHPK - correspondent of Russell Bedford International*

Aurela Gjokutaj
*Al-Tax Studio*

Eduart Gjokutaj
*Al-Tax Studio*

Shirli Gorenca
*Kalo & Associates*

Luan Gosnishti
*Alb BB Auditing SHPK - correspondent of Russell Bedford International*

Mateo Gosnishti
*Alb BB Auditing SHPK - correspondent of Russell Bedford International*

Emel Haxhillari
*Kalo & Associates*

Blerina Hilaj
*A&B Business Consulting*

Shpati Hoxha
*Hoxha, Memi & Hoxha*

Elona Hoxhaj
*Boga & Associates Tirana*

Xhet Hushi
*Kalo & Associates*

Evis Jani
*Drakopoulos Law Firm*

Evandro Janka
*Bozo & Associates Law Firm*

Ilir Johollari
*Hoxha, Memi & Hoxha*

Sabina Lalaj
*Boga & Associates Tirana*

Dorian Kashuri
*Kalo & Associates*

Erlind Kodhelaj
*Boga & Associates Tirana*

Renata Leka
*Boga & Associates Tirana*

Dorjana Maliqi
*A&B Business Consulting*

Andi Memi
*Hoxha, Memi & Hoxha*

Aigest Milo
*Kalo & Associates*

Blerta Nesho
*Wolf Theiss*

Loreta Peci
*PwC Albania*

Florian Piperi
*OPTIMA Legal and Financial*

Artila Rama
*Boga & Associates Tirana*

Loriana Robo
*Kalo & Associates*

Anisa Rrumbullaku
*Kalo & Associates*

Ergis Sefa
*ERG Managerial*

Enkelejd Seitllari
*Kalo & Associates*

Ardjana Shehi
*Kalo & Associates*

Elda Shuraja
*Hoxha, Memi & Hoxha*

Majlinda Sulstarova
*Tonucci & Partners*

Besa Tauzi
*Boga & Associates Tirana*

Paul Tobin
*PwC Bulgaria*

Ketrin Topçiu
*Bozo & Associates Law Firm*

Ened Topi
*Boga & Associates Tirana*

Fioralba Trebicka
*Hoxha, Memi & Hoxha*

Alketa Uruçi
*Boga & Associates Tirana*

Gerhard Velaj
*Boga & Associates Tirana*

Silva Velaj
*Boga & Associates Tirana*

Aspasi Xhori
*CEZ Shperndarje sh.a*

Selena Ymeri
*Hoxha, Memi & Hoxha*

Enida Zeneli
*Bozo & Associates Law Firm*

## ALGERIA

Branka Achari-Djokic
*Banque d'Algérie*

Salima Aloui
*Law Firm Goussanem & Aloui*

Mohamed Atbi
*Etude Notariale Mohamed Atbi*

Djamila Azzouz
*Cabinet d'Audit Azzouz - correspondent of Russell Bedford International*

Salim Azzouz
*Cabinet d'Audit Azzouz - correspondent of Russell Bedford International*

Khodja Bachir
*SNC Khodja & Co.*

Samir Benslimane
*Cabinet Benslimane*

Adnane Bouchaib
*Bouchaib Law Firm*

Amin Bouhaddi
*Entreprise Bouhaddi*

Selima Daadouche
*Lefèvre Pelletier & associés*

Mohamed Dhif
*Centre National du Registre du Commerce*

Said Dib
*Banque d'Algérie*

Nicolas Granier
*Landwell & Associés*

Ould Hocine
*Studio A*

Goussanem Khaled
*Law Firm Goussanem & Aloui*

Arezki Khelout
*Ministère des Finances - Direction Générale du Domaine National*

Maya Laichoubi
*Ghellal & Mekerba*

Mohamed Lanouar
*Lefèvre Pelletier & associés*

Karine Lasne
*Landwell & Associés*

Vincent Lunel
*Lefèvre Pelletier & associés*

Bournissa Mehdi
*Landwell & Associés*

Sid-Ahmed Mekerba
*Ghellal & Mekerba*

Mohamed Mokrane
*Ministère des Finances - Direction Générale du Domaine National*

Fares Ouzegdouh
*Transport Port Logistics & Solutions*

Ahmed Rahou
*Ministère des Finances - Direction Générale du Domaine National*

Mourad Seghir
*Ghellal & Mekerba*

Mohamed Smati
*Avocat*

Benabid Mohammed Tahar
*Cabinet Mohammed Tahar Benabid*

## ANGOLA

*Ernst & Young*

*Lourdes Caposso Fernandes & Associados*

Alexandre Caldas Menezes
*Caldas Menezes*

Pedro Calixto
*PwC Angola*

Anacleta Cipriano
*FBL Advogados*

Miguel Conceição
*RGT- Advogados Associados*

Miguel de Avillez Pereira
*Abreu Advogados*

Patricia Dias
*AVM Advogados*

Beatriz Ferreira de Andrade dos Santos
*Banco Nacional de Angola*

Adérito Figueira
*Ministério da Energia e Águas*

Berta Grilo
*FBL Advogados*

Jacinto José
*EDEL-EP*

Victor Leonel
*Ordem dos Arquitectos*

Teresinha Lopes
*FBL Advogados*

Zinga Lourença Correia João
*EDEL-EP*

1. PwC refers to the network of member firms of PricewaterhouseCoopers International Limited (PwCIL), or, as the context requires, individual member firms of the PwC network. Each member firm is a separate legal entity and does not act as agent of PwCIL or any other member firm. PwCIL does not provide any services to clients. PwCIL is not responsible or liable for the acts or omissions of any of its member firms nor can it control the exercise of their professional judgment or bind them in any way. No member firm is responsible or liable for the acts or omissions of any other member firm nor can it control the exercise of another member firm's professional judgment or bind another member firm or PwCIL in any way.

Arlete Maia
*CFRA Advogados Associados*

Guirec Malfait
*SDV-AMI Angola Lda*

Vitor Marques da Cruz
*MC&A, in association with MVA - Mota Veiga Advogados*

Vanessa Mendes
*NTA - Noronha Tiny Advogados*

Marcos Neto
*Banco Nacional de Angola*

Luis Miguel Nunes
*AVM Advogados*

Janota Nzogi
*EDEL-EP*

Sofia Oliveira
*FBL Advogados*

Eduardo Paiva
*PwC Angola*

José Paxe
*IRSE - Instituto Regulador do Sector Eléctrico*

Nair Pitra
*CFRA Advogados Associados*

Laurinda Prazeres Cardoso
*FBL Advogados*

João Robles
*F. Castelo Branco & Associados*

Tatiana Serrao
*FBL Advogados*

Cristina Teixeira
*PwC Angola*

Kiluange Tiny
*NTA - Noronha Tiny Advogados*

Ludmilo Tiny
*NTA - Noronha Tiny Advogados*

N'Gunu Tiny
*CFRA Advogados Associados*

Antônio Vicente Marques
*AVM Advogados*

### ANTIGUA AND BARBUDA

Ricki Camacho
*Antigua & Barbuda Intellectual Property & Commerce (ABIPCO)*

Eleanor R. Clark
*Clarke & Clarke*

Neil Coates
*PwC Antigua*

Brian D'Ornellas
*OBM International, Antigua Ltd.*

Joy Dublin
*James & Associates*

Vernon Edwards Jr.
*Freight Forwarding & Deconsolidating*

Robert Giraldo
*CaribTrans*

Sherelyn Hughes Thomas
*Antigua and Barbuda Investment Authority*

Alfred McKelly James
*James & Associates*

Lenworth Johnson
*Johnson Gardiner*

Lisa M. John Weste
*Thomas, John & Co.*

Hugh C. Marshall
*Marshall & Co.*

Gloria Martin
*Francis Trading Agency Limited*

Girvan Pigott
*Antigua Public Utility Authority*

Septimus A. Rhudd
*Rhudd & Associates*

Stacy A. Richards-Anjo
*Richards & Co.*

Andrea Roberts
*Roberts & Co.*

Cathrona Samuel
*Antigua Public Utility Authority*

Lestroy Samuel
*Antigua and Barbuda Investment Authority*

Patricia Simon-Forde
*Chambers Patricia Simon-Forde*

Marsha Thomas
*PwC Antigua*

Hesketh Williams
*Ministry of Labor*

### ARGENTINA

Ignacio Acedo
*Gonzalez & Ferraro Mila*

Fernando Aguinaga
*Zang, Bergel & Viñes Abogados*

Lisandro A. Allende
*Brons & Salas Abogados*

Ignacio E. Aramburu
*Estudio Moltedo*

Natalia Artmann
*Alfaro Abogados*

Ariadna Artopoulos
*M. & M. Bomchil*

Alejo Baca Castex
*G. Breuer*

Vanesa Balda
*Vitale, Manoff & Feilbogen*

Gonzalo Carlos Ballester
*J.P. O'Farrell Abogados*

Néstor J. Belgrano
*M. & M. Bomchil*

Nicolás Belgrano
*M. & M. Bomchil*

Sebastián Bittner
*Jebsen & Co.*

Ignacio Fernández Borzese
*Luna Requena & Fernández Borzese Tax Law Firm*

Mariano Bourdieu
*Severgnini Robiola Grinberg & Larrechea*

Nicolás Bühler
*Hope, Duggan & Silva*

Adriana Paola Caballero
*Wiener Soto Caparrós*

Federico Carenzo
*Leonhardt, Dietl, Graf & von der Fecht*

Mariano E. Carricart
*Fornieles Law Firm*

Luciano Cativa
*Luna Requena & Fernández Borzese Tax Law Firm*

Pablo L. Cavallaro
*Estudio Cavallaro Abogados*

Guadalupe Cores
*Quattrini, Laprida & Asociados*

Roberto H. Crouzel
*Estudio Beccar Varela*

María Amalia Cruz
*Zang, Bergel & Viñes Abogados*

Valeria D'Alessandro
*Marval, O'Farrell & Mairal, member of Lex Mundi*

Nicolás de Ezcurra
*Estudio Beccar Varela*

Nicolás Debernardi
*Hope, Duggan & Silva*

Carola Del Rio
*Severgnini Robiola Grinberg & Larrechea*

Oscar Alberto del Río
*Central Bank of Argentina*

Julio C. Durand
*Cassagne Abogados*

Andrés Edelstein
*PwC Argentina*

Joaquín Eppens
*Murray, Anguillesi, Guyot, Rossi & Sirito de Zavalía*

Daniel Escolá
*Quattrini, Laprida & Asociados*

Juan M. Espeso
*Jebsen & Co.*

Pablo Ferraro Mila
*Gonzalez & Ferraro Mila*

Diego M. Fissore
*G. Breuer*

Alejandro D. Fiuza
*K&L Gates LLP New York*

Victoria Funes
*M. & M. Bomchil*

Martín Gastaldi
*Estudio Beccar Varela*

Giselle Rita Geuna
*Alfaro Abogados*

Juan Jose Glusman
*PwC Argentina*

María Soledad Gonzalez
*Marval, O'Farrell & Mairal, member of Lex Mundi*

Eugenia Goya
*Zang, Bergel & Viñes Abogados*

Matías Grinberg
*Severgnini Robiola Grinberg & Larrechea*

Sandra S. Guillan
*De Dios & Goyena Abogados Consultores*

Daniel Intile
*Daniel Intile & Asoc. - member of Russell Bedford International*

Martín Jebsen
*Jebsen & Co.*

Luciano José Nístico
*J.P. O'Farrell Abogados*

Santiago Laclau
*Marval, O'Farrell & Mairal, member of Lex Mundi*

Federico Hernán Laprida
*Quattrini, Laprida & Asociados*

Sofía Leggiero
*Severgnini Robiola Grinberg & Larrechea*

Bastiana Locurscio
*Rattagan, Macchiavello Arocena & Peña Robirosa Abogados*

Alvaro Luna Requena
*Luna Requena & Fernández Borzese Tax Law Firm*

Dolores Madueño
*Jebsen & Co.*

Juan Manuel Magadan
*PwC Argentina*

Rodrigo Marchan
*MetA*

María Lucila Marchini
*Estudio Beccar Varela*

Gonzalo María Gros
*J.P. O'Farrell Abogados*

Pedro Mazer
*Alfaro Abogados*

Diego Melfi
*Estudio Beccar Varela*

Maria Fernanda Mierez
*Estudio Beccar Varela*

José Oscar Mira
*Central Bank of Argentina*

Jorge Miranda
*Clippers S.A.*

Miguel P. Murray
*Murray, Anguillesi, Guyot, Rossi & Sirito de Zavalía*

Pablo Murray
*Fiorito Murray & Diaz Cordero*

Damián Mauricio Najenson
*Estudio Spota*

Alfredo Miguel O'Farrell
*Marval, O'Farrell & Mairal, member of Lex Mundi*

Gonzalo Oliva Beltran
*Llerena Amadeo, Dondo & Oliva Beltrán*

Javier M. Petrantonio
*M. & M. Bomchil*

Alejandro Poletto
*Estudio Beccar Varela*

Luis Ponsati
*J.P. O'Farrell Abogados*

José Miguel Puccinelli
*Estudio Beccar Varela*

Federico José Reibestein
*Reibestein & Asociados*

Miguel Remmer
*Estudio Beccar Varela*

Armando Ricci
*Zang, Bergel & Viñes Abogados*

Flavia Ríos
*J.P. O'Farrell Abogados*

Sebastián Rodrigo
*Alfaro Abogados*

Andrés Sebastián Rojas
*Estudio Beccar Varela*

Fernanda Sabbatini
*Wiener Soto Caparrós*

Jorge Sanchez Diaz
*Ecobamboo S.A.*

Esteban Aguirre Saravia
*Luna Requena & Fernández Borzese Tax Law Firm*

Mariela Sas
*M. & M. Bomchil*

Pablo Staszewski
*Staszewski & Asoc.*

Maria Alejandra Stefanich
*Marval, O'Farrell & Mairal, member of Lex Mundi*

Javier Tarasido
*Severgnini Robiola Grinberg & Larrechea*

Adolfo Tombolini
*Daniel Intile & Asoc. - member of Russell Bedford International*

Martín Torres Girotti
*M. & M. Bomchil*

María Paola Trigiani
*Alfaro Abogados*

Susana Urresti
*Edesur Electricidad Distribuidora Sur S.A.*

Hernan Verly
*Alfaro Abogados*

Paz Villamil
*Rattagan, Macchiavello Arocena & Peña Robirosa Abogados*

Saúl Zang
*Zang, Bergel & Viñes Abogados*

Joaquín Emilio Zappa
*J.P. O'Farrell Abogados*

Carlos Zima
*PwC Argentina*

### ARMENIA

Yelena Adamyan
*PHP Audit*

Armen Alaverdyan
*State Revenue Committee of the Government of the Republic of Armenia*

Ruzan Alaverdyan
*Ministry of Urban Development*

Sevak Aleksanyan
*Investment Law Group LLC*

Armen Arzumanyan
*FinStab LLC*

Sedrak Asatryan
*Concern-Dialog Law Firm*

Albert Babayan
*Ministry of Economy of Armenia*

Karapet Badalyan
*Prudence Legal*

Sayad S. Badalyan
*Investment Law Group LLC*

Haykaz Bakhshetsyan
*Elite Group*

Vardan Bezhanyan
*Law Faculty, Yerevan State University*

Abgar Budaghyan
*Public Services Regulatory Commission of Armenia*

Artyom Chakhalyan
*Logicon Development LLC*

Vahe Chibukhchyan
*Ministry of Economy of Armenia*

Vahe Danielyan
*Ministry of Economy of Armenia*

Kristina Dudukchyan
*KPMG*

Aikanush Edigaryan
*Trans-Alliance*

Gagik Galstyan
*Horizon 95*

Koryun Gevorgyan
*Ministry of Economy of Armenia*

Vahe Ghavalyan
*Paradigma Armenia CJSC*

Hayk Ghazazyan
*KPMG*

Suren Gomtsyan
*Concern-Dialog Law Firm*

Armine Grigoryan
*The State Committee of the Real Property Cadastre of the Government of the Republic of Armenia*

Narek Grigoryan
*The State Committee of the Real Property Cadastre of the Government of the Republic of Armenia*

Tigran Grigoryan
*Ameria CJSC*

Sargis H. Martirosyan
*Trans-Alliance*

Gevorg Hakobyan
*Concern-Dialog Law Firm*

Meri Hambardzumyan
*Armenia Judical Department*

Davit Harutyunyan
*PwC Armenia*

Isabella Hovhannisyan
*EBRD Business Support Office*

Davit Iskandarian
*HSBC Bank*

Paruyr Jangulyan
*Ministry of Economy of Armenia*

Vahram Jotyan
*Gosselin*

Tigran Jrbashyan
*Ameriabank CJSC*

Artashes F. Kakoyan
*Investment Law Group LLC*

Vahe G. Kakoyan
*Investment Law Group LLC*

Arshak Karapetyan
*Investment Law Group LLC*

Georgi Khachatryan
*Ameria CJSC*

Aida Khachaturian

Karen Khachaturyan
*The State Committee of the Real Property Cadastre of the Government of the Republic of Armenia*

Marine Khchoyan
*Logicon Development LLC*

Tigran Kocharyan
*Compact Real Estate Agency LLC*

Karen Martirosyan
*Ameria CJSC*

Lilit Martirosyan
*Hovnanian International Ltd.*

Lilit Matevosyan
*PwC Armenia*

Arsen Matikyan
*CMA CGM*

Robin McCone
*PwC Armenia*

Armen Melkumyan
*Prudence Legal*

Gurgen Migranovich Minasyan
*Union of Builders of Armenia*

Armen Mkoyan
*Elite Group*

Gagik Mkrtchyan
*Technometre LLC*

Vahe Movsisyan
*Investment Law Group LLC*

Ashot Musayan
*The State Committee of the Real Property Cadastre of the Government of the Republic of Armenia*

Nerses Nersisyan
*PwC Armenia*

Artur Nikoyan
*Trans-Alliance*

Anna Nubaryan
*Ameria CJSC*

Aram Orbelyan
*Ministry of Justice*

Anahit Petrosyan
*Paradigma Armenia CJSC*

Karen Petrosyan
*Investment Law Group LLC*

Naira Petrosyan
*Paradigma Armenia CJSC*

Vahe Petrosyan
*Logicon Development LLC*

Aram Poghosyan
*Grant Thornton LLP*

Arman Porsughyan
*Ameria CJSC*

Gagik Sahakyan
*Ameriabank CJSC*

David Sargsyan
*Ameria CJSC*

Ruben Shahmuradyan
*Comfort R&V*

Suzanna Shamakhyan
*Concern-Dialog Law Firm*

Gayane Shimshiryan

Hakob Tadevosyan
*Grant Thornton LLP*

Artur Tunyan
*Judicial Reform Project*

Lilit Tunyan
*FINCA Universal Credit Organization CJSC*

Araik Vardanyan
*Chamber of Commerce and Industry of the Republic of Armenia*

Arman Yesayan
*Alfa System Technologies*

Aram Zakaryan
*ACRA Credit Bureau*

## AUSTRALIA

*Allen & Overy*

*Fayman International Pty. Ltd.*

*Veda Advantage*

Zeallie Ainsworth
*Clifford Chance*

Elizabeth Allen
*PwC Australia*

Lynda Brumm
*PwC Australia*

David Buda
*RBHM Commercial Lawyers*

Chris Camillin
*Holman Webb Lawyers*

Alicia Castillo
*Alicia Castillo Wealthing Group*

Joe Catanzariti
*Clayton Utz, member of Lex Mundi*

Greg Channell
*Department of Lands*

Gaibrielle Cleary
*Gould Ralph Pty Ltd. - member of Russell Bedford International*

Tim Cox
*PwC Australia*

Philip Crawford
*Henry Davis York*

Mark Dalby
*Office of State Revenue, NSW Treasury*

Anne Davis
*Clayton Utz, member of Lex Mundi*

Jenny Davis
*EnergyAustralia*

Warren Davis
*Gadens Lawyers*

Chaz Dheer
*Marque Lawyers*

Kelly Dickson
*M+K Lawyers*

Robert Downing
*Macpherson + Kelley Lawyers*

Sam Eichenbaum
*M+K Lawyers*

Ian Farmer
*PwC Australia*

Nicole Flint
*Arnold Bloch Leibler*

Grant Guenther
*M+K Lawyers*

Owen Hayford
*Clayton Utz, member of Lex Mundi*

Jason Henniker
*EnergyAustralia*

Erica Henshilwood
*Marque Lawyers*

David Hopwood
*M+K Lawyers*

Amelia Horvath
*Clifford Chance*

Ian Humphreys
*Ashurst LLP*

Jennifer Ingram
*Clayton Utz, member of Lex Mundi*

Stephen Jauncey
*Henry Davis York*

Melissa Kirby
*Honeywell*

Paul Kirton
*M+K Lawyers*

Rachel Kong
*Marque Lawyers*

Przemek Kucharski
*Allens Arthur Robinson*

David Larish
*King & Wood Mallesons*

Chi-Yung Lee
*M+K Lawyers*

John Lobban
*Ashurst LLP*

Prue Long
*M+K Lawyers*

Suzy Madar
*King & Wood Mallesons*

John Martin
*Thomson Playford*

Melody Martin
*Ashurst LLP*

Mitchell Mathas
*Norton Rose*

Nathan Mattock
*Marque Lawyers*

Nicholas Mavrakis
*Clayton Utz, member of Lex Mundi*

Des Mooney
*Department of Lands*

Louise Murphy
*Marque Lawyers*

Aparna Nanayakkara
*Allens Arthur Robinson*

William Nerlich
*M+K Lawyers*

Claudia Newman-Martin
*King & Wood Mallesons*

Meredith Paynter
*King & Wood Mallesons*

Mark Pistilli
*Clifford Chance*

Michael Quinlan
*Allens Arthur Robinson*

John Reid
*Office of State Revenue, NSW Treasury*

Bob Ronai

Amber Sharp
*Marque Lawyers*

Marisha Steinberg
*King & Wood Mallesons*

Damian Sturzaker
*Marque Lawyers*

Allira Swick
*Marque Lawyers*

Nick Thomas
*Clayton Utz, member of Lex Mundi*

Rosie Thomas
*King & Wood Mallesons*

Robert Tracy
*Henry Davis York*

Simon Truskett
*Clayton Utz, member of Lex Mundi*

David Twigg
*EnergyAustralia*

## AUSTRIA

*Austrian Regulatory Authority*

*Vienna Business Agency*

*Wien Kanal*

Clemens Baerenthaler
*DLA Piper Weiss-Tessbach Rechtsanwälte GmbH*

Georg Bahn
*Freshfields Bruckhaus Deringer*

Constantin Benes
*Schoenherr*

Georg Brandstetter
*Brandstetter Pritz & Partner*

Doris Buxbaum
*Heger & Partner*

Bruno Clemente Palma
*PwC Austria*

Martin Eckel
*e|n|w|c Natlacen Walderdorff Cancola Rechtsanwälte GmbH*

Agnes Eigner
*Brandstetter Pritz & Partner*

Tibor Fabian
*Binder Grösswang Rechtsanwälte GmbH*

Julian Feichtinger
*CHSH Cerha Hempel Spiegelfeld Hlawati*

Ferdinand Graf
*Graf & Pitkowitz Rechtsanwälte GmbH*

Andreas Hable
*Binder Grösswang Rechtsanwälte GmbH*

Tina Hausensteiner
*bpv Hügel Rechtsanwälte OG*

Friedrich Helml
*SCWP Schindhelm Austria*

Alexander Hofmann
*RA Dr. Alexander Hofmann, LL.M.*

Lothar Hofmann
*HLAW*

Alexander Isola
*Graf & Pitkowitz Rechtsanwälte GmbH*

Rudolf Kaindl
*Koehler, Kaindl, Duerr & Partner, Civil Law Notaries*

Alexander Klauser
*Brauneis Klauser Prändl Rechtsanwälte GmbH*

Rudolf Krickl
*PwC Austria*

Barbara Luger
*Freshfields Bruckhaus Deringer*

Peter Madl
*Schoenherr*

Wolfgang Messeritsch
*Oesterreichische Nationalbank*

Gerald Mitteregger
*International Logistic Gateway*

Gerhard Muggenhuber
*BEV - Federal Office of Metrology & Surveying*

Elke Napokoj
*bpv Hügel Rechtsanwälte OG*

Felix Neuwirther
*Freshfields Bruckhaus Deringer*

Christian Pöchlinger
*PwC Austria*

Barbara Pogacar
*bpv Hügel Rechtsanwälte OG*

Martina Raczova
*Graf & Pitkowitz Rechtsanwälte GmbH*

Ulla Reisch
*Urbanek Lind Schmied Reisch Rechtsanwälte OG*

Georg Schima
*Kunz Schima Wallentin Rechtsanwälte OG, member of Ius Laboris*

Stephan Schmalzl
*Graf & Pitkowitz Rechtsanwälte GmbH*

Ernst Schmidt
*Halpern & Prinz*

Christian Schuppich
*CHSH Cerha Hempel Spiegelfeld Hlawati*

Reinhard Schwarz
*International Logistic Gateway*

Franz Schwarzinger
*Revisionstreuhand - member of Russell Bedford International*

Günther Sedlacek
*Oesterreichische Nationalbank*

Wolfgang Tichy
*Schoenherr*

Thomas Trettnak
*CHSH Cerha Hempel Spiegelfeld Hlawati*

Christoph Twaroch
*Technical University Vienna*

Wolfgang Vanas
*Graf & Pitkowitz Rechtsanwälte GmbH*

Birgit Vogt-Majarek
*Kunz Schima Wallentin Rechtsanwälte OG, member of Ius Laboris*

Gerhard Wagner
*KSV 1870*

Lukas A Weber
*Brauneis Klauser Prändl Rechtsanwälte GmbH*

Thomas Zottl
*Freshfields Bruckhaus Deringer*

Christian Zwick
*Binder Grösswang Rechtsanwälte GmbH*

## AZERBAIJAN

*OMNI Law Firm*

Aliagha Akhundov
*Baker & McKenzie - CIS, Limited*

Elnur Aliyev
*BHM Baku Law Centre LLC*

Rashid Aliyev
*Baker & McKenzie - CIS, Limited*

Sevinj Aliyeva
*MGB Law Offices*

Jamil Alizada
*Baker & McKenzie - CIS, Limited*

Aykhan Asadov
*Baker & McKenzie - CIS, Limited*

Ismail Askerov
*MGB Law Offices*

Esmer Atakishiyeva
*Azerbaijan Global Logistic*

Anar Baghirov
*BHM Baku Law Centre LLC*

Natavan Baghirova
*BM Morrison Partners Law Firm*

Samir Balayev
*Unibank*

Johanna Cronin
*BHM Baku Law Centre LLC*

Sevil Gasimova
*Baker & McKenzie - CIS, Limited*

Abbas Guliyev
*Baker & McKenzie - CIS, Limited*

Arif Guliyev
*PwC Azerbaijan*

Gulnar Gurbanova
*BHM Baku Law Centre LLC*

Elchin Habibov
*Central Bank of Azerbaijan*

Samir Hadjiyev
*MICHAEL WILSON & PARTNERS LTD.*

Nigar Hajiyeva
*BAKER & MCKENZIE - CIS, LIMITED*

Gulshan Hasanova
*BHM BAKU LAW CENTRE LLC*

Elmar Huseynov
*BLUE WATER SHIPPING LTD.*

Zaur Huseynov
*OJSC BAKIELEKTRIKSHEBEKE*

Jeyhun Huseynzada
*PWC AZERBAIJAN*

Ruhiyya Isayeva
*SALANS*

Delara Israfilova
*BM MORRISON PARTNERS LAW FIRM*

Vagif Karimli
*BAKER & MCKENZIE - CIS, LIMITED*

Fuad Karimov
*KERMUR SPECIALIZED BUREAU OF ADVOCATES*

Emin Karimov

Rena Khalilova
*DELOITTE LLP*

Ferid Madatli
*BM MORRISON PARTNERS LAW FIRM*

Kamal Mamedzade
*SALANS*

Javanshir Mammadov
*GRATA LAW FIRM*

Faiq S. Manafov
*UNIBANK*

Daniel Matthews
*BAKER & MCKENZIE - CIS, LIMITED*

Farhad Mirzayev
*BM MORRISON PARTNERS LAW FIRM*

Ruslan Mukhtarov
*BM MORRISON PARTNERS LAW FIRM*

Atakishi Nadirov
*PWC AZERBAIJAN*

Mammad Nazaraliyev
*STATE OIL COMPANY OF AZERBAIJAN REPUBLIC*

Naida Sadigova
*SALANS*

Ali Samedov
*AZERBAIJAN GLOBAL LOGISTIC*

Natig Shirinov
*MINISTRY OF TAXES*

Elvira Sirajzada
*DELOITTE LLP*

Mehman Sultanov
*BHM BAKU LAW CENTRE LLC*

Sona Tagieva
*SALANS*

Kamil Valiyev
*STATE OIL COMPANY OF AZERBAIJAN REPUBLIC*

Murad Yahyayev
*UNIBANK*

Ulvia Zeynalova-Bockin
*SALANS*

### BAHAMAS, THE

*MCKINNEY, BANCROFT & HUGHES*

David F. Allen
*BAHAMAS LAW CHAMBERS*

Kevin Basden
*BAHAMAS ELECTRICITY CORPORATION*

Natasha Bosfield
*LENNOX PATON*

Rodney W. Braynen
*DESIGN HÄUS*

Tara Cooper Burnside
*HIGGS & JOHNSON*

Surinder Deal

Craig G. Delancy
*THE COMMONWEALTH OF THE BAHAMAS, MINISTRY OF WORKS & TRANSPORT*

Amos J. Ferguson Jr.
*FERGUSON ASSOCIATES & PLANNERS*

Wendy Forsythe
*IMPORT EXPORT BROKERS LTD.*

Vann P. Gaitor
*HIGGS & JOHNSON*

Kenneth L. Lightbourne
*GRAHAM, THOMPSON & CO.*

Portia Nicholson
*HIGGS & JOHNSON*

Andrew G.S O'Brien II
*GLINTON, SWEETING,O'BRIEN LAW FIRM*

Sophie Rolle
*LENNOX PATON*

Castino D. Sands
*LENNOX PATON*

Rochelle Sealy
*PWC BAHAMAS*

Kevin Seymour
*PWC BAHAMAS*

Burlington Strachan
*BAHAMAS ELECTRICITY CORPORATION*

Jody Wells
*LENNOX PATON*

### BAHRAIN

*ELECTRICITY & WATER AUTHORITY*

*ERNST & YOUNG*

Najma Abdul-Redha Hassan
*MINISTRY OF MUNICIPALITIES AND URBAN PLANNING*

Amel Al Aseeri
*ZEENAT AL MANSOORI & ASSOCIATES*

Eman Al Haji
*TALAL ABU GHAZALEH LEGAL (TAG-LEGAL)*

Zeenat Al Mansoori
*ZEENAT AL MANSOORI & ASSOCIATES*

Reem Al Rayes
*ZEENAT AL MANSOORI & ASSOCIATES*

Mohamed Al-Ahmadi
*BAHRAIN INVESTORS CENTER*

Haider Al-Noaimi
*MOHAMED SALAHUDDIN CONSULTING ENGINEERING BUREAU*

Raju Alagarsamy
*HASSAN RADHI & ASSOCIATES*

Shaji Alukkal
*PANALPINA WORLD TRANSPORT LLP*

Rahiel Bhikhie
*PWC BAHRAIN*

Michael Durgavich
*ASAR - AL RUWAYEH & PARTNERS*

Ken Healy
*PWC BAHRAIN*

Hessa Hussain
*THE BENEFIT COMPANY*

Seema Isa Al-Thawadi
*MINISTRY OF MUNICIPALITIES AND URBAN PLANNING*

Jawad Habib Jawad
*BDO JAWAD HABIB*

Shereen Karimi
*TALAL ABU GHAZALEH LEGAL (TAG-LEGAL)*

Ebrahim Karolia
*PWC BAHRAIN*

Ronald Langat
*HAYA RASHED AL KHALIFA*

Saifuddin Mahmood
*HASSAN RADHI & ASSOCIATES*

Abdul-Haq Mohammed
*TROWERS & HAMLINS*

Eman Omar
*QAYS H. ZU'BI ATTORNEYS & LEGAL CONSULTANTS*

Hassan Ali Radhi
*HASSAN RADHI & ASSOCIATES*

Najib Saade
*ASAR - AL RUWAYEH & PARTNERS*

Mohamed Salahuddin
*MOHAMED SALAHUDDIN CONSULTING ENGINEERING BUREAU*

Thamer Salahuddin
*MOHAMED SALAHUDDIN CONSULTING ENGINEERING BUREAU*

Cecile Scaros
*QAYS H. ZU'BI ATTORNEYS & LEGAL CONSULTANTS*

Esmond Hugh Stokes
*HATIM S. ZU'BI & PARTNERS*

Baiju Thomas
*AGILITY LOGISTICS*

Hatim S. Zu'bi
*HATIM S. ZU'BI & PARTNERS*

### BANGLADESH

Zainul Abedin
*A. QASEM & CO.*

Afrin Akhter
*A. QASEM & CO.*

Sharmin Akter
*AMIR & AMIR LAW ASSOCIATES, MEMBER OF LEX MUNDI*

K. M. Tanzib Alam
*TANJIB UL ALAM AND ASSOCIATES*

Md. Shafiul Alam
*THE HONGKONG AND SHANGHAI BANKING CORPORATION LTD.*

Noorul Azhar
*AZHAR & ASSOCIATES*

A.S.A. Bari
*A.S. & ASSOCIATES*

Anirban Bhowmik
*BANK OF BANGLADESH*

Taslim Uddin Bhuiyan
*AMIR & AMIR LAW ASSOCIATES, MEMBER OF LEX MUNDI*

Gouranga Chakraborty
*BANK OF BANGLADESH*

Jamilur Reza Choudhury

Nasirud Doulah
*DOULAH & DOULAH ADVOCATES*

Shamsud Doulah
*DOULAH & DOULAH ADVOCATES*

K. M. A. Halim
*UPRIGHT TEXTILE SUPPORTS*

Mirza Quamrul Hasan
*ADVISER'S LEGAL ALLIANCE FIRM*

Farhana Hossain
*ZOHA ZAMAN KABIR RASHID & CO., CHARTERED ACCOUNTANTS*

Arif Imtiaz
*FM ASSOCIATES*

M. Amir-Ul Islam
*AMIR & AMIR LAW ASSOCIATES, MEMBER OF LEX MUNDI*

Ariful Islam
*BHUIYAN ISLAM & ZAIDI*

Md Aminul Islam
*CITY APPAREL-TEX CO.*

Seema Karim
*AMIR & AMIR LAW ASSOCIATES, MEMBER OF LEX MUNDI*

Sohel Kasem
*A. QASEM & CO.*

Asif Khan
*A. QASEM & CO.*

Sayeed Khan
*A.S. & ASSOCIATES*

Qazi Mahtab-uz-Zaman

Shahjahan Mia
*DHAKA ELECTRICITY SUPPLY COMPANY LTD. (DESCO)*

Mohammad Moniruzzaman
*THE LAW COUNSEL*

A.I.M. Monsoor

Sultana Nasrin
*AMIR & AMIR LAW ASSOCIATES, MEMBER OF LEX MUNDI*

Eva Quasem
*AMIR & AMIR LAW ASSOCIATES, MEMBER OF LEX MUNDI*

Ahmedur Rahim
*REGISTRAR, JOINT STOCK COMPANIES & FIRMS*

Al Amin Rahman
*FM ASSOCIATES*

Ferdaus Rahman
*A.S. & ASSOCIATES*

Tarek Rashid
*ZOHA ZAMAN KABIR RASHID & CO., CHARTERED ACCOUNTANTS*

Abdus Samad
*A.S. & ASSOCIATES*

Imran Siddiq
*THE LAW COUNSEL*

Taposh
*ENERGYPAC ENGINEERING LTD.*

Sabrina Zarin
*FM ASSOCIATES*

### BARBADOS

Ramone Alleyne
*CLARKE GITTENS FARMER*

Ricardo Anderson
*SRM ARCHITECTS LTD.*

Alicia Archer
*ARTEMIS LAW*

Patricia Boyce
*EVERSON R. ELCOCK & CO. LTD.*

Andrew F. Brathwaite
*AFB CONSULTING*

Anthony Brooks
*TONY BROOKS ARCHITECTS LTD.*

George Browne
*TOWN AND COUNTRY DEVELOPMENT PLANNING OFFICE*

Louis Christie
*TMR SALES & SERVICE LTD.*

Berkeley Clark
*BJS CUSTOMS SERVICE INC.*

Grady M. Clarke
*CARIBBEAN CREDIT BUREAU*

Heather A. Clarke
*CORPORATE AFFAIRS AND INTELLECTUAL PROPERTY OFFICE*

Joy-Ann Clarke
*LAND REGISTRY DEPARTMENT*

Horace Cobham
*RBC ROYAL BANK*

Andrew Cox
*MINISTRY OF LABOR AND SOCIAL SECURITY*

Madam Justice Maureen Crane-Scott
*SUPREME COURT OF BARBADOS*

Sherica J. Mohammed Cumberbatch
*CARRINGTON & SEALY*

Adrian W. Cummins
*CARRINGTON & SEALY*

Mark Cummins
*TOWN AND COUNTRY DEVELOPMENT PLANNING OFFICE*

Marcel El-Daher
*DAHER & ASSOCIATES*

Adrian M. Elcock
*EVERSON R. ELCOCK & CO. LTD.*

Antonio Elcock
*EVERSON R. ELCOCK & CO. LTD.*

Andrew C. Ferreira
*CHANCERY CHAMBERS*

Lorenzo Forde
*PWC BARBADOS*

Basil A. Giles
*YEARWOOD AND BOYCE*

Stanton Gittens
*STANGITTS LIMITED*

Adam Godson
*ROTHERLY CONSTRUCTION INC.*

Anice C.N. Granville
*LEX CARIBBEAN*

Yolande F. Howard
*MINISTRY OF LABOR AND SOCIAL SECURITY*

Russ Jones
*PWC BARBADOS*

Ruan C. Martinez
*BCF*

Jenevieve Maynard
*INN CHAMBERS*

David McCollin
*LAND REGISTRY DEPARTMENT*

Jennifer R. Murray
*THE BANK OF NOVA SCOTIA*

Percy Murrell
*P CUSTOMS BROKERS AIR SEA AND LAND TRANSPORT INC.*

Ricardo Norville
*MINISTRY OF LABOR AND SOCIAL SECURITY*

Noel M. Nurse
*THE BOOTH STEAMSHIP CO. (B'DOS) LTD.*

Laurel Odle
*PWC BARBADOS*

Gina D. Patrick
*TOWN AND COUNTRY DEVELOPMENT PLANNING OFFICE*

Sheridan A. Reece
*CARRINGTON & SEALY*

P.E. Serrao
*FITZWILLIAM, STONE & ALCAZAR*

Joe Steinbok
*ROTHERLY CONSTRUCTION INC.*

Kaye A. Williams
*MERIDIAN LAW*

Stephen Worme
*THE BARBADOS LIGHT AND POWER COMPANY LTD.*

### BELARUS

Amir Al-Haidar
*REVERA CONSULTING GROUP*

Tatiana Aleksnina
*CHSH CERHA HEMPEL SPIEGELFELD HLAWATI*

Alexey Anischenko
*SORAINEN*

Aliaksandr Anisovich
*PROMAUDIT*

Kiryl Apanasevich
*VLASOVA MIKHEL & PARTNERS*

Dmitry Arkhipenko
*REVERA CONSULTING GROUP*

Alexander Artsiukhevich
*JURZNAK LAW FIRM LLC*

Dzmitry Barouka
*Arzinger & Partners International Law Firm*

Irina A. Belskaya
*The Supreme Economic Court of the Republic of Belarus*

Vladimir G. Biruk
*Capital Group*

Evgeniya Borisevich

Ekaterina V. Borovtsova
*The Supreme Economic Court of the Republic of Belarus*

Alexander Botian
*Borovtsov & Salei Law Offices*

Sergey Chistyakov
*Stepanovski, Papakul and Partners Ltd.*

Alexey Daryin
*Revera Consulting Group*

Sergey Dubovik
*National Bank of the Republic of Belarus*

Tatiana Emelianova
*Vlasova Mikhel & Partners*

Andrej Ermolenko
*Vlasova Mikhel & Partners*

Alena Gavdur
*Arzinger & Partners International Law Firm*

Kirill Golovko
*Revera Consulting Group*

Evgenia Goriounova
*Borovtsov & Salei Law Offices*

Tatiana Guretskaya
*Revera Consulting Group*

Oleg Gvozd
*PwC Belarus*

Elena Hmeleva
*Businessconsult Law Firm*

Antonina Ivanova
*Law Firm DICSA*

Marina Kalinouskaya
*Jurznak Law Firm LLC*

Alina Kalinovskaya

Uljana Karpekina
*Revera Consulting Group*

Dmitry Khalimonchyk
*Jurznak Law Firm LLC*

Maria Khomenko
*PwC Belarus*

Sergey Khostovich
*GS Plus*

Alexander Khrapoutski
*Sysouev, Bondar, Khrapoutski Law Firm*

Alexander Kirilenko
*Agency of Ternaround Technologies*

Nina Knyazeva
*Businessconsult Law Firm*

Irina Koikova
*Law Firm DICSA*

Alexander Korsak
*Arzinger & Partners International Law Firm*

Dmitry Kovalchik
*Stepanovski, Papakul and Partners Ltd.*

Anna Kozlova
*BNT Legal & Tax*

Sergey G. Krasovsky
*The Supreme Economic Court of the Republic of Belarus*

Olga Kuchinskaya
*Vlasova Mikhel & Partners*

Alexandra Kuchminskaya
*Revera Consulting Group*

Anastasiya Kudryakova
*National Cadastral Agency*

Elena Lefter
*Arzinger & Partners International Law Firm*

Alexander Ließem
*BNT Legal & Tax*

Sergei Makarchuk
*CHSH Cerha Hempel Spiegelfeld Hlawati*

Sergei Makarchuk
*CHSH Cerha Hempel Spiegelfeld Hlawati*

Mikalai Markounik
*Vlasova Mikhel & Partners*

Sergey Mashonsky
*Arzinger & Partners International Law Firm*

Dmitry Matveyev
*Law Group Argument*

Tatiana I. Melnik
*The Supreme Economic Court of the Republic of Belarus*

Konstantin Mikhel
*Vlasova Mikhel & Partners*

Dmitry Montik
*Individual Entrepreneur*

Helen Mourashko
*Revera Consulting Group*

Valiantsina Neizvestnaya
*Audit and Consulting Ltd., Belarus*

Anna Nikolaeva
*Revera Consulting Group*

Sergei Odintsov
*PwC Belarus*

Yulia Ovseichyk
*Revera Consulting Group*

Volha Parfenchyk
*CHSH Cerha Hempel Spiegelfeld Hlawati*

Ekaterina Pastukhovich
*National Bank of the Republic of Belarus*

Anastasiya Pavliuchenko
*Revera Consulting Group*

Olga Pepenina
*Glimstedt*

Vladimir Aleksandrovich Polishuk
*Profelektroproekt*

Olga Prokopova
*National Bank of the Republic of Belarus*

Alexandr Putyato
*Revera Consulting Group*

Inesa Safronava
*PwC Belarus*

Maksim Salahub
*Vlasova Mikhel & Partners*

Vassili I. Salei
*Borovtsov & Salei Law Offices*

Volha Samasiuk
*Belarus State University*

Yury Samkov
*Borovtsov & Salei Law Offices*

Elena Sapego
*Stepanovski, Papakul and Partners Ltd.*

Kristina Shibeko

Yulia Shuba
*Borovtsov & Salei Law Offices*

Dmitry Skorodulin
*Belarus State University*

Anna Skorodulina
*Jurznak Law Firm LLC*

Sergey Strelchik
*Valex Consult*

Alla Sundukova
*Ministry of Taxes and Duties Belarus*

Natalia Talai
*Vlasova Mikhel & Partners*

Alesia Tsekhanava
*Law Firm DICSA*

Natalia Ulasevich
*Glimstedt*

Eugenia Urodnich
*Glimstedt*

Elena Usenia
*Arzinger & Partners International Law Firm*

Sviatlana Valuyeva
*Stepanovski, Papakul and Partners Ltd.*

Alexander Vasilevsky
*Valex Consult*

Oleg Veremeychik
*National Bank of the Republic of Belarus*

Igor Verkhovodko
*Businessconsult Law Firm*

Dmitry Viltovsky
*Arzinger & Partners International Law Firm*

Irina Voronchuk
*Arzinger & Partners International Law Firm*

Alexey Voronchuk
*Revera Consulting Group*

Maria Yurieva
*Sorainen*

Ekaterina Zabello
*Vlasova Mikhel & Partners*

Olga Zdobnova
*Vlasova Mikhel & Partners*

Dmitri Zikratsky
*Revera Consulting Group*

Maxim Znak
*Jurznak Law Firm LLC*

Nadezhda Znak
*Jurznak Law Firm LLC*

## BELGIUM

*Centre Administratif de la Ville de Bruxelles*

*Stibbe*

*Wouters, Van Merode & Co. - member of Russell Bedford International*

Hubert André-Dumont
*McGuire Woods LLP*

Patrick Bissot
*National Bank of Belgium*

Géraldine Blairvacq
*SPF Finances - AGDP*

Erik Bomans
*Deminor International SCRL*

Hakim Boularbah
*Liedekerke Wolters Waelbroeck Kirkpatrick, member of Lex Mundi*

Yves Brosens
*DLA Piper UK LLP*

Adriaan Dauwe
*Altius*

Astrid de Bandt
*Deminor International SCRL*

Koenraad De Bie
*PwC Belgium*

Esther De Raymaeker
*DLA Piper UK LLP*

Kris De Schutter
*Loyens & Loeff*

Didier De Vliegher
*NautaDutilh*

Frank Dierckx
*PwC Belgium*

Camille Dümm
*National Bank of Belgium*

Jürgen Egger
*Laga*

Aline Etienne
*NautaDutilh*

Alain François
*Eubelius Attorneys*

Conny Grenson
*Eubelius Attorneys*

Jean-Luc Hagon
*Loyens & Loeff*

Thomas Hürner
*National Bank of Belgium*

An Jacobs
*Liedekerke Wolters Waelbroeck Kirkpatrick, member of Lex Mundi*

Grégoire Jakhian
*Loyens & Loeff*

Olivia Ledoux
*NautaDutilh*

Erika Leenknecht
*Eubelius Attorneys*

Stephan Legein
*Federal Public Service Finance*

Luc Legon
*PwC Belgium*

Axel Maeterlinck
*Simont Braun*

Philippe Massart
*Sibelga*

Glenn Moolenschot
*Eubelius Attorneys*

Dominique Mougenot
*Commercial Court Mons*

Peter Neefs
*National Bank of Belgium*

Sabrina Otten
*PwC Belgium*

Timothy Speelman
*McGuire Woods LLP*

Damien Stas de Richelle
*DLA Piper UK LLP*

Nicolas Stoffels
*PwC Belgium*

Jan Van Celst
*DLA Piper UK LLP*

Erwin van de Velde
*SPF Finances - AGDP*

Bart Van Rossum
*B.T.V.*

Sibylle Vandenberghe
*PwC Belgium*

Grégory Vandenbussche
*Aren Architects and Engineers sprl*

Tom Vantroyen
*Altius*

Robert Vermetten
*Transport & Project Logistics*

Ivan Verougstraete
*Cour de Cassation*

Katrien Vorlat
*Stibbe*

Bram Vuylsteke
*Notary Bram Vuylsteke*

Christian Willems
*Loyens & Loeff*

## BELIZE

Emil Arguelles
*Arguelles & Company LLC*

John Avery
*Public Utilities Commission*

José A. Bautista
*PKF International*

Emory K. Bennett
*Young's Engineering Consultancy Ltd.*

Herbert Bradley
*Herbert Bradley Custom house brokers*

Christopher Coye
*Courtenay Coye LLP*

Julius Espat
*Strukture Architects*

Sherman Ferguson
*Belize Electricity Ltd.*

Velda Flowers
*Belize Companies and Corporate Affairs Registry*

Gian C. Gandhi
*International Financial Services Commission*

Celina Gill
*Belize Electricity Ltd.*

Glenn D. Godfrey S.C.
*Glenn D. Godfrey & Co LLP*

C. Victor Lewis
*Public Utilities Commission*

Reynaldo F. Magana
*Frontier International Business Services Limited*

Tania Moody
*Barrow & Williams*

Vanessa Retreage
*W.H. Courtenay & Co.*

Patricia Rodriguez
*Belize Companies and Corporate Affairs Registry*

Oscar Sabido S.C.
*Sabido & Company*

Saidi Vaccaro
*Arguelles & Company LLC*

Ryan Wrobel
*Wrobel & Co., Attorneys-at-Law*

Carlton Young
*Young's Engineering Consultancy Ltd.*

## BENIN

*Cabinet John W. Ffooks & Co.*

Safia Abdoulaye
*Cabinet d'Huissier de Justice*

Ganiou Adechy
*Etude de Me Ganiou Adechy*

A. Abdou Kabir Adoumbou
*Cabinet Maître Rafikou Alabi*

Saïdou Agbantou
*Cabinet d'Avocats*

Rodolphe Kadoukpe Akoto
*Coman S.A.*

Sybel Akuesson
*Fiduciaire Conseil et Assistance (FCA)*

Ahmadou Al Aminou Lo
*BCEAO*

Rafikou Agnila Alabi
*Cabinet Maître Rafikou Alabi*

Françoise Amoussou
*Nouvelle Vision*

Jacques Moïse Atchade
*Cabinet de Maître Atchade*

Charles Badou
*Cabinet d'Avocat Charles Badou*

Is-Dine Bouraima
*Guichet Unique de Formalisation des Entreprises*

Alice Codjia-Sohouenou
*Cabinet d'Avocats Alice Codjia Sohouénou*

Michel Djossouvi
OFFICE NOTARIAL OLAGNIKA SALAM

Guy Médard Agbo Fayemi
CABINET D'ARCHITECTURE ARCADE
INTERNATIONAL

Jean Claude Gnamien
PwC CÔTE D'IVOIRE

Irène Grimaud
CABINET D'AVOCATS

Taïrou Mama
SOCIÉTÉ INTERNATIONALE DE TRANSIT
TOURÉ

Jérémie Missihoun
CABINET D'HUISSIER DE JUSTICE

Emmanuella Moulod
PwC CÔTE D'IVOIRE

Taoïdi Osseni
SOCIÉTÉ BÉNINOISE D'ENERGIE
ELECTRIQUE

Olagnika Salam
OFFICE NOTARIAL OLAGNIKA SALAM

Hermann Senou
ENTREPRISE GÉNÉRALE DE
CONSTRUCTION MACKHO

Didier Sterlingot
BOLLORÉ AFRICA LOGISTICS

Nelly Tagnon Gambor
FIDUCIAIRE CONSEIL ET ASSISTANCE
(FCA)

Dominique Taty
PwC CÔTE D'IVOIRE

Jean-Bosco Todjinou
ECOPLAN SARL

José Tonato
IMPACT CONSULTANTS

Fousséni Traoré
PwC CÔTE D'IVOIRE

Francine Vittin
OFFICE NOTARIAL OLAGNIKA SALAM

Zacharie Yalo
MAIRIE DE LA VILLE DE COTONOU

Emmanuel Yehouessi
BCEAO

Brignon Zizindohoue

## BHUTAN

Loknath Chapagai
MINISTRY OF ECONOMIC AFFAIRS

Tashi Chenzom
MINISTRY OF LABOUR AND HUMAN
RESOURCES

Eden Dema
ROYAL MONETARY AUTHORITY OF
BHUTAN

Bhim L. Dhungel
ZORIG CONSULTANCY

Kencho Dorji
LEKO PACKERS

Lhundub Dorji
EAST - WEST CONSTRUCTION

Ugyen Dorji
DRUK INTEGRATED GREEN BUILDINGS

Chheku Dukpa
CONSTRUCTION ASSOCIATION OF
BHUTAN

N. B. Gurung
GLOBAL LOGISTICS

Sonam Gyeltshen
BHUTAN POWER CORPORATION LTD.

Deki Kesang

Shera Lhendup
SAYANG LAW CHAMBERS

Sonam Lhundrup
DRUK HOLDING AND INVESTMENTS

Tashi Pem

Dorji Phuntsho
ROYAL SECURITIES EXCHANGE OF
BHUTAN LTD.

T. B. Rai
ZORIG CONSULTANCY

Yeshey Selden
MINISTRY OF ECONOMIC AFFAIRS

Govinda Sharma
THIMPHU CITY CORPORATION

Dorji Tshering
BHUTAN POWER CORPORATION LTD.

Gem Tshering
BHUTAN POWER CORPORATION LTD.

Sonam Tshering
MINISTRY OF FINANCE

Wang Tshering
PCT CONSULTANCY & CONSTRUCTION

Deki Wangmo
BHUTAN NATIONAL BANK

Karma Yeshey
MINISTRY OF ECONOMIC AFFAIRS

## BOLIVIA

Fernando Aguirre
BUFETE AGUIRRE SOC. CIV.

Ignacio Aguirre
BUFETE AGUIRRE SOC. CIV.

Carolina Aguirre Urioste
BUFETE AGUIRRE SOC. CIV.

David Alcózer
CRIALES, URCULLO & ANTEZANA

Christian Amestegui
ASESORES LEGALES CP

Daniela Aragones Cortez
SANJINÉS & ASOCIADOS SOC. CIV.
ABOGADOS

Eduardo Aramayo
PwC BOLIVIA

Miguel Angel Ardúz Ayllón
ELECTROPAZ S.A.

Johnny Arteaga Chavez

Maria del Carmen Ballivián
C.R. & F. ROJAS, MEMBER OF LEX
MUNDI

Fernando Bedoya
C.R. & F. ROJAS, MEMBER OF LEX
MUNDI

Cristian Bustos
FERRERE ATTORNEYS

Walter B. Calla Cardenas
COLEGIO DEPARTAMENTAL DE
ARQUITECTOS DE LA PAZ

Jose Callau
FERRERE ATTORNEYS

Mauricio Costa du Rels
WÜRTH KIM COSTA DU RELS

Jose Luis Diaz Romero
SERVICIOS GENERALES EN ELECTRICIDAD
Y CONSTRUCCIÓN (SGEC)

Salomon Eid
FERRERE ATTORNEYS

Isabel Ferrufino
FERRERE ATTORNEYS

Kattia Galdo
FERRERE ATTORNEYS

Roberto Gomez-Justiniano
SALAZAR, SALAZAR & ASOCIADOS,
SOC. CIV.

Primitivo Gutiérrez
GUEVARA & GUTIÉRREZ S.C.

Ana Carola Guzman Gonzales
SALAZAR, SALAZAR & ASOCIADOS,
SOC. CIV.

Jaime M. Jiménez Alvarez
COLEGIO DE INGENIEROS ELECTRICISTAS Y
ELECTRÓNICOS LA PAZ

Rodrigo Jimenez-Cusicanqui
SALAZAR, SALAZAR & ASOCIADOS,
SOC. CIV.

Paola Justiniano Arias
SANJINÉS & ASOCIADOS SOC. CIV.
ABOGADOS

Julio César Landívar Castro
GUEVARA & GUTIÉRREZ S.C.

César Lora Moretto
PwC BOLIVIA

Alejandra Bernal Mercado
C.R. & F. ROJAS, MEMBER OF LEX
MUNDI

Ariel Morales Vasquez
C.R. & F. ROJAS, MEMBER OF LEX
MUNDI

Ana Carola Muñoz
WÜRTH KIM COSTA DU RELS

Jaime Muñoz-Reyes G.
CORPORATIVE LAW BOLIVIA
CONSULTORES ASOCIADOS

Pablo Ordonez
AYOROA & ORDONEZ

Alejandro Peláez Kay
INDACOCHEA & ASOCIADOS

Mariana Pereira Nava
INDACOCHEA & ASOCIADOS

Orlando Pérez
ELECTROPAZ S.A.

Carlos Pinto
FERRERE ATTORNEYS

Oscar Antonio Plaza Ponte Sosa
ENTIDAD DE SERVICIOS DE
INFORMACIÓN ENSERBIC S.A.

Patricio Rojas
C.R. & F. ROJAS, MEMBER OF LEX
MUNDI

Mariela Rojas de Hamel
ENTIDAD DE SERVICIOS DE
INFORMACIÓN ENSERBIC S.A.

Sergio Salazar-Machicado
SALAZAR, SALAZAR & ASOCIADOS,
SOC. CIV.

Fernando Salazar-Paredes
SALAZAR, SALAZAR & ASOCIADOS,
SOC. CIV.

Sandra Salinas
C.R. & F. ROJAS, MEMBER OF LEX
MUNDI

Mariela Sanchez
SUPERINTENDENCIA DE BANCOS Y
ENTIDADES FINANCIERAS

Rodolfo Raúl Sanjinés Elizagoyen
SANJINÉS & ASOCIADOS SOC. CIV.
ABOGADOS

Jorge Nelson Serrate
WÜRTH KIM COSTA DU RELS

Javier Urcullo
CRIALES, URCULLO & ANTEZANA

Ramiro Velasco
COLEGIO DE INGENIEROS ELECTRICISTAS Y
ELECTRÓNICOS LA PAZ

Karla Würth
WÜRTH KIM COSTA DU RELS

## BOSNIA AND
HERZEGOVINA

Samir Bajrović
LAW OFFICE FEMIL CURT (PART OF
DLA PIPER GROUP)

Fedja Bicakcic
KN KARANOVIĆ & NIKOLIĆ

Dario Biščević
DB SCHENKER

Petar Bosnić
USAID TAX AND FISCAL PROJECT IN
BiH (TAF)

Mubera Brković
PwC BOSNIA AND HERZEGOVINA

Stevan Dimitrijevic
KN KARANOVIĆ & NIKOLIĆ

Višnja Dizdarević
MARIĆ & CO LAW FIRM

Anel Droce
KEBO & GUZIN

Dina Duraković Morankić
LAW OFFICE DURAKOVIC

Stefan Dusanic
KN KARANOVIĆ & NIKOLIĆ

Entezam Dzubur
MARIĆ & CO LAW FIRM

Dzemila Gavrankapetanović
BEKIR GAVRANKAPETANOVIĆ, KOLDŽO
DAMIR AND KUKIĆ EMIR

Adis Gazibegović
CMS REICH-ROHRWIG HAINZ D.O.O.

Azer Guzin
KEBO & GUZIN

Semir Guzin
KEBO & GUZIN

Dulizara Hadzimustafic
FERK (REGULATORY COMMISSION
FOR ELECTRICITY IN THE FEDERATION OF
BOSNIA AND HERZEGOVINA)

Senada Havić Hrenovica
LRC CREDIT BUREAU

Nusmir Huskić
HUSKIC LAW OFFICE

Amra Isic
MARIĆ & CO LAW FIRM

Arela Jusufbasic-Goloman
LAWYERS OFFICE TKALCIC-
DULIC, PREBANIC, RIZVIC &
JUSUFBASIC-GOLOMAN

Lejla Kaknjo
PKF INTERNATIONAL

Nedžada Kapidžić
NOTARY

Miro Kebo
KEBO & GUZIN

Damir Koldžo
BEKIR GAVRANKAPETANOVIĆ, KOLDŽO
DAMIR AND KUKIĆ EMIR

Anja Margetić
CENTRAL BANK OF BOSNIA AND
HERZEGOVINA

Branko Marić
MARIĆ & CO LAW FIRM

Davorin Marinkovic
KN KARANOVIĆ & NIKOLIĆ

Adnan Mataradžija
MERFI, D.O.O. DRUŠTVO ZA REVIZIJU
SARAJEVO

Sead Miljković
WOLF THEISS D.O.O.

Monija Nogullo
FERK (REGULATORY COMMISSION
FOR ELECTRICITY IN THE FEDERATION OF
BOSNIA AND HERZEGOVINA)

Mehmed Omeragić
COVJEK I PROSTOR

Indir Osmić
CMS REICH-ROHRWIG HAINZ D.O.O.

Đorđe Racković
CENTRAL BANK OF BOSNIA AND
HERZEGOVINA

Predrag Radovanović
MARIĆ & CO LAW FIRM

Alma Ramezic
PwC BOSNIA AND HERZEGOVINA

Nedžida Salihović-Whalen
CMS REICH-ROHRWIG HAINZ D.O.O.

Hasib Salkić
JUMP LOGISTICS D.O.O.

Arjana Selimić
JP ELEKTROPRIVREDA BiH PODRUŽNICA
ELEKTRODISTRIBUCIJA SARAJEVO

Nihad Sijerčić
KN KARANOVIĆ & NIKOLIĆ

Maja Šimunac
WOLF THEISS D.O.O.

Bojana Tkalčić-Djulić
LAWYERS OFFICE TKALCIC-
DULIC, PREBANIC, RIZVIC &
JUSUFBASIC-GOLOMAN

Vildana Uščuplić
WOLF THEISS D.O.O.

Edin Zametica
DERK (STATE ELECTRICITY REGULATORY
COMMISSION)

## BOTSWANA

COLLINS NEWMAN & CO.

Jeffrey Bookbinder
BOOKBINDER BUSINESS LAW

Ofentse Chifedi
HOYA REMOVALS & FREIGHT

Edward W. Fasholé-Luke II
LUKE & ASSOCIATES

Snoeky Gobopaone Kebakile
MINISTRY OF LABOUR AND HOME
AFFAIRS

Godfrey Madanha
CHOCHOLOZA BUILDING CONSTRUCTION
PTY. LTD.

Jonathan Maphepa
GABORONE CITY COUNCIL

Finola McMahon
OSEI-OFEI SWABI & CO.

Tsametse Mmolai
BOTSWANA STOCK EXCHANGE

Neo Thelma Moatlhodi

Moilwa
ZISMO ENGINEERING (PTY) LTD.

Segametsi Mothibedi
GABORONE CITY COUNCIL

Mmatshipi Motsepe
MANICA AFRICA PTY. LTD.

Rajesh Narasimhan
GRANT THORNTON LLP

Buhle Ncube
LUKE & ASSOCIATES

Kwadwo Osei-Ofei
OSEI-OFEI SWABI & CO.

Chabo Peo
BOOKBINDER BUSINESS LAW

Anura Suren Perera
PwC BOTSWANA

Butler Phirie
PwC BOTSWANA

Samuel Rathedi
MINISTRY OF ENVIRONMENT, WILDLIFE
AND TOURISM

Claudio Rossi
SHARPS ELECTRICAL (PTY) LTD.

Daniel Swabi
OSEI-OFEI SWABI & CO.

Onkemetse Thomas
BOTSWANA STOCK EXCHANGE

Frederick Webb
ARMSTRONGS ATTORNEYS

Sipho Ziga
ARMSTRONGS ATTORNEYS

## BRAZIL

ERNST & YOUNG

EXPERTNESS BRAZIL FREIGHT
FORWARDING & CONSULTING LTDA.

Marina Agueda
DE LUCA, DERENUSSON, SCHUTTOFF E
AZEVEDO ADVOGADOS

Antônio Aires
*Demarest e Almeida Advogados*

Kleber Altale
*Machado Meyer Sendacz e Opice Advogados*

Flávia Cristina Altério
*KLA-Koury Lopes Advogados*

Lúcia Aragao
*Veirano Advogados*

Ubajara Arcas Dias
*Gasparini, De Cresci e Nogueira de Lima Advogados*

Bruna Argento
*Machado Meyer Sendacz e Opice Advogados*

Bruno Balduccini
*Pinheiro Neto Advogados*

Priscyla Barbosa
*Veirano Advogados*

Júlio Henrique Batista
*Guerra e Batista Advogados*

Roberta Bessa
*Machado Meyer Sendacz e Opice Advogados*

Paula Bichuete
*Rayes & Fagundes Advogados*

Camila Biral
*Demarest e Almeida Advogados*

Adriano Borges
*De Vivo, Whitaker, Castro e Gonçalves Advogados*

Carlos Braga
*Souza, Cescon, Barrieu & Flesch Advogados*

Danilo Breve
*Souza, Cescon, Barrieu & Flesch Advogados*

Sérgio Bronstein
*Veirano Advogados*

Paulo Campana
*Felsberg, Pedretti, Mannrich e Aidar Advogados e Consultores Legais*

Renato Canizares
*Demarest e Almeida Advogados*

Érika Carvalho
*Souza, Cescon, Barrieu & Flesch Advogados*

Ramon Castilho
*Souza, Cescon, Barrieu & Flesch Advogados*

Veridiana Celestino
*Veirano Advogados*

Eduardo Chaves
*Rayes & Fagundes Advogados*

Alexandre Clapis
*Machado Meyer Sendacz e Opice Advogados*

Ricardo E. Vieira Coelho
*Pinheiro Neto Advogados*

Jarbas Contin
*PwC Brazil*

Adriana Correa
*Souza, Cescon, Barrieu & Flesch Advogados*

Gilberto Deon Corrêa Junior
*Veirano Advogados Porto Alegre*

Bruno Costa Altenfelder Silva Mesquita
*Gasparini, De Cresci e Nogueira de Lima Advogados*

Bruno Henrique Coutinho de Aguiar
*Rayes & Fagundes Advogados*

Anderson Bispo da Silva
*Guerra e Batista Advogados*

Gabriela da Silva Brandão
*Ministry of Mines and Energy*

Gisela da Silva Freire
*Porto Advogados*

Adriana Daiuto
*Demarest e Almeida Advogados*

João Luis Ribeiro de Almeida
*Demarest e Almeida Advogados*

Anderson Rivas de Almeida
*Guerra e Batista Advogados*

Rafael de Carvalho Passaro
*Machado Meyer Sendacz e Opice Advogados*

Rafael De Conti
*De Conti Law Office*

Aldo de Cresci Neto
*Gasparini, De Cresci e Nogueira de Lima Advogados*

João Claudio De Luca
*De Luca, Derenusson, Schuttoff e Azevedo Advogados*

Marcelo Viveiros de Moura
*Pinheiro Neto Advogados*

Marília de Paula
*De Vivo, Whitaker, Castro e Gonçalves Advogados*

Andreza de Souza Ribeiro
*Souza, Cescon, Barrieu & Flesch Advogados*

Nádia Demoliner Lacerda
*Mesquita Barros Advogados, member of Ius Laboris*

Eduardo Depassier
*Loeser e Portela Advogados*

Ana Luisa Derenusson
*De Luca, Derenusson, Schuttoff e Azevedo Advogados*

José Ricardo dos Santos Luz Júnior
*Duarte Garcia, Caselli Guimarães e Terra Advogados*

Brigida Melo e Cruz
*Pinheiro Neto Advogados*

João Paulo F.A. Fagundes
*Rayes & Fagundes Advogados*

Vanessa Felício
*Veirano Advogados*

Iara Ferfoglia Gomes Dias
*Machado Meyer Sendacz e Opice Advogados*

Raphael Fernandes da Silveira Polito
*Rayes & Fagundes Advogados*

Alexsander Fernandes de Andrade
*Duarte Garcia, Caselli Guimarães e Terra Advogados*

Oswaldo Fernandes Neto
*De Luca, Derenusson, Schuttoff e Azevedo Advogados*

Isabelle Ferrarini Bueno
*Veirano Advogados*

Glaucia Ferreira
*Demarest e Almeida Advogados*

José Fidalgo
*De Luca, Derenusson, Schuttoff e Azevedo Advogados*

Rafael Figueiredo
*Souza, Cescon, Barrieu & Flesch Advogados*

Guilherme Filardi
*De Luca, Derenusson, Schuttoff e Azevedo Advogados*

Silvia Fiszman
*Machado Meyer Sendacz e Opice Advogados*

Paulo Roberto Fogarolli Filho
*Duarte Garcia, Caselli Guimarães e Terra Advogados*

Clarissa Freitas
*Machado Meyer Sendacz e Opice Advogados*

Rafael Gagliardi
*Demarest e Almeida Advogados*

Bruna Luiza Gambogi Bertozzi
*Gasparini, De Cresci e Nogueira de Lima Advogados*

Alessandra Ganz
*Veirano Advogados*

Thiago Giantomassi Medeiros
*Demarest e Almeida Advogados*

Michelle Giraldi Lacerda
*PwC Brazil*

Jorge Eduardo Gouvêa Vieira
*Gouvêa Vieira Advogados*

Vanessa Grosso da Silveria Lardosa
*Gouvêa Vieira Advogados*

Joao Mauricio Gumiero
*Deloitte Touche Tohmatsu*

Eduardo Ferraz Guerra
*Guerra e Batista Advogados*

Enrique Hadad
*Loeser e Portela Advogados*

Ricardo Higashitani
*KLA-Koury Lopes Advogados*

Carlos Alberto Iacia
*PwC Brazil*

Marcelo Inglez de Souza
*Demarest e Almeida Advogados*

Fernando Koury Lopes
*KLA-Koury Lopes Advogados*

Miguel Kreling
*Pinheiro Neto Advogados*

Vilma Kutomi
*Demarest e Almeida Advogados*

Sergio André Laclau
*Xavier Bragança Advogados*

Flávio Lantelme
*Prefeitura da Cidade de Sao Paulo*

Juliano Lazzarini Moretti
*Lazzarini Moretti Advogados*

José Augusto Leal
*Castro, Barros, Sobral, Gomes Advogados*

Alexandre Leite
*Souza, Cescon, Barrieu & Flesch Advogados*

Fernando Loeser
*Loeser e Portela Advogados*

Ricardo Loureiro
*Serasa S.A.*

Eduardo Luise Gonzalez Bronzatti
*Pinheiro Guimarães Advogados*

Marina Maccabelli
*Demarest e Almeida Advogados*

Tiago Machado Cortez
*KLA-Koury Lopes Advogados*

João Gabriel A. L. Clark Magon
*Demarest e Almeida Advogados*

Estêvão Mallet
*Mallet e Advogados Associados*

Camila Mansur
*Lazzarini Moretti Advogados*

André Marques
*Pinheiro Neto Advogados*

Laura Massetto Meyer
*Pinheiro Guimarães Advogados*

Eduardo Augusto Mattar
*Pinheiro Guimarães Advogados*

Felipe Oliveira Mavignier
*Gasparini, De Cresci e Nogueira de Lima Advogados*

Marianne Mendes Webber
*Souza, Cescon, Barrieu & Flesch Advogados*

Sarah Mila Barbassa
*Souza, Cescon, Barrieu & Flesch Advogados*

Renata Moreira Lima
*Lazzarini Moretti Advogados*

Gustavo Morel
*Veirano Advogados*

Renata Morelli
*Rayes & Fagundes Advogados*

Giorgia Nagalli
*Souza, Cescon, Barrieu & Flesch Advogados*

Cássio S. Namur
*Souza, Cescon, Barrieu & Flesch Advogados*

Marcelo Natale
*Deloitte Touche Tohmatsu*

Diogo Nebias
*Souza, Cescon, Barrieu & Flesch Advogados*

Jorge Nemr
*Leite, Tosto e Barros*

Walter Nimir
*De Vivo, Whitaker, Castro e Gonçalves Advogados*

João Paulo Nogueira Barros
*Gouvêa Vieira Advogados*

Flávio Pinto Nunes
*ThyssenKrupp CSA Siderurgica do Atlantico*

Daniel Oliveira
*Souza, Cescon, Barrieu & Flesch Advogados*

Evany Oliveira
*PwC Brazil*

João Otávio Pinheiro Olivério
*Campos Mello Advogados, in cooperation with DLA Piper*

Andréa Oricchio Kirsh
*Cunha Oricchio Ricca Lopes Advogados*

Gyedre Palma Carneiro de Oliveira
*Souza, Cescon, Barrieu & Flesch Advogados*

Eloisa Paulino
*Souza, Cescon, Barrieu & Flesch Advogados*

Rogerio Rabelo Peixoto
*Banco Central do Brasil*

Leila Pigozzi Alves
*De Luca, Derenusson, Schuttoff e Azevedo Advogados*

Luanda Pinto Backheuser
*De Luca, Derenusson, Schuttoff e Azevedo Advogados*

Durval Portela
*Loeser e Portela Advogados*

Daniela Prieto
*Veirano Advogados*

Dario Rabay
*Souza, Cescon, Barrieu & Flesch Advogados*

Eliane Ribeiro Gago
*Duarte Garcia, Caselli Guimarães e Terra Advogados*

Laura Ribeiro Vissotto
*1º Cartório de Notas de São José dos Campos*

Viviane Rodrigues
*Souza, Cescon, Barrieu & Flesch Advogados*

Cezar Roedel

Maristela Rossetti
*Xavier Bragança Advogados*

César Rossi Machado
*Demarest e Almeida Advogados*

Lia Roston
*Rayes & Fagundes Advogados*

Gustavo Rotta
*Deloitte Touche Tohmatsu*

Luis Augusto Roux Azevedo
*De Luca, Derenusson, Schuttoff e Azevedo Advogados*

José Samurai Saiani
*Machado Meyer Sendacz e Opice Advogados*

Sérgio Savi
*Castro, Barros, Sobral, Gomes Advogados*

Carolina Schreier
*KLA-Koury Lopes Advogados*

Sabine Schuttoff
*De Luca, Derenusson, Schuttoff e Azevedo Advogados*

Gabriel Seijo
*Souza, Cescon, Barrieu & Flesch Advogados*

Donizetti A. Silva
*DAS Consultoria*

Beatriz Souza
*Souza, Cescon, Barrieu & Flesch Advogados*

Walter Stuber
*Walter Stuber Consultoria Jurídica*

Paula Surerus
*Xavier Bragança Advogados*

Rodrigo Takano
*Machado Meyer Sendacz e Opice Advogados*

Marcelo Tendolini Saciotto
*Rayes & Fagundes Advogados*

Milena Tesser
*Rayes & Fagundes Advogados*

Marcos Tiraboschi
*De Luca, Derenusson, Schuttoff e Azevedo Advogados*

Ivandro Trevelim
*Souza, Cescon, Barrieu & Flesch Advogados*

Priscila Trevisan
*Rayes & Fagundes Advogados*

Luiz Fernando Valente De Paiva
*Pinheiro Neto Advogados*

Ronaldo C. Veirano
*Veirano Advogados*

Rafael Vitelli Depieri
*1º Cartório de Notas de São José dos Campos*

Karina Vlahos
*De Luca, Derenusson, Schuttoff e Azevedo Advogados*

José Carlos Wahle
*Veirano Advogados*

Eduardo Guimarães Wanderley
*Veirano Advogados*

Thiago Wscieklica
*Souza, Cescon, Barrieu & Flesch Advogados*

Celso Xavier
*Demarest e Almeida Advogados*

Karin Yamauti Hatanaka
*Souza, Cescon, Barrieu & Flesch Advogados*

Carolina Zanolo
*Machado Meyer Sendacz e Opice Advogados*

Alessandra Zequi Salybe de Moura
*Souza, Cescon, Barrieu & Flesch Advogados*

## BRUNEI DARUSSALAM

*HSE Engineering SDN BHD*

Ahmad Basuni Abbas

Hafizah Alkaff
*Akitek SAA*

Jonathan Cheok
*Cheok Advocates & Solicitors*

Robin Cheok
*Cheok Advocates & Solicitors*

Danny Chua
*Brunei Transporting Company*

Mohamad Daud Ismail
*Daud Ismail and Company*

Nur al-Ain Haji Abdullah
*Attorney General's Chambers*

Saipol Hj Abd Razak
*Attorney General's Chambers*

Zaleha Hj Mat Zain
*Attorney General's Chambers*

Zuleana Kassim
*Lee Corporatehouse Associates*

Alice Khan
*Attorney General's Chambers*

Cynthia Kong
*Widdows Kong & Associates*

Kin Chee Lee
*Lee Corporatehouse Associates*

Lennon Lee
*PwC Singapore*

Christina Lim
*Cheok Advocates & Solicitors*

Kelvin Lim
*K. Lim & Co.*

Siew Yen Lim
*The Judicial Department*

Colin Ong
*Dr. Colin Ong Legal Services*

Pg Yusuf Pg Hj Mat Salleh
*Attorney General's Chambers*

Mariani Hj Sabtu
*Ministry of Industry and Primary Resources Building*

Martin Sinnung Jr.
*Brunei Transporting Company*

Shazali Sulaiman
*KPMG*

Ting Tiu Pheng
*Arkitek Ting*

Cecilia Wong
*Tricor (B) Sdn Bhd*

## BULGARIA

Svetlin Adrianov
*Penkov, Markov & Partners*

Ekaterina Aleksova
*PwC Bulgaria*

Anton Andreev
*Schoenherr*

Stefan Angelov
*V Consulting Bulgaria*

Rusalena Angelova
*Djingov, Gouginski, Kyutchukov & Velichkov*

Iva Baeva
*Legalex*

Svetlana Balabanova
*TravelInn Ltd.*

Ganka Belcheva
*Belcheva & Associates Law Office*

Ilian Beslemeshki
*Georgiev, Todorov & Co.*

Plamen Borissov
*Borissov & Partners*

Christopher Christov
*Penev LLP*

Lyudmila Chulkova
*Penev LLP*

Maria Danailova
*Danailova, Todorov and Partners Law Firm*

Kostadinka Deleva
*Gugushev & Partners*

Alexandra Doytchinova
*Schoenherr*

Silvia Dulevska
*Bulgarian National Bank*

Daniela Dzabarova
*IKRP Rokas & Partners*

Maria Endreva
*Dobrev, Kinkin & Lyutskanov*

Slavcho Georgiev
*Penev LLP*

Atanas Georgiev
*Public Services OOD*

Marieta Getcheva
*PwC Bulgaria*

Matea Gospodinova
*Djingov, Gouginski, Kyutchukov & Velichkov*

Ralitsa Gougleva
*Djingov, Gouginski, Kyutchukov & Velichkov*

Stefan Gugushev
*Gugushev & Partners*

Tatyana Hristova
*Legalex*

Velyana Hristova
*Penkov, Markov & Partners*

Ginka Iskrova
*PwC Bulgaria*

Angel Kalaidjiev
*Kalaidjiev & Georgiev*

Yavor Kambourov
*Kambourov & Partners*

Irena Karpe
*Kambourov & Partners*

Rositsa Kebedjieva
*Penkov, Markov & Partners*

Hristina Kirilova
*Kambourov & Partners*

Diana Kiskinova
*Tax Account Ltd.*

Nikolay Kolev
*Boyanov & Co.*

Donko Kolev
*Raiffeisen Real Estate Ltd.*

Ilya Komarevski
*Tsvetkova, Bebov and Partners*

Hristiana Krivoshieva
*Economou International Shipping Agency Limited*

Tsvetan Krumov
*Schoenherr*

Stephan Kyutchukov
*Djingov, Gouginski, Kyutchukov & Velichkov*

Dessislava Lukarova
*Arsov Natchev Ganeva*

Jordan Manahilov
*Bulgarian National Bank*

Dimitrinka Metodieva
*Gugushev & Partners*

Slavi Mikinski
*Legalex*

Blagomir Minov
*Tsvetkova, Bebov and Partners*

Tzvetoslav Mitev
*Georgiev, Todorov & Co.*

Vladimir Natchev
*Arsov Natchev Ganeva*

Yordan Naydenov
*Boyanov & Co.*

Neli Nedkova
*Wolf Theiss*

Nedyalka Novakova
*Boyanov & Co.*

Yulia Peeva
*Rex Consulting Ltd. – member of Russell Bedford International*

Lilia Pencheva
*Experian Bulgaria EAD*

Sergey Penev
*Penev LLP*

Daniela Petkova
*Dobrev, Kinkin & Lyutskanov*

Veselka Petrova
*Tsvetkova, Bebov and Partners*

Gergana Popova
*Georgiev, Todorov & Co.*

Alexander Rangelov
*PwC Bulgaria*

Svetoslav Shterev
*Virtus*

Julian Spassov
*McGregor & Partners*

Irina Stoeva
*Stoeva, Kuyumdjieva & Vitliemov*

Roman Stoyanov
*Penkov, Markov & Partners*

Margarita Stoyanova
*Kambourov & Partners*

Vessela Tcherneva Yankova
*V Consulting Bulgaria*

Yordan Terziev
*Arsov Natchev Ganeva*

Aleksandrina Terziyska
*Gugushev & Partners*

Kaloyan Todorov
*Danailova, Todorov and Partners Law Firm*

Svilen Todorov
*Todorov & Doykova Law Firm*

Lily Trifonova
*Rex Consulting Ltd. – member of Russell Bedford International*

Georgi Tzvetkov
*Djingov, Gouginski, Kyutchukov & Velichkov*

Kamena Valcheva
*Tsvetkova, Bebov and Partners*

Miroslav Varnaliev
*Unimasters Logistics Plc.*

Venzi Vassilev
*Rex Consulting Ltd. – member of Russell Bedford International*

Marina Voynova
*Kalaidjiev & Georgiev*

Katya Yurukova
*Penkov, Markov & Partners*

## BURKINA FASO

*Bolloré Africa Logistics*

*Cabinet Benoît J. Sawadogo*

*Cabinet John W. Ffooks & Co.*

*JFA Afrique*

Pierre Abadie
*Cabinet Pierre Abadie*

Ahmadou Al Aminou Lo
*BCEAO*

Seydou Balama
*Etude Maître Balama Seydou*

Joséphine Bassolet
*SONABEL*

Flora Josiane Bila
*SCPA Yaguibou & Yanogo*

Aimé Bonkoungou
*SONABEL*

Serge Damiba
*Archi Consult*

Denis Dawende
*Office Notarial Me Jean Celestin Zoure*

Moumouni Diarra
*SONABEL*

Seydou Diarra

Jean Claude Gnamien
*PwC Côte d'Ivoire*

Jean Bedel Gouba
*SONABEL*

Karim Ilboudo
*CEFAC*

Olé Alain KAM
*Dembs Associates Sarl*

Issaka Kargougou
*Maison de l'Entreprise du Burkina Faso*

Barthélémy Kere
*Cabinet d'Avocats Barthélemy Kere*

Gilbert Kibtonré
*CEFAC*

Clarisse Kienou
*Maison de l'Entreprise du Burkina Faso*

Alain Gilbert Koala
*Ordre des Architectes du Burkina*

Vincent Armand Kobiané
*ARDI – Architectes Conseils*

Moumouny Kopiho
*Cabinet d'Avocats Moumouny Kopiho*

Raphaël Kouraogo
*SONABEL*

Ange Laure M'Pow
*SCPA Yaguibou & Yanogo*

Adeline Messou
*PwC Côte d'Ivoire*

Emmanuella Mouloud
*PwC Côte d'Ivoire*

S. Al Nadia
*Cabinet d'Avocats Moumouny Kopiho*

Moussa Ouedraogo
*SCPA Yaguibou & Yanogo*

Oumarou Ouedraogo
*Cabinet Ouedraogo*

Roger Omer Ouédraogo
*Association Professionnelle des Transitaires & Commissionnaires en Douane Agréés*

Alain Serge Paré
*Cabinet Yaguibou & Yanogo*

Bénéwendé S. Sankara
*Cabinet Maître Sankara*

Hermann Lambert Sanon
*Groupe Hage*

Adama Saouadogo
*ONEA*

Dieudonné Sawadogo
*Cabinet d'Avocats Moumouny Kopiho*

Olga Tamini
*SCPA Yaguibou & Yanogo*

Dieudonné Tapsoba
*Secrétariat Général du Ministère de l'Habitat et de l'Urbanisme*

Dominique Taty
*PwC Côte d'Ivoire*

Moussa Traore
*Maison de l'Entreprise du Burkina Faso*

Fousséni Traoré
*PwC Côte d'Ivoire*

Bouba Yaguibou
*SCPA Yaguibou & Yanogo*

Emmanuel Yehouessi
*BCEAO*

Francis Zagre
*SONABEL*

K. Cyrille Zangre
*Cabinet d'Avocats Moumouny Kopiho*

Bogore Zongo
*Chambre Nationale des Huissiers de Justice du Burkina Faso*

Sylvie Zongo
*Cabinet Pierre Abadie*

## BURUNDI

Joseph Bahizi
*Banque de la République du Burundi*

Jean De Dieu Basabakwinshi
*IMATCO*

Mélance Bukera
*Burundi General Services*

Ange Gakundwakazi
*GPO Partners Burundi correspondent firm of Deloitte*

Gerard Handika
*GPO Partners Burundi correspondent firm of Deloitte*

Augustin Mabushi
*A & JN Mabushi Cabinet d'Avocats*

René Claude Madebari
*Mkono & Co Advocates*

Rodrigue Majambere
*Intercontact Services*

Trust Manjengwah
*Wintertons Law firm*

Anatole Miburo
*Cabinet Anatole Miburo*

Ildephonse Nahimana
*Banque de la République du Burundi*

Patrick Ndayishimiye

Albert Ndereyimana
*GETRA*

Gregoire Nduwimana
*SDV Transami Burundi*

Bonaventure Nicimpaye
*Intercontact Services*

Lambert Nigarura
*Mkono & Co Advocates*

Charles Nihangaza

Montfort Nininahazwe
*SEACO*

Gustave Niyonzima
*Mkono & Co Advocates*

Prosper Niyoyankana

Jean-Marie Niyubahwe
*Sénat du Burundi*

Jocelyne Ntibangana
*Cabinet de Maître Ntibangana*

Antoine Ntisigana
*SODETRA Ltd.*

Happy Ntwari
*Mkono & Co Advocates*

Patrick-Didier Nukuri

François Nyamoya
*Avocat à la Cour*

Gilbert L.P. Nyatanyi
*Mkono & Co Advocates*

Déogratias Nzemba
*Avocat à la Cour*

Willy Rubeya
*Rubeya & Co – Advocates*

Benjamin Rufagari
*GPO Partners Burundi*
*correspondent firm of Deloitte*

Thierry Rujerwaka
*Laboratoire National du Bâtiment et des Travaux Publics (LNBTP) Burundi*

Isaac Rwankineza
*Entreprise BTCE*

Fabien Segatwa
*Etude Me Segatwa*

Gabriel Sinarinzi
*Cabinet Me Gabriel Sinarinzi*

Audace Sunzu
*REGIDESO*

Egide Uwimana
*Tribunal du Travail de Bujumbura*

**CAMBODIA**
*Cambodia Commercial Bank*

*Ernst & Young*

Chanmalise Bun
*PwC Cambodia*

Kosal Chan
*Acleda Bank Plc.*

Kearath Chan
*Linehaul Express (Cambodia) Co., Ltd.*

Phanin Cheam
*Municipality of Phnom Penh Bureau of Urban Affairs*

Rithy Chey
*BNG Legal*

Sokcheng Chou
*Arbitration Council Foundation*

Susanna Coghlan
*AAA Cambodia Ltd.*

Antoine Fontaine
*Bun & Associates*

Leanghor Hak
*Linehaul Express (Cambodia) Co., Ltd.*

Hour Naryth Hem
*BNG Legal*

Sokpheaneath Huon
*Cambodian Federation of Employers and Business Associations*

Phalla Im
*CBD Partner & Consultancy*

Sophealeak Ing
*Bun & Associates*

Visal Iv
*Electricite du Cambodge*

Phoung Wattey Kemnay
*BNG Legal*

Chhorpornpisey Keo
*Acleda Bank Plc.*

Sambath Kheang
*Acleda Bank Plc.*

Vansok Khem
*Arbitration Council Foundation*

Y Manou
*BNG Legal*

Sokvirak Pheang
*PwC Cambodia*

Thea Pheng
*BNG Legal*

Sotheaphal Pho
*Sciaroni & Associates*

Matthew Rendall
*Sciaroni & Associates*

Sovan Sa
*Attorney-at-Law*

Muny Samreth
*PwC Cambodia*

Chanthy Sin
*Linehaul Express (Cambodia) Co., Ltd.*

Chea Sinhel
*Electricite du Cambodge*

Vannarith Siv
*B.N.G. - Advocates & Solicitors*

Billie Jean Slott
*Sciaroni & Associates*

Lor Sok
*Arbitration Council Foundation*

Chamnan Som
*Cambodian Federation of Employers and Business Associations*

Ny Som
*SDV Logistics*

Sinoun Sous
*Arbitration Council Foundation*

Vannaroth Sovann
*BNG Legal*

Ousaphea Suos
*Acleda Bank Plc.*

Rathvisal Thara
*BNG Legal*

Sopymakara Thong
*Arbitration Council Foundation*

Heng Thy
*PwC Cambodia*

Janvibol Tip
*Tip & Partners*

Sokhan Uch
*Acleda Bank Plc.*

Bun Youdy
*Bun & Associates*

Potim Yun
*DFDL Mekong Law Group*

**CAMEROON**
*Cabinet John W. Ffooks & Co.*

Armelle Silvana Abel (epse) Piskopanis
*Legal Power Law Firm*

Roland Abeng
*The Abeng Law Firm*

Rosine Pauline Amboa
*Legal Power Law Firm*

Armand Atono
*AES Sonel*

Caroline Barla
*CEBCRÉA*

Thomas Didier Remy Batoumbouck
*CADIRE*

Pierre Bertin Simbafo
*BICEC*

David Boyo
*Boyo & Patimark LLP*

Olivier Buquet
*Bolloré Africa Logistics*

Joseph Dibabo
*Bolloré Africa Logistics*

Anne Marie Diboundje Njocke
*Cabinet Diboundje Njocke & Associés*

Paul Marie Djamen
*Mobile Telephone Networks Cameroon (MTN)*

Tognia Djanko
*Cabinet Tognia et Associes*

Aurélien Djengue Kotte
*Cabinet Ekobo*

Laurent Dongmo
*Jing & Partners*

Régine Dooh Collins
*Etude Me Régine Dooh Collins*

Hyacinthe Clément Fansi Ngamou
*SCP Ngassam Njike & Associes*

Oréol Marcel Fetue
*Nimba Conseil SARL*

Isabelle Fomukong
*Cabinet d'Avocats Fomukong*

Georges Fopa
*GIEA*

Philippe Fouda Fouda
*BEAC Cameroon*

Nicaise Ibohn
*The Abeng Law Firm*

Samuel Iyug Iyug
*Groupement des Entreprises de Frêt et Messagerie du Cameroun (GEFMCAM)*

Paul T. Jing
*Jing & Partners*

Eugène Romeo Kengne Sikadi
*Nimba Conseil SARL*

Michel Kangmeni
*Cabinet Auditec-Foirier*

Julienne Kengue Piam
*Nimba Conseil SARL*

Jean Aime Kounga
*Cabinet d'Avocats Abeng Roland*

Merlin Arsene Kouogang
*Cabinet d'Avocats Fomukong*

Emmanuel Loga
*Bolloré Africa Logistics*

Thyerine Divine Masso Siche
*Boyo & Patimark LLP*

Alain Serges Mbebi
*CADIRE*

Augustin Yves Mbock Keked
*CADIRE*

Martial Mbongue Mpallawoh
*Legal Power Law Firm*

Patrick Menyeng Manga
*The Abeng Law Firm*

Jules Minamo
*Karvan Finance*

Nitua Tabot Moliki
*Legal Power Law Firm*

Marie Agathe Ndeme
*CADIRE*

Bernard Ngaibe
*The Abeng Law Firm*

Virgile Ngassam Njiké
*SCP Ngassam Njike & Associes*

Francine Ngninkeu Yonda
*Atanga Law Office*

Marie-Andrée Ngwe
*Cabinet Maître Marie Andrée Ngwe*

Joel Penda
*The Abeng Law Firm*

Olivier Priso
*Ville de Douala Communauté Urbaine de Douala*

Sylvester Qui
*Boyo & Patimark LLP*

Noupoue Ngaffa Richard
*Legal Power Law Firm*

Abane Stanley
*The Abeng Law Firm*

Willy Ndie Tadmi
*Legal Power Law Firm*

Walson Emmanuel Tanwie
*Atanga Law Office*

Magloire Tchande
*PricewaterhouseCoopers Tax & Legal SARL*

Pierre Morgant Tchuikwa
*CADIRE*

Nadine Tinen
*PricewaterhouseCoopers Tax & Legal SARL*

Duga Titanji
*Duga & Co. Law Firm*

Tamfu Ngarka Tristel Richard
*Legal Power Law Firm*

Eliane Yomsi
*Karvan Finance*

Philippe Zouna
*PwC Cameroun*

**CANADA**
*Fraser Export*

*Toronto Hydro*

*TransUnion Canada*

Saad Ahmad
*Blakes, Cassels & Graydon LLP, member of Lex Mundi*

David Bish
*Torys LLP*

Ann Borooah
*Toronto City Hall*

Colin L. Campbell
*Superior Court of Justice of Ontario*

Sally Chieng
*Thompson, Ahern & Co. Ltd.*

Adrian Cochrane
*Blakes, Cassels & Graydon LLP, member of Lex Mundi*

John Craig
*Heenan Blaikie LLP, member of Ius Laboris*

Rod Davidge
*Osler, Hoskin & Harcourt LLP*

Isabelle Foley
*Corporations Canada*

Paul Gasparatto
*Ontario Energy Board*

Marlow Gereluk
*Norton Rose Canada LLP*

Yoine Goldstein
*McMillan LLP*

Pamela S. Hughes
*Blakes, Cassels & Graydon LLP, member of Lex Mundi*

Armando Iannuzzi
*Kestenberg Rabinowicz Partners LLP - member of Russell Bedford International*

Gloria Kim
*PwC Canada*

Harris Kligman
*Kestenberg Rabinowicz Partners LLP - member of Russell Bedford International*

Joshua Kochath
*Comage Container Lines*

Christopher Kong
*PwC Canada*

Jay Lefton
*Borden Ladner Gervais LLP*

Susan Leslie
*First Canadian Title*

Terry McCann
*MLG Enterprises Ltd.*

William McCarthy
*First Canadian Title*

Dave McKechnie
*McMillan LLP*

Patricia Meehan
*PwC Canada*

William Northcote
*Shibley Righton LLP*

Alfred Page
*Borden Ladner Gervais LLP*

Eric Paton
*PwC Canada*

Antonin Pribetic
*Steinberg Morton Hope & Israel LLP*

Thomas Provost
*McMillan LLP*

Bruce Reynolds
*Borden Ladner Gervais LLP*

Damian Rigolo
*Osler, Hoskin & Harcourt LLP*

Tony Rodrigues
*SDV Logistics*

Gaynor Roger
*Shibley Righton LLP*

Nicholas Scheib
*McMillan LLP*

Lincoln Schreiner
*PwC Canada*

Elliot Smith
*Osler, Hoskin & Harcourt LLP*

Shane Todd
*Heenan Blaikie LLP, member of Ius Laboris*

Dmitry Uduman
*PwC Canada*

Randal S. Van de Mosselaer
*Norton Rose Canada LLP*

Sharon Vogel
*Borden Ladner Gervais LLP*

George Waggot
*McMillan LLP*

Andrea White
*Shibley Righton LLP*

**CAPE VERDE**
David Almada
*D. Hopffer Almada & Associados*

Bruno Andrade Alves
*PwC Portugal*

Salete Alves
*SAMP - Sociedades de Advogados*

Quilda Domingas Andrade Canto
*AUDITEC - Auditores & Consultores*

Joana Andrade Correia
*Raposo Bernardo & Associados*

Denise Barreto
*PwC Portugal*

Liver Canuto
*PwC Portugal*

Ana Catarina Carnaz
*PwC Portugal*

Ana Raquel Costa
*PwC Portugal*

Ilídio Cruz
*Ilidio Cruz & Associados-Sociedade de Advogados RL*

Manuel de Pina
*SAMP - Sociedades de Advogados*

Victor Adolfo de Pinto Osório
*Attorney-at-Law*

John Duggan
*PwC Portugal*

Sofia Ferreira Enriquez
*Raposo Bernardo & Associados*

Florentino Jorge Fonseca Jesus
*Engineer*

João Gomes
*D. Hopffer Almada & Associados*

António Gonçalves
*JD Advogados*

Francisco Guimarães Melo
*PwC Portugal*

Julio Martins Junior
*Raposo Bernardo & Associados*

João Medina
*Neville de Rougemont & Associados*

Francisco Guimarães Melo
*PwC Portugal*

Ana Pinto Morais
*PwC Portugal*

Catarina Nunes
*PwC Portugal*

João Pereira
*FPS*

José Manuel Pinto Monteiro
*Advogados & Jurisconsultos*

Nelson Raposo Bernardo
*Raposo Bernardo & Associados*

Armando J.F. Rodrigues
*PwC Cape Verde*

Aguinaldo Rosario

José Rui de Sena
*Agência de Despacho aduaneiro Ferreira e Sena Lda*

Henrique Semedo Borges
*Law Firm Semedo Borges*

Luís Filipe Sousa
*PwC Portugal*

José Spinola
*FPS*

Frantz Tavares
*INOVE - Consultores Empresariais*

Mario Alberto Tavares
*Municipality of Praia*

Tereza Teixeira B. Amado
*Amado & Medina Advogadas*

Liza Helena Vaz
*PwC Portugal*

Leendert Verschoor
*PwC Portugal*

## CENTRAL AFRICAN REPUBLIC

*Cabinet John W. Ffooks & Co.*

*SDV Logistics*

Jean Christophe Bakossa
*L'ordre Centrafricain des Architectes*

Paul Bangonalia
*Guichet Unique de Formalités des Entreprises (GUFE)*

Jean-Noël Bangue
*Cour de Cassation de Bangui*

Blaise Banguitoumba
*ENERCA (Energie Centrafricaine)*

Maurice Dibert- Dollet
*Ministère de la Justice*

Désiré Blaise Dinguita
*Guichet Unique de Formalités des Entreprises (GUFE)*

Christiane Doraz-Serefessenet
*Cabinet Notaire Doraz-Serefessenet*

Emile Doraz-Serefessenet
*Cabinet Notaire Doraz-Serefessenet*

Jean-Pierre Douzima
*Agence Centrafricaine pour la Formation Professionnelle et l'Emploi (ACFPE)*

Marie-Edith Douzima-Lawson
*Cabinet Douzima et Ministère de la fonction publique*

Philippe Fouda Fouda
*BEAC Cameroon*

Dolly Gotilogue
*Avocate à la Cour*

Cyr Gregbanda
*Bamelec*

Marious Guibaut Metongo
*Transimex Centrafrique*

Jean Paul Maradas Nado
*Ministère de l'Urbanisme*

Mauricette Monthe-Psimhis
*Cabinet d'Avocats & Juristes Associés*

Yves Namkomokoina
*Tribunal de Commerce de Bangui*

Jacob Ngaya
*Ministère des Finances - Direction Générale des Impôts et des Domaines*

François Sabegala
*Guichet Unique de Formalités des Entreprises (GUFE)*

Ghislain Samba Mokamanede
*Bamelec*

Nicolas Tiangaye
*Nicolas Tiangaye Law Firm*

Salifou Yende
*Transimex Centrafrique*

Jonas Zonaita
*Guichet Unique de Formalités des Entreprises (GUFE)*

## CHAD

*Cabinet John W. Ffooks & Co.*

Dana Abdelkader Waya
*Cabinet Notarial Bongoro*

Adoum Daoud Adoum Haroun
*SCGADA et Fils*

Abdelkerim Ahmat
*SDV Logistics*

Théophile B. Bongoro
*Cabinet Notarial Bongoro*

Oscar d'Estaing Deffosso
*PricewaterhouseCoopers Tax & Legal SARL*

Thomas Dingamgoto
*Cabinet Thomas Dingamgoto*

Nadmian Dionmian
*Cabinet d'avocats Djaibe et associés*

Ernest Djagba Balandi
*BEAC - Chad*

Mahamat Ousman Djidda
*Architectural*

N'Doningar Djimasna
*Faculté de Droit, Université de N'Djamena*

Philippe Fouda Fouda
*BEAC Cameroon*

Delphine K. Djiraibe
*Avocate à la Cour*

Francis Kadjilembaye
*Cabinet Thomas Dingamgoto*

Gérard Leclaire
*Architectural*

Béchir Madet
*Office Notarial*

Hayatte N'Djiaye
*Profession Libérale*

Issa Ngarmbassa
*Etude Me Issa Ngar mbassa*

Tchouafiene Pandare
*Cabinet Notarial Bongoro*

Gilles Schwarz
*SDV Logistics*

Ahmat Senoussi
*Architectural*

Nadine Tinen
*PricewaterhouseCoopers Tax & Legal SARL*

Massiel Toudjoum Melyoel
*Office Notarial*

Masrangue Trahogra
*Cabinet d'Avocats Associés*

Issouf Traore
*Imperial Tobacco*

Abdoulaye Yacouba
*Mairie de N'Djamena*

Sobdibé Zoua
*Cabinet Sobdibe Zoua*

## CHILE

Leticia Acosta Aguirre
*Redlines Group*

Alejandra Anguita Avaria
*Superintendencia de Quiebras*

Josefina Montenegro Araneda
*Superintendencia de Quiebras*

Luis Avello
*PwC Chile*

Angeles Barría
*Philippi, Yrarrazaval, Pulido & Brunner, Abogados Ltda*

Enrique Benitez Urrutia
*Urrutia & Cía*

Jorge Benitez Urrutia
*Urrutia & Cía*

Carolina Benito Kelly
*Núñez Muñoz & Cía Ltda. Abogados*

Mario Bezanilla
*Alcaíno Rodríguez Abogados*

Manuel Brunet Bofill
*Cámara Chilena de la Construcción*

Rodrigo Cabrera Ortiz
*Chilectra*

Javier Carrasco
*Núñez Muñoz & Cía Ltda. Abogados*

Héctor Carrasco
*Superintendencia de Bancos y Instituciones Financieras Chile*

Paola Casorzo
*Philippi, Yrarrazaval, Pulido & Brunner, Abogados Ltda*

Andrés Chirgwin
*Chirgwin Recart*

María Alejandra Corvalán
*Yrarrázaval, Ruiz-Tagle, Goldenberg, Lagos & Silva*

Francisco della Maggiora
*Urenda, Rencoret, Orrego y Dörr*

Fernando Echeverria
*Cámara Chilena de la Construcción*

Alejandro Eliash
*Cámara Chilena de la Construcción*

Claudia Paz Escobar
*Chirgwin Recart*

Cristián S. Eyzaguirre
*Eyzaguirre & Cía.*

Maria Teresa Fernandez
*Bahamondez, Alvarez & Zegers*

Nicolás García
*Núñez Muñoz & Cía Ltda. Abogados*

Cristian Garcia-Huidobro
*Boletin Comercial*

Raúl Gómez Yáñez
*Urenda, Rencoret, Orrego y Dörr*

Eugenio Gonzalez
*Philippi, Yrarrazaval, Pulido & Brunner, Abogados Ltda*

José Gutiérrez
*PwC Chile*

Sofía Haupt
*Alessandri & Compañía*

Cristian Hermansen Rebolledo
*ACTIC Consultores*

Jorge Hirmas
*Albagli Zaliasnik Abogados*

Javier Hurtado
*Cámara Chilena de la Construcción*

Fernando Jamarne
*Alessandri & Compañía*

Michel Laurie
*PwC Chile*

Jose Luis Letelier
*Cariola Diez Perez-Copatos & Cia*

Macarena Letelier
*Urenda, Rencoret, Orrego y Dörr*

María Esther López Di Rubba
*Fiscalía Banco de Chile*

Gianfranco Lotito
*Claro & Cía., member of Lex Mundi*

Carolina Masihy
*Carey y Cía Ltda.*

Consuelo Maze
*Núñez Muñoz & Cía Ltda. Abogados*

Ignacio Mehech
*Núñez Muñoz & Cía Ltda. Abogados*

Pablo Menchaca
*Cariola Diez Perez-Copatos & Cia*

Enrique Munita
*Philippi, Yrarrazaval, Pulido & Brunner, Abogados Ltda*

Rodrigo Muñoz
*Núñez Muñoz & Cía Ltda. Abogados*

Cristian Olavarria
*Philippi, Yrarrazaval, Pulido & Brunner, Abogados Ltda*

Alberto Oltra
*DHL Global Forwarding*

Sergio Orrego
*Urenda, Rencoret, Orrego y Dörr*

Felipe Ossa
*Claro & Cía., member of Lex Mundi*

Gerardo Ovalle Mahns
*Yrarrázaval, Ruiz-Tagle, Goldenberg, Lagos & Silva*

Luis Parada Hoyl
*Bahamondez, Alvarez & Zegers*

Pablo Paredes
*Albagli Zaliasnik Abogados*

Gonzalo Paredes
*Núñez Muñoz & Cía Ltda. Abogados*

Miguel Pavez B.
*Russell Bedford Chile - member of Russell Bedford International*

Carmen Paz Cruz Lozano

Daniela Peña Fergadiott
*Barros & Errázuriz*

Alberto Pulido A.
*Philippi, Yrarrazaval, Pulido & Brunner, Abogados Ltda*

Felipe Rencoret
*Urenda, Rencoret, Orrego y Dörr*

Gonzalo Rencoret
*Urenda, Rencoret, Orrego y Dörr*

Ursula Retamal Marquez
*Superintendencia de Quiebras*

Alfonso Reymond Larrain
*Chadwick & Aldunate Abogados*

Sebastián Riesco
*Eyzaguirre & Cía.*

Constanza Rodriguez
*Philippi, Yrarrazaval, Pulido & Brunner, Abogados Ltda*

Edmundo Rojas García
*Conservador de Bienes Raíces y Comercio de Santiago*

Nelson Contador Rosales
*Nelson Contador y Cia. Abogados*

Alvaro Rosenblut
*Albagli Zaliasnik Abogados*

Marco Salgado
*Alcaíno Rodríguez Abogados*

Andrés Sanfuentes
*Philippi, Yrarrazaval, Pulido & Brunner, Abogados Ltda*

Francisco Selamé
*PwC Chile*

Cristián Sepúlveda
*Barros & Errázuriz*

Marcela Silva
*Philippi, Yrarrazaval, Pulido & Brunner, Abogados Ltda*

Luis Fernando Silva Ibañez
*Yrarrázaval, Ruiz-Tagle, Goldenberg, Lagos & Silva*

Alan Smith
*Agencia de Aduana Smith y Cía. Ltda.*

Grethel Soler
*Núñez Muñoz & Cía Ltda. Abogados*

Victor Tavera
*Chilectra*

Ricardo Tisi L.
*Cariola Diez Perez-Copatos & Cia*

Esteban Tomic Errázuriz
*Cruz & Cia. Abogados*

Carlos Torres
*Redlines Group*

Salvador Valdes
*Carey y Cía Ltda.*

Sebastián Valdivieso
*Yrarrázaval, Ruiz-Tagle, Goldenberg, Lagos & Silva*

Matias Varas
*Yrarrázaval, Ruiz-Tagle, Goldenberg, Lagos & Silva*

Nicolás Velasco Jenschke
*Superintendencia de Quiebras*

Jorge Vial
*Urenda, Rencoret, Orrego y Dörr*

Kenneth Werner
*Agencia de Aduana Jorge Vio y Cía. Ltda*

Arturo Yrarrázaval Covarrubias
*Yrarrázaval, Ruiz-Tagle, Goldenberg, Lagos & Silva*

Jean Paul Zalaquett
*Chilectra*

Matías Zegers
*Bahamondez, Alvarez & Zegers*

## CHINA

Bjarne Bauer
*Sofia Group*

Russell Brown
*LehmanBrown*

Daniel Chan
*DLA Piper Hong Kong*

Rico Chan
*Baker & McKenzie*

Donald Chen
*Ningbo Sunsea Apparel*

Elliott Youchun Chen
*Jun Ze Jun Law Offices*

Grace Cheng
*Capitallaw & Partners*

Jie Chen
*Jun He Law Office, member of Lex Mundi*

Weili Ding
*Jun He Law Office, member of Lex Mundi*

**Zhitong Ding**
*Credit Reference Center of People's Bank of China*

**Yu Du**
*MMLC Group*

**Wei Gao**
*Beijing V&T Law Firm*

**Alexander Gong**
*Baker & McKenzie*

**Joanna Guo**
*Zhong Lun Law Firm*

**William He**
*Zhong Lun Law Firm*

**Vivian Ho**
*Baker & McKenzie*

**Jing Hu**
*Noronha Advogados*

**Jinquan Hu**
*King & Wood Mallesons Lawyers*

**Brenda Jiang**
*Ningbo Sunsea Apparel*

**Jiao Jiao**
*Jun He Law Office, member of Lex Mundi*

**Audry Li**
*Zhong Lun Law Firm*

**Mark Li**
*Zhong Lun Law Firm*

**Qing Li**
*Jun He Law Office, member of Lex Mundi*

**Jane Liang**
*King & Wood Mallesons Lawyers*

**Grace Liu**
*Hua-Ander CPAs - member of Russell Bedford International*

**Zhiqiang Liu**
*King & Wood Mallesons Lawyers*

**Lucy Lu**
*King & Wood Mallesons Lawyers*

**Xiaoli Ma**
*Jun He Law Office, member of Lex Mundi*

**Matthew Mui**
*PwC China*

**Matthew Murphy**
*MMLC Group*

**Lei Niu**
*Zhong Lun Law Firm*

**Andrea Ren**
*Mayer Brown JSM*

**Jane Ren**
*Zhong Lun Law Firm*

**Mark Rockwood**
*Nicobar Group*

**Stephen Rynhart**
*Jones Lang LaSalle*

**Han Shen**
*Davis Polk & Wardwell*

**Jessie Tang**
*Global Star Logistics (China) Co., Ltd.*

**Terence Tung**
*Mayer Brown JSM*

**Fenghe Wang**
*Dacheng Law Offices*

**Guoqi Wang**
*Hua-Ander CPAs - member of Russell Bedford International*

**Jinghua Wang**
*Jun He Law Office, member of Lex Mundi*

**Thomas Wang**
*JoinWay Lawfirm*

**Xiaolei Wang**
*Credit Reference Center of People's Bank of China*

**Max Wong**
*Jones Lang LaSalle*

**Anthea Wong**
*PwC China*

**Kent Woo**
*Guangda Law Firm*

**Bruce Wu**
*Jiangsu Hongteng Food Co., Ltd.*

**Christina Wu**
*Capitallaw & Partners*

**Tony Wu**
*JoinWay Lawfirm*

**Changrong Xu**
*Baker Botts LLP*

**Meng Xu**
*Beijing V&T Law Firm*

**Hua Xuan**
*MMLC Group*

**Flora Yang**
*Baker & McKenzie*

**Ricky Yiu**
*Baker & McKenzie*

**Hai Yong**
*Baker & McKenzie*

**Natalie Yu**
*Shu Jin Law Firm*

**Xia Yu**
*MMLC Group*

**Jianan Yuan**
*Jun He Law Office, member of Lex Mundi*

**Sarah Zhang**
*Hogan Lovells*

**Yi Zhang**
*King & Wood Mallesons Lawyers*

**Johnny Zhao**
*Shanghai Wealth Finance Consulting Ltd.*

**Alina Zhu**
*Zhong Lun Law Firm*

**Judy Zhu**
*Mayer Brown JSM*

**Roy Zhu**
*Zhong Lun Law Firm*

**Viviane Zhu**
*Dacheng Law Offices*

**Roy Zou**
*Hogan Lovells*

## COLOMBIA

*EINCE Ltda.*

*Notaría 13 de Bogotá*

*Notaría 41 de Bogotá*

**Enrique Alvarez**
*Jose Lloreda Camacho & Co.*

**Napoleon Alvarez**
*Colegio de Registradores de Instrumentos Públicos de Colombia*

**Jaime Mauricio Angulo Sanchez**
*Computec - DataCrédito*

**Alexandra Arbeláez Cardona**
*Russell Bedford Colombia - member of Russell Bedford International*

**María Alejandra Arboleda**
*Posse Herrera & Ruiz*

**Fabio Ardila**
*Gómez-Pinzón Zuleta Abogados S.A.*

**Jorge Mauricio Arenas Sanchez**
*Codensa S.A. ESP*

**Juan Sebastián Arias**
*Brigard & Urrutia, member of Lex Mundi*

**Jose Luis Ariza Vargas**
*Superintendence of Notaries and Registries*

**Bernardo Avila**
*Parra, Rodríguez & Cavelier S.A.S.*

**Catherine Baena**
*Cavelier Abogados*

**Luis Alfredo Barragán**
*Brigard & Urrutia, member of Lex Mundi*

**Aurora Barroso**
*Parra, Rodríguez & Cavelier S.A.S.*

**Martha Bonett**
*Cavelier Abogados*

**Gloria María Borrero Restrepo**
*Corporación Excelencia en la Justicia*

**Leonardo Calderón Perdomo**
*Colegio de Registradores de Instrumentos Públicos de Colombia*

**Carolina Camacho**
*Posse Herrera & Ruiz*

**Claudia Marcela Camargo Arias**
*PwC Colombia*

**Pablo Cárdenas**
*Brigard & Urrutia, member of Lex Mundi*

**Erick Camilo Castellanos Reyes**
*Jose Lloreda Camacho & Co.*

**Felipe Cuberos**
*Prieto & Carrizosa S.A.*

**Maria Cristina Cuestas**
*DHL Global Forwarding*

**Andrés de la Rosa**
*Cavelier Abogados*

**María Alejandra de los Ríos**
*Jose Lloreda Camacho & Co.*

**Lorena Diaz**
*Jose Lloreda Camacho & Co.*

**Juliana Duque**
*Parra, Rodríguez & Cavelier S.A.S.*

**Jairo Flechas**
*GENELEC Ltda.*

**Carlos Fradique-Méndez**
*Brigard & Urrutia, member of Lex Mundi*

**Luis Hernando Gallo Medina**
*Gallo Medina Abogados Asociados*

**Natalia García**
*Jose Lloreda Camacho & Co.*

**Yamile Andrea Gómez**
*Productos Stahl de Colombia S.A.*

**Francisco González**
*Parra, Rodríguez & Cavelier S.A.S.*

**Santiago Gutiérrez**
*Jose Lloreda Camacho & Co.*

**Mónica Hernández**
*Prieto & Carrizosa S.A.*

**Jhovanna Jiménez**
*Brigard & Urrutia, member of Lex Mundi*

**Carlos Mario Lafaurie Escorce**
*PwC Colombia*

**Jorge Lara-Urbaneja**
*Lara Consultores*

**Alejandro Linares-Cantillo**
*Gómez-Pinzón Zuleta Abogados S.A.*

**Eduardo Mantilla-Serrano**
*M&M Trade and Law*

**María Fernanda Martínez**
*Cavelier Abogados*

**David Mejía**
*Jose Lloreda Camacho & Co.*

**Luis Mendoza**
*Jose Lloreda Camacho & Co.*

**Catalina Menjura**
*Posse Herrera & Ruiz*

**Ricardo Molano**
*Posse Herrera & Ruiz*

**Luis Gabriel Morcillo-Méndez**
*Brigard & Urrutia, member of Lex Mundi*

**Juan Carlos Moreno Peralta**
*Rodriguez Retamoso & Associates*

**Francisco Javier Morón López**
*Parra, Rodríguez & Cavelier S.A.S.*

**Enrique Jose Nates Guerra**
*Superintendence of Notaries and Registries*

**María Neira Tobón**
*Holguín, Neira & Pombo Abogados*

**Tonia Orozco**
*Brigard & Urrutia, member of Lex Mundi*

**Adriana Carolina Ospina Jiménez**
*Brigard & Urrutia, member of Lex Mundi*

**Alvaro Parra**
*Parra, Rodríguez & Cavelier S.A.S.*

**Silvia Patiño**
*Cavelier Abogados*

**Mónica Pedroza Garcés**
*Corporación Excelencia en la Justicia*

**Juan Sebastián Peredo**
*Jose Lloreda Camacho & Co.*

**Carolina Posada**
*Posse Herrera & Ruiz*

**Raul Quevedo**
*Jose Lloreda Camacho & Co.*

**Irma Isabel Rivera**
*Brigard & Urrutia, member of Lex Mundi*

**Bernardo Rodriguez**
*Parra, Rodríguez & Cavelier S.A.S.*

**Maria Andrea Rodriguez**
*ABC Cargo Logistics S.A.*

**Maria Isabel Rodriguez**
*Posse Herrera & Ruiz*

**Henry Javier Rodriguez Jiménez**
*Cavelier Abogados*

**Liliana Maria Rodriguez Retamoso**
*Rodriguez Retamoso & Associates*

**Daniel Rothstein**
*Parra, Rodríguez & Cavelier S.A.S.*

**Paula Samper Salazar**
*Gómez-Pinzón Zuleta Abogados S.A.*

**Nadia Sánchez**
*Jose Lloreda Camacho & Co.*

**Edna Sarmiento**
*Cavelier Abogados*

**Pablo Sierra**
*Posse Herrera & Ruiz*

**Carlos Silva**
*Cavelier Abogados*

**Carlos Arturo Silva Burbano**
*Cavelier Abogados*

**Paola Spada**
*Corporación Excelencia en la Justicia*

**Raúl Alberto Suárez Arcila**

**Diana Talero**
*Superintendency of Corporation*

**Jose Alejandro Torres**
*Posse Herrera & Ruiz*

**Angela Carolina Vaca**
*PwC Colombia*

**Patricia Vergara**
*Gómez-Pinzón Zuleta Abogados S.A.*

**Daniela Vergel**
*Cárdenas & Cárdenas*

**Adriana Zapata**
*Cavelier Abogados*

**Alberto Zuleta**
*Cárdenas & Cárdenas*

**Diana Zuleta**
*Parra, Rodríguez & Cavelier S.A.S.*

## COMOROS

**Chabani Abdallah Halifa**
*Groupe Hassanati Soilihi - Groupe Hasoil*

**Said Ahmed Aboudou**
*Toping*

**Hilmy Aboudsaid**
*Comores Cargo International*

**Abdillahe Ahamed Ahamada**
*Direction Générale des Impôts*

**Yassian Ahamed**
*Direction de l'Energie*

**Bahassani Ahmed**
*Cabinet d'Avocat Bahassani*

**Harimia Ahmed Ali**
*Cabinet Me Harimia*

**Mbaraka Al Ibrahim**
*Service de l'Urbanisme Comoros*

**Omar Said Allaoui**
*E.C.D.I.*

**Mouzaoui Amroine**
*Organisation Patronale des Comores*

**Moustoifa Assoumani**
*Etude Maître Chouzour Loutfi*

**Zahara Assoumani**
*Etude de Maîtres Binti Oumouri et Zahara Assoumani*

**Said Ali Said Athouman**
*Union of the Chamber of Commerce*

**Issilam Bambi**
*Appro Build*

**Ali Mohamed Choibou**
*Etude Maître Choibou*

**Remy Grondin**
*Vitogaz Comores*

**Ali Hadidi Hanima**
*Etude Maître Choibou*

**Adili Hassani**
*Electricité et Eau des Comores*

**Elyachourtu Ali Hila**
*Conseil en Finance*

**Haroussi Idrissa**
*Tribunal de Première Instance de Moroni*

**Youssouf Ismael**
*Direction Générale des Impots*

**Said Bacar Kaab**
*Préfecture Moroni*

**Faouzi Mohamed Lakj**
*Tribunal de Commerce Comoros*

**Chouzour Loutfi**
*Etude Maître Chouzour Loutfi*

**Abdillah Maoulana**
*Customs Comoros*

**Mohamed Mbechezi**
*Codetrans*

**Abdoulbastoi Moudjahidi**
*Club OHADA Comores*

**Farahati Moussa**
*Organisation Patronale des Comores*

**Ibrahim A. Mzimba**
*Cabinet Mzimba Avocats*

**Binti Oumouri**
*Etude de Maitres Binti Oumouri et Zahara Assoumani*

Mohamed Youssouf
*Etude Maître Abdourazak*

### CONGO, DEM. REP.
*Cabinet d'Architecte Marc Perazzone*

*Société Nationale d'Electricité (SNEL)*

Michel Alenda
*Klam & Partners Avocats*

Boniface Baluti
*Cabinet Ntoto*

Romain Battajon
*Cabinet Battajon*

Prince Bintene
*Cabinet Masamba*

Jean Adolphe Bitenu
*ANAPI*

Guillaume Bononge Litobaka
*Rocat*

Deo Bukayafwa
*MBM Conseil*

Nicaise Chikuru Munyiogwarha
*Chikuru & Associés*

Jean-Paul Dambana
*Socodam*

Nanan Diasivi
*Cabinet Irénée Falanka*

Andy Diata
*PwC*

Prosper Djuma Bilali
*Cabinet Masamba*

Irénée Falanka
*Cabinet Irénée Falanka*

Patrick Gérenthon
*SDV Logistics*

Ida Jiazet
*Klam & Partners Avocats*

Emery Kalamba
*Kalamba & Associes*

Vincent Kangulumba Mbambi
*André & Vincent Avocats Associés*

Benoit Kapila
*SDV Logistics*

Robert Katambu
*Cabinet Robert Katambu & Associés*

Arly Khuty
*Avocat*

Dolores Sonia Kimpwene
*Cabinet Madudu Sulubika*

Phistian Kubangusu Makiese
*Cabinet Masamba*

Emmanuel Le Bras
*PwC*

Jean-Délphin Lokonde Mvulukunda
*Cabinet Masamba*

Francis Lugunda Lubamba
*Cabinet Lukombe & Les Avocats*

Serge Mwankana Lulu
*Avocat*

Vital Lwanga Bizanbila
*Cabinet Vital Lwanga*

Aubin Mabanza
*Klam & Partners Avocats*

Béatrice Mabanza
*Klam & Partners Avocats*

Roger Masamba Makela
*Cabinet Masamba*

Cyril Emery Masiala
*Cabinet Irénée Falanka*

Tanayi Mbuy-Mbiye
*Cabinet Mbuy-Mbiye & Associés*

Karine Milandu Mia Vamosi
*Cabinet Irénée Falanka*

Marie-Thérèse Moanda
*Klam & Partners Avocats*

Didier Mopiti
*MBM Conseil*

Gérard Mosolo
*MBM Conseil*

Louman Mpoy
*Mpoy Louman & Associés*

Emery Mukendi Wafwana
*Cabinet Emery Mukendi Wafwana & Associés*

Freddy Mulamba Senene
*Cabinet Munkindji*

Hilaire Mumvudi Mulangi
*Ministère de l'Urbanisme et de l'Habitat*

Jacques Munday
*Cabinet Ntoto*

Ilunga Israel Ndambi
*S.I.E.C. SPRL*

Anthony Nkinzo
*PwC*

Victorine Bibiche Nsimba Kilembe
*Barreau de Kinshasa/Matete*

Jean Thomas Ntelu
*Cabinet Irénée Falanka*

Marcel Ntoto
*Cabinet Ntoto*

Leon Nzimbi
*PwC Congo (Democratic Republic of.)*

Otton Oligo Mbelia Kanalia
*ANAPI*

Abdoulaye G. Ouane
*Klam & Partners Avocats*

Jean-Louis Paquet
*Atelier d' Architecture*

Destin Pelete
*DHL Global Forwarding*

Christie Madudu Sulubika
*Cabinet Madudu Sulubika*

Sylvie Tshilanda Kabongo
*Cabinet Madudu Sulubika*

Nadine Mundala Walo
*Cabinet Madudu Sulubika*

### CONGO, REP.
*Cabinet John W. Ffooks & Co.*

*SNE (Société Nationale d'Electricité)*

Patrice Bazolo
*PwC*

Prosper Bizitou
*PwC*

Antoine Bokolo Joue
*CAP Architects*

Morin Boris
*Transporter*

Claude Coelho
*Cabinet d'Avocats Claude Coelho*

Mohammad Daoudou
*PwC*

Mathias Essereke
*Cabinet d'Avocats Mathias Essereke*

Philippe Fouda Fouda
*BEAC Cameroon*

Gaston Gapo
*Atelier d'Architecture et d'Urbanisme*

François Grimaud
*PwC*

Moise Kokolo
*PwC*

Pascal Kouo
*Sogeco - ETDE Congo*

Emmanuel Le Bras
*PwC*

Salomon Louboula
*Etude Notariale Louboula*

Jean Prosper Mabassi
*Ordre National des Avocats du Congo Barreau de Brazzaville*

Zahour Mbemba
*Lawyer*

Jean Paul Moliso Samba
*SOCAB*

Robert Ngabou
*CAP Architects*

Regina Nicole Okandza Yoka
*Direction Générale des Impôts*

Armand Robert Okoko
*Cabinet Armand Robert Okoko*

Alpha Zingamoko
*PwC*

### COSTA RICA
Aisha Acuña
*Lexincorp Costa Rica*

Gloriana Alvarado
*Pacheco Coto*

Arnoldo André
*Andre Tinoco Abogados*

Alejandro Antillon
*Pacheco Coto*

Carlos Araya
*Quiros Abogados Central Law*

Carlos Arias
*Oller Abogados*

Luis Diego Barahona
*PwC Costa Rica*

Carlos Barrantes
*PwC Costa Rica*

Ignacio Beirute
*Quiros Abogados Central Law*

Alejandro Bettoni Traube
*Doninelli & Doninelli - Asesores Jurídicos Asociados*

Michael Bruce
*ACZALAW*

Oswald Bruce
*ACZALAW*

Eduardo Calderón-Odio
*BLP Abogados*

Adriana Castro
*BLP Abogados*

Luis Manuel Castro
*BLP Abogados*

Silvia Chacon
*Alfredo Fournier & Asociados*

Roberto Esquivel
*Oller Abogados*

Freddy Fachler
*Pacheco Coto*

Elizabeth Fallas
*Quiros Abogados Central Law*

Irene Fernández
*LEX Counsel*

Neftali Garro
*BLP Abogados*

Miguel Golcher Valverde
*Colegio de Ingenieros Electricistas, Mecánicos e Industriales*

Andrea González
*BLP Abogados*

David Gutierrez

Jorge Guzmán
*LEX Counsel*

Roy Guzman Ramirez
*Compañía Nacional de Fuerza y Luz*

Milena Hidalgo
*Teletec S.A.*

Randall Zamora Hidalgo
*Costa Rica ABC*

Ernesto Hütt Crespo
*Facio & Cañas, member of Lex Mundi*

Anneth Jimenez
*BLP Abogados*

Vivian Jiménez
*Oller Abogados*

Elvis Eduardo Jiménez Gutiérrez
*Superintendencia General de Entidades Financieras*

Margarita Libby Hernandez
*Margarita Libby y Asociados S.A.*

Carlos Marin Castro
*Ministerio de Comercio Exterior*

Ivannia Méndez Rodríguez
*Oller Abogados*

Gabriela Miranda
*Oller Abogados*

Jaime Molina
*Proyectos ICC S.A.*

Jorge Montenegro
*SCGMT Arquitectura y Diseño*

Eduardo Montoya Solano
*Superintendencia General de Entidades Financieras*

Cecilia Naranjo
*LEX Counsel*

Tomas Nassar
*Pacheco Coto*

Olman Núñez
*Teletec S.A.*

Sergio Pérez
*Lexincorp Costa Rica*

Mainor Quesada
*Teletec S.A.*

Mauricio Quiros
*Quiros Abogados Central Law*

Rafael Quiros
*Quiros Abogados Central Law*

Ana Quiros Vaglio
*TransUnion*

Ricardo Rodriguez
*Quiros Abogados Central Law*

Manrique Rojas
*Lexincorp Costa Rica*

Miguel Ruiz Herrera
*LEX Counsel*

Jose Luis Salinas
*SCGMT Arquitectura y Diseño*

Luis Sánchez
*Facio & Cañas, member of Lex Mundi*

Fernando Sanchez Castillo
*Russell Bedford Costa Rica / ABBQ Consultores, S.A. - member of Russell Bedford International*

Luis Sibaja
*LEX Counsel*

Ronny Michel Valverde Mena
*Extrusiones de Aluminio S.A.*

Alonso Vargas
*Lexincorp Costa Rica*

Daniela Vargas
*PwC Costa Rica*

Marianela Vargas
*PwC Costa Rica*

Stanley Villegas
*Decisa*

Jafet Zúñiga Salas
*Superintendencia General de Entidades Financieras*

### CÔTE D'IVOIRE
*Cabinet John W. Ffooks & Co.*

*Ordre des Géometres Expert de la Côte d'Ivoire*

Ahmadou Al Aminou Lo
*BCEAO*

Claude Aman
*Bolloré Africa Logistics*

Ika Raymond Any-Gbayere
*Any Ray & Partners*

Landry Baguy

Lassiney Kathann Camara
*CLK Avocats*

Asman César
*Cabinet N'Goan, Asman & Associés*

Aminata Cone
*SCPA Dogué-Abbé Yao & Associés*

Issa Diabaté
*Koffi & Diabaté*

Junior Doukoure
*Any Ray & Partners*

Dorothée K. Dreesen
*Etude Maître Dreesen*

Stéphane Eholie
*SIMAT*

Bertrand Fleury
*Bolloré Africa Logistics*

Liadé Vaudy Gbetibouo
*CLK Avocats*

Koupo Gnoleba
*Ministère de la Construction*

Claude-Andrée Groga
*Cabinet Jean-François Chauveau*

Barnabe Kabore
*NOVELEC Sarl*

Noel Koffi
*Cabinet Noël Y. Koffi*

Fatoumata Konate Toure-B.
*Etude de Me Konate Toure-B. Fatoumata*

Mahoua Kone
*Etude de Maître Kone Mahoua*

N'Dri Marielle-Ange Kouakou
*CLK Avocats*

Arsène Dablé Kouassi
*SCPA Dogué-Abbé Yao & Associés*

Tape Likane
*Cabinet N'Goan, Asman & Associés*

Charlotte-Yolande Mangoua
*Etude de Maître Mangoua*

Adeline Messou
*PwC Côte d'Ivoire*

Georges N'Goan
*Cabinet N'Goan, Asman & Associés*

Patricia N'guessan
*Cabinet Jean-François Chauveau*

Jacques Otro
*Conseil National de l'Ordre des Architectes*

Athanase Raux
*Cabinet Raux, Amien & Associés*

Koffi Raymond
*SIMAT*

Simon Dognima Silué
*Bile-Aka, Brizoua-Bi & Associés*

Dominique Taty
*PwC Côte d'Ivoire*

Fousséni Traoré
*PwC Côte d'Ivoire*

Jean Christian Turkson
*CIE*

Kotokou Kouakou Urbain
*ATK*

Emmanuel Yehouessi
*BCEAO*

Léon Désiré Zalo
*Ministère d'Etat, Ministère de l'Agriculture*

Seydou Zerbo
*SCPA Dogué-Abbé Yao & Associés*

## CROATIA

Boris Andrejaš
*Babić & Partners*

Andrea August
*Financial Agency - Centre for HITRO.HR*

Emir Bahtijarević
*Divjak, Topić & Bahtijarević*

Hrvoje Bardek
*CMS Legal*

Ivo Bijelić
*PwC Croatia*

Zoran Bohaček
*Croatian Banking Association*

Marko Borsky
*Divjak, Topić & Bahtijarević*

Linda Brčić
*Divjak, Topić & Bahtijarević*

Lana Brlek
*PwC Croatia*

Belinda Čačić
*Čačić & Partners*

Ivan Ćuk
*Vukmir & Associates*

Saša Divjak
*Divjak, Topić & Bahtijarević*

Anela Dizdarević
*Sihtar Attorneys at Law*

Ronald Given
*Wolf Theiss*

Tonka Gjoić
*Glinska & Mišković Ltd.*

Ivan Gjurgjan
*Gjurgjan & Šribar Radić Law Firm*

Krešimir Golubić
*Golmax d.o.o.*

Tom Hadzija
*Korper & Partneri Law Firm*

Lidija Hanžek
*HROK d.o.o.*

Branimir Iveković
*Iveković Law Office*

Irina Jelčić
*Hanžeković & Partners Ltd., member of Lex Mundi*

Ivica Jelovcic
*Damco*

Saša Jovičić
*Wolf Theiss*

Sanja Jurković
*PwC Croatia*

Branko Kirin
*Čačić & Partners*

Ozren Kobsa
*Divjak, Topić & Bahtijarević*

Anita Krizmanić
*Mačešić & Partners, Odvjetnicko drustvo*

Krešimir Ljubić
*Odvjetničko društvo Leko i Partneri*

Andrea Lončar
*Glinska & Mišković Ltd.*

Marko Lovrić
*Divjak, Topić & Bahtijarević*

Dina Lukac
*Leko i Partneri Attorneys at Law*

Miroljub Mačešić
*Mačešić & Partners, Odvjetnicko drustvo*

Josip Marohnić
*Glinska & Mišković Ltd.*

Domagoj Matica
*Čačić & Partners*

Andrej Matijevich
*Matijevich Law Office*

Igor Mirosevic
*Divjak, Topić & Bahtijarević*

Tomislav Pedišić
*Vukmir & Asociates*

Miroslav Plašćar
*Žurić i Partneri*

Marko Praljak
*Praljak & Svić*

Hrvoje Radić
*Gjurgjan & Šribar Radić Law Firm*

Kristina Rihtar
*Law Office Vidan*

Gordan Rotkvić
*PwC Croatia*

Davor Rukonić
*Divjak, Topić & Bahtijarević*

Boris Šarović
*Šavorić & Partners*

Ana Sihtar
*Sihtar Attorneys at Law*

Andrej Skočić
*Mervis d.o.o. - member of Russell Bedford International*

Vladimir Skočić
*Mervis d.o.o. - member of Russell Bedford International*

Manuela Špoljarić
*Odvjetničko društvo Leko i Partneri*

Irena Šribar Radić
*Gjurgjan & Šribar Radić Law Firm*

Lidija Subašić
*Odvjetničko društvo Leko i Partneri*

Stjepan Šutija
*Babić & Partners*

Marin Svić
*Praljak & Svić*

Zoran Tasić
*CMS Legal*

Tena Tomek
*Divjak, Topić & Bahtijarević*

Branka Tutek
*Jurić and Partners Attorneys at Law*

Ivana Urem
*Assono Ltd. Croatia*

Hrvoje Vidan
*Law Office Vidan*

Željko Vrban
*HEP Distribution System Operator Ltd.*

Zrinka Vrtarić
*CMS Legal*

Mario Vukelić
*High Commercial Court of the Republic of Croatia*

Marin Vukovrić
*Divjak, Topić & Bahtijarević*

Gorana Vukušić
*Leko i Partneri Attorneys at Law*

## CYPRUS

*Electricity Authority of Cyprus*

Alexandros Alexandrou
*Tornaritis Law Firm*

Achilleas Amvrosiou
*Artemis Bank Information Systems Ltd.*

Andreas Andreou
*Cyprus Global Logistics*

George Antoniades
*Gantoni General Enterprises*

Pavlos Aristodemou
*Aristodemou Loizides Yiolitis LLC*

Anja Arsalides
*Cyprus Investment Promotion Agency*

Antonis Christodoulides
*PwC Cyprus*

Kypros Chrysostomides
*Dr. K. Chrysostomides & Co. LLC*

Achilleas Demetriades
*Lellos P Demetriades Law Office LLC*

Tatia Efstathiou
*P.G. Economides & Co Limited - member of Russell Bedford International*

Lefteris S. Eleftheriou
*Cyprus Investment Promotion Agency*

Marios Eliades
*M.Eliades & Partners LLC*

Elena Frixou
*Artemis Bank Information Systems Ltd.*

Olga Gaponova
*Deloitte LLP*

Elvira Georgiou
*Antis Triantafyllides & Sons LLC*

Marios Hadjigavriel
*Antis Triantafyllides & Sons LLC*

Iacovos Hadjivarnavas
*Famagusta Chamber of Commerce and Industry*

Samantha G. Hellicar
*Antis Triantafyllides & Sons LLC*

Marina Ierokipiotou
*Antis Triantafyllides & Sons LLC*

Christina Ioannidou
*Ioannides Demetriou LLC*

George Karakannas
*Ch.P. Karakannas Electrical Ltd.*

Melina Karaolia
*M.Eliades & Partners LLC*

Harris Kleanthous
*Deloitte LLP*

Kleanthis Kleanthous
*Ministry of Interior*

Christina Koronis
*PwC Cyprus*

Christina Kotsapa
*Antis Triantafyllides & Sons LLC*

Nicholas Ktenas
*Andreas Neocleous & Co. Legal Consultants*

Olga Lambrou
*Mouaimis & Mouaimis Advocates*

Pieris M. Markou
*Deloitte LLP*

Costas Mavrocordatos
*PwC Cyprus*

Phivos Michaelides
*Ioannides Demetriou LLC*

Panayotis Mouaimis
*Mouaimis & Mouaimis Advocates*

George Mouskides
*FOX Smart Estate Agency*

Demetris Nicolaou
*Aristodemou Loizides Yiolitis LLC*

Varnavas Nicolaou
*PwC Cyprus*

Themis Panayi
*Cyprus Stock Exchange*

Georgios Papadopoulos
*M.Eliades & Partners LLC*

Stella Papadopoulou
*Ministry of Interior*

Chrysilios Pelekanos
*PwC Cyprus*

Marios Pelekanos
*Mesaritis Pelekanos Architects - Engineers*

Ioanna Petrou
*PwC Cyprus*

Maria Petsa
*Cyprus Stock Exchange*

Yiannos Pipis
*Nice Day Developers*

Kritonas Savvides
*Nice Day Developers*

Lambros Soteriou
*Michael Kyprianou & Co. LLC*

Criton Tornaritis
*Tornaritis Law Firm*

Stelios Triantafyllides
*Antis Triantafyllides & Sons LLC*

Irene Tziakouri
*PwC Cyprus*

Christiana Vassiliou
*Antis Triantafyllides & Sons LLC*

Xenios Xenopoulos
*Lawyer*

Savvas Yiordamlis
*Ioannides Demetriou LLC*

## CZECH REPUBLIC

*Allen & Overy (Czech Republic) LLP, organizační složka*

Vladimír Ambruz
*Ambruz & Dark*

Michaela Baranyková
*Euro-Trend, s.r.o. - member of Russell Bedford International*

Libor Basl
*Baker & McKenzie*

Stanislav Bednár
*Peterka & Partners*

Tomáš Běhounek
*BNT - Pravda & Partner, s.r.o.*

Stanislav Beran
*Peterka & Partners*

Jan Beres
*Kocian Solc Balastik, Advokátní Kancelář, s.r.o.*

Martin Bohuslav
*Ambruz & Dark*

Michal Buchta
*Ambruz & Dark*

Jiří Černý
*Peterka & Partners*

Ivan Chalupa
*Squire, Sanders & Dempsey, v.o.s. Advokátní Kancelář*

Peter Chrenko
*PwC Czech Republic*

Pavel Cirek
*Energy Regulator Office Czech Republic*

Jakub Cisar
*DLA Piper Prague LLP*

Martin Dančišin
*Glatzová & Co.*

Matěj Daněk
*PRK Partners s.r.o. Advokátní Kancelář*

Dagmar Dubecka
*Kocian Solc Balastik, Advokátní Kancelář, s.r.o.*

Tomáš Elbert
*White & Case*

Robert Elefant
*PwC Czech Republic*

Tereza Erényi
*PRK Partners s.r.o. Advokátní Kancelář*

Michal Forýtek
*Kinstellar*

Jakub Hajek
*Ambruz & Dark*

Michal Hanko
*Bubnik, Myslil & Partners*

Jarmila Hanzalová
*PRK Partners s.r.o. Advokátní Kancelář*

Vít Horáček
*Glatzová & Co.*

Radek Horký
*Notary Chamber, Czech Republic*

Pavel Jakab
*Peterka & Partners*

Kateřina Jarolímková
*Notářská komora České republiky*

Ludvik Juřička
*Ambruz & Dark*

Jitka Korejzova
*PRK Partners s.r.o. Advokátní Kancelář*

Adela Krbcová
*Peterka & Partners*

Martin Krechler
*Glatzová & Co.*

Tomáš Kren
*White & Case*

Aleš Kubáč
*Ambruz & Dark*

Petr Kucera
*CCB - Czech Credit Bureau*

Zdeněk Kučera
*Baker & McKenzie*

Petr Kuhn
*White & Case*

Lukas Lejcek
*BDP-Wakestone s.r.o.*

Zuzana Luklová
*Ambruz & Dark*

Ondrej Machala
*Notary Chamber, Czech Republic*

Ondřej Mánek
*Wolf Theiss Advokáti s.r.o.*

Jiří Markvart
*Ambruz & Dark*

Peter Maysenhölder
*BNT - Pravda & Partner, s.r.o.*

Petr Měšťánek
*Kinstellar*

Veronika Mistova
*PRK Partners s.r.o. Advokátní Kancelář*

Pavlína Mišutová
*White & Case*

Vojtech Mlynar
*White & Case*

Miroslava Mojžišová
*Ambruz & Dark*

Lenka Mrazova
*PwC Czech Republic*

David Musil
*PwC Czech Republic*

Jarmila Musilova
*Czech National Bank*

Lenka Navrátilová
*Ambruz & Dark*

Lenka Nemcova
*Ambruz & Dark*

Marketa Penazova
*Ambruz & Dark*

Igor Pieš
*Baker & McKenzie*

Jan Procházka
*Ambruz & Dark*

Markéta Protivankova
*Vejmelka & Wünsch, s.r.o.*

Zdenek Rosicky
*Squire, Sanders & Dempsey, v.o.s. Advokátní Kancelář*

Kamila Rychtarova
*White & Case*

Petra Schneiderova
*Ambruz & Dark*

Václav Semrád
*Wolf Theiss Advokáti s.r.o.*

Paul Sestak
*Wolf Theiss Advokáti s.r.o.*

Dana Sládečková
*Czech National Bank*

Ladislav Smejkal
*White & Case*

Erik Steger
*Wolf Theiss Advokáti s.r.o.*

Martin Štěpaník
*Peterka & Partners*

Paul Stewart
*PwC Czech Republic*

Marek Švehlík
*Švehlí & Mikuláš Advokáti s.r.o.*

Stanislav Travnicek
*Energy Regulator Office Czech Republic*

Růžena Trojánková
*Kinstellar*

Klara Valentova
*Ambruz & Dark*

Daniel Vitouš
*Ambruz & Dark*

Ludek Vrána
*Vrána & Pelikán*

Vaclav Zaloudek
*White & Case*

## DENMARK
*Center for Construction*

Elsebeth Aaes-Jørgensen
*Norrbom Vinding, member of Ius Laboris*

Niels Bang
*Gorrissen Federspiel*

Peter Bang
*Plesner*

Thomas Bang
*Lett Law Firm*

Ole Borch
*Bech-Bruun Law Firm*

Frants Dalgaard-Knudsen
*Plesner*

Pia Dalziel
*Miller Rosenfalck LLP*

Mogens Ebeling
*Bruun & Hjejle*

Anne Birgitte Gammeljord
*Gorrissen Federspiel*

Ata Ghilassi
*Kromann Reumert, member of Lex Mundi*

Anne Louise Haack Andersen
*Lett Law Firm*

Merry Hansen
*Plesner*

Annette Hastrup
*Magnusson*

Heidi Hoelgaard
*Experian Northern Europe*

Mette Højberg
*Bech-Bruun Law Firm*

Peter Honoré
*Kromann Reumert, member of Lex Mundi*

Jens Steen Jensen
*Kromann Reumert, member of Lex Mundi*

Hans-Peter Jørgensen
*Gorrissen Federspiel*

Eva Kaya
*Advokatgruppen*

Lars Kjaer
*Bech-Bruun Law Firm*

Mette Klingsten
*Bech-Bruun Law Firm*

Alexander Troeltzsch Larsen
*Bech-Bruun Law Firm*

Mikkel Stig Larsen
*Kromann Reumert, member of Lex Mundi*

Susanne Schjølin Larsen
*Kromann Reumert, member of Lex Mundi*

Jesper Avnborg Lentz
*Gorrissen Federspiel*

Morten Bang Mikkelsen
*PwC Denmark*

Lita Misozi Hansen
*PwC Denmark*

Andreas Nielsen
*Bruun & Hjejle*

Susanne Norgaard
*PwC Denmark*

Anders Ørskov Melballe
*Accura Advokataktieselskab*

Carsten Pedersen
*Bech-Bruun Law Firm*

Lars Lindencrone Petersen
*Bech-Bruun Law Firm*

Jannick Prehn Brøndum
*Bruun & Hjejle*

Sisse Riis-Hansen
*Kromann Reumert, member of Lex Mundi*

Steen Rosenfalck
*Miller Rosenfalck LLP*

Michael Schebye Larsen
*Gorrissen Federspiel*

Louise Krarup Simonsen
*Kromann Reumert, member of Lex Mundi*

Martin Sørensen
*2M El-installation A/S*

Kim Trenskow
*Kromann Reumert, member of Lex Mundi*

Søren Vasegaard Andreasen
*Advokatgruppen*

Anders Worsøe
*Magnusson*

## DJIBOUTI
*Electricité de Djibouti*

Ouloufa Ismail Abdo
*Office Djiboutien de la Propriété Industrielle et Commerciale (ODPIC)*

Nima Ali Warsama
*Banque pour le Commerce et l'Industrie - Mer Rouge (BCI MR)*

Mourad Farah

Malik Garad
*Banque Centrale de Djibouti*

Mohamed Ali Houssein
*Direction de l'Habitat et de l'Urbanisme*

Ismael Mahamoud
*Universite de Djibouti*

Fatouma Mahamoud Hassan

Alain Martinet
*Cabinet d'Avocats Martinet & Martinet*

Marie-Paule Martinet
*Cabinet d'Avocats Martinet & Martinet*

Oubah Mohamed Omar
*Société Maritime L. Savon & Ries*

Abdallah Mohammed Kamil
*Etude Maître Mohammed Kamil*

Ahmed Osman
*Banque Centrale de Djibouti*

Lantosoa Hurfin Ralaiarinosy
*Cosmezz Sarl Djibouti*

## DOMINICA
*Anthony Astaphan Chambers*

Wilmot Alexander
*Dev Trading Ltd.*

Rene Akobi Butcher
*Isidore & Associates LLP*

Jo-Anne Commodore
*Supreme Court Registry*

Marvlyn Estrado
*KPB Chartered Accountants*

Joelle A.V. Harris
*Harris & Harris*

Sandra Julien
*Companies and Intellectual Property Office*

Alick C. Lawrence
*Lawrence Alick C. Chambers*

Charlene Mae Magnaye
*PwC St. Lucia*

Severin McKenzie
*McKenzie Architectural & Construction Services Inc.*

Richard Peterkin
*PwC St. Lucia*

Joan K.R. Prevost
*Prevost & Roberts*

Vernanda Raymond
*House of Assembly*

Eugene G. Royer
*Eugene G. Royer Chartered Architect*

Jason Timothy
*DOMLEC*

Anya Trim
*PwC St. Lucia*

Ossie Walsh
*Supreme Court Registry*

Dawn Yearwood
*Yearwood Chambers*

## DOMINICAN REPUBLIC

Rhadys Abreu de Polanco
*Union Internacional del Notariado Latino*

Maria Teresa Acta
*Headrick Rizik Alvarez & Fernández*

Jennifer Beauchamps
*Jiménez Cruz Peña*

Luis Eduardo Bernard
*González & Coiscou*

Laura Bobea
*Medina & Rizek, Abogados*

Joanna M. Bonnelly Ginebra
*Squire, Sanders & Dempsey LLP*

Ana Isabel Caceres
*Troncoso y Caceres*

Giselle Castillo
*Superintendencia de Bancos*

Ramon Ceballos
*Ceballos & Sánchez, Ingeniería y Energía, C. por A.*

Milvio Coiscou
*González & Coiscou*

Leandro Corral
*Estrella & Tupete*

José Cruz Campillo
*Jiménez Cruz Peña*

Marcos de León
*Superintendencia de Bancos*

Sarah de León Perelló
*Headrick Rizik Alvarez & Fernández*

Raúl De Moya
*Arquitectura & Planificación*

Juan Carlos De Moya
*González & Coiscou*

Rosa Díaz
*Jiménez Cruz Peña*

Alejandro Fernández de Castro
*PwC Dominican Republic*

Mary Fernández Rodríguez
*Headrick Rizik Alvarez & Fernández*

Milagros Figuereo
*Job, Báez, Soto & Associates - member of Russell Bedford International*

Jose Ernesto Garcia A.
*Transglobal Logistic*

Melissa Gilbert
*Jiménez Cruz Peña*

Pablo Gonzalez Tapia
*González & Coiscou*

Luis Heredia Bonetti
*Russin & Vecchi, LLC*

Luis J. Jiménez
*Jiménez Cruz Peña*

José Ramón Logroño Morales
*Logroño Aquino Durán & Logroño*

Fernando Marranzini
*Headrick Rizik Alvarez & Fernández*

Carlos Marte
*Agencia de Comercio Exterior CM*

Jesús Geraldo Martínez
*Superintendencia de Bancos*

Fabiola Medina
*Medina & Rizek, Abogados*

Laura Medina
*Jiménez Cruz Peña*

Doris Miranda
*González & Coiscou*

Ramon Ortega
*PwC El Salvador*

Edward Piña Fernandez
*Biaggi & Messina*

Julio Pinedo
*PwC Dominican Republic*

Maria Portes
*Castillo y Castillo*

Alejandro Miguel Ramirez Suzaña
*Ramirez Suzaña & Asoc.*

Katherine Rosa
*Jiménez Cruz Peña*

Wendy Sánchez
*TransUnion Dominican Republic*

Carolina Silié
*Headrick Rizik Alvarez & Fernández*

Juan Tejeda
*PwC Dominican Republic*

Ana Gisselle Valerio
*Troncoso y Caceres*

Jeannerette Vergez
*Job, Báez, Soto & Associates - member of Russell Bedford International*

Vilma Verras Terrero
*Jiménez Cruz Peña*

Chery Zacarías
*Medina & Rizek, Abogados*

## ECUADOR
*MZ Sistemas Electricos y Electronicos*

Pablo Aguirre
*PwC Ecuador*

Natalia Almeida-Oleas
*Pérez, Bustamante y Ponce, member of Lex Mundi*

Diego Cabezas-Klaere
*Cabezas & Cabezas-Klaere*

Sandra Cevallos
*Pérez, Bustamante y Ponce, member of Lex Mundi*

Pablo Chiriboga Dechiara
*Puente Reyes & Galarza Attorneys At Law Cia. Ltda.*

Fernando Coral
*Panalpina World Transport LLP*

Renato Coronel
*Pinto & Garcés Asoc. Cía Ltda - member of Russell Bedford International*

Fernando Del Pozo Contreras
*Gallegos, Valarezo & Neira*

Martín Galarza Lanas
*Puente Reyes & Galarza Attorneys At Law Cia. Ltda.*

Leopoldo González R.
*Paz Horowitz Robalino Garcés Abogados*

Jaime Gordillo
*PwC Ecuador*

Veronica Jaramillo
*Panalpina World Transport LLP*

Rubby Lucero
*Cabezas & Cabezas-Klaere*

Carlos Alberto Maldonado Terneus
*Empresa Eléctrica Quito SA*

Juan Manuel Marchán
*Pérez, Bustamante y Ponce, member of Lex Mundi*

Luis Marin-Tobar
*Pérez, Bustamante y Ponce, member of Lex Mundi*

Sansone Massimiliano

Eduardo Montero

Francisco Javier Naranjo Grijalva
*Paz Horowitz Robalino Garcés Abogados*

Esteban Ortiz
*Pérez, Bustamante y Ponce, member of Lex Mundi*

Jorge Paz Durini
*Paz Horowitz Robalino Garcés Abogados*

Bruno Pineda-Cordero
*Pérez, Bustamante y Ponce, member of Lex Mundi*

Daniel Pino Arroba
*Coronel y Pérez*

Ramiro Pinto
*Pinto & Garcés Asoc. Cía Ltda - member of Russell Bedford International*

Patricia Ponce Arteta
*Bustamante & Bustamante*

Juan Carlos Proaño
*Panalpina World Transport LLP*

Angel Alfonso Puente Reyes
*Puente Reyes & Galarza Attorneys at Law Cia. Ltda.*

Juan José Puente Reyes
*Puente Reyes & Galarza Attorneys at Law Cia. Ltda.*

Sandra Reed
*Pérez, Bustamante y Ponce, member of Lex Mundi*

Amparo Romero
*Romero Arteta Ponce*

Diego Romero
*Romero Arteta Ponce*

Gustavo Romero
*Romero Arteta Ponce*

José Romero

Hugo Arias Salgado

Montserrat Sánchez
*Coronel y Pérez*

Carlos Serrano

Paulina Viteri

**EGYPT, ARAB REP.**
*Talal Abu Ghazaleh Legal (TAG-Legal)*

Abdel Aal Aly
*Afifi World Transport Alexandria*

Naguib Abadir
*Nacita Corporation*

Mostafa Abd El Rahim
*Al Kamel Law Office*

Ghada Abdel Aziz
*Ibrachy & Dermarkar Law Firm*

Ibrahim Mustafa Ibrahim Abdel Khalek
*General Authority for Investment GAFI*

Ahmed Abdel Warith
*AAW Consulting Engineers*

Ahmed Abou Ali
*Hassouna & Abou Ali*

Gamal Abou Ali
*Hassouna & Abou Ali*

Hazem Ahmed Fathi
*Hassouna & Abou Ali*

Abd El Wahab Aly Ibrahim
*Abd El Wahab Sons*

Sarah Ammar
*Al Kamel Law Office*

Sayed Ammar
*Al Kamel Law Office*

Lilihane Atlam
*Al Kamel Law Office*

Khaled Balbaa
*KPMG*

Louis Bishara
*Bishara Textile & Garment Manufacturing Co.*

Karim Dabbous
*Sherif Dabbous - member of Russell Bedford International*

Sherif Dabbous
*Sherif Dabbous - member of Russell Bedford International*

Sameh Dahroug
*Ibrachy & Dermarkar Law Firm*

Amal Afifi Dawood
*SNR Denton Wilde Sapte & Co*

Amany El Bagoury
*Al Kamel Law Office*

Hanan El Dib
*Al-Ahl Firm*

Ahmed El Gammal
*Shalakany Law Office, member of Lex Mundi*

Mohamed Refaat El Houshi
*The Egyptian Credit Bureau I-Score*

Hassan El Maraashly
*AAW Consulting Engineers*

Amr El Monayer
*PwC Egypt*

Amina El Oteify
*Shalakany Law Office, member of Lex Mundi*

Khaled El Shalakany
*Shalakany Law Office, member of Lex Mundi*

Sally El Shalakany
*Shalakany Law Office, member of Lex Mundi*

Passant El Tabei
*PwC Egypt*

Abd-Allah El-Shazly
*Egyptian Public Prosecution*

Soheir Elbanna
*Ibrachy Law Firm*

Karim Elhelaly
*Al-Ahl Firm*

Ashraf Elibrachy
*Ibrachy Law Firm*

Rana Elnahal
*Ibrachy Law Firm*

Mostafa Elshafei
*Ibrachy Law Firm*

Karim Emam
*PwC Egypt*

Hassan Fahmy
*Ministry of Investment*

Mariam Fahmy
*Shalakany Law Office, member of Lex Mundi*

Tarek Gadallah
*Ibrachy Law Firm*

Samir Ghareeb
*Office of the Minister of State for Local Development*

Zeinab Saieed Gohar
*Central Bank of Egypt*

Ahmed Hantera
*Egyptian Public Prosecution*

Mohamed Hashish
*TELELAWS*

Maha Hassan
*Afifi World Transport Alexandria*

Tarek Hassib
*Al Kamel Law Office*

Omneia Helmy
*Egyptian Center for Economic Studies*

Mohamed Hisham Hassan
*Ministry of Investment*

Ahmed Hossam
*PwC Egypt*

Stephan Jäger
*Amereller Rechtsanwälte*

Mohamed Kamal
*Shalakany Law Office, member of Lex Mundi*

Salma Kamal
*Shalakany Law Office, member of Lex Mundi*

Mohanad Khaled
*BDO, Khaled & Co*

Shahira Khaled
*Al Kamel Law Office*

Taha Khaled
*BDO, Khaled & Co*

Ussama Khattab
*Bridges To Business*

Adel Kheir
*Adel Kheir Law Office*

Lobna Magdy
*Shalakany Law Office, member of Lex Mundi*

Mustafa Makram
*BDO, Khaled & Co*

Amr Mohamed
*Ministry of Investment*

Marwa Omara
*TELELAWS*

Ingy Rasekh
*MENA Associates, member of Amereller Rechtsanwälte*

Menha Samy
*Ibrachy & Dermarkar Law Firm*

Mohamed Serry
*Serry Law Office*

Abdallah Shalash
*Abdallah Shalash & Co.*

Ramy Shalash
*Abdallah Shalash & Co.*

Abdelrahman Sherif
*MENA Associates, member of Amereller Rechtsanwälte*

Omar Sherif
*Shalakany Law Office, member of Lex Mundi*

Sharif Shihata
*Shalakany Law Office, member of Lex Mundi*

Shaimaa Solaiman
*Challenge Law Firm*

Frédéric Soliman
*TELELAWS*

Amira Thabet
*Sherif Dabbous - member of Russell Bedford International*

Randa Tharwat
*Nacita Corporation*

Ehab Yehia
*Egyptian Public Prosecution*

Tarek Zahran
*Al Kamel Law Office*

Mohsen Ziko
*Al Kamel Law Office*

Mona Zobaa
*Ministry of Investment*

**EL SALVADOR**
*AES El Salvador*

*Alsicorp Group*

Miguel Angel
*Ale Cargo S.A. de C.V.*

Aida Arguello de Morera
*Ministry of Labor and Social Welfare*

Francisco Armando Arias Rivera
*Arias & Muñoz*

Francisco José Barrientos
*Francisco Jose Barrientos, S.A. de C.V.*

Hazel Alexandra Cabezas
*Aguilar Castillo Love*

Carlos Roberto Alfaro Castillo
*Aguilar Castillo Love*

Walter Chávez
*Gold Service*

David Claros
*García & Bodán*

Luis Alfredo Cornejo
*Cornejo & Umaña, Ltda. de C.V. - member of Russell Bedford International*

Porfirio Diaz Fuentes
*DLM, Abogados, Notarios & Consultores*

Lorena Dueñas
*Superintendencia del Sistema Financiero*

Ericka Elias
*PwC El Salvador*

Camila Escobar
*Lexincorp*

Enrique Escobar
*Lexincorp*

Roberta Gallardo de Cromeyer
*Arias & Muñoz*

Yudy Guerrero
*Gold Service*

Carlos Henriquez
*Gold Service*

America Hernandez
*Ale Cargo S.A. de C.V.*

Benjamín Valdez Iraheta
*Benjamín Valdez & Asociados*

Luis Lievano
*Asociacion de Ingenieros y Arquitectos*

Thelma Dinora Lizama de Osorio
*Superintendencia del Sistema Financiero*

Hegel Lopez
*PwC El Salvador*

Mario Lozano
*Arias & Muñoz*

Astrud María Meléndez
*Asociación Protectora de Créditos de El Salvador (PROCREDITO)*

Antonio R. Mendez Llort
*Romero Pineda & Asociados, member of Lex Mundi*

Miriam Eleana Mixco Reyna
*Gold Service*

Jocelyn Mónico
*Francisco Jose Barrientos, S.A. de C.V.*

Fernando Montano
*Arias & Muñoz*

Mario Moran
*M. Representaciones*

Jose Navas
*All World Cargo, S.A. de C.V.*

Ramon Ortega
*PwC El Salvador*

Iris Palma
*OEA*

Carlos Pastrana
*Colegio de Arquitectos de El Salvador*

Jose Polanco
*Lexincorp*

Ana Patricia Portillo Reyes
*Guandique Segovia Quintanilla*

Carlos Roberto Rodriguez
*Consortium Centro América Abogados*

Flor de Maria Rodriguez
*Arias & Muñoz*

Otto Rodríguez
*Benjamín Valdez & Asociados*

Roxana Romero
*Romero Pineda & Asociados, member of Lex Mundi*

Jaime Salinas
*García & Bodán*

Oscar Samour
*Consortium Centro América Abogados*

Alonso V. Saravia
*Asociación Salvadoreña de Ingenieros y Arquitectos (ASIA)*

Benjamín M. Valdez Tamayo
*Benjamín Valdez & Asociados*

Manuel Telles Suvillaga
*Lexincorp*

Luis Tevez
*Benjamín Valdez & Asociados*

Oscar Torres
*García & Bodán*

Mauricio Antonio Urrutia
*Superintendencia del Sistema Financiero*

Julio Vargas
*García & Bodán*

Rene Velasquez
*Arias & Muñoz*

Osmin Vizcarra
*DLM, Abogados, Notarios & Consultores*

**EQUATORIAL GUINEA**
*CIGESA*

*Ernst & Young*

Gabriel Amugu
*Interactivos GE*

N.J. Ayuk
*Centurion LLP*

Philippe Beziat
*SDV Logistics*

Ana Margarita Bibang Nnegue
*BEAC - Equatorial Guinea*

Francisco Campos Braz
*Solege*

Angel-Francisco Ela Ngomo Nchama
*Solege*

Philippe Fouda Fouda
*BEAC Cameroon*

Eddy Garrigo
*PwC Equatorial Guinea*

Marcel Juetsop

Sébastien Lechêne
*PwC Equatorial Guinea*

Angel Mba Abeso
*Centurion LLP*

Tomás Engono Mba López
*Segesa (Sociedad de Electricidad de Guinea Ecuatorial)*

Ezequiel Robbe Mbila
*CCEI Bank GE*

Paulino Mbo Obama
*Oficina de estudios - ATEG*

Maria Luz Ndjondjo Andrada
*Centurion LLP*

Gustavo Ndong Edu
*Afri Logistics*

Antonio-Pascual Oko Ebobo
*Attorney-at-Law*

Jacinto Ona
*Centurion LLP*

Juan Carlos Ondo
*Equatorial Guinea Constitutional Court*

Elena Pedrero Polán
*PwC Côte d'Ivoire*

Dominique Taty
*PwC Côte d'Ivoire*

Vincent Tekam

Deeana Rochelle Wilson Edjang
*Centurion LLP*

## ERITREA

Ali Reza Abdolhussein
*Elmi Olindo & Co. PLC - General Contractor*

Senai Andemariam
*University of Asmara*

Tadesse Beraki

Biniam Fessehazion Ghebremichael
*Eritrean Airlines*

Tesfai Ghebrehiwet
*Department of Energy*

Berhane Gila-Michael
*Berhane Gila-Michael Law Firm*

Kebreab Habte Michael
*Kebreab Habte Michael Legal Consulting*

Mebrahtom Habtemariam

Mulgheta Hailu
*Teferi Berhane & Mulgheta Hailu Law Firm*

Tekeste Mesghenna
*MTD Enterprises PLC*

Akberom Tedla
*Chamber of Commerce*

Isac Tesfazion

## ESTONIA

*Estonian Logistics and Freight Forwarding Association*

Ott Aava
*Attorneys at Law BORENIUS*

Juulika Aavik
*BNT Klauberg Kraukliis Advokaadibüroo*

Angela Agur
*MAQS Law Firm Estonia Tallinn*

Risto Agur
*Advokaadibüroo SORAINEN AS*

Katrin Altmets
*Advokaadibüroo SORAINEN AS*

Airi Asperk
*Konkurentsiamet Estonian Competition Authority*

Aet Bergmann
*BNT Klauberg Kraukliis Advokaadibüroo*

Jane Eespõld
*Advokaadibüroo SORAINEN AS*

Diana Freivald
*Ministry of Justice*

Helen Ginter
*Advokaadibüroo SORAINEN AS*

Külli Haab
*Konkurentsiamet Estonian Competition Authority*

Kristjan Hänni
*Kawe Kapital*

Annika Jaanson
*Attorneys at Law BORENIUS*

Ulla Jürimäe
*Advokaadibüroo SORAINEN AS*

Andres Juss
*Estonian Land Board*

Marko Kairjak
*Varul*

Erica Kaldre
*Hough, Hutt & Partners OU*

Helerin Kaldvee
*Raidla Lejins & Norcous*

Kadri Kallas
*Advokaadibüroo SORAINEN AS*

Jevgeni Kazutkin
*Hough, Hutt & Partners OU*

Igor Kostjuk
*Hough, Hutt & Partners OU*

Andreas Kotsjuba
*Attorneys at Law BORENIUS*

Villu Kõve
*Estonian Supreme Court*

Tanja Kriisa
*PwC Estonia*

Piia Kulm
*Lextal Law Office*

Kaido Künnapas
*MAQS Law Firm Estonia Tallinn*

Peeter Kutman
*Attorneys at Law BORENIUS*

Marika Kütt
*Raidla Lejins & Norcous*

Gerda Liik
*Raidla Lejins & Norcous*

Karin Madisson
*Advokaadibüroo SORAINEN AS*

Tiina Maldre
*Konkurentsiamet Estonian Competition Authority*

Veiko Meos
*Krediidiinfo A.S.*

Jaanus Mody
*Attorneys at Law BORENIUS*

Margus Mugu
*Attorneys at Law Borenius*

Jaana Nõgisto
*Law Office Nordeus*

Irina Nossova
*Varul*

Arne Ots
*Raidla Lejins & Norcous*

Karl J. Paadam
*Advokaadibüroo SORAINEN AS*

Loori Paadik
*Ministry of Justice*

Karina Paatsi
*Attorneys at Law Borenius*

Priit Pahapill
*Attorneys at Law BORENIUS*

Sven Papp
*Raidla Lejins & Norcous*

Evelin Pärn-Lee
*MAQS Law Firm Estonia Tallinn*

Kirsti Pent
*Law Office Nordeus*

Tarmo Peterson
*Varul*

Maria Pihlak
*Advokaadibüroo SORAINEN AS*

Sigrid Polli

Ants Ratas
*CF&S AS*

Piret Saartee
*Ministry of Justice*

Katrin Sarap
*MAQS Law Firm Estonia Tallinn*

Villi Tõntson
*PwC Estonia*

Veikko Toomere
*MAQS Law Firm Estonia Tallinn*

Neve Uudelt
*Raidla Lejins & Norcous*

Erle Uus
*KPMG*

Ingmar Vali
*Registrite ja infosüsteemide Keskus*

Triin Väljaots
*Advokaadibüroo SORAINEN AS*

Hannes Vallikivi
*Law Office Tark Grunte Sutkiene*

Ivo Vanasaun

Paul Varul
*Varul*

Peeter Viirsalu
*Varul*

Ago Vilu
*PwC Estonia*

Urmas Volens
*Advokaadibüroo SORAINEN AS*

## ETHIOPIA

*Ernst & Young*

Siraj Ahmed
*Packford International*

Abdella Ali
*Abdella Ali Law Office*

Wubetu Assefa
*Bunna International Bank*

Teklu Assefa Damte
*Teklu Assefa*

Adamseled Belay
*Zemen Bank*

Teshome Gabre-Mariam Bokan
*Teshome Gabre-Mariam Bokan Law Firm*

Semere Wolde Bonge
*National Bank of Ethiopia*

Kumlachew Dagne

Samuel Demke
*Delnessahou Tadesse - Counselor and Attorney at Law*

Berhane Ghebray
*Berhane Ghebray & Associates*

Solomon Gizaw
*HST Consulting*

Asheber Hailesilassie
*Trans Ethiopia PLC - TEPLCO*

Getu Jemaneh
*HST Consulting*

Belay Kebede Alemu
*Ethiopian Insurance Corporation*

Zekarias Keneaa
*Addis Ababa University*

Yitbarek Medhin
*Building Permits and Inspection Authority of Addis Ababa*

Tewodros Meheret
*Addis Ababa University*

Misrak Mengehsa
*Packford International*

Molla Mengistu
*Addis Ababa University*

Alem Mengsteab
*Ethiopian General Installation Supply*

Meiklit Seifu
*Delnessahou Tadesse - Counselor and Attorney at Law*

Mathewos Shamo
*Independent Consultant*

Ameha Sime
*Ameha Sime B.C.*

Delnessahou Tadesse
*Delnessahou Tadesse - Counselor and Attorney at Law*

Mesfin Tafese
*Mesfin Tafese Law Office*

Eyasu Tequame
*Jehoiachin Techno Pvt. Ltd. Co.*

Dagnachew Tesfaye
*Dagnachew Tesfaye Law Office*

Amanuel Teshome
*Aman & Partners*

Amsalah Tsehaye
*Amsale Tsehaye & Associates Law Office*

Solomon Areda Waktolla
*First Instance Federal Court*

Tameru Wondmagegnehu

Teferi Zewdu
*Trans Ethiopia PLC - TEPLCO*

## FIJI

David Aidney
*Williams & Gosling Ltd.*

Eddielin Almonte
*PwC Fiji*

Jon Apted
*Munro Leys*

Nehla Basawaiya
*Munro Leys*

Mahendra Chand
*Munro Leys*

William Wylie Clarke
*Howards Lawyers*

Delores Elliott
*Data Bureau Limited*

Dilip Jamnadas
*Jamnadas and Associates*

Jerome Kado
*PwC Fiji*

Besant Kumar
*Fiji Electricity Authority*

Roneel Lal
*Williams & Gosling Ltd.*

Brenda Nanius
*Siwatibau & Sloan*

Jon Orton
*Orton Architects*

Pradeep Patel
*PKF International*

Ramesh Prakash
*Mishra Prakash & Associates*

Nilesh Prasad
*Mitchell, Keil & Associates*

Ramesh Prasad Lal
*Carpenters Shipping*

Abhi Ram
*Companies Registrar*

Ronlyn Sahib
*Siwatibau & Sloan*

Varun Shandil
*Munro Leys*

Om Dutt Sharma
*Fiji Electricity Authority*

Shelvin Singh
*Parshotam & Co.*

Atunaisa Siwatibau
*Siwatibau & Sloan*

James Sloan
*Siwatibau & Sloan*

Narotam Solanki
*PwC Fiji*

Shayne Sorby
*Munro Leys*

Seini Tinaikoro
*Cromptons Solicitors*

Vulisere Tukama
*Suva City Council*

Chirk Yam
*PwC Fiji*

Glenis Yee
*Munro Leys*

Eddie Yuen
*Williams & Gosling Ltd.*

## FINLAND

*PwC Finland*

Ville Ahtola
*Castrén & Snellman Attorneys Ltd.*

Manne Airaksinen
*Roschier Attorneys Ltd.*

Tuomo Åvall
*Wabuco Oy - member of Russell Bedford International*

Claudio Busi
*Castrén & Snellman Attorneys Ltd.*

Esa Halmari
*Hedman Partners*

Pekka Halme
*National Land Survey of Finland*

Johanna Haltia-Tapio
*Hannes Snellman LLC*

Joni Hatanmaa
*Hedman Partners*

Seppo Havia
*Dittmar & Indrenius*

Leenamaija Heinonen
*Roschier Attorneys Ltd.*

Mia Hukkinen
*Roschier Attorneys Ltd.*

Nina Isokorpi
*Roschier Attorneys Ltd.*

Lauri Jääskeläinen
*Building Control Department of the City of Helsinki*

Pekka Jaatinen
*Castrén & Snellman Attorneys Ltd.*

Juuso Jokela
*Suomen Asiakastieto Oy*

Tanja Jussila
*Waselius & Wist*

Mika Karpinnen
*Hannes Snellman LLC*

Aki Kauppinen
*Roschier Attorneys Ltd.*

Sakari Kauppinen
*National Board of Patents & Registration*

Suvi Knaapila
*Dittmar & Indrenius*

Tiina Komppa
*Hannes Snellman LLC*

Mikko Korhonen
*Helen Sähköverkko Oy*

Jouni Lehtinen
*Helen Sähköverkko Oy*

Petteri Leinonen
*Geodis Wilson Finland Oy*

Jan Lilius
*Hannes Snellman LLC*

Patrik Lindfors
*Lindfors & Co, Attorneys-at-Law Ltd.*

Patrick Lindgren
*Law office ADVOCARE*

Tuomas Lukkarinen
*National Land Survey of Finland*

Anna Lumijärvi
*Krogerus Attorneys Ltd.*

Kimmo Mettälä
*Krogerus Attorneys Ltd.*

Ville Mykkänen
*Wabuco Oy - member of Russell Bedford International*

Juha-Pekka Nuutinen

Linda Nyman
*Waselius & Wist*

Elina Pesonen
*Castrén & Snellman Attorneys Ltd.*

Ilkka Pesonen
*Wabuco Oy - member of Russell Bedford International*

Aino Saarilahti
*Attorneys-At-Law Juridia Ltd*

Helena Viita
*Roschier Attorneys Ltd.*

Anna Vuori
*Hedman Partners*

Marko Vuori
*Krogerus Attorneys Ltd.*

Gunnar Westerlund
*Roschier Attorneys Ltd.*

## FRANCE

Claire Adenis-Lamarre
*Miller Rosenfalck LLP*

Jean-Marc Albiol
*Hogan Lovells*

Nicolas Barberis
*Ashurst LLP*

Andrew Booth
*Andrew Booth Architect*

Franck Buffaud
*Delsol Avocats*

Stéphanie Chatelon
*Taj, member of Deloitte Touche Tohmatsu Limited*

Michel Combe
*Landwell & Associés*

Patricia de Suzzoni
*Commission de Régulation de l'Energie*

Nicolas Deshayes
*AJAssociés*

Jean-Marc Dufour
*France eCommerce International*

Olivier Everaere
*Agence Epure SARL*

Benoit Fauvelet
*Banque de France*

Ingrid Fauvelière
*Gide Loyrette Nouel, member of Lex Mundi*

Cécile Gilliet
*Vatier & Associés*

Thierry Gomot
*Banque de France*

Kevin Grossmann
*Cabinet Kevin Grossmann*

Philippe Guibert
*FIEEC*

Carol Khoury
*Jones Day*

Daniel Arthur Laprès
*Avocat à la Cour d'Appel de Paris*

Vanessa Li
*Hogan Lovells*

Julien Maire du Poset
*Smith Violet*

Jean-Louis Martin
*Jones Day*

Nathalie Morel
*Mayer Brown*

Laurence Mounier
*Vatier & Associés*

Sabine Paul
*Miller Rosenfalck LLP*

Arnaud Pédron
*Taj, member of Deloitte Touche Tohmatsu Limited*

Arnaud Pelpel
*Pelpel Avocats*

Caroline Poncelet
*Mayer Brown*

Camille Potier
*Mayer Brown*

Emmanuelle Ries
*Miller Rosenfalck LLP*

Hugues Roux
*Banque de France*

Pierre Roux
*Ashurst LLP*

Carole Sabbah
*Mayer Brown*

Jennifer Sachetat
*Ashurst LLP*

Diane Sénéchal
*Ashurst LLP*

Isabelle Smith Monnerville
*Smith Violet*

Marlène-Johanne Suberville
*Delsol Avocats*

Salli Anne Swartz
*Artus Wise*

Jean Luc Vallens
*Cour d'Appel de Colmar*

Philippe Xavier-Bender
*Gide Loyrette Nouel, member of Lex Mundi*

Claire Zuliani
*Transparence – member of Russell Bedford International*

## GABON

*Cabinet John W. Ffooks & Co.*

*Etude Maître Gey Bekale*

*Municipalité de Libreville*

*Panalpina World Transport*

Marcellin Massila Akendengue
*Société d'Energie et d'Eau du Gabon (SEEG)*

Itchola Mano Alade
*Cabinet d'Avocats Itchola & Abganrin*

Marie Carmel Ketty Ayimambenwe

Madeleine Berre
*Deloitte Juridique et Fiscal*

Daniel Chevallon
*Matelec*

Augustin Fang

Philippe Fouda Fouda
*BEAC Cameroon*

Michael Jeannot
*Matelec*

Athanase Ndoye Loury
*Syndic Judiciaire*

Pélagie Massamba Mouckocko
*PricewaterhouseCoopers Tax & Legal SA*

Jean Mbagou

Abel Mouloungui
*Etude Maître Abel Mouloungui*

Jean Hilaire Moussavou
*Fumu Technologie*

Célestin Ndelia
*Etude Maître Ndelia Célestin*

Ruben Mindonga Ndongo

Thierry Ngomo
*ARCHi Pro International*

François Nguema Ebane
*Cabinet Atelier 5A*

Lubin Ntoutoume
*Cabinet SCP Ntoutoume et Mezher*

Josette Cadie Olendo

César Apollinaire Ondo Mve
*Mettre Cour de Cassation du Gabon*

Marie-Jose Ongo Mendou
*Business Consulting*

Laurent Pommera
*PricewaterhouseCoopers Tax & Legal SA*

Christophe A. Relongoué
*PricewaterhouseCoopers Tax & Legal SA*

## GAMBIA, THE

*PwC Ghana*

Lamin A.K Touray
*Attorney General Chambers of Gambia*

Alpha Amadou Barry
*DT Associates, Independent Correspondence Firm of Deloitte Touche Tohmatsu Limited*

Abdul Aziz Bensouda
*Amie Bensouda & Co.*

Amie N.D. Bensouda
*Amie Bensouda & Co.*

Roy Chalkley

Ida Denise Drameh
*Ida D. Drameh & Associates*

Fatoulili Drammeh
*Trust Bank Ltd.*

Frederick Forster
*Judiciary of The Gambia*

Jon Goldy
*Amie Bensouda & Co.*

Cherno Alieu Jallow
*DT Associates, Independent Correspondence Firm of Deloitte Touche Tohmatsu Limited*

Edrissa Jarjue
*National Water and Electricity Company Ltd.*

Lamin S. Jatta
*DT Associates, Independent Correspondence Firm of Deloitte Touche Tohmatsu Limited*

Sulayman M. Joof
*S.M. Joof Agency*

Nani Juwara
*National Water and Electricity Company Ltd.*

Momodou F. K. Kolley
*Development Control Unit – Department of Physical Planning and Housing*

Pa M. M. N'jie
*Trust Bank Ltd.*

Adama Samba
*Value Engineering Construction*

Mary Abdoulie Samba-Christensen
*Legal Practitioner*

Hawa Sisay-Sabally
*Lawyer*

Saliou Taal
*Temple Legal Practitioners*

## GEORGIA

Zviad Akhvlediani
*Akvlediani Business Consulting LLC – correspondent of Russell Bedford International*

Irakli Apkhadze
*Chancellery of the Government of Georgia*

Irakli Asapini
*ITM Global Logistics*

Nino Bakakuri
*Nodia, Urumashvili & Partners*

Niko Bakashvili
*Bakashvili and Company*

Nino Begalishvili
*Colibri Law Firm*

Lily Begiashvili
*Georgia Revenue Service*

Revaz Beridze
*Eristavi Law Group*

Koba Bobokhidze
*Mgaloblishvili, Kipiani, Dzidziguri (MKD) Law Firm*

Bondo Bolkvadze
*Deloitte Overseas Consulting Projects*

Temur Bolotashvili
*USAID Economic Prosperity Initiative*

Michael Cowgill
*American Chamber of Commerce*

Kakha Damenia
*Gutidze Damenia Chantladze Solutions*

Maia Darsalia
*Tbilisi City Court, Chamber of Civil Cases*

Teymur Gamrekelashvili
*Telasi*

Rusudan Gergauli
*LPA LLC Law Firm*

Nata Ghibradze
*LPA LLC Law Firm*

Ilia Giorgadze
*ARCI Architecture & Development*

Erekle Glurjidze
*DLA Piper Georgia LP*

Lasha Gogiberidze
*BGI Legal*

Gega Gogichashvili
*Chancellery of the Government of Georgia*

Gocha Gogishvili
*Amirashvili, Gogishvili & Shengelia AGS*

Mamuka Gordeziani
*ITM Global Logistics*

Kakhaber Grubelashvili
*Akvlediani Business Consulting LLC – correspondent of Russell Bedford International*

Giorgi Gulua
*Bakashvili and Company*

Nana Gurgenidze
*LPA LLC Law Firm*

Izabela Gutidze
*Gutidze Damenia Chantladze Solutions*

Batu Gvasalia
*National Agency of Public Registry*

Rusudan Gvazava
*BGI Legal*

Gia Jandieri
*New Economic School*

Revaz Javelidze
*Colibri Law Firm*

Aleksandre Kacharava
*Chancellery of the Government of Georgia*

David Kakabadze

Grigol Kakauridze
*Ministry of Economic Development*

Irakli Kandashvili

Givi Karchava
*Lasare Ltd.*

Mari Khardziani
*National Agency of Public Registry*

Anastasia Kipiani
*PwC Georgia*

Nika Kirkitadze
*National Bureau of Enforcement*

Sergi Kobakhidze
*PwC Georgia*

Tamar Kobakhidze
*Cargo Logistics Group*

Eteri Kritskhali
*Amirashvili, Gogishvili & Shengelia AGS*

Aieti Kukava
*Alliance Group Holding*

Tamar Kvintradze
*Getsadze & Pateishvili LLC*

Tamara Lakerbaya
*Eristavi Law Group*

Sergo Lasareshvili
*Lasare Ltd.*

Vakhtang Lejava
*Chancellery of the Government of Georgia*

Archil Lezhava
*LPA LLC Law Firm*

Mirab-Dmitry Lomadze

Robin McCone
*PwC Georgia*

Manana Meshishvili
*Eristavi Law Group*

Ekaterina Meskhidze
*National Agency of Public Registry*

Roin Migriauli
*Law Office Migriauli & Partners*

Nino Mirtskhulava
*Poti Sea Port Corporation*

Kakhaber Nariashvili

Merab Narmania
*Chancellery of the Government of Georgia*

Zaza Nemsadze
*Chancellery of the Government of Georgia*

Levan Nikoladze
*LPA LLC Law Firm*

Lasha Nodia
*Nodia, Urumashvili & Partners*

Giorgi Otaridze
*LPA LLC Law Firm*

Vakhtang Paresishvili
*DLA Piper Georgia LP*

Levan Pavlenishvili
*PwC Georgia*

Joseph Salukvadze
*Tbilisi State University*

Natia Samushia
*Chancellery of the Government of Georgia*

Irakli Sarjveladze
*Poti Sea Port Corporation*

Manzoor Shah
*Globalink Logistics Group*

Manana Shurghulaia
*Agency for Free Trade and Competition*

Zaza Simaev
*Eleco Ltd.*

Eka Siradze
*Colibri Law Firm*

Irakli Siradze
*Gutidze Damenia Chantladze Solutions*

Rusudan Sreseli
*Gutidze Damenia Chantladze Solutions*

David Sukiasov
*Eleco Ltd.*

Avto Svanidze
*DLA Piper Georgia LP*

Giorgi Tavartkiladze
*Deloitte LLP*

Levan Tektumanidze
*Andreas Sofocleaous & Co.*

Tamara Tevdoradze
*BGI Legal*

Sergo Tsikarishvili
*National Agency of Public Registry*

Zviad Voshakidze
*Telasi*

Georgi Zedginidze
*Eristavi Law Group*

## GERMANY

Gabriele Apfelbacher
*Cleary Gottlieb Steen & Hamilton LLP*

Stephan Bank
*Cleary Gottlieb Steen & Hamilton LLP*

Henning Berger
*White & Case*

Jennifer Bierly
*GSK Stockmann + Kollegen*

Arnd Böken
*Graf von Westphalen Rechtsanwälte Partnerschaft*

Simeon-Tobias Bolz
*Heussen Rechtsanwaltsgesellschaft mbH*

Elena Bratanova
*Cleary Gottlieb Steen & Hamilton LLP*

Claus-Dieter Braun
*SCHUFA Holding AG*

Michael Brems
*Cleary Gottlieb Steen & Hamilton LLP*

Thomas Büssow
*PwC Germany*

Lorenz Czajka
*Graf von Westphalen Rechtsanwälte Partnerschaft*

Andreas Eckhardt
*PricewaterhouseCoopers Legal Aktiengesellschaft Rechtsanwaltsgesellschaft*

Dieter Endres
*PwC Germany*

Sigrun Erber-Faller
*Notare Erber-Faller und Voran*

Shahzadi Firdous
*Graf von Westphalen Rechtsanwälte Partnerschaft*

Mathias Fischer
*Latham & Watkins LLP*

Alexander Freiherr von Aretin
*Graf von Westphalen Rechtsanwälte Partnerschaft*

Michael Frühmorgen
*Heussen Rechtsanwaltsgesellschaft mbH*

Björn Gaul
*CMS Hasche Sigle*

Markus J. Goetzmann
*C·B·H Rechtsanwälte*

Andrea Gruss
*Merget + Partner*

Klaus Günther
*Oppenhoff & Partner*

Robert Gutte
*Cleary Gottlieb Steen & Hamilton LLP*

Marc Alexander Häger
*Oppenhoff & Partner*

Rüdiger Harms
*Cleary Gottlieb Steen & Hamilton LLP*

Götz-Sebastian Hök
*Dr. Hök Stieglmeier & Partner*

Markus Jakoby
*Jakoby Rechtsanwälte*

Helmuth Jordan
*JordanRechtsanwalts GmbH*

Henrik Kirchhoff
*GSK Stockmann + Kollegen*

Britta Klatte
*SCHUFA Holding AG*

Johann Klein
*Beeh & Happich GmbH – member of Russell Bedford International*

Steffen Koch
*Wienberg Wilhelm*

Dirk Kohlenberg
*PricewaterhouseCoopers Legal Aktiengesellschaft Rechtsanwaltsgesellschaft*

Jörg Kraffel
*White & Case*

Markus Krüger
*Latham & Watkins LLP*

Holger Kühl
*Graf von Westphalen Rechtsanwälte Partnerschaft*

Carsten Liersch
*Graf von Westphalen Rechtsanwälte Partnerschaft*

Peter Limmer
*Notare Dr. Limmer & Dr. Friederich*

Burkhard Lindenlaub
*MBS Logistics*

Frank Lohrmann
*Cleary Gottlieb Steen & Hamilton LLP*

Roland Maaß
*Latham & Watkins LLP*

Thomas Stefan Malik
*Heussen Rechtsanwaltsgesellschaft mbH*

Robert Manger
*PricewaterhouseCoopers Legal Aktiengesellschaft Rechtsanwaltsgesellschaft*

Jan Geert Meents
*DLA Piper UK LLP*

Werner Meier
*Cleary Gottlieb Steen & Hamilton LLP*

Daniel Meier-Greve
*PricewaterhouseCoopers Legal Aktiengesellschaft Rechtsanwaltsgesellschaft*

Thomas Miller
*Heussen Rechtsanwaltsgesellschaft mbH*

Eike Najork
*C·B·H Rechtsanwälte*

Dirk Otto
*Norton Rose LLP*

Daniel Panajotow
*Cleary Gottlieb Steen & Hamilton LLP*

Laura Pfirrmann
*Cleary Gottlieb Steen & Hamilton LLP*

John Piotrowski
*Jakoby Rechtsanwälte*

Marlena Polic
*PricewaterhouseCoopers Legal Aktiengesellschaft Rechtsanwaltsgesellschaft*

Peter Polke
*Cleary Gottlieb Steen & Hamilton LLP*

Thomas Poss
*Latham & Watkins LLP*

Sebastian Prügel
*White & Case*

Christina Reifelsberger
*Heussen Rechtsanwaltsgesellschaft mbH*

Angela Reimer
*Diaz Reus & Targ LLP*

Wilhelm Reinhardt
*Latham & Watkins LLP*

Carl Renner
*DLA Piper UK LLP*

Alexander Reus
*Diaz Reus & Targ LLP*

Philipp Ruehland
*PricewaterhouseCoopers Legal Aktiengesellschaft Rechtsanwaltsgesellschaft*

Christoph Schauenburg
*Cleary Gottlieb Steen & Hamilton LLP*

Johannes Schmidt
*Cleary Gottlieb Steen & Hamilton LLP*

Sönke Schröder
*SALGER Rechtsanwälte*

Ulrich Schroeder
*Graf von Westphalen Rechtsanwälte Partnerschaft*

Volker Schwarz
*Heussen Rechtsanwaltsgesellschaft mbH*

Kirstin Schwedt
*Linklaters LLP*

Ingrid Seitz
*Deutsche Bundesbank*

Hyeon-Won Song
*PwC Germany*

Kai Sebastian Staak
*PricewaterhouseCoopers Legal Aktiengesellschaft Rechtsanwaltsgesellschaft*

Volker Staehr
*EF-ES-WE Elektroanlagen GmbH*

Susanne Stellbrink
*PwC Germany*

Dieter Straub
*CMS Hasche Sigle*

Tobias Taetzner
*PwC Germany*

Nora Thies
*Graf von Westphalen Rechtsanwälte Partnerschaft*

Arne Vogel
*PricewaterhouseCoopers Legal Aktiengesellschaft Rechtsanwaltsgesellschaft*

Heiko Vogt
*Panalpina Welttransport GmbH*

Katharina von Rosenstiel
*Orrick Hölters & Elsing*

Peter Voss
*Interglobal Shipping GmbH*

Raimund E. Walch
*Wendler Tremml Rechtsanwälte*

Annekatren Werthmann-Feldhues
*PricewaterhouseCoopers Legal Aktiengesellschaft Rechtsanwaltsgesellschaft*

Hartmut Wicke
*Notare Rudolf Spoerer & Dr. Hartmut Wicke, LL. M.*

Stefan Wirsch
*Latham & Watkins LLP*

Gerlind Wisskirchen
*CMS Hasche Sigle*

Boris Witt
*Cleary Gottlieb Steen & Hamilton LLP*

Uwe Witt
*PricewaterhouseCoopers Legal Aktiengesellschaft Rechtsanwaltsgesellschaft*

Christian Zeissler
*C·B·H Rechtsanwälte*

## GHANA

Gillian Ablorh-Quarcoo
*Bentsi-Enchill, Letsa & Ankomah, member of Lex Mundi*

George K. Acquah
*Expresso Telecom Ghana*

Stephen N. Adu
*Public Utilities Regulatory Commission of Ghana*

Rene Adu Junior
*Lawfields Consulting*

George Ahiafor
*XDSDATA Ghana Ltd.*

Kweku Ainuson

Nana Akonu G. P. Amartey
*Andah and Andah Chartered Accountants*

Nene Amegatcher
*Sam Okudzeto & Associates*

Kennedy Paschal Anaba
*Lawfields Consulting*

Kweku Brebu Andah
*Andah and Andah Chartered Accountants*

Wilfred Kwabena Anim-Odame
*Land Commission*

Adwoa S. Asamoah-Addo
*Nana Akuoku Sarpong & Partners*

Fred Asiamah-Koranteng
*Bank of Ghana*

Selma Awumbila
*Bentsi-Enchill, Letsa & Ankomah, member of Lex Mundi*

Gideon Ayi-Owoo
*PwC Ghana*

Ellen Bannerman
*Bruce-Lyle Bannerman & Associates*

Ras Afful Davis
*Climate Shipping & Trading*

Clifford Gershon Fiadjoe
*Andah and Andah Chartered Accountants*

Emmanuel Fiati
*Public Utilities Regulatory Commission of Ghana*

Frank Fugar
*College of Architecture and Planning*

Roland Horsoo
*Crown Agents Ltd.*

Matilda Idun-Donkor
*Reindorf Chambers*

Adam Imoru Ayarna
*Cademse International*

Sophie Mutebi Kayemba
*PwC Ghana*

Emmanuel Kissi-Boateng
*Public Utilities Regulatory Commission of Ghana*

Rosa Kudoadzi
*Bentsi-Enchill, Letsa & Ankomah, member of Lex Mundi*

George Kwatia
*PwC Ghana*

Margaret Laryea
*Laryea, Laryea & Co. P.C.*

Frank N. Akowuah
*Bentsi-Enchill, Letsa & Ankomah, member of Lex Mundi*

Wordsworth Odame Larbi
*Lands Commission*

Rexford Oppong
*Knust*

Jacob Saah
*Saah & Co.*

Frank Sarpong
*Fame Shipping Agency*

Doris Tettey
*Town and Country Planning Department*

Darcy White
*PwC Ghana*

Dorothy Sena Woanya
*Laryea, Laryea & Co. P.C.*

## GREECE

Sophia Ampoulidou
*Drakopoulos Law Firm*

Rita Anthouli
*K | P Law Firm*

George Apostolakos
*Apostolakos Architects*

Amalia Balla
*Potamitis Vekris*

Marilena Bellou

Constantin Calavros
*Calavros & Partners*

Stefanos Charaktiniotis
*Zepos & Yannopoulos Law Firm, member of Lex Mundi*

Ira Charisiadou
*Charisiadou Law Office*

Margarita Christodoulatou

Theodora Christodoulou
*KLC Law Firm*

Alkistis - Marina Christofilou
*IKRP Rokas & Partners*

Evangelia Christopoulou - Stamelou
*Notary*

Vasiliki Christou
*KLC Law Firm*

Vassilis Chryssomalis
*Sarantitis Law Firm*

Sotiris Constantinou
*Grant Thornton LLP*

Theodora D. Karagiorgou
*Koutalidis Law Firm*

Nikos Daskalakis
*Hellenic Confederation of Professionals, Craftsmen and Merchants*

Eleni Dikonimaki
*Teiresias S.A. Interbanking Information Systems*

Anastasia Dritsa
*Kyriakides Georgopoulos & Daniolos Issaias Law Firm*

Alkiviadis Feresidis
*Ministry of Justice*

Efstathia Fetsi
*K | P Law Firm*

Margarita Flerianou
*Economou International Shipping Agencies*

Dionysia I. Gamvrakis
*Sarantitis Law Firm*

John Gavanozis
*J.G. Tech*

Dionysios Gavounelis
*K | P Law Firm*

Dimitra Georgaraki
*TaxExperts*

Chris Geroulanos
*Ministry of Development*

Dimitris V. Hatzihristidis
*Electrical Engineer*

Peter Kapasouris
*Teiresias S.A. Interbanking Information Systems*

Evangelos Karaindros
*Evangelos Karaindros Law Firm*

Artemis Karathanassi
*PwC Greece*

Catherine M. Karatzas
*Karatzas & Partners*

Constantine Karydis
*PwC Greece*

Rita Katsoula
*PotamitisVekris*

Constantinos Klissouras
*K | P Law Firm*

Ioanna Kombou
*Elias Paraskevas Attorneys 1933*

Zacharoula Konstantinidi
*PwC Greece*

Nikolaos Konstantinidis
*BDO*

Panos Koromantzos
*Bahas, Gramatidis & Partners*

Olga Koromilia
*PwC Greece*

Dimitris Kyparissis
*TT Helenic Postbank*

Tom Kyriakopoulos
*Kelemenis & Co.*

Thomas Lamnidis
*KLC Law Firm*

Vassiliki G. Lazarakou
*Zepos & Yannopoulos Law Firm, member of Lex Mundi*

Konstantinos Logaras
*Zepos & Yannopoulos Law Firm, member of Lex Mundi*

Christos Makris

Panagiotis Manalopoulos
*Militzer & Münch*

Antonis Mantonanakis
*Panmonotiki Prostasia*

Smaro V. Markou
*Alpha Bank*

Evangelia Martinovits
*IKRP Rokas & Partners*

Emmanuel Mastromanolis
*Zepos & Yannopoulos Law Firm, member of Lex Mundi*

John Mazarakos
*Elias Paraskevas Attorneys 1933*

Alexandros N. Metaxas
*Sarantitis Law Firm*

Mike Michopoulos
*Tech KM S.A.*

Theodora G. Monochartzi
*Sarantitis Law Firm*

Athena Moraiti
*Athena Moraiti Law Office*

Efi Moucha
*Militzer & Münch*

Konstantinos Nanopoulos
*TaxExperts*

Anthony Narlis
*Calberson SA*

Kyriakos Oikonomou
*Ministry of Justice*

Panayis Panagiotopoulos
*Kremmydas-Doris & Associates Law Firm*

Elena Papachristou
*Zepos & Yannopoulos Law Firm, member of Lex Mundi*

Konstantinos Papadiamantis
*PotamitisVekris*

Alexios Papastavrou
*PotamitisVekris*

Dimitris E. Paraskevas
*Elias Paraskevas Attorneys 1933*

Michalis Pattakos
*Zepos & Yannopoulos Law Firm, member of Lex Mundi*

Spiros Pilios
*Phoenix*

Katerina Politi
*Kyriakides Georgopoulos & Daniolos Issaias Law Firm*

Stathis Potamitis
*Potamitis-Vekris*

Ioanna Poulakou
*Zepos & Yannopoulos Law Firm, member of Lex Mundi*

Constantine D. Poulios
*Ministry of Development*

Vicky Psaltaki
*Sarantitis Law Firm*

Vicky Psaltis
*PotamitisVekris*

Mary Psylla
*PwC Greece*

Terina Raptis
*Sarantitis Law Firm*

Vasiliki Salaka
*Karatzas & Partners*

Despina D. Samara
*Calavros & Partners*

Harry Stamelos
*Harry Stamelos Law Office and Partners*

Anastasia Stamou
*Athens Exchange SA*

Ioanna Stamou
*K | P Law Firm*

Alexia Stratou
*Kremalis Law Firm, member of Ius Laboris*

Fotini Trigazi
*Notary*

Antonios Tsavdaridis
*IKRP Rokas & Partners*

Elena Tsertsigianni

Chryssi Tsirogianni

Panagiota D. Tsitsa

Ioannis Vekris
*PotamitisVekris*

Kalliopi Vlachopoulou
*Kelemenis & Co.*

Ioannis Xenopoulos
*BDO*

Vicky Xourafa
*Kyriakides Georgopoulos & Daniolos Issaias Law Firm*

## GRENADA

*Lewis & Renwick*

W.R. Agostini
*Agostini W.R. Fcca*

James Bristol
*Henry, Henry & Bristol*

Ruggles Ferguson
*Ciboney Chambers*

Cyrus Griffith
*Labour Department*

Annette Henry
*Ministry of Legal Affairs*

Keith Hosten
*Hosten's (Electrical Services) Ltd.*

Winston Hosten
*Hosten's (Electrical Services) Ltd.*

Christopher Husbands
*National Water and Sewage Authority*

Henry Joseph
*PKF International*

Psyche Julien
*St. Louis Service*

Dickon Mitchell
*Grant Joseph & Co., member of Lex Mundi*

Niel Noel
*Henry Hudson - Phillips & Co.*

Valentino Sawney
*Tradship International*

David R. Sinclair
*Sinclair Enterprises Limited*

Lisa Telesford
*Supreme Court Registry*

Shireen Wilkinson
*Wilkinson, Wilkinson & Wilkinson*

Daniella Williams Mitchell
*Danny Williams & Co.*

Selwyn Woodroffe
*Consulting Engineers Partnership Ltd.*

## GUATEMALA

*A.D. Sosa & Soto*

Rodolfo Alegría Toruno
*Carrillo & Asociados*

Rafael Alvarado-Riedel
*Consortium-Rodríguez, Archila, Castellanos, Solares & Aguilar, S.C.*

Pedro Aragón
*Aragón & Aragón*

Mario R. Archila Cruz
*Consortium-Rodríguez, Archila, Castellanos, Solares & Aguilar, S.C.*

Oscar Arriaga
*Comisión Nacional de Energía Eléctrica*

Elías Arriaza
*Consortium-Rodríguez, Archila, Castellanos, Solares & Aguilar, S.C.*

Ruby María Asturias Castillo
*ACZALAW*

María de los Angeles Barillas Buchhalter
*Saravia & Muñoz*

Amaury Barrera
*City Hall of Guatemala City*

Jorge Rolando Barrios
*Bonilla, Montano, Toriello & Barrios*

Alejandra Bermúdez
*Consortium-Rodríguez, Archila, Castellanos, Solares & Aguilar, S.C.*

Maria del Pilar Bonilla
*Bonilla, Montano, Toriello & Barrios*

Guillermo Bonillo
*Bonilla, Montano, Toriello & Barrios*

Jean Paul Brichaux
*Asociación de Exportadores de Café (ADEC)*

Mario Adolfo Búcaro Flores
*Díaz-Durán & Asociados Central Law*

Rodrigo Callejas Aquino
*Carrillo & Asociados*

José Alfredo Cándido Durón
*Superintendencia de Bancos*

Juan Pablo Carrasco de Grote
*Díaz-Durán & Asociados Central Law*

Ana Gisela Castillo Aparicio
*Saravia & Muñoz*

Juan Carlos Castillo Chacón
*Aguilar Castillo Love*

Luis Pedro Cazali Leal
*Palacios & Asociados*

Fanny de Estrada
*Asociación Guatemalteca de Exportadores*

Gerardo Alberto de León
*FEDECOCAGUA*

Anabella de León Ruiz
*Registro General de la Propiedad de Guatemala*

Karla de Mata
*CPS Logistics*

Juan Manuel Díaz Duran Mendez
*Díaz-Durán & Asociados Central Law*

Edwin Leonel Diéguez Alvarado
*Registro General de la Propiedad de Guatemala*

Ana Sofia Escriba Barnoya
*Consortium-Rodríguez, Archila, Castellanos, Solares & Aguilar, S.C.*

Hugo Daniel Figueroa Estrada
*Superintendencia de Bancos*

Héctor Flores
*City Hall of Guatemala City*

Lorena Isabel Flores Estrada
*Díaz-Durán & Asociados Central Law*

Rodolfo Fuentes
*Protectora de Crèdito Comercial*

Paola Galich
*Mayora & Mayora S.C.*

Rafael Garavito
*Bufete Garavito*

Wendy Janeth Garcia Miranda
*Russell Bedford Guatemala / García Sierra y Asociados, S.C. - member of Russell Bedford International*

Ileana Liset González Bolaños
*Saravia & Muñoz*

Erick Gordillo
*City Hall of Guatemala City*

Miguel Angel Gualim
*City Hall of Guatemala City*

Andrés Hernández
*Carrillo & Asociados*

Carlos Guillermo Herrera
*Registro General de la Propiedad de Guatemala*

Raúl Stuardo Juárez Leal
*Superintendencia de Bancos*

Christian Lanuza
*Díaz-Durán & Asociados Central Law*

Nils Leporowski
*Asociación Nacional del Café*

María Isabel Luján Zilbermann
*Quiñones, Ibargüen, Luján & Mata S.C.*

Víctor Manuel Mancilla Castro
*Superintendencia de Bancos*

Marco Antonio Martinez
*CPS Logistics*

Estuardo Mata Palmieri
*Quiñones, Ibargüen, Luján & Mata S.C.*

Eduardo Mayora Alvarado
*Mayora & Mayora S.C.*

Edgar Mendoza
*PwC Guatemala*

Gonzalo Menendez Gonzalez
*Lexincorp*

Christian Michelangeli
*Carrillo & Asociados*

Guillermo Montano
*Transactel (Barbados.) Inc.*

Edvin Montoya
*Lexincorp*

Anajoyce Oliva
*City Hall of Guatemala City*

Marco Palacios
*Bardeli & Palacios*

Marco Antonio Palacios
*Palacios & Asociados*

Maria Jose Pepio Pensabene
*Cámara Guatemalteca de la Construcción*

Rita Pérez
*Aragón & Aragón*

Francisco Pilona
*City Hall of Guatemala City*

Melida Pineda
*Carrillo & Asociados*

Evelyn Rebuli
*Quiñones, Ibargüen, Luján & Mata S.C.*

Marco Tulio Reyna
*Cámara Guatemalteca de la Construcción*

Alfredo Rodríguez Mahuad
*Consortium-Rodríguez, Archila, Castellanos, Solares & Aguilar, S.C.*

Rodrigo Salguero
*PwC Guatemala*

Salvador A. Saravia Castillo
*Saravia & Muñoz*

Salvador Augusto Saravia Mendoza
*Saravia & Muñoz*

Klamcy Solorzano
*City Hall of Guatemala City*

José Augusto Toledo Cruz
*Arias & Muñoz*

Arelis Torres de Alfaro
*Superintendencia de Bancos*

Elmer Vargas
*ACZALAW*

Maria del Rosario Yaquian
*Quiñones, Ibargüen, Luján & Mata S.C.*

## GUINEA

*Cabinet John W. Ffooks & Co.*

Camara Aly Badara

Aminatou Bah
*Transco SA & Aqua Marine SA*

Thierno Amadou Tidiane Bah

Aminata Bah Tall
*Transco SA & Aqua Marine SA*

Mouhamed Lamine Bayo
*APIP*

Lousseny Cisse
*Transco SA & Aqua Marine SA*

John Delahaye
*SOCOPAO - SDV*

Ahmadou Diallo
*Chambre des Notaires*

Djenabou Diallo
*Transco SA & Aqua Marine SA*

Mohamed Kadialiou Diallo
*Electricité de Guinée*

El Hajj Barry Djoudja
*AICHFEET*

Adama Skel Fofana

Soukeina Fofana
*Banque Centrale de Guinée (BCRG)*

Joachim Gbilimou

Yannick Gui
ANY RAY PARTNERS

Abdel Aziz Kaba
TRANSCO SA & AQUA MARINE SA

Lansana Kaba
CARIG

Mbalou Keita
TRIBUNAL DE PREMIÈRE INSTANCE DE
KALOUM

Mariama Ciré Keita Diallo
TRANSCO SA & AQUA MARINE SA

Nounké Kourouma
ADMINISTRATION ET CONTRÔLE DES
GRANDS PROJETS

Avit Kpoghomou
NIMBA CONSEIL SARL

Fofana Naby Moussa
BANQUE CENTRALE DE GUINÉE
(BCRG)

Guy Piam
TRANSCO SA & AQUA MARINE SA

Raffi Raja
CABINET KOÛMY

Amadou Salif Kébé
CABINET AVOCAT SALIF KÉBÉ

Lansana Salif Soumah

Abdourahamane Tounkara
GUINÉE CONSULTING

Aboubacar Salimatou Toure
NTM AREEBA GUINEE S.A.

Fatoumata Yari Soumah
Yansane
OFFICE NOTARIAL

### GUINEA-BISSAU

ELECTRICIDADE E AGUAS DA
GUINE-BISSAU

Ahmadou Al Aminou Lo
BCEAO

José Alves Té
MINISTÉRIO DA JUSTIÇA

Humiliano Alves Cardoso
GABINETE ADVOCACIA

Adelaida Mesa D'Almeida
JURISCONTA SRL

Djamila Mary Pereira Gomes
ARQUITECTONICA LDA

Emilfreda M. de Oliveira
ECOBANK

Miguel Mango
AUDI - CONTA LDA

Vitor Marques da Cruz
MC&A - SOCIEDADE DE ADVOGADOS,
RL

Francisco Mendes
MINISTRY OF FOREIGN AFFAIRS

Teresa Pala Schwalbach
MC&A - SOCIEDADE DE ADVOGADOS,
RL

Eduardo Pimentel
CENTRO DE FORMALIZAÇÃO DE
EMPRESAS

Sydney Pinto
DP-ACU

Fernando Tavares
TRANSMAR SERVICES

Djunco Suleiman Ture
MUNICIPALITY OF BISSAU

Carlos Vamain
GOMES & VAMAIN ASSOCIADOS

Emmanuel Yehouessi
BCEAO

### GUYANA

Marcel Bobb
FRASER, HOUSTY & YEARWOOD
ATTORNEYS-AT-LAW

Ashton Chase
LAW OFFICE OF ASHTON CHASE
ASSOCIATES

Desmond Correia
CORREIA & CORREIA LTD.

Lucia Desir-John
D & J SHIPPING SERVICES

Marlon Gonsalves
RODRIGUES ARCHITECTS LTD.

Orin Hinds
ORIN HINDS & ASSOCIATES ARCH. LTD.

Teni Housty
FRASER, HOUSTY & YEARWOOD
ATTORNEYS-AT-LAW

Rexford Jackson
SINGH, DOODNAUTH LAW FIRM

Kashir Khan

Rakesh Latchana
RAM & MCRAE CHARTERED
ACCOUNTANTS

Alexis Monize
GUYANA OFFICE FOR INVESTMENT

Enrique Monize
LAND REGISTRY

Manzoor Nadir
DIGICOM

R.N. Poonai
POONAI & POONAI

Christopher Ram
RAM & MCRAE CHARTERED
ACCOUNTANTS

Vishwamint Ramnarine
PFK BARCELLOS, NARINE & CO.

Albert Rodrigues
RODRIGUES ARCHITECTS LTD.

Shantel Scott
FRASER, HOUSTY & YEARWOOD
ATTORNEYS-AT-LAW

Shaundell Stephenson
OFFICE OF THE PRIME MINISTER

Gidel Thomside
NATIONAL SHIPPING CORPORATION LTD.

Josephine Whitehead
CAMERON & SHEPHERD

Troy Williams
RAM & MCRAE CHARTERED
ACCOUNTANTS

Roger Yearwood
BRITTON, HAMILTON & ADAMS

### HAITI

MÉROVÉ-PIERRE - CABINET
D'EXPERTS-COMPTABLES

Jean Baptiste Brown
BROWN LEGAL GROUP

Martin Camille Cangé
ELECTRICITÉ D'HAÏTI

Monique César Guillaume
PAGS - CABINET D'EXPERTS
COMPATBLES

Djacaman Charles
CABINET GASSANT

Robinson Charles
BANQUE DE LA RÉPUBLIQUE D'HAITI

Inelor Dorval

Lucien Fresnel
CABINET GASSANT

Enerlio Gassant
CABINET GASSANT

Giordani Gilbert Emile
ETUDE BRISSON CASSAGNOL

Marc Hebert Ignace
BANQUE DE LA RÉPUBLIQUE D'HAITI

Raphaël Izmery
GBS GENERAL BUILDING SYSTEMS

Luciner Joseph
MAIRIE DE PETIONVILLE

Robert Laforest
CABINET LAFOREST

Camille Leblanc
CABINET LEBLANC & ASSOCIÉS

Ludwig Leblanc
CABINET LEBLANC & ASSOCIÉS

Wilhelm E. Lemke Jr.
ENMARCOLDA (D'ADESKY.)

Roberson Louis
CABINET GASSANT

Kathia Magloire
CABINET GASSANT

Joseph Paillant
BUCOFISC

Micosky Pompilus
CABINET D'AVOCATS CHALMERS

Leon Saint -Louis
AVOCAT

Margarette Sanon
BANQUE DE LA RÉPUBLIQUE D'HAITI

Michel Succar
SUCCAR AND ASSOCIATES

Salim Succar
CABINET LISSADE

Antoine Turnier
FIRME TURNIER - COMPTABLE
PROFESSIONNELS AGRÉÉS CONSEILS DE
DIRECTION

### HONDURAS

CNBS - COMISION NACIONAL DE
BANCOS Y SEGUROS

EMPRESA NACIONAL DE ENERGÍA
ELÉCTRICA

José Antonio Abate
ABAS CONSULTORES

Juan José Alcerro Milla
AGUILAR CASTILLO LOVE

Jose Miguel Alvarez
CONSORTIUM CENTRO AMÉRICA
ABOGADOS

José Simón Azcona
INMOBILIARIA ALIANZA SA

Adrián Burgos
CONSORTIUM CENTRO AMÉRICA
ABOGADOS

César Augusto Cabrera Zapata
TRANSUNION

Fredy Castillo
GARCÍA & BODÁN

Jaime Alberto Colindres Rosales
DYCELES S DE R.L.

Graciela Cruz
GARCÍA & BODÁN

Víctor Manuel Cuadra Burlero
CONSTRUCTORA URBE

Gilda Espinal Veliz
ASJ - ASOCIACION PARA UNA
SOCIEDAD MAS JUSTA

Oscar Armando Girón
ASOCIACIÓN HONDUREÑA DE
COMPAÑÍAS Y REPRESENTANTES
NAVIEROS (AHCORENA)

Jessica Handal
ARIAS & MUÑOZ

Juan Diego Lacayo González
AGUILAR CASTILLO LOVE

Evangelina Lardizábal
ARIAS & MUÑOZ

Guadalupe Martinez Casas
CENTRAL LAW MEDINA, ROSENTHAL &
ASOCIADOS

Claribel Medina
CENTRAL LAW MEDINA, ROSENTHAL &
ASOCIADOS

Jesús Humberto Medina-Alva
CENTRAL LAW MEDINA, ROSENTHAL &
ASOCIADOS

Juan Carlos Mejía Cotto
INSTITUTO DE LA PROPIEDAD

Iván Alfredo Vigíl Molina
ABOGADO

Ricardo Montes Belot
ARIAS & MUÑOZ

Ramón E. Morales
PwC HONDURAS

Vanessa Oquelí
GARCÍA & BODÁN

Danna Paredes
PwC HONDURAS

José Ramón Paz
CONSORTIUM CENTRO AMÉRICA
ABOGADOS

Marco Ponce
CENTRAL LAW MEDINA, ROSENTHAL &
ASOCIADOS

Milton Rivera
PwC HONDURAS

José Rafael Rivera Ferrari
CONSORTIUM CENTRO AMÉRICA
ABOGADOS

Enrique Rodriguez Burchard
AGUILAR CASTILLO LOVE

Fanny Rodríguez del Cid
ARIAS & MUÑOZ

René Serrano
ARIAS & MUÑOZ

Gricelda Urquía
TransUnion

Armando Urtecho López
COHEP (CONSEJO HONDUREÑO DE LA
EMPRESA PRIVADA)

Roberto Manuel Zacarías
Urrutia
ZACARÍAS & ASOCIADOS

Mario Rubén Zelaya
ENERGÍA INTEGRAL S. DE R.L. DE C.V.

Carlos Zuniga
IRÍAS & ASOCIADOS - CORRESPONDENT
OF RUSSELL BEDFORD INTERNATIONAL

### HONG KONG SAR, CHINA

ALLEN & OVERY

GUANGDONG AND HONG KONG FEEDER
ASSOCIATION LTD.

Duncan Abate
MAYER BROWN JSM

Albert P.C. Chan
THE HONG KONG POLYTECHNIC
UNIVERSITY

Kenneth Chan
HONG KONG ECONOMIC & TRADE
OFFICE

Nicholas Chan
SQUIRE SANDERS

Rico Chan
BAKER & MCKENZIE

Wendy O. Chan
FAIRBAIRN CATLEY LOW & KONG

Vashi Chandiramani
EXCELLENCE INTERNATIONAL

Beverly Cheung
MAYER BROWN JSM

Winnie Cheung
THE LAND REGISTRY OF HONG KONG

Michael Chiang
MCAA LTD.

Stephanie Chiu
MAYER BROWN JSM

Robert Chu
ECONOMIC ANALYSIS AND BUSINESS
FACILITATION UNIT

Tony Chu
VICTON REGISTRATIONS LTD.

Jimmy Chung
JAMES NGAI & PARTNERS CPA LIMITED
- MEMBER OF RUSSELL BEDFORD
INTERNATIONAL

Vicky Chung
GILT CHAMBERS

Joshua Cole
MALLESONS STEPHEN JACQUES

Keith Man Kei Ho
WILKINSON & GRIST

Vivian Ho
BAKER & MCKENZIE

Basil Hwang
DECHERT

Salina Ko
APL

Peter Kwon
ASHURST LLP

Billy Lam
MAYER BROWN JSM

Christie Lam
HONG KONG FINANCIAL SECRETARY

Cindy Lam
THE LAND REGISTRY OF HONG KONG

Lauren Lau
KLC KENNIC LUI & CO

Candas Lee
EDMUND W. H. CHOW & CO

Juliana Lee
MAYER BROWN JSM

Alice Leung
CUSTOMS AND EXCISE DEPARTMENT

Dennis Li
SIMON REID-KAY & ASSOCIATES

Tommy Li
EDMUND W. H. CHOW & CO

Kennic L H Lui
KLC KENNIC LUI & CO

Psyche S.F. Luk
FAIRBAIRN CATLEY LOW & KONG

Louise Ng
SQUIRE SANDERS

Kok Leong Ngan
CLP POWER HONG KONG LIMITED

Kenneth Poon
THE LAND REGISTRY OF HONG KONG

Martinal Quan
METOPRO ASSOCIATES LIMITED

Yash A. Rana
GOODWIN PROCTER LLP

Kim Rooney
GILT CHAMBERS

Matthias Schemuth
ASHURST LLP

Eric Tang
ASIA BUSINESS SERVICE LIMITED

Hong Tran
MAYER BROWN JSM

Anita Tsang
PwC HONG KONG

Derek Tsang
MAYER BROWN JSM

Laurence Tsong
TransUnion HONG KONG

Paul Tsui
*Hong Kong Association of Freight Forwarding & Logistics Ltd. (HAFFA)*

Leung Wan
*Inland Revenue Department, HKSAR*

Yeeling Wan
*Stephenson Harwood*

Christopher Whiteley
*Ashurst LLP*

Agnes Wong
*Companies Registry, HKSAR*

Bill Wong
*Hong Kong Economic & Trade Office*

Chester Wong
*Mayer Brown JSM*

Fergus Wong
*PwC Hong Kong*

Patrick Wong
*Mayer Brown JSM*

Winston Yau
*Oriental Business Services Limited*

Ricky Yiu
*Baker & McKenzie*

Hai Yong
*Baker & McKenzie*

Peter Yu
*PwC Hong Kong*

Frank Yuen
*KLC Kennic Lui & Co*

## HUNGARY

*Cargo-Partner*

*Jones Lang LaSalle*

Mark Balastyai
*Futureal Group*

Diana Balazs
*PwC Hungary*

Péter Bárdos
*Law Firm Dr. Péter and Rita Bárdos*

Marianna Bártfai
*BDO Hungary*

Sándor Békési
*Partos & Noblet Hogan Lovells*

Péter Berethalmi
*Nagy és Trócsányi Law Office, member of Lex Mundi*

Hedi Bozsonyik
*Szecskay Attorneys at Law*

Beata Bujnoczki
*Reti, Antall and Partners Law Firm*

Zsuzsanna Cseri
*Cseri & Partners Law Firm*

Gábor Dohány
*Partos & Noblet Hogan Lovells*

Gabriella Erdos
*PwC Hungary*

Tamás Esze
*BPV | Jádi Németh Attorneys at Law*

Agnes Fábry
*PRK Partners / Fábry Law Office*

György Fehér
*PRK Partners / Fábry Law Office*

Hajnalka Fekó
*BPV | Jádi Németh Attorneys at Law*

Éva Fülöp
*BPV | Jádi Németh Attorneys at Law*

Gyula Gábriel
*Bogsch & Partners*

Ernő Garamvölgyi
*Budapest IX District Municipality*

Éva Gargya
*Nagy és Trócsányi Law Office, member of Lex Mundi*

Anna Gáspár
*Build-Econ Ltd.*

Csaba Attila Hajdu
*BNT Szabó Tom Burmeister Ügyvédi Iroda*

Tamas Halmos
*Partos & Noblet Hogan Lovells*

Dóra Horváth
*Reti, Antall and Partners Law Firm*

István Illés
*Reti, Antall and Partners Law Firm*

Norbert Izer
*PwC Hungary*

Andrea Jádi Németh
*BPV | Jádi Németh Attorneys at Law*

Dorottya Kovacsics
*Partos & Noblet Hogan Lovells*

Petra Lencs
*Cseri & Partners Law Firm*

László Mohai
*Mohai Law Office*

András Multas
*Partos & Noblet Hogan Lovells*

Robert Nagy
*BISZ Central Credit Information (PLC)*

Sándor Németh
*Szecskay Attorneys at Law*

Christopher Noblet
*Partos & Noblet Hogan Lovells*

István Sándor
*Kelemen, Meszaros, Sandor & Partners*

Tamas Sotet
*International Logistic Gateway*

Krisztina Stachó
*BPV | Jádi Németh Attorneys at Law*

Gergely Szabó
*Reti, Antall and Partners Law Firm*

Tibor Szabó
*Reti, Antall and Partners Law Firm*

Ágnes Szent-Ivány
*Sándor Szegedi Szent-Ivány Komáromi Eversheds*

Viktória Szilágyi
*Nagy és Trócsányi Law Office, member of Lex Mundi*

Angéla Szőke
*BDO Hungary*

Adrienn Tar
*Szecskay Attorneys at Law*

Ágnes Tigelmann
*BPV | Jádi Németh Attorneys at Law*

Ádám Tóth
*Dr. Tóth Ádám Közjegyzői Iroda*

Gábor Varga
*BISZ Central Credit Information (PLC)*

Réka Vizi-Magyarosi
*BNT Szabó Tom Burmeister Ügyvédi Iroda*

Blanka Zombori
*PwC Hungary*

Antónia Zsigmond
*BPV | Jádi Németh Attorneys at Law*

## ICELAND

*PwC Iceland*

*Reykjavik Municipal Building Control Office*

Karen Bragadóttir
*Tollstjóri - Directorate of Customs*

Eymundur Einarsson
*Endurskoðun og ráðgjöf ehf - member of Russell Bedford International*

Ólafur Eiríksson
*LOGOS, member of Lex Mundi*

Skuli Th. Fjeldsted
*Fjeldsted, Blöndal & Fjeldsted*

Benedikt Geirsson
*ISTAK*

Erlendur Gíslason
*LOGOS, member of Lex Mundi*

Guðrún Guðmundsdóttir
*Jónar Transport*

Reynir Haraldsson
*Jónar Transport*

Hörður Davíð Harðarson
*Tollstjóri - Directorate of Customs*

Margrét Hauksdóttir
*Registers Iceland*

Stefan Ingimarsson
*Fulltingi Legal Services*

Sigrun Helga Johannsdottir
*Fulltingi Legal Services*

Erlingur E. Jónasson
*ISTAK*

Hróbjartur Jónatansson
*Jónatansson & Co. Legal Services*

Jóhanna Áskels Jónsdóttir
*PricewaterhouseCoopers Legal ehf*

Thora Jónsdóttir
*Juris Law office*

Jóhann Magnús Jóhannsson
*LOGOS, member of Lex Mundi*

Benedetto Nardini
*BBA Legal*

Dagbjört Oddsdóttir
*BBA Legal*

Kristján Pálsson
*Jónar Transport*

Ásgeir Á. Ragnarsson
*BBA Legal*

Eyvindur Sólnes
*CATO Lögmenn*

Jóhannes Stephensen
*Creditinfo Iceland*

Gunnar Sturluson
*LOGOS, member of Lex Mundi*

Rúnar Svavar Svavarsson
*Orkuveita Reykjavíkur, Distribution-Electrical System*

Stefán A. Svensson
*Juris Law office*

Steinþór Þorsteinsson
*Tollstjóri - Directorate of Customs*

## INDIA

Jolly Abraham
*Desai & Diwanji*

Mahima Ahluwalia
*Trilegal*

Lzafeer Ahmad
*Trilegal*

Fraser Alexander
*Juris Corp*

P. V. Balasubramaniam
*BFS Legal*

Ashish Banga
*Juris Corp*

Sumant Batra
*Kesar Dass B & Associates*

Neeraj Bhagat
*Neeraj Bhagat & Co.*

M.L Bhakta
*Kanga & Co.*

Pradeep Bhandari
*Proteam Consulting Private Limited*

Sushil Bhasin
*Bhasin International*

Saurav Bhattacharya
*PwC India*

Rewati Bobde
*Juris Corp*

Nidhi Bothra
*Vinod Kothari & Co., Company Secretaries*

Leena Chacko
*Amarchand & Mangaldas & Suresh A. Shroff & Co.*

Rajarshi Chakrabarti
*Kochhar & Co.*

Harshala Chandorkar
*Credit Information Bureau Ltd.*

Prashant Chauhan
*Advocate*

Daizy Chawla
*Singh & Associates, Advocates and Solicitors*

Manjula Chawla
*Phoenix Legal*

Arzineh Chinoy
*Desai & Diwanji*

Harish Chugh
*Param Overseas*

Sachin Chugh
*Singhi Chugh & Kumar, Chartered Accountants*

Ketan Dalal
*PwC India*

Vishwang Desai
*Desai & Diwanji*

Devendra Deshmukh
*Khaitan & Co.*

Monika Deshmukh
*Desai & Diwanji*

Prashant Dharia
*Anant Industries*

Farida Dholkawala
*Desai & Diwanji*

Ashwin Didwania
*New Globe Logistik Pvt. Ltd.*

Thambi Durai
*T. Durai & Co.*

Ferdinand Duraimanickam
*BFS Legal*

Ritika Ganju
*Phoenix Legal*

Rahul Garg
*PwC India*

Tavishi Garg
*Majmudar & Co.*

Sameer Guha
*Trilegal*

Trupti Guha
*Kochhar & Co.*

Atul Gupta
*Trilegal*

Ruchira Gupta
*The Juris Sociis*

Akil Hirani
*Majmudar & Co.*

Ashok Jain
*Runtai Industry Co. Ltd.*

Yogesh Jare
*Suhasini Impex*

H. Jayesh
*Juris Corp*

Dharmendra Johari
*Stonex Inc.*

Rajat Joneja
*KNM & Partners, Law Offices*

Sumeet Kachwaha
*Kestenberg Rabinowicz Partners LLP - member of Russell Bedford International*

Rupen Kanawala
*Juris Corp*

Megha Kapoor
*Singh & Associates, Advocates and Solicitors*

Jayesh Karandikar
*Kochhar & Co.*

Rajas Kasbekar
*Little & Co.*

Kripi Kathuria
*Phoenix Legal*

Charandeep Kaur
*Trilegal*

Paramjeet Kaur
*Param Overseas*

Mitalee Kaushal

Shahriar Khan
*Crown Agents Ltd.*

Ravinder Komaragiri
*The Tata Power Company Limited*

Anuraag Kothari
*Trilegal*

Vinod Kothari
*Vinod Kothari & Co., Company Secretaries*

Harsh Kumar
*Singhi Chugh & Kumar, Chartered Accountants*

Mukesh Kumar
*KNM & Partners, Law Offices*

Vikram Kumar
*Supply Source India*

Dilip Kumar Niranjan
*Singh & Associates, Advocates and Solicitors*

Manoj Kumar Singh
*Singh & Associates, Advocates and Solicitors*

Vijay Kumar Singh
*Singh & Associates, Advocates and Solicitors*

Shreedhar Kunte
*Sharp and Tannan - member of Russell Bedford International*

C.K.N. Kuppuraajha
*Shri Abinaya Mercantiles Private Limited*

Harjeet Lall
*Axon Partners LLP*

Nitesh Latwal
*Corporate Professionals*

Chandni Lochan
*Trilegal*

Rajiv K. Luthra
*Luthra & Luthra*

Sarika Malhotra
*PwC India*

Aditi Manchanda
*Juris Corp*

Som Mandal
*Fox Mandal & Co.*

Vipender Mann
*KNM & Partners, Law Offices*

Vaishali Manubarwala
*Desai & Diwanji*

Avadesh Marthur
*Harsh Impex*

Atul Mehta
*Mehta & Mehta*

Dara Mehta
*Little & Co.*

Dipti Mehta
*MEHTA & MEHTA*

Jitesh Mehta
*SOURCE INDIA*

Preeti G. Mehta
*KANGA & CO.*

Vishal Mehta
*MEHTA & MEHTA*

Dhiraj Mhetre
*DESAI & DIWANJI*

Sharad Mishra
*NEO MULTIMEDIAN*

Saurabh Misra
*SAURABH MISRA & ASSOCIATES, ADVOCATES*

Ananya Mitra
*JURIS CHAMBERS*

Moiz Motiwala
*SHARP AND TANNAN - MEMBER OF RUSSELL BEDFORD INTERNATIONAL*

Mustafa Motiwala
*JURIS CORP*

Shyamal Mukherjee
*PwC INDIA*

Sudip Mullick
*KHAITAN & CO.*

Vaidehi Naik
*PHOENIX LEGAL*

Puja Nalam
*BMR LEGAL*

Gunita Pahwa
*SINGH & ASSOCIATES, ADVOCATES AND SOLICITORS*

Dharmesh Panchal
*PwC INDIA*

Madhav Pande

Janak Pandya
*NISHITH DESAI ASSOCIATES*

Tejas R. Parekh
*NISHITH DESAI ASSOCIATES*

Vijayta Parmar
*SINGH & ASSOCIATES, ADVOCATES AND SOLICITORS*

Barasha Pathak
*JURIS CORP*

Sanjay Patil
*BDH INDUSTRIES LIMITED*

Dhruv Paul
*TRILEGAL*

Bhadrinath Madhusudan Pogul
*KALKI INTERNATIONAL*

Madhavi Pogul
*KALKI INTERNATIONAL*

Madhusudan Venkatesh Pogul
*KALKI INTERNATIONAL*

Nitin Potdar
*J. SAGAR ASSOCIATES, ADVOCATES & SOLICITORS*

M. Prabhakaran
*CONSULTA JURIS*

Ajay Raghavan
*TRILEGAL*

Ravishankar Raghavan
*MAJMUDAR & CO.*

Palaniandavan Ramasamy
*BFS LEGAL*

Ashok Ramgir
*HARSH IMPEX*

Harsh Ramgir
*HARSH IMPEX*

Dipak Rao
*SINGHANIA & PARTNERS LLP SOLICITORS & ADVOCATES*

Abhishek A. Rastogi
*PwC INDIA*

Richie Sancheti
*NISHITH DESAI ASSOCIATES*

Ramani Seshadri

Brinda Shah
*MEHTA & MEHTA*

Manav Shah
*KOCHHAR & CO.*

Sonali Sharma
*JURIS CORP*

S.D. Sharma
*PARAM OVERSEAS*

Varnika Sharma
*JURIS CORP*

K.M. Aasim Shehzad
*BFS LEGAL*

Shivanand Shenoy
*SIDDHI FOAMS*

Vikram Shroff
*NISHITH DESAI ASSOCIATES*

Ravinder Pal Singh
*INTERNATIONAL SURGICAL INDS.*

Mukesh Singhal
*KNM & PARTNERS, LAW OFFICES*

Ankit Singhi
*CORPORATE PROFESSIONALS*

Vinay Sirohia
*AXON PARTNERS LLP*

Veena Sivaramakrishnan
*JURIS CORP*

Harshita Srivastava
*NISHITH DESAI ASSOCIATES*

P.N. Swaroop
*MODERN CARGO SERVICES PVT. LTD.*

Anil Tanwar
*PARAM OVERSEAS*

Rajesh Tayal
*KNM & PARTNERS, LAW OFFICES*

Mahesh Thaker
*MJ CO., LTD.*

Chetan Thakkar
*KANGA & CO.*

Vishnu Thakkar
*PwC INDIA*

Piyush Thareja
*NEERAJ BHAGAT & CO.*

Kanishka Tyagi
*KESAR DASS B & ASSOCIATES*

Rahul Tyagi
*FOX MANDAL & CO.*

Navratan Uppal

Ajay Verma
*JURIS CHAMBERS*

Hemant Vijay Pandya
*MEHTA & MEHTA*

Rajat Vohra
*TRILEGAL*

Saral Kumar Yadav
*SAADHAAR MARKETING PVT.LTD.*

Pooja Yedukumar
*JURIS CORP*

## INDONESIA

*JAKARTA PROVINCE'S BUILDING SUPERVISION & ADMINISTRATION OFFICE*

Adi Ariantara
*JAKARTA INVESTMENT AND PROMOTION BOARD*

Hamud M. Balfas
*ALI BUDIARDJO, NUGROHO, REKSODIPUTRO, MEMBER OF LEX MUNDI*

Fabian Buddy Pascoal
*HANAFIAH PONGGAWA & PARTNERS*

Ita Budhi
*PwC INDONESIA*

Prianto Budi
*PT PRATAMA INDOMITRA KONSULTAN - MEMBER OF RUSSELL BEDFORD INTERNATIONAL*

Tony Budidjaja
*BUDIDJAJA & ASSOCIATES LAW OFFICES*

Harri Budiman
*FRANS WINARTA & PARTNERS*

Jimmy Charles
*PT HYPER MEGA SHIPPING*

Juni Dani
*BUDIDJAJA & ASSOCIATES LAW OFFICES*

Utari Dyah Kusuma
*BRIGITTA I. RAHAYOE & PARTNERS*

Sani Eka Duta
*BANK INDONESIA*

Donny Fadilah
*BAHAR & PARTNERS*

Renita Girsang
*YAN APUL & REKAN*

Widigdya Sukma Gitaya
*WSG TAX ADVISOR*

Ayik Gunadi
*ALI BUDIARDJO, NUGROHO, REKSODIPUTRO, member of LEX MUNDI*

Iqbal Hadromi
*HADROMI & PARTNERS*

Dedet Hardiansyah
*BUDIMAN AND PARTNERS*

Jonathan Hariandja
*FRANS WINARTA & PARTNERS*

Muhaimin Ibnu Hasan
*MAKARIM & TAIRA S.*

Michael Hasian Giovanni
*BRIGITTA I. RAHAYOE & PARTNERS*

Erwandi Hendarta
*HADIPUTRANTO, HADINOTO & PARTNERS*

Firman Setia Herwanto
*INDONESIAN INSTITUTE OF ARCHITECTS*

Mohammad Kamal Hidayat

Alexander Augustinus Hutauruk
*HADIPUTRANTO, HADINOTO & PARTNERS*

Brigitta Imam Rahayoe
*BRIGITTA I. RAHAYOE & PARTNERS*

Robert Buana Jaya
*BUDIDJAJA & ASSOCIATES LAW OFFICES*

Mirza Karim
*KARIMSYAH LAW FIRM*

Galinar R. Kartakusuma
*MAKARIM & TAIRA S.*

Herry N. Kurniawan
*ALI BUDIARDJO, NUGROHO, REKSODIPUTRO, member of LEX MUNDI*

Rudy Kusmanto
*MAKARIM & TAIRA S.*

Winita E. Kusnandar
*KUSNANDAR & CO.*

Arno F. Rizaldi Kwok
*KUSNANDAR & CO.*

Edward N. Lontoh
*LONTOH & PARTNERS LAW OFFICE*

Rudhy A. Lontoh
*LONTOH & PARTNERS LAW OFFICE*

Noorfina Luthfiany
*BANK INDONESIA*

Ferry P. Madian
*ALI BUDIARDJO, NUGROHO, REKSODIPUTRO, member of LEX MUNDI*

Ella Melany
*HANAFIAH PONGGAWA & PARTNERS*

Karen Mills
*KARIMSYAH LAW FIRM*

Nico Mooduto
*SOEWITO SUHARDIMAN EDDYMURTHY KARDONO*

Norma Mutalib
*MAKARIM & TAIRA S.*

Alexander Nainggolan
*HADROMI & PARTNERS*

Suria Nataadmadja
*SURIA NATAADMADJA & ASSOCIATES*

Mia Noni Yuniar
*BRIGITTA I. RAHAYOE & PARTNERS*

Meiske Panggabean
*BAHAR & PARTNERS*

Ay Tjhing Phan
*PwC INDONESIA*

Denny Rahmansyah
*SOEWITO SUHARDIMAN EDDYMURTHY KARDONO*

Sophia Rengganis
*PwC INDONESIA*

Adrio Rivadi
*KUSNANDAR & CO.*

Isyana W. Sadjarwo
*NOTARIS & PEJABAT PEMBUOT AKIO TANOH*

Gatot Sanyoto
*KUSNANDAR & CO.*

Nur Asyura Anggini Sari
*BANK INDONESIA*

Marinza Savanthy
*WIDYAWAN & PARTNERS*

Natasha A. Sebayang
*SOEWITO SUHARDIMAN EDDYMURTHY KARDONO*

Arie Setiawan
*PT SAHABAT UTAMA INDONESIA*

Kevin Omar Sidharta
*ALI BUDIARDJO, NUGROHO, REKSODIPUTRO, member of LEX MUNDI*

Ricardo Simanjuntak
*RICARDO SIMANJUNTAK & PARTNERS*

Terman Siregar
*JAKARTA INVESTMENT AND PROMOTION BOARD*

Yukiko Lyla Usman Tambunan
*BANK INDONESIA*

S.H. Anggra Syah Reza Tengku
*ALI BUDIARDJO NUGROHO, member of LEX MUNDI REKSODIPUTRO*

Christian Teo
*CHRISTIAN TEO & ASSOCIATES*

Yuliana Tjhai
*BAHAR & PARTNERS*

Hanum Ariana Tobing
*BUDIDJAJA & ASSOCIATES LAW OFFICES*

Gatot Triprasetio
*WIDYAWAN & PARTNERS*

Runi Tusita
*PwC INDONESIA*

Pudji Wahjuni Purbo
*MAKARIM & TAIRA S.*

Ilham Wahyu
*ALI BUDIARDJO, NUGROHO, REKSODIPUTRO, member of LEX MUNDI*

Sony Panji Wicaksono
*BANK INDONESIA*

Fransiska Ade Kurnia Widodo
*BUDIDJAJA & ASSOCIATES LAW OFFICES*

Aditya Kesha Wijayanto
*WIDYAWAN & PARTNERS*

Frans Winarta
*FRANS WINARTA & PARTNERS*

## IRAN, ISLAMIC REP.

Hamid Reza Adabi
*STATE ORGANIZATION FOR REGISTRATION OF DEEDS & PROPERTIES OF ISLAMIC REPUBLIC OF IRAN*

Nazem Ahmadian Nasrabadi
*STATE ORGANIZATION FOR REGISTRATION OF DEEDS & PROPERTIES OF ISLAMIC REPUBLIC OF IRAN*

Hamede Akhavan
*SECURITIES AND EXCHANGE ORGANIZATION OF IRAN*

Gholam Ali Asghari
*GREAT TEHRAN ELECTRICITY DISTRIBUTION COMPANY (GTEDC)*

Hamid Berenjkar
*OFFICE OF HAMID BERENJKAR*

Morteza Dezfoulian
*MORTEZA*

Mahmoud Ebadi Tabrizi
*LAW OFFICES M. EBADI TABRIZI & ASSOCIATES ATTORNEYS AT LAW*

Maryam Ebrahimi
*TEHRAN STOCK EXCHANGE (TSE)*

Mona Ebrahimi
*IMIDRO*

Mahmoud Eskandari
*IRAN TRADE PROMOTION ORGANIZATION*

Shirzad Eslami
*OJE LAW OFFICE*

Hossein Fahimi
*SECURITIES AND EXCHANGE ORGANIZATION OF IRAN*

Zahra Farzaliyan
*STATE ORGANIZATION FOR REGISTRATION OF DEEDS & PROPERTIES OF ISLAMIC REPUBLIC OF IRAN*

Hengameh Fazeli Daie Zangi
*STATE ORGANIZATION FOR REGISTRATION OF DEEDS & PROPERTIES OF ISLAMIC REPUBLIC OF IRAN*

Nassim Jahanbani
*GREAT TEHRAN ELECTRICITY DISTRIBUTION COMPANY (GTEDC)*

Mohammad Jalili
*IRAN CREDIT SCORING*

Farid Kani
*ATIEH ASSOCIATES*

Behnam Khatami
*ATIEH ASSOCIATES*

Amir Kheirollahy
*HT CO., LTD.*

Gholam Reza Malekshoar
*CENTRAL BANK OF THE ISLAMIC REPUBLIC OF IRAN*

Seyed Ali Mirshafiei
*TEHRAN CHAMBER OF COMMERCE, INDUSTRY AND MINES*

Fatemeh Sadat Mirsharifi
*MINISTRY OF COMMERCE*

Seyedeh Fatemeh Moghimi
*SADID BAR INT TRANSPORT*

Mozaffar Mohammadian
*TEEMA BAR INTERNATIONAL TRANSPORT*

Babak Namazi
*ATIEH ASSOCIATES*

Rasoul Nowrouzi
*IRAN TRADE PROMOTION ORGANIZATION*

Ahmad Parkhideh
*IRAN CHAMBER OF COMMERCE*

Mohammad Reza Pasban
*ALLAME TABATABAEI UN.- IRANIAN CENTRAL BAR ASSOCIATION*

Farmand Pourkarim
*TEHRAN MUNICIPALITY*

Mariam Sahrabin
*KHADEM GROUP*

Ahmad Shabanifard
*BASTAN HONAR NAMA*

Cyrus Shafizadeh
*ATIEH ASSOCIATES*

Farzan Shirvanbeigi
*TEHRAN MUNICIPALITY*

Rajat Ratan Sinha
*RCS PVT. LTD. BUSINESS ADVISORS GROUP*

Mohammad Soltani
*SECURITIES AND EXCHANGE ORGANIZATION OF IRAN*

Abbas Taghipour
*CENTRAL BANK OF THE ISLAMIC REPUBLIC OF IRAN*

Ebrahim Tavakoli
*TAVAKOLI & SHAHABI*

Meghdad Torabi
*TAVAKOLI & SHAHABI*

Vrej Torossian
*TOROSSIAN, AVANESSIAN & ASSOCIATE*

Abdolamir Yaghouti
*GREAT TEHRAN ELECTRICITY DISTRIBUTION COMPANY (GTEDC)*

**IRAQ**

*ERNST & YOUNG*

*GEZAIRI TRANSPORT IRAQI COMPANY LTD.*

*IRAQI ASSOCIATION OF SECURITIES DEALERS*

Faik Abdul Rasool
*IRAQI INSTITUTE FOR ECONOMIC REFORM*

Emad Abdullatif
*IRAQI INSTITUTE FOR ECONOMIC REFORM*

Marie Antoinette Airut
*AIRUT LAW OFFICES*

Omar Al Nemer
*TALAL ABU GHAZALEH LEGAL (TAG-LEGAL)*

Ahmed Al-Jannabi
*MENA ASSOCIATES, MEMBER OF AMERELLER RECHTSANWÄLTE*

Jafar Albadran
*IRAQI INSTITUTE FOR ECONOMIC REFORM*

Mazin Albadran
*IRAQI INSTITUTE FOR ECONOMIC REFORM*

Mustafa Alshawi
*IRAQI INSTITUTE FOR ECONOMIC REFORM*

Florian Amereller
*AMERELLER RECHTSANWÄLTE*

Munther B. Hamoudi
*AL ATTAR REAL ESTATE OFFICE*

Duraid Basil
*IRAQI INSTITUTE FOR ECONOMIC REFORM*

Thomas David
*PANALPINA GULF*

Husam Addin Hatim

Stephan Jäger
*AMERELLER RECHTSANWÄLTE*

Imad Makki
*AL QARYA GROUP CO.*

Mudher Mohammed Salih
*IRAQ CENTRAL BANK*

Omar Moneer
*TALAL ABU GHAZALEH LEGAL (TAG-LEGAL)*

Auday Najim Ali
*ASHUR INTERNATIONAL BANK*

Ahmed Salih Al-Janabi
*MENA ASSOCIATES, MEMBER OF AMERELLER RECHTSANWÄLTE*

Claus Schmidt
*PANALPINA GULF*

Abdelrahman Sherif
*MENA ASSOCIATES, MEMBER OF AMERELLER RECHTSANWÄLTE*

Khaled Yaseen

Ilza Zwein
*AIRUT LAW OFFICES*

**IRELAND**

*ESB NETWORKS*

Margaret Austin
*EUGENE F. COLLINS SOLICITORS*

Michael Bergin
*PwC IRELAND*

Finola Boyle
*EUGENE F. COLLINS SOLICITORS*

Alan Browning
*LK SHIELDS SOLICITORS, MEMBER OF IUS LABORIS*

John Comerford
*COONEY CAREY - MEMBER OF RUSSELL BEDFORD INTERNATIONAL*

Eoin Cunneen
*LK SHIELDS SOLICITORS, MEMBER OF IUS LABORIS*

Richard Curran
*LK SHIELDS SOLICITORS, MEMBER OF IUS LABORIS*

Kiara Daly
*DANIEL MURPHY SOLICITORS*

Laura Daly
*LK SHIELDS SOLICITORS, MEMBER OF IUS LABORIS*

Gavin Doherty
*EUGENE F. COLLINS SOLICITORS*

Eoghan Doyle
*PHILIP LEE*

Ray Duffy
*THE PROPERTY REGISTRATION AUTHORITY*

Frank Flanagan
*MASON HAYES+CURRAN*

Sarah Gallagher
*DILLON EUSTACE*

Aileen Gittens
*ARTHUR COX, MEMBER OF LEX MUNDI*

Paul Gough
*EUGENE F. COLLINS SOLICITORS*

Sinéad Greene
*LK SHIELDS SOLICITORS, MEMBER OF IUS LABORIS*

William Johnston
*ARTHUR COX, MEMBER OF LEX MUNDI*

Jonathan Kelly
*PHILIP LEE*

Maeve Larkin
*ARTHUR COX, MEMBER OF LEX MUNDI*

MaryLiz Mahony
*ARTHUR COX, MEMBER OF LEX MUNDI*

Gavin McGuire
*PHILIP LEE*

Kevin Meehan
*COMPASS MARITIME LTD.*

Shane Neville
*LK SHIELDS SOLICITORS, MEMBER OF IUS LABORIS*

Michael O'Connor
*MATHESON ORMSBY PRENTICE*

Deirdre O'Mahony
*ARTHUR COX, MEMBER OF LEX MUNDI*

Maurice Phelan
*MASON HAYES+CURRAN*

Sinead Power
*IRISH CREDIT BUREAU*

Jilian Pringle
*OLM CONSULTANCY*

Brendan Sharkey
*REDDY CHARLTON*

Gavin Simons
*DANIEL MURPHY SOLICITORS*

Lorcan Tiernan
*DILLON EUSTACE*

Mark Traynor
*A&L GOODBODY*

Joe Tynan
*PwC IRELAND*

Colm Walsh
*IRISH INTERNATIONAL FREIGHT ASSOCIATION*

Maeve Walsh
*REDDY CHARLTON*

Emma Weld-Moore
*DANIEL MURPHY SOLICITORS*

**ISRAEL**

*A. MOSKOVITS & SONS LTD.*

Ofer Bar-On
*SHAVIT BAR-ON GAL-ON TZIN YAGUR, LAW OFFICES*

Jacob Ben-Chitrit
*YIGAL ARNON & CO.*

Moshe Ben-Yair
*PUBLIC UTILITY AUTHORITY-ELECTRICITY*

Jeremy Benjamin
*GOLDFARB SELIGMAN & CO.*

Marina Benvenisti
*RUTH CARGO*

Yitzchak Chikorel
*DELOITTE LLP*

Doron Cohon
*RAVEH, RAVID & CO CPAS - MEMBER OF RUSSELL BEDFORD INTERNATIONAL*

Danny Dilbary
*GOLDFARB SELIGMAN & CO.*

Tuvia Geffen
*NASDCHITZ, BRANDES & CO.*

Ido Gonen
*GOLDFARB SELIGMAN & CO.*

Amos Hacmun
*HESKIA-HACMUN LAW FIRM*

Liron HaCohen
*YIGAL ARNON & CO.*

Yossi Katsav
*RUTH CARGO*

Zeev Katz
*PwC ISRAEL*

Vered Kirshner
*PwC ISRAEL*

Adam Klein
*GOLDFARB SELIGMAN & CO.*

Gideon Koren
*GIDEON KOREN & CO. LAW OFFICES*

Orna Kornreich-Cohen
*SHAVIT BAR-ON GAL-ON TZIN YAGUR, LAW OFFICES*

Meira Kowalsky
*EFRAT-KOWALSKY ARCHITECTS*

Michael Lagon
*THE ISRAEL ELECTRIC CORPORATION LTD.- DAN DISTRICT*

Benjamin Leventhal
*GIDEON FISHER & CO.*

Michelle Liberman
*S. HOROWITZ & CO., MEMBER OF LEX MUNDI*

Danielle Loewenstein
*S. HOROWITZ & CO., MEMBER OF LEX MUNDI*

Rotem Muntner
*RUTH CARGO*

Meir Nussbaum
*DELOITTE LLP*

Mirit Reif
*HACOHEN WOLF LAW OFFICES*

Liat Rothschild
*GOLDFARB SELIGMAN & CO.*

Gerry Seligman
*PwC ISRAEL*

Edward Shtaif
*THE ISRAEL ELECTRIC CORPORATION LTD.- DAN DISTRICT*

Daniel Singerman
*BUSINESS DATA ISRAEL + PERSONAL CHECK*

Maya Tiomkin
*EFRAT-KOWALSKY ARCHITECTS*

Daphna Tsarfaty
*GOLDFARB SELIGMAN & CO.*

Eylam Weiss
*WEISS-PORAT & CO.*

Zeev Weiss
*WEISS-PORAT & CO.*

Dave Wolf
*HACOHEN WOLF LAW OFFICES*

**ITALY**

Marianna Abbaticchio
*RISTUCCIA & TUFARELLI*

Marco Sebastiano Accorrà
*TLS - ASSOCIAZIONE PROFESSIONALE DI AVVOCATI E COMMERCIALISTI*

Fabrizio Acerbis
*PwC ITALY*

Mario Altavilla
*UNIONCAMERE*

Federico Antich
*STUDIO DELL'AVVOCATO ANTICH*

Stefano Aprile
*PENAL COURT OF ROME*

Roberto Argeri
*CLEARY GOTTLIEB STEEN & HAMILTON LLP*

Gaetano Arnò
*TLS - ASSOCIAZIONE PROFESSIONALE DI AVVOCATI E COMMERCIALISTI*

Romina Ballanca
*TLS - ASSOCIAZIONE PROFESSIONALE DI AVVOCATI E COMMERCIALISTI*

Paola Barazzetta
*TLS - ASSOCIAZIONE PROFESSIONALE DI AVVOCATI E COMMERCIALISTI*

Lamberto Barbieri
*CRIF S. P. A.*

Giuseppe Battaglia
*PORTOLANO CAVALLO STUDIO LEGALE*

Vlad Beffa
*STUDIO SAVOIA*

Susanna Beltramo
*STUDIO LEGALE BELTRAMO*

Stefano Biagioli
*TLS - ASSOCIAZIONE PROFESSIONALE DI AVVOCATI E COMMERCIALISTI*

Giampaolo Botta
*SPEDIPORTO - ASSOCIAZIONE SPEDIZIONIERI CORRIERI E TRASPORTATORI DI GENOVA*

Giuseppe Broccoli
*BDA STUDIO LEGALE*

Sergio Calderara
*ALMAVIVA S.P.A. - DIREZIONE AFFARI LEGALI*

Gianluca Cambareri
*TONUCCI & PARTNERS, IN ALLIANCE WITH MAYER BROWN LLP*

Stefano Cancarini
*TLS - ASSOCIAZIONE PROFESSIONALE DI AVVOCATI E COMMERCIALISTI*

Alessandro Cardia
*GRIECO E ASSOCIATI*

Cecilia Carrara
*LEGANCE*

Paolo Carta
*ACEA S.P.A.*

Fausto Caruso
*NCTM - STUDIO LEGALE ASSOCIATO*

Gennaro Cassiani
*GC ARCHITECTURE BURO*

Lucia Ceccarelli
*PORTOLANO CAVALLO STUDIO LEGALE*

Giorgio Cherubini
*PIROLA PENNUTO ZEI & ASSOCIATI*

Domenico Colella
*PORTOLANO CAVALLO STUDIO LEGALE*

Fabrizio Colonna
*LCA - LEGA COLUCCI E ASSOCIATI*

Mattia Colonnelli de Gasperis
*COLONNELLI DE GASPERIS STUDIO LEGALE*

Dorella Concadoro
*PORTOLANO CAVALLO STUDIO LEGALE*

Barbara Corsetti
*PORTOLANO CAVALLO STUDIO LEGALE*

Filippo Corsini
*CHIOMENTI STUDIO LEGALE*

Barbara Cortesi
*STUDIO LEGALE GUASTI*

Domenica Cotroneo
*TLS - ASSOCIAZIONE PROFESSIONALE DI AVVOCATI E COMMERCIALISTI*

Massimo Cremona
*PIROLA PENNUTO ZEI & ASSOCIATI*

Salvatore Cuzzocrea
*TLS - ASSOCIAZIONE PROFESSIONALE DI AVVOCATI E COMMERCIALISTI*

Antonio De Martinis
*SPASARO DE MARTINIS LAW FIRM*

Raffaella De Martinis
*SPASARO DE MARTINIS LAW FIRM*

Francesca De Paolis
*INTERNATIONAL CENTRE FOR DISPUTE RESOLUTION*

Claudio Di Falco
*CLEARY GOTTLIEB STEEN & HAMILTON LLP*

Antonella Di Maria
*M&M ASSOCIATI*

Massimiliano Di Tommaso
*CLEARY GOTTLIEB STEEN & HAMILTON LLP*

Emanuele Ferrari
*STUDIO NOTARILE FERRARI*

Maddalena Ferrari
*STUDIO NOTARILE FERRARI*

Guiseppe Ferrelli
*STUDIO LEGALE SINATRA*

Paola Flora
*STUDIO LEGALE ASSOCIATO AD ASHURST LLP*

Alberto Forte
*NOTAIO FORTE*

Pier Andrea Fré Torelli Massini
*CARABBA & PARTNERS*

Linda Nicoletta Frigo
*GRUPPO PAM S.P.A.*

Paolo Gallarati
*NCTM - STUDIO LEGALE ASSOCIATO*

Andrea Gangemi
*PORTOLANO CAVALLO STUDIO LEGALE*

Enrica Maria Ghia
*GHIA LAW FIRM*

Lucio Ghia
*Ghia Law Firm*

Vincenzo Fabrizio Giglio
*Giglio & Scofferi Studio legale del lavoro*

Andrea Grappelli
*Tonucci & Partners, in alliance with Mayer Brown LLP*

Antonio Grieco
*Grieco e Associati*

Tommaso Gualco
*Bre-engineering srl*

Valentino Guarini
*TLS - Associazione Professionale di Avvocati e Commercialisti*

Federico Guasti
*Studio Legale Guasti*

Giovanni Izzo
*Abbatescianni Studio Legale e Tributario*

Ignazio la Candia
*Pirola Pennuto Zei & Associati*

Enrico Lodi
*CRIF S. P. A.*

Cesare Lombrassa
*Studio Legale Lombrassa*

Artemisia Lorusso
*Tonucci & Partners, in alliance with Mayer Brown LLP*

Francesco Losappio
*TLS - Associazione Professionale di Avvocati e Commercialisti*

Paolo Lucarini
*PwC Italy*

Stefano Macchi di Cellere
*Jones Day*

Matteo Magistrelli
*Portolano Cavallo Studio Legale*

Fabrizio Mariotti
*Studio Legale Beltramo*

Laura Marretta
*Romolotti Marretta*

Donatella Martinelli
*Studio Legale Associato Tommasini e Martinelli*

Pietro Masi
*Portolano Cavallo Studio Legale*

Gennaro Mazzuoccolo
*Norton Rose*

Laura Mellone
*Bank of Italy*

Regina Meo
*Portolano Cavallo Studio Legale*

Andrea Messuti
*LCA - Lega Colucci e Associati*

Mario Miccoli
*Notaio Miccoli*

Luca Milan
*Studio Associato Giannessi Milan*

Nunzia Moliterni
*Jones Lang LaSalle*

Marco Monaco Sorge
*Tonucci & Partners, in alliance with Mayer Brown LLP*

Micael Montinari
*Portolano Cavallo Studio Legale*

Eliana Morandi
*Studio Notarile Eliana Morandi*

Daniela Morante
*Milan Chamber of Arbitration*

Valeria Morosini
*Toffoletto e Soci Law Firm, member of Ius Laboris*

Gianmatteo Nunziante
*Nunziante Magrone*

Francesco Nuzzolo
*PwC Italy*

Ferdinando Offredi
*VENOSTA R.E. S.rl*

Aldo Olivo
*Architect*

Fabiana Padroni
*Ristuccia & Tufarelli*

Luciano Panzani
*Torino Court of First Instance*

Giovanni Patti
*Abbatescianni Studio Legale e Tributario*

Yan Pecoraro
*Portolano Cavallo Studio Legale*

Federica Peres
*Portolano Cavallo Studio Legale*

Davide Petris
*Portolano Cavallo Studio Legale*

Martina Pivetti
*TLS - Associazione Professionale di Avvocati e Commercialisti*

Laura Prosperetti
*Cleary Gottlieb Steen & Hamilton LLP*

Giuseppe Ramondelli
*Ramondelli e Associati Studio legale Notarile*

Marianna Ristuccia
*Ristuccia & Tufarelli*

Tommaso Edoardo Romolotti
*Romolotti Marretta*

Silvia Sandrin
*Studio Legale associato ad Ashurst LLP*

Filippo Savoia
*Studio Savoia*

Azzurra Scasso
*Spediporto - Associazione Spedizionieri Corrieri e Trasportatori di Genova*

Mario Scofferi
*Giglio & Scofferi Studio legale del lavoro*

Susanna Servi
*Carabba & Partners*

Massimiliano Silvetti
*Nunziante Magrone*

Carlo Sinatra
*Studio Legale Sinatra*

Pierluigi Sodini
*Unioncamere*

Piervincenzo Spasaro
*Spasaro De Martinis Law Firm*

Elisa Sulcis
*Studio Legale Sinatra*

Maria Antonietta Tanico
*Studio Legale Tanico*

Andrea Tedioli
*Tedioli Law Firm*

Francesca Tironi
*TLS - Associazione Professionale di Avvocati e Commercialisti*

Giacinto Tommasini
*Studio Legale Associato Tommasini e Martinelli*

Stefano Tresca
*T and Partners*

Luca Tufarelli
*Ristuccia & Tufarelli*

Laura Tumolo
*NCTM - Studio Legale Associato*

Rachele Vacca de Dominicis
*Grieco e Associati*

Mario Valentini
*Pirola Pennuto Zei & Associati*

Elisabetta Ventrella
*BDA Studio Legale*

Antonio Virgallita
*TLS - Associazione Professionale di Avvocati e Commercialisti*

Angelo Zambelli
*Dewey & LeBoeuf*

Bruno Benvenuto Zerbini
*Studio Legale Beltramo*

Filippo Zucchinelli
*TLS - Associazione Professionale di Avvocati e Commercialisti*

## JAMAICA

*Attorney General's Office, Jamaica*

*Ernst & Young*

Cheronne Allen
*Jamaica Promotions Corporation (JAMPRO)*

Judith Allen
*KPMG Jamaica*

Malene Alleyne
*Myers, Fletcher & Gordon, member of Lex Mundi*

Francine Blair
*National Environment & Planning Agency*

Mitzie W. Gordon Burke-Green
*Jamaica Trading Services Ltd.*

Raymond Campbell
*KPMG Jamaica*

Colleen Coleman-Wright
*LEX Caribbean*

Eric Alexander Crawford
*PwC Jamaica*

Lincoln A.C. Eatmon
*Dunn Cox Attorneys-At-Law*

Vitus Evans
*Jamaica Exporters Association*

Natalie Farrell-Ross
*Myers, Fletcher & Gordon, member of Lex Mundi*

Nicole Foga
*Foga Daley*

Yvonne Godfrey
*Deloitte & Touche Chartered Accountants*

Gavin Goffe
*Myers, Fletcher & Gordon, member of Lex Mundi*

Lisa-Ann S. Grant
*Ministry of Labour and Social Security*

Lissa L. Grant
*Pride Jamaica*

Carla-Anne Harris Roper
*Ministry of Labour and Social Security*

Kerry-Ann Heavens
*Myers, Fletcher & Gordon, member of Lex Mundi*

Corrine N. Henry
*Myers, Fletcher & Gordon, member of Lex Mundi*

Roger Hinds
*The Shipping Association of Jamaica*

Wilbert Hoo
*Jamaica Mechanical & Electrical Engineering*

Alicia P. Hussey
*Myers, Fletcher & Gordon, member of Lex Mundi*

Donovan Jackson
*Nunes, Scholefield DeLeon & Co*

Peter Knight
*National Environment & Planning Agency*

Viralee Latibeaudiere
*Jamaica's Tax Administration at the Ministry of Finance & Public Service*

Joan Lawla
*Manager, Academician*

Jerome I. Lee
*Dunn Cox Attorneys-At-Law*

Grace Lindo
*Nunes, Scholefield DeLeon & Co*

Melinda Lloyd
*Jamaica Public Service Company Limited*

Karen McHugh
*PwC Jamaica*

Marlene McIntosh
*Fersan*

Andrine McLaren
*Kingston and St. Andrew Corporation*

Alton E. Morgan
*Legis-Alton E.Morgan & Co. Attorneys-at-Law*

Janet E. Morrison
*Dunn Cox Attorneys-At-Law*

Viveen Morrison
*PwC Jamaica*

Dana Morrison Dixon
*Jamaica Promotions Corporation (JAMPRO)*

Gary Parker
*Jamaica Promotions Corporation (JAMPRO)*

Gina Phillipps Black
*Myers, Fletcher & Gordon, member of Lex Mundi*

Norman Rainford
*KPMG Jamaica*

Judith Ramlogan
*Companies Office of Jamaica*

Stephan Rampair
*West Indies Home Contractors*

Hilary Reid
*Myers, Fletcher & Gordon, member of Lex Mundi*

Venice Ricketts
*Jamaica Inland Revenue Department*

Corah Ann Robertson-Sylvester
*Seaboard Freight and Shipping*

Milton J. Samuda
*Samuda & Johnson Attorneys-at-law*

Norman Shand
*Kingston and St. Andrew Corporation*

Bernard Shepherd
*LEX Caribbean*

Stephanie Sterling
*Myers, Fletcher & Gordon, member of Lex Mundi*

Douglas Stiebel
*Stiebel & Company Limited*

Marjorie Straw
*Jamaica Promotions Corporation (JAMPRO)*

Paul Tai
*Nunes, Scholefield DeLeon & Co*

Lorraine Thomas
*LTN Logistics International Co. Ltd.*

Denzil Thorpe
*Ministry of Labour and Social Security*

Junior Waugh
*Jamaica Society of Customs Brokers*

Patricka Wiggan Chambers
*Jamaica Customs Department*

Donovan Wignal
*Mairtrans International Logistics Ltd.*

Sophia Williams
*National Land Agency*

Maia Wilson
*LEX Caribbean*

Angelean Young-Daley
*Jamaica Public Service Company Limited*

## JAPAN

*Ernst & Young*

*PwC Japan*

*Tokyo Electric Power Company Inc.*

Miho Arimura
*Hatasawa & Wakai Law Firm*

Marie Eguchi
*Atsumi & Sakai*

Toyoki Emoto
*Atsumi & Sakai*

Tatsuya Fukui
*Atsumi & Sakai*

Shinnosuke Fukuoka
*Nishimura & Asahi*

Beppu Fumiya
*Nishimura & Asahi*

Mika Haga
*Davis & Takahashi*

Tamotsu Hatasawa
*Hatasawa & Wakai Law Firm*

Akiko Hiraoka
*Atsumi & Sakai*

Takashi Hirose
*Oh-Ebashi LPC & Partners*

Hiroyasu Horimoto
*City-Yuwa Partners*

Katsuo Hosoyama
*Azabu Aiwa & Co.*

Yuko Ishida
*Nishimura & Asahi*

Michiya Iwasaki
*Atsumi & Sakai*

Tomomi Kagawa

Yosuke Kanegae
*Oh-Ebashi LPC & Partners*

Chie Kasahara
*Atsumi & Sakai*

Takahiro Kato
*Nishimura & Asahi*

Kohei Kawamura
*Nishimura & Asahi*

Yasuyuki Kuribayashi
*City-Yuwa Partners*

Yukie Kurosawa
*O'Melveny & Myers LLP*

Yoji Maeda
*O'Melveny & Myers LLP*

Nobuaki Matsuoka
*Osaka International Law Offices*

Toshio Miyatake
*Adachi, Henderson, Miyatake & Fujita*

Michihiro Mori
*Nishimura & Asahi*

Masahiro Murashima
*Kitahama Partners*

Hirosato Nabika
*City-Yuwa Partners*

Masahiro Nakatsukasa
*Chuo Sogo Law Office, P.C.*

Hiroyuki Ota
*Chuo Sogo Law Office, P.C.*

Takashi Saito
*City-Yuwa Partners*

Yuka Sakai
*City-Yuwa Partners*

Sara Sandford
*Garvey Schubert Barer Law Firm*

Rieko Sasaki
*Atsumi & Sakai*

Takefumi Sato
*Anderson Mori & Tomotsune*

Tetsuro Sato
*Baker & McKenzie*

Yoshihito Shibata
*Bingham McCutchen Murase, Sakai & Mimura Foreign Law Joint Enterprise*

Tomoko Shimomukai
*Nishimura & Asahi*

Hiroaki Shinomiya
*Davis & Takahashi*

Hisako Shiotani
*Atsumi & Sakai*

Kentaro Shoji
*O'Melveny & Myers LLP*

Sachiko Sugawara
*Atsumi & Sakai*

Yuri Suzuki
*Atsumi & Sakai*

Hiroaki Takahashi
*Davis & Takahashi*

Mikio Tasaka
*Nittsu Research Institute and Consulting, Inc.*

Atsushi Tempaku
*Nippon Express Co., Ltd.*

Junichi Tobimatsu
*Mori Hamada & Matsumoto*

Yoshito Tsuji
*Obayashi Corporation*

Yoshiki Tsurumaki
*Atsumi & Sakai*

Kenji Utsumi
*Nagashima Ohno & Tsunematsu*

Jun Yamada
*Anderson Mori & Tomotsune*

Michi Yamagami
*Anderson Mori & Tomotsune*

Akio Yamamoto
*Kajima Corporation*

Yusuke Yukawa
*Nishimura & Asahi*

**JORDAN**

*Ernst & Young*

*Social Security Corporation*

Hassan Abdullah
*The Jordanian Electric Power Co. Ltd. (JEPCO)*

Mazen Abu Alghanam

Hayja'a Abu AlHayja'a
*Hayja'a*

Nayef Abu Alim
*Premier Law Firm LLP*

Deema Abu Zulaikha
*Hayja'a*

Ibrahim Abunameh
*Abunameh & Partners Law Firm*

Maha Al Abdallat
*Central Bank of Jordan*

Omar Al Sawadha
*Hammouri & Partners*

Mohammad Al Smadi
*International Business Legal Associates*

Eman M. Al-Dabbas
*International Business Legal Associates*

Razan Al-Hosban
*Ali Sharif Zu'bi, Advocates & Legal Consultants, member of Lex Mundi*

Sabri S. Al-Khassib
*Amman Chamber of Commerce*

Ala Al-Louzi
*Hammouri & Partners*

Mohammad Al-Said
*Nathan Associates*

Omar Aljazy
*Aljazy & Co. Advocates & Legal Consultants*

Khaled Asfour
*Ali Sharif Zu'bi, Advocates & Legal Consultants, member of Lex Mundi*

Michael T. Dabit
*Michael T. Dabit & Associates*

Richard Davidsen
*Aqaba Container Terminal Co. (ACT)*

Anwar Elliyan
*The Jordanian Electric Power Co. Ltd. (JEPCO)*

Tariq Hammouri
*Hammouri & Partners*

Lubna Hawamdeh
*Ali Sharif Zu'bi, Advocates & Legal Consultants, member of Lex Mundi*

George Hazboun
*Hazboun & Co. for International Legal Business Consultations*

Reem Hazboun
*Hazboun & Co. for International Legal Business Consultations*

Tayseer Ismail
*East Echo Co.*

Emad Karkar
*PwC Jordan*

Basel Kawar
*Kawar Transport & Transit Kargo*

Hussein Kofahy
*Central Bank of Jordan*

Rasha Laswi
*Zalloum & Laswi Law Firm*

Firas Malhas
*International Business Legal Associates*

Daniah Murad
*Ali Sharif Zu'bi, Advocates & Legal Consultants, member of Lex Mundi*

Nizar Musleh
*Hazboun & Co. for International Legal Business Consultations*

Omar B. Naim
*National Construction Company*

Sami Naimat
*Khalifeh & Partners Lawyers*

Laith Nasrawin
*Aljazy & Co. Advocates & Legal Consultants*

Khaldoun Nazer
*Khalifeh & Partners Lawyers*

Main Nsair
*Nsair & Partners - Lawyers*

Mutasem Nsair
*Nsair & Partners - Lawyers*

Osama Y. Sabbagh
*The Jordanian Electric Power Co. Ltd. (JEPCO)*

Fouad Shaban
*Ali Sharif Zu'bi, Advocates & Legal Consultants, member of Lex Mundi*

Stephan Stephan
*PwC Jordan*

Mohammed Tarawneh

Mahmoud Wafa

Azzam Zalloum
*Zalloum & Laswi Law Firm*

Salma Zibdeh
*Ali Sharif Zu'bi, Advocates & Legal Consultants, member of Lex Mundi*

Malek Zreiqat
*Ali Sharif Zu'bi, Advocates & Legal Consultants, member of Lex Mundi*

**KAZAKHSTAN**

Yerkin Abdrakhmanov
*PwC Kazakhstan*

Askar Abubakirov
*Aequitas Law Firm*

Bulat Ahmetov
*Arhico Arhstudio*

Zulfiya Akchurina
*Grata Law Firm*

Aktan Akhmetov
*First Credit Bureau*

Botagoz Aliakbarova
*Olympex Advisers*

Zhabelov Alim
*Panalpina World Transport LLP*

Uzakbay Aytzhanov
*Atameken Holding*

Nailya Azizova
*Panalpina World Transport LLP*

Rahat Baisuanov
*Signum Law Firm*

Amir Begdesenov
*Sayat Zholshy & Partners*

Jypar Beishenalieva
*Michael Wilson & Partners Ltd.*

Joel Benjamin
*SNR Denton Kazakhstan Limited*

Arman Berdalin
*Sayat Zholshy & Partners*

Aidyn Bikebayev
*Sayat Zholshy & Partners*

Richard Bregonje
*PwC Kazakhstan*

Yelena Bychkova
*Aequitas Law Firm*

Irina Chen
*M&M Logistics*

Shaimerden Chikanayev
*Grata Law Firm*

Richard Chudzynski
*Michael Wilson & Partners Ltd.*

Oksana Danilova
*RBS*

Aida Daulenova
*BMF Group LLP*

Dina Daumova
*Grata Law Firm*

Minyailova Dinara
*Aricargo*

Ardak Dyussembayeva
*Aequitas Law Firm*

Indira Eleusizova
*Sayat Zholshy & Partners*

Vladimir P. Furman
*BMF Group LLP*

Sevil Gassanova
*Norton Rose*

Shestakov Gennady
*Kazakhstan Logistics Service*

Alexandr Giros
*Aristan Project Management Group (APMG)*

Evgeniy Gonov
*I.P. Petrova*

Ali Imanalin
*Grata Law Firm*

Semion Issyk
*Aequitas Law Firm*

Kamil Jambakiyev
*Norton Rose*

Thomas Johnson
*SNR Denton Kazakhstan Limited*

Mariyash Kabikenova
*Rehabilitation Manager*

Elena Kaeva
*PwC Kazakhstan*

Marina Kahiani
*Grata Law Firm*

Alibek Kaliyev
*Aristan Project Management Group (APMG)*

Andrey Kim
*Kuehne & Nagel Kazakhstan*

Marina Kolesnikova
*Grata Law Firm*

Yerbol Konarbayev
*SNR Denton Kazakhstan Limited*

Askar Konysbayev
*Grata Law Firm*

Anna Kravchenko
*Grata Law Firm*

Natalya Kulagina
*M&M Logistics*

Alina Larina
*M&M Logistics*

Irina Latipova
*Marka Audit ACF LLP*

Madina Lavrenova
*Signum Law Firm*

Aigerim Malikova
*PwC Kazakhstan*

Vsevolod Markov
*BMF Group LLP*

Yessen Massalin
*Olympex Advisers*

Bolat Miyatov
*Grata Law Firm*

Saida Moldasheva
*Cruz Logistics*

Toregali Muhamedzhanov
*Rehabilitation Manager*

Abdul-Gaziz Mukashev
*BDO*

Assel Mukhambekova
*Grata Law Firm*

Elena Murzabekova
*Kuehne & Nagel Kazakhstan*

Daniyar Mussakhan
*Norton Rose*

Assel Mussina
*SNR Denton Kazakhstan Limited*

Abylkhair Nakipov
*Signum Law Firm*

Nazira Nurbayeva
*PwC Kazakhstan*

Berik Nurgaziyev
*Aristan Project Management Group (APMG)*

Saktagana Nurmahanov
*Rehabilitation Manager*

Zhanar Ordabayeva
*BMF Group LLP*

Yuliya V. Petrenko
*BMF Group LLP*

Nikolay Popov
*BDO*

Elvis Roberts
*Cruz Logistics*

Olga Salimova
*ORIS Law Firm*

Talgat Sariev
*Signum Law Firm*

Kuanysh Sarsenbayev
*Olympex Advisers*

Ruslan Serkebulanov
*Rehabilitation Manager*

Alzhan Stamkulov
*Synergy Partners Law Firm*

Nurzhan Stamkulov
*Synergy Partners Law Firm*

Timur Suleymanov
*Grata Law Firm*

Bolatkhan Turtbajev
*Alatau Zharyk*

Amir Tussupkhanov
*ORIS Law Firm*

Alida Tuyebekova
*Michael Wilson & Partners Ltd.*

Shakhrukh Usmanov
*Grata Law Firm*

Zhaniya Ussen
*Assistance, LLC Law Firm*

Yekaterina V. Kim
*Michael Wilson & Partners Ltd.*

Marla Valdez
*SNR Denton Kazakhstan Limited*

Vitaliy Vodolazkin
*Sayat Zholshy & Partners*

Arlan Yerzhanov
*Grata Law Firm*

Yerzhan Yessimkhanov
*Grata Law Firm*

Marina Yudina
*Panalpina World Transport LLP*

Kogarshin Zhamikanova
*Rehabilitation Manager*

Adeliya Zhunussova
*SNR Denton Kazakhstan Limited*

Sofiya Zhylkaidarova
*Signum Law Firm*

Anton Zinoviev
*Booz Allen Hamilton*

**KENYA**

*Metropol Corporation Ltd.*

Oliver Fowler
*Kaplan & Stratton*

Peter Gachuhi
*Kaplan & Stratton*

Edmond Gichuru
*Post Bank*

William Ikutha Maema
*Iseme, Kamau & Maema Advocates*

Shellomith Irungu
*Anjarwalla & Khanna Advocates*

Milly Jalega
*Iseme, Kamau & Maema Advocates*

Benson Kamau
*PwC Kenya*

Hamish Keith
*Daly & Figgis Advocates*

Peter Kiara
*Architect*

Jinaro Kibet
*Ochieng, Onyango, Kibet & Ohaga*

Timothy Kiman
*Siginon Freight Ltd.*

Morris Kimuli
*B.M. Musau & Co. Advocates*

Meshack T. Kipturgo
*Siginon Freight Ltd.*

Owen Koimburi
KOKA KOIMBURI & CO., MEMBER OF MAZARS

David Lekerai
ISEME, KAMAU & MAEMA ADVOCATES

Victor Majani
CROWE HORWATH EA, MEMBER
CROWE HORWATH INTERNATIONAL

Bakari Mangale
NATIONAL ENVIRONMENT
MANAGEMENT AUTHORITY

James Mburu Kamau
ISEME, KAMAU & MAEMA ADVOCATES

Mansoor A. Mohamed
RUMAN SHIP CONTRACTORS LIMITED

Bernard Muange
ANJARWALLA & KHANNA ADVOCATES

John Muoria
WARUHIU K'OWADE & NG'ANG'A
ADVOCATES

Murigu Murithi
ARCS AFRICA

Benjamin Musau
B.M. MUSAU & CO. ADVOCATES

Wachira Ndege
CREDIT REFERENCE BUREAU AFRICA
LTD.

Mbage Ng'ang'a
WARUHIU K'OWADE & NG'ANG'A
ADVOCATES

Joseph Ng'ang'ira
DALY & FIGGIS ADVOCATES

Killian Ngala
MEDITERRANEAN SHIPPING COMPANY
(MSC), OCEANFREIGHT (E.A.) LTD.

James Ngomeli
THE KENYA POWER AND LIGHTING
COMPANY LTD.

Kenneth Njuguna
PwC KENYA

Conrad Nyukuri
CHUNGA ASSOCIATES

Denis Augustine Onyango
FRONTIER DESIGNS

Cephas Osoro
CROWE HORWATH EA, MEMBER
CROWE HORWATH INTERNATIONAL

Prakash
MASTER POWER SYSTEMS LTD.

Don Priestman
THE KENYA POWER AND LIGHTING
COMPANY LTD.

Sonal Sejpal
ANJARWALLA & KHANNA ADVOCATES

Rajesh Shah
PwC KENYA

Deepen Shah
WALKER KONTOS ADVOCATES

David Tanki
LAN-X AFRICA LTD.

Joseph Taracha
CENTRAL BANK OF KENYA

Harpreet Ubhi
DALY & FIGGIS ADVOCATES

Peter Wahome
PwC KENYA

Nicholas Wambua
B.M. MUSAU & CO. ADVOCATES

Angela Waweru
KAPLAN & STRATTON

## KIRIBATI

Kibae Akaaka
MINISTRY OF FINANCE

Neiran Areta
MINISTRY OF COMMERCE, INDUSTRY
AND COOPERATIVES

Kenneth Barden
ATTORNEY-AT-LAW

Rengaua Bauro
MINISTRY OF FINANCE

Taake Cama
MINISTRY OF FINANCE

Kiata Tebau Kabure
KK & SONS

Seri Kautuntamoa
REGISTRY OF COMPANIES

Paul McLaughlin
CA'BELLA BETIO CONSTRUCTION

Moaniti Teuea
JOYCE SHIPPING LINE

Eliza Tokataake
BETIO TOWN COUNCIL

Isikeli Tuituku
ANZ BANK (KIRIBATI) LTD.

## KOREA, REP.

Won-Mo Ahn
AHN & CHANG

Jong-Hyun Baek
JEIL BROKER

Sang Mi Baek
SHIN & KIM

Jennifer Min-Sook Chae
KOREA CREDIT BUREAU

Kyoung Soo Chang
SHIN & KIM

Han-Jun Chon
SAMIL PRICEWATERHOUSECOOPERS

Eui Jong Chung
BAE, KIM & LEE LLC

Seok Jong Chung
SUPREME COURT OF KOREA

Jong Ki Hong
HWANG MOK PARK P.C.

C.W. Hyun
KIM & CHANG

James I.S. Jeon
SOJONG PARTNERS

Goo-Chun Jeong
KOREA CUSTOMS SERVICE

Jeong Hwa Jeong
SHIN & KIM

Hwan-Chul Jeung
SAMIL PRICEWATERHOUSECOOPERS

Bo Moon Jung
KIM & CHANG

Sang Wook Kang
KOREAN ELECTRICAL CONTRACTORS
ASSOCIATION

Young-Ju Kang
SOJONG PARTNERS

Byung-Tae Kim
SHIN & KIM

Eun-Kyung Kim
KOREA CREDIT BUREAU

Hyo-Sang Kim
KIM & CHANG

Ji Yeoun Kim
HWANG MOK PARK P.C.

Jinsoon Kim
AGL CO., LTD.

Jung-In Kim
KOREA CREDIT BUREAU

Kwang Soo Kim
WOOSUN ELECTRIC COMPANY LTD.

Stephan Kim
SOJONG PARTNERS

Sung Won (David) Kim
HANARO TNS

Wan-Seok Kim
SAMIL PRICEWATERHOUSECOOPERS

Wonhyung Kim
YOON & YANG LLC

Yoon Young Kim
HWANG MOK PARK P.C.

Joong Hoon Kwak
LEE & KO

Ji-Ha Kwon
KOREA CREDIT BUREAU

Hee-Ryoung Lee
SOJONG PARTNERS

Hongyou Lee
PANALPINA IAF LTD.

Hye Jeong Lee
AHNSE LAW OFFICES

Jin-Young Lee
SAMIL PRICEWATERHOUSECOOPERS

Jong Ho Lee
SOJONG PARTNERS

Kwon H. Lee
HANJIN SHIPPING CO. LTD.

Kyu Wha Lee
LEE & KO

Sang-don Lee
SHIN & KIM

Sang-Woon Lee
KOREA CUSTOMS SERVICE

Seung Yoon Lee
KIM & CHANG

Sung Whan Lee
AHNSE LAW OFFICES

Jul-Ki Lim
KOREA CREDIT BUREAU

Chul-Gue Maeng
KOREA CUSTOMS SERVICE

Soogeun Oh
EWHA WOMANS UNIVERSITY

Yon-Kyun Oh
KIM & CHANG

Joo Seok Paik
SOJONG PARTNERS

Sang Il Park
HWANG MOK PARK P.C.

Soo-Hwan Park
SAMIL PRICEWATERHOUSECOOPERS

Yong Seok Park
SHIN & KIM

Jeong Seo
KIM & CHANG

Mi-Jin Shin
KIM & CHANG

Philippe Shin
SHIN & KIM

Bong Woo Song
HANJIN SHIPPING CO. LTD.

Jiwon Suh
MINISTRY OF STRATEGY AND FINANCE

Kiwon Suh
CHEON JI ACCOUNTING CORPORATION
- MEMBER OF RUSSELL BEDFORD
INTERNATIONAL

Huh Uoung-uhk
KEPCO ECONOMY MANAGEMENT
RESEARCH INSTITUTE (KEMRI)

Ju-Hyun Yoo
SHIN & KIM

## KOSOVO

KOSOVO ENERGY CORPORATION J.S.C.

TAX ADMINISTRATION OF KOSOVO

USAID SYSTEMS FOR ENFORCING
AGREEMENTS AND DECISIONS (SEAD)
PROGRAM

Serton Ajeti
IPAK

Albert Avdiu
KOSOVO JUDICIAL COUNCIL
SECRETARIAT

Agon Baruti
KOMTEL PROJECT ENGINEERING

Arsim Behrami
ALBERT ISLAMI & PARTNERS

Ardiana Bunjaku
SOCIETY OF CERTIFIED ACCOUNTANTS
AND AUDITORS OF KOSOVO (SCAAK)

Shyqiri Bytyqi
VALA CONSULTING

Muzafer Çaka
KOSOVO CADASTRAL AGENCY

Burim Cena
BDO KOSOVA LLC

Fadil Dalipi
VNV STUDIO INC.

Faton Demaj
SHEGA PRO

Amir Dërmala
BDO KOSOVA LLC

Agron S. Dida
KOMTEL PROJECT ENGINEERING

Atdhe Dika
KALO & ASSOCIATES

Muhamed Disha
IPAK

Sokol Elmazaj
BOGA & ASSOCIATES TIRANA

Mirjeta Emini
BOGA & ASSOCIATES

Rezak Fetai

Lorena Gega
PwC ALBANIA

Fazli Gjonbalaj
LIGJI LAW FIRM

Maliq Gjyshinca
INTEREUROPA KOSOVA LLC

Valon Hasani
INTERLEX ASSOCIATES LLC

Ahmet Hasolli
KALO & ASSOCIATES

Rrahim Hoxha
ISARS

Naim Huruglica
KOSOVO CUSTOMS

Virtyt Ibrahimaga
LAW FIRM IBRAHIMAGA OSAMNI
TIGANI

Albert Islami
ALBERT ISLAMI & PARTNERS

Besarta Kllokoqi
BOGA & ASSOCIATES

Vegim Kraja
KALO & ASSOCIATES

Naim Krasniqi
LIGJI LAW FIRM

Sabina Lalaj
BOGA & ASSOCIATES TIRANA

Valdrin Lluka
IPAK

Florim Maxharraj
CENTRAL BANK OF THE REPUBLIC OF
KOSOVO

Murat Meha
KOSOVO CADASTRAL AGENCY

Fitore Mekaj
BOGA & ASSOCIATES

Bajram Morina

Fitim Mucaj
4M GROUP LTD.

Ilir Murseli
MURSELI ARCHITECTS & PARTNERS

Lekë Musa
BU & PARTNERS

Arben Mustafa
INTEREUROPA KOSOVA LLC

Bernard Nikaj
MINISTRY OF TRADE AND INDUSTRY

Gazmend Nushi
KALO & ASSOCIATES

Valdet Osmani
ARCHITECT ASSOCIATION OF KOSOVO

Dastid Pallaska
PALLASKA & ASSOCIATES

Gazmend Pallaska
PALLASKA & ASSOCIATES

Loreta Peci
PwC ALBANIA

Denis Pitarka
KOSOVO CADASTRAL AGENCY

Bujar Prestreshi
USAID KOSOVO PRIVATE ENTERPRISE
PROGRAM (KPEP)

Ilaz Ramajli
RAMAJLI & PARTNERS CO.

Vigan Rogova
ETHEM ROGOVA LAW FIRM

Ariana Rozhaja
VALA CONSULTING

Valentina Salihu
VALA CONSULTING

Suzana Sejdiu
COMMERCIAL COURT KOSOVO

Shiqeri Spahiu
MUNICIPALITY OF PRISHTINA

Dardan Sylaj
KOSOVA CHAMBER OF COMMERCE

Elez Sylaj
KOSOVA CHAMBER OF COMMERCE

Flakron Sylejmani
LAW FIRM IBRAHIMAGA OSAMNI
TIGANI

Bardha Tahiri
ALBERT ISLAMI & PARTNERS

Kreshnik Thaqi
IPAK

Anita Tigani
LAW FIRM IBRAHIMAGA OSAMNI
TIGANI

Paul Tobin
PwC BULGARIA

Valon Ukaj
CIMAROSTI

Gëzim Xharavina
ARCHITECTURAL, DESIGN AND
ENGINEERING

Petrit Zeka
BU & PARTNERS

Ruzhdi Zenelaj
PwC

Shaha Zylfiu
CENTRAL BANK OF THE REPUBLIC OF
KOSOVO

## KUWAIT

Labeed Abdal
THE LAW FIRM OF LABEED ABDAL

Hossam Abduel Fetouh

Lina A.K. Adlouni
KIPCO ASSET MANAGEMENT
COMPANY K.S.C

Hussein Mohammed Hassan
Ahmed
ABDULLAH KH. AL-AYOUB &
ASSOCIATES, MEMBER OF LEX MUNDI

Abdullah Musfir Al Hayyan
KUWAIT UNIVERSITY

Homoud Al Mutawa
SMP LAW FIRM

Faten Al Naqeeb
*ALI & PARTNERS*

Faisal Al Sarraf
*SMP LAW FIRM*

Abdullah Al-Ayoub
*ABDULLAH KH. AL-AYOUB & ASSOCIATES, member of LEX MUNDI*

Omar Hamad Yousuf Al-Essa
*THE LAW OFFICE OF AL-ESSA & PARTNERS*

Nada F. A. Al-Fahad
*GEC DAR*

Mishari M. Al-Ghazali
*THE LAW OFFICES OF MISHARI AL-GHAZALI*

Aiman Alaraj
*KEO INTERNATIONAL CONSULTANTS*

Reema Ali
*ALI & PARTNERS*

Akusa Batwala
*ASAR – AL RUWAYEH & PARTNERS*

Abdullah Bin Ali
*PACKAGING AND PLASTIC INDUSTRIES CO. (KSC)*

Nada Bourahmah
*THE LAW OFFICES OF MISHARI AL-GHAZALI*

Fouad Douglas
*PRICEWATERHOUSECOOPERS AL-SHATTI & CO.*

Mohammed Eissa
*ASAR – AL RUWAYEH & PARTNERS*

Charbel Fadel
*ASAR – AL RUWAYEH & PARTNERS*

Sam Habbas
*ASAR – AL RUWAYEH & PARTNERS*

Mazen A. Khoursheed
*PACKAGING AND PLASTIC INDUSTRIES CO. (KSC)*

Chirine Krayem Moujaes
*THE LAW OFFICES OF MISHARI AL-GHAZALI*

Dany Labaky
*THE LAW OFFICE OF AL-ESSA & PARTNERS*

Mohammed Maamoun
*PACKAGING AND PLASTIC INDUSTRIES CO. (KSC)*

Medhat Mubarak
*THE LAW OFFICES OF MISHARI AL-GHAZALI*

Sasidhara Panicker
*SMP LAW FIRM*

Hanaa Razzouqi
*CREDIT INFORMATION NETWORK*

Abdul Qayyum Saeed
*GHF LAWYERS*

Ibrahim Sattout
*ASAR – AL RUWAYEH & PARTNERS*

Sherif Shawki
*PRICEWATERHOUSECOOPERS AL-SHATTI & CO.*

Prateek Shete
*ABDULLAH KH. AL-AYOUB & ASSOCIATES, member of LEX MUNDI*

### KYRGYZ REPUBLIC

Alexander Ahn
*KALIKOVA & ASSOCIATES LAW FIRM*

Shuhrat Akhmatakhunov
*KALIKOVA & ASSOCIATES LAW FIRM*

Gulnara Akhmatova
*INTERNATIONAL BUSINESS COUNCIL*

Niyazbek Aldashev
*LORENZ INTERNATIONAL LAW FIRM*

Ruslan Alybayev
*BIOR*

Rahman Asylbekov
*OAO KYRGYZGIPROSTROY*

Kerim Begaliev
*COLIBRI LAW FIRM*

Bakytbek Djusupbekov
*DEPARTMENT OF CADASTRE AND REGISTRATION OF RIGHTS ON IMMOVABLE PROPERTY*

Samara Dumanaeva
*LORENZ INTERNATIONAL LAW FIRM*

Akjoltoi Elebesova
*CREDIT INFORMATION BUREAU ISHENIM*

Leyla Gulieva
*LORENZ INTERNATIONAL LAW FIRM*

Gribkova Irina
*TRANSSYSTEM LTD.*

Nurbek Ismankulov
*M&M TRANSPORT LOGISTIC SERVICES*

Amanbek Kebekov
*DEPARTMENT OF CADASTRE AND REGISTRATION OF RIGHTS ON IMMOVABLE PROPERTY*

Aleksandr Klishevich
*ARHSTROYPROEKT*

Svetlana Lebedeva
*LORENZ INTERNATIONAL LAW FIRM*

Marina Lim
*KALIKOVA & ASSOCIATES LAW FIRM*

Asel Momoshova
*KALIKOVA & ASSOCIATES LAW FIRM*

Taalay Choroevich Murzakulov
*COLISEUM*

Aigul Myrzabekova
*LORENZ INTERNATIONAL LAW FIRM*

Almas Nakipov
*PwC KAZAKHSTAN*

Dmitry No
*PARTNER LAW FIRM*

Karlygash Ospankulova
*KALIKOVA & ASSOCIATES LAW FIRM*

Kubanychbek Sagaliev
*PwC KAZAKHSTAN*

Erkin Sakiev

Kanat Seidaliev
*COLIBRI LAW FIRM*

Tatyana Shapovalova

Elvira Sharshekeeva
*COLIBRI LAW FIRM*

Saken Shayakhmetov
*PwC KAZAKHSTAN*

Anna Shirshova
*CUSTOMS CARGO SERVICE LTD.*

Mirgul Smanalieva
*PARTNER LAW FIRM*

Ruslan Sulaimanov
*KALIKOVA & ASSOCIATES LAW FIRM*

Ulan Tilenbaev
*KALIKOVA & ASSOCIATES LAW FIRM*

Daniyar Ubyshev
*PARTNER LAW FIRM*

Gulnara Uskenbaeva
*AUDIT PLUS*

Azim Usmanov
*COLIBRI LAW FIRM*

Ali Ramazanovich Vodyanov
*ELECTROSILA*

### LAO PDR

Gnoykham Aphayalath

John Biddle
*LS HORIZON LIMITED (LAO)*

Xaynari Chanthala
*LS HORIZON LIMITED (LAO)*

Sithong Chanthasouk

Lasonexay Chanthavong
*DFDL MEKONG LAW GROUP*

Chatchai Chanyuttasart
*HUNG HUANG (LAO) LOGISTICS CO.,LTD.*

Brennan Coleman
*DFDL MEKONG LAW GROUP*

Aristotle David
*DFDL MEKONG LAW GROUP*

William D. Greenlee Jr.
*DFDL MEKONG LAW GROUP*

Duangkamol Ingkapattanakul
*DFDL MEKONG LAW GROUP*

Litsamy Latsavong

Varavudh Meesaiyati
*PRICEWATERHOUSECOOPERS (LAO) LTD.*

Phanthasak Mingnakhone

Somlack Nhoybouakong
*LAO FREIGHT FORWARDER CO. LTD.*

Vongphacnanh Onepaseuth
*DFDL MEKONG LAW GROUP*

Somphone Phasavath
*LAO FREIGHT FORWARDER CO. LTD.*

Thavorn Rujivanarom
*PwC THAILAND*

Sivath Sengdouangchanh
*R&T KHOUN MUANG LAO CO.,LTD.*

Senesakoune Sihanouvong
*DFDL MEKONG LAW GROUP*

Valloph Sisopha

Phonexay Southiphong
*DESIGN GROUP CO LTD.*

### LATVIA

*COLLIERS INTERNATIONAL*

Ilze Abika
*SKUDRA & UDRIS LAW OFFICES*

Martins Aljens
*RAIDLA LEJINS & NORCOUS*

Svetlana Beitane
*ESTMA LTD.*

Eva Berlaus
*SORAINEN*

Jevgenija Brike
*STATE SOCIAL INSURANCE AGENCY*

Kristine Bumbure
*PwC LATVIA*

Andis Burkevics
*SORAINEN*

Andis Čonka
*LATVIJAS BANKA*

Ingrida Dimina
*PwC LATVIA*

Valters Diure
*LAWIN*

Zane Džule
*ATTORNEYS AT LAW BORENIUS*

Baiba Felsberga
*STATE SOCIAL INSURANCE AGENCY*

Valters Gencs
*GENCS VALTERS LAW FIRM*

Andris Ignatenko
*ESTMA LTD.*

Janis Irbe
*LATVENERGO AS, SADALES TIKLS*

Zinta Jansons
*LAWIN*

Andris Jekabsons
*LEXTAL*

Sandis Jermuts
*PUBLIC UTILITIES COMMISSION LATVIA*

Julija Jerneva
*VARUL*

Aris Kakstans
*EVERSHEDS BITĀNS*

Inese Kalvane
*STATE EMPLOYMENT AGENCY*

Irina Kostina
*LAWIN*

Gunda Leite
*GENCS VALTERS LAW FIRM*

Dainis Leons
*SADALES TĪKLS AS*

Alisa Leškoviča
*SORAINEN*

Alla Lichkovska
*LATVIAN INSOLVENCY ADMINISTRATION*

Indrikis Liepa
*ATTORNEYS AT LAW BORENIUS*

Irina Olevska
*ATTORNEYS AT LAW BORENIUS*

Baiba Orbidane
*LAWIN*

Zane Paeglite
*SORAINEN*

Kristine Parsonse
*ECB SIA - correspondent of RUSSELL BEDFORD INTERNATIONAL*

Galina Pitulina
*ECB SIA - correspondent of RUSSELL BEDFORD INTERNATIONAL*

Baiba Plaude
*LAW OFFICES BLUEGER & PLAUDE*

Katrine Plavina
*VARUL*

Lāsma Rugāte
*SORAINEN*

Jevgenijs Salims
*RAIDLA LEJINS & NORCOUS*

Anita Sondore
*GENCS VALTERS LAW FIRM*

Mihails Špika
*JSC DZINTARS*

Sarmis Spilbergs
*LAWIN*

Zane Štālberga - Markvarte
*MARKVARTE LEXCHANGE LAW OFFICE*

Girts Strazdins
*VARUL*

Ruta Teresko
*AZ SERVICE LTD.*

Edgars Timpa
*STATE LABOUR INSPECTORATE*

Maija Tipaine
*RAIDLA LEJINS & NORCOUS*

Ziedonis Udris
*SKUDRA & UDRIS LAW OFFICES*

Maris Vainovskis
*EVERSHEDS BITĀNS*

Agate Ziverte
*PwC LATVIA*

Daiga Zivtina
*LAWIN*

### LEBANON

*ELECTRICITÉ DU LIBAN*

*KORDAHI ESTABLISHMENT COMPANY*

Hanan Abboud
*PwC LEBANON*

Nadim Abboud
*LAW OFFICE OF A. ABBOUD & ASSOCIATES*

Suzane AbiKhalil
*PwC LEBANON*

Wassim Abou Nader
*MENA CITY LAWYERS*

Wadih Abou Nasr
*PwC LEBANON*

Samir Ali Ahmad
*AA ARCHITECTS*

Karen Baroud
*PwC LEBANON*

Jean Baroudi
*BAROUDI & ASSOCIATES*

Tarek Baz
*HYAM G. MALLAT LAW FIRM*

Katia Bou Assi
*MOGHAIZEL LAW OFFICE*

Nayla Chemaly
*MENA CITY LAWYERS*

Najib Choucair
*CENTRAL BANK OF LEBANON*

Alice Choueiri
*MENA CITY LAWYERS*

Sanaa Daakour
*MENA CITY LAWYERS*

Aline Dantziguian
*CHAMBER OF COMMERCE, INDUSTRY & AGRICULTURE OF BEIRUT*

Michel Doueihy
*BADRI AND SALIM EL MEOUCHI LAW FIRM, member of INTERLEGES*

Hanadi El Hajj
*MENA CITY LAWYERS*

Sarah Fakhry
*BADRI AND SALIM EL MEOUCHI LAW FIRM, member of INTERLEGES*

Hadi Fathallah
*ESCO FATHALLAH & CO.*

Izzat Fathallah
*ESCO FATHALLAH & CO.*

Dania George
*PwC LEBANON*

Abdallah Hayek
*HAYEK GROUP*

Alexa Hechaime
*HECHAIME LAW FIRM*

Wajih Hechaime
*HECHAIME LAW FIRM*

Walid Honein
*BADRI AND SALIM EL MEOUCHI LAW FIRM, member of INTERLEGES*

Dany Issa
*MOGHAIZEL LAW OFFICE*

Fady Jamaleddine
*MENA CITY LAWYERS*

Elie Kachouh
*ELC TRANSPORT SERVICES SAL*

Georges Kadige
*KADIGE & KADIGE LAW FIRM*

Michel Kadige
*KADIGE & KADIGE LAW FIRM*

Lea Kai
*MENA CITY LAWYERS*

Najib Khattar
*KHATTAR ASSOCIATES*

Georges Mallat
*HYAM G. MALLAT LAW FIRM*

Nabil Mallat
*HYAM G. MALLAT LAW FIRM*

Rachad Medawar
*OBEID & MEDAWAR LAW FIRM*

Fadi Moghaizel
*MOGHAIZEL LAW OFFICE*

Mirvat Mostafa
*MENA CITY LAWYERS*

Myriam Moughabghab
*BADRI AND SALIM EL MEOUCHI LAW FIRM, member of INTERLEGES*

Andre Nader
*NADER LAW OFFICE*

Rana Nader
*NADER LAW OFFICE*

Toufic Nehme
*Law Offices of Albert Laham*

Mireille Richa
*Tyan & Zgheib Law Firm*

Jihan Rizk Khattar
*Khattar Associates*

Jihad Rizkallah
*Badri and Salim El Meouchi Law Firm, member of Interleges*

Samir Safa
*Baroudi & Associates*

Joseph Safar
*Hayek Group*

Rached Sarkis
*Consultant*

Antoine Sfeir
*Badri and Salim El Meouchi Law Firm, member of Interleges*

Mona Sfeir
*Hyam G. Mallat Law Firm*

Rami Smayra
*Smayra Law Office*

George Tannous *
*Beirut International Movers*

Bassel Tohme
*MENA City Lawyers*

Nady Tyan
*Tyan & Zgheib Law Firm*

Rania Yazbeck
*Tyan & Zgheib Law Firm*

### LESOTHO

*Archiplan Studio*

*Harley & Morris*

*Registrar-General*

Mark Badenhorst
*PwC South Africa*

Thakane Chimombe
*Naledi Chambers Inc.*

Paul De Chalain
*PwC South Africa*

Fumane Khabo
*Labour Court*

Gerhard Gouws
*NedBank Lesotho Ltd.*

M. Hoohlo
*High Court*

Lebereko Lethobane
*Labour Court Lesotho*

Realeboha Makamane
*High Court*

Tseliso Daniel Makhaphela
*Land Administration Authority*

Thakane Makume
*Lesotho Electricity Company (Pty) Ltd.*

Moeketsi Marumo
*PowerConsult (Pty) Ltd.*

Leoma Matamne
*Molepe Quantity Surveyors*

Kolisang Mochesane Lepholisa
*Du Preez Liebetrau & Co.*

Denis Molyneaux
*Webber Newdigate*

Tseliso Monaphathi
*High Court*

Phillip Mophethe
*Phillips Clearing & Forwarding Agent (Pty) Ltd.*

Molemo Motseki
*Ultimate Solution*

Bulane None
*Ultimate Solution*

Poulo Nono
*The Legal Voice*

Theodore Ntlatlapa
*DNT Architects*

Pulane Ramonene
*NedBank Lesotho Ltd.*

Duduzile Seamatha
*Sheeran & Associates*

Tiisetso Sello-Mafatle
*Sello-Mafatle Attorneys*

Lindiwe Sephomolo
*L. Sephomolo Chambers*

Mooresi Tau Thabane
*Mofolo, Tau - Thabane and Co.*

Phoka Thene

Sehaba Thibeli
*Triangle Freight*

George Thokoa
*Maseru Electro Services Pty Ltd.*

Refiloe Thulo
*K. R. Consultants*

### LIBERIA

*Jafain Consortium*

*Liberia Law Services*

Andrew Anderson
*Gentle Clearing & Forwarding Ltd.*

Gideon Ayi-Owoo
*PwC Ghana*

Khalil Azar
*Beever Company*

Golda A. Bonah
*Sherman & Sherman*

F. Augustus Caesar Jr.
*Caesar Architects, Inc.*

Henry Reed Cooper
*Cooper & Togbah Law Office*

Frank Musah Dean
*Dean & Associates*

Fonsia Donzo
*Central Bank of Liberia*

Christine Sonpon Freeman
*Cooper & Togbah Law Office*

Paul Greene
*Ministry of Finance*

Anthony Henry
*Cuttington University Graduate School*

Cyril Jones
*Jones & Jones*

Mohamedu F. Jones
*Liberian Legal International Inc.*

Abu Kamara
*Ministry of Commerce & Industry*

Monkpeh Karr
*Frontier Logistics*

Samuel T. K. Kortimai
*Cooper & Togbah Law Office*

Samuel F. Kpakio
*Ministry of Public Works*

George Kwatia
*PwC Ghana*

Marie Norman
*City Corporation of Monrovia*

Christiana Osei-Mensah
*PwC Ghana*

Sylvester Rennie
*Cooper & Togbah Law Office*

Kwame L. Richardson
*Odebrecht*

Lasana Sasay
*Ministry of Public Works*

Nancy Seeboe
*National Custom Brokers Association of Liberia*

Amos Siebo
*Ministry of State for Presidential Affairs*

Pierre Valentin Tchol Kaldjob
*PwC Ghana*

Benjamin M. Togbah
*Cooper & Togbah Law Office*

G. Lahaison Waritay
*Ministry of Public Works*

Darcy White
*PwC Ghana*

Melvin Yates
*Compass Inc., Clearing and Forwarding*

### LITHUANIA

*Bank of Lithuania*

Tomas Ambrasas
*Tark Grunte Sutkiene*

Loreta Andziulyte
*Proventuslaw LT*

Dovile Aukstuolyte
*Ecovis Miskinis, Kvainauskas ir partneriai advokatu kontora*

Pavel Balbatunov

Petras Baltusevičius
*DSV Transport UAB*

Donatas Baranauskas
*Vilniaus Miesto 14 - Asis Notaru Biuras*

Šarūnas Basijokas
*Glimstedt*

Vilius Bernatonis
*Tark Grunte Sutkiene*

Renata Beržanskienė
*Sorainen*

Andrius Bogdanovičius
*JSC Creditinfo Lietuva*

Dovile Cepulyte
*Law Firm LAWIN*

Giedre Cerniauske
*Law Firm LAWIN*

Giedre Dailidenaite
*Varul*

Giedre Domkute
*AAA Baltic Service Company -Law firm*

Dalia Foigt-Norvaišienė
*Attorneys at Law BORENIUS*

Rimante Gentvilaite
*Varul*

Yvonne Goldammer
*BNT Heemann Klauberg Krauklis APB*

Simas Gudynas
*Law Firm LAWIN*

Arturas Gutauskas
*Ecovis Miskinis, Kvainauskas ir partneriai advokatu kontora*

Frank Heemann
*BNT Heemann Klauberg Krauklis APB*

Eglė Jankauskaitė
*Glimstedt*

Indrė Jonaitytė
*Law Firm LAWIN*

Ieva Kairytė
*PwC Lithuania*

Povilas Karlonas
*Sorainen*

Inga Karulaityte-Kvainauskiene
*Proventuslaw LT*

Romualdas Kasperavičius
*State Enterprise Centre of Registers*

Jonas Kiauleikis
*Attorneys at Law BORENIUS*

Jurgita Kiškiūnaitė
*Law Firm Zabiela, Zabielaite & Partners*

Kristina Kriščiūnaitė
*PwC Lithuania*

Ronaldas Kubilius
*PwC Lithuania*

Egidijus Kundelis
*PwC Lithuania*

Žilvinas Kvietkus
*Raidla Lejins & Norcous*

Gytis Malinauskas
*Sorainen*

Linas Margevicius
*Legal Bureau of Linas Margevicius*

Rūta Matonienė
*Vilnius City Municipality*

Vaidotas Melynavicius
*AAA Baltic Service Company -Law firm*

Tomas Mieliauskas
*Law Firm Foresta*

Ana Mikuliene
*Proventuslaw LT*

Bronislovas Mikūta
*State Enterprise Centre of Registers*

Jurate Misionyte
*Tark Grunte Sutkiene*

Asta Misiukiene
*Ministry of Economy*

Žygimantas Pacevičius
*Attorneys at Law BORENIUS*

Rytis Paukste
*Law Firm LAWIN*

Algirdas Pekšys
*Sorainen*

Angelija Petrauskienė
*Vilnius City Municipality*

Aidas Petrosius
*State Enterprise Centre of Registers*

Lina Radavičienė
*Law Firm LAWIN*

Justina Rakauskaitė
*Glimstedt*

Lina Ramanauskaite

Marius Rindinas
*Law Firm Zabiela, Zabielaite & Partners*

Andrius Šidlauskas
*Attorneys at Law BORENIUS*

Rimantas Simaitis
*Raidla Lejins & Norcous*

Diana Skripetiene
*State Enterprise Centre of Registers*

Alius Stamkauskas
*UAB Elmonta*

Jonas Stamkauskas
*UAB Elmonta*

Marius Stračkaitis
*Lithuanian Notary Chamber*

Ieva Tarailiene
*State Enterprise Centre of Registers*

Vilija Vaitkutė Pavan
*Law Firm LAWIN*

Darius Zabiela
*Law Firm Zabiela, Zabielaite & Partners*

Audrius Žvybas
*Glimstedt*

### LUXEMBOURG

*Allen & Overy Luxembourg*

*PwC Luxembourg*

*Service de l'Urbanisme Police des Bâtisses*

Sebastien Bos
*OPF Partners*

Eleonora Broman
*Loyens & Loeff*

Guy Castegnaro
*Ius Laboris Luxembourg, CASTEGNARO*

Gérard Eischen
*Chamber of Commerce of the Grand-Duchy of Luxembourg*

Annie Elfassi
*Loyens & Loeff*

Ambroise Foerster
*Loyens & Loeff*

Peggy Goossens
*Pierre Thielen Avocats*

Alain Grosjean
*Bonn & Schmitt*

Vincent Hieff
*Chamber of Commerce of the Grand-Duchy of Luxembourg*

Véronique Hoffeld
*Loyens & Loeff*

Paul Hoffmann
*Creos Luxembourg S.A.*

Christian Jungers
*Kleyr Grasso Associes*

Tom Loesch
*Etude Loesch*

Nathalie Mangen
*Bonn & Schmitt*

Marc Meyer
*Creos Luxembourg S.A.*

Marco Peters
*Creos Luxembourg S.A.*

Judith Raijmakers
*Loyens & Loeff*

Sandra Rapp
*Kleyr Grasso Associes*

Jean-Luc Schaus
*Pierre Thielen Avocats*

Roger Schintgen
*Paul Wurth S.A. Société anonyme*

Alex Schmitt
*Bonn & Schmitt*

Danielle Schmit
*Creos Luxembourg S.A.*

Alessandro Sorcinelli
*Linklaters*

### MACEDONIA, FYR

Natasa Andrevska
*National Bank of the Republic of Macedonia*

Zlatko Antevski
*Lawyers Antevski*

Aleksandra Arsoska
*IKRP Rokas & Partners*

Rubin Atanasoski
*Timelproject Engineering*

Benita Beleshkova
*IKRP Rokas & Partners*

Dragan Blažev
*Timelproject Engineering*

Dejan Bogdanovski
*Republic of Macedonia, Municipality of Ilinden*

Slavica Bogoeva
*Macedonian Credit Bureau AD Skopje*

Viktor Bogorojceski
*Stojkoska Attorney at law*

Ema Cubrinovska
*Energo Dizajn*

Ljupco Cubrinovski
*Energo Dizajn*

Andrej Dameski
*PwC Macedonia*

Julijana Dimitrievska
*Republic of Macedonia, Municipality of Ilinden*

Mile Doldurov
*Stojkoska Attorney at Law*

Ljupco Georgievski
*Agency for Real Estate Cadastre*

Marijana Gjoreska
*Central Registry of the Republic of Macedonia*

Sonja Gjurevska
*Cakmakova Advocates*

Zoranco Griovski
*Republic of Macedonia, Municipality of Ilinden*

Werner Hengst
*EVN Macedonia*

Biljana Ickovska
*Law Office Nikolovski & Associates*

Aleksandar Ickovski
*Tax & Legal Consultant*

Maja Jakimovska
*Cakmakova Advocates*

Dragana Jashevic
*Law Office Nikolovski & Associates*

Aneta Jovanoska Trajanovska
*Lawyers Antevski*

Lenche Karpuzovska
*EVN Macedonia*

Dejan Knezović
*Law Office Knezovic & Associates*

Vancho Kostadinovski
*Central Registry of the Republic of Macedonia*

Antonio Kostanov
*Enforcement Agent Republic of Macedonia*

Aleksandra Kostovska
*Stojkoska Attorney at Law*

Ivana Lekic
*PwC Macedonia*

Miroslav Marchev
*PwC Macedonia*

Mirjana Markovska
*Stojkoska Attorney at Law*

Oliver Mirchevski
*EVN Macedonia*

Irena Mitkovska
*Lawyers Antevski*

Martin Monevski
*Monevski Law Firm*

Valerjan Monevski
*Monevski Law Firm*

Elena Mucheva
*National Bank of the Republic of Macedonia*

Svetlana Neceva
*Law Office Pepeljugoski*

Marina Nikoloska
*Cakmakova Advocates*

Marija Nikolova
*Law Office Knezovic & Associates*

Vesna Nikolovska
*Law Office Nikolovski & Associates*

Goran Nikolovski
*Law Office Nikolovski & Associates*

Zlatko Nikolovski
*Notary Chamber of R. of Macedonia*

Martin Odzaklieski
*Ministry of Transport and Communications*

Vasil Pavloski
*Ministry of Economy*

Valentin Pepeljugoski
*Law Office Pepeljugoski*

Sonja Peshevska
*Law Office Pepeljugoski*

Zorica Pulejkova
*Republic of Macedonia Notary Public*

Viktor Ristovski
*Cakmakova Advocates*

Ljubica Ruben
*Mens Legis Law Firm*

Biljana Saraginova
*Monevski Law Firm*

Simonida Shosholceva-Giannitsakis
*IKRP Rokas & Partners*

Milica Shutova
*Cakmakova Advocates*

Alexander Sipek
*EVN Macedonia*

Ivica Smilevski
*Chamber of Bankruptcy Managers of the Republic of Macedonia*

Ljupka Stojanovska
*Law Office Nikolovski & Associates*

Zika Stojanovski
*Republic of Macedonia, Municipality of Ilinden*

Suzana Stojkoska
*Stojkoska Attorney at Law*

Margareta Taseva
*Cakmakova Advocates*

Dragica Tasevska
*National Bank of the Republic of Macedonia*

Stefan Trost
*EVN Macedonia*

Vladimir Vasilevski
*BETASPED D.O.O.*

Tome Velkovski
*Ministry of Economy*

Zlatko Veterovski
*Customs Administration*

Milica Zafirova
*Stojkoska Attorney at Law*

## MADAGASCAR

*Bureau de Liaison SGS*

*Cabinet John W. Ffooks & Co.*

*Cabinet SIGMA Consulting*

Eric Robson Andriamiahaja
*Economic Development Board of Madagascar*

Tsiry Andriamisamanana
*Madagascar Conseil International*

Andriamanalina Andrianjaka
*Office Notarial de Tamatave*

Wasoudeo Balloo
*KPMG Madagascar*

Yves Duchateau
*SDV Logistics*

Raphaël Jakoba
*Madagascar Conseil International*

Hanna Keyserlingk
*Cabinet HK Jurifisc*

Jean Claude Liong
*KPMG Madagascar*

Pascaline R. Rasamoeliarisoa
*Delta Audit Deloitte*

Julie R. Ratsimisetra
*Groupement des Entreprises Franches et Partenaires (GEFP)*

Sahondra Rabenarivo
*Madagascar Law Offices*

Pierrette Rajaonarisoa
*SDV Logistics*

Serge Lucien Rajoelina
*Jiro Sy Rano Malagasy (JIRAMA)*

Tojo Rakotomamonjy
*Etude Razanadrakoto Rija*

Danielle Rakotomanana
*Cabinet Rakotomanana*

Heritiana Rakotosalama
*Legislink Consulting*

Mamisoa Rakotosalama
*Legislink Consulting*

Lanto Tiana Ralison
*PwC Madagascar*

Martial Ralison
*Jiro Sy Rano Malagasy (JIRAMA)*

Gérard Ramarijaona
*Prime Lex*

Roland Ramarijaona
*Delta Audit Deloitte*

Laingo Ramarimbahoaka
*Madagascar Conseil International*

Heritiana Rambeloson
*Jiro Sy Rano Malagasy (JIRAMA)*

Zakazo Ranaivoson
*Cabinet de Conseils d'Entreprises*

William Randrianarivelo
*PwC Madagascar*

Sahondra Rasoarisoa
*Delta Audit Deloitte*

Michael Ratrimo
*Madagascar International Container Terminal Services Ltd.*

Mahery Ratsimandresy
*Prime Lex*

Théodore Raveloarison
*JARY - Bureau d'Etudes Architecture Ingenierie*

Andry Nirina Ravelojaona
*Banque Centrale de Madagascar*

Andriamisa Ravelomanana
*PwC Madagascar*

Jean Marcel Razafimahenina
*Delta Audit Deloitte*

Rija Nirina Razanadrakoto
*Etude Razanadrakoto Rija*

Rivolala Razanatsimba
*Jiro Sy Rano Malagasy (JIRAMA)*

Ida Soamiliarimana
*Madagascar Conseil International*

## MALAWI

*Malawi Revenue Authority*

*Manica Africa Pty. Ltd.*

Dino Amritlal Raval
*Wilson & Morgan*

Kevin M. Carpenter
*PwC Malawi*

Richard Chakana
*2PS Cargo Co.*

Joseph Chavula
*First Merchant Bank Ltd.*

Marshal Chilenga
*TF & Partners*

Gautoni D. Kainja
*Kainja & Dzonzi*

Chimwemwe Kalua
*Golden & Law*

Dannie J. Kamwaza
*Kamwaza Design Partnership*

Frank Edgar Kapanda
*High Court of Malawi*

Andrews Katuya
*Dowell & Jones, Attorneys-at-Law*

Shabir Latif
*Sacranie, Gow & Co.*

Alfred Majamanda
*Mbendera & Nkhono Associates*

James Masumbu
*Tembenu, Masumbu & Co.*

Raphael Mhone
*Racane Associates*

Vyamala Moyo
*PwC Malawi*

Charles Mvula
*DUMA Electrics - Control Systems and Energy Management*

Davis Njobvu
*Savjani & Co.*

Dinker A. Raval
*Wilson & Morgan*

## MALAYSIA

*Bank Negara Malaysia*

*Integrated Logistics Solutions Sdn Bhd*

*Port Klang Authorities*

Halimi Abd Manaf
*Ministry of Housing and Local Government*

Nor Azimah Abdul Aziz
*Companies Commission of Malaysia*

Abdul Karim Abdul Jalil
*Malaysia Department of Insolvency*

Mohammad Rohaimy Abdul Rahim
*Ministry of International Trade and Industry*

Sonia Abraham
*Azman, Davidson & Co.*

Wilfred Abraham
*Zul Rafique & Partners, Advocate & Solicitors*

Alwizah Al-Yafii Ahmad Kamal
*Zaid Ibrahim & Co (ZICO)*

Dato' Abdul Halim Ain
*Department of Director General of Land & Mines*

Dato' Sh. Yahya bin Sh. Mohamed Almurisi
*Ministry of Human Resource*

Adrian Azlan
*Westports Malaysia Sdn Bhd*

Mohd Azlan B. Mohd Radzi
*Land & Mines Office*

Anita Balakrishnan
*Shearn Delamore & Co.*

Abdul Murad Bin Che Chik

KC Chan
*Freight Transport Network Sdn. Bhd.*

Hong Yun Chang
*Tay & Partners*

Ar Teoh Chee Wui

Ruban Chelliah
*Stanco and Ruche Consulting*

Andrew Ean Vooi Chiew
*Lee Hishammuddin Allen & Gledhill*

Tze Keong Chung
*CTOS Data Systems Sdn Bhd*

Walter Culas
*Air Freight Forwarders Association of Malaysia (AFAM)*

Nadesh Ganabaskaran
*Zul Rafique & Partners, Advocate & Solicitors*

Tiew Hai San
*Ministry of Federal Territories and Urban Wellbeing*

Dato' Hashim Hamzah
*Federal Court of Malaysia*

Betty Hasan
*Ministry of Human Resource*

Ramli Hazra Izadi
*LKMD Architecture*

Ang Seng Hing
*Ushamas Forwarding (M) Sdn. Bhd.*

Hj. Hasim Hj. Ismail
*Land & Mines Office*

Hung Hoong
*Shearn Delamore & Co.*

Rohani Ismail
*Session Court Kuala Lumpur*

Norhaiza Jemon
*Companies Commission of Malaysia*

Kumar Kanagasabai
*Skrine, member of Lex Mundi*

Kumar Kanagasingam
*Lee Hishammuddin Allen & Gledhill*

Kesavan Karuppiah
*Ministry of Human Resource*

Azemi Kasim
*Department of Director General of Land & Mines*

Geeta Kaur
*SDV Transport*

Teh Wai Keong
*Equatorial Logistics Sdn Bhd.*

Chuan Keat Khoo
*PwC Malaysia*

Loh Kok Leong
*Russell Bedford LC & Company - member of Russell Bedford International*

Christopher Lee
*Christopher Lee & Co.*

Bernard Lim
*PHK Management Services Sdn Bhd*

Koon Huan Lim
*Skrine, member of Lex Mundi*

Seok Hua Lim
*North Port (Malaysia) Bhd*

Len Toong Low
*North Port (Malaysia) Bhd*

Ir. Bashir Ahamed Maideen
*Nadi Consult Era Sdn Bhd*

Alias Marjoh
*Kuala Lumpur City Hall*

Chuah Meng Sim
*Russell Bedford LC & Company - member of Russell Bedford International*

Rokiah Mhd Noor
*Companies Commission of Malaysia*

Adura Mizan
*Companies Commission of Malaysia*

Zuhaidi Mohd Shahari
*Azmi & Associates*

Saran Nair
*CIMB Group*

Marina Nathan
*Companies Commission of Malaysia*

Oy Moon Ng
*CTOS Data Systems Sdn Bhd*

Swee Kee Ng
*Shearn Delamore & Co.*

Shahri Omar
*North Port (Malaysia) Bhd*

Allison Ong
*Azman, Davidson & Co.*

Hock An Ong
*KPMG*

Aminah BT Abd. Rahman
*Ministry of Housing and Local Government*

Sakaya Johns Rani
*PwC Malaysia*

Sugumar Saminathan
*MALAYSIA PRODUCTIVITY CORPORATION*

Andy Seo

Fiona Sequerah
*CHRISTOPHER LEE & CO.*

Chan Kum Siew
*MALAYSIA PRODUCTIVITY CORPORATION*

Hadiman Bin Simin
*MINISTRY OF HOUSING AND LOCAL
GOVERNMENT*

Rishwant Singh
*ZUL RAFIQUE & PARTNERS, ADVOCATE
& SOLICITORS*

Sukhbir Singh
*M & N MANAGEMENT CONSULTANTS*

Kenneth Tiong
*THE ASSOCIATED CHINESE CHAMBERS
OF COMMERCE AND INDUSTRY OF
MALAYSIA (ACCCIM)*

Sugumaran Vairavappillai
*TENAGA NASIONAL BERHAD*

Heng Choon Wan
*PwC MALAYSIA*

Chee Lin Wong
*SKRINE, MEMBER OF LEX MUNDI*

Keat Ching Wong
*ZUL RAFIQUE & PARTNERS, ADVOCATE
& SOLICITORS*

Clifford Eng Hong Yap
*PwC MALAYSIA*

## MALDIVES

Mohamed Abdul Azeez
*AIMA CONSTRUCTION COMPANY
PVT LTD.*

Mohamed Ahsan
*ArchEng STUDIO PVT LTD.*

Yamuna Amaraperuma
*KPMG*

Arafath
*GLOBAL CARGO CARE*

Jatindra Bhattray
*PwC MALDIVES*

Asma Chan-Rahim
*SHAH, HUSSAIN & CO. BARRISTERS &
ATTORNEYS*

Mohamed Fahad
*GLOBAL CARGO CARE*

Mohamed Fizan
*SHAH, HUSSAIN & CO. BARRISTERS &
ATTORNEYS*

Charith Gunathilaka
*KPMG*

Mohamed Hameed
*ANTRAC PVT. LTD.*

Shamila Jayasekera
*KPMG*

Laila Manik
*SHAH, HUSSAIN & CO. BARRISTERS &
ATTORNEYS*

Prasanta Misra
*PwC MALDIVES*

Abdul Samad Mohamed
*SMD AUDIT & CONSULTANCY*

Ahmed Murad
*MAZLAN & MURAD LAW ASSOCIATES*

Jagath Perera
*KPMG*

Mazlan Rasheed
*MAZLAN & MURAD LAW ASSOCIATES*

Sam
*GLOBAL CARGO CARE*

Ishan Sampath
*KPMG*

Shuaib M. Shah
*SHAH, HUSSAIN & CO. BARRISTERS &
ATTORNEYS*

Upul Shantha
*KPMG*

Mizna Shareef
*SHAH, HUSSAIN & CO. BARRISTERS &
ATTORNEYS*

Abdul Mallik Thoufeeg
*STELCO*

## MALI

*CABINET JOHN W. FFOOKS & CO.*

*DAMCO*

Ahmadou Al Aminou Lo
*BCEAO*

Oumar Bane
*JURIFIS CONSULT*

Amadou Camara
*SCP CAMARA TRAORÉ*

Céline Camara Sib
*ETUDE ME CELINE CAMARA SIB*

Boubacar Coulibaly
*MATRANS*

Elvis Danon
*PwC CÔTE D'IVOIRE*

Fatoumata D. Diarra
*AFRICAN LEGAL & TAX MALI
(ALT-MALI)*

Aboubacar S. Diarrah
*MINISTÈRE DE LA JUSTICE, GARDE DES
SCEAUX*

Fatimata Dicko Zouboye

Djibril Guindo
*JURIFIS CONSULT*

Maiga Seydou Ibrahim
*CABINET D'AVOCATS SEYDOU IBRAHIM
MAIGA*

Awa Kane
*MATRANS*

Mamadou Ismaïla Konate
*JURIFIS CONSULT*

Amadou Maiga
*MAIRIE DU MALI*

Maiga Mamadou
*AGENCE NATIONALE D'ASSISTANCE
MEDICALE*

Adeline Messou
*PwC CÔTE D'IVOIRE*

Bérenger Y. Meuke
*JURIFIS CONSULT*

Keita Zeïnabou Sacko
*API MALI*

Alassane T. Sangaré
*NOTARY*

Djibril Semega
*CABINET SEAG CONSEIL*

Désiré Sidibé
*ETUDE ME CELINE CAMARA SIB*

Toumani Sidibe
*MINISTÈRE DES AFFAIRES ETRANGÈRES
ET DE LA COOPÉRATION INTERNATIONALE*

Perignama Sylla
*ARCHITECT DE/AU*

Dominique Taty
*PwC CÔTE D'IVOIRE*

Imirane A. Touré
*DIRECTION NATIONALE DE L'URBANISME
ET DE L'HABITAT*

Alassane Traoré
*ICON SARL*

Fousséni Traoré
*FwC CÔTE D'IVOIRE*

Mahamadou Traore

Emmanuel Yehouessi
*BCEAO*

## MALTA

Shawn Agius
*INLAND REVENUE DEPARTMENT*

Alexia Albani
*BANK OF VALLETTA*

Randolph Aquilina
*INLAND REVENUE DEPARTMENT*

Matthew Attard
*GANADO & ASSOCIATES – ADVOCATES*

John Bonello
*SCERRI & BONELLO ADVOCATES*

Leonard Bonello
*GANADO & ASSOCIATES – ADVOCATES*

Paul Bonello
*MINISTRY OF FINANCE DEPARTMENT
OF CUSTOMS*

Caroline Borg
*MALTA FREEPORT TERMINALS LIMITED*

Kris Borg
*DR KRIS BORG & ASSOCIATES
– ADVOCATES*

Maria Clara Borg
*EMD ADVOCATES*

Mario Raymond Borg
*INLAND REVENUE DEPARTMENT*

Katrina Borg Cardona
*MALTA ENTERPRISE*

Joseph P. Brincat
*MINISTRY OF FINANCE DEPARTMENT
OF CUSTOMS*

Ann M. Bugeja
*CSB ADVOCATES*

George Bugeja
*GANADO & ASSOCIATES – ADVOCATES*

Adrian Cachia
*MALTA FREEPORT TERMINALS LIMITED*

André Camilleri
*MALTA FINANCIAL SERVICES AUTHORITY
(MFSA)*

Kenneth Camilleri
*CHETCUTI CAUCHI ADVOCATES*

Paul Camilleri
*PAUL CAMILLERI & ASSOCIATES*

Simon Camilleri
*CREDITINFO*

Joseph Caruana
*MALTA FINANCIAL SERVICES AUTHORITY
(MFSA)*

David Cassar
*MALTA ENVIRONMENT & PLANNING
AUTHORITY (MEPA)*

Jean-Philippe Chetcuti
*CHETCUTI CAUCHI ADVOCATES*

Maria Chetcuti Cauchi
*CHETCUTI CAUCHI ADVOCATES*

Jeanette Ciantar
*FENECH & FENECH ADVOCATES*

Edward Dalmas
*MALTA FINANCIAL SERVICES AUTHORITY
(MFSA)*

Edward DeBono
*FENECH & FENECH ADVOCATES*

Sergio Ebejer
*INLAND REVENUE DEPARTMENT*

Italo Ellul
*EMD ADVOCATES*

Hilda Ellul-Mercer
*DR KRIS BORG & ASSOCIATES
– ADVOCATES*

Alfred Farrugia
*WORLD EXPRESS LOGISTICS*

David Felice
*ARCHITECTURE PROJECT*

Ramon Fiott
*MALTA ENTERPRISE*

George Francalanza
*MALTA ENTERPRISE*

Antoine S Galea
*ENEMALTA CORPORATION*

Matthew Galea Debono
*CSB ADVOCATES*

Neville Gatt
*PwC*

Christabelle Gauci
*CSB ADVOCATES*

Mark Gauci
*OCCUPATIONAL HEALTH AND SAFETY
AUTHORITY (OHSA)*

Keith German
*LAND REGISTRY*

Joseph Ghio
*FENECH & FENECH ADVOCATES*

Steve Gingell
*PwC*

Joseph Grech
*MALTA ENTERPRISE*

Marisa Grech
*LAND REGISTRY*

Sandro Grech
*SG MALTA LIMITED – CORRESPONDENT
OF RUSSELL BEDFORD INTERNATIONAL*

Karl Grech Orr
*GANADO & ASSOCIATES – ADVOCATES*

Peter Grima
*ENEMALTA CORPORATION*

Stefan Grima
*BANK OF VALLETTA*

Josef Laferla
*SCERRI & BONELLO ADVOCATES*

Kevin Loughborough
*COBRA INSTALLATIONS*

Adrian Mallia
*MALTA FREEPORT TERMINALS LIMITED*

Chris Mallia
*GANADO & ASSOCIATES – ADVOCATES*

Allan Micallef
*ENEMALTA CORPORATION*

Priscilla Mifsud Parker
*CHETCUTI CAUCHI ADVOCATES*

Henri Mizzi
*CAMILLERI PREZIOSI*

Robert Mizzi
*GANADO & ASSOCIATES – ADVOCATES*

John Paris
*CREDITINFO*

Reynold Portelli
*MALTA FREEPORT TERMINALS LIMITED*

Julienne Portelli Demajo
*GANADO & ASSOCIATES – ADVOCATES*

Dion Buhagiar Said
*SMS LOGISTICS*

Claude Sapiano
*LAND REGISTRY*

Albert Scerri
*MINISTRY OF FINANCE DEPARTMENT
OF CUSTOMS*

Joseph Scicluna
*SCICLUNA & ASSOCIATES*

Simon Scicluna
*SCICLUNA & ASSOCIATES*

Andrei Vella
*CAMILLERI PREZIOSI*

Noel Vella
*DEPARTMENT OF INDUSTRIAL AND
EMPLOYMENT RELATIONS*

Simone Vella Lenicker
*ARCHITECTURE PROJECT*

Austin Walker
*MALTA ENVIRONMENT & PLANNING
AUTHORITY (MEPA)*

Mark Wirth
*PwC*

Angelo Xuereb
*AX HOLDINGS*

Quentin Zahra
*EUROFREIGHT*

Silvana Zammit
*CHETCUTI CAUCHI ADVOCATES*

Andrew J. Zammit
*CSB ADVOCATES*

John Zarb
*PwC*

## MARSHALL ISLANDS

*BANK OF MARSHALL ISLANDS*

*MARSHALLS ENERGY COMPANY*

Helkena Anni
*MARSHALL ISLANDS REGISTRY*

Kenneth Barden
*ATTORNEY-AT-LAW*

Raquel De Leon
*MARSHALL ISLANDS SOCIAL SECURITY
ADMINISTRATION*

Jerry Kramer
*PACIFIC INTERNATIONAL, INC.*

James McCaffrey
*THE MCCAFFREY FIRM, LTD.*

Dennis Reeder
*RMI RECEIVERSHIPS*

Liz Rodick
*EZ PRICE MART*

Scott H. Stege
*LAW OFFICES OF SCOTT STEGE*

Anthony Tomlinson
*BECA INTERNATIONAL CONSULTANTS
LTD.*

Bori Ysawa
*ROBERT REIMERS ENTERPRISES, INC.*

## MAURITANIA

Mohamed Salem Abdy
*CABINET D'AVOCATS SALEM ABDY*

Moussa Aw
*BSD & ASSOCIÉS*

Tidiane Bal
*BSD & ASSOCIÉS*

Mohamed El Hassen Boukhreiss
*DIRECTION DES DOMAINES, DE
L'ENREGISTREMENT ET DU TIMBRE*

Hamoud Ismail
*SMPN*

Cheikany Jules
*CHEIKHANY JULES LAW OFFICE*

Abdou M'Bodj
*COMMUNAUTÉ URBAINE DE
NOUAKCHOTT*

Wedou Mohamed
*MAURIHANDLING*

Bekaye Ould Abdelkader
*MINISTÈRE DE LA FONCTION PUBLIQUE,
DU TRAVAIL ET DE LA MODERNISATION
DE L'ADMINISTRATION*

Mine Ould Abdoullah
*CABINET D'AVOCAT OULD ABDOULLAH*

Ishagh Ould Ahmed Miské
*CABINET ISHAGH MISKE*

Mohamed Ould Bouddida
*ETUDE MAÎTRE MOHAMED OULD
BOUDDIDA*

Abdellahi Ould Charrouck
*ATELIER ARCHITECTURE ET DESIGN*

Brahim Ould Daddah
*CABINET DADDAH CONSEILS*

Brahim Ould Ebety
*LAWYER*

Mohamed Mahmoud Ould Mohamedou
*GENISERVICES*

Ahmed Ould Radhi
*BANQUE CENTRALE DE MAURITANIE*

Abdel Fettah Ould Sidi Mohamed
*SOCIÉTÉ MAURITANIENNE D'ÉLECTRICITÉ (SOMELEC)*

Aliou Sall
*ASSURIM CONSULTING*

Aissetou Sy
*BSD & ASSOCIÉS*

Dominique Taty
*PwC CÔTE D'IVOIRE*

## MAURITIUS

Ryan Allas
*PwC MAURITIUS*

Anishah Aujayeb
*JURISTCONSULT CHAMBERS*

Mohamed Iqbal Belath
*BANK OF MAURITIUS*

Vanesha Babooa Bissonauth
*DE COMARMOND & KOENIG*

Jean-François Boisvenu
*BLC CHAMBERS*

Urmila Boolell
*BANYMANDHUB BOOLELL CHAMBERS*

James Boucher
*HSBC*

Nicolas Carcasse
*DAGON INGENIEUR CONSEIL LTÉE*

Jagwantsing Chetlall
*GAMMA*

Jaimie Chiniah
*BANYMANDHUB BOOLELL CHAMBERS*

D.P. Chinien
*REGISTRAR OF COMPANIES AND BUSINESSES, OFFICE OF THE REGISTRAR OF COMPANIES*

Vincent Chong Leung
*UTILIS CORPORATE SERVICE*

Sandy Chuong
*GEROUDISGLOVER GHURBURRUN*

Chandansingh Chutoori
*DAGON INGENIEUR CONSEIL LTÉE*

Martine de Fleuriot de la Colinière
*DE COMARMOND & KOENIG*

Catherine de Rosnay
*LEGIS & PARTNERS*

Shalinee Dreepaul-Halkhoree
*JURISTCONSULT CHAMBERS*

Sapna Dwarka
*BANYMANDHUB BOOLELL CHAMBERS*

Robert Ferrat
*LEGIS & PARTNERS*

Yannick Fok
*GEROUDISGLOVER GHURBURRUN*

Poonam Geemul
*BANYMANDHUB BOOLELL CHAMBERS*

Gavin Glover
*GEROUDISGLOVER GHURBURRUN*

J. Gilbert Gnany
*THE MAURITIUS COMMERCIAL BANK LIMITED*

Arvin Halkhoree
*NS MANAGEMENT LTD.*

Mikash Hassamal
*GEROUDISGLOVER GHURBURRUN*

Marc Hein
*JURISTCONSULT CHAMBERS*

Reshma Hurday
*KROSS BORDER TRUST SERVICES LTD. - MEMBER OF RUSSELL BEDFORD INTERNATIONAL*

Nitish Hurnaum
*GEROUDISGLOVER GHURBURRUN*

Thierry Koenig
*DE COMARMOND & KOENIG*

Anthony Leung Shing
*PwC MAURITIUS*

Jayram Luximon
*CEB*

Malcolm Moller
*APPLEBY GLOBAL*

Ramdas Mootanah
*ARCHITECTURE & DESIGN LTD.*

R. Mungly-Gulbul
*SUPREME COURT*

Loganayagan Munian
*ARTISCO INTERNATIONAL*

Mushtaq Namdarkhan
*BLC CHAMBERS*

Marie Cristelle Joanna Parsooramen
*BANYMANDHUB BOOLELL CHAMBERS*

Priscilla Pattoo-Mungur
*JURISTCONSULT CHAMBERS*

Siv Potayya
*WORTELS LEXUS*

Nicolas Pougnet
*BUILDING AND CIVIL ENGINEERING CO LTD.*

Iqbal Rajahbalee
*BLC CHAMBERS*

Vivekanand Ramburun
*MAURITIUS REVENUE AUTHORITY*

André Robert
*ATTORNEY-AT-LAW*

Wenda Sawmynaden
*CABINET DE NOTAIRE SAWMYNADEN*

Gilbert Seeyave
*DCDM FINANCIAL SERVICES LTD.*

Sentokee
*CITY COUNCIL OF PORT LOUIS*

Gaetan Siew
*LAMPOTANG & SIEW ARCHITECTS LTD.*

Deviantee Sobarun
*MINISTRY OF FINANCE & ECONOMIC DEVELOPMENT*

Chitra Soobagrah
*GEROUDISGLOVER GHURBURRUN*

Oudesh Suddul
*KROSS BORDER TRUST SERVICES LTD. - MEMBER OF RUSSELL BEDFORD INTERNATIONAL*

Vikash Takoor
*BANK OF MAURITIUS*

Parikshat Teeluck
*DAMCO LOGISTICS (MAURITIUS)*

Shamina Toofanee
*PwC MAURITIUS*

Natasha Towokul-Jiagoo
*JURISTCONSULT CHAMBERS*

## MEXICO
*NDA*

Gustavo I. Alarcón Caballero
*BAKER & MCKENZIE*

Areli Archundia
*GALAZ, YAMAZAKI, RUIZ URQUIZA, S.C., MEMBER OF DELOITTE TOUCHE TOHMATSU LIMITED*

Rafael Barragan Mendoza
*COMAD, S.C.*

Guillermo Barragan Toledo
*GONZALEZ CALVILLO, S.C.*

Ana Rosa Bobadilla
*GONZALEZ CALVILLO, S.C.*

Gilberto Calderon
*GALAZ, YAMAZAKI, RUIZ URQUIZA, S.C., MEMBER OF DELOITTE TOUCHE TOHMATSU LIMITED*

Carlos Cano
*PwC MEXICO*

Oscar O. Cano
*ADEATH LOGISTICS S.A. DE C.V.*

Santiago Carrillo
*RITCH MUELLER, S.C.*

María Casas López
*BAKER & MCKENZIE*

Hermilo Ceja
*COMISIÓN FEDERAL DE ELECTRICIDAD*

Carlos Chávez
*GALICIA Y ROBLES, S.C.*

Ernesto Chávez
*INTERCONTINENTAL NETWORK SERVICES*

Rodrigo Conesa
*RITCH MUELLER, S.C.*

Eduardo Corzo Ramos
*HOLLAND & KNIGHT-GALLÁSTEGUI Y LOZANO, S.C.*

Jose Covarrubias-Azuela
*SOLORZANO, CARVAJAL, GONZALEZ Y PEREZ-CORREA, S.C.*

Elvira Creel
*SECRETARÍA DE ENERGÍA*

Cecilia Curiel
*SÁNCHEZ DEVANNY ESEVERRI, S.C.*

Miguel de la Fuente
*NADER, HAYAUX & GOEBEL*

Oscar de La Vega
*LITTLER DE LA VEGA Y CONDE, S.C.*

Jorge de Presno
*BASHAM, RINGE Y CORREA, MEMBER OF IUS LABORIS*

Nicolas del Olmo
*NDA*

Luis Enrique Díaz Mirón S.
*BUFETE DIAZ MIRÓN*

Carlos Ramon Diaz Sordo
*LOPEZ VELARDE, HEFTYE Y SORIA, S.C.*

Carlos Diez Garcia
*GONZALEZ CALVILLO, S.C.*

Felipe Dominguez P.
*MOORE STEPHENS OROZCO MEDINA, S.C.*

Mariana Eguiarte Morett
*SÁNCHEZ DEVANNY ESEVERRI, S.C.*

Lourdes Elizondo
*RITCH MUELLER, S.C.*

Dolores Enriquez
*PwC MEXICO*

Miguel Espitia
*BUFETE INTERNACIONAL*

Roberto Fagoaga
*SÁNCHEZ DEVANNY ESEVERRI, S.C.*

Lucía Fernández
*GONZALEZ CALVILLO, S.C.*

Pedro Flores Carillo
*MOORE STEPHENS OROZCO MEDINA, S.C.*

Julio Flores Luna
*GOODRICH, RIQUELME Y ASOCIADOS*

Manuel Galicia
*GALICIA Y ROBLES, S.C.*

Mauricio Gamboa
*TRANSUNION DE MEXICO SA SIC*

Emilio García
*SÁNCHEZ DEVANNY ESEVERRI, S.C.*

Jose Martin Garcia
*GALAZ, YAMAZAKI, RUIZ URQUIZA, S.C., MEMBER OF DELOITTE TOUCHE TOHMATSU LIMITED*

Mauricio Garza Bulnes
*J.A. TREVIÑO ABOGADOS S.A. DE C.V.*

Hans Goebel
*NADER, HAYAUX & GOEBEL*

Patricia Gonzalez
*PwC MEXICO*

Marisol González Echevarría
*SÁNCHEZ DEVANNY ESEVERRI, S.C.*

Eugenia González Rivas
*GOODRICH, RIQUELME Y ASOCIADOS*

Luis Enrique Graham
*CHADBOURNE & PARKE LLP*

Mario Alberto Gutiérrez
*PwC MEXICO*

Yves Hayaux-du-Tilly
*NADER, HAYAUX & GOEBEL*

Roberto Hernandez Garcia
*COMAD, S.C.*

Angélica Huacuja
*CHADBOURNE & PARKE LLP*

Agustin Humann
*SÁNCHEZ DEVANNY ESEVERRI, S.C.*

Mauricio Hurtado
*PwC MEXICO*

Jose Ricardo Ibarra Cordova
*SÁNCHEZ DEVANNY ESEVERRI, S.C.*

Maria Isoard
*RITCH MUELLER, S.C.*

Jorge Jimenez
*LOPEZ VELARDE, HEFTYE Y SORIA, S.C.*

Jorge Jiménez
*RUSSELL BEDFORD MÉXICO - MEMBER OF RUSSELL BEDFORD INTERNATIONAL*

Diana Juárez Martínez
*BAKER & MCKENZIE*

Alfredo Kupfer-Dominguez
*SÁNCHEZ DEVANNY ESEVERRI, S.C.*

Ricardo León-Santacruz
*SÁNCHEZ DEVANNY ESEVERRI, S.C.*

Alfonso Lopez Lajud
*GONZALEZ CALVILLO, S.C.*

Julio Luna Castillo
*COLEGIO DE INGENIEROS MECÁNICOS Y ELECTRICISTAS (CIME)*

Daniel Maldonado
*SÁNCHEZ DEVANNY ESEVERRI, S.C.*

Lucia Manzo
*GALICIA Y ROBLES, S.C.*

Esteban Maqueo Barnetche
*MAQUEO ABOGADOS, S.C.*

José Antonio Marquez González
*NOTARY PUBLIC #2*

Bernardo Martínez Negrete
*GALICIA Y ROBLES, S.C.*

Carla E. Mendoza Pérez
*BAKER & MCKENZIE*

Carlos E. Montemayor
*PwC MEXICO*

Erika Mora
*SÁNCHEZ DEVANNY ESEVERRI, S.C.*

Guillermo Moran
*GALAZ, YAMAZAKI, RUIZ URQUIZA, S.C., MEMBER OF DELOITTE TOUCHE TOHMATSU LIMITED*

Oscar Moreno Silva
*GONZALEZ CALVILLO, S.C.*

Enrique Muñoz
*GONZALEZ CALVILLO, S.C.*

Eloy F. Muñoz M.
*IMEYEL SOLUCIONES INTEGRALES, S.A. DE C.V.*

Manuel Najera
*NDA*

Jorge Narváez Hasfura
*BAKER & MCKENZIE*

Marco Nava
*PwC MEXICO*

Isabel Nuñez
*GONZALEZ CALVILLO, S.C.*

Diego Ortiz
*PwC MEXICO*

Juan Manuel Ortiz
*PwC MEXICO*

Arturo Pedromo
*GALICIA Y ROBLES, S.C.*

Arturo Perdomo
*GALICIA Y ROBLES, S.C.*

Eduardo Perez Armienta
*MOORE STEPHENS OROZCO MEDINA, S.C.*

Gerardo Perez Monter
*COLEGIO DE INGENIEROS MECÁNICOS Y ELECTRICISTAS (CIME)*

Fernando Perez-Correa
*SOLORZANO, CARVAJAL, GONZALEZ Y PEREZ-CORREA, S.C.*

Pablo Perezalonso Eguía
*RITCH MUELLER, S.C.*

Guillermo Piecarchic
*PMC & ASOCIADOS*

Jose Piecarchic Cohen
*PMC & ASOCIADOS*

Gizeh Polo Ballinas
*CREEL, GARCÍA-CUÉLLAR, AIZA Y ENRIQUEZ, S.C.*

Jose Antonio Postigo-Uribe
*SÁNCHEZ DEVANNY ESEVERRI, S.C.*

Daniel Puente
*J.A. TREVIÑO ABOGADOS S.A. DE C.V.*

David Puente-Tostado
*SÁNCHEZ DEVANNY ESEVERRI, S.C.*

Alvaro Quintana
*ALVARO QUINTANA S.C.*

Brindisi Reyes
*RITCH MUELLER, S.C.*

Eduardo Reyes Díaz-Leal
*BUFETE INTERNACIONAL*

Héctor Reyes Freaner
*BAKER & MCKENZIE*

Claudia Ríos
*PwC MEXICO*

Jose Ignacio Rivero
*GONZALEZ CALVILLO, S.C.*

Cecilia Rojas
*GALICIA Y ROBLES, S.C.*

Ivonne M. Rojas Rangel
*PMC & ASOCIADOS*

Luis M. Sada-Beltrán
*SÁNCHEZ DEVANNY ESEVERRI, S.C.*

Raúl Sahagun
*BUFETE INTERNACIONAL*

Ana Cristina Sanchez
*SECRETARÍA DE ENERGÍA*

Lucero Sánchez de la Concha
*BAKER & MCKENZIE*

Cristina Sanchez Vebber
*SÁNCHEZ DEVANNY ESEVERRI, S.C.*

Cristina Sánchez-Urtiz
*MIRANDA & ESTAVILLO, S.C.*

Francisco Santoyo
*COMISIÓN FEDERAL DE ELECTRICIDAD*

Monica Schiaffino Pérez
*LITTLER DE LA VEGA Y CONDE, S.C.*

Ernesto Silvas
*SÁNCHEZ DEVANNY ESEVERRI, S.C.*

Pietro Straulino-Rodriguez
*SÁNCHEZ DEVANNY ESEVERRI, S.C.*

Juan Francisco Torres Landa Ruffo
*BARRERA, SIQUEIROS Y TORRES LANDA, S.C.*

Jaime A. Treviño
*J.A. TREVIÑO ABOGADOS*

Maribel Trigo Aja
GOODRICH, RIQUELME Y ASOCIADOS

Rafael Vallejo
GONZALEZ CALVILLO, S.C.

Layla Vargas Muga
GOODRICH, RIQUELME Y ASOCIADOS

Jose Villa Ramirez
COMAD, S.C.

Guillermo Villaseñor
SÁNCHEZ DEVANNY ESEVERRI, S.C.

Claudio Villavicencio
GALAZ, YAMAZAKI, RUIZ URQUIZA,
S.C., member of DELOITTE TOUCHE
TOHMATSU LIMITED

Humberto Zapien
GALAZ, YAMAZAKI, RUIZ URQUIZA,
S.C., member of DELOITTE TOUCHE
TOHMATSU LIMITED

## MICRONESIA, FED. STS.

BANK OF FSM

FSM DEVELOPMENT BANK

POHNPEI TRANSFER & STORAGE, INC.

Sweeter Aaron
FOREIGN INVESTMENT BOARD, POHNPEI
STATE GOVERNMENT

Kenneth Barden
ATTORNEY-AT-LAW

Marstella Jack
LAWYER

Simon Lihpai
DIVISION OF FORESTRY & MARINE
CONSERVATION

Quirino Loyola
FOREIGN INVESTMENT BOARD, POHNPEI
STATE GOVERNMENT

Sisananto Loyola
POHNPEI STATE ENVIRONMENTAL
PROTECTION AGENCY

Silberio S. Mathias
MICROPC

Douglas Nelber
POHNPEI STATE DEPARTMENT OF LANDS
AND NATURAL RESOURCES

Kevin Palep
OFFICE OF THE REGISTRAR OF
CORPORATIONS

Ronald Pangelinan
A&P ENTERPRISES, INC.

Kevin Pelep
FOREIGN INVESTMENT BOARD, POHNPEI
STATE GOVERNMENT

Bendura Rodriquez
FOREIGN INVESTMENT BOARD, POHNPEI
STATE GOVERNMENT

Salomon Saimon
MICRONESIAN LEGAL SERVICES
CORPORATION

## MOLDOVA

ICS RED UNION FNOSA S.A.

Brian Arnold
PwC MOLDOVA

Victor Burac
VICTOR BURAC LAW FIRM

Andrei Caciurenco
ACI PARTNERS LAW OFFICE

Octavian Cazac
TURCAN CAZAC

Svetlana Ceban
PwC MOLDOVA

Vitalie Ciofu
GLADEI & PARTNERS

Vera Coslet
VICTOR BURAC LAW FIRM

Sergiu Dumitrasco
PwC MOLDOVA

Serghei Filatov
ACI PARTNERS LAW OFFICE

Iulia Furtuna
TURCAN CAZAC

Ana Galus
TURCAN CAZAC

Roger Gladei
GLADEI & PARTNERS

Silvia Grosu
PwC MOLDOVA

Andrian Guzun
SCHOENHERR

Vladimir Iurkovski
SCHOENHERR

Roman Ivanov
VERNON DAVID & ASSOCIATES

Valentin Kiba
ELIA SA.

Boyan Kolev
SRL CONSTRUCTPROJECT

Cristina Martin
ACI PARTNERS LAW OFFICE

Georgeta Mincu
IOM

Alexandru Munteanu
INTREPRINDEREA CU CAPITAL STRAIN
PRICEWATERHOUSECOOPERS LEGAL SRL

Oxana Novicov
NATIONAL UNION OF JUDICIAL
OFFICERS

Igor Odobescu
ACI PARTNERS LAW OFFICE

Aelita Orhei
GLADEI & PARTNERS

Vladimir Palamarciuc
TURCAN CAZAC

Ilona Panurco
INTREPRINDEREA CU CAPITAL STRAIN
PRICEWATERHOUSECOOPERS LEGAL SRL

Carolina Parcalab
ACI PARTNERS LAW OFFICE

Vladimir Plehov
MARITIMTRANS

Igor Popa
POPA & ASOCIATII LAWYERS

Dimitru Popescu
INTREPRINDEREA CU CAPITAL STRAIN
PRICEWATERHOUSECOOPERS LEGAL SRL

Victor Rusu
GLADEI & PARTNERS

Olga Saveliev
TURCAN CAZAC

Alexandru Savva
TURCAN CAZAC

Foca Silviu
BIROUL DE CREDIT - MOLDOVA

Viorel Sirghi
BSMB LEGAL COUNSELLORS

Mariana Stratan
TURCAN CAZAC

Ruslan Surugiu
NATIONAL ENERGY REGULATORY
AGENCY OF THE REPUBLIC OF MOLDOVA

Elena Talmazan
SC CONTABIL PRINCIPAL SRL

Alexander Tuceac
TURCAN CAZAC

Alexander Turcan
TURCAN CAZAC

Tatiana Vasiliu
VERNON DAVID & ASSOCIATES

## MONGOLIA

PwC MONGOLIA

Munkhjargal Baashuu
GTs ADVOCATES LLC

Telenged Baast
MONLOGISTICS WORLDWIDE LLC

Bolortsogoo Baldandorj
ULAANBAATAR ELECTRICITY
DISTRIBUTION NETWORK COMPANY

Buyantogos Baljinnyam
ANDERSON AND ANDERSON LLP

Batdelger
FEA ENERGY MONGOLIA

Badarch Bayarmaa
MAHONEY LIOTTA

Ebone. M Bishop
ANDERSON AND ANDERSON LLP

Batzaya Bodikhuu
ANAND & BATZAYA ADVOCATES
LAW FIRM

David C. Buxbaum
ANDERSON AND ANDERSON LLP

Khatanbat Dashdarjaa
ARLEX CONSULTING SERVICES

Zoljargal Dashnyam
GTs ADVOCATES LLC

Uyanga del Sol
TSETS

Enkhgerel Deleg
ANDERSON AND ANDERSON LLP

Ganbaatar
FEA ENERGY MONGOLIA

Uuganbayar Ganbaatar
TRANSGATE CO., LTD.

Batbayar Jigmedsuren
UB TRANS LLC

Undram Lhagvasuren
ANAND & BATZAYA ADVOCATES
LAW FIRM

Zolbayar Luvsansharav
TSETS

Daniel Mahoney
MAHONEY LIOTTA

Bayarmanla Manljav
GTs ADVOCATES LLC

Odonhuu Muuzee
TSETS

Batragchaa Ragchaa
A&A GLOBAL LAW FIRM

Norovtseren Sanjmyatav
ARLEX CONSULTING SERVICES

Tsolmon Shar
TSOLMON PARTNERS

Baatarsuren Sukhbaatar
THE BANK OF MONGOLIA

Arslaa Urjin
ULAANBAATAR ELECTRICITY
DISTRIBUTION NETWORK COMPANY

Paul Weifnnbach
ANAND & BATZAYA ADVOCATES
LAW FIRM

Misheel Zorig
ARLEX CONSULTING SERVICES

## MONTENEGRO

Aleksandar Adamovic
PACORINI MONTENEGRO

Bojana Andrić
ČELEBIĆ

Veselin Anđušić
ČELEBIĆ

Marija Bojović
BOJOVIĆ DAŠIĆ KOJOVIĆ

Bojana Bošković
MINISTRY OF FINANCE

Dragan Ćorac
LAW OFFICE VUJAČIĆ

Marija Crnogorac
KN KARANOVIĆ & NIKOLIĆ

Savo Djurović
ADRIATIC MARINAS D.O.O.

Dragan Draca
PwC SERBIA

Vuk Drašković
BOJOVIĆ DAŠIĆ KOJOVIĆ

Božidar Gogić
MONTECCO INC D.O.O.

Milorad Janjević
LAW OFFICE VUJAČIĆ

Maja Jokanović
MINISTRY OF ECONOMY

Nada Jovanović
CENTRAL BANK OF MONTENEGRO

Srđan Kalezić
TAX AUTHORITY MONTENEGRO

Radoš-Lolo Kastratović
ADVOKATSKA KANCELARIJA

Ana Krsmanović
MINISTRY OF FINANCE

Sefko Kurpejović
MINISTRY OF FINANCE

Krzysztof Lipka
PwC SERBIA

Nebojša Nikitović
PROINSPECT++

Ivan Nikolic
BOJOVIĆ DAŠIĆ KOJOVIĆ

Goran Nikolić
MINISTRY OF ECONOMY

Predrag Pavličić
MONTECCO INC D.O.O.

Nenad Pavličić
PAVLIČIĆ LAW OFFICE

Nikola Perović
PLANTAŽE

Uros Popovic
BOJOVIĆ DAŠIĆ KOJOVIĆ

Ana Radivojević
PwC SERBIA

Radmila Radoičić
LAW OFFICE VUJAČIĆ

Miladin Radošević
LAW FIRM RADOŠEVIĆ

Slobodan Radovic
BAST D.O.O

Ivan Radulović
MINISTRY OF FINANCE

Vesna Radunović
R&P AUDITING

Dragan Rakočević
COMMERCIAL COURT OF PODGORICA

Milena Roncević
KN KARANOVIĆ & NIKOLIĆ

Itana Scekic
HARRISONS SOLICITORS

Velimir Strugar
EPCG AD NIKŠIĆ

Jelena Vojinović
MINISTRY OF FINANCE

Saša Vujačić
LAW OFFICE VUJAČIĆ

Jelena Vujisić
LAW OFFICE VUJAČIĆ

Lana Vukmirovic-Misic
HARRISONS SOLICITORS

Sandra Zdravkovic
MONTECCO INC D.O.O.

## MOROCCO

Sidimohamed Abouchikhi
EXPERIAN

Lamya Alami
CABINET DE NOTAIRE ALAMI

Fassi-Fihri Bassamat
BASSAMAT & ASSOCIÉE

Hamid Ben Elfadil
CENTRE RÉGIONAL D'INVESTISSEMENT

Said Benjelloun
ABOUAKIL, BENJELLOUN & MAHFOUD
AVOCATS

Azel-arab Benjelloun
AGENCE D'ARCHITECTURE D'URBANISME
ET DE DECORATION

Karim Benkirane
ESPACE TRANSIT

Mohamed Benkirane
ESPACE TRANSIT

Myriam Emmanuelle Bennani
AMIN HAJJI & ASSOCIÉS ASSOCIATION
D'AVOCATS

Saad Beygrine
CABINET DE NOTAIRE ALAMI

Khalid Boumichi
TECNOMAR

Johan Bruneau
CMS BUREAU FRANCIS LEFEBVRE

Richard Cantin
JURISTRUCTURES - PROJECT
MANAGEMENT & LEGAL ADVISORY
SERVICES LLP

Mahat Chraibi
PwC ADVISORY MAROC

Driss Debbagh
KETTANI ASSOCIÉS

Merieme Diouri
ETUDE DE NOTARIAT MODERNE

Sarah El Couhen
ETUDE DE NOTARIAT MODERNE

Driss Ettaki
ADMINISTRATION DES DOUANES ET
IMPOTS INDIRECTS

Youssef Fassi Fihri
FYBA LAWYERS

Nasser Filali
ZIMAG

Fatima Zahrae Gouttaya
ETUDE DE NOTARIAT MODERNE

Zohra Hasnaoui
HASNAOUI LAW FIRM

Ahmad Hussein
TALAL ABU GHAZALEH LEGAL
(TAG-LEGAL)

Bahya Ibn Khaldoun
UNIVERSITÉ M.V. SOUISSI RABAT,
MAROC

Ali Kettani
KETTANI ASSOCIÉS

Mehdi Kettani
KETTANI ASSOCIÉS

Nadia Kettani
KETTANI LAW FIRM

Rita Kettani
KETTANI ASSOCIÉS

Nabyl Lakhdar
ADMINISTRATION DES DOUANES ET
IMPOTS INDIRECTS

Béatrice Larrègle
EXPERIAN

Amine Mahfoud
AMINE MAHFOUD NOTAIRE

Anis Mahfoud
ABOUAKIL, BENJELLOUN & MAHFOUD
AVOCATS

Noureddine Marzouk
PwC ADVISORY MAROC

Abdelkhalek Merzouki
ADMINISTRATION DES DOUANES ET
IMPOTS INDIRECTS

Kamal Nasrollah
AUGUST & DEBOUZY AVOCATS

Nesrine Roudane
*Nero Boutique Law Firm*

Laetitia Saulais
*August & Debouzy Avocats*

Ghalia Sebti
*Ait Manos*

Houcine Sefrioui
*Etude de Notariat Moderne*

Nadia Tajouidi
*Etude de Notariat Moderne*

Marc Veuillot
*CMS Bureau Francis Lefebvre*

Khalil Yassir
*Yassir Khalil Studio*

**MOZAMBIQUE**
*Electricidade de Moçambique E.P.*

Eunice Ali
*CGA & Associados, Advogados*

Carolina Balate
*PwC Mozambique*

José Manuel Caldeira
*Sal & Caldeira Advogados, Lda.*

Eduardo Calú
*Sal & Caldeira Advogados, Lda.*

Alexandra Carvalho Monjardino
*Attorney-at-Law*

Sandra Clifton
*AVM Advogados Mozambique*

Avelar Da Silva
*Intertek International Ltd.*

Thera Dai
*CGA & Associados, Advogados*

Alberto de Deus
*Macurru Law, Sociedade Unipessoal, Lda*

Elisio De Sousa
*Fernanda Lopes & Associados Advogados*

Carlos de Sousa e Brito
*Carlos de Sousa e Brito & Associados*

Tiago Dias José
*MGRA & Associados*

Fulgêncio Dimande
*Manica Freight Services S.A.R.L*

Rita Donato
*Couto Graça e Associados*

Telmo Ferreira
*Couto Graça e Associados*

Pinto Fulane
*Banco de Moçambique*

Xiluva Gonçalves Nogueira da Costa
*Sal & Caldeira Advogados, Lda.*

Jorge Graça
*CGA - Couto, Graça e Associados, Sociedade de Advogados*

Victoria Gundanhane
*SDV Moçambique SA*

Agnaldo Laice
*Damco*

Rute Langa
*Couto Graça e Associados*

Daniel Lobo Antunes
*Carlos de Sousa e Brito & Associados*

Rui Loforte
*CGA - Couto, Graça e Associados, Sociedade de Advogados*

Fernanda Lopes
*Fernanda Lopes & Associados Advogados*

Gimina Luís Mahumana
*Sal & Caldeira Advogados, Lda.*

Marla Mandlate
*Sal & Caldeira Advogados, Lda.*

Vítor Marques da Cruz
*FCB&A in association with Law & Mark, Advogados e Consultores Law & Mark, Lda*

João Martins
*PwC Mozambique*

Gonçalo Meneses
*Carlos de Sousa e Brito & Associados*

Monica Moti Guerra
*CGA & Associados, Advogados*

Álvaro Pinto Basto
*CGA - Couto, Graça e Associados, Sociedade de Advogados*

Malaika Ribeiro
*PwC Mozambique*

Bilal Ismail Seedat
*B'ilm Consulting*

Paula Castro Silveira
*Raposo Bernardo & Associados*

Ricardo Veloso
*VMP - Veloso, Mendes, Pato e Associados*

**NAMIBIA**
*Namibia Real Estate*

*Woker Freight Services*

Joos Agenbach
*Koep & Partners*

Mark Badenhorst
*PwC South Africa*

Tiaan Bazuin
*Namibian Stock Exchange*

Ronnie Beukes
*City of Windhoek Electricity Department*

Clifford Bezuidenhout
*Engling, Stritter & Partners*

Benita Blume
*H.D. Bossau & Co.*

Hanno D. Bossau
*H.D. Bossau & Co.*

Lorna Celliers
*BDO Spencer Steward (Namibia)*

Esi Chase
*Advocate*

Helené Cronje
*H.D. Bossau & Co.*

Jana-Marie De Bruyn
*BDO Spencer Steward (Namibia)*

Paul De Chalain
*PwC South Africa*

Ferdinand Diener
*City of Windhoek Electricity Department*

Marcha Erni
*TransUnion*

Hans-Bruno Gerdes
*Engling, Stritter & Partners*

Amanda Gous
*PwC Namibia*

Ismeralda Hangue
*Deeds Office*

Stefan Hugo
*PwC Namibia*

Jaco Jacobs
*Ellis Shilengudwa*

Mignon Klein
*G.F. Köpplinger Legal Practitioners*

Frank Köpplinger
*G.F. Köpplinger Legal Practitioners*

Norbert Liebich
*Transworld Cargo (PTY) Ltd.*

John D. Mandy
*Namibian Stock Exchange*

Brigitte Nependa
*H.D. Bossau & Co.*

Riana Oosthuizen
*BDO Spencer Steward (Namibia)*

Axel Stritter
*Engling, Stritter & Partners*

Andreas Vaatz
*Andreas Vaatz & Partners*

Hugo Van den Berg
*Koep & Partners*

Ockhuizen Welbert
*Namibia Water Corporation (NamWater)*

Renate Williamson
*Koep & Partners*

**NEPAL**

Anil Chandra Adhikari
*Credit Information Bureau Ltd. Nepal*

Sulakshan Adhikari
*Shangri-La Freight Pvt. Ltd.*

Lalit Aryal
*LA & Associates Chartered Accountants*

Tulasi Bhatta
*Unity Law Firm & Consultancy*

Tankahari Dahal
*Niraula Law Chamber & Co.*

Devendra Dongol
*Kathmandu Metropolitan City*

Ajay Ghimire
*Apex Law Chamber*

Sunil Gupta
*Lawyer*

Navin Kejriwal

Ananda Raj Khanal
*Nepal Telecommunications Authority*

Gourish K. Kharel
*KTO Inc.*

Parsuram Koirala
*Koirala & Associates*

Tek Narayan Kunwar
*Makanwpur District Court*

Arpana Lama
*CSC & Co.*

Bharat Lamsal
*Kathmandu District Court*

Amir Maharjan
*SAFE Consulting Architects & Engineers Pvt. Ltd.*

Lumb Mahat
*CSC & Co.*

Ashok Man Kapali
*Shangri-La Freight Pvt. Ltd.*

Purna Man Napit
*NIC Bank*

Matrika Niraula
*Niraula Law Chamber & Co.*

Rajan Niraula
*Niraula Law Chamber & Co.*

Purnachitra Pradhan
*Karja Suchana Kendra Ltd. (CIB)*

Deepak K. Shrestha
*Nepal Investment Bank*

P. L. Shrestha
*Evergreen Cargo Services Pvt. Ltd.*

Rajeshwor Shrestha
*Sinha - Verma Law Concern*

Suman Lal Shrestha
*H.R. Logistic Pvt Ltd.*

Baburam Subedi
*Nepal Electricity Authority*

Ram Chandra Subedi
*Apex Law Chamber*

Mahesh Kumar Thapa
*Sinha - Verma Law Concern*

**NETHERLANDS**
*Municipality - South District Office*

Joost Achterberg
*Kennedy Van der Laan*

Jan Biemans
*De Brauw Blackstone Westbroek*

Karin W.M. Bodewes
*Baker & McKenzie*

Sytso Boonstra
*PwC Netherlands*

Roland Brandsma
*PwC Netherlands*

Martin Brink
*Van Benthem & Keulen NV*

Margriet de Boer
*De Brauw Blackstone Westbroek*

Taco de Lange
*Lexence*

Robert de Vries
*Bosselaar & Strengers Advocaten*

Rolef de Weijs
*Houthoff Buruma*

Hans de Wilde
*KAB Accountants & Belastingadviseurs - member of Russell Bedford International*

Wilfrank Driesprong
*Stichting Bureau Krediet Registratie*

Arnold Fajel
*Merzario BV*

Ingrid Greveling
*NautaDutilh Attorneys*

Ruud Hermans
*De Brauw Blackstone Westbroek*

Mark Huijzen
*Simmons & Simmons LLP*

Niels Huurdeman
*Houthoff Buruma*

Bas Jongtien
*Bosselaar & Strengers Advocaten*

Marcel Kettenis
*PwC Netherlands*

Edwin Kleefstra
*KAB Accountants & Belastingadviseurs - member of Russell Bedford International*

Christian Koedam
*PwC Netherlands*

Filip Krsteski
*Van Doorne N.V.*

Andrej Kwitowski
*AKADIS b.v.*

Stefan Leening
*PwC Netherlands*

Allard Meine Jansen
*Allard Architecture*

Matthias Noorlander
*Office of Energy Regulation*

Peter Plug
*Office of Energy Regulation*

Johan Polet
*Simmons & Simmons LLP*

Peter Radema
*Merzario BV*

Mark G. Rebergen
*De Brauw Blackstone Westbroek*

Hugo Reumkens
*Van Doorne N.V.*

Maayke Rooijendijk
*De Brauw Blackstone Westbroek*

Rutger Schimmelpenninck
*Houthoff Buruma*

Stéphanie Spoelder
*Baker & McKenzie*

Michiel Stoove
*Bosselaar & Strengers Advocaten*

Natusia Szeliga
*Baker & McKenzie*

Fedor Tanke
*Baker & McKenzie*

Maarten Tinnemans
*De Brauw Blackstone Westbroek*

Jaap Jan Trommel
*NautaDutilh Attorneys*

Annet van Balen
*Bosselaar & Strengers Advocaten*

Helene van Bommel
*PwC Netherlands*

Leonard Van den Ende
*Baker & McKenzie*

Berdieke van den Hoek
*Bosselaar & Strengers Advocaten*

Jos van der Schans
*De Brauw Blackstone Westbroek*

Florentine van der Schrieck
*De Brauw Blackstone Westbroek*

Gert-Jan van Gijs
*VAT Logistics (Ocean Freight) BV*

Sjaak van Leeuwen
*Stichting Bureau Krediet Registratie*

Christian Van Megchelen
*Stibbe*

Jan van Oorschot
*Liander*

Petra van Raad
*PwC Netherlands*

Rodolfo Van Vlooten
*Kennedy Van der Laan*

Frédéric Verhoeven
*Houthoff Buruma*

Janine Verweij
*Office of Energy Regulation*

Reinout Vriesendorp
*De Brauw Blackstone Westbroek*

Frank Werger
*PwC Netherlands*

Stephan Westera
*Lexence*

Marcel Willems
*Kennedy Van der Laan*

Berto Winters
*De Brauw Blackstone Westbroek*

Marleen Zandbergen
*NautaDutilh Attorneys*

Christiaan Zijderveld
*Simmons & Simmons LLP*

**NEW ZEALAND**
*Inland Revenue Department*

*New Zealand Customs Service*

Connor Archbold
*Bell Gully*

Geoff Bevan
*Chapman Tripp*

Justin Cameron
*Lowndes Associates - Corporate and Commercial Law Specialists*

Shelley Cave
*Simpson Grierson, member of Lex Mundi*

Philip Coombe
*Panalpina World Transport LLP*

Ross Crotty
*Lowndes Associates - Corporate and Commercial Law Specialists*

John Cuthbertson
*PwC New Zealand*

Daniel De Vries
*Veda Advantage*

Kerr Dewe
*Lowndes Associates - Corporate and Commercial Law Specialists*

Joanne Dickson
*Simpson Grierson, member of Lex Mundi*

Igor Drinkovic
*Minter Ellison Rudd Watts*

Vince Duffin
*Vector Electricity*

Catherine Fonseca
*PwC New Zealand*

Koustabh Gadgil
*Investment New Zealand (a division of New Zealand Trade and Enterprise)*

Lowry Gladwell
*Bell Gully*

Matt Kersey
*Russell McVeagh*

Greg King
*Jackson Russell*

Mahesh Lala
*Jackson Russell*

Kate Lane
*Minter Ellison Rudd Watts*

Leroy Langeveld
*Simpson Grierson, member of Lex Mundi*

John Lawrence
*Auckland City Council*

Mark Lowndes
*Lowndes Associates - Corporate and Commercial Law Specialists*

Mandy McDonald
*Ministry of Economic Development*

Andrew Minturn
*Qualtech International Ltd.*

Robert Muir
*Land Information New Zealand*

Michael O'Brien
*Hesketh Henry Lawyers*

Catherine Otten
*New Zealand Companies Office*

Mihai Pascariu
*Minter Ellison Rudd Watts*

John Powell
*Russell McVeagh*

David Quigg
*Quigg Partners*

Jim Roberts
*Hesketh Henry Lawyers*

Silvana Schenone
*Minter Ellison Rudd Watts*

Howard Thomas
*Lowndes Associates - Corporate and Commercial Law Specialists*

Ben Thomson
*Simpson Grierson, member of Lex Mundi*

Amy Tiong
*PwC New Zealand*

Ben Upton
*Simpson Grierson, member of Lex Mundi*

Mike Whale
*Lowndes Associates - Corporate and Commercial Law Specialists*

Jessica Wilsher
*Lowndes Associates - Corporate and Commercial Law Specialists*

Richard Wilson
*Jackson Russell*

## NICARAGUA

*Exportadora Atlantic S.A*

Bertha Argüello de Rizo
*Arias & Muñoz*

Rosa Baca
*García & Bodán*

Marco Baldizón
*Disnorte-Dissur (Union Fenosa)*

Minerva Adriana Bellorín Rodríguez
*ACZALAW*

Marco Benavente
*García & Bodán*

Flavio Andrés Berríos Zepeda
*Multiconsult & CIA Ltda.*

Carlos Alberto Bonilla López
*Superintendencia de Bancos*

Orlando Cardoza
*Bufete Juridico Obregon y Asociados*

Thelma Carrion
*Aguilar Castillo Love*

Ramón Castro
*Arias & Muñoz*

Yuri Fernando Cerrato Espinoza
*Alvarado y Asociados, member of Lex Mundi*

Dorisabel Conrado
*Consortium Taboada y Asociados*

Sergio David Corrales Montenegro
*García & Bodán*

Juan Carlos Cortes
*PwC Nicaragua*

Eugenia Cruz
*CETREX*

Brenda Darce
*CETREX*

Gloria Maria de Alvarado
*Alvarado y Asociados, member of Lex Mundi*

Terencio Garcia Montenegro
*García & Bodán*

Engelsberth Gómez
*Pro Nicaragua*

Denis González Torres
*G.E. Electromecánica & Cia Ltda.*

Claudia Guevara
*Aguilar Castillo Love*

Federico Gurdian
*García & Bodán*

Marianela Gutierrez
*Aguilar Castillo Love*

Gerardo Hernandez
*Consortium Taboada y Asociados*

María Fernanda Jarquín
*Arias & Muñoz*

María José Peña
*Disnorte-Dissur (Union Fenosa)*

Eduardo Lacayo
*TransUnion*

José Mejía
*García & Bodán*

Jorge Molina Lacayo
*CETREX*

Roberto Montes
*Arias & Muñoz*

Soraya Montoya Herrera
*Molina & Asociados Central Law*

Jeanethe Morales Núñez
*Superintendencia de Bancos*

Amilcar Navarro Amador
*García & Bodán*

Francisco Ortega
*Francisco Ortega & Asociados*

Ramon Ortega
*PwC El Salvador*

Róger Pérez Grillo
*Arias & Muñoz*

Alonso Porras
*ACZALAW*

Mazziel Rivera
*ACZALAW*

Ana Teresa Rizo Briseño
*Arias & Muñoz*

Erwin Rodriguez
*PwC Nicaragua*

Patricia Rodríguez
*Multiconsult & CIA Ltda.*

Alfonso José Sandino Granera
*Consortium Taboada y Asociados*

Rodrigo Taboada
*Consortium Taboada y Asociados*

Carlos Téllez
*García & Bodán*

Diogenes Velasquez
*ACZALAW*

## NIGER

*Cabinet John W. Ffooks & Co.*

*Maersk S.A.*

Kassoum Abari
*Ville de Niamey*

Ahmadou Al Aminou Lo
*BCEAO*

Takoubakoye Aminata
*Millennium Challenge Account*

Mamoudou Aoula
*Ministère de l'Urbanisme, de l'Habitat et du Cadastre*

Sidi Sanoussi Baba Sidi
*Cabinet d'Avocats Souna-Coulibaly*

Joël Broux
*Bolloré Africa Logistics*

Moussa Coulibaly
*Cabinet d'Avocats Souna-Coulibaly*

Moussa Dantia
*Centre des Formalites des Entreprises*

Abdou Djando
*EMTEF*

Jean Claude Gnamien
*PwC Côte d'Ivoire*

Souley Hammi Illiassou

Moussa Gros Ibrahim
*Millennium Challenge Account*

Seybou Issifi
*Ville de Niamey*

Bernar-Oliver Kouaovi
*Cabinet Kouaovi*

Diallo Rayanatou Loutou
*Cabinet Loutou - Architectes*

Boubacar Nouhou Maiga
*ENGE*

Saadou Maiguizo
*Bureau d'Etudes Techniques d'Assistance et de Surveillance en Construction Civile*

Ari Malla
*Millennium Challenge Account*

Marie-Virginie Mamoudou
*Chambre Nationale des Notaires du Niger*

Issaka Manzo
*EGTC*

André Abboh Joseph Monso
*PwC Côte d'Ivoire*

Amadou Moussa
*Millennium Challenge Account*

Moukaïla Nouhou Hamani
*Cour Suprême*

Sahabi Oumarou
*Themis International Consultants*

Daouda Samna
*S.C.P.A. Mandela*

Abdou Moussa Sanoussi
*ENGE*

Dominique Taty
*PwC Côte d'Ivoire*

Idrissa Tchernaka
*Etude d'Avocats Marc Le Bihan & Collaborateurs*

Fousséni Traoré
*PwC Côte d'Ivoire*

Hamado Yahaya
*Societe Civile Professionnelle d'Avocats Yankori et associés*

Emmanuel Yehouessi
*BCEAO*

## NIGERIA

*Sterling Partnership*

Ijeoma Abalogu
*Gbenga Biobaku & Co*

Mohammed K. Abdulsalam
*GITRAS Ltd.*

Innocent Abidoye
*Nnenna Ejekam Associates*

Lemea Abina
*Sterling Partnership*

Oluseyi Abiodun Akinwunmi
*Akinwunmi & Busari Legal Practitioners*

Olaleye Adebiyi
*WTS Adebiyi & Associates*

Kentuadei Adefe

Kunle Adegbite
*Canaan Solicitors*

Steve Adehi
*Steve Adehi and Co*

Olufunke Adekoya
*AELEX, Legal Practitioners & Arbitrators*

Korode Adeola
*WTS Adebiyi & Associates*

Tolulope Aderemi
*Perchstone & Graeys*

Ademola Adesalu
*CRC Credit Bureau Limited*

Adekunle Adewale
*Jackson, Etti & Edu*

Yetunde Adewale
*Akinwunmi & Busari Legal Practitioners*

Daniel Agbor
*Udo Udoma & Belo-Osagie*

Kunle Ajagbe
*Perchstone & Graeys*

Olaoluwa Ajala
*Gbenga Biobaku & Co*

Koyin Ajayi
*Olaniwun Ajayi LP*

Barbara Ufuoma Akpotaire
*Dream Yard Project Inc.*

Overaye Brodrick Akpotaire
*LIDUD Nigeria Ltd.*

Folake Alabi
*Olaniwun Ajayi LP*

Jonathan Aluju
*Olaniwun Ajayi LP*

Segun Aluko
*Aluko & Oyebode*

Godwin Amadi
*Alliance Law Firm*

Owolabi Animashaun
*Scotech Universal Resources Limited*

Ifeoma Anwuta
*Punuka Attorneys & Solicitors*

Sola Arifayan
*Ikeyi & Arifayan*

Temitayo Arikenbi
*CRC Credit Bureau Limited*

Ige Asemudara
*Punuka Attorneys & Solicitors*

Esther Atoyebi
*Okonjo, Odiawa & Ebie*

Ayodeji Balogun
*Tony Elumelu Foundation*

Ngozi Chianakwalam
*Legal Standard Consulting*

Stanley Chikwendu
*AELEX, Legal Practitioners & Arbitrators*

Chinwe Chiwete
*Punuka Attorneys & Solicitors*

Peter Crabb
*Nnenna Ejekam Associates*

Rebecca Dokun
*Aluko & Oyebode*

Judith Egbeadumah
*Perchstone & Graeys*

Colin Egemonye
*Colin Egemonye & Associates*

Emmanuel Egwuagu
*Obla & Co.*

Oyindamola Ehiwere
*Udo Udoma & Belo-Osagie*

Nnenna Ejekam
*Nnenna Ejekam Associates*

Mary Ekemezie
*Udo Udoma & Belo-Osagie*

Nelson Ekere
*1st Attorneys*

Samuel Etuk
*1st Attorneys*

Marcellina Eya Abang
*Nigerian Electricity Regulatory Commission (NERC)*

Chris Eze
*Nnenna Ejekam Associates*

Adanma Ezegbulam
*WTS Adebiyi & Associates*

Anse Agu Ezetah
*Chief Law Agu Ezetah & Co.*

Kenechi Ezezika
*Ikeyi & Arifayan*

Babatunde Fagbohunlu
*Aluko & Oyebode*

Omowumi Fajemiroye
*Olaniwun Ajayi LP*

Olawale Fapohunda
*Ikeyi & Arifayan*

Olubunmi Fayokun
*Aluko & Oyebode*

Bimbola Fowler-Ekar
*Jackson, Etti & Edu*

Justice Idehen-Nathaniel
*Perchstone & Graeys*

Chimezie Iheakweazu
*Chikwem Chambers*

Chidinma Ihemedu
*Alliance Law Firm*

Agent Benjamin Ihua-Maduenyi
*Ihua & Ihua*

Nduka Ikeyi
*Ikeyi & Arifayan*

Okorie Kalu
*Punuka Attorneys & Solicitors*

Jelilat Kareem
*CRC Credit Bureau Limited*

Adetola Lawal
*Okonjo, Odiawa & Ebie*

Ishaya Livinus Etsu
*Nigerian Electricity Regulatory Commission (NERC)*

Nnenna Nwaokobia
*Nnenna Ejekam Associates*

Kenechi Nwizu
*Ikeyi & Arifayan*

Tochi Nwogu
*Punuka Attorneys & Solicitors*

Wole Obayomi
*KPMG*

V. Uche Obi
*Alliance Law Firm*

Godwin Obla
*Obla & Co.*

Oluwakemi Oduntan
*Jade & Stone Solicitors*

Tari Ofongo

Nelson Ogbuanya
*Nocs Consults*

Godson Ogheneochuko
*Udo Udoma & Belo-Osagie*

Ozofu Ogiemudia
*Udo Udoma & Belo-Osagie*

Yvonne Ogunoiki
*Ikeyi & Arifayan*

Ayodeji Ojo
*Jackson, Etti & Edu*

Titilayo Oke
*PwC Nigeria*

Ifedayo Oke-Lawal
*Perchstone & Graeys*

Oghenetekevwe Okobiah
*Jackson, Etti & Edu*

Christine Okokon
*Udo Udoma & Belo-Osagie*

Patrick Okonjo
*Okonjo, Odiawa & Ebie*

Dozie Okwuosah
*Central Bank of Nigeria*

Ololade Oladipupo
*Alliance Law Firm*

Adefunke Oladosu
*Akinwunmi & Busari Legal Practitioners*

Titilola Olateju
*Okonjo, Odiawa & Ebie*

Adebayo Ologe
*Perchstone & Graeys*

Ayotunde Ologe
*Synergy Legal Practitioners and Consultants*

Afolasade Olowe
*Jackson, Etti & Edu*

Oladipo Olukuewu
*Oladipo Olukuewu & Company*

Patrick Omeke
*Columbia University School of Law*

Jennifer Omozuwa
*Perchstone & Graeys*

Ekundayo Onajobi
*Udo Udoma & Belo-Osagie*

Fred Onuobia
*G. Elias & Co. Solicitors and Advocates*

Nnamdi Oragwu
*Punuka Attorneys & Solicitors*

Donald Orji
*Jackson, Etti & Edu*

Tunde Osasona
*Whitestone Worldwide Ltd.*

Yewande Oshile
*Aluko & Oyebode*

Olufemi Ososanya
*HLB Z.O. Ososanya & Co.*

Abraham Oyakhilome
*First & First International Agencies*

Taiwo Oyedele
*PwC Nigeria*

Tade Oyewunmi
*Alliance Law Firm*

Bukola Oyinlola
*Perchstone & Graeys*

Tunde Popoola
*CRC Credit Bureau Limited*

Titilola Rotifa
*Okonjo, Odiawa & Ebie*

Taofeek Shittu
*Ikeyi & Arifayan*

Adeola Sunmola
*Udo Udoma & Belo-Osagie*

Olufemi Sunmonu
*Femi Sunmonu & Associates, Solicitors*

Olubukola Thomas
*Perchstone & Graeys*

Chima Polly Ubechu
*Cenoux Logistics Ltd.*

Aniekan Ukpanah
*Udo Udoma & Belo-Osagie*

Adamu M. Usman
*F.O. Akinrele & Co.*

Edward Vera-Cruz
*Gbenga Biobaku & Co*

## NORWAY

*Advokatfirmaet Hjort DA, member of Ius Laboris*

*Agency for Planning and Building Services*

Eli Aasheim
*Wiersholm Law Office AS*

Sverre Ardø
*Experian*

Jan L. Backer
*Wikborg, Rein & Co.*

Guro Bakke Haga
*PwC Norway*

Stig Berge
*Advokatfirmaet Thommessen AS*

Jacob S. Bjønnes-Jacobsen
*Grette Law Firm DA*

Margrethe Buskerud Christoffersen
*Advokatfirmaet Thommessen AS*

Tron Dalheim
*Arntzen de Besche Advokatfirma AS*

Magnar Danielsen
*Ministry of the Environment*

Lars Davidsen
*Hafslund*

Åsne Dingsør Haukvik
*Advokatfirmaet Schjødt AS*

Knut Ekern
*PwC Norway*

Lars Eliassen
*The Bronnoysund Register Center*

Turid Ellingsen
*Statens Kartverk*

Simen Aasen Engebretsen
*Deloitte LLP*

Jan Erik Bauge
*Simonsen Advokatfirma DA*

Inger Eline Eriksen
*Grette Law Firm DA*

Claus R. Flinder
*Simonsen Advokatfirma DA*

Marius Moursund Gisvold
*Wikborg, Rein & Co.*

Hede Glimsdall
*Homble Olsby advokatfirma AS*

Maria Therese Haga
*Grette Law Firm DA*

Ruth Haile Tesfazion
*Grette Law Firm DA*

Odd Hylland
*PwC Norway*

Thomas Urdal Johnsen
*Wikborg, Rein & Co.*

Bjørn H. Kise
*Advokatfirma Vogt & Wiig AS*

Charlotte Kristensen
*PwC Norway*

Knut Martinsen
*Advokatfirmaet Thommessen AS*

Karl Erik Nedregotten
*PwC Norway*

Halfdan Nitter
*Nitter AS - correspondent of Russell Bedford International*

Ole Kristian Olsby
*Homble Olsby advokatfirma AS*

Lars S. Haugstvedt
*Wiersholm Law Office AS*

Camilla Schøyen Breibøl
*Wiersholm Law Office AS*

Ståle Skutle Arneson
*Advokatfirma Vogt & Wiig AS*

Oyvind Vagan
*The Bronnsund Register Center*

Ida Winters
*Homble Olsby advokatfirma AS*

## OMAN

Hamad Al Abri
*Muscat Electricity Distribution Company*

Zahir Abdulla Al Abri
*Muscat Electricity Distribution Company*

Zubaida Fakir Mohamed Al Balushi
*Central Bank of Oman*

Salman Ali Al Hattali
*Muscat Electricity Distribution Company*

Hanaan Al Marhuby
*PwC Oman*

Amer Al Rawas
*Omantel*

Said bin Saad Al Shahry
*SASLO - Said Al Shahry & Partners*

Majid Al Toky
*Trowers & Hamlins*

Khalid Khamis Al-Hashmi
*Muscat Municipality*

Zaid Al-Khattab
*Talal Abu Ghazaleh Legal (TAG-Legal)*

Ahmed al-Mukhaini
*SASLO - Said Al Shahry & Partners*

Ibrahim Albri
*Muscat Municipality*

Hilal Almayahi
*Muscat Municipality*

Mohamed Alrashdi
*Muscat Municipality*

Mohammed Alshahri
*Mohammed Alshahri & Associates*

Russell Aycock
*PwC Oman*

David Augustus Ball
*SASLO - Said Al Shahry & Partners*

Mahmoud Bilal
*SASLO - Said Al Shahry & Partners*

Yacoob Bin Salim Abdullah Al-Oufy
*Meyer-Reumann & Partners*

Sadaf Buchanan
*SNR Denton & Co.*

Akanksha Choubey
*SNR Denton & Co.*

Francis D'Souza
*BDO Jawad Habib*

Nasser A. Elhaidib
*Trowers & Hamlins*

Jamie Gibson
*Trowers & Hamlins*

Hussein
*Muscat Electricity Distribution Company*

Catherine Jaskiewicz
*Meyer-Reumann & Partners*

Robert Kenedy
*Curtis Mallet - Prevost, Colt & Mosle LLP*

Philip Keun
*SNR Denton & Co.*

Kenneth Macfarlane
*PwC Oman*

Jose Madukakuzhy
*Khimji Ramdas*

Siham Mahgoub
*SASLO - Said Al Shahry & Partners*

Pushpa Malani
*PwC Oman*

Krishnadas Mathilakath
*Bank Muscat*

Yashpal Mehta
*BDO Jawad Habib*

Haleem Mohammed
*SNR Denton & Co.*

Subha Mohan
*Curtis Mallet - Prevost, Colt & Mosle LLP*

Ahmed Naveed Farooqui
*Oman Cables Industry (SAOG)*

Bruce Palmer
*Curtis Mallet - Prevost, Colt & Mosle LLP*

Raghavendra Pangala
*Semac & Partners LLC*

George Sandars
*SNR Denton & Co.*

Rajshekhar Singh
*Bank Muscat*

Ganesan Sridhar
*Bank Muscat*

Roy Thomas
*Oman Cables Industry (SAOG)*

## PAKISTAN

Elsa Abbasi
*Abraham & Sarwana*

Sh. Farooq Abdullah
*Abraham & Sarwana*

Ali Jafar Abidi
*State Bank of Pakistan*

Masooma Afzal
*Haseeb Law Associates*

Mirza Taqi Ud Din Ahmad
*A.F. Ferguson & Co., Chartered Accountants, a member firm of PwC network*

Nadeem Ahmad
*Orr, Dignam & Co., Advocates*

Waheed Ahmad
*Maxim International Law Firm*

Anwaar Ahmed
*Securities and Exchange Commission of Pakistan*

Jawad Ahmed
*Muhammad Farooq & Co. Chartered Accountants*

Nasir Mehmood Ahmed
*Bunker Logistics*

Syed Akhter Ahmed
*Pyramid Pakistan*

Syed Asif Ali
*Pyramid Pakistan*

Syed Nasir Ali Gilani
*Zafar & Associates LLP*

Uzma Anwar
*Zafar & Associates LLP*

Sarah Arshad
*Surridge & Beecheno*

Armughan Ashfaq
*Surridge & Beecheno*

Hasnain Ashraf
*AQLAAL Advocates*

Khwaja Shaheryar Aziz
*A.F. Ferguson & Co., Chartered Accountants, a member firm of PwC network*

Major Javed Bashir
*Greenfields International*

Waheed Chaudhary
*LEGIS INN Attorneys & Corporate Consultants*

Fouad Rashid Dar
*Target Logistics Intl. (PVT) Ltd.*

Faisal Daudpota
*Khalid Daudpota & Co.*

Harish Dhamania
*Pyramid Pakistan*

Zaki Ejaz
*Zaki & Zaki Advocates and Solicitors*

Salman Faisal
*Haseeb Law Associates*

Ikram Fayaz
*Qamar Abbas & Co.*

Kausar Fecto
*Kausar Fecto & Co. Chartered Accountants*

Tahseen Ghani
*Hussain Home Textile*

Irfan Haider
*Pyramid Pakistan*

Asim Hameed Khan
*Ivon Trading Company Pvt. Ltd.*

Asma Hameed Khan
*Surridge & Beecheno*

Rashid Ibrahim
*A.F. Ferguson & Co., Chartered Accountants, a member firm of PwC network*

Samson Iqbal
*My Cargo Pvt. Ltd.*

Hasan Irfan Khan
*Irfan & Irfan*

Fiza Islam
*LEGIS INN Attorneys & Corporate Consultants*

Muzaffar Islam
*LEGIS INN Attorneys & Corporate Consultants*

Masooma Jaffer
*Abraham & Sarwana*

Mujtaba Jamal
*Mujtaba Jamal Law Associates*

Tariq Nasim Jan
*Datacheck Pvt. Ltd.*

Rubina Javed
*Texperts International*

M Javed Hassan
*Texperts International*

Aftab Ahmed Khan
*Surridge & Beecheno*

Arif Khan
*Qamar Abbas & Co.*

Sara IHayat
*Mujtaba Jamal Law Associates*

Farah Malik
*Haseeb Law Associates*

Muhammad Aslam Memon
*United Agencies*

Moazzam Mughal
*Boxing Winner*

Uzma Munir
*Hassan Kaunain Nafees*

Faiza Muzaffar
*LEGIS INN Attorneys & Corporate Consultants*

Jamal Panhwar
*Travel and Culture Services*

Abdul Rahman
*Qamar Abbas & Co.*

Zaki Rahman
*Ebrahim Hosain, Advocates and Corporate Counsel*

Ameeruddin Rana
*Abraham & Sarwana*

Tariq Saeed Rana
*Surridge & Beecheno*

Abdur Razzaq
*Qamar Abbas & Co.*

Jawad A. Sarwana
*Abraham & Sarwana*

Huma Shah
*M/s Sheikh Shah Rana & Ijaz*

Muhammad Siddique
*Securities and Exchange Commission of Pakistan*

Safdar Syed
*Abraham & Sarwana*

Muhammad Ashraf Tiwana
*AQLAAL Advocates*

Mian Haseeb ul Hassan
*Haseeb Law Associates*

Chaudhary Usman
*Ebrahim Hosain, Advocates and Corporate Counsel*

Saleem uz Zaman
*Saleem uz Zaman & Co.*

Javed Ahmed Vohra
*Fair Brothers International*

Fareed Yaldram
*Mujtaba Jamal Law Associates*

Muhammad Yousuf
*Haider Shamsi & Co., Chartered Accountants*

Ilyas Zafar
*Zafar & Associates LLP*

Akhtar Zaidi
*Zain Consulting*

Vaqar Zakaria
*Hagler Bailley Pakistan (Pvt) Ltd*

Amer Zia
*KESC*

### PALAU

*Bureau of Public Works*

*Palau Public Utility Corporation*

Maggy Antonio
*Koror Planning and Zoning Office*

Kenneth Barden
*Attorney-at-Law*

Cristina Castro
*Western Caroline Trading Co.*

Yukiwo P. Dengokl
*Dengokl, Dimitruk & Nakamura*

Rachel Dimitruk
*Dengokl, Dimitruk & Nakamura*

Suzanne Finney
*Palau Historic Preservation Office*

Sterlina Gabriel
*Bureau of Land and Surveys*

William Keldermans
*Palau Shipping Company, Inc.*

Kevin N. Kirk
*The Law Office of Kirk and Shadel*

Kuniwo Nakamura
*Belau Transfer & Terminal Co. Group*

Ramsey Ngiraibai
*Koror Planning and Zoning Office*

Lily Rdechor
*Palau Environmental Quality Protection Board*

Techur Rengulbai
*Bureau of Public Works*

William L. Ridpath
*William L. Ridpath, Attorney at Law*

David Shadel
*The Law Office of Kirk and Shadel*

Peter C. Tsao
*Western Caroline Trading Co.*

### PANAMA

Aristides Anguizola
*Morgan & Morgan*

Mercedes Araúz de Grimaldo
*Morgan & Morgan*

Gilberto Arosemena
*Arosemena Noriega & Contreras*

Amanda Barraza de Wong
*PwC Panama*

Jovani Bermudez
*Fire Department of Panama City*

Gustavo Adolfo Bernal
*Sociedad Panameña de Ingenieros y Arquitectos*

Javier Bouche
*Union Fenosa - EDEMET - EDECHI*

Jose A. Bozzo
*Garrido & Garrido*

Luis Carlos Bustamante
*Panamá Soluciones Logísticas Int. - PSLI*

Hernando Carrasquilla
*Registro Público de Panamá*

Irene Carrizo
*Ministry of Economy and Finances*

Luis Chalhoub
*Icaza, Gonzalez-Ruiz & Aleman*

Maria Lourdes Chanis
*CAPAC (Cámara Panameña de la Construcción)*

Aurelia Chen
*Mossack Fonseca & Co.*

Julio Cesar Contreras III
*Arosemena Noriega & Contreras*

Rigoberto Coronado
*Mossack Fonseca & Co.*

Eduardo De Alba
*Arias Fábrega & Fábrega*

Ana Belen de Zeimetz
*Eskildsen & Eskildsen*

M. Ducasa
*Arosemena Noriega & Contreras*

Manuel Ducasa
*Arosemena Noriega & Contreras*

Ricardo Eskildsen Morales
*Eskildsen & Eskildsen*

Mailyn Espinosa
*PwC Panama*

Michael Fernandez
*CAPAC (Cámara Panameña de la Construcción)*

Nicole Fernandez
*PwC Panama*

Jorge García
*ANAM*

Jorge Garrido
*Garrido & Garrido*

William Gonzales
*PwC Panama*

Yamileth Herrera
*Morgan & Morgan*

Anny Jordan
*CAPAC (Cámara Panameña de la Construcción)*

Andres Kosmas
*KPMG*

Ricardo Lachman
*Morgan & Morgan*

Ivette Elisa Martínez Saenz
*Patton, Moreno & Asvat*

Jair Montufar
*KPMG*

Erick Rogelio Muñoz
*Sucre, Arias & Reyes*

Boris Nuñez
*Registro Público de Panamá*

Ramon Ortega
*PwC El Salvador*

Maximiliano Quintero Domínguez
*Patton, Moreno & Asvat*

Ricardo Rocha
*KPMG*

Mario Rognoni
*Arosemena Noriega & Contreras*

Luz María Salamina
*Asociación Panameña de Crédito*

Carla Salvatierra
*Dirección de Obras y Construcciones Municipio de Panama*

Verónica Sinisterra
*Arosemena Noriega & Contreras*

Edwin Solis
*Panalpina World Transport LLP*

Raul Soto
*Arosemena Noriega & Contreras*

Ricardo Tribaldos Hernández
*Ministry of Economy and Finances*

Marlaine Tuñón
*Ministerio de Comercio e Industria*

Camilo Valdes

Ramón Varela
*Morgan & Morgan*

Juan Manuel Vasquez
*Dirección de Obras y Construcciones Municipio de Panama*

Carlos Villalobos
*Icaza, Gonzalez-Ruiz & Aleman*

### PAPUA NEW GUINEA

*PT Sea Horse Pacific - PNG*

Marjorie Andrew
*Consultative Implementation & Monitoring Council*

Whitman Atasoa
*PNG Power Ltd.*

Paul Barker
*Consultative Implementation & Monitoring Council*

Simon Bendo
*Department of Lands and Physical Planning*

Moses Billy
*Billy Architects*

David Caradus
*PwC Papua New Guinea*

Richard Flynn
*Ashurst LLP*

Vanessa Geita
*PwC Papua New Guinea*

Iboko Haraka
*Eltech Engineering Services Ltd.*

Kevin Hebou
*Morea Customs Agencies*

Stevens Kami
*Gadens Lawyers*

Timothy Koris
*PNG Power Ltd.*

Sarah Kuman
*Allens Arthur Robinson*

John Leahy
*Leahy Lewin Nutley Sullivan Lawyers*

Bruce Mackinlay
*Credit & Data Bureau Limited*

Nigel Merrick
*Warner Shand Lawyers Lae*

Vaughan Mills
*Allens Arthur Robinson*

Antonia Nohou
*PwC Papua New Guinea*

Lou Pipi
*NCDC Municipality*

Jason Reclamado
*Eltech Engineering Services Ltd.*

Ian Shepherd
*Ashurst LLP*

Thomas Taberia
*Leahy Lewin Nutley Sullivan Lawyers*

Tyson Yapao
*Allens Arthur Robinson*

### PARAGUAY

*Administración Nacional de Electricidad*

Magalí Rodríguez Alcalá
*Berkemeyer, Attorneys & Counselors*

Perla Alderete
*Vouga & Olmedo Abogados*

Florinda Benitez
*Notary public*

Enrique Benítez
*BDO Rubinsztein & Guillén*

Luis Alberto Breuer
*Berkemeyer, Attorneys & Counselors*

Esteban Burt
*Peroni, Sosa, Tellechea, Burt & Narvaja, member of Lex Mundi*

Laura Cabrera
*Vouga & Olmedo Abogados*

Lorena Dolsa
*Berkemeyer, Attorneys & Counselors*

Estefanía Elicetche
*Peroni, Sosa, Tellechea, Burt & Narvaja, member of Lex Mundi*

Natalia Enciso Benitez
*Notary public*

Bruno Fiorio Carrizosa
*Fiorio, Cardozo & Alvarado*

Juan Bautista Fiorio Gimenez
*Fiorio, Cardozo & Alvarado*

Veronica Franco
*Ferrere Abogados*

Néstor Gamarra
*Servimex SACI*

Jorge Guillermo Gomez
*PwC Paraguay*

Nadia Gorostiaga
*PwC Paraguay*

Carl Thomas Gwynn
*Gwynn & Gwynn - Legal Counselling and Translations*

Norman Gwynn
*Gwynn & Gwynn - Legal Counselling and Translations*

Jorge Jimenez Rey
*Banco Central del Paraguay*

Pablo Livieres Guggiari
*Estudio Jurídico Livieres Guggiari*

Nestor Loizaga
*Ferrere Abogados*

Augusto César Mengual Mazacotte
*Fiorio, Cardozo & Alvarado*

María Esmeralda Moreno
*Moreno Ruffinelli & Asociados*

Natalia Oddone
*Berkemeyer, Attorneys & Counselors*

Rocío Penayo
*Moreno Ruffinelli & Asociados*

Yolanda Pereira
*Berkemeyer, Attorneys & Counselors*

María Antonia Ramírez de Gwynn
*Gwynn & Gwynn - Legal Counselling and Translations*

Natalio Rubinsztein
*BDO Rubinsztein & Guillén*

Jorge Saba
*Fiorio, Cardozo & Alvarado*

Mauricio Salgueiro
*Vouga & Olmedo Abogados*

Guillermo Sarubbi
*Vouga & Olmedo Abogados*

Federico Silva
*Ferrere Abogados*

Ruben Taboada
*PwC Paraguay*

Ernesto Velázquez-Argaña
*Fiorio, Cardozo & Alvarado*

Lia Zanotti
*Peroni, Sosa, Tellechea, Burt & Narvaja, member of Lex Mundi*

### PERU

*PLFA & CIA Abogados, Asesores y Consultores*

*Sociedad Agricola Drokasa*

Jose Aguado
*Payet, Rey, Cauvi Abogados*

Walter Aguirre
*Aguirre Abogados & Asesores*

Marco Antonio Alarcón Piana
*Estudio Luis Echecopar García S.R.L.*

Alfonso Alvarez Calderón
*Estudio Alvarez Calderon*

Guilhermo Auler
*Jorge Avendaño & Forsyth Abogados*

Adriana Aurazo
*Russell Bedford Perú / Barzola & Asociados S.C. - member of Russell Bedford International*

Raul Barrios
*Barrios & Fuentes Abogados*

Maritza Barzola
*Russell Bedford Perú / Barzola & Asociados S.C. - member of Russell Bedford International*

Stephany Giovanna Bravo de Rueda Arce
*Ransa*

Jorge Calle
*Rubio Leguía Normand*

Liliana Callirgos
*Barrios & Fuentes Abogados*

Renzo Camaiora
*Gallo Barrios Pickmann*

Katherine Carranza
*PwC Peru*

José Castillo
*Russell Bedford Perú / Barzola & Asociados S.C. - member of Russell Bedford International*

Fernando Castro
*Muñiz, Ramírez, Peréz-Taiman & Olaya Abogados*

Cecilia Catacora
*Estudio Olaechea, member of Lex Mundi*

Alessandra Cocchella
*Rubio Leguía Normand*

Joanna Dawson
*Estudio Olaechea, member of Lex Mundi*

Ricardo de la Piedra
*Estudio Olaechea, member of Lex Mundi*

Alfonso De Los Heros Pérez Albela
*Estudio Luis Echecopar García S.R.L.*

Ginnette Deneumostier Carbonell
*CONUDFI*

Paula Devescovi
*Barrios & Fuentes Abogados*

Juan Carlos Durand Grahammer
*Durand Abogados*

Hugo Espinoza Rivera
*SUNARP*

Guillermo Ferrero
*Estudio Ferrero Abogados*

Mariana Franco
*Estudio Ferrero Abogados*

Luis Fuentes
*Barrios & Fuentes Abogados*

Jorge Fuentes
*Rubio Leguía Normand*

Carlos Gallardo Torres
*General Agency of Public Income Policy*

Javier Garcia
*Oficina de la Secretaria Tecnica de Calidad*

Juan García Montúfar
*Rubio Leguía Normand*

Pamela Goyzueta
*Equifax Peru S.A.*

Cecilia Guzmán-Barrón
*Gallo Barrios Pickmann*

Giuliana Higuchi
*Barrios & Fuentes Abogados*

Jose Antonio Honda
*Estudio Olaechea, member of Lex Mundi*

César Ballón Izquierdo
*Ransa*

Paul Jasaui
*Agencia San Remo*

Juan Carlos Leon

Gianfranco Linares
*Muñiz, Ramírez, Peréz-Taiman & Olaya Abogados*

German Lora
*Payet, Rey, Cauvi Abogados*

Juan Maranon
*PwC Peru*

Milagros Maravi Sumar
*Rubio Leguía Normand*

Carlos Martínez
*Rubio Leguía Normand*

Ricardo Martinez Alvarez
*ACREDITA S.A.C.*

Carlos Martínez Ebell
*Rubio Leguía Normand*

Jesús Matos
*Estudio Olaechea, member of Lex Mundi*

Jorge Mogrovejo
*Superintendency of Banking, Insurance and Private Pension Fund Administrator*

Ronaldo Moreno-Aramburú
*Barrios & Fuentes Abogados*

Javier Mori Cockburn
*Equifax Peru S.A.*

Miguel Mur
*PwC Peru*

Jorge Olcese
*Superintendency of Banking, Insurance and Private Pension Fund Administrator*

Lilian Oliver
*SUNARP*

Ariel Orrego-Villacorta
*Barrios & Fuentes Abogados*

Jorge Ortiz
*SUNARP*

Marco Palacios
*Bardeli & Palacios*

Max Panay Cuya
*SUNARP*

Mario Pereda
*Jorge Avendaño & Forsyth Abogados*

Adolfo Pinillos
*Miranda & Amado Abogados*

Lucianna Polar
*Estudio Olaechea, member of Lex Mundi*

Maribel Príncipe
*Rubio Leguía Normand*

María José Puertas
*Gallo Barrios Pickmann*

Bruno Marchese Quintana
*Rubio Leguía Normand*

Carlos Javier Rabanal Sobrino
*Durand Abogados*

Amilcar Ramos
*Equifax Peru S.A.*

Fernando M. Ramos
*Barrios & Fuentes Abogados*

Jorge Reategui
*Estudio Ferrero Abogados*

Sonia L. Rengifo
*Barrios & Fuentes Abogados*

Alonso Rey Bustamante
*Payet, Rey, Cauvi Abogados*

Jose M. Reyes
*Barrios & Fuentes Abogados*

Yulissa Rivero
*Jorge Avendaño & Forsyth Abogados*

Guillermo Acuña Roeder
*Rubio Leguía Normand*

Jose Rosas
*Lima Chamber of Commerce*

Lucy Ruiz
*OCR Aduanas*

Emil Ruppert
*Rubio Leguía Normand*

Carolina Sáenz Llanos
*Rubio Leguía Normand*

Mateo Salinas
*Estudio Olaechea, member of Lex Mundi*

Adolfo Sanabria
*Muñiz, Ramírez, Peréz-Taiman & Olaya Abogados*

Arturo Ruiz Sanchez
*Rubio Leguía Normand*

Paola Joselyn Sánchez Alfaro
*Ransa*

Victor Scarsi
*Luz del Sur*

Martin Serkovic
*Estudio Olaechea, member of Lex Mundi*

Hugo Silva
*Rodrigo, Elías, Medrano Abogados*

Liliana Tsuboyama Shiohama
*Estudio Luis Echecopar García S.R.L.*

Daniel Ulloa
*Rebaza, Alcazar & De Las Casas Abogados Financieros*

Carlos Urbina Cárcamo
*Ransa*

Jack Vainstein
*Vainstein & Ingenieros S.A.*

Erick Valderrama Villalobos
*PwC Peru*

José Antonio Valdez
*Estudio Olaechea, member of Lex Mundi*

Omar Valle
*Barrios & Fuentes Abogados*

Edwin Vilca
*PwC Peru*

Manuel Villa-García
*Estudio Olaechea, member of Lex Mundi*

Agustín Yrigoyen
*García Sayán Abogados*

Gustavo Zanabria
*General Agency of Foreign Economic Matters, Competition and Private Investment*

Hector Zegarra
*Payet, Rey, Cauvi Abogados*

Heidy Zuzunaga
*Aguirre Abogados & Asesores*

## PHILIPPINES
*Ernst & Young*

Jazmin Banal
*Romulo, Mabanta, Buenaventura, Sayoc & de los Angeles, member of Lex Mundi*

Manuel Battallones
*BAP Credit Bureau, Inc.*

Antonio T. Bote
*International Consolidator Philippines, Inc.*

Alexander Cabrera
*Isla Lipana & Co.*

Ciriaco S. Calalang
*Calalang Law Offices*

Ernesto Caluya Jr.
*Jimenez Gonzales Bello Valdez Caluya & Fernandez*

Mylene Capangcol
*Department of Energy*

Cecile Margaret Caro
*SyCip Salazar Hernandez & Gatmaitan*

Bryant Casiw
*Baker & McKenzie*

Domingo Castillo
*SyCip Salazar Hernandez & Gatmaitan*

Jon Edmarc Castillo
*SyCip Salazar Hernandez & Gatmaitan*

Sandhya Marie Castro
*Romulo, Mabanta, Buenaventura, Sayoc & de los Angeles, member of Lex Mundi*

Kenneth Chua
*Quisumbing Torres, member firm of Baker & McKenzie International*

Barbra Jill Clara
*SyCip Salazar Hernandez & Gatmaitan*

Juan Paolo Colet
*Castillo Laman Tan Pantaleon & San Jose*

Emerico O. de Guzman
*Angara Abello Concepcion Regala & Cruz Law Offices (ACCRALAW)*

Dino de los Angeles
*Romulo, Mabanta, Buenaventura, Sayoc & de los Angeles, member of Lex Mundi*

Anthony Dee
*SyCip Salazar Hernandez & Gatmaitan*

Rafael del Rosario
*Romulo, Mabanta, Buenaventura, Sayoc & de los Angeles, member of Lex Mundi*

Juana M. Dela Cruz
*International Consolidator Philippines, Inc.*

Redel Domingo
*MERALCO*

Rachel Follosco
*Follosco Morallos & Herce*

Catherine Franco
*Quisumbing Torres, member firm of Baker & McKenzie International*

Gilberto Gallos
*Angara Abello Concepcion Regala & Cruz Law Offices (ACCRALAW)*

Geraldine S. Garcia
*Follosco Morallos & Herce*

Andres Gatmaitan
*SyCip Salazar Hernandez & Gatmaitan*

Nicole Dawn Gavine
*Isla Lipana & Co.*

Victor Genuino
*MERALCO*

Vicente Gerochi
*SyCip Salazar Hernandez & Gatmaitan*

Gwen Grecia-de Vera
*Puyat, Jacinto & Santos Law Office*

Jessica Hilado
*Puyat, Jacinto & Santos Law Office*

Tadeo F. Hilado
*Angara Abello Concepcion Regala & Cruz Law Offices (ACCRALAW)*

Thea Marie Jimenez
*Quasha Ancheta Pena & Nolasco*

Carina Laforteza
*SyCip Salazar Hernandez & Gatmaitan*

Hiyasmin Lapitan
*SyCip Salazar Hernandez & Gatmaitan*

Benjamin Lerma
*Romulo, Mabanta, Buenaventura, Sayoc & de los Angeles, member of Lex Mundi*

Esther Claudine F. Lim
*Angara Abello Concepcion Regala & Cruz Law Offices (ACCRALAW)*

Erich H. Lingad
*International Consolidator Philippines, Inc.*

Ronald Mark Lleno
*SyCip Salazar Hernandez & Gatmaitan*

Roberto Locsin
*International Container Terminal Services, Inc.*

Eleanor Lucas Roque
*Punongbayan & Araullo*

Bhong Paulo Macasaet
*SyCip Salazar Hernandez & Gatmaitan*

Yolanda Mendoza-Eleazar
*Castillo Laman Tan Pantaleon & San Jose*

Maria Teresa Mercado-Ferrer
*SyCip Salazar Hernandez & Gatmaitan*

Marianne Miguel
*SyCip Salazar Hernandez & Gatmaitan*

Jose Salvador Mirasol
*Romulo, Mabanta, Buenaventura, Sayoc & de los Angeles, member of Lex Mundi*

Jesusito G. Morallos
*Follosco Morallos & Herce*

Freddie Naagas
*SCM Creative Concepts Inc.*

Jomini C. Nazareno
*Romulo, Mabanta, Buenaventura, Sayoc & de los Angeles, member of Lex Mundi*

Amanda Nograles
*Romulo, Mabanta, Buenaventura, Sayoc & de los Angeles, member of Lex Mundi*

Leonid C. Nolasco
*Castillo Laman Tan Pantaleon & San Jose*

Carla Ortiz
*Romulo, Mabanta, Buenaventura, Sayoc & de los Angeles, member of Lex Mundi*

Maria Christina Ortua
*SyCip Salazar Hernandez & Gatmaitan*

Ma. Minerva Paez-Collantes
*Jimenez Gonzales Bello Valdez Caluya & Fernandez*

Benedicto Panigbatan
*SyCip Salazar Hernandez & Gatmaitan*

Emmanuel C. Paras
*SyCip Salazar Hernandez & Gatmaitan*

Senen Quizon
*Punongbayan & Araullo*

Elaine Patricia S. Reyes
*Angara Abello Concepcion Regala & Cruz Law Offices (ACCRALAW)*

Ricardo J. Romulo
*Romulo, Mabanta, Buenaventura, Sayoc & de los Angeles, member of Lex Mundi*

Lea L. Roque
*Punongbayan & Araullo*

Neptali Salvanera
*Angara Abello Concepcion Regala & Cruz Law Offices (ACCRALAW)*

Froilan Savet
*MERALCO*

Abigail D. Sese
*Castillo Laman Tan Pantaleon & San Jose*

Felix Sy
*Baker & McKenzie*

Sheryl Tanquilut
*Romulo, Mabanta, Buenaventura, Sayoc & de los Angeles, member of Lex Mundi*

Carlos Martin Tayag
*Romulo, Mabanta, Buenaventura, Sayoc & de los Angeles, member of Lex Mundi*

Herman Tinoyan
*Isla Lipana & Co.*

Anna Bianca Torres
*Puyat, Jacinto & Santos Law Office*

Patrick Tovey
*International Container Terminal Services, Inc.*

Glenn T. Tuazon
*Romulo, Mabanta, Buenaventura, Sayoc & de los Angeles, member of Lex Mundi*

Shirley Velasquez
*Puyat, Jacinto & Santos Law Office*

Peter Young
*International Container Terminal Services, Inc.*

Maria Winda Ysibido
*Isla Lipana & Co.*

Redentor C. Zapata
*Quasha Ancheta Pena & Nolasco*

Gil Roberto Zerrudo
*Quisumbing Torres, member firm of Baker & McKenzie International*

## POLAND

*Agencja Transportowa Makro Service*

*Allen & Overy, A. Pędzich sp.k.*

*Bird & Bird Maciej Gawroński sp.k.*

*Business & Law Blog*

*Jolanta Barej Notary*

*Małgorzata Morelowska-Mamińska Notary*

*PwC Poland*

*Rejestr Dłużników ERIF Biuro Informacji Gospodarczej S.A.*

Michał Anastasiu
*Kancelaria Prawa Gospodarczego i Ekologicznego dr Bartosz Draniewicz*

Grzegorz Banasiuk
*Gide Loyrette Nouel Poland Warsaw*

Michal Barłowski
*Wardyński & Partners*

Ewelina Bartnik
*MultiBank S.A.*

Michal Białobrzeski
*Hogan Lovells (Warszawa) LLP*

Anna Bochnia
*DLA Piper Wiater sp.k.*

Aleksander Borowicz
*Biuro Informacji Kredytowej S.A.*

Sławomir Boruc
*Baker & McKenzie*

Urszula Brzezińska
*Blackstones*

Piotr Brzeziński
*Gide Loyrette Nouel Poland Warsaw*

Tomasz Chentosz
*Baker & McKenzie*

Pawel Cupriak
*Paweł Cupriak Notary*

Agnieszka Czarnecka
*KPT Tax Advisors*

Tomasz Czech
*Raiffeisen Bank Polska S.A.*

Michał Dąbrowski
*Ministry of Justice*

Andrzej Dmowski
*Russell Bedford DZO Sp. z.o.o. - member of Russell Bedford International*

Bartosz Draniewicz
*Kancelaria Prawa Gospodarczego i Ekologicznego dr Bartosz Draniewicz*

Mateusz Dróżdż
*Gide Loyrette Nouel Poland Warsaw*

Edyta Dubikowska
*Squire Sanders Święcicki Krześniak sp.k.*

Rafal Dziedzic
*Gide Loyrette Nouel Poland Warsaw*

Piotr Falarz
*DLA Piper Wiater sp.k.*

Agnieszka Fedor
*WKB Wiercinski, Kwiecinski, Baehr*

Krzysztof Feluch
*Wierzbowski Eversheds, member of Eversheds International Ltd.*

Marek Firlej
*Ministry of Finance*

Joanna Gasowski
*Wierzbowski Eversheds, member of Eversheds International Ltd.*

Lech Giliciński
*Wierzbowski Eversheds, member of Eversheds International Ltd.*

Michał Gliński
*Wardyński & Partners*

Rafał Godlewski
*Wardyński & Partners*

Paweł Grześkowiak
*Gide Loyrette Nouel Poland Warsaw*

Łukasz Hejmej
*White & Case W. Daniłowicz, W. Jurcewicz i Wspólnicy - Kancelaria Prawna sp.k.*

Mariusz Hildebrand
*BIG InfoMonitor SA*

Magdalena Inglot
*White & Case W. Daniłowicz, W. Jurcewicz i Wspólnicy - Kancelaria Prawna sp.k.*

Witold Jarzyński
*Magnusson*

Joanna Jasiewicz
*Gide Loyrette Nouel Poland Warsaw*

Jakub Jędrzejak
*WKB Wiercinski, Kwiecinski, Baehr*

Adam Jerzykowski
*Wardyński & Partners*

Magdalena Kalińska
*WKB Wiercinski, Kwiecinski, Baehr*

Rafał Kamiński
*White & Case W. Daniłowicz, W. Jurcewicz i Wspólnicy - Kancelaria Prawna sp.k.*

Tomasz Kański
*Sołtysiński Kawecki & Szlęzak*

Katarzyna Kapuścińska
*Ministry of Justice*

Iwona Karasek-Wojciechowicz
*Jagiellonian University*

Mariusz Każuch
*Ministry of Finance*

Karol Kołowski
*Law Firm Domański Zakrzewski Palinka*

Katarzyna Konstanty
*Nikiel & Partners Law Office*

Olga Koszewska
*Chadbourne & Parke LLP*

Agnieszka Kowalska
*Gide Loyrette Nouel Poland Warsaw*

Kinga Kowalska
*Gide Loyrette Nouel Poland Warsaw*

Ewa Łachowska - Brol
*Wierzbowski Eversheds, member of Eversheds International Ltd.*

Konrad Piotr Lewandowski

Marta Liberda - Stembalska
*Krajowy Rejestr Długów Biuro Informacji Gospodarczej S.A.*

Agnieszka Lisiecka
*Wardyński & Partners*

Wojciech Łuczka
*Hogan Lovells (Warszawa) LLP*

Anna Krystyna Machulak
*Baker & McKenzie*

Paweł Mazurkiewicz
*MDDP Michalik Dłuska Dziedzic i Partnerzy*

Sebastian Michalik
*Cargo-Partner spedycja sp. z.o.o.*

Tomasz Michalik
*MDDP Michalik Dłuska Dziedzic i Partnerzy*

Anna Misiak
*MDDP Michalik Dłuska Dziedzic i Partnerzy*

Magdalena Moczulska
*Wardyński & Partners*

Michal Niemirowicz-Szczytt
*bnt Neupert Zamorska & Partnerzy sp.j.*

Michał Nowacki
*Wardyński & Partners*

Justyna Nowak
*Baker & McKenzie*

Dariusz Okolski
*Okolski Law Office*

Krystyna Olczak
*Russell Bedford DZO Sp. z.o.o. - member of Russell Bedford International*

Anita Ołdakowska

Krzysztof Pawlak
*Sołtysiński Kawecki & Szlęzak*

Weronika Pelc
*Wardyński & Partners*

Alexandra Pereira dos Reis
*Raposo Bernardo & Associados*

Łukasz Piebiak
*Regional Court in Warsaw*

Tomasz Połeć
*KPT Tax Advisors*

Adrian Praczuk
*Ministry of Finance*

Bartłomiej Raczkowski
*Bartłomiej Raczkowski Kancelaria Prawa Pracy*

Piotr Sadownik
*Gide Loyrette Nouel Poland Warsaw*

Katarzyna Sarek
*Bartłomiej Raczkowski Kancelaria Prawa Pracy*

Alicja Sarna
*MDDP Michalik Dłuska Dziedzic i Partnerzy*

Piotr Siciński
*Piotr Siciński Notary*

Karol Skibniewski
*Sołtysiński Kawecki & Szlęzak*

Zbigniew Skórczyński
*Chadbourne & Parke LLP*

Michał Steinhagen
*Wardyński & Partners*

Ewelina Stobiecka
*Taylor Wessing, e|n|v|c*

Peter Święcicki
*Squire Sanders Święcicki Krześniak sp. k.*

Aleksandra Sypek
*KPT Tax Advisors*

Izabela Szczygielska
*WKB Wiercinski, Kwiecinski, Baehr*

Łukasz Szegda
*Wardyński & Partners*

Paweł Szmurło
*Nikiel & Partners Law Office*

Maciej Szwedowski
*Squire Sanders Święcicki Krześniak sp. k.*

Anna Tarasiuk-Flodrowska
*Hogan Lovells (Warszawa) LLP*

Dariusz Tokarczuk
*Gide Loyrette Nouel Poland Warsaw*

Katarzyna Trzaska
*Baker & McKenzie*

Sylwia Tylenda
*Raposo Bernardo & Associados*

Dominika Wagrodzka
*bnt Neupert Zamorska & Partnerzy sp.j.*

Dariusz Wasylkowski
*Wardyński & Partners*

Joanna Wierzejska
*Law Firm Domański Zakrzewski Palinka*

Anna Wietrzyńska
*DLA Piper Wiater sp.k.*

Robert Windmill
*Windmill Gąsiewski & Roman Law Office*

Steven Wood
*Blackstones*

Tomasz Zabost
*ProLogis*

Małgorzata Zamorska
*bnt Neupert Zamorska & Partnerzy sp.j.*

Katarzyna Zarębska
*White & Case W. Daniłowicz, W. Jurcewicz i Wspólnicy - Kancelaria Prawna sp.k.*

Grażyna Zaremba
*Russell Bedford DZO Sp. z o.o. - member of Russell Bedford International*

Tomasz Zasacki
*Wardyński & Partners*

Magdalena Zwolińska
*Bartłomiej Raczkowski Kancelaria Prawa Pracy*

Sylwester Zydowicz
*Taylor Wessing, e|n|v|c*

## PORTUGAL

Joana Abreu
*Abreu Advogados*

Paula Alegria Martins
*Mouteira Guerreiro, Rosa Amaral & Associados - Sociedade de Advogados R.L.*

Bruno Andrade Alves
*PwC Portugal*

Nuno Alves Mansilha
*Miranda Correia Amendoeira & Associados - Sociedade de Advogados RL*

Rogério Alves Vieira
*Associação dos Transitários de Portugal - APAT*

Joana Andrade Correia
*Raposo Bernardo & Associados*

Filipa Arantes Pedroso
*Morais Leitão, Galvão Teles, Soares da Silva & Associados, member of Lex Mundi*

Miguel Azevedo
*J & A Garrigues, S.L.P*

Diana Bandeira
*Pedro Raposo & Associados*

João Banza
*PwC Portugal*

João Nuno Barrocas
*Barrocas Advogados*

Manuel P. Barrocas
*Barrocas Advogados*

Irina Bartman Ferreira
*PwC Portugal*

Marco Bicó da Costa
*Credinformações/ Equifax*

Zita Brito Limpo
*Pedro Raposo & Associados*

Vicente Caldeira Pires
*Pedro Raposo & Associados*

Fernando Cardoso da Cunha
*Gali Macedo & Associados*

Fernando Carmo
*CÂMARA Despachantes Oficiais*

Tiago Castanheira Marques
*Abreu Advogados*

Susana Cebola
*Instituto dos Registos e do Notariado*

Paula Coelho
*PwC Portugal*

Marcelo Correia Alves
*Barrocas Advogados*

Joaquim Correia Teixeira
*EDP Distribuição - Energia, SA*

Andreia Damásio
*Pedro Raposo & Associados*

Miguel de Avillez Pereira
*Abreu Advogados*

João Cadete de Matos
*Banco de Portugal*

Carlos de Sousa e Brito
*Carlos de Sousa e Brito & Associados*

Cristina Dein
*Dein Advogados*

João Duarte de Sousa
*J & A Garrigues, S.L.P*

Jaime Esteves
*PwC Portugal*

Bruno Ferreira
*J & A Garrigues, S.L.P*

Sofia Ferreira Enriquez
*Raposo Bernardo & Associados*

Ana Filipa Ribeiro
*PwC Portugal*

Nélson Freitas
*PwC Portugal*

Nuno Pimentel Gomes
*Abreu Advogados*

Patricia Gomes
*Morais Leitão, Galvão Teles, Soares da Silva & Associados, member of Lex Mundi*

Tania Gomes
*Neville de Rougemont & Associados*

Paulo Henriques
*P. Henriques - Consultoria, Lda.*

Inga Kilikeviciene
*KPL Legal*

Tiago Lemos
*PLEN - Sociedade de Advogados, RL*

Diogo Léonidas Rocha
*J & A Garrigues, S.L.P*

Daniel Lobo Antunes
*Carlos de Sousa e Brito & Associados*

Jorge Pedro Lopes
*Polytechnic Institute of Bragança*

Helga Lopes Ribeiro
*Mouteira Guerreiro, Rosa Amaral & Associados - Sociedade de Advogados R.L.*

Tiago Gali Macedo
*Gali Macedo & Associados*

Ana Margarida Maia
*Miranda Correia Amendoeira & Associados - Sociedade de Advogados RL*

Francisco José Maia Coelho
*AICCOPN-Associação dos Industriais da Construção Civil e Obras Públicas*

Pedro Manuel Niza
*PwC Portugal*

Miguel Marques dos Santos
*J & A Garrigues, S.L.P*

Isabel Martínez de Salas
*J & A Garrigues, S.L.P*

Francisco Guimarães Melo
*PwC Portugal*

Susana Melo
*Grant Thornton LLP*

Anabela Mendes
*PwC Portugal*

Joaquim Luis Mendes
*Grant Thornton LLP*

Gonçalo Meneses
*Carlos de Sousa e Brito & Associados*

Ana Pinto Morais
*PwC Portugal*

João Moucheira
*Instituto dos Registos e do Notariado*

António Mouteira Guerreiro
*Mouteira Guerreiro, Rosa Amaral & Associados - Sociedade de Advogados R.L.*

Vânia Nicolau
*Pedro Raposo & Associados*

Rita Nogueira Neto
*J & A Garrigues, S.L.P*

Catarina Nunes
*PwC Portugal*

Vitorino Oliveira
*Instituto dos Registos e do Notariado*

António Luís Pereira Figueiredo
*Instituto dos Registos e do Notariado*

Acácio Pita Negrão
*PLEN - Sociedade de Advogados, RL*

Rita Pitacas
*Pedro Raposo & Associados*

Margarida Ramalho
*Associação de Empresas de Construção, Obras Públicas e Serviços*

Nelson Raposo Bernardo
*Raposo Bernardo & Associados*

Maria João Ricou
*Cuatrecasas, Gonçalves Pereira*

Filomena Rosa
*Instituto dos Registos e do Notariado*

Francisco Salgueiro
*Neville de Rougemont & Associados*

Miguel Santana
*Miranda Correia Amendoeira & Associados - Sociedade de Advogados RL*

Pedro Santos
*Grant Thornton LLP*

Raquel Santos
*Morais Leitão, Galvão Teles, Soares da Silva & Associados, member of Lex Mundi*

Filipe Santos Barata
*Gómez-Acebo & Pombo Abogados, S.L.P. Sucursal em Portugal*

Susana Santos Valente
*Pedro Raposo & Associados*

Cristina Serrazina
*Pedro Raposo & Associados*

Ana Sofia Silva
*Cuatrecasas, Gonçalves Pereira*

Cláudia Silva Nunes
*Pedro Raposo & Associados*

Luís Filipe Sousa
*PwC Portugal*

Carmo Sousa Machado
*Abreu Advogados*

Rui Souto
*Pedro Raposo & Associados*

João Paulo Teixeira de Matos
*J & A Garrigues, S.L.P*

Ricardo Veloso
*VMP - Veloso, Mendes, Pato e Associados*

Antônio Vicente Marques
*AVM Advogados*

## PUERTO RICO (U.S.)

Viviana Aguilu
*PwC Puerto Rico*

Alfredo Alvarez-Ibañez
*O'Neill & Borges*

Salvador Antonetti
*O'Neill & Borges*

Vicente Antonetti
*Goldman Antonetti & Córdova PSC*

Juan Aquino
*O'Neill & Borges*

Antonio A. Arias-Larcada
*McConnell Valdés LLC*

Luis Ariza
*ABF Freight Systems, Inc.*

James A. Arroyo
*TransUnion De Puerto Rico*

Vanessa Badillo
*O'Neill & Borges*

Pedro Barcelo

Hermann Bauer
*O'Neill & Borges*

Nikos Buxeda Ferrer
*Adsuar Muñiz Goyco Seda & Pérez-Ochoa, PSC*

Edward Calvesbert
*Departamento de Desarrollo Económico Puerto Rico*

Adriana Capacete
*O'Neill & Borges*

Jorge Capó Matos
*O'Neill & Borges*

Vanessa Carballido
*O'Neill & Borges*

Solymar Castillo-Morales
*Goldman Antonetti & Córdova PSC*

Samuel Céspedes Jr.
*McConnell Valdés LLC*

Odemaris Chacon
*William Estrella | Attorneys & Counselors*

Walter F. Chow
*O'Neill & Borges*

Miguel A. Cordero
*Puerto Rico Electric Power Authority*

Myrtelena Diaz-Pedrosa
*Adsuar Muñiz Goyco Seda & Pérez-Ochoa, PSC*

Veronica Duran
*Banco Popular de Puerto Rico*

Antonio Escudero
*McConnell Valdés LLC*

Alfonso Fernandez
*Ivyport Logistical Services Inc.*

David Freedman
*O'Neill & Borges*

Julio Galindez
*FPV & Galíndez, PSC - member of Russell Bedford International*

Virginia Gomez
*Puerto Rico Electric Power Authority*

William Gutierrez
*Banco Popular de Puerto Rico*

Pedro Janer
*CMA Architects & Engineers LLP*

Gabriel Maldonado
*Quiñones & Sánchez, PSC*

Oswald Maldonado
*Laparkan*

Rubén M. Medina-Lugo
*Cancio, Nadal, Rivera & Díaz*

Oscar O. Meléndez - Sauri
*Malley Tamargo & Meléndez-Sauri, LLC*

Juan Carlos Méndez
*McConnell Valdés LLC*

Jose Morales
*Sun Air Expedite Service*

Julio Pereira
*Platinum Cargo Logistics*

Thelma Rivera
*Goldman Antonetti & Córdova PSC*

Victor Rodriguez
*Multitransport & Marine Co.*

Victor Rodriguez
*PwC Puerto Rico*

Ana Margarita Rodríguez
*O'Neill & Borges*

Victor R. Rodríguez
*O'Neill & Borges*

Loudres Rodriguez-Morera

Edgardo Rosa-Ortiz
*FPV & Galíndez, PSC - member of Russell Bedford International*

Jorge M. Ruiz Montilla
*McConnell Valdés LLC*

Patricia Salichs
*McConnell Valdés LLC*

Alejandro Siguerea
*Quiñones & Sánchez, PSC*

Eduardo Tamargo
*Malley Tamargo & Meléndez-Sauri, LLC*

Paola Ubiñas
*O'Neill & Borges*

Carlos Valldejuly
*O'Neill & Borges*

Tania Vazquez Maldonado
*Banco Popular de Puerto Rico*

Raúl Vidal y Sepúlveda
*Department of Economic Development and Commerce*

Travis Wheatley
*O'Neill & Borges*

## QATAR

Abdelmoniem Abutiffa
*Qatar International Law Firm*

Hani Al Naddaf
*Al Tamimi & Company Advocates & Legal Consultants*

Khalifa Al-Moselmani
*Doha Court of First Instance*

Rashed Albuflasa
*Panalpina Qatar WLL*

Clarine Assaf
*Badri and Salim El Meouchi Law Firm, member of Interleges*

Monita Barghachieh
*Patton Boggs LLP*

Sleiman Dagher
*Badri and Salim El Meouchi Law Firm, member of Interleges*

Fouad El Haddad
*Clyde & Co.*

Chadia El Meouchi
*Badri and Salim El Meouchi Law Firm, member of Interleges*

Ömer Elmas
*AGA-MEP Contracting & Engineering Co. LLC*

Sami Fakhoury
*Al Tamimi & Company Advocates & Legal Consultants*

Sarah Fakhry
*Badri and Salim El Meouchi Law Firm, member of Interleges*

Mohamed Fouad
*Sultan Al-Abdulla & Partners*

Robert Hager
*Patton Boggs LLP*

Walid Honein
*Badri and Salim El Meouchi Law Firm, member of Interleges*

Ahmed Jaafir
*Al Tamimi & Company Advocates & Legal Consultants*

Marie-Anne Jabbour
*Badri and Salim El Meouchi Law Firm, member of Interleges*

Marc Jreidini
*Badri and Salim El Meouchi Law Firm, member of Interleges*

Maryline Kalaydjian
*Badri and Salim El Meouchi Law Firm, member of Interleges*

Upuli Kasturiarachchi
*PwC Qatar*

Sajid Khan
*PwC Qatar*

Frank Lucente
*Al Tamimi & Company Advocates & Legal Consultants*

Mustafa Mahmoud
*Supreme Judiciary Council, Qatar*

Seem Maleh
*Al Tamimi & Company Advocates & Legal Consultants*

Elias Matni
*Badri and Salim El Meouchi Law Firm, member of Interleges*

Declan Mordaunt
*PwC Qatar*

Rita Moukarzel
*Badri and Salim El Meouchi Law Firm, member of Interleges*

Ahmed Tawfik Nassim
*Ahmed Tawfik & Co. Certified Public Accountant*

Charbel Neaman
*Clyde & Co.*

Sujani Nisansala
*PwC Qatar*

Mike Palmer
*Patton Boggs LLP*

Lyka Rom
*Ahmed Tawfik & Co. Certified Public Accountant*

David Salt
*Clyde & Co.*

Mohammad Sami
*Al Sulaiti, Attorneys, Legal Consultants & Arbitrators, MENA City Lawyers*

Zain Al Abdin Sharar
*Qatar Financial Markets Authority (QFMA)*

Abdul Aziz Mohammed Sorour
*Ministry of Justice*

Terence G.C. Witzmann
*HSBC*

## ROMANIA

*ANRE*

Nicolaie Adam
*Țuca Zbârcea & Asociații*

Andrei Albulescu
*Țuca Zbârcea & Asociații*

Adelina Anghel
*Gebrueder Weiss Romania SRL*

Cosmin Anghel
*Clifford Chance Badea SCA*

Gabriela Anton
*Țuca Zbârcea & Asociații*

Andrei Badiu
*3B Expert Audit - member of Russell Bedford International*

Irina Elena Bănică
*POP PEPA SCA Attorneys- at- Law*

Alexandra Barac
*POP PEPA SCA Attorneys- at- Law*

Paula Boteanu
*DLA Piper Dinu SCA*

Vlad Cercel
*Țuca Zbârcea & Asociații*

Alin Chitu
*Țuca Zbârcea & Asociații*

Victor Ciocîltan
*Oancea Ciocîltan & Asociatii*

Raluca Coman
*Clifford Chance Badea SCA*

Oana Cornescu
*Țuca Zbârcea & Asociații*

Dorin Coza
*Sulica Protopopescu Vonica*

Sergius Crețu
*Țuca Zbârcea & Asociații*

Alex Cristea
*Țuca Zbârcea & Asociații*

Radu Damaschin
*Nestor Nestor Diculescu Kingston Petersen*

Rebeca Dan
POP PEPA SCA ATTORNEYS-AT-LAW

Crina Danila
MUŞAT & ASOCIAŢII

Peter De Ruiter
PwC ROMANIA

Adrian Deaconu
TAXHOUSE SRL

Georgiana Descultu
PwC ROMANIA

Luminita Dima
NESTOR NESTOR DICULESCU KINGSTON
PETERSEN

Rodica Dobre
PwC ROMANIA

Ion Dragulin
NATIONAL BANK OF ROMANIA

Laura Adina Duca
NESTOR NESTOR DICULESCU KINGSTON
PETERSEN

Serban Epure
BIROUL DE CREDIT

Georgiana Evi
CLIFFORD CHANCE BADEA SCA

Adriana Gaspar
NESTOR NESTOR DICULESCU KINGSTON
PETERSEN

Monica Georgiadis
DLA PIPER DINU SCA

Sergiu Gidei
D&B DAVID ŞI BAIAS LAW FIRM

Laura Gradinescu
DLA PIPER DINU SCA

Daniela Gramaticescu
NESTOR NESTOR DICULESCU KINGSTON
PETERSEN

Mihai Guia
LINA & GUIA SCA

Horia Hispas
ŢUCA ZBÂRCEA & ASOCIAŢII

Ana-Maria Hritcu
SULICA PROTOPOPESCU VONICA

Cristina Iacobescu
POP PEPA SCA ATTORNEYS-AT-LAW

Iulian Iosif
MUŞAT & ASOCIAŢII

Diana Emanuela Ispas
NESTOR NESTOR DICULESCU KINGSTON
PETERSEN

Crenguta Leaua
LEAUA & ASOCIATII

Cristian Lina
LINA & GUIA SCA

Edita Lovin
RETIRED JUDGE OF ROMANIAN SUPREME
COURT OF JUSTICE

Ileana Lucian
MUŞAT & ASOCIAŢII

Andreea-Maria Lupulet
POP PEPA SCA ATTORNEYS-AT-LAW

Smaranda Mandrescu
POP PEPA SCA ATTORNEYS-AT-LAW

Dumitru Viorel Manescu
NATIONAL UNION OF CIVIL LAW
NOTARIES OF ROMANIA

Gelu Maravela
MUŞAT & ASOCIAŢII

Carmen Medar
D&B DAVID ŞI BAIAS LAW FIRM

Raluca Mihaila
PwC ROMANIA

Cătălina Mihăilescu
ŢUCA ZBÂRCEA & ASOCIAŢII

Ana Mirea
CLIFFORD CHANCE BADEA SCA

Tiberius Mitu-Dumitrescu
OANCEA CIOCÎLTAN & ASOCIATII

Amalia Musat
DLA PIPER DINU SCA

Mona Musat
MUŞAT & ASOCIAŢII

Razvan Nanescu
NESTOR NESTOR DICULESCU KINGSTON
PETERSEN

Adriana Neagoe
NATIONAL BANK OF ROMANIA

Manuela Marina Nestor
NESTOR NESTOR DICULESCU KINGSTON
PETERSEN

Theodor Catalin Nicolescu
NICOLESCU & PERIANU LAW FIRM

Tudor Oancea
OANCEA CIOCÎLTAN & ASOCIATII

Marius Pătrăşcanu
MUŞAT & ASOCIAŢII

Steven Pepa
POP PEPA SCA ATTORNEYS-AT-LAW

Laurenţiu Petre
SĂVESCU VOINESCU ŞI ASOCIAŢII

Monica Pirvulescu
POP PEPA SCA ATTORNEYS-AT-LAW

Ana Maria Placintescu
MUŞAT & ASOCIAŢII

Carolina Pletniuc
LINA & GUIA SCA

Claudiu Pop
POP PEPA SCA ATTORNEYS-AT-LAW

Eugen Pop

Alina Elena Popescu
MUŞAT & ASOCIAŢII

Mariana Popescu
NATIONAL BANK OF ROMANIA

Tiberiu Potyesz
BITRANS LTD.

Monica Preotescu
NESTOR NESTOR DICULESCU KINGSTON
PETERSEN

Sebastian Radocea
ŢUCA ZBÂRCEA & ASOCIAŢII

Cristian Radu
ŢUCA ZBÂRCEA & ASOCIAŢII

Laura Radu
STOICA & ASOCIAŢII - SOCIETATE
CIVILĂ DE AVOCAŢI

Alexandra Rimbu
MUŞAT & ASOCIAŢII

Angela Rosca
TAXHOUSE SRL

Adrian Rotaru
CLIFFORD CHANCE BADEA SCA

Andrei Săvescu
SĂVESCU VOINESCU ŞI ASOCIAŢII

Valentin Serban
SALANS MOORE & ASOCIATII SCA

Catalina Sodolescu
NESTOR NESTOR DICULESCU KINGSTON
PETERSEN

Alexandru Stanciu
LEAUA & ASOCIATII

Anca Stanciulescu
LAW OFFICES CORNEL TABARTA

Lorena Stanciulescu
LAW OFFICES CORNEL TABARTA

Sorin Corneliu Stratula
STRATULA MOCANU & ASOCIATII

Mariana Sturza
ŢUCA ZBÂRCEA & ASOCIAŢII

Miruna Suciu
MUŞAT & ASOCIAŢII

Roxana Talasman
NESTOR NESTOR DICULESCU KINGSTON
PETERSEN

Florin Tineghe
DLA PIPER DINU SCA

Andra Trantea
DLA PIPER DINU SCA

Oana Tudorache
PwC ROMANIA

Anca Maria Ulea
MUŞAT & ASOCIAŢII

Ionut Ursache
PwC ROMANIA

Cristina Vedel
POP PEPA SCA ATTORNEYS-AT-LAW

Cristina Virtopeanu
NESTOR NESTOR DICULESCU KINGSTON
PETERSEN

## RUSSIAN FEDERATION

Andrei Afanasiev
BAKER & MCKENZIE - CIS, LIMITED

Marat Agabalyan
HERBERT SMITH CIS LLP

Mike Allen
RUSSIAN CONSULTING LLC

Julia Andreeva
CAPITAL LEGAL SERVICES LLC

Anatoly E. Andriash
NORTON ROSE (CENTRAL EUROPE) LLP

Mikhail Anosov
CAPITAL LEGAL SERVICES LLC

Irina Anyukhina
ALRUD LAW FIRM

Igor Arakelov
ALRUD LAW FIRM

Stefan Bah
PUBLISHING HOUSE CUSTOMS
TERMINALS

Konstantin Baranov
CMS LEGAL

Elena Barikhnovskaya
SALANS

Derek Bloom
CAPITAL LEGAL SERVICES LLC

Egor Bogdanov
GIDE LOYRETTE NOUEL, MEMBER OF
LEX MUNDI

Julia Borozdna
PEPELIAEV GROUP

Sergey Budylin
ROCHE & DUFFAY

Maria Bykovskaya
GIDE LOYRETTE NOUEL, MEMBER OF
LEX MUNDI

David Cranfield
CMS LEGAL

George Darasselia
NORTON ROSE (CENTRAL EUROPE) LLP

Irina Davidovskaya
CHAMBER OF TAX ADVISERS OF RUSSIA

Andrey Demusenko
RUSSIAN CONSULTING LLC

Irina Dmitrieva
WHITE & CASE LLC

Oleg Ganeles

Roman Golovatsky
DLA PIPER RUS LIMITED

Maria Gorban
GIDE LOYRETTE NOUEL, MEMBER OF
LEX MUNDI

Inna Havanova
CHAMBER OF TAX ADVISERS OF RUSSIA

Maria Ivakina
ALRUD LAW FIRM

Ivan Ivanov
FINEC

Anton Kalanov
INTEREXPERTIZA LLC, MEMBER OF AGN
INTERNATIONAL

Pavel Karpunin
CAPITAL LEGAL SERVICES LLC

Ekaterina Karunets
BAKER & MCKENZIE - CIS, LIMITED

Alexander Khretinin
HERBERT SMITH CIS LLP

Ruslan Kiss
RUSSIAN LOGISTICS PROVIDER

Olga Konkova
ABU ACCOUNTING SERVICES

Anastasia Konovalova
NORTON ROSE (CENTRAL EUROPE) LLP

Oksana Kostenko
CMS LEGAL

Alyona Kozyreva
NORTON ROSE (CENTRAL EUROPE) LLP

Alyona Kucher
DEBEVOISE & PLIMPTON LLP

Artem Kukin
YUST

Victoria Kushner
PEPELIAEV GROUP

Olga Laletina

David Lasfargue
GIDE LOYRETTE NOUEL, MEMBER OF
LEX MUNDI

Stepan Lubavsky
FINEC

Dmitry Lyakhov
RUSSIN & VECCHI, LLC

Igor N. Makarov
BAKER & MCKENZIE - CIS, LIMITED

Anna Maximenko
DEBEVOISE & PLIMPTON LLP

Mikhail Morozov

Igor Nevsky
MIKHAILOV & PARTNERS - MEMBER OF
RUSSELL BEDFORD INTERNATIONAL

Elena Novikova
ALRUD LAW FIRM

Elena Ogawa
LEVINE BRIDGE

Aleksandr Panarin
LOGISTIC SERVICE

Sergey Pankov
ABU ACCOUNTING SERVICES

Andrey Panov
MONASTYRSKY, ZYUBA, STEPANOV &
PARTNERS

Roman Peikrishvili
TNB-LINE

Andrey Pestov
ZAO 2B2

Sergey Petrachkov
ALRUD LAW FIRM

Oleg Petrov
CMS LEGAL

Olga Pimanova
ALRUD LAW FIRM

Sergey Pozdnyakov
ZAO ZNAK

Evgeny Saklakov
WHITE & CASE LLC

André Scholz
RÖDL & PARTNER

Vladimir Shikin
NATIONAL BUREAU OF CREDIT
HISTORIES

Ksenia Sidorova
YUST

Maria Sinyavskaya
CMS LEGAL

Victoria Sivachenko
ALRUD LAW FIRM

Alexey Soldatov
ABU ACCOUNTING SERVICES

Julia Solomkina
LEVINE BRIDGE

Maria Solovykh
ALRUD LAW FIRM

Ekaterina Starostina
NATIONAL BUREAU OF CREDIT
HISTORIES

Tatiana Stepanenko
RUSSIAN CONSULTING LLC

Valentina Subbotina
INTEREXPERTIZA LLC, MEMBER OF AGN
INTERNATIONAL

Victoria Subocheva
RUSSIN & VECCHI, LLC

Vitaliy Survillo
PUBLIC NATIONWIDE ORGANIZATION
BUSINESS RUSSIA

Ivetta Tchistiakova-Berd
GIDE LOYRETTE NOUEL, MEMBER OF
LEX MUNDI

Ivan Tertychny
NORTON ROSE (CENTRAL EUROPE) LLP

Pavel Timofeev
HANNES SNELLMAN LLC

Daria Trozanova
LEVINE BRIDGE

Alexander Tsakoev
NORTON ROSE (CENTRAL EUROPE) LLP

Olga Yudina
CMS LEGAL

Vladislav Zabrodin
CAPITAL LEGAL SERVICES LLC

Julia Zasukhina
NORTON ROSE (CENTRAL EUROPE) LLP

Andrey Zavalishin
CMS LEGAL

Marina Zaykova
CLOSED STOCK COMPANY STS ENERGY

Andrey Zelenin
LIDINGS LAW FIRM

Evgeny Zhilin
YUST

## RWANDA

BRALIRWA LTD.

NATIONAL BANK OF RWANDA

Alberto Basomingera
CABINET D'AVOCATS MHAYIMANA

Pierre Célestin Bumbakare
RWANDA REVENUE AUTHORITY

Eric Cyaga
K-SOLUTIONS AND PARTNERS

Claudine Gasarabwe
GASARABWE CLAUDINE & ASSOCIES

Patrick Gashagaza
GPO PARTNERS RWANDA LIMITED, AN
INDEPENDENT CORRESPONDENT FIRM OF
DELOITTE TOUCHE TOHMATSU

Felix Gatanazi
EWSA

Jean Havugimana
ECODESEP LTD.

Suzanne Iyakaremye
SDV TRANSAMI

Francois Xavier Kalinda
UNIVERSITÉ NATIONALE DU RWANDA

Désiré Kamanzi
KAMANZI, NTAGANIRA & ASSOCIATES

Marcellin Kamanzi
*Bureau d'Etudes d'Architecture et de Réalisation (BEAR)*

Julien Kavaruganda
*K-Solutions and Partners*

Rodolphe Kembukuswa
*SDV Transami*

Bernice Kimacia
*PwC*

Isaïe Mhayimana
*Cabinet d'Avocats Mhayimana*

Joseph Mpunga
*Rwanda Development Board*

Donatien Mucyo
*Mucyo & Associés*

Paul Frobisher Mugambwa
*PwC Uganda*

Alexandre Mugenzangabo
*Mucyo & Associés*

Richard Mugisha
*Trust Law Chambers*

Léopold Munderere
*Cabinet d'Avocats-Conseils*

Pothin Muvara

Ernest Mwiza
*Town Nice View*

Jean Kizito Niyonshuti
*Kamanzi, Ntaganira & Associates*

Martin Nkurunziza
*GPO Partners Rwanda Limited, an Independent Correspondent Firm of Deloitte Touche Tohmatsu*

Marie Ange Nsengimana
*Kamanzi, Ntaganira & Associates*

Jean Claude Nsengiyumva
*Tribunal de Commerce de Nyarugenge*

Paul Pavlidis
*Credit Reference Bureau Africa Ltd.*

Lucien Ruterana
*EWSA*

Etienne Ruzibiza

Sandrali Sebakara
*Bureau d'Etudes CAEDEC*

Florence Umurungi
*Freight Logistic Services Ltd.*

Ravi Vadgama
*Credit Reference Bureau Africa Ltd.*

## SAMOA

*Electric Power Corporation*

*Leavai Law*

Mike Betham
*Transam Ltd.*

Ferila Brown
*Planning and Urban Management Agency*

Lawrie Burich
*Quantum Contrax Ltd*

Murray Drake
*Drake & Co.*

Ruby Drake
*Drake & Co.*

Fiona Ey
*Clarke Ey Lawyers*

Heather Ikenasio-Heather
*Ministry of Natural Resources & Environment*

Siŝiŝi Aumua Isaia Lameko
*Ministry of Commerce, Industry and Labour*

Sala Isitolo Leota
*Public Accountant*

Arthur R. Penn
*Lesa ma Penn*

Faletasi Sao
*Samoe Realty Estate*

Wilber Stewart
*Stewart Architecture*

Grace Stowers
*Stevensons Lawyers*

Shan Shiraz Ali Usman
*Tradepac Marketing Ltd.*

Sieni Voorwinden
*Manager Legal*

## SÃO TOMÉ AND PRÍNCIPE

*Guiché Único Para Empresas*

Eudes Aguiar
*Aguiar & Pedronho Studio*

André Aureliano Aragão
*Jurisconsulta & Advogado*

Helder Batista
*Despachante Helder Batista*

Sukayna Braganca
*Banco Internacional de São Tomé e Príncipe*

Celiza Deus Lima
*JPALMS Advogados*

Saul Fonseca
*Miranda Correia Amendoeira & Associados - Sociedade de Advogados RL*

Amadeu Goncalves
*Manuel Roque Ltda.*

Pedro Guiomar
*Supermaritime São Tomé*

Fernando Lima da Trindade
*Ministry of Publics Works, Geographical-Cadastre, Natural Resources, and Environment*

Vítor Marques da Cruz
*FCB&A in association with Posser da Costa & Associados*

Idalina Martinho
*Despachante Helder Batista*

Raul Mota Cerveira
*Miranda Correia Amendoeira & Associados - Sociedade de Advogados RL*

João Branco Pedro
*National Laboratory of Civil Engineering*

Ana Rijo
*Miranda Correia Amendoeira & Associados - Sociedade de Advogados RL*

Hugo Rita
*Terra Forma*

Ana Roque
*Manuel Roque Ltda.*

José Manuel Roque
*Manuel Roque Ltda.*

Cláudia Santos Malaquias
*Miranda Correia Amendoeira & Associados - Sociedade de Advogados RL*

Nayda Silveira D'Almeida
*AVM Advogados Portugal*

Rui Veríssimo
*Soares Da Costa*

Teresa Veríssimo
*Soares Da Costa*

Antônio Vicente Marques
*AVM Advogados*

## SAUDI ARABIA

*Electricity & Co-Generation Regulatory Authority*

*Talal bin Naif Al-Harbi Law Firm*

Abdulaziz Abdullatif
*Al-Soaib Law Firm*

Asad Abedi
*The Alliance of Abbas F. Ghazzawi & Co. and Hammad, Al-Mehdar & Co.*

Fayyaz Ahmad
*Jones Lang LaSalle*

Naeem Akhtar
*Capital Logistics & Transport*

Amer Abdulaziz Al Amr
*DLA Piper*

Majed Al Hedayan
*Chamber of Commerce & Industry*

Omar Al Saab
*Law Office of Mohanned Bin Saud Al-Rasheed in association with Baker Botts LLP*

Fouad Mohammed Al-Abdulqader
*Saudi Electricity Company*

Gihad Al-Amri
*Dr. Mohamed Al-Amri & Co.*

Naïm Al-Chami
*Talal Abu Ghazaleh Legal (TAG-Legal)*

Sulaiman R. Al-Fraih
*Al-Fraih Law Office*

Mohammed Al-Ghamdi
*Fulbright & Jaworski LLP*

Abdullah Al-Hashim
*Al-Jadaan & Partners Law Firm*

Tala Al-Hejailan
*DLA Piper*

Mohammed Al-Jadaan
*Al-Jadaan & Partners Law Firm*

Yousef A. Al-Joufi
*Al-Joufi Law Firm*

Fahad I. Al-Khudairy
*Fadha Engineering Consultants*

Nabil Abdullah Al-Mubarak
*Saudi Credit Bureau - SIMAH*

Lamia Abdulaziz Al-Ogailee
*Fulbright & Jaworski LLP*

Ayedh Al-Otaibi
*Saudi Arabian General Investment Authority*

Ahmed A. Al-Sabti
*Saudi Arabian General Investment Authority*

Abdullatif Bin Abdullah Al-Shelash
*Dar Al-Arkan*

Mohammed Al-Soaib
*Al-Soaib Law Firm*

Turki M. AlBallaa
*The Law Office of Bander Alnogaithan*

Fayez Aldebs
*PwC Saudi Arabia*

Omar AlHoshan
*AlHoshan CPAs & Consultants - correspondent of Russell Bedford International*

Bander A. Alnogaithan
*The Law Office of Bander Alnogaithan*

Wicki Andersen
*Baker Botts LLP*

Abdul Moeen Arnous
*Law Office of Hassan Mahassni*

Arwa Aulaqi
*Bafakih & Nassief*

Karim Aziz

Wael Fadl Bafakih
*Bafakih & Nassief*

John Balouziyeh
*SNR Denton*

Kamal El-Batnigi
*KPMG*

Majdi El-Shami
*Omrania & Associates*

Imad El-Dine Ghazi
*Law Office of Hassan Mahassni*

Rahul Goswami
*Law Office of Hassan Mahassni*

Shadi Haroon
*Law Office of Mohanned Bin Saud Al-Rasheed in association with Baker Botts LLP*

John Harris
*Jones Lang LaSalle*

Kenny Hawsey
*PwC Saudi Arabia*

Chadi F. Hourani
*Hourani & Associates*

Amgad Husein
*SNR Denton*

Samer Jamhour
*Talal Abu Ghazaleh Legal (TAG-Legal)*

Mohammad Kamran Sial
*KPMG*

Zaid Mahayni
*Law Office of Hassan Mahassni*

Waheed M. Mallisho
*Al Rashid Trading & Contracting Company*

Rukn Eldeen Mohammed
*Omrania & Associates*

Nadine Murshid
*Bafakih & Nassief*

Eyad R. Reda
*DLA Piper*

Mustafa Saleh
*EMDAD Arriyadh*

Abdul Shakoor
*Globe Marine Services Co.*

Archana Sinha
*RCS Pvt. Ltd Business Advisors Group*

Peter Stansfield
*Al-Jadaan & Partners Law Firm*

Neil Sturgeon
*Dr. Mohamed Al-Amri & Co.*

Sameh M. Toban
*Toban, Attorneys at law & legal Advisors*

Mohammed Yaghmour
*PwC Saudi Arabia*

Natasha Zahid
*Baker Botts LLP*

Abdul Aziz Zaibag
*Alzaibag Consultants*

Soudki Zawaydeh
*PwC Saudi Arabia*

## SENEGAL

*Bolloré Africa Logistics*

*Cabinet John W. Ffooks & Co.*

Ahmadou Al Aminou Lo
*BCEAO*

Marie Ba
*BDO*

Magatte Dabo
*Transfret Dakar*

Ibrahima Diagne
*Gainde 2000*

Amadou Dioulidé Diallo
*Ministère de l'Urbanisme et de l'Assainissement*

Fidèle Dieme
*Senelec*

Adoul Aziz Dieng
*Centre de Gestion Agréé de Dakar*

Issa Dione
*Senelec*

Fodé Diop
*Art Ingegierie Afrique*

Amadou Diop
*Gainde 2000*

Khadijatou Fary Diop Thiombane
*Cabinet Jurafrik Conseil en Affaires (JCA)*

Amadou Drame
*Cabinet d'Avocat Cheikh Fall*

Cheikh Fall
*Cabinet d'Avocat Cheikh Fall*

Aïssatou Fall
*PricewaterhouseCoopers Tax & Legal SA*

Bakary Faye
*BDS*

Seynabou Faye
*Cabinet d'Avocat Cheikh Fall*

Moustapha Faye
*Société Civile Professionnelle d'Avocats François Sarr & Associés*

Elehadji Madiop Feme
*COSELEC*

Antoine Gomis
*SCP Senghor & Sarr, Notaires Associés*

Sylvie Gomis
*SCP Senghor & Sarr, Notaires Associés*

Matthias Hubert
*PricewaterhouseCoopers Tax & Legal SA*

Abdou Dialy Kane
*Cabinet Maître Abdou Dialy Kane*

Mahi Kane
*PricewaterhouseCoopers Tax & Legal SA*

Mouhamed Kebe
*Geni & Kebe*

Ousseynou Lagnane
*BDS*

Moussa Mbacke
*Etude Notariale Moussa Mbacke*

Mamadou Mbaye
*SCP Mame Adama Gueye & Associés*

Dame Mbaye
*Transfret Dakar*

Ibrahima Mbodj
*Avocat à la Cour*

Aly Mar Ndiaye
*Commission de Régulation du Secteur de l'Electricité*

Ndéné Ndiaye

Moustapha Ndoye
*Avocat à la Cour*

Joséphine Ngom
*PricewaterhouseCoopers Tax & Legal SA*

Babacar Sall
*BDS*

Mbacké Sene
*Senelec*

Fatma Sene
*Société Civile Professionnelle d'Avocats François Sarr & Associés*

Daniel-Sédar Senghor
*SCP Senghor & Sarr, Notaires Associés*

Codou Sow-Seck
GENI & KEBE

Ibra Thiombane
CABINET JURAFRIK CONSEIL EN AFFAIRES
(JCA)

Sokna Thiombane
CABINET JURAFRIK CONSEIL EN AFFAIRES
(JCA)

Baba Traore
TRANSFRET DAKAR

Emmanuel Yehouessi
BCEAO

### SERBIA
TRIMO INZENJERING D.O.O.

Milos Andjelkovic
WOLF THEISS

Aleksandar Andrejic
PRICA & PARTNERS LAW OFFICE

Marija Bojović
BOJOVIĆ DAŠIĆ KOJOVIĆ

Bojana Bregovic
WOLF THEISS

Milan Brkovic
ASSOCIATION OF SERBIAN BANKS

Marina Bulatovic
WOLF THEISS

Ana Čalić
PRICA & PARTNERS LAW OFFICE

Ivan Cavdarevic
PRICA & PARTNERS LAW OFFICE

Jovan Cirkovic
HARRISON SOLICITORS

Vladimir Dabić
THE INTERNATIONAL CENTER FOR
FINANCIAL MARKET DEVELOPMENT

Dejan Davidovic
NINKOVIĆ LAW OFFICE

Vera Davidović
MARIĆ, MALIŠIĆ & DOSTANIĆ O.A.D.
CORRESPONDENT LAW FIRM OF GIDE
LOYRETTE NOUEL

Simon Dayes
CMS CAMERON MCKENNA

Nikola Djordjevic
LAW OFFICES JANKOVIĆ, POPOVIĆ
& MITIĆ

Uroš Djordjević
ŽIVKOVIĆ & SAMARDŽIĆ LAW OFFICE

Nemanja Djukic
ŽIVKOVIĆ & SAMARDŽIĆ LAW OFFICE

Jelena Kuveljic Dmitric
LAW OFFICES ZECEVIC & LUKIC

Veljko Dostanic
MARIĆ, MALIŠIĆ & DOSTANIĆ O.A.D.
CORRESPONDENT LAW FIRM OF GIDE
LOYRETTE NOUEL

Dragan Draca
PwC SERBIA

Vuk Drašković
BOJOVIĆ DAŠIĆ KOJOVIĆ

Jelena Gazidova
LAW OFFICES JANKOVIĆ, POPOVIĆ
& MITIĆ

Danica Gligorijevic
PRICA & PARTNERS LAW OFFICE

Milanka Jaric
PRICA & PARTNERS LAW OFFICE

Dejan Jeremić
REPUBLIC GEODETIC AUTHORITY

Aleksandra Jović
CMS CAMERON MCKENNA

Nemanja Kačavenda
A.D. INTEREUROPA, BELGRADE

Tatjana Kaplanovic
JETSET REAL ESTATE AGENCY

Dimitrios Katsaros
IKRP ROKAS & PARTNERS

Nikola Kliska
MARIĆ, MALIŠIĆ & DOSTANIĆ O.A.D.
CORRESPONDENT LAW FIRM OF GIDE
LOYRETTE NOUEL

Vidak Kovacevic
WOLF THEISS

Ivan Krsikapa
NINKOVIĆ LAW OFFICE

Dejan Krstic
FREE LANCE LEGAL CONSULTANT

Zach Kuvizić
KUVIZIC & TADIC LAW OFFICE

Krzysztof Lipka
PwC SERBIA

Rastko Malisic
MARIĆ, MALIŠIĆ & DOSTANIĆ O.A.D.
CORRESPONDENT LAW FIRM OF GIDE
LOYRETTE NOUEL

Aleksandar Mančev
PRICA & PARTNERS LAW OFFICE

Ines Matijević-Papulin
HARRISON SOLICITORS

Dimitrije Nikolić
CARGO T. WEISS D.O.O.

Djurdje Ninković
NINKOVIĆ LAW OFFICE

Bojana Noskov
WOLF THEISS

Jelena Obradović
ŽIVKOVIĆ & SAMARDŽIĆ LAW OFFICE

Darija Ognjenović
PRICA & PARTNERS LAW OFFICE

Igor Oljačić
ADVOKATSKA KANCELARIJA OLJAČIĆ

Vladimir Perić
PRICA & PARTNERS LAW OFFICE

Mihajlo Prica
PRICA & PARTNERS LAW OFFICE

Ana Radivojević
PwC SERBIA

Oliver Radosavljevic
MARIĆ, MALIŠIĆ & DOSTANIĆ O.A.D.
CORRESPONDENT LAW FIRM OF GIDE
LOYRETTE NOUEL

Stojan Semiz
CMS CAMERON MCKENNA

Dragana Stanojević
USAID BUSINESS ENABLING PROJECT
(BY CARDNO EMERGING MARKETS
USA)

Milica Steljić
ADVOKATSKA KANCELARIJA OLJAČIĆ

Petar Stojanović
JOKSOVIC, STOJANOVIC AND PARTNERS

Zoran Teodosijević
LAW OFFICES JANKOVIĆ, POPOVIĆ
& MITIĆ

Ana Tomic
JOKSOVIC, STOJANOVIC AND PARTNERS

Snežana Tošić
SERBIAN BUSINESS REGISTERS AGENCY

Sanja Vesic
A.D. INTEREUROPA, BELGRADE

Andreja Vrazalic
MORAVČEVIĆ, VOJNOVIĆ &
ZDRAVKOVIĆ U SARADNJI SA
SCHONHERR

Milenko Vucaj
PD ELEKTRODISTRIBUCIJA BEOGRAD
D.O.O.

Srećko Vujaković
MORAVČEVIĆ, VOJNOVIĆ &
ZDRAVKOVIĆ U SARADNJI SA
SCHONHERR

Tanja Vukotić Marinković
SERBIAN BUSINESS REGISTERS AGENCY

Miloš Vulić
PRICA & PARTNERS LAW OFFICE

Miloš Živković
ŽIVKOVIĆ & SAMARDŽIĆ LAW OFFICE

### SEYCHELLES
ERNST & YOUNG

INTERNATIONAL LAW & CORPORATE
SERVICES LTD.

PUBLIC UTILITIES CORPORATION

Gerry Adam
MAHE SHIPPING CO. LTD.

Clifford Andre
P&A ASIA

Jules Baker
MINISTRY OF LABOUR AND HUMAN
RESOURCES DEVELOPMENT

Lucienne Charlette
SEYCHELLES REGISTRAR GENERAL

Andre D. Ciseau
SEYCHELLES PORTS AUTHORITY

Alex Ellenberger
LOCUS ARCHITECTURE PTY. LTD.

Gerard Esparon
MINISTRY OF NATIONAL DEVELOPMENT

Malcolm Moller
APPLEBY GLOBAL

Margaret Nourice
STAMP DUTY COMMISSION

Brian Orr
MEJ ELECTRICAL

Divino Sabino
PARDIWALLA TWOMEY LABLACHE

Kieran B. Shah
BARRISTER & ATTORNEY-AT-LAW

### SIERRA LEONE
Gideon Ayi-Owoo
PwC GHANA

Abdul Akim Bangura
ASSOCIATION OF CLEARING AND
FORWARDING AGENCIES SIERRA LEONE

Mohamed Sahid Bangura
MACAULEY, BANGURA & CO.

Philip Bangura
BANK OF SIERRA LEONE

Desmond Dalton Beckley
DALTTECH / DESMI ENTERPRISES

Cheryl Blake
B&J PARTNERS

Sonia Browne
CLAS LEGAL

Emile Carr
LEONE CONSULTANTS

Delphine Caulker
MINISTRY OF WORKS HOUSING AND
INFRASTRUCTURE (MWH&I)

Beatrice Chaytor
CLAS LEGAL

Kpana M. Conteh
NATIONAL REVENUE AUTHORITY

Michaela Kadijatu Conteh
WRIGHT & CO.

Sahid Conteh
NATIONAL REVENUE AUTHORITY

Abu Bakr Dexter
E.E.C. SHEARS-MOSES & CO.

Mariama Dumbuya
RENNER THOMAS & CO., ADELE
CHAMBERS

Joseph Fofanah
OFFICE OF THE ADMINISTRATOR AND
REGISTRAR GENERAL (OARG)

Manilius Garber
JARRETT-YASKEY, GARBER &
ASSOCIATES: ARCHITECTS (JYGA)

Eke Ahmed Halloway
HALLOWAY & PARTNERS

Donald Jones
MINISTRY OF LANDS, COUNTRY
PLANNING AND THE ENVIRONMENT

Francis Kaifala
WRIGHT & CO.

Mariama Seray Kallay
GOVERNMENT OF SIERRA LEONE

Raymond Fleance Kamara
NATIONAL REVENUE AUTHORITY

Georgiana Karim
CLAS LEGAL

Shiaka Kawa
EDRA CONSULTANCY

Adekunle Milton King
PETROLEUM RESOURCES UNIT

Baimba Koroma
MINISTRY OF WORKS HOUSING AND
INFRASTRUCTURE (MWH&I)

Francis Kpukumu
MINISTRY OF WORKS HOUSING AND
INFRASTRUCTURE (MWH&I)

Millicent Lewis-Ojumu
CLAS LEGAL

Corneleius Max-Williams
DESTINY SHIPPING AGENCIES AND
CLEARING AND FORWARDING AGENCIES

Mohamed Pa Momoh Fofanah
EDRINA CHAMBERS

Rev. Dan Oalmer
NATIONAL POWER AUTHORITY

Christopher J. Peacock
SERPICO TRADING ENTERPRISES

Kargbo Santigie
A+S BUSINESS CENTRE

Augustine Santos Kamara
NATIONAL REVENUE AUTHORITY

Julia Sarkodie-Mensah

Horatio Sawyer
MINISTRY OF WORKS HOUSING AND
INFRASTRUCTURE (MWH&I)

Nana Adjoa Anaisewa Sey
PwC GHANA

Fatmata Sorie
WRIGHT & CO.

Valisius Thomas
ADVENT CHAMBERS

Alhaji Timbo
NATIONAL POWER AUTHORITY

Darcy White
PwC GHANA

Franklyn Williams
SIERRA LEONE BUSINESS FORUM LTD.

Yada Williams
YADA WILLIAMS AND ASSOCIATE

Claudius Williams-Tucker
KPMG

Rowland Wright
WRIGHT & CO.

### SINGAPORE
ALLEN & GLEDHILL LLP

DP INFORMATION NETWORK PTE. LTD.

WONG TAN & MOLLY LIM LLC

Lim Ah Kuan
SP POWERGRID LTD.

Matthew Bubb
ASHURST LLP

Ronald Cai
MINISTRY OF MANPOWER

Shi-Chien Chia
MINISTRY OF TRADE & INDUSTRY

Hooi Yen Chin
POLARIS LAW CORPORATION

Koon Fun Chin
URBAN REDEVELOPMENT AUTHORITY

Ng Chin Lock
SP POWERGRID LTD.

Paerin Choa
TSMP LAW CORPORATION

Douglas Chow
MINISTRY OF TRADE & INDUSTRY

Beng Chye Chua
RAJAH & TANN LLP

Kit Min Chye
TAN PENG CHIN LLC

Joseph Foo
THE NATIONAL ENVIRONMENT AGENCY

Sandy Foo
DREW NAPIER

Chi Duan Gooi
DONALDSON & BURKINSHAW

Tan Guan Wah
MULTI-LINES ENGINEERING PTE LTD.

Yvonne Hill
YEO-LEONG & PEH LLC

Irene Ho
BUILDING & CONSTRUCTION
AUTHORITY

Moana Jagasia
SINGAPORE CUSTOMS

Wong Kum Hoong
ENERGY MARKET AUTHORITY

Ashok Kumar

K. Latha
ACCOUNTING & CORPORATE
REGULATORY AUTHORITY, ACRA

Yvonne Lay
MINISTRY OF FINANCE

Eng Beng Lee
RAJAH & TANN LLP

Grace Lee
SINGAPORE CUSTOMS

James Leong
SUBORDINATE COURTS

Yik Wee Liew
WONG PARTNERSHIP LLP

Eugene Lim
DONALDSON & BURKINSHAW

Kexin Lim
PwC SINGAPORE

William Lim
CREDIT BUREAU SINGAPORE PTE LTD.

Olivine Lin
DONALDSON & BURKINSHAW

Madan Mohan
YEO-LEONG & PEH LLC

Eddee Ng
TAN KOK QUAN PARTNERSHIP

Max Ng
POLARIS LAW CORPORATION

Shawn Poon
TAN KOK QUAN PARTNERSHIP

See Tiat Quek
PwC SINGAPORE

Teck Beng Quek
LAND TRANSPORT AUTHORITY

Shari Rasanayagam
KINETICA PTE. LTD., IN ASSOCIATION
WITH KELVIN CHIA PARTNERSHIP

Alan Ross
PwC SINGAPORE

Kaveeta Sandhu
DREW NAPIER

David Sandison
PwC SINGAPORE

Wei Hurng Sio
PUBLIC UTILITIES BOARD

Angeline Soh
*ACCOUNTING & CORPORATE REGULATORY AUTHORITY, ACRA*

Douglas Tan
*STEVEN TAN PAC - MEMBER OF RUSSELL BEDFORD INTERNATIONAL*

Hak Khoon Tan
*ENERGY MARKET AUTHORITY*

Pei Luan Tan
*DONALDSON & BURKINSHAW*

Sharon Tay
*DONALDSON & BURKINSHAW*

Shara Tay
*MINISTRY OF MANPOWER*

Siu Ing Teng
*SINGAPORE LAND AUTHORITY*

Magdalene Teo-Yong
*DONALDSON & BURKINSHAW*

Keith Tnee
*TAN KOK QUAN PARTNERSHIP*

Siew Kwong Wong
*ENERGY MARKET AUTHORITY*

Jennifer Yeo
*YEO-LEONG & PEH LLC*

Isaac Yong
*FIRE SAFETY & SHELTER DEPARTMENT*

Stefanie Yuen Thio
*TSMP LAW CORPORATION*

## SLOVAK REPUBLIC

Martina Behuliaková
*GEODESY, CARTOGRAPHY AND CADASTRE AUTHORITY OF THE SLOVAK REPUBLIC*

Peter Bollardt
*ČECHOVÁ & PARTNERS, MEMBER OF LEX MUNDI AND WSG*

Ján Budinský
*SLOVAK CREDIT BUREAU, S.R.O.*

Peter Cavojsky
*CLS ČAVOJSKY & PARTNERS, S.R.O.*

Katarína Čechová
*ČECHOVÁ & PARTNERS, MEMBER OF LEX MUNDI AND WSG*

Kristina Čermáková
*PETERKA & PARTNERS*

Elena Červenová
*WHITE & CASE S.R.O.*

Matus Chmelo
*PETERKA & PARTNERS*

Ema Cveckova
*DEDÁK & PARTNERS*

Jana Fabianová
*ČECHOVÁ & PARTNERS, MEMBER OF LEX MUNDI AND WSG*

Matej Firicky
*WHITE & CASE S.R.O.*

Juraj Fuska
*WHITE & CASE S.R.O.*

Petronela Galambosova
*PANALPINA SLOVAKIA, S.R.O.*

Simona Haláková
*ČECHOVÁ & PARTNERS, MEMBER OF LEX MUNDI AND WSG*

Peter Hodál
*WHITE & CASE S.R.O.*

Vladimir Ivanco
*WHITE & CASE S.R.O.*

Miroslav Jalec
*ZAPADOSLOVENSKA ENERGETIKA, A.S.*

Tomáš Kamenec
*DEDÁK & PARTNERS*

Veronika Keszeliova
*ČECHOVÁ & PARTNERS, MEMBER OF LEX MUNDI AND WSG*

Roman Konrad
*PROFINAM, S.R.O.*

Miroslav Kopac
*NATIONAL BANK OF SLOVAKIA*

Katarina Leitmannová
*GEODESY, CARTOGRAPHY AND CADASTRE AUTHORITY OF THE SLOVAK REPUBLIC*

Maria Malovcova
*PwC SLOVAKIA*

Jozef Malý
*DETVAI LUDIK MALÝ UDVAROS*

Přemysl Marek
*PETERKA & PARTNERS*

Tomáš Maretta
*ČECHOVÁ & PARTNERS, MEMBER OF LEX MUNDI AND WSG*

Nadezda Niksova
*GEODESY, CARTOGRAPHY AND CADASTRE AUTHORITY OF THE SLOVAK REPUBLIC*

Jaroslav Niznansky
*JNC LEGAL S.R.O.*

Katarína Nováková
*MONAREX AUDIT CONSULTING*

Katarína Novotná
*PETERKA & PARTNERS*

Veronika Pázmányová
*WHITE & CASE S.R.O.*

Ladislav Pompura
*MONAREX AUDIT CONSULTING*

Simona Rapavá
*WHITE & CASE S.R.O.*

Ľubomír Šatka
*WHITE & CASE S.R.O.*

Christiana Serugova
*PwC SLOVAKIA*

Michal Simunic
*ČECHOVÁ & PARTNERS, MEMBER OF LEX MUNDI AND WSG*

Lucia Skubáková
*MONAREX AUDIT CONSULTING*

Jaroslav Škubal
*PRK PARTNERS S.R.O.*

Michaela Špetková
*GEODESY, CARTOGRAPHY AND CADASTRE AUTHORITY OF THE SLOVAK REPUBLIC*

Andrea Štefančíková
*PETERKA & PARTNERS*

Lubica Suhajova
*PwC SLOVAKIA*

Andrea Šupáková
*DETVAI LUDIK MALÝ UDVAROS*

Zdenka Švingalová
*MONAREX AUDIT CONSULTING*

Stanislava Valientová
*WHITE & CASE S.R.O.*

Otakar Weis
*PwC SLOVAKIA*

Ladislav Záhumenský
*WHITE & CASE S.R.O.*

Dagmar Zukalová
*ZUKALOVÁ - ADVOKÁTSKA KANCELÁRIA S.R.O.*

## SLOVENIA
*ENERGY AGENCY OF THE REPUBLIC OF SLOVENIA*

Marjan Babič
*AGENCY OF THE REPUBLIC OF SLOVENIA FOR PUBLIC LEGAL RECORDS AND RELATED SERVICES*

Erika Braniselj
*NOTARY OFFICE BRANISELJ*

Akos Burjan
*PwC SLOVENIA*

Biljana Čamber Pavli
*AVBREHT, ZAJC & PARTNERS*

Franc Cmok
*FABIANI, PETROVIČ, JERAJ, O.P. D.O.O. IN COOPERATION WITH CMS REICH-ROHRWIG HAINZ*

Nada Drobnic
*KPMG*

Marina Ferfolja Howland
*FERFOLJA, LJUBIC IN PARTNERJI*

Ana Filipov
*FABIANI, PETROVIČ, JERAJ, O.P. D.O.O. IN COOPERATION WITH CMS REICH-ROHRWIG HAINZ*

Alenka Gorenčič
*DELOITTE LLP*

Mira Goršič
*PwC SLOVENIA*

Eva Gostisa
*LAW OFFICE JADEK & PENSA D.N.O. - O.P., WITH THE SUPPORT OF ERNST & YOUNG*

Hermina Govekar Vičič
*KREDITNI BIRO SISBON, D.O.O.*

Masa Grgurevic Alcin
*SUPREME COURT OF THE REPUBLIC OF SLOVENIA*

Barbara Guzina
*DELOITTE LLP*

Rajko Hribar
*ELEKTRO LJUBLJANA D.D.*

Damjana Iglič
*BANK OF SLOVENIA*

Dunja Jandl
*CMS REICH-ROHRWIG HAINZ*

Andrej Jarkovic
*LAW FIRM JANEŽIČ & JARKOVIČ LTD.*

Jernej Jeraj
*FABIANI, PETROVIČ, JERAJ, O.P. D.O.O. IN COOPERATION WITH CMS REICH-ROHRWIG HAINZ*

Roman Jesenko
*ELEKTRO LJUBLJANA D.D.*

Vita Korinšek
*CITY STUDIO*

Miro Košak
*NOTARY OFFICE KOŠAK*

Brigita Kraljič
*CMS REICH-ROHRWIG HAINZ*

Marko Kranjc
*CMS REICH-ROHRWIG HAINZ*

Tjaša Lahovnik
*ODVETNIKI ŠELIH & PARTNERJI*

Vatovec Lea
*CMS REICH-ROHRWIG HAINZ*

Aleš Lunder
*CMS REICH-ROHRWIG HAINZ*

Jera Majzelj
*ODVETNIKI ŠELIH & PARTNERJI*

Darja Malogorski
*KPMG*

Matjaž Miklavčič
*SODO D.O.O.*

Eva Mozina
*MIRO SENICA IN ODVETNIKI*

Mojca Muha
*MIRO SENICA IN ODVETNIKI*

Jure Nikolič
*CARGO-PARTNER*

Ela Omersa
*CMS REICH-ROHRWIG HAINZ*

Irena Ostojic
*CITY STUDIO*

Pavle Pensa
*LAW OFFICE JADEK & PENSA D.N.O. - O.P., WITH THE SUPPORT OF ERNST & YOUNG*

Nataša Pipan Nahtigal
*ODVETNIKI ŠELIH & PARTNERJI*

Petra Plevnik
*MIRO SENICA IN ODVETNIKI*

Igor Podbelsek
*ELEKTRO LJUBLJANA D.D.*

Bojan Podgoršek
*NOTARIAT*

Jan Poniž
*DATA D.O.O*

Magda Posavec
*KPMG*

Marija Remic
*AGENCY OF THE REPUBLIC OF SLOVENIA FOR PUBLIC LEGAL RECORDS AND RELATED SERVICES*

Kostanca Rettinger
*KREDITNI BIRO SISBON, D.O.O.*

Marijana Ristevski
*PwC SLOVENIA*

Patricija Rot
*LAW OFFICE JADEK & PENSA D.N.O. - O.P., WITH THE SUPPORT OF ERNST & YOUNG*

Savic Sanja
*DELOITTE LLP*

Andreja Škofič-Klanjšček
*DELOITTE LLP*

Petra Smolnikar
*SCHOENHERR*

Branka Španič
*LAW OFFICE JADEK & PENSA D.N.O. - O.P., WITH THE SUPPORT OF ERNST & YOUNG*

Maja Stojko
*MIRO SENICA IN ODVETNIKI*

Jožef Strmšek
*BANK OF SLOVENIA*

Gregor Strojin
*SUPREME COURT OF THE REPUBLIC OF SLOVENIA*

Melita Trop
*MIRO SENICA IN ODVETNIKI*

Urša Volk
*AGENCY OF THE REPUBLIC OF SLOVENIA FOR PUBLIC LEGAL RECORDS AND RELATED SERVICES*

Katja Wostner
*BDO SVETOVANJE D.O.O.*

Anka Zagar
*CARGO-PARTNER*

## SOLOMON ISLANDS

Dayson Boso
*OFFICE OF THE CHIEF MAGISTRATE*

Don Boykin
*PACIFIC ARCHITECTS LTD.*

Chris Farakii
*GLOBAL LAWYERS, BARRISTERS & SOLICITORS*

Michael Ipo
*WHITLAM K TOGAMAE LAWYERS*

Thomas Kama
*SOL - LAW*

John Keniapisia
*LAWYER*

Judah Kulabule
*SOLOMON ISLANDS PORTS AUTHORITY*

Veronica Manedika
*MINISTRY OF COMMERCE, INDUSTRY, LABOR AND IMMIGRATION*

Dennis McGuire
*SOL - LAW*

Ruth Moore
*MINISTRY OF FINANCE AND TREASURY*

Richard Muaki
*HIGH COURT OF SOLOMON ISLANDS*

Norman Nicholls
*SOLOMON ISLANDS ELECTRICITY AUTHORITY*

Maurice Nonipitu
*KRAMER AUSENCO*

Andrew Norrie
*BRIDGE LAWYERS*

Nele Paia
*OFFICE OF THE CHIEF MAGISTRATE*

Haelo Pelu
*MINISTRY OF JUSTICE AND LEGAL AFFAIRS*

Wilson Henry Rano
*RANO & COMPANY, BARRISTERS & SOLICITORS*

Peter Rockson
*COMMODITY EXPORT MARKETING AUTHORITY*

Roselle R. Rosales
*PACIFIC ARCHITECTS LTD.*

Livingston Saepio
*HONIARA CITY COUNCIL*

Leonard Saii
*SPARK ELECTRICAL SERVICES*

Martin B. Sam
*SOLOMON ISLANDS ELECTRICITY AUTHORITY*

Gregory Joseph Sojnocki
*MORRIS & SOJNOCKI CHARTERED ACCOUNTANTS, WITH THE SUPPORT OF ERNST & YOUNG*

Gerald Stenzel
*TRADCO SHIPPING*

Selwyn Takana
*MINISTRY OF FINANCE AND TREASURY*

Whitlam K. Togamae
*WHITLAM K TOGAMAE LAWYERS*

Jackson Vaikota
*MINISTRY OF JUSTICE AND LEGAL AFFAIRS*

Penny Vaughn
*PwC UNITED STATES*

Pamela Wilde
*MINISTRY FOR JUSTICE AND LEGAL AFFAIRS*

Yolande Yates
*GOH & PARTNERS*

## SOUTH AFRICA
*ADAMS & ADAMS*

*Q & N WEST EXPORT TRADING HOUSE*

Nicolaos Akritidis
*PARADIGM ARCHITECTS*

Ross Alcock
*EDWARD NATHAN SONNENBERGS INC.*

Rovina Asray
*BOWMAN GILFILLAN INC.*

Kavisha Baboolal
*GARLICKE & BOUSFIELD INC.*

Claire Barclay
*CLIFFE DEKKER HOFMEYR INC.*

Natascha Belford
*WHITE & CASE LLP*

Boitumelo Bogatsu
*GARLICKE & BOUSFIELD INC.*

Johan Botes
*CLIFFE DEKKER HOFMEYR INC.*

Edward Brooks
*ACTIVATE ARCHITECTURE (PTY) LTD.*

Bless Cedric
*UMAR'S ELECTRICAL*

Beric Croome
*EDWARD NATHAN SONNENBERGS INC.*

Haydn Davies
*WEBBER WENTZEL*

Gretchen de Smit
*EDWARD NATHAN SONNENBERGS INC.*

Desiree
*Forwarding African Transport Services (Pty) Ltd.*

Tim Desmond
*Garlicke & Bousfield Inc.*

Steve Donninger
*Rawlins Wales & Partners*

Claire Fawbert
*TransUnion*

Elise Gibson
*Grosskopff Lombart Huyberechts & Associates Architects*

Tim Gordon-Grant
*Bowman Gilfillan Inc.*

Kim Goss
*Bowman Gilfillan Inc.*

Jenna Hamilton
*White & Case LLP*

Caron Harris
*Forwarding African Transport Services (Pty) Ltd.*

Julian Jones
*Cliffe Dekker Hofmeyr Inc.*

Gillian Lumb
*Cliffe Dekker Hofmeyr Inc.*

Kyle Mandy
*PwC South Africa*

Khaya Mantengu
*Cliffe Dekker Hofmeyr Inc.*

Joey Mathekga
*CIPRO (Companies & IPR Registration Office)*

Duncan McMeekin
*Bowman Gilfillan Inc.*

Gabriel Meyer
*Norton Rose*

Glory Moumakwe
*CIPRO (Companies & IPR Registration Office)*

Twaambo Muleza
*Bowman Gilfillan Inc.*

Sanelisiwe Nyasulu
*Garlicke & Bousfield Inc.*

Nancy Prohl
*Edward Nathan Sonnenbergs Inc.*

Eamonn David Quinn
*Attorney-at-Law*

Hansuya Reddy
*Deneys Reitz Inc. / Africa Legal*

Mark Ross
*PwC South Africa*

Mytha Sajiwan
*TransUnion*

Andres Sepp
*Office of the Chief Registrar of Deeds*

Richard Shein
*Bowman Gilfillan Inc.*

Mathew Shepherd
*Patron Air*

Themba Sikhosana
*Cliffe Dekker Hofmeyr Inc.*

Archana Sinha
*RCS Pvt. Ltd Business Advisors Group*

Rajat Ratan Sinha
*RCS Pvt. Ltd Business Advisors Group*

Jane Strydom
*TransUnion*

Roxanna Valayathum
*Mervyn Taback Incorporated*

Muhammed Vally
*Edward Nathan Sonnenbergs Inc.*

Dawid Van der Berg
*BDO Spencer Steward Southern African Co-Ordination (Pty) Limited*

Naomi Van der Merwe
*BDO Spencer Steward Southern African Co-Ordination (Pty) Limited*

Nicky van der Weshuizen
*Edward Nathan Sonnenbergs Inc.*

Stefan Vosloo
*Eskom*

Allen West
*Department of Rural Development and Land Reform*

St Elmo Wilken
*Mervyn Taback Incorporated*

Andrew Wood
*Grosskopff Lombart Huyberechts & Associates Architects*

Ralph Zulman
*Supreme Court of Appeal of South Africa*

## SPAIN

*Allen & Overy*

Basilio Aguirre
*Registro de la Propiedad de España*

Angel Alonso Hernández
*Uría & Menéndez, member of Lex Mundi*

Elena Álvarez Fernández
*Addient*

José Luis Amérigo Sánchez
*Gómez-Acebo & Pombo Abogados*

Joana Andrade Correia
*Raposo Bernardo & Associados*

Nuria Armas
*Banco de España*

Ana Armijo
*Ashurst LLP*

Cristina Ayo Ferrándiz
*Uría Menéndez*

Denise Bejarano
*Pérez - Llorca*

Alfonso Benavides
*Clifford Chance*

Andrés Berral
*Clifford Chance*

Vicente Bootello
*J & A Garrigues, S.L.P*

Agustín Bou
*Jausas*

Héctor Bouzo Cortejosa
*Solcaisur S.L.*

Laura Camarero
*Baker & McKenzie*

Julio Cano Guillamón
*Asociacion/Colegio Nacional de Ingenieros del ICAI*

Ignacio Castrillón Jorge
*Iberdrola S.A.*

Francisco Conde Viñuelas
*Cuatrecasas, Gonçalves Pereira*

Jaume Cornudella i Marques
*PwC Spain*

Juan Jose Corral Moreno
*Cuatrecasas, Gonçalves Pereira*

Miguel Cruz Amorós
*PwC Spain*

Rossanna D'Onza
*Baker & McKenzie*

Almudena del Río Galán
*Colegio de Registradores de la Propiedad y Mercantiles de España*

Agustín Del Río Galeote
*Gómez-Acebo & Pombo Abogados*

Iván Delgado González
*Pérez - Llorca*

Antonio Fernández
*J & A Garrigues, S.L.P*

Idoya Fernandez Elorza
*Cuatrecasas, Gonçalves Pereira*

Sofia Ferreira Enriquez
*Raposo Bernardo & Associados*

Guillermo Frühbeck
*Dr. Frühbeck Abogados S.L.P*

Ignacio García Errandonea
*J & A Garrigues, S.L.P*

Valentín García González
*Cuatrecasas, Gonçalves Pereira*

Borja García-Alamán
*J & A Garrigues, S.L.P*

Luis Giménez Godosar
*Giménez Torres & Yúfera Abogados*

Juan Ignacio Gomeza Villa
*Notario de Bilbao*

Carlos Gonzalez Gutierrez-Barquin
*Asociación Española de la Industria Eléctrica*

Esther González Pérez
*Uría & Menéndez, member of Lex Mundi*

Marta Hernáez
*Baker & McKenzie*

Carlos Hernández
*Metropolitana de Aduanas y Transportes & Icontainers.com*

Joaquín Rodriguez Hernández
*Colegio de Registradores*

Jorge Hernandez
*Equifax Iberica*

Alejandro Huertas León
*J & A Garrigues, S.L.P*

Jaime Llopis
*Cuatrecasas, Gonçalves Pereira*

Marina Lorente
*J & A Garrigues, S.L.P*

Álvaro Lucini Mateo
*Notaría Perales-Farrés*

Joaquin Macias
*Ashurst LLP*

Alberto Manzanares
*Ashurst LLP*

Juan Carlos Marhuenda Gómez
*TLACORP*

Susana Marimón Charola
*Gómez-Acebo & Pombo Abogados*

Daniel Marín
*Gómez-Acebo & Pombo Abogados*

Ana Martín
*J & A Garrigues, S.L.P*

Jorge Martín - Fernández
*Clifford Chance*

Aida Martin Andres
*Giménez Torres & Yúfera Abogados*

Gabriel Martínez
*Russell Bedford España Auditores y Consultores, S.L. - member of Russell Bedford International*

Antonio Méndez
*Altius S.A. Madrid*

Alberto Monreal Lasheras
*PwC Spain*

Eva Mur Mestre
*PwC Spain*

Nicolás Nogueroles Peiró
*Colegio de Registradores de la Propiedad y Mercantiles de España*

Ana Novoa
*Baker & McKenzie*

Carla Palau Segura
*Gómez-Acebo & Pombo Abogados*

Carlos Pardo
*Giménez Torres & Yúfera Abogados*

Daniel Parejo
*J & A Garrigues, S.L.P*

Óscar Parra
*Giménez Torres & Yúfera Abogados*

Pedro Pérez-Llorca Zamora
*Pérez - Llorca*

Nelson Raposo Bernardo
*Raposo Bernardo & Associados*

Maria Redondo
*Baker & McKenzie*

Guillermo Rodrigo García
*Clifford Chance*

Déborah Rodríguez
*Clifford Chance*

Noemi Rodriguez Alonso
*Sagardoy Abogados, member of Ius Laboris*

Eduardo Rodríguez-Rovira
*Uría & Menéndez, member of Lex Mundi*

Javier Romeu
*TIBA Internacional, S.A.*

Javier Ruz Cerezo
*Montealto*

Álvaro Ryan Murua
*Iberdrola S.A.*

Iñigo Sagardoy de Simón
*Sagardoy Abogados, member of Ius Laboris*

Ignacio Sánchez-Vizcaino Valdés
*Giménez Torres & Yúfera Abogados*

Eduardo Santamaría Moral
*J & A Garrigues, S.L.P*

Ramón Santillán
*Banco de España*

Pablo Santos
*Gómez-Acebo & Pombo Abogados*

Cristina Soler
*Gómez-Acebo & Pombo Abogados*

Raimon Tagliavini
*Uría Menéndez*

Francisco Téllez de Gregorio
*J & A Garrigues, S.L.P*

Adrián Thery
*J & A Garrigues, S.L.P*

Ivan Tintore Subirana
*Metropolitana de Aduanas y Transportes & Icontainers.com*

Roberto Tojo Thomas de Carranza
*Clifford Chance*

Alejandro Valls
*Baker & McKenzie*

Juan Verdugo
*J & A Garrigues, S.L.P*

Fernando Vives
*J & A Garrigues, S.L.P*

## SRI LANKA

*Freight Links International (Pte) Ltd.*

*Registrar General*

Ayomi Aluwihare-Gunawardene
*F.J. & G. De Saram, member of Lex Mundi*

Nihal Sri Ameresekere
*Consultants 21 Ltd.*

Gerard David
*SJMS Associates*

Savantha De Saram
*D.L. & F. De Saram*

Chamari de Silva
*F.J. & G. De Saram, member of Lex Mundi*

Kolitha Dissanayake
*F.J. & G. De Saram, member of Lex Mundi*

Sadhini Edirisinghe
*F.J. & G. De Saram, member of Lex Mundi*

Nilmini Ediriweera
*Julius & Creasy*

Chamindi Ekanayake
*Nithya Partners*

Amila Fernando
*Julius & Creasy*

Anjali Fernando
*F.J. & G. De Saram, member of Lex Mundi*

Jivan Goonetilleke
*D.L. & F. De Saram*

Naomal Goonewardena
*Nithya Partners*

P. Mervyn Gunasekera
*LAN Management Development Service*

Priyanthi Guneratne
*F.J. & G. De Saram, member of Lex Mundi*

Thilanka Namalie Haputhanthrie
*Julius & Creasy*

Dharshika Herath Gunarathna
*Sudath Perera Associates*

Sonali Jayasuriya
*D.L. & F. De Saram*

Tudor Jayasuriya
*F.J. & G. De Saram, member of Lex Mundi*

Shamalie Jayatunge
*Tiruchelvam Associates*

Sanjaya Jayawardene
*Progressive Design Associates*

Mahes Jeyadevan
*PwC Sri Lanka*

Yudhishtran Kanagasabai
*PwC Sri Lanka*

Neelakandan Kandiah
*Murugesu & Neelakandan*

Janaka Lakmal
*Credit Information Bureau Ltd.*

Ishara Madarasinghe
*F.J. & G. De Saram, member of Lex Mundi*

Sasikala Mayadunne
*Sudath Perera Associates*

Kaushalya Meedeniya
*Sudath Perera Associates*

Fathima Amra Mohamed
*Sudath Perera Associates*

Asiri Perera
*MIT Cargo (Pvt) Ltd.*

Jagath Perera
*MIT Cargo (Pvt) Ltd.*

Sudath Perera
*Sudath Perera Associates*

Lilangi Randeni
*F.J. & G. De Saram, member of Lex Mundi*

Hiranthi Ratnayake
*PwC Sri Lanka*

Paul Ratnayeke
*Paul Ratnayeke Associates*

Neluka Seneviratne
*Julius & Creasy*

Shane Silva
*Julius & Creasy*

Bharatha Subasinghe
*D. P. R. Consultants (Pvt) Limited*

J.M. Swaminathan
*Julius & Creasy*

Bandula S. Tilakasena
*Ceylon Electricity Board*

Shehara Varia
*F.J. & G. De Saram, member of Lex Mundi*

Charmalie Weerasekera
*Sudath Perera Associates*

John Wilson
*John Wilson Partners*

Tilak Wimalagunaratne
*Julius & Creasy*

## ST. KITTS AND NEVIS
*St. Kitts Electricity Department*

Michella Adrien
*The Law Offices of Michella Adrien*

Launlia Archibald
*Customs and Excise Department*

Rublin Audain
*Audain & Associates*

Nicholas Brisbane
*Brisbane O'Garro Alvaranga*

Neil Coates
*PwC Antigua*

Tamara Daniel
*Henderson Legal Chambers*

Jan Dash
*Liburd and Dash*

Kennedy de Silva
*Customs and Excise Department*

K. Gregory Hardtman
*Hardtman & Associates*

Rodney Harris
*Customs and Excise Department*

Marsha T. Henderson
*Henderson Legal Chambers*

Dahlia Joseph
*Daniel Brantley & Associates*

Mahailia Pencheon
*PwC Antigua*

Sandrine Powell-Huggins
*Henderson Legal Chambers*

Nervin Rawlins
*Inland Revenue Authority*

Larkland M. Richards
*Larkland M. Richards & Associates*

Reginald Richards
*R & R Electrical Engineering Air Conditioning & Refrigeration Services Ltd.*

Arlene Ross-Daisley
*Lex Caribbean*

Tavo Sargeant
*Customs and Excise Department*

Warren Thompson
*Construction Management and Consulting Agency Inc (CMCAI)*

Charles Walwyn
*PwC Antigua*

Leonora Walwynlaw
*WalwynLaw*

Collin Williams
*Royal Logistics*

## ST. LUCIA
*Lucelec*

Clive Antoine
*Ministry of Communications Works Transport and Public Utilities*

Thaddeus M. Antoine
*Francis & Antoine*

Gerard Bergasse
*Tropical Shipping*

Shannon Chitolie
*Gordon & Gordon Co.*

Swithin Donelly
*Ministry of Economic Affairs, Economic Planning & National Development*

Peter I. Foster
*Peter I. Foster & Associates*

Peterson D. Francis
*Peterson D. Francis Worldwide Shipping & Customs Services Ltd.*

Carol J. Gedeon
*Chancery Chambers*

Ulric George
*Tropical Shipping*

Michael B.G. Gordon
*Gordon & Gordon Co.*

Claire Greene-Malaykhan
*Peter I. Foster & Associates*

Anderson Lake
*Bank of Saint Lucia Limited*

Charlene Mae Magnaye
*PwC St. Lucia*

Bradley Paul
*Bradley Paul Associates*

Richard Peterkin
*PwC St. Lucia*

Eldris Pierre-Mauricette
*Tropical Shipping*

Candace Polius
*Nicholas John & Co.*

Catherine Sealys
*Procurement Services International*

Michael Sewordor
*Ministry of Communications Works Transport and Public Utilities*

Anya Trim
*PwC St. Lucia*

Leandra Gabrielle Verneuil
*Chambers of Jennifer Remy & Associates*

Andie A. Wilkie
*Gordon & Gordon Co.*

Brenda M. Williams
*BDO St. Lucia*

## ST. VINCENT AND THE GRENADINES

Kay R.A. Bacchus-Browne
*Kay Bacchus-Browne Chambers*

Aurin Bennett
*Aurin Bennett Architects*

Allan P. Burke
*Perry's Customs and Shipping Agency, Ltd.*

Bernadine Dublin
*Labour Department*

Tamara Gibson-Marks
*High Court Registrar*

Errol E. Layne
*Errol E. Layne Chambers*

Isaac Legair
*Dennings*

Charlene Mae Magnaye
*PwC St. Lucia*

Moulton Mayers
*Moulton Mayers Architects*

Richard Peterkin
*PwC St. Lucia*

Martin Sheel
*Commerce & Intellectual Property Office (CIPO)*

Andrea Young-Lewis
*Commerce & Intellectual Property Office (CIPO)*

## SUDAN
*Tristar*

Omer Abdel Ati
*Omer Abdel Ati Solicitors*

Abdalla Abuzeid
*Abdalla A. Abuzeid & Associates*

Mohamed Ibrahim Adam
*Dr. Adam & Associates*

Ahmed Ahmed Elmohtar Adbdelhammed
*Mahmoud Elsheikh Omer & Associates Advocates*

Al Fadel Ahmed Al Mahdi
*Al Mahdi Law Office*

Abdalla Bashir Ibrahim Alataya
*Mahmoud Elsheikh Omer & Associates Advocates*

Nour Eldin A. Idris
*Mahmoud Elsheikh Omer & Associates Advocates*

Ahmed Mahdi
*Mahmoud Elsheikh Omer & Associates Advocates*

Nafisa Omer
*Omer Abdel Ati Solicitors*

Rayan Omer
*Omer Abdel Ati Solicitors*

Amel M. Sharif
*Mahmoud Elsheikh Omer & Associates Advocates*

## SURINAME
*Handels-, Krediet- en Industrie Bank (Hakrinbank) N.V.*

G. Clide Cambridge
*Paramaribo Custom Broker & Packer*

Anoeschka Debipersad
*A.E. Debipersad & Associates*

Marcel K. Eyndhoven
*N.V. Energiebedrijven Suriname*

Johan Kastelein
*Kastelein Design*

B.M. Oemraw
*N.V. Global Expedition*

Joanne Pancham
*Chamber of Commerce & Industry*

Adiel Sakoer
*N.V. Global Expedition*

Inder Sardjoe
*N.V. Easy Electric*

Dennis Singh
*Deloitte Suriname*

Prija Soechitram
*Chamber of Commerce & Industry*

Albert D. Soedamah
*Lawfirm Soedamah & Associates*

Radjen A. Soerdjbalie
*Notariaat R.A. Soerdjbalie*

Carol-Ann Tjon-Pian-Gi
*Lawyer & Sworn Translator*

Jennifer van Dijk-Silos
*Law Firm Van Dijk-Silos*

Carel van Hest
*Carel van Hest Architecten N.V.*

Dayenne Wielingen - Verwey
*Vereniging Surinaams Bedrijfsleven, Suriname Trade & Industry Association*

Andy Wong
*N.V. Energiebedrijven Suriname*

## SWAZILAND
*Office of the Registrar Swaziland*

*TransUnion ITC*

Eddie Chiringah
*DHL*

Susanne DeBeer
*MNS Group*

Veli Dlamini
*Interfreight Pty. Ltd.*

Phumlile Tina Khoza
*Standard Bank*

Mbuso Kingsley
*Lang Mitchell Associates*

Paul Lewis
*PwC Swaziland*

Andrew Linsey
*PwC Swaziland*

Zodwa Mabuza
*Federation of Swaziland Employers and Chamber of Commerce*

Nhlanhla Maphanga
*Lang Mitchell Associates*

Sabelo Masuku
*Maphanga Howe Masuku Nsibande*

Mduduzi Mtsetfwa
*Swaziland Electricity Company*

Bongani Mtshali
*Federation of Swaziland Employers and Chamber of Commerce*

George Mzungu
*M&E Consulting Engineers*

Zakes Nkosi
*Federation of Swaziland Employers and Chamber of Commerce*

Knox Nxumalo
*Robinson Bertram*

Emmanuel Ofori
*Kobla Quashie and Associates*

Kobla Quashie
*Kobla Quashie and Associates*

John Resting
*Bicon Consulting Engineers*

José Rodrigues
*Rodrigues & Associates*

Bongani Simelane
*Municipal Council of Mbabane*

Muzi Simelane
*Waring Simelane*

Manene Thwala
*Thwala Attorneys*

Bradford Mark Walker
*Brad Walker Architects*

## SWEDEN
*Vattenfall Eldistribution AB*

Stig Åkerman
*Boverket- Swedish National Board of Housing, Building and Planning*

Nicklas Anth
*Panalpina AB*

Martin Bergander
*Gärde Wesslau Advokatbyrå*

Simon Bergström
*Hammarskiöld & Co.*

Mats Berter
*MAQS Law Firm*

Karl Björlin
*Advokatfirman Lindahl*

Helena Brännvall
*Advokatfirman Vinge KB, member of Lex Mundi*

Alexander Broch
*Öresunds Redovisning AB*

Sandra Carlén
*MAQS Law Firm Advokatbyrå AB*

Ake Dahlqvist
*UC*

Jenny Dangré
*Advokatfirman Vinge KB, member of Lex Mundi*

Martin Ekdahl
*PwC Sweden*

Anna Eklund
*Swedish Association of Local Authorities and Regions*

Peder Hammarskiöld
*Hammarskiöld & Co.*

Lars Hartzell
*Elmzell Advokatbyrå AB, member of Ius Laboris*

Emil Hedberg
*Roschier Sweden*

Erik Hygrell
*Wistrand Advokatbyrå*

Anders Isgren
*Baker & McKenzie*

Magnus Johnsson
*PwC Sweden*

Almira Kashani
*Miller Rosenfalck LLP*

Niklas Körling
*Setterwalls Advokatbyrå*

Caroline Lagergréen
*Elmzell Advokatbyrå AB, member of Ius Laboris*

Jasmine Lawson
*PwC Sweden*

Rikard Lindahl
*Advokatfirman Vinge KB, member of Lex Mundi*

Inger Lindhe
*Lantmäteriet*

Jens Malmqvist
*Advokatfirman Lindahl*

Andréa Nicolin
*Advokatfirman Vinge KB, member of Lex Mundi*

Eric Ödling
*Advokatfirman Vinge KB, member of Lex Mundi*

Ola Lo Olsson
*Elmzell Advokatbyrå AB, member of Ius Laboris*

Karl-Arne Olsson
*Gärde Wesslau Advokatbyrå*

Mattias Örnulf
*Hökerberg & Söderqvist Advokatbyrå KB*

Sara Ribbeklint
*MAQS Law Firm Advokatbyrå AB*

Jesper Schönbeck
*Advokatfirman Vinge KB, member of Lex Mundi*

Lennart Svantesson
*PwC Sweden*

Bo Thomaeus
*Gärde Wesslau Advokatbyrå*

Astrid Trolle Adams
*Miller Rosenfalck LLP*

Albert Wållgren
*Advokatfirman Vinge KB, member of Lex Mundi*

## SWITZERLAND
*Baudirektion Kanton Zürich*

*Ernst & Young*

Rashid Bahar
*Bär & Karrer AG*

Beat M. Barthold
*Froriep Renggli*

Marc Bernheim
*Staiger, Schwald & Partner Ltd.*

Frédéric Bétrisey
*Baker & McKenzie*

Sébastien Bettschart
*ABELS AVOCATS*

Myriam Büchi-Bänteli
*PwC SWITZERLAND*

Lucas Bühlmann
*PwC SWITZERLAND*

Andrea Cesare Canonica
*SWISS CUSTOMS*

Sonia de la Fuente
*ABELS AVOCATS*

Fiona Deucher
*ALTENBURGER LTD. LEGAL AND TAX*

Stefan Eberhard
*ABELS AVOCATS*

Suzanne Eckert
*WENGER PLATTNER*

Andrea Elvedi
*VISCHER ATTORNEYS AT LAW*

Jana Essebier
*VISCHER AG*

Benjamin Fehr
*PwC SWITZERLAND*

Peter Flückiger
*ECONOMIESUISSE*

Robert Furter
*PESTALOZZI, MEMBER OF LEX MUNDI*

Gaudenz Geiger
*STAIGER, SCHWALD & PARTNER LTD.*

Debora Ghilardotti
*MOLINO ADAMI GALANTE*

Erwin Griesshammer
*VISCHER ATTORNEYS AT LAW*

Olivier Hari
*SCHELLENBERG WITTMER*

Nicolas Herzog
*HERZOG & GOZZI*

Mark W. Hippenmeyer
*ALTENBURGER LTD. LEGAL AND TAX*

Jakob Hoehn
*PESTALOZZI, MEMBER OF LEX MUNDI*

Patrick Hünerwadel
*LENZ & STAEHELIN*

David Jenny
*VISCHER AG*

Michael Kramer
*PESTALOZZI, MEMBER OF LEX MUNDI*

Andrea Molino
*MOLINO ADAMI GALANTE*

Georg Naegeli
*HOMBURGER*

Roland Niklaus
*NCMB NOTAIRES ASSOCIÉS*

Gema Olivar Pascual
*PwC SWITZERLAND*

Daniela Reinhardt
*PwC SWITZERLAND*

Joseph Riedweg
*AUDICONSULT SA - MEMBER OF RUSSELL BEDFORD INTERNATIONAL*

Patricia Roberty
*VISCHER AG*

Guy-Philippe Rubeli
*PESTALOZZI, MEMBER OF LEX MUNDI*

Marc Schenk
*PwC SWITZERLAND*

Daniel Schmitz
*PwC SWITZERLAND*

Roland Stadler
*MIGROS-GENOSSENSCHAFTS-BUND*

Meinrad Vetter
*ECONOMIESUISSE*

Patrick Weber
*EKZ ELEKTRIZITÄTSWERKE DES KANTONS ZÜRICH*

Marc Widmer
*FRORIEP RENGGLI*

## SYRIAN ARAB REPUBLIC

*ERNST & YOUNG*

Maysa Abu Baker
*CENTRAL BANK OF SYRIA*

Sulafah Akili
*MINISTRY OF ECONOMY & TRADE*

Boulos Al Ashhab
*AUDITING CONSULTING ACCOUNTING CENTER*

Mouazza Al Ashhab
*AUDITING CONSULTING ACCOUNTING CENTER*

Bisher Al-Houssami
*AL-ISRAA INTERNATIONAL FREIGHT FORWARDER*

Ahnaf Al-Sarraj

Tarek AlHamwi
*KARAWANI LAW OFFICE*

Serene Almaleh
*KARAWANI LAW OFFICE*

Ghada Armali
*SARKIS & ASSOCIATES*

Mohammad Khaled Darwicheh
*TALAL ABU GHAZALEH LEGAL (TAG-LEGAL)*

Nuhad Dimashkiyyah
*UNDP*

Anas Ghazi
*MEETHAK - LAWYERS & CONSULTANTS*

Ebraheem Ziad Habeeb

Abdul Raouf Hamwi
*CIVIL ENGINEERING OFFICE*

Osama Karawani
*KARAWANI LAW OFFICE*

Raed Karawani
*KARAWANI LAW OFFICE*

Mazen N. Khaddour
*INTERNATIONAL LEGAL BUREAU*

Loubna Khoury
*AUDITING CONSULTING ACCOUNTING CENTER*

Moussa Mitry
*UNIVERSITY OF DAMASCUS / LOUKA & MITRY LAW OFFICE*

Gabriel Oussi
*OUSSI LAW FIRM*

Yasser Quwaider
*TALAL ABU GHAZALEH LEGAL (TAG-LEGAL)*

Housam Safadi
*SAFADI BUREAU*

Fadi Sarkis
*SARKIS & ASSOCIATES*

## TAIWAN, CHINA

*YANG & ASSOCIATES CONSULTING ENGINEERS*

Olivier Beydon
*YANGMING PARTNERS*

Mark Brown
*WINKLER PARTNERS*

Jersey Chang
*PRICEWATERHOUSECOOPERS LEGAL*

Victor Chang
*LCS & PARTNERS*

Edgar Y. Chen
*TSAR & TSAI LAW FIRM, MEMBER OF LEX MUNDI*

Hui-ling Chen
*WINKLER PARTNERS*

Nicholas V. Chen
*PAMIR LAW GROUP*

Yo-Yi Chen
*FORMOSA TRANSNATIONAL*

Chun-Yih Cheng
*FORMOSA TRANSNATIONAL*

Chia Yi Chiang
*PRICEWATERHOUSECOOPERS LEGAL*

Ying-Che Chiu
*TAIPEI CITY GOVERNMENT*

Yu-Chung Chiu
*MINISTRY OF THE INTERIOR*

Cindy Chou
*CHEN, SHYUU & PUN*

Dennis Chou
*EIGER LAW*

Peter Dernbach
*WINKLER PARTNERS*

Rosamund Fan
*PwC TAIWAN*

Philip T. C. Fei
*FEI & CHENG ASSOCIATES*

Steven Go
*PwC TAIWAN*

Mark Harty
*LCS & PARTNERS*

James Hong
*CHEN, SHYUU & PUN*

Sophia Hsieh
*TSAR & TSAI LAW FIRM, MEMBER OF LEX MUNDI*

Barbara Hsu
*SDV LOGISTICS*

Robert Hsu
*SDV LOGISTICS*

Tony Hsu
*PAMIR LAW GROUP*

Margaret Huang
*LCS & PARTNERS*

T.C. Huang
*HUANG & PARTNERS*

Ya-Ting Huang
*FORMOSA TRANSNATIONAL*

Charlotte J. Lin
*LCS & PARTNERS*

Joan Jing
*PRICEWATERHOUSECOOPERS LEGAL*

Nathan Kaiser
*EIGER LAW*

Chih-Shan Lee
*WINKLER PARTNERS*

Michael D. Lee
*PAMIR LAW GROUP*

Vivian Lee
*HUANG & PARTNERS*

Yu Lee
*TAIPEI CITY GOVERNMENT*

Che-Wei Liang
*JUDICIAL YUAN*

Justin Liang
*BAKER & MCKENZIE*

Frank Lin
*REXMED INDUSTRIES CO., LTD.*

Lilian Lin
*FINANCIAL SUPERVISORY COMMISSION, BANKING BUREAU*

Ming-Yen Lin
*DEEP & FAR, ATTORNEYS-AT-LAW*

Nelson J Lin
*HUANG & PARTNERS*

Nicole M. Lin
*TAI E INTERNATIONAL PATENT & LAW OFFICE*

Rich Lin
*LCS & PARTNERS*

Yishian Lin
*PwC TAIWAN*

Mark Ohlson
*YANGMING PARTNERS*

Lawrence S. Ong
*PRICEWATERHOUSECOOPERS LEGAL*

Patrick Pai-ChiangChu
*LEE AND LI*

J. F. Pun
*CHEN, SHYUU & PUN*

Tanya Y. Teng
*HUANG & PARTNERS*

Bee Leay Teo
*BAKER & MCKENZIE*

C.F. Tsai
*DEEP & FAR, ATTORNEYS-AT-LAW*

Eric Tsai
*PRICEWATERHOUSECOOPERS LEGAL*

Joe Tseng
*LCS & PARTNERS*

Sean Tung
*LCS & PARTNERS*

Chao-Yu Wang
*YANGMING PARTNERS*

Richard Watanabe
*PwC TAIWAN*

Ja Lin Wu
*COUNCIL FOR ECONOMIC PLANNING & DEVELOPMENT*

Pei-Yu Wu
*BAKER & MCKENZIE*

Quiao-ling Wu
*DEEP & FAR, ATTORNEYS-AT-LAW*

Alex Yeh
*LCS & PARTNERS*

Shih-Ming You
*MINISTRY OF THE INTERIOR*

## TAJIKISTAN

*NATIONAL BANK OF TAJIKISTAN*

*TAJIKHYDROELEKTROMONTAJ*

Bakhtiyor Abdulloev
*ABM TRANS SERVICE LLC*

Zarrina Adham
*HUMO AND PARTNERS*

Zulfiya Akchurina
*GRATA LAW FIRM*

Shavkat Akhmedov
*AKHMEDOV, AZIZOV & ABDULHAMIDOV ATTORNEYS*

Farhad Azizov
*AKHMEDOV, AZIZOV & ABDULHAMIDOV ATTORNEYS*

Denis Bagrov
*COLIBRI LAW FIRM*

Abdulbori Baybayev
*LAW FIRM LEX*

Jienshoh Bukhoriev
*USAID BEI BUSINESS ENVIRONMENT IMPROVEMENT PROJECT (BY PRAGMA CORPORATION)*

Yunus Ernazarov
*AKHMEDOV, AZIZOV & ABDULHAMIDOV ATTORNEYS*

Sobir Abduvaliyevich Haitov
*AGROINVESTBANK*

Amirhonov Ilhom
*ABM TRANS SERVICE LLC*

Elena Kaeva
*PwC KAZAKHSTAN*

Assel Khamzina
*PwC KAZAKHSTAN*

Parviz Kuliev
*MASHVARAT LIMITED LIABILITY COMPANY*

Farhod Mirfozilov
*BARKI TOJIK*

Rahmon Muratov
*KN IBRAKOM FZCO.*

Jamshed Rahmonberdiev
*SOMON CAPITAL JSC*

Ravshan Rashidov
*LAW FIRM LEX*

Zimfera Rizvanova
*REPUBLICAN COMMITTEE OF LABOR UNION OF TAJIKISTAN*

Emin Sanginov
*MINISTRY OF LABOR & SOCIAL PROTECTION*

Marina Shamilova
*LEGAL CONSULTING GROUP*

Kamila Tursunkulova
*PwC KAZAKHSTAN*

Azim Usmanov
*COLIBRI LAW FIRM*

Aliya Utegaliyeva
*PwC KAZAKHSTAN*

Arlan Yerzhanov
*GRATA LAW FIRM*

Abdurakhmon Yuldoshev
*MINISTRY OF LABOR & SOCIAL PROTECTION*

## TANZANIA

*ERNST & YOUNG*

*ISHENGOMA, KARUME, MASHA & MAGAI ADVOCATES*

Abdul Abdallah
*CRB AFRICA LEGAL*

UmmiKulthum Abdallah
*AKO LAW IN ASSOCIATION WITH CLYDE & CO.*

Zukra Ally
*PwC TANZANIA*

Said Athuman
*TANZANIA REVENUE AUTHORITY*

Aloys Bahebe
*LA LAW ASSOCIATES ADVOCATES*

Tadjidine Ben Mohamed
*AVOCAT À LA COUR*

Ibrahim Bendera
*M & B LAW CHAMBERS*

Albina Burra
*MINISTRY OF LANDS & HUMAN SETTLEMENTS DEVELOPMENT*

Vijendra J. Cholera
*PKF ACCOUNTANTS & BUSINESS ADVISOR TANZANIA*

Magori Cosmas
*TRADE FACILITATION UNIT, CUSTOMS*

Moses Dancan
*GAPCS*

Theresia Dominic
*UNIVERSITY OF DAR ES SALAAM*

Esteriano Emmanuel Mahingila
*MINISTRY OF INDUSTRY & TRADE*

Bosco R. Gadi
*MINISTRY OF INDUSTRY & TRADE*

Santosh Gajjar
*SUMAR VARMA ASSOCIATES*

Christopher Giattas
*REX ATTORNEYS*

Syed Hasan
*RAIS SHIPPING SERVICES (TANZANIA) LTD.*

Beatus Idana
*PKF ACCOUNTANTS & BUSINESS ADVISOR TANZANIA*

Lincoln P. Irungu
*DL SHIPPING COMPANY LTD.*

Protase R. G. Ishengoma
*ISHENGOMA, KARUME, MASHA & MAGAI ADVOCATES*

Edward John Urio
*TANZANIA FREIGHT FORWARDERS ASSOCIATION*

John R. Kahyoza
*HIGH COURT OF TANZANIA COMMERCIAL DIVISION*

Kamanga K. Kapinga
*CRB AFRICA LEGAL*

Wilbert B. Kapinga
*MKONO & CO ADVOCATES*

Edward Kateka
*CRB AFRICA LEGAL*

David Kibebe
*EPITOME ARCHITECTS*

Shani Kinswaga
*PwC TANZANIA*

Barney Laseko
*PRIVATE SECTOR DEVELOPMENT AND INVESTMENT DIVISION, PRIME MINISTERS OFFICE*

Simon Lazaro
*MINISTRY OF LANDS & HUMAN SETTLEMENTS DEVELOPMENT*

Amalia Lui
*FB ATTORNEYS*

Christine M.S. Shekidele
*TANZANIA REVENUE AUTHORITY*

Victoria Makani
*VELMA LAW CHAMBERS*

Robert Makaramba
*HIGH COURT OF TANZANIA COMMERCIAL DIVISION*

Hyacintha Benedict Makileo
*NATIONAL CONSTRUCTION COUNCIL*

G.O.L. Masangwa
*MOLLEL ELECTRICAL CONTRACTORS LTD.*

Lydia Massawe
*BLUELINE ATTORNEYS*

Peter S. Matinde
*PSM ARCHITECTS CO. LTD.*

Sophia Mgonja
*TANESCO LTD.*

Nyaga Mawalla
*MAWALLA & ASSOCIATES ADVOCATES*

Ayoub Mftaya
*NEXLAW ADVOCATES*

Lucia Minde
*AKO LAW IN ASSOCIATION WITH CLYDE & CO.*

Steven Mlote
*ENGINEERS REGISTRATION BOARD*

Angela Mndolwa
*AKO LAW IN ASSOCIATION WITH CLYDE & CO.*

Chris Mnyanga
*MINISTRY OF LANDS & HUMAN SETTLEMENTS DEVELOPMENT*

George Mpeli Kilindu
*REX ATTORNEYS*

Khalfan Msumi
*M & B LAW CHAMBERS*

Octavian Mushukuma
*CRB AFRICA LEGAL*

Bumi Mwaisaka
*MINISTRY OF LANDS & HUMAN SETTLEMENTS DEVELOPMENT*

Gerald Mwakipesile
*MINISTRY OF LANDS & HUMAN SETTLEMENTS DEVELOPMENT*

Lugano J.S. Mwandambo
*REX ATTORNEYS*

Shabani Mwatawala
*PSM ARCHITECTS CO. LTD.*

Gerald Nangi
*FB ATTORNEYS*

Maningo Nassoro
*NATIONAL CONSTRUCTION COUNCIL*

Stephen Ngatunga
*TANZANIA FREIGHT FORWARDERS ASSOCIATION*

Alex Thomas Nguluma
*REX ATTORNEYS*

Sweetbert Nkuba
*LEXGLOBE LLP TANZANIA*

Neema Nyiti
*CRB AFRICA LEGAL*

Cyril Pesha
*CRB AFRICA LEGAL*

Katarina T. Revocati
*HIGH COURT OF TANZANIA COMMERCIAL DIVISION*

Frederick Ringo
*ADEPT CHAMBERS*

Charles R.B. Rwechungura
*CRB AFRICA LEGAL*

Emmy Salewi
*NORPLAN TANZANIA LIMITED*

Amish Shah
*ADEPT CHAMBERS*

Rishit Shah
*PwC TANZANIA*

Thadeus J. Shio
*CQS SERVICES LIMITED*

Geoffrey Sikira
*CRB ATTORNEYS*

Aliko Simon
*AKO LAW IN ASSOCIATION WITH CLYDE & CO.*

Eve Hawa Sinare
*REX ATTORNEYS*

Richard Sisa
*GAPCS*

Joseph T. Tango
*CQS SERVICES LIMITED*

David Tarimo
*PwC TANZANIA*

Reginald Tarimo
*BANK OF TANZANIA*

Mustafa Tharoo
*ADEPT CHAMBERS*

Joseph Thomas Klerruu
*MINISTRY OF LANDS & HUMAN SETTLEMENTS DEVELOPMENT*

Sarah Thomas Massamu
*ADEPT CHAMBERS*

Irene Mutalemwa Woerle
*MKONO & CO ADVOCATES*

Sinare Zaharan
*REX ATTORNEYS*

**THAILAND**

Janist Aphornratana
*PwC THAILAND*

Roi Bak
*DEJ-UDOM & ASSOCIATES*

Chanakarn Boonyasith
*SIAM CITY LAW OFFICES LTD.*

Chalee Chantanayingyong
*SECURITIES AND EXCHANGE COMMISSION*

Chinnavat Chinsangaram
*WEERAWONG, CHINNAVAT & PEANGPANOR LTD.*

Wachakorn Chiramongkolkul
*PwC THAILAND*

Kanphassorn Chotwathana
*PwC THAILAND*

Ramin Chuayriang
*METROPOLITAN ELECTRICITY AUTHORITY*

David Duncan
*TILLEKE & GIBBINS*

Alexandre Dupont
*LAW SOLUTIONS LTD.*

Jennifer Erickson
*TILLEKE & GIBBINS*

Frederic Favre
*VOVAN & ASSOCIES*

Seetha Gopalakrishnan
*PwC THAILAND*

Amélie Guardiola
*VOVAN & ASSOCIES*

Yothin Intaraprasong
*CHANDLER & THONG-EK*

Muncharee Ittipalin
*APL*

Tanach Kanjanasiri
*DLA THAILAND LLP*

Chaiwat Keratisuthisathorn
*TILLEKE & GIBBINS*

Suwat Kerdphon
*DEPARTMENT OF LANDS*

Natchar Leedae
*ALLENS ARTHUR ROBINSON / SIAM PREMIER INTERNATIONAL LAW OFFICE LIMITED*

William Lehane
*ALLENS ARTHUR ROBINSON / SIAM PREMIER INTERNATIONAL LAW OFFICE LIMITED*

Sakchai Limsiripothong
*WEERAWONG, CHINNAVAT & PEANGPANOR LTD.*

Steven Miller
*MAYER BROWN JSM*

Surapol Opasatien
*NATIONAL CREDIT BUREAU CO. LTD.*

Nipa Pakdeechanuan
*DEJ-UDOM & ASSOCIATES*

Tanadee Pantumkomol
*CHANDLER & THONG-EK*

Thidarat Patjaisomboon
*APL*

Santhapat Periera
*TILLEKE & GIBBINS*

Thawatchai Pittayasophon
*SECURITIES AND EXCHANGE COMMISSION*

Thunsamorn Pochjanapanichakul
*VICKERY & WORACHAI LTD.*

Ratana Poonsombudlert
*CHANDLER & THONG-EK*

Cynthia M. Pornavalai
*TILLEKE & GIBBINS*

Supan Poshyananda
*SECURITIES AND EXCHANGE COMMISSION*

Somboonpoonpol Pratumporn
*SIAM CITY LAW OFFICES LTD.*

Chitchai Punsan
*TILLEKE & GIBBINS*

Sahachthorn Putthong
*RATCHABURI ELECTRICITY GENERATING HOLDING PCL.*

Anake Rattanajitbanjong
*TILLEKE & GIBBINS*

Panuwat Rattanawechasit
*DLA THAILAND LLP*

Suraphon Rittipongchusit
*DLA THAILAND LLP*

Thavorn Rujivanarom
*PwC THAILAND*

Arnon Rungthanakarn
*SIAM CITY LAW OFFICES LTD.*

Maythawee Sarathai
*MAYER BROWN JSM*

Maprang Sombatthai
*DLA THAILAND LLP*

Kowit Somwaiya
*LAWPLUS LTD.*

Pattanapong Srinam
*DLA THAILAND LLP*

Pornchai Srisawang
*TILLEKE & GIBBINS*

Rachamarn Suchitchon
*SECURITIES AND EXCHANGE COMMISSION*

Picharn Sukparangsee
*SIAM CITY LAW OFFICES LTD.*

Luxsiri Supakijjanusorn
*SIAM CITY LAW OFFICES LTD.*

Naddaporn Suwanvajukkasikij
*LAWPLUS LTD.*

Hunt Talmage
*CHANDLER & THONG-EK*

Jinjutha Techakumphu
*SIAM CITY LAW OFFICES LTD.*

Kobkit Thienpreecha
*TILLEKE & GIBBINS*

Paisan Tulapornpipat
*BLUE OCEAN LOGISTICS CO., LTD.*

Sutharm Valaisathien
*INTERNATIONAL LEGAL COUNSELLORS*

Pattara Vasinwatanapong
*VICKERY & WORACHAI LTD.*

Harold K. Vickery Jr.
*VICKERY & WORACHAI LTD.*

Patcharaporn Vinitnuntarat
*SIAM CITY LAW OFFICES LTD.*

Pimvimol Vipamaneerut
*TILLEKE & GIBBINS*

Auradee Wongsaroj
*CHANDLER & THONG-EK*

Ahmet Yesilkaya
*TILLEKE & GIBBINS*

Somchai Yungkarn
*CHANDLER & THONG-EK*

**TIMOR-LESTE**

*BANCO CENTRAL DE TIMOR-LESTE (BCTL)*

*EDTL*

*MINISTRY OF INFRASTRUCTURE*

*MINISTRY OF JUSTICE*

*MINISTRY OF TOURISM, TRADE AND INDUSTRY (MTCI)*

*PORT AUTHORITY*

Fernando Afonso da Silva
*KAI WATU KMANEK CONSULTANT LDA*

Lidia Ardita

Regina Azevedo Pinto
*CRA TIMOR*

Luis Carvalho
*ENGINEER*

Sofia Neves Cruz
*CRA TIMOR*

Joana Custoias
*MIRANDA CORREIA AMENDOEIRA & ASSOCIADOS*

Brigida da Silva
*CUSTOMS, TIMOR-LESTE MINISTRY OF FINANCE*

Sahe da Silva
*LAWYER*

Tiago Dias
*CRA TIMOR*

Paulo Duarte
*TRIBUNAL DE DILI - TIMOR*

Alejandro Garcia
*CUSTOMS, TIMOR-LESTE MINISTRY OF FINANCE*

Renato Guerra de Almeida
*MIRANDA CORREIA AMENDOEIRA & ASSOCIADOS*

Ashish Gupta
*NATIONAL INSURANCE TIMOR-LESTE S.A. (NITL)*

Tommy Hariyanto

Jackson Lay
*PALM SPRING ESTATE*

João Leite
*MIRANDA CORREIA AMENDOEIRA & ASSOCIADOS*

Naomi Leong
*DELOITTE LLP*

Shirley Ng
*VICTORIAN EMPLOYER'S CHAMBER OF COMMERCE AND INDUSTRY (VECCI)*

Tony O'Connor
*MINISTRY OF FINANCE*

Cornelio Pacheco
*JVK INTERNATIONAL MOVERS*

Mick C. Payze
*SHIPPING & FREIGHT ENTERPRISES PTY LTD.*

Alexandre Pita Soares
*CRA TIMOR*

Tjia Soh Siang
*TJIA & TCHAI ASSOCIATES*

Melisa Silva Caldas
*CRA TIMOR*

Petrus Supriyatno

Kim Tchia
*STARTEC ENTERPRISES*

Fernando Torrao
*CAIXA GERAL DE DEPOSITOS (CGD)*

Ronel Valente
*ROCKY CONSTRUCTIONS*

Collin Yap
*NATIONAL INSURANCE TIMOR-LESTE S.A. (NITL)*

**TOGO**

*AGENCE EPAUC NOUVELLE*

*CABINET JOHN W. FFOOKS & CO.*

Jean-Marie Adenka
*CABINET ADENKA*

Edzodzi Délato Adonsou
*DIRECTION DE L'HABITAT ET DU PATRIMOINE IMMOBILIER*

Koudzo Mawuéna Agbemaple
*AUTORITÉ DE RÉGLEMENTATION DU SECTEUR DE L'ELECTRICITÉ*

Kokou Gadémon Agbessi
*CABINET LUCREATIF*

Fo-Koffi Wolassé Agboli
*AQUEREBURU AND PARTNERS CABINET D'AVOCATS*

Prosper Gato Amegnido
*GROUPE GATO*

Martial Akakpo
*SCP MARTIAL AKAKPO & ASSOCIÉS*

Ahmadou Al Aminou Lo
*BCEAO*

Coffi Alexis Aquereburu
*AQUEREBURU AND PARTNERS CABINET D'AVOCATS*

Cécile Assogbavi
*ETUDE NOTARIALE ASSOGBAVI*

Sylvanus Dodzi Awutey
*CABINET LUCREATIF*

Koli-Yidaou Bako
*COMPAGNIE ENERGIE ELECTRIQUE DU TOGO (CEET)*

Tiem Bolidja
*COMPAGNIE ENERGIE ELECTRIQUE DU TOGO (CEET)*

Customer Service Department
*TOGO TÉLÉCOM*

Sockna Diaby
*PwC CÔTE D'IVOIRE*

Koffi Joseph Dogbevi
*CABINET LUCREATIF*

Simon Dogbo
*DAMCO TOGO*

Akouvi Thérèse Donu
*SCP MARTIAL AKAPO & ASSOCIÉS*

Messan Raphael Ekoue
Hagbonon
*CENTRE D'ETUDES D'ARCHITECTURE ET
D'URBANISME*

Komlan Cyrille Houssin
*SCP MARTIAL AKAPO & ASSOCIÉS*

Kodjo John Kokou
*CABINET D'AVOCATS JOHN KOKOU*

Atchroe Leonard Johnson
*SCP AQUEREBURU & PARTNERS*

Komivi Kassegne
*COMPAGNIE ENERGIE ELECTRIQUE DU
TOGO (CEET)*

Bleounou Komlan
*AVOCAT À LA COUR*

Hokaméto Kpenou
*AUTORITÉ DE RÉGLEMENTATION DU
SECTEUR DE L'ELECTRICITÉ*

Alain Kofi Kumodzi
*CPF & BELBIN*

Adeline Messou
*PwC CÔTE D'IVOIRE*

Kissao Napo
*COMPAGNIE ENERGIE ELECTRIQUE DU
TOGO (CEET)*

Yawovi Negbegble
*AUTORITÉ DE RÉGLEMENTATION DU
SECTEUR DE L'ELECTRICITÉ*

Adoko Pascal
*TRIANGLE CONSTRUCTEUR*

Olivier Pedanou
*CABINET LUCREATIF*

Nourou Sama
*COMPAGNIE ENERGIE ELECTRIQUE DU
TOGO (CEET)*

Galolo Soedjede
*CABINET DE MAÎTRE GALOLO SOEDJEDE*

Hoédjéto Tonton Soedjede
*CABINET DE MAÎTRE GALOLO SOEDJEDE*

Dominique Taty
*PwC CÔTE D'IVOIRE*

Mouhamed Tchassona Traore
*ETUDE ME MOUHAMED TCHASSONA
TRAORE*

Inès Mazalo Tekpa
*CABINET LUCREATIF*

Fousséni Traoré
*PwC CÔTE D'IVOIRE*

Komi Tsakadi
*CABINET DE ME TSAKADI*

Emmanuel Yehouessi
*BCEAO*

Edem Amétéfé Zotchi
*SCP MARTIAL AKAPO & ASSOCIÉS*

## TONGA

Inoke Afu
*PACIFIC FINANCE & INVESTMENT LTD.*

Rosamond Bling
*MINISTRY OF LANDS, SURVEY, NATURAL
RESOURCES & ENVIRONMENT*

Lord Dalgety
*ELECTRICITY COMMISSION*

Paula Feaomoeata
*SUPREME COURT*

Taniela Fonna
*KRAMER AUSENCO TONGA*

Kolotia Fotu
*MINISTRY OF LABOUR, COMMERCE AND
INDUSTRIES*

Nailasikau Halatuituia
*MINISTRY OF LANDS, SURVEY, NATURAL
RESOURCES & ENVIRONMENT*

Aminiasi Kefu
*CROWN LAW*

Peni Lavakeiaho Makoni
*MINISTRY OF WORKS*

Fisilau Leone
*KRAMER AUSENCO TONGA*

Rod Lowe
*TONGA POWER LTD.*

Temaleti Manakovi Patiulu
*SUPREME COURT*

Salesi Mataele
*OCEANTRANZ TONGA LTD.*

Sione Tomasi Naite Fakahua
*FAKAHUA-FA'OTUSIA & ASSOCIATES*

Laki M. Niu
*LAKI NIU OFFICES*

Michael O'Shannassy
*INLAND REVENUE TONGA*

Sipiloni Raass
*JAIMI ASSOCIATES - ARCHITECTS*

Jemma San Jose
*ELECTRICITY COMMISSION*

Alani Schaumkel
*DATELINE TRANS- AM SHIPPING*

Dana Stephenson
*STEPHENSON ASSOCIATES*

Ralph Stephenson
*STEPHENSON ASSOCIATES*

Hiva Tatila
*TONGA DEVELOPMENT BANK*

Alisi Numia Taumoepeau
*TMP LAW*

Fine Tohi
*DATELINE TRANS- AM SHIPPING*

Lesina Tonga
*LESINA TONGA LAW FIRM*

Distquaine P. Tu'ihalamaka
*MINISTRY OF LABOUR, COMMERCE AND
INDUSTRIES*

Jennifer Tupou
*JKCA*

Kisione Tupou
*JKCA*

Petunia Tupou
*FUNGATEIKI LAW OFFICE*

John Fanua Uele
*MINISTRY OF LANDS, SURVEY, NATURAL
RESOURCES & ENVIRONMENT*

Christine Uta'atu
*UTA'ATU & ASSOCIATES*

Lepaola B. Vaea
*INLAND REVENUE TONGA*

Jone Vuli
*WESTPAC BANK OF TONGA*

Dianna Warner
*SKIP'S CUSTOM JOINERY LTD.*

Paul Wilkinson
*WESTPAC BANK OF TONGA*

## TRINIDAD AND TOBAGO

*ERNST & YOUNG*

Israiell Ali
*TRINIDAD & TOBAGO ELECTRICITY
COMMISSION*

Michael Andrew
*INTERNATIONAL CARGO SERVICES
LIMITED*

Harjinder S. Atwal
*REGULATED INDUSTRIES COMMISSION*

Steve Beckles
*DELOITTE LLP*

Ashrini Beharry
*J.D. SELLIER & CO.*

Cecil Camacho
*JOHNSON, CAMACHO & SINGH*

Tiffany Castillo
*M. HAMEL-SMITH & CO., MEMBER OF
LEX MUNDI*

Stacy Lee Daniell
*M. HAMEL-SMITH & CO., MEMBER OF
LEX MUNDI*

Hadyn-John Gadsby
*J.D. SELLIER & CO.*

Nadia Henriques
*M. HAMEL-SMITH & CO., MEMBER OF
LEX MUNDI*

Melissa Inglefield
*M. HAMEL-SMITH & CO., MEMBER OF
LEX MUNDI*

Nadia Sharon Kangaloo
*FITZWILLIAM STONE FURNESS-SMITH
& MORGAN*

Glenn A. Khan
*REGULATED INDUSTRIES COMMISSION*

Keomi Lourenco
*M. HAMEL-SMITH & CO., MEMBER OF
LEX MUNDI*

Ann-Marie Mahabir
*M. HAMEL-SMITH & CO., MEMBER OF
LEX MUNDI*

Nigel Marcham
*NITEC ELECTRICAL CONTRACTORS, LTD.*

Imtiaz Mohammed
*DELTA ELECTRICAL CONTRACTORS, LTD.*

Nalini Mohansingh
*CARGO CONSOLIDATORS AGENCY LTD.*

David Montgomery
*D. MONTGOMERY & CO. -
CORRESPONDENT OF RUSSELL BEDFORD
INTERNATIONAL*

Dean Nieves
*TRANSUNION*

Marjorie Nunez
*LEX CARIBBEAN*

Steven M. Paul
*J.D. SELLIER & CO.*

Fanta Punch
*M. HAMEL-SMITH & CO., MEMBER OF
LEX MUNDI*

Ramdath Dave Rampersad
*DELOITTE LLP*

Kelvin Ramsook
*TRINIDAD & TOBAGO ELECTRICITY
COMMISSION*

Danzel Reid
*TRINIDAD & TOBAGO ELECTRICITY
COMMISSION*

Myrna Robinson-Walters
*M. HAMEL-SMITH & CO., MEMBER OF
LEX MUNDI*

Walter Rochester
*PwC*

Colin Sabga
*M. HAMEL-SMITH & CO., MEMBER OF
LEX MUNDI*

Alice Salandy
*GSAL DESIGNS LTD.*

Gregory Salandy
*GSAL DESIGNS LTD.*

Stephen A. Singh
*JOHNSON, CAMACHO & SINGH*

Karen Vanaik
*LEX CARIBBEAN*

Jonathan Walker
*M. HAMEL-SMITH & CO., MEMBER OF
LEX MUNDI*

Allyson West
*PwC*

Grantley Wilshire
*M. HAMEL-SMITH & CO., MEMBER OF
LEX MUNDI*

Jude Xavier
*CARGO CONSOLIDATORS AGENCY LTD.*

Phillip Xavier
*CARGO CONSOLIDATORS AGENCY LTD.*

## TUNISIA

Samir Abdelly
*ABDELLY & ASSOCIES*

Ilhem Abderrahim
*SOCIÉTÉ TUNISIENNE DE L'ELECRICITÉ ET
DU GAZ (STEG)*

Mohamed Ammar
*SOCIÉTÉ TUNISIENNE DE L'ELECRICITÉ ET
DU GAZ (STEG)*

Mohamed Moncef Barouni
*ACR*

Adly Bellagha
*ADLY BELLAGHA & ASSOCIATES*

Hend Ben Achour
*ADLY BELLAGHA & ASSOCIATES*

Ismail Ben Farhat
*ADLY BELLAGHA & ASSOCIATES*

Wassim Ben Mahmoud
*ARCHITECT*

Leila Ben Mbarek
*LEGALYS*

Abdelfetah Benahji
*FERCHIOU & ASSOCIÉS*

Manel Bondi
*PwC TUNISIA*

Salaheddine Caid Essebsi
*CAID ESSEBSI AND PARTNERS LAW FIRM*

Salma Chaari
*ABDELLY & ASSOCIES*

Elyes Chafter
*CHAFTER RAOUADI LAW FIRM*

Zine el Abidine Chafter
*CHAFTER RAOUADI LAW FIRM*

Afef Challouf
*SOCIÉTÉ TUNISIENNE DE L'ELECRICITÉ ET
DU GAZ (STEG)*

Abdelmalek Dahmani
*DAHMANI TRANSIT INTERNATIONAL*

Mohamed Derbel
*BDO*

Mohamed Lotfi El Ajeri
*EL AJERI LAWYERS, PARTENAIRE DE DS
AVOCATS*

Yassine El Hafi
*ADLY BELLAGHA & ASSOCIATES*

Myriam Escheikh
*LEGALYS*

Abderrahmen Fendri
*PwC TUNISIA*

Noureddine Ferchiou
*FERCHIOU & ASSOCIÉS*

Slim Gargouri
*CPA*

Imene Hanafi
*LEGALYS*

Anis Jabnoun
*GIDE LOYRETTE NOUEL, MEMBER OF
LEX MUNDI*

Atf Jebali Nasri
*LEGALYS*

Badis Jedidi
*GIDE LOYRETTE NOUEL, MEMBER OF
LEX MUNDI*

Najla Jezi
*ACR*

Sami Kallel
*KALLEL & ASSOCIATES*

Faycal Karoui
*SOCIÉTÉ TUNISIENNE DE L'ELECRICITÉ ET
DU GAZ (STEG)*

Larbi Khedira
*CHAFTER RAOUADI LAW FIRM*

Mabrouk Maalaoui
*PwC TUNISIA*

Dina Magroun
*EL AJERI LAWYERS, PARTENAIRE DE DS
AVOCATS*

Sarah Mebazaa
*COMETE ENGINEERING*

Radhi Meddeb
*COMETE ENGINEERING*

Rahma Meddeb
*GIDE LOYRETTE NOUEL, MEMBER OF
LEX MUNDI*

Faouzi Mili
*MILI AND ASSOCIATES*

Slah Minaoui
*BANQUE CENTRALE DE TUNISIE*

Imen Nouira
*CONSERVATION FONCIÈRE TUNISIA*

Olfa Othmane
*BANQUE CENTRALE DE TUNISIE*

Habiba Raouadi
*CHAFTER RAOUADI LAW FIRM*

Hédi Rezgui
*SOCIÉTÉ TUNISIENNE DE L'ELECRICITÉ ET
DU GAZ (STEG)*

Koubaa Rym
*CRK*

Nizar Sdiri
*NIZAR SDIRI LAW FIRM*

Saber Souid
*CHAFTER RAOUADI LAW FIRM*

## TURKEY

Emre Akarkarasu
*PwC TURKEY*

Basak Akin
*AYDAŞ LIMAN KURMAN ATTORNEYS
AT LAW*

Deniz Akman
*BENER LAW OFFICE, MEMBER OF IUS
LABORIS*

Sezin Akoğlu
*PEKIN & PEKIN*

Müjdem Aksoy
*CERRAHOĞLU LAW FIRM*

Seza Ceren Aktaş
*PRICEWATERCOOPERS*

Simge Akyüz
*DEVRES LAW OFFICE*

Inci Alaloglu
*TABOGLU & DEMIRHAN*

Kenan Alpdündar
*CENTRAL BANK OF THE REPUBLIC OF
TURKEY*

Ekin Altıntaş
*PwC TURKEY*

Selin Barlin Aral
*PAKSOY LAW FIRM*

Ilkay Arslantaslı
*KPMG*

Cinar Aslan
*SEDAS*

Melis Atasagun
*PEKIN & BAYAR LAW FIRM*

Melis Avunduk
*PRICEWATERCOOPERS*

Aybike Aygun
*SARIIBRAHIMOĞLU LAW OFFICE*

Basak Aygun
*DÜLGER LAW FIRM*

Elvan Aziz
*PAKSOY LAW FIRM*

Derya Baksı
*TARLAN – BAKSI LAW FIRM*

Z. İlayda Balkan
*ADMD LAW FIRM*

Naz Bandik
*ÇAKMAK AVUKATLIK BÜROSU*

Serra Başoğlu Gürkaynak
*Mehmet Gün & Partners*

Ayça Bayburan
*ADMD Law Firm*

Pelin Baysal
*Mehmet Gün & Partners*

Nergis Beşiroğlu
*Cerrahoğlu Law Firm*

Ayşe Eda Biçer
*Çakmak Avukatlık Bürosu*

Taner Gokmen Bolayir
*Serap Zuvin Law Offices*

Nehize Boran Demir
*PricewaterCoopers*

Gulnur Camcı
*Somay Hukuk Bürosu*

Esin Çamlıbel
*Turunç Law Office*

Uraz Canbolat
*Cerrahoğlu Law Firm*

Maria Lianides Çelebi
*Bener Law Office, member of Ius Laboris*

Ipek Merve Çelik
*Pekin & Pekin*

M. Fadlullah Cerrahoğlu
*Cerrahoğlu Law Firm*

Emel Çetin
*Paksoy Law Firm*

Orçun Çetinkaya
*Mehmet Gün & Partners*

Alisya Bengi Danisman
*Mehmet Gün & Partners*

Okan Demirkan
*Kolcuoglu Kolcuoglu Attorneys at Law*

Orkun Deniz
*Kredit Kayıt Bureau*

Pınar Denktaş
*Pekin & Pekin*

Kazım Derman
*Kredit Kayıt Bureau*

Emine Devres
*Devres Law Office*

Ahmet İlker Doğan
*Çakmak Avukatlık Bürosu*

Didem Doğar
*Paksoy Law Firm*

Murat Volkan Dülger
*Dülger Law Firm*

Dilara Duman
*Duman Law Office*

Safa Mustafa Durakoğlu
*Çakmak Avukatlık Bürosu*

Pelin Ecevit
*Serap Zuvin Law Offices*

Burcak Er
*Bati Shipping and Trading S.A.*

Gökben Erdem Dirican
*Pekin & Pekin*

Onur Ergun
*Taboglu & Demirhan*

Gokce Erkaya
*Jones Lang LaSalle*

Mehmet Esendal Çam
*Kavlak Law Firm*

Umurcan Gago
*PwC Turkey*

Nigar Gökmen
*Çakmak Avukatlık Bürosu*

Sabiha Nur Göllü
*Bener Law Office, member of Ius Laboris*

Osman Nuri Gönenç
*Central Bank of the Republic of Turkey*

Gunhan Gonul
*Çakmak Avukatlık Bürosu*

Zeki Gunduz
*PwC Turkey*

Remzi Orkun Guner
*ADMD Law Firm*

Ömer Gürbüz
*Mehmet Gün & Partners*

Ayşegül Gürsoy
*Cerrahoğlu Law Firm*

Gülşah Güven
*Dülger Law Firm*

Tugce Hepsusler
*PricewaterCoopers*

Ece Ilter
*PwC Turkey*

Gül Incesulu
*Çakmak Avukatlık Bürosu*

Baris Kalayci
*Mehmet Gün & Partners*

Ibrahim Kara
*Kredit Kayıt Bureau*

Firat Baris Kavlak
*Kavlak Law Firm*

Aslan Kaya
*DMF System International, member of Russell Bedford International*

Betül Kencebay
*YASED - International Investors Association*

Burak Kepkep
*Kepkep International Legal Counseling*

Asena Aytug Keser
*Mehmet Gün & Partners*

İklim Kiliç
*Sarıibrahimoğlu Law Office*

Özlem Kızıl Voyvoda
*Çakmak Avukatlık Bürosu*

Çiğdem Koğar
*Central Bank of the Republic of Turkey*

Burcak Kurt
*Somay Hukuk Bürosu*

Ümit Kurt
*Jones Lang LaSalle*

Mert Kutlar
*ADMD Law Firm*

Altan Liman
*Aydaş Liman Kurman Attorneys at Law*

Orhan Yavuz Mavioğlu
*ADMD Law Firm*

Dilek Menteş
*Cerrahoğlu Law Firm*

Şila Muratoğlu
*Bayırlı & Muratoğlu Law Firm*

Melis Oget Koc
*Serap Zuvin Law Offices*

Gülçin Özlem Oğuzlar
*Turunç Law Office*

Ozgecan Oksuz
*Özel & Özel Attorneys At Law*

M. Bigen Onder
*Cerrahoğlu Law Firm*

Neşe Onder
*Mehmet Gün & Partners*

Mert Oner
*KPMG*

Selin Özdamar
*Salans*

Caner Özen
*Özel & Özel Attorneys At Law*

Okşan Özkan
*PricewaterCoopers*

Gokhan Ozmen
*Birsel Law Offices*

Özlem Özyiğit
*YASED - International Investors Association*

Serkan Pamukkale
*Birsel Law Offices*

Ahmed Pekin
*Pekin & Pekin*

Ferhat Pekin
*Pekin & Bayar Law Firm*

Çağatay Pekyorur
*Pekin & Pekin*

Batuhan Şahmay
*Bener Law Office, member of Ius Laboris*

Bilge Saltan
*Dülger Law Firm*

Selim Sarıibrahimoğlu
*Sarıibrahimoğlu Law Office*

Selim S. Seçkin
*Aydınlıoğlu Lawfirm*

Ömer Kayhan Seyhun
*Central Bank of the Republic of Turkey*

Sezil Simsek
*PricewaterCoopers*

M. Ufuk Söğütlüoğlu
*Deloitte LLP*

Sera Somay
*Somay Hukuk Bürosu*

Selda Soyoz
*Presidency of Revenue Administration*

Çağıl Sünbül
*PricewaterCoopers*

Esin Taboğlu
*Taboglu & Demirhan*

Aylin Tarlan Tüzemen
*Tarlan – Baksi Law Firm*

Özben Tekdal
*PwC Turkey*

Elif Tezcan Bayırlı
*Bayırlı & Muratoğlu Law Firm*

Filiz Toprak
*Mehmet Gün & Partners*

Noyan Turunç
*Turunç Law Office*

Ibrahim Tutar
*Penetra Consulting and Auditing*

Ürün Ülkü
*ADMD Law Firm*

Ayse Unal
*Turunç Law Office*

Furkan Ünal
*PGlobal Global Advisory and Training Services Ltd.*

Hazal Ungan
*Pekin & Pekin*

Barış Yalçın
*PwC Turkey*

Selcen Yalçın
*Mehmet Gün & Partners*

Ayşegül Yalçınmani Merler
*Cerrahoğlu Law Firm*

Beril Yayla
*Mehmet Gün & Partners*

A.Çağrı Yıldız
*ADMD Law Firm*

Cağatay Yılmaz
*Yılmaz Law Offices*

Rana Yılmaz
*Yılmaz Law Offices*

Murat Yülek
*PGlobal Global Advisory and Training Services Ltd.*

Izzet Zakuto
*Somay Hukuk Bürosu*

Serap Zuvin
*Serap Zuvin Law Offices*

**UGANDA**

*Ernst & Young*

Claire Amanya
*Kampala Associated Advocates*

Leria Arinaitwe
*Sebalu & Lule Advocates and Legal Consultants*

Doreen Atuhurra
*PwC Uganda*

Justine Bagyenda
*Bank of Uganda*

Bernard Baingana
*PwC Uganda*

Matovu Emmy
*Marma Technical Services*

Sarfaraz Jiwani
*Seyani Brothers & Co. (U) Ltd.*

Lwanga John Bosco
*Marma Technical Services*

Charles Kalu Kalumiya
*Kampala Associated Advocates*

Francis Kamulegeya
*PwC Uganda*

Phillip Karugaba
*MMAKS Advocates*

Edwin Karugire
*Kiwanuka & Karugire Advocates*

Baati Katende
*Katende, Ssempebwa & Co. Advocates*

David Katende
*EnviroKAD*

Sim K. Katende
*Katende, Ssempebwa & Co. Advocates*

Peter Kauma
*Kiwanuka & Karugire Advocates*

Kiryowa Kiwanuka
*Kiwanuka & Karugire Advocates*

Brigitte Kusiima Byarugaba
*Shonubi, Musoke & Co. Advocates*

Ida Kussima
*Katende, Ssempebwa & Co. Advocates*

Hakim Lugemwa
*Uganda Entrepreneurs Business Foundation*

Michael Malan
*Compuscan CRB Ltd.*

Paul Mbuga
*Sebalu & Lule Advocates and Legal Consultants*

John Mpambala
*Kampala City Council*

Andrew Munanura Kamuteera
*Sebalu & Lule Advocates and Legal Consultants*

Peters Musoke
*Shonubi, Musoke & Co. Advocates*

Rachel Mwanje Musoke
*MMAKS Advocates*

Benon Mutambi
*Electricity Regulatory Authority*

Jimmy M. Muyanja
*Muyanja & Associates*

Noah Mwesigwa
*Shonubi, Musoke & Co. Advocates*

Plaxeda Namirimu
*PwC Uganda*

Sophia Nampijja
*Katende, Ssempebwa & Co. Advocates*

Kassim Ngude

Diana Ninsiima
*MMAKS Advocates*

James Kagiri Njoroge
*Price & King Certified Public Accountants*

Eddie Nsamba-Gayiiya
*Consultant Surveyors and Planners*

William Okello

Silver Adowa Owaraga
*Magezi, Ibale & Co. Advocates*

Enoch Sabiiti
*Stema Associates*

Moses Segawa
*Sebalu & Lule Advocates and Legal Consultants*

Lawrence Sengendo
*Kampala City Council*

Alan Shonubi
*Shonubi, Musoke & Co. Advocates*

Manish Siyani
*Seyani Brothers & Co. (U) Ltd.*

Charles Lwanga Ssemanda

Obed Tindyebwa
*Grand & Noble, Certified Public Accountants*

Ambrose Turyahabwe
*DHL Global Forwarding (u) Ltd.*

Isaac Walukagga
*MMAKS Advocates*

**UKRAINE**

Yaroslav Abramov
*ILF Integrites*

Oleg Y. Alyoshin
*Vasil Kisil & Partners*

Andrey Astapov
*Astapov Lawyers International Law Group*

Viktoriya Baliuk
*Vasil Kisil & Partners*

Ron J. Barden
*PwC Ukraine*

Olena Basanska
*CMS Cameron McKenna*

Irina Batmanova
*Salans*

Yevgen Blok
*ILF Integrites*

Timur Bondaryev
*Arzinger & Partners*

Lilia Boulakh
*DLA Piper Ukraine LLC*

Alexander Buryak
*PwC Ukraine*

Serhiy Chorny
*Baker & McKenzie*

Vladimir Didenko
*Egorov Puginsky Afanasiev & Partners*

Dmytro Donets
*DLA Piper Ukraine LLC*

Igor Dykunskyy
*BNT & Partner*

Julia Goptarenko
*Chalas and Partners Law Firm*

Oleksandra Gorak
*DLA Piper Ukraine LLC*

Volodymyr Grabchak
*Arzinger & Partners*

Sergiy Gryshko
*CMS Cameron McKenna*

Valeriia Gudiy
*Ilyashev & Partners*

Maryna Ilchuk
*ARZINGER & PARTNERS*

Olga Ivaniv
*VASIL KISIL & PARTNERS*

Jon Johannesson
*IBCH*

Tetiana Kanashchuk
*GLEEDS UKRAINE LLC*

Victoria Kaplan
*CMS CAMERON MCKENNA*

Oleksii Kharitonov
*INYURPOLIS LAW FIRM*

Vitalii Khilko
*CMS CAMERON MCKENNA*

Ivanna Khonina
*KUZMINSKY & PARTNERS ATTORNEYS AT LAW LLC*

Natalya Kim
*CHADBOURNE & PARKE LLP*

Andriy Kirmach
*CHADBOURNE & PARKE LLP*

Olena Kochergina
*KONNOV & SOZANOVSKY*

Sergei Konnov
*KONNOV & SOZANOVSKY*

Maksym Kopeychykov
*ILYASHEV & PARTNERS*

Denys Kulgavyi
*SALANS*

Oleksandr Kurdydyk
*DLA PIPER UKRAINE LLC*

Tatyana Kuzmenko
*ASTAPOV LAWYERS INTERNATIONAL LAW GROUP*

Oles Kvyat
*ASTERS*

Mariana Legotska
*ASTERS*

Borys Lobovyk
*KONNOV & SOZANOVSKY*

Mykola Lomachynskyy
*GLEEDS UKRAINE LLC*

Olga Lubiv
*KPMG*

Anastasiya Lytvynenko
*KIBENKO, ONIKA & PARTNERS LAW FIRM*

Angela Mahinova
*SAYENKO KHARENKO*

Oleksandr Maydanyk
*EGOROV PUGINSKY AFANASIEV & PARTNERS*

Oleg Mazur
*CHADBOURNE & PARKE LLP*

Arsenyy Milyutin
*EGOROV PUGINSKY AFANASIEV & PARTNERS*

Vadim Mizyakov
*ASTERS*

Anna Moliboga
*KPMG*

Nataliya Mykolska
*SAYENKO KHARENKO*

Lurii Nekliaiev
*EGOROV PUGINSKY AFANASIEV & PARTNERS*

Sergiy Onishchenko
*CHADBOURNE & PARKE LLP*

Ruslan Ostapenko
*CMS CAMERON MCKENNA*

Oleksandr Padalka
*ASTERS*

Magdalena Patryk
*PwC UKRAINE*

Mikhail Pergamenshik
*KONNOV & SOZANOVSKY*

Alexey Pokotylo
*KONNOV & SOZANOVSKY*

Andriy Pozhidayev
*ASTERS*

Dmytro Pshenychnyuk
*DLA PIPER UKRAINE LLC*

Mariana Pyskun
*PwC UKRAINE*

Yuliana Revyuk
*KPMG*

Dmytro Rylovnikov
*DLA PIPER UKRAINE LLC*

Vadym Samoilenko
*ASTERS*

Marina Savchenko
*ASTAPOV LAWYERS INTERNATIONAL LAW GROUP*

Vladimir Sayenko
*SAYENKO KHARENKO*

Olga Serbul
*LAW FIRM IP & C. CONSULT, LLC*

Alla Shevchenko
*BNT & PARTNER*

Dmytro Shevchenko
*ARZINGER & PARTNERS*

Oleg Shevchuk
*PROXEN & PARTNERS*

Hanna Shtepa
*BAKER & MCKENZIE*

Anzhelika Shtukaturova
*SALANS*

Dmitry Sichkar
*KONNOV & SOZANOVSKY*

Markian B. Silecky
*SALANS*

Anna Sisetska
*VASIL KISIL & PARTNERS*

Evgen Solovyov
*ILYASHEV & PARTNERS*

Eugene Starikov
*INYURPOLIS LAW FIRM*

Andriy Stetsenko
*CMS CAMERON MCKENNA*

Iryna Stratiuk
*KPMG*

Yaroslav Teklyuk
*VASIL KISIL & PARTNERS*

Svitlana Teush
*ARZINGER & PARTNERS*

Anna Tkachenko
*SALANS*

Dmytro Tkachenko
*DLA PIPER UKRAINE LLC*

Zakhar Tropin
*PROXEN & PARTNERS*

Olena Tsybukh
*CHALAS AND PARTNERS LAW FIRM*

Olena Verba
*ARZINGER & PARTNERS*

Oleksandr Vygovskyy
*ASTERS*

Zeeshan Wani
*GLOBALINK TRANSPORTATION & LOGISTICS WORLDWIDE LLP*

Artur Yalovyy
*I_F INTEGRITES*

Olexiy Yanov
*LAW FIRM IP & C. CONSULT, LLC*

Anna Yarenko
*ASTAPOV LAWYERS INTERNATIONAL LAW GROUP*

Yulia Yashenkova
*ASTAPOV LAWYERS INTERNATIONAL LAW GROUP*

Galyna Zagorodniuk
*DLA PIPER UKRAINE LLC*

Galina Zagorodnyuk
*DLA PIPER UKRAINE LLC*

Tatiana Zamorska
*KPMG*

Anton Zinchuk
*INYURPOLIS LAW FIRM*

## UNITED ARAB EMIRATES
*GRIFFINS*

Qurashi Elsheikh Abdulghani Qurashi
*DUBAI MUNICIPALITY*

Khalid Abdulla
*AL MASHAWEER TRANSPORT*

Farid Ahmadi
*NATIONAL TRADING AND DEVELOPMENT EST.*

Yakud Ahmed
*ORCHID GULF*

Abdul Amir Ahmed abdulla Kodarzi
*JALAL AHMED GROUP*

Vinayak Ahuja
*APPAREL GROUP*

Kara Ajani
*TROWERS & HAMLINS LLP*

Mariam S.A. Al Afridi
*DUBAI WORLD*

Najeeb Mohammed Al Ali
*EMIRATES COMPETITIVENESS COUNCIL*

Mahmood Al Bastaki
*DUBAI TRADE*

Obaid Saif Atiq Al Falasi
*DUBAI ELECTRICITY AND WATER AUTHORITY*

Muzafar Al Haj
*GENERAL PENSION & SOCIAL SECURITY AUTHORITY*

Alya Hussain Al Hammadi
*DUBAI TRADE*

Abdulla Saif Al Kaabi
*DEPARTMENT OF ECONOMIC DEVELOPMENT – DUBAI*

Basil T. Al Kilani
*DUBAI WORLD*

Malik Al Madani
*EMIRATES COMPETITIVENESS COUNCIL*

Ahmed Al Mazrouei
*EMCREDIT*

Marwan Abdulla Al Mohammad
*DUBAI MUNICIPALITY*

Alya Al Mulla
*EMIRATES COMPETITIVENESS COUNCIL*

Habib M. Al Mulla
*HABIB AL MULLA & CO.*

Salah El Dien Al Nahas
*HADEL AL DHAHIRI & ASSOCIATES*

Saif Al Shamsi
*THE LEGAL GROUP*

Mohammed Abdulrahman Al Sharhan
*GENERAL PENSION & SOCIAL SECURITY AUTHORITY*

Yousuf Al Sharif
*YOUSUF AL SHARIF ASSOCIATES, ADVOCATES & LEGAL CONSULTANTS*

Essam Al Tamimi
*AL TAMIMI & COMPANY ADVOCATES & LEGAL CONSULTANTS*

Saeed Al-Hamiz
*CENTRAL BANK OF THE UAE*

Yousef Al-Suwaidi
*DUBAI COURTS*

Ibrahim Alhossani
*DUBAI COURTS*

Deepak Amin
*INCHCAPE SHIPPING SERVICES*

Adnan Amiri
*BAKER BOTTS LLP*

Wicki Andersen
*BAKER BOTTS LLP*

Sunil Anto
*MODERN FREIGHT COMPANY LLC*

Marcos Arocha
*EMIRATES COMPETITIVENESS COUNCIL*

Manavalan Arumugam
*EROS GROUP*

Mohammed Ather
*FARZANA TRADING*

T. Suresh Babu
*LANDMARK GROUP*

Srinivas Balla
*GREEN PORT SHIPPING AGENCY*

Elmugtaba Bannaga
*BIN SUWAIDAN ADVOCATES & LEGAL CONSULTANTS*

Prakash Bhanushali
*ALSAHM AL SAREE TRANSPORT & CLEARING*

Hiten Bhatia
*SILVER LINE TRANSPORTATION*

Jennifer Bibbings
*TROWERS & HAMLINS LLP*

Hammad Mohd. Bin Hammad
*GENERAL PENSION & SOCIAL SECURITY AUTHORITY*

Rashid Bin Humaidan
*DUBAI ELECTRICITY AND WATER AUTHORITY*

Maryam Bin Lahej
*DUBAI COURTS*

Mazen Boustany
*HABIB AL MULLA & CO.*

Lori-Ann Campbell
*HADEF & PARTNERS*

R. Chandran
*SEA BRIDGE SHIPPING CO. LLC*

Sudesh Chaturvedi
*GULF AGENCY COMPANY LLC*

Ravindranath Chowdhary
*ARTY TRANSPORT CO LLC*

Noreen Crasto
*SONY GULF*

Bipin Daniel
*MODERN FREIGHT COMPANY LLC*

Shirish Deshpande
*ARABIAN AUTOMOBILES*

Abdullah Ebedin
*YOUSUF AL SHARIF ASSOCIATES, ADVOCATES & LEGAL CONSULTANTS*

Rony Eid
*HABIB AL MULLA & CO.*

Mohammed El Ghul
*HABIB AL MULLA & CO.*

Ashfat Farhan
*AIR SOLUTIONS FZE*

Jim Fernandes
*ALLIED TRANSPORT ESTABLISHMENT*

Senil George
*NATIONAL TRADING AND DEVELOPMENT EST.*

Samer Hamzeh
*TROWERS & HAMLINS LLP*

Jayaram Hariharan
*VASCO GLOBAL MARITIME*

David Harris
*DUBAI FOREIGN INVESTMENT OFFICE*

Mohamed Hassan Ali Al Sherif
*FARZANA TRADING*

Barton Hoggard
*HADEF & PARTNERS*

Ashiq Hussain
*DUBAI TRADE*

Ali Ibrahim
*EMCREDIT*

Viji John
*FREIGHT SYSTEMS*

Iman Kaiss
*TROWERS & HAMLINS LLP*

Aarthi Kannan
*ARTY TRANSPORT CO LLC*

Mohamed Khalifa
*GENERAL PENSION & SOCIAL SECURITY AUTHORITY*

Naeem Khan
*MOHAMMED ESHAQ TRADING COMPANY*

Salim Ahmed Khan
*DUBAI TRADE*

Shahid M. Khan
*BUSIT AL ROKEN & ASSOCIATES*

Jai Kishan Khushaldasani
*JMD CLEARING & FORWARDING*

Khaled Kilani
*ARAMEX EMIRATES LLC*

Rola Kobeissi
*EMCREDIT*

Vipul Kothari
*KOTHARI AUDITORS & ACCOUNTANTS*

Solafa Kouta
*SHARAF SHIPPING AGENCY*

B.S. Krishna Moorthy
*LANDMARK GROUP*

Rajiv Krishnan
*FARZANA TRADING*

Anil Kumar
*MODERN FREIGHT COMPANY LLC*

Rajeev Kumar
*AL YOUSUF ELECTRONICS*

Ravi Kumar
*DUBAI TRADE*

Senthil Kumar
*GLG SHIPPING*

John Kunjappan
*MAERSK KANOO LLC*

Asherf Kunjimoidu
*AL YOUSUF ELECTRONICS*

Charles S. Laubach
*AFRIDI & ANGELL, MEMBER OF LEX MUNDI*

P.S. Liaquath
*SHARAF SHIPPING AGENCY*

Sohail Maklai
*MOHAMMED ESHAQ TRADING COMPANY*

Gagan Malhotra
*DUBAI TRADE*

Srikrishnan Mannapara
*SONY GULF*

Premanand Maroly
*VASCO GLOBAL MARITIME*

Harish Matabonu
*ARTY TRANSPORT CO LLC*

Chandru Mirchandani
*JUMBO ELECTRONICS CO. LLC*

Sharnooz Mohammed
*DHL GLOBAL FORWARDING*

Faysal (Fakhr-Eddine) Mokadem
*EMIRATES COMPETITIVENESS COUNCIL*

Ottavia Molinari
*MOLINARI LEGAL CONSULTANCY*

Roland Monteath
*AGILITY GLOBAL LOGISTICS*

Abdulqader Mossa
*DUBAI COURTS*

Badih Moukarzel
*HUQOOQ LEGAL PRACTICE*

Pretish P.N
*MODERN FREIGHT COMPANY LLC*

Ravi Parambott
*IAL Logistics Emirates LLC*

Jagdish Parulekar
*Al Habtoor Motors*

Vijendra Vikram Singh Paul
*Talal Abu Ghazaleh Legal
(TAG-Legal)*

Elise PaulHus
*Habib Al Mulla & Co.*

Biju Pillai
*DHL Global Forwarding*

Jaya Prakash
*Al Futtaim Logistics*

V. Prakash
*Al Tajir Glass Industries*

Lal Premarathne
*DHL Global Forwarding*

Praveen Pudhuvail
*Dubai Express LLC (Freightworks
Branch)*

Hera Qazi
*The Legal Group*

Samer Qudah
*Al Tamimi & Company Advocates
& Legal Consultants*

Yusuf Rafiudeen
*Dubai Electricity and Water
Authority*

Sujaya Rao
*DHL Global Forwarding*

Dean Rolfe
*PwC United Arab Emirates*

Shoeb Saher
*Habib Al Mulla & Co.*

Kamarudeen Sahib
*Al Habtoor Motors*

Nisrine Salam
*Dubai Foreign Investment Office*

Mohammed Ahmed Saleh
*Dubai Municipality*

Khalid Mohamed Saleh Al Mulla
*Dubai Municipality*

Mohammed Ahmed Saqer
*General Pension & Social Security
Authority*

Claus Schmidt
*Panalpina Gulf*

Herbert Schroder
*Emcredit*

Derrick Sequeira
*Kuehne + Nagel LLC*

Dilip Shadavani
*Al Habtoor Motors*

M. Vivekanand Shetty
*Eros Group*

Shailen Shukla
*Jumbo Electronics Co. LLC*

N.K. Sidharthan
*National Trading and Development
Est.*

Sreekumar Sivasankaran
*Globelink West Star Shipping LLC*

Douglas Smith
*Habib Al Mulla & Co.*

Wayne Smith
*Al Futtaim Logistics*

Johnson Soans
*Extron Electronics M.E*

Suresh
*X-Architects*

Pervez Tatary
*Green Port Shipping Agency*

Taha Tawawala
*Al Suwaidi & Company*

Mohammed Sultan Thani
*Dubai Land Department*

Hamad Thani Mutar
*Dubai Courts*

Nitin Tirath
*Dubai Trade*

Suresh Vallu
*Diamond Shipping Services*

P.M Valsalan
*Mubarak & Sons Transport*

Justin Varghese
*Al Futtaim Logistics*

Gary Watts
*Al Tamimi & Company Advocates
& Legal Consultants*

Rania Youssef
*Habib Al Mulla & Co.*

Natasha Zahid
*Baker Botts LLP*

Nawal Zemni
*Yousuf Al Sharif Associates,
Advocates & Legal Consultants*

## UNITED KINGDOM

*Ofgem*

*White & Black Legal LLP*

Zainul Ahmad
*PwC*

Simon Allison
*Mayer Brown International LLP*

Imran Badat
*Veritas Solicitors LLP*

Tilly Baderin
*PricewaterhouseCoopers Legal LLP*

Hannah Belton
*QualitySolicitors Redkite*

Sally Booth
*Simmons & Simmons LLP*

David Bridge
*Simmons & Simmons LLP*

Oliver Browne
*Latham & Watkins LLP*

Connor Cahalane
*Mayer Brown International LLP*

Sebastian Cameron
*Cleary Gottlieb Steen & Hamilton
LLP*

Michael Canvin
*Crown Agents Ltd.*

Jonathan Dawe
*Grant Dawe LLP*

Kathryn Donovan
*Latham & Watkins LLP*

Lindsay Edkins
*Weil, Gotshal & Manges LLP*

Nick Francis
*PwC United Kingdom*

Alice Fraser
*Cleary Gottlieb Steen & Hamilton
LLP*

Kelvin Goh
*Simmons & Simmons LLP*

Simon Graham
*Latham & Watkins LLP*

Tony Grant
*Grant Dawe LLP*

Donald Gray
*Darwin Gray LLP*

Helen Hall
*DLA Piper UK LLP*

Jillian Hastings
*Department for Communities and
Local Government*

Neville Howlett
*PwC United Kingdom*

Stephen Hubner
*Shepherd & Wedderburn*

Simon Jay
*Cleary Gottlieb Steen & Hamilton
LLP*

Jolita Kajtazi
*Grant Dawe LLP*

Chandini Kanwar
*Latham & Watkins LLP*

Susan Kennedy
*Latham & Watkins LLP*

Gillian Key-Vice
*Experian Ltd.*

Christoph Klenner
*ACCIS - Association of Consumer
Credit Information Suppliers*

Rebecca Knight
*PwC United Kingdom*

Shinoj Koshy
*Cleary Gottlieb Steen & Hamilton
LLP*

Kristin Kufel
*Baker & McKenzie*

Pascal Lalande
*Her Majesty's Land Registry*

Mushtak Macci
*Lubbock Fine - member of Russell
Bedford International*

Neil Maclean
*Shepherd & Wedderburn*

Neil Magrath
*UK Power Networks*

Christopher Mallon
*Skadden, Arps, Slate, Meagher &
Flom LLP*

Emily Marshall
*Cleary Gottlieb Steen & Hamilton
LLP*

Kate Matthews
*Stevens & Bolton LLP*

Charles Mayo
*Simmons & Simmons LLP*

Adam McCarron
*Baker & McKenzie*

Martin Michalski
*Baker & McKenzie*

Neil Munroe
*ACCIS - Association of Consumer
Credit Information Suppliers*

Idris Natha
*Veritas Solicitors LLP*

Frances Okosi
*Baker & McKenzie*

Chris Perkins
*PricewaterhouseCoopers Legal LLP*

Stewart Perry
*Clyde & Co.*

Steve Pocock
*Crown Agents Ltd.*

Alex Rogan
*Skadden, Arps, Slate, Meagher &
Flom LLP*

Renuka Sharma
*Clyde & Co.*

Andrew Shutter
*Cleary Gottlieb Steen & Hamilton
LLP*

Sandra Simoni
*Department for Communities and
Local Government*

Lisa Slevin
*DLA Piper UK LLP*

Richard Smith
*Mayer Brown International LLP*

Stacey-Jo Smith
*Companies House*

Spencer Stevenson
*British International Freight
Association*

Caroline Taylor
*Latham & Watkins LLP*

Lance Terry
*Glanvilles Solicitors*

Mehboob Vadiya
*Veritas Solicitors LLP*

Stephanie Walker
*PricewaterhouseCoopers Legal LLP*

Stephanie Warren
*Latham & Watkins LLP*

Geoffrey Wilkinson
*Wilkinson Construction
Consultants*

Sally Willcock
*Weil, Gotshal & Manges LLP*

Andrew Wilson
*Andrew Wilson & Co*

## UNITED STATES

*Allen & Overy LLP*

*Business & Law Blog*

*TransUnion*

Stephen Anderson
*PwC United States*

Phillip Anzalone
*Atelier Architecture 64, PLLC*

Pamy J. S. Arora
*Cornell Group, Inc*

Luke A. Barefoot
*Cleary Gottlieb Steen & Hamilton
LLP*

Richard Baumann
*Morrison Cohen LLP*

G. Carlo
*Corporate Solvency Stress Testing
Advisors L3C*

Victor Chiu
*Cleary Gottlieb Steen & Hamilton
LLP*

Richard Conza
*Cleary Gottlieb Steen & Hamilton
LLP*

Brendan Cyr
*Cleary Gottlieb Steen & Hamilton
LLP*

James Denn
*New York State Public Service
Commission*

Vilas Dhar
*Dhar Law, LLP*

Joshua L. Ditelberg
*Seyfarth Shaw LLP*

Lindsay Dunn
*Cleary Gottlieb Steen & Hamilton
LLP*

Irma Foley
*Orrick, Herrington & Sutcliffe LLP*

Daphney François
*Cleary Gottlieb Steen & Hamilton
LLP*

Patrick Fuller
*Cleary Gottlieb Steen & Hamilton
LLP*

Anita Gambhir
*Cornell Group, Inc*

Robert Goethe
*Cornell Group, Inc*

Daniel Gottfried
*Rogin Nassau LLC*

Boris Grosman
*L & B Electrical International*

Thomas Halket
*Halket Weitz LLP*

Adam Heintz
*Morrison and Foerster*

Nancy Israel
*Law Office of Nancy D. Israel*

Neil Jacobs
*NI Jacobs & Associates*

Christopher Andrew Jarvinen
*Berger Singerman*

Charles L. Kerr
*Morrison and Foerster*

Joshua Kochath
*Comage Container Lines*

Arthur Kohn
*Cleary Gottlieb Steen & Hamilton
LLP*

Walter Krauklis
*Jarvis International Freight, Inc*

Michael Lazerwitz
*Cleary Gottlieb Steen & Hamilton
LLP*

Bradford L. Livingston
*Seyfarth Shaw LLP*

Dave Lucia
*Security Cargo Network, Inc.*

A Edward Major
*A Edward Major,
Counsellors-at-Law*

Kerry Mohan
*Seyfarth Shaw LLP*

Kelly J. Murray
*PwC United States*

David Newberg
*Collier, Halpern, Newberg,
Nolletti, & Bock*

Samuel Nolen
*Richards, Layton & Finger, P.A.,
member of Lex Mundi*

Sean O'Neal
*Cleary Gottlieb Steen & Hamilton
LLP*

Jeffrey Penn
*Cleary Gottlieb Steen & Hamilton
LLP*

William Peters
*Corporate Solvency Stress Testing
Advisors L3C*

Igor Putilov
*Link Lines Logistics Inc*

Stephen Raslavich
*United States Bankruptcy Court*

Damian Ridealgh
*Ashurst LLP*

Sandra Rocks
*Cleary Gottlieb Steen & Hamilton
LLP*

Jack Rose
*Ashurst LLP*

Kenneth Rosen
*University of Alabama School
of Law*

Manuel Santiago
*Milrose Consultants, Inc.*

Helen Skinner
*Cleary Gottlieb Steen & Hamilton
LLP*

David Smith
*Cleary Gottlieb Steen & Hamilton
LLP*

David Snyder
*Snyder & Snyder, LLP*

F.W. Turner
*Turner & Turner*

Edna Udobong
*Liberty University School of Law*

Penny Vaughn
*PwC United States*

Frank Wolf
*Corporate Solvency Stress Testing
Advisors L3C*

## URURUGUAY
## URUGUAY

**Isabel Abarno**
*Olivera Abogados*

**Juan Achugar**
*Banco Central del Uruguay*

**Marta Alvarez**
*Administración Nacional de Usinas y Transmisión Eléctrica (UTE)*

**Bernardo Amorín**
*Olivera Abogados*

**Sebastián Arcia**
*Arcia Storace Fuentes Medina Abogados*

**Cecilia Arias**
*Guyer & Regules, member of Lex Mundi*

**Alicia Badanian**
*Estudio Bergstein*

**Fernando Bado**
*Estudio Dr. Mezzera*

**Pablo Balao Gay**
*Panalpina World Transport*

**Martín Balmaceda**
*Estudio Bergstein*

**Leticia Barrios Bentancourt**
*Estudio Bergstein*

**Ady Beitler**
*Estudio Bergstein*

**Juan Bonet**
*Guyer & Regules, member of Lex Mundi*

**Sofia Borba**
*Sofia Borba*

**Virginia Brause**
*Jiménez de Aréchaga, Viana & Brause*

**Ricardo Marcelo Bregani**
*Estudio Blanco & Etcheverry*

**Luis Burastero Servetto**
*Luis Burastero & Asoc.*

**Martín Colombo**
*Ferrere Abogados*

**Leonardo Couto**
*Jose Maria Facal & Co.*

**Jorge De Vita**
*Jorge De Vita Studio*

**María Durán**
*Hughes & Hughes*

**Maria Jose Echinope**
*Jiménez de Aréchaga, Viana & Brause*

**Noelia Eiras**
*Hughes & Hughes*

**Gabriel Ejgenberg**
*Estudio Bergstein*

**Pilar Etcheverry**
*Guyer & Regules, member of Lex Mundi*

**Agustín Etcheverry Reyes**
*Estudio Blanco & Etcheverry*

**Analía Fernández**
*Estudio Bergstein*

**Javier Fernández Zerbino**
*Bado, Kuster, Zerbino & Rachetti*

**Hector Ferreira**
*Hughes & Hughes*

**Juan Federico Fischer**
*Fischer & Schickendantz*

**Federico Florin**
*Guyer & Regules, member of Lex Mundi*

**Sergio Franco**
*PwC Uruguay*

**Andres Fuentes**
*Arcia Storace Fuentes Medina Abogados*

**Diego Galante**
*Galante & Martins*

**Pablo Galmarini**
*Galmarini*

**Enrique Garcia Pini**
*Administración Nacional de Usinas y Transmisión Eléctrica (UTE)*

**Nelson Alfredo Gonzalez**
*SDV Uruguay*

**Andrés Hessdörfer**
*Arcia Storace Fuentes Medina Abogados*

**Marcela Hughes**
*Hughes & Hughes*

**Maria Ibarra**
*Stavros Moyal y Asociados - member of Russell Bedford International*

**Ignacio Imas**
*Ferrere Abogados*

**Ariel Imken**
*Superintendencia de Servicios Financieros - Banco Central del Uruguay*

**Alfredo Inciarte Blanco**
*Estudio Pérez del Castillo, Inciarte, Gari Abogados*

**Richard Iturria**
*Bado, Kuster, Zerbino & Rachetti*

**Elías Mantero**
*Olivera Abogados*

**Enrique Martínez Schickendantz**
*Asociación de Despachantes de Aduana del Uruguay*

**Leonardo Melos**
*Estudio Bergstein*

**Ricardo Mezzera**
*Estudio Dr. Mezzera*

**Matilde Milicevic Santana**
*Equifax - Clearing de Informes*

**Pamela Moreira**
*Ferrere Abogados*

**Matias Morgare**
*SDV Uruguay*

**Pablo Mosto**
*Administración Nacional de Usinas y Transmisión Eléctrica (UTE)*

**Pablo Moyal**
*Stavros Moyal y Asociados - member of Russell Bedford International*

**Agustin Muzio**
*PwC Uruguay*

**Juan Martín Olivera**
*Olivera Abogados*

**María Concepción Olivera**
*Olivera Abogados*

**Ricardo Olivera García**
*Olivera Abogados*

**Federico Otegui**
*PwC Uruguay*

**Domingo Pereira**
*Estudio Bergstein*

**Hugo Pereira**
*Arcia Storace Fuentes Medina Abogados*

**Alli Rebollo**
*Stiler*

**Alejandro Santi Estefan**
*Olivera Abogados*

**Carolina Sarroca**
*Arcia Storace Fuentes Medina Abogados*

**Eliana Sartori**
*PwC Uruguay*

**Beatriz Spiess**
*Guyer & Regules, member of Lex Mundi*

**Dolores Storace**
*Arcia Storace Fuentes Medina Abogados*

**Alejandro Taranto**
*Estudio Taranto*

**Maria Jose Tegiacchi**
*Jiménez de Aréchaga, Viana & Brause*

**Ana Inés Terra**
*Estudio Bergstein*

**Evangelina Torres**
*Jiménez de Aréchaga, Viana & Brause*

**Augusto Tricotti**
*Softron*

**Juan Ignacio Troccoli**
*Fischer & Schickendantz*

**Diego Viana**
*Jiménez de Aréchaga, Viana & Brause*

**Gerardo Viñoles**
*Viñoles Arquitect Studio*

## UZBEKISTAN
*Globalink Logistics Group*

*PwC Mongolia*

*PwC Uzbekistan*

*Uzbekenergo*

**Askar K. Abdusagatov**
*OOO Progress-Development*

**Mels Akhmedov**
*BAS Law Firm*

**Natalya Apukhtina**
*SNR Denton Wilde Sapte & Co*

**Renata Gafarova**
*M & M*

**Irina Gosteva**
*SNR Denton Wilde Sapte & Co*

**Nodir B. Hakimov**
*European Elite Construction*

**Nail Hassanov**
*Leges Advokat Law Firm*

**Mouborak Kambarova**
*SNR Denton Wilde Sapte & Co*

**Babur Karimov**
*Grata Law Firm*

**Khurshid Kasimdzhanov**
*M & M*

**Alisher T. Kasimov**
*European Elite Construction*

**Nurali Eshibaevich Khalmuratov**
*National Institute of Credit Information of Central Bank of the Republic of Uzbekistan*

**Davron Khasanov**
*Mukhamedjanov & Partners Law Firm*

**Oscar Khusnullin**
*Holos*

**Tatyana Lee**
*Legalmax Law Firm*

**Ibrahim Mukhamedjanov**
*Mukhamedjanov & Partners Law Firm*

**Behruz Nizamutdinov**
*M & M*

**Valeriya Ok**
*Legalmax Law Firm*

**Mirzaaziz Ruziev**
*Grata Law Firm*

**Azamat Salaev**
*Chamber of Commerce & Industry of the Republic of Uzbekistan*

**Alexander Samborsky**
*National Centre of Geodesy & Cartography*

**Nizomiddin Shakhabutdinov**
*Leges Advokat Law Firm*

**Petros Tsakanyan**
*Azizov & Partners*

**Aziz Turdibaev**
*M & M*

**Nodir Yuldashev**
*Grata Law Firm*

## VANUATU
*Department of Environmental Protection & Conservation (DEPC)*

*Entreprise Dinh Van Tu*

*Fr8 Logistics Ltd.*

*Vanuatu Financial Services Commission*

**Barry Amoss**
*South Sea Shipping Ltd.*

**Loïc Bernier**
*Caillard & Kaddour*

**Andy Cottam**
*National Bank of Vanuatu*

**Frederic Derousseau**
*Vate Electrics*

**David Hudson**
*Hudson & Sugden*

**Jonathan Law**
*Law Partners*

**Colin B. Leo**
*Colin Bright Leo Lawyers*

**Philippe Mehrenberger**
*UNELCO*

**Mark Pardoe**
*South Sea Shipping Ltd.*

**Harold Qualao**
*Qualao Consulting Ltd. QCL*

**Katua Rezel**
*Department of Lands, Surveys & Records*

**Martin Saint Hilaire**
*Cabinet AJC, an independent correspondent member of DFK International*

**Mark Stafford**
*Barrett & Partners*

**Mandes Tangaras**
*Municipality of Port Vila*

## VENEZUELA, RB
**Jorge Acedo-Prato**
*Hoet Pelaez Castillo & Duque*

**Tamara Adrian**
*Adrian & Adrian*

**Juan Enrique Aigster**
*Hoet Pelaez Castillo & Duque*

**Servio T. Altuve Jr.**
*Servio T. Altuve R. & Asociados*

**Carlos Bachrich Nagy**
*De Sola Pate & Brown, Abogados - Consultores*

**Arturo De Sola Lander**
*De Sola Pate & Brown, Abogados - Consultores*

**Juan Domingo Cordero**
*Baker & McKenzie*

**Carlos Domínguez Hernández**
*Hoet Pelaez Castillo & Duque*

**Carlos Flores**
*Computec - DataCrédito Venezuela*

**Selma Flores Ferreira**

**Jose Garcia**
*PwC Venezuela*

**Jose Alfredo Giral**
*Baker & McKenzie*

**Lynne H. Glass**
*Despacho de Abogados miembros de Norton Rose, S.C.*

**Ybeth Gonzalez**
*Baker & McKenzie*

**Andres Gonzalez Crespo**
*Casas Rincon Gonzalez Rubio & Asociados*

**Diego Gonzalez Crespo**
*Casas Rincon Gonzalez Rubio & Asociados*

**Enrique Gonzalez Rubio**
*Casas Rincon Gonzalez Rubio & Asociados*

**Andres Felipe Guevara**
*Baker & McKenzie*

**Alfredo Hurtado**
*Hurtado Esteban & Asociados - member of Russell Bedford International*

**Maigualida Ifill**
*PwC Venezuela*

**Enrique Itriago**
*Rodriguez & Mendoza*

**Gabriela Longo**
*Palacios, Ortega y Asociados*

**Ana Lugo**
*Hoet Pelaez Castillo & Duque*

**Maritza Meszaros**
*Baker & McKenzie*

**Patricia Milano Hernández**
*De Sola Pate & Brown, Abogados - Consultores*

**Lorena Mingarelli Lozzi**
*De Sola Pate & Brown, Abogados - Consultores*

**John R. Pate**
*De Sola Pate & Brown, Abogados - Consultores*

**Thomas J. Pate Páez**
*De Sola Pate & Brown, Abogados - Consultores*

**Fernando Pelaez-Pier**
*Hoet Pelaez Castillo & Duque*

**Bernardo Pisani**
*Rodriguez & Mendoza*

**Juan Carlos Pró-Rísquez**
*Despacho de Abogados miembros de Norton Rose, S.C.*

**José Alberto Ramirez**
*Hoet Pelaez Castillo & Duque*

**Francisco Seijas**
*Americas Interactiva*

**Laura Silva Aparicio**
*Hoet Pelaez Castillo & Duque*

**Raúl Stolk Nevett**
*Hoet Pelaez Castillo & Duque*

**Oscar Ignacio Torres**
*Travieso Evans Arria Rengel & Paz*

**Sara Trimboli**
*Baker & McKenzie*

**John Tucker**
*Hoet Pelaez Castillo & Duque*

**Carlos Velandia Sanchez**
*Asociación Venezolana de Derecho Registral "AVEDER"*

**José Vivas**

## VIETNAM
*Panalpina World Transport LLP*

**Katrina Alday**
*VILAF - Hong Duc Law Firm*

**Hong Ngan Anh**
*Indochine Counsel*

**Nguyen Anh Thu**
*University of Economics and Business, VNU*

Ken Atkinson
*GRANT THORNTON LLP*

Pham Nghiem Xuan Bac
*VISION & ASSOCIATES*

Pham Quoc Bao
*HO CHI MINH CITY POWER CORPORATION (EVN HCMC)*

Frederick Burke
*BAKER & MCKENZIE*

Samantha Campbell
*GIDE LOYRETTE NOUEL, MEMBER OF LEX MUNDI*

Giles Thomas Cooper
*DUANE MORRIS LLC*

Thi Thu Quyen Dang
*EPLEGAL*

Trong Hieu Dang
*VISION & ASSOCIATES*

Nguyen Dang Viet
*BIZCONSULT LAW FIRM*

Van Dinh Thi Quynh
*PwC VIETNAM*

Linh Do
*KTC ASSURANCE & BUSINESS ADVISORS - MEMBER OF RUSSELL BEDFORD INTERNATIONAL*

Linh Doan
*LVN & ASSOCIATES*

Ngoan Doan
*GRANT THORNTON LLP*

Dang The Duc
*INDOCHINE COUNSEL*

Minh Duong
*ALLENS ARTHUR ROBINSON*

Thanh Long Duong
*ALIAT LEGAL*

Tieng Thu Duong
*VISION & ASSOCIATES*

Huong Duong Thi Mai
*LUATVIET - ADVOCATES & SOLICITORS*

Ngoc Hai Ha
*BAKER & MCKENZIE*

Thu Ha

Quang Ha Dang
*GIDE LOYRETTE NOUEL, MEMBER OF LEX MUNDI*

Giang Ha Thi Phuong
*PwC VIETNAM*

Kevin B. Hawkins
*MAYER BROWN JSM*

Hoa Hoang
*LVN & ASSOCIATES*

Tam Hoang
*KTC ASSURANCE & BUSINESS ADVISORS - MEMBER OF RUSSELL BEDFORD INTERNATIONAL*

Nguyen Hoang Kim Oanh
*BAKER & MCKENZIE*

Bui Ngoc Hong
*INDOCHINE COUNSEL*

Le Hong Phong
*BIZCONSULT LAW FIRM*

Nguyen Thi Hong Van
*YKVN*

Tran Quang Huy
*VILAF - HONG DUC LAW FIRM*

Kim Ngoan Huynh
*GIDE LOYRETTE NOUEL, MEMBER OF LEX MUNDI*

Tuong Long Huynh
*GIDE LOYRETTE NOUEL, MEMBER OF LEX MUNDI*

Jean Claude Junin
*SDV LOGISTICS*

Hai Long Khuat
*INDOCHINE COUNSEL*

Tho Khuc Duong
*LUATVIET - ADVOCATES & SOLICITORS*

Tran Trung Kien
*S&B LAW*

Matt King
*ASIAN TIGERS TRANSPO INTERNATIONAL LTD.*

Milton Lawson
*FRESHFIELDS BRUCKHAUS DERINGER*

Anh Tuan Le
*CREDIT INFORMATION CENTRE - STATE BANK OF VIETNAM*

Phuc Le Hong
*LUATVIET - ADVOCATES & SOLICITORS*

Thuy Le Nguyen Huy
*INDOCHINE COUNSEL*

Phuoc Le Van
*HO CHI MINH CITY POWER CORPORATION (EVN HCMC)*

Le Thi Loc
*YKVN*

Nguyen Phan Manh Long
*HUNG & PARTNERS*

Tien Ngoc Luu
*VISION & ASSOCIATES*

Le Thi Luyen
*HO CHI MINH CITY POWER CORPORATION (EVN HCMC)*

Tran Dinh Muoi
*SEAREFICO*

Duy Minh Ngo
*VB LAW*

Thuy Ngo Quang
*NT TRADE LAW LLC*

Bui Thi Thanh Ngoc
*DS AVOCATS*

Dao Nguyen
*MAYER BROWN JSM*

Duy Ninh Nguyen
*NAM TIEN ARCHITECTURE & CONSULTANTS*

Hong Hai Nguyen
*DUANE MORRIS LLC*

Huong Nguyen
*MAYER BROWN JSM*

Khai Nguyen
*GRANT THORNTON LLP*

Linh D. Nguyen
*VILAF - HONG DUC LAW FIRM*

Minh Tuan Nguyen
*VIET PREMIER LAW LTD.*

Oanh Nguyen
*BAKER & MCKENZIE*

Quoc Phong Nguyen
*ALIAT LEGAL*

Thanh Hai Nguyen
*BAKER & MCKENZIE*

Tien Hoa Nguyen
*S&B LAW*

Trang Nguyen
*CREDIT INFORMATION CENTRE - STATE BANK OF VIETNAM*

Tram Nguyen Huyen
*GIDE LOYRETTE NOUEL, MEMBER OF LEX MUNDI*

Tam Nguyen Tinh
*GIDE LOYRETTE NOUEL, MEMBER OF LEX MUNDI*

Long Nguyen Vinh
*LUATVIET - ADVOCATES & SOLICITORS*

Eddie O'Shea
*MAYER BROWN JSM*

Hung Duy Pham
*KTC ASSURANCE & BUSINESS ADVISORS - MEMBER OF RUSSELL BEDFORD INTERNATIONAL*

Viet D. Phan
*LUATPVD*

Vu Anh Phan
*INDOCHINE COUNSEL*

Hyunh Truong Que Phuong
*PRIME CONSTRUCTION & TRADING CO, LTD.*

Cristian Predan

Truong Nhat Quang
*YKVN*

Nguyen Que Tam
*CHEN SHAN & PARTNERS*

Yee Chung Seck
*BAKER & MCKENZIE*

Chau Ta
*DFDL MEKONG LAW GROUP*

Tran Thi Than Niem
*DFDL MEKONG LAW GROUP*

Le Thi Nhat Linh
*BAN MAI CO. LTD.*

Nhung Thieu Hong
*PwC VIETNAM*

Tan Heng Thye
*CHEN SHAN & PARTNERS*

Antoine Toussaint
*GIDE LOYRETTE NOUEL, MEMBER OF LEX MUNDI*

Binh Minh Tran
*VIETIN BANK*

Chi Anh Tran
*BAKER & MCKENZIE*

Quang Tuong Tran
*INDOCHINE COUNSEL*

Bac Tran Phuong
*LUATVIET - ADVOCATES & SOLICITORS*

Nguyen Thu Trang
*S&B LAW*

Nam Hoai Truong
*INDOCHINE COUNSEL*

Vo Huu Tu
*INDOCHINE COUNSEL*

Nguyen Anh Tuan
*DP CONSULTING LTD.*

Ngo Thanh Tung
*VILAF - HONG DUC LAW FIRM*

Chi Vo Ngoc Phuong
*GIDE LOYRETTE NOUEL, MEMBER OF LEX MUNDI*

Anh Thu Vu
*MAYER BROWN LLP*

Dzung Vu
*LVN & ASSOCIATES*

Thang Vu
*BAKER & MCKENZIE*

Le Vu Anh
*PwC VIETNAM*

Son Ha Vuong
*VISION & ASSOCIATES*

Matthew Williams
*MAYER BROWN JSM*

## WEST BANK AND GAZA

Kareem Abdel Hadi
*JEDICO*

Hani Abdel Jaldeh

Salha Aboushi
*PwC*

Murad Abu Mwis
*MINISTRY OF NATIONAL ECONOMY*

Ata Al Biary

Haytham L. Al-Zubi
*AL-ZUBI LAW OFFICE, ADVOCATES & LEGAL CONSULTANTS*

Mohammad Amarneh

Moayad Amouri
*PwC*

Nada Atrash
*ARCHITECTURE & DESIGN*

Hanna Atrash
*CMG*

Nizam Ayoob
*MINISTRY OF NATIONAL ECONOMY*

Ali Faroun
*PALESTINIAN MONETARY AUTHORITY*

George Handal
*BETHLEHEM FREIGHT*

Samir Hulileh
*PADICO HOLDINGS*

Hiba I. Husseini
*HUSSEINI & HUSSEINI*

Mohamed Khader
*LAUSANNE TRADING CONSULTANTS*

Zahi Khouri
*NATIONAL BEVERAGES COMPANY*

Munib Masri
*PADICO HOLDINGS*

Nabil A. Mushahwar
*LAW OFFICES OF NABIL A. MUSHAHWAR*

Absal Nusseibeh
*HUSSEINI & HUSSEINI*

Michael F. Orfaly
*PwC*

Wael Sa'adi
*PwC*

Samir Sahhar
*OFFICE OF SAMIR SAHHAR*

Nadeem Shehadeh
*A.F. & R. SHEHADEH LAW OFFICE*

Maysa Sirhan
*PALESTINIAN MONETARY AUTHORITY*

## YEMEN, REP.

Khalid Abdullah
*SHEIKH MOHAMMED ABDULLAH SONS (EST. 1927)*

Tariq Abdullah
*LAW OFFICES OF SHEIKH TARIQ ABDULLAH*

Shafiq Adat
*LAW OFFICES OF SHEIKH TARIQ ABDULLAH*

Khaled Al Buraihi
*KHALED AL BURAIHI FOR ADVOCACY & LEGAL SERVICES*

Yaser Al-Adimi
*ABDUL GABAR A. AL-ADIMI FOR CONSTRUCTION & TRADE*

Hamzah Al-Anesi
*DR. HAMZAH SHAHER LAW FIRM*

Mohamed Taha Hamood Al-Hashimi
*MOHAMED TAHA HAMOOD & CO.*

Abdulkader Al-Hebshi
*ADVOCACY AND LEGAL CONSULTATIONS OFFICE (ALCO)*

Ali Al-Hebshi
*ADVOCACY AND LEGAL CONSULTATIONS OFFICE (ALCO)*

Rashad Khalid Al-Howiadi

Mohamed Ali
*MAS FREIGHT INTERNATIONAL*

Abdulla Farouk Luqman
*LUQMAN LEGAL ADVOCATES & LEGAL CONSULTANTS*

Esam Nadeesh
*ADVOCACY AND LEGAL CONSULTATIONS OFFICE (ALCO)*

Sami Abdullah Sabeha
*SAS FOR CARGO SERVICES*

Yousra Salem
*LUQMAN LEGAL ADVOCATES & LEGAL CONSULTANTS*

Khaled Mohammed Salem Ali
*LUQMAN LEGAL ADVOCATES & LEGAL CONSULTANTS*

Muhammad Saqib
*MOHAMED TAHA HAMOOD & CO.*

Khaled Hassan Zaid
*YEMEN CHAMBER OF SHIPPING*

## ZAMBIA

Chewe K. Bwalya
*D.H. KEMP & CO.*

Mwelwa Chibesakunda
*CHIBESAKUNDA & COMPANY, MEMBER OF DLA PIPER GROUP*

Sydney Chisenga
*CORPUS LEGAL PRACTITIONERS*

Emmanuel Chisenga Chulu
*PwC ZAMBIA*

Eddie Musonda Chunga
*MINISTRY OF LAND*

Harjinder Dogra
*PwC ZAMBIA*

Arshad A. Dudhia
*MUSA DUDHIA & COMPANY*

Robin Durairajah
*CHIBESAKUNDA & COMPANY, MEMBER OF DLA PIPER GROUP*

Charles Haanyika
*UTILINK LIMITED*

Diane Harrington
*SDV LOGISTICS*

Mubanga Kangwa
*CHIBESAKUNDA & COMPANY, MEMBER OF DLA PIPER GROUP*

Mutale Kasonde
*CHIBESAKUNDA & COMPANY, MEMBER OF DLA PIPER GROUP*

Mumba Makumba
*PACRA*

Sylvester Mashamba
*NATIONAL COUNCIL FOR CONSTRUCTION*

Clyde Mbazima
*CHIBESAKUNDA & COMPANY, MEMBER OF DLA PIPER GROUP*

Bonaventure Mbewe
*BARCLAYS BANK*

Jyoti Mistry
*PwC ZAMBIA*

Gerald Mkandawire
*SDV LOGISTICS*

Mwape Mondoloka
*BARCLAYS BANK*

Michael Mwape Moono

Mutule Museba
*CORPUS LEGAL PRACTITIONERS*

Eustace Ng'oma
*CHIBESAKUNDA & COMPANY, MEMBER OF DLA PIPER GROUP*

Kanti Patel
*CHRISTOPHER, RUSSELL COOK & CO.*

Solly Patel
*CHRISTOPHER, RUSSELL COOK & CO.*

Aleksandar Perunicic
*SDV LOGISTICS*

Rodwyn Peterson
*CHIBESAKUNDA & COMPANY, MEMBER OF DLA PIPER GROUP*

Miriam Sabi
*ZRA-CUSTOMER SERVICE CENTER*

John Serlemitsos
*PLATINUM GOLD EQUITY*

Valerie Sesia
*CUSTOMIZED CLEARING AND FORWARDING LTD.*

Juliana Shoko Chilombo
*Ministry of Land*

Mildred Stephenson
*Credit Reference Bureau Africa
Ltd.*

Johannas Steyn
*Apollo Enterprises Ltd.*

Liu Yang
*SDV Logistics*

Enos Zulu
*PACRA*

### ZIMBABWE

*BCHOD and Partners*

Richard Beattie
*The Stone/Beattie Studio*

Tim Boulton
*Manica Africa Pty. Ltd.*

Peter Cawood
*PwC Zimbabwe*

Innocent Chagonda
*Atherstone & Cook*

Benjamin Chikowero
*Gutu & Chikowero*

Grant Davies
*Manica Africa Pty. Ltd.*

Beloved Dhlakama
*Dhlakama B. Attorneys*

Paul Fraser
*Lofty & Fraser*

Obert Chaurura Gutu
*Gutu & Chikowero*

R.T. Katsande
*Zimbabwe Electricity Transmission
& Distribution Company*

Peter Lloyd
*Gill, Godlonton & Gerrans*

Manuel Lopes
*PwC Zimbabwe*

Memory Mafo
*Scanlen & Holderness*

Mordecai Pilate Mahlangu
*Gill, Godlonton & Gerrans*

Vimbai Makora
*Gutu & Chikowero*

Gertrude Maredza
*Gutu & Chikowero*

David Masaya
*PwC Zimbabwe*

Gloria Mawarire
*Mawere & Sibanda Legal
Practitioners*

Jim McComish
*Pearce McComish Architects*

Lloyd Mhishi
*Dube, Manikai and Hwacha Legal
Practitioners - DMH Commercial
Law Chambers*

Honour P. Mkushi
*Sawyer & Mkushi*

Evans Talent Moyo
*Scanlen & Holderness*

Sternford Moyo
*Scanlen & Holderness*

Alec Muchadehama
*Mbidzo Muchadehama & Makoni*

Benjamin Mukandi
*Freight World (Pvt) Ltd.*

T. Muringani
*Speartec*

Ostern Mutero
*Sawyer & Mkushi*

Alec Tafadzwa Muza
*Mawere & Sibanda Legal
Practitioners*

Namatirai Muzarakuza
*Gutu & Chikowero*

Phathisile Paula Ncube
*Mawere & Sibanda Legal
Practitioners*

Maxwell Ngorima
*BDO Tax & Advisory Services
(Pvt) Ltd.*

Vanani Nyangulu
*V.S. Nyangulu & Associates*

Archford Rutanhira
*Scanlen & Holderness*

Unity Sakhe
*Kantor & Immerman*